AF412621

Studies in the History of Art
Published by the National Gallery of Art,
Washington

This series includes: Studies in the History of
Art, collected papers on objects in the Gallery's
collections and other art-historical studies
(formerly Report and Studies in the History of
Art); Monograph Series I, a catalogue of stained
glass in the United States; Monograph Series II,
on conservation topics; and Symposium Papers
(formerly Symposium Series), the proceedings of
symposia sponsored by the Center for Advanced
Study in the Visual Arts at the National Gallery
of Art.

[1] *Report and Studies in the History of Art*, 1967
[2] *Report and Studies in the History of Art*, 1968
[3] *Report and Studies in the History of Art*, 1969
     [In 1970 the National Gallery of Art's annual
     report became a separate publication.]
[4] *Studies in the History of Art*, 1972
[5] *Studies in the History of Art*, 1973
     [The first five volumes are unnumbered.]
 6   *Studies in the History of Art*, 1974
 7   *Studies in the History of Art*, 1975
 8   *Studies in the History of Art*, 1978
 9   *Studies in the History of Art*, 1980
10   *Macedonia and Greece in Late Classical and
     Early Hellenistic Times*, edited by Beryl Barr-
     Sharrar and Eugene N. Borza. Symposium Series
     I, 1982
11   *Figures of Thought: El Greco as Interpreter of
     History, Tradition, and Ideas*, edited by
     Jonathan Brown, 1982
12   *Studies in the History of Art*, 1982
13   *El Greco: Italy and Spain*, edited by Jonathan
     Brown and José Manuel Pita Andrade.
     Symposium Series II, 1984
14   *Claude Lorrain, 1600–1682: A Symposium*,
     edited by Pamela Askew. Symposium Series III,
     1984
15   *Stained Glass before 1700 in American
     Collections: New England and New York
     (Corpus Vitrearum Checklist I)*, compiled by
     Madeline H. Caviness et al. Monograph Series I,
     1985
16   *Pictorial Narrative in Antiquity and the Middle
     Ages*, edited by Herbert L. Kessler and Marianna
     Shreve Simpson. Symposium Series IV, 1985
17   *Raphael before Rome*, edited by James Beck.
     Symposium Series V, 1986
18   *Studies in the History of Art*, 1985
19   *James McNeill Whistler: A Reexamination*,
     edited by Ruth E. Fine. Symposium Papers VI,
     1987
20   *Retaining the Original: Multiple Originals,
     Copies, and Reproductions*. Symposium Papers
     VII, 1989
21   *Italian Medals*, edited by J. Graham Pollard.
     Symposium Papers VIII, 1987
22   *Italian Plaquettes*, edited by Alison Luchs.
     Symposium Papers IX, 1989
23   *Stained Glass before 1700 in American
     Collections: Mid-Atlantic and Southeastern
     Seaboard States (Corpus Vitrearum Checklist
     II)*, compiled by Madeline H. Caviness et al.
     Monograph Series I, 1987
24   *Studies in the History of Art*, 1990
25   *The Fashioning and Functioning of the British
     Country House*, edited by Gervase Jackson-
     Stops et al. Symposium Papers X, 1989

26   *Winslow Homer*, edited by Nicolai Cikovsky, Jr.
     Symposium Papers XI, 1990
27   *Cultural Differentiation and Cultural Identity
     in the Visual Arts*, edited by Susan J. Barnes and
     Walter S. Melion. Symposium Papers XII, 1989
28   *Stained Glass before 1700 in American
     Collections: Midwestern and Western States
     (Corpus Vitrearum Checklist III)*, compiled by
     Madeline H. Caviness et al. Monograph Series I,
     1989
29   *Nationalism in the Visual Arts*, edited by
     Richard A. Etlin. Symposium Papers XIII, 1991
30   *The Mall in Washington, 1791–1991*, edited by
     Richard Longstreth. Symposium Papers XIV, 1991
31   *Urban Form and Meaning in South Asia:
     The Shaping of Cities from Prehistoric to
     Precolonial Times*, edited by Howard Spodek
     and Doris Meth Srinivasan. Symposium Papers
     XV, 1993
32   *New Perspectives in Early Greek Art*, edited by
     Diana Buitron-Oliver. Symposium Papers XVI,
     1991
33   *Michelangelo Drawings*, edited by Craig Hugh
     Smyth. Symposium Papers XVII, 1992
34   *Art and Power in Seventeenth-Century Sweden*,
     edited by Michael Conforti and Michael
     Metcalf. Symposium Papers XVIII (withdrawn)
35   *The Architectural Historian in America*, edited
     by Elisabeth Blair MacDougall. Symposium
     Papers XIX, 1990
36   *The Pastoral Landscape*, edited by John Dixon
     Hunt. Symposium Papers XX, 1992
37   *American Art around 1900*, edited by Doreen
     Bolger and Nicolai Cikovsky, Jr. Symposium
     Papers XXI, 1990
38   *The Artist's Workshop*, edited by Peter M.
     Lukehart. Symposium Papers XXII, 1993
39   *Stained Glass before 1700 in American
     Collections: Silver-Stained Roundels and
     Unipartite Panels (Corpus Vitrearum Checklist
     IV)*, compiled by Timothy B. Husband.
     Monograph Series I, 1991
40   The Feast of the Gods: *Conservation,
     Examination, and Interpretation*, by David Bull
     and Joyce Plesters. Monograph Series II, 1990
41   *Conservation Research*. Monograph Series II,
     1993
42   *Conservation Research: Studies of Fifteenth- to
     Nineteenth-Century Tapestry*, edited by Lotus
     Stack. Monograph Series II, 1993
43   Eius Virtutis Studiosi: *Classical and
     Postclassical Studies in Memory of Frank
     Edward Brown*, edited by Russell T. Scott and
     Ann Reynolds Scott. Symposium Papers XXIII,
     1993
44   *Intellectual Life at the Court of Frederick II
     Hohenstaufen*, edited by William Tronzo,
     Symposium Papers XXIV, 1994
45   *Titian 500*, edited by Joseph Manca. Symposium
     Papers XXV, 1994
46   *Van Dyck 350*, edited by Susan J. Barnes and
     Arthur K. Wheelock, Jr. Symposium Papers
     XXVI, 1994
47   *The Formation of National Collections of Art
     and Archaeology*, edited by Gwendolyn Wright.
     Symposium Papers XXVII*
48   *Monarca della Pittura: Piero and His Legacy*,
     edited by Marilyn Aronberg Lavin. Symposium
     Papers XXVIII*
49   *Architectural Sculpture in Fifth-Century
     Greece*, edited by Diana Buitron-Oliver.
     Symposium Papers XXIX*

---

*Forthcoming

Van Dyck 350

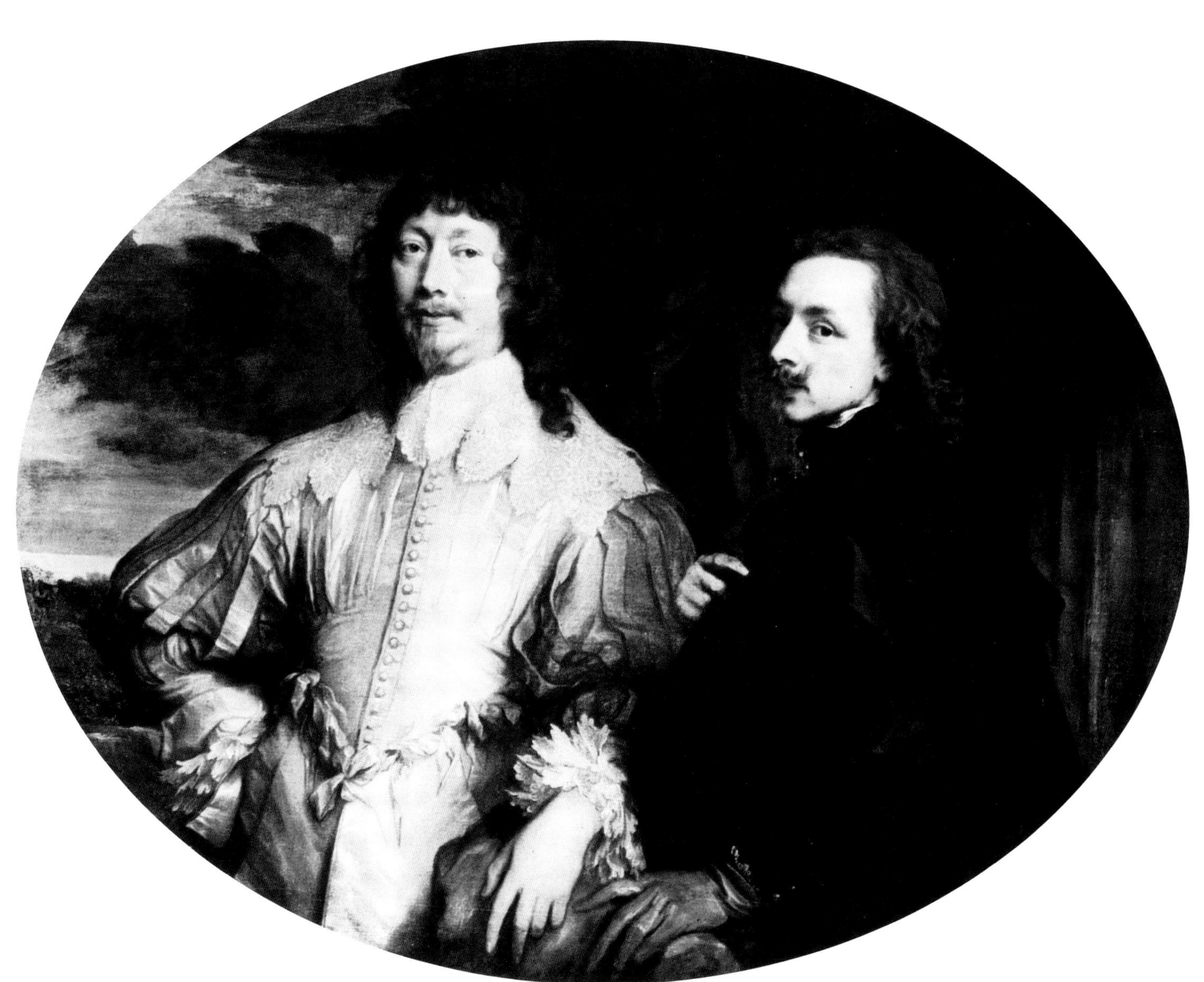

STUDIES IN THE HISTORY OF ART · 46 ·

Center for Advanced Study in the Visual Arts

Symposium Papers XXVI

Van Dyck 350

Edited by Susan J. Barnes and Arthur K. Wheelock, Jr.

National Gallery of Art, Washington

Distributed by the University Press of New England

Hanover and London

Distributed by the University Press of New England, 23 South Main Street, Hanover, New Hampshire 03755

Abstracted by RILA (International Repertory of the Literature of Art), Williamstown, Massachusetts 01267

Proceedings of the symposium "Van Dyck 350," sponsored by the Center for Advanced Study in the Visual Arts and the Department of Art History, University of Maryland at College Park, 8–9 February 1991

ISSN 0091-7338
ISBN 0-89468-201-6

Frontispiece: Anthony van Dyck, *Sir Endymion Porter and Van Dyck,* c. 1635, oil on canvas
Museo del Prado, Madrid

Endpapers: Anthony van Dyck brings action against Adriaen Diericx and Lancelot Lancelots to protect the rights of his younger brothers and sisters, 13 September 1617
City archives, Antwerp

Contents

Preface

In February 1991 the Center for Advanced Study in the Visual Arts and the department of art history at the University of Maryland at College Park jointly sponsored a symposium entitled "Van Dyck 350." Twelve papers were delivered in Washington and at College Park. The gathering was held in conjunction with the exhibition *Anthony van Dyck,* organized by the National Gallery of Art to commemorate the 350th anniversary of the artist's death.

This volume reflects current research into Van Dyck's artistic production, patronage, and influence; registers new archival evidence on the artist's early career; and addresses issues of attribution. The breadth of topics is testimony to the varied career and international influence of this Flemish master, and affirms the continued scholarly interest in and broad appeal of Anthony van Dyck. The fourteen papers here include supplemental essays by David Freedberg, Marzia Cataldi Gallo, and Julius S. Held. Reinhold Baumstark was not able to prepare his paper for publication.

The symposium was planned in consultation with Susan J. Barnes, deputy director and chief curator of the Dallas Museum of Art, and Arthur K. Wheelock, Jr., curator of northern baroque painting at the National Gallery. They served as curators of the Van Dyck exhibition and kindly agreed to edit the symposium papers for publication, as well as to write the introduction and afterword. The cosponsoring institutions would like to express their appreciation to Egbert Haverkamp-Begemann of the Institute of Fine Arts, New York University; John Martin, emeritus professor of art, Princeton University; and Susan J. Barnes and Arthur K. Wheelock, Jr. for serving as moderators of the symposium sessions.

The Center for Advanced Study in the Visual Arts was founded in 1979, as part of the National Gallery of Art, to foster study of the history, theory, and criticism of art, architecture, and urbanism through programs of meetings, research, publication, and fellowships. The symposium series within Studies in the History of Art, of which this is the twenty-sixth volume, is designed to document scholarly meetings sponsored under the auspices of the Center for Advanced Study. The series also is intended to stimulate further research and scholarly debate. A summary of published and forthcoming titles may be found on the opening leaf of this volume. Many of the publications result from collaborations between the Center for Advanced Study and sister institutions, including universities, museums, and research institutions.

HENRY A. MILLON
Dean, Center for Advanced Study in the Visual Arts

SUSAN J. BARNES
Dallas Museum of Art

ARTHUR K. WHEELOCK, Jr.
National Gallery of Art

Introduction

Many scholars in the United States and abroad have been at work on aspects of Van Dyck's oeuvre, and it was gratifying to bring together at a symposium this group of voices and viewpoints. The papers gathered here represent a spectrum of issues and methods. Some focus on questions of attribution or of studio method, others on cultural context or fundamental archival research. Indeed, some of the most significant archival discoveries on the artist in a century are presented, and they come from each of the regions in which the itinerant Van Dyck was active: Antwerp, Genoa, and England.

In this brief overview, we have summarized the major thrust of each author's paper. The essays are organized in approximate chronological fashion, beginning with Katlijne Van der Stighelen's archival study on the young Van Dyck. The volume concludes with an afterword, a reflection on the *Anthony van Dyck* exhibition at the National Gallery of Art.[1]

For over a hundred years the biographies of Van Dyck have been based on the documents published by Frans Joseph van den Branden in 1883 and L. Galesloot in 1868. Henceforth they will rely on Van der Stighelen's research in the Antwerp archives and the conclusions she has drawn. Her discoveries about Van Dyck's artist forebears give us an entirely new understanding of the origins and speedy recognition of Van Dyck's own talent. Other documents about his father's changing financial fortunes help explain Van Dyck's known early legal actions with regard to his family and, perhaps, the motives for his precocious professional activity. Finally, Van der Stighelen brings to the ongoing discourse about Van Dyck's early work with studio assistants actual archival evidence about the ownership and occupants of the studio in which he worked, which was named the Dom van Ceulen.

Justus Müller Hofstede's study focuses on a single, if complex, object: the Chatsworth Sketchbook. Since its publication in 1966, the Chatsworth Sketchbook has become widely accepted as by Van Dyck. It is regarded both as important documentation for Van Dyck's early studies and style and as evidence for the contents of one of Rubens' lost sketchbooks. Müller Hofstede lays out the first serious challenge to this attribution, positing instead that the Chatsworth Sketchbook was drawn by an unknown young artist working in Rubens' orbit in the later 1630s.

The nature of Van Dyck's relationship, both personal and professional, with Peter Paul Rubens at various stages of his career is the subject of Julius S. Held's essay. In his assessment of documentary evidence and later legends, Held examines the reasons Van Dyck was so often perceived as a dependent follower of Rubens even after he had achieved his own preeminence as an artist.

We know from Giovanni Pietro Bellori, our most reliable seventeenth-century source about Van Dyck's Roman sojourns in 1622 and 1623, that preeminent among the young painter's patrons in Rome were cardinals Bentivoglio and Maffeo Barberini, the latter of whom would soon become Pope Urban VIII. David Freedberg has recognized another member of that powerful circle, Virginio Cesarini, as the sitter of a half-length portrait in the Hermitage. Linked by birth to the major families of Roman society and by his own interests and achievements to Galileo, among other leading figures, Cesarini made significant contributions in science, literature, and philosophy before his life was cut short by illness, whose traces Van Dyck's portrait recorded. Through his biographical account of Cesarini's life, Freedberg evokes the richness of early seventeenth-century Roman intellectual life.

Three contributions focus on Van Dyck's activity in Genoa, particularly in portraiture, and bring new archival evidence to bear. Michael Jaffé proposes the addition of two paintings to Van Dyck's Italian corpus. He also has succeeded in naming the sitters in the group portrait in the Palazzo Durazzo-Pallavicini. Such identifications are rare indeed, because of the movement of paintings within Genoa and their subsequent dispersal. Piero Boccardo explains this phenomenon, along with other aspects of collecting by members of the Genoese patriciate. His study sheds particular light on Van Dyck's relations with the two branches of the Balbi family, whom his discoveries reveal to be the painter's greatest Italian patrons. The history of Italian costume has relied heavily on datable painted portraits, because of the paucity of surviving examples. Marzia Cataldi Gallo brings many new sources to bear on this subject, including contemporary law, literature, and sermons, as well as archival evidence. Her study, which articulates the role of costume in early seventeenth-century Italian aristocratic society in general, also gives a particular feel for the daily lives and social values of Van Dyck's Genoese sitters.

Problems of attribution exist at all phases of Van Dyck's career, but particularly during the artist's second Antwerp period. The lack of documentation about workshop practice during this period makes it difficult to draw firm conclusions about paintings at the fringe of Van Dyck's accepted oeuvre. Arnout Balis, having identified a number of such paintings, demonstrates how an understanding of the broader artistic context of the period provides a framework for dealing with attribution. In one instance he identifies a grisaille panel based on a Van Dyck composition as a model for an engraving by Hendrik Snyers, which was then published by Abraham van Diepenbeeck. By knowing that Van Diepenbeeck had hired Snyers to engrave copies he had made, Balis is able to propose that Van Diepenbeeck was the artist of the work in question. In another instance, Balis has associated stylistic characteristics and individual figures in a disputed painting with those in drawings by Willem Panneels. Panneels, about whom little is known, has recently been identified as the author of the bulk of the drawings after Rubens, known as the Rubens Cantoor, that are housed in the royal print room in Copenhagen. The relationships Balis has discovered between this painting and Panneels' distinctive drawings raise the possibility that other paintings in the orbit of Rubens and Van Dyck might have been executed by this shadowy figure.

The existence of such derivative paintings speaks, to a certain extent, to the impact of Van Dyck's distinctive imagery and style on his contemporaries. Hans Vlieghe expands on this issue in his essay with his assessment of the character of Van Dyck's fame. Despite the important commissions he received and his international reputation, Vlieghe finds that Van Dyck was not as influential in Flanders during his lifetime as has sometimes been supposed. To begin with, the prices that he commanded for his altarpieces and portraits during his second Antwerp period were about average for an established painter, but certainly substantially lower than those received by Rubens. It was only after he returned to Brussels and Antwerp in 1634/1635 as a court painter that his reputation seemed to peak, a conclusion based not only on the prices he then demanded for his work, but also on an engraving by Paulus Pontius after Erasmus Quellinus that depicts Van Dyck together with Rubens, rather as joint princes of Antwerp painting.

By tracing the character of Van Dyck's influence in the compositions and painting styles of other Flemish artists, Vlieghe is able to identify different generational responses to Van Dyck's work. Older painters, such as Cornelis de Vos, Gaspar de Crayer, and Jacob van Oost the Elder, adapted compositional motifs but not Van Dyck's style. For example, even when De Crayer introduced elongated figures into his altarpieces to emulate Van Dyck's emotional type of religious imagery, he did not adapt Van Dyck's distinctive handling of paint but continued in a manner that emphasized plasticity of forms and local coloring. While Jan Boeckhorst, who was just slightly younger than Van Dyck, was able to assimilate Van Dyck's style to a remarkable degree, it was only a later generation of artists, including Thomas Willeboirts Bosschaert and Gonzales Coques, who took as their starting point Van Dyck's tender and emotional late style of painting. Whether these artists actually trained with Van Dyck is not known, in part because Van Dyck was not required to register his students when he was court painter in Brussels from about 1628 to 1630. While other artists of a later generation, including Pieter Thijs and Lucas Franchoys II, also worked in a Van Dyckian style, Vlieghe stresses that many painters remained relatively unaffected by Van Dyck's work and continued to paint within the tradition of Rubens.

One of the least known aspects of Van Dyck's career was his contact with the Dutch court in The Hague in the early 1630s. Amy Walsh proposes that Van Dyck, no less than Rubens, was understood as an important political asset by the Infanta Isabella, who may well have sent her court painter to Frederik Hendrik in 1631 to paint portraits of the prince of Orange and his family as a good-will gesture at a time when the archduchess was seeking to establish a truce with the Netherlands. Van Dyck's role as an emissary may well have been why the artist brought as gifts portraits of the archduchess and Maria de' Medici, who was living in exile in Brussels.

Walsh further examines Van Dyck's relationships with the court in the broader context of Frederik Hendrik's collection and his own dynastic ambitions. Frederik Hendrik, she argues, used his collections to create an image of a prosperous and idyllic court, dynastically related to heroes of the past whose exploits paralleled those of mythological heroes. Frederik Hendrik also collected paintings for political reasons; he hung devotional paintings in private quarters, for example, to demonstrate to Catholic visitors that he could be sympathetic to Catholic concerns. In all these respects Van Dyck's paintings were ideally suited to Frederik Hendrik's needs, and the prince of Orange continued to acquire them long after Van Dyck's departure for England and even after the artist's death.

While the court of Charles I was far more sophisticated than the one Van Dyck had witnessed in The Hague, the underlying realization that painting could serve the aspirations of the court was comparable in both places. In London, however, the court and the monarchy were glorified by poets and playwrights as well. Just how Van Dyck and his paintings were received by Caroline poets, among them Robert Herrick, Richard Lovelace, Edmund Waller, and Abraham Cowley, is the focus of Graham Parry's essay. Parry notes that while poetry traditionally had been viewed in England as an art form superior to painting, Van Dyck's elegant and animated portrait style transformed that appraisal. Not only were his portraits often cited for their high standard of achievement, but they were occasionally even celebrated for creating a sense of the individual that was unattained in poetry.

The adulatory tone created by poems, masques, and paintings for the court of Charles I had certain distinctive characteristics. Charles was generally portrayed as an active and enterprising monarch, ever watchful and in charge of events. Although Charles preferred to be represented in armor, the mood conveyed was one of effortless conquest, as though his very presence were sufficient to prevail over any opposition. Whether in poetry, the masque, or painting, the message projected was that the country was safe in Stuart hands. Paralleling such concerns were efforts to enhance the ideal of civility within English society. In this respect, as well, Van Dyck played an important role, as his works helped give visual expression to the aesthetic of grace that Caroline poets were urging on the English court.

This aesthetic is highly visible in Van Dyck's portrait of Lord George Stuart, Seigneur d'Aubigny, in the National Portrait Gallery, London, the subject of Malcolm Rogers' essay. Rogers uses this portrait as a vehicle for identifying a number of the stylistic characteristics of Van Dyck's English period: the comparatively wide range of colors, which includes blues, pinks, yellows, and greens; the more romantic treatment of dress, characterized by flowing robes that convey an effect of timelessness and nobility; the preference for the comparatively intimate format of three-quarter length portraits and friendship portraits; and, finally, the prevalence of landscape as a setting for sitters, a development associated with the English fashion for pastoral poetry and drama. Specifically, in the case of the portrait of Lord George Stuart, Rogers examines the circumstances of the sitter's life and his relationship to the court as a framework for determining the meaning of the inscription, ME FIRMIOR AMOR ("love is stronger than I am"), and the symbolic elements in the landscape.

The issue of patronage, of course, is a fundamental one throughout Van Dyck's life, particularly as the artist seems to have been so adept at responding to the wishes and aspirations of those for whom he worked. Jeremy Wood examines in depth Van Dyck's relationship with one of his most important patrons, and one of the most distinguished collectors of the day, Algernon Percy, 10th earl of Northumberland. Working in large part from extensive family inventories, which are published here for the first time, Wood examines Northumberland's specific interest in Van Dyck's work as well as the broad character of the earl's collection, which included major sixteenth-century Italian paintings, particularly those of Titian, and antique sculpture. Not only was Northumberland a major patron of Van Dyck, commissioning four family portraits from the artist, but he continued to acquire paintings by the master until the 1660s. At least eight of these latter works were portraits of females that hung together in a picture gallery, perhaps in emulation of the duke of Mantua's "Gallery of Beauties," or that assembled by Philip, Lord Wharton, at Upper Winchendon. The importance of Van Dyck's paintings to the earl can also be measured by the fact that Northumberland had copies made of them by the cura-

tor of his collection, Symon Stone, which were then given away as gifts.

One of the most complex issues to be confronted in Van Dyck scholarship concerns the Iconography. This group of portrait prints, executed by nine printmakers, was published in Van Dyck's name in 1645, some five years after the artist's death. As Joaneath Spicer explains in her essay, there is no consensus on how this "series" of prints came into being, its purpose, or even its content. Many questions exist about the relationship of these prints to Van Dyck's paintings, as well as to his drawings, and to a large group of oil studies, not all of which are generally accepted as being by the master. Spicer looks at this material in a systematic way, from the meaning of the term *pinxit*, which often appears on the prints, to the use of oil sketches as preparatory models for engravings. She has established patterns in Van Dyck's working procedure that help place the prints in a more consistent framework within Van Dyck's oeuvre. It appears that Van Dyck's concept for the project evolved as he worked on this venture, from c. 1630, when he first conceived it, until the last years of his life. While the artist almost certainly intended the series to consist of three parts: depictions of princes, men of letters, and painters and sculptors, it seems that the completed project had not yet been realized at his death. Some of the most distinguished royalty of the day, most notably Charles I, was not included in the publication of 1645. Although Van Dyck's untimely death prevented him from bringing this ambitious project to conclusion, the subsequent publications of the Iconography were instrumental in spreading Van Dyck's renown as one of the foremost painters of his day.

NOTE

1. *Anthony van Dyck*, National Gallery of Art, Washington, 11 November 1990–24 February 1991. Arthur K. Wheelock, Jr., et al., *Anthony van Dyck* [exh. cat., National Gallery of Art] (Washington, 1990).

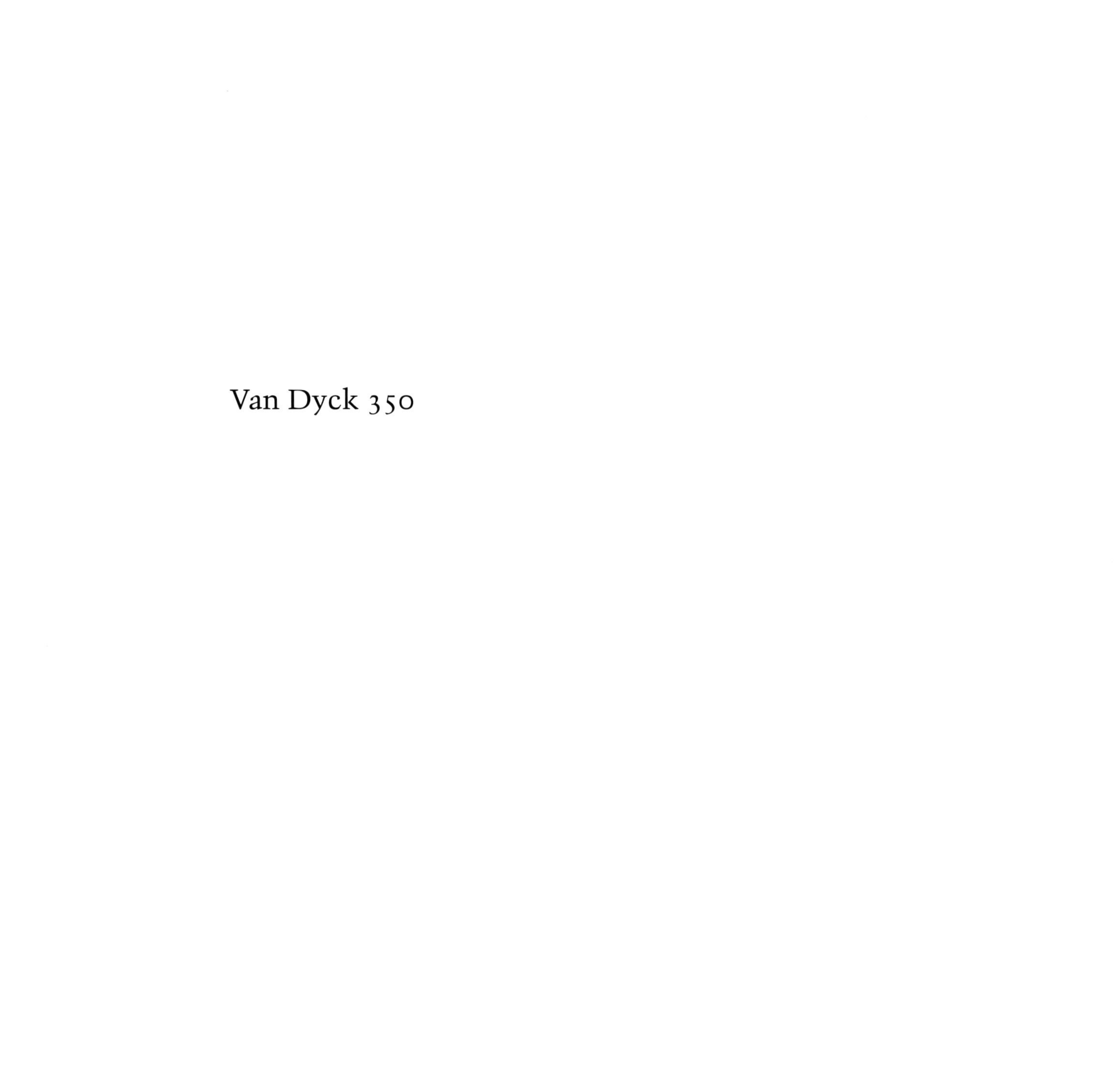

Van Dyck 350

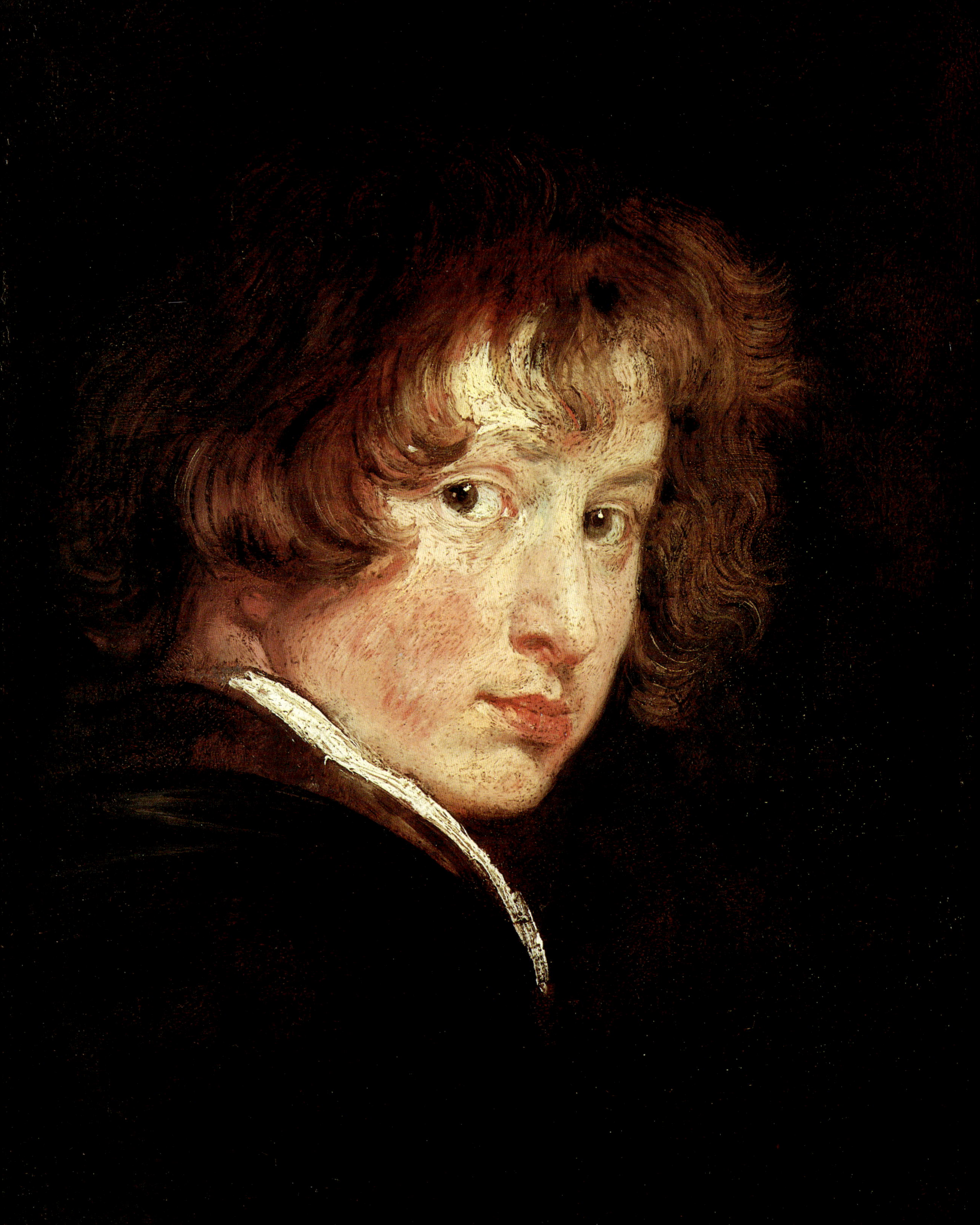

KATLIJNE VAN DER STIGHELEN
Catholic University, Louvain

Young Anthony: Archival Discoveries Relating to Van Dyck's Early Career

An inquiry into the way in which Anthony van Dyck became a painter first requires an investigation of the well-known biographical sources. The literature on Van Dyck during his first period in Antwerp is based largely on F. J. van den Branden's *Geschiedenis der Antwerpsche schilderschool*,[1] published in 1883, in which, however, only a few direct quotations from source material appear. A few years earlier, in 1868, L. Galesloot had published in the *Annales de l'Académie d'Archéologie de Belgique* a few documents[2] dealing with the famous legal case of 1660/1662, in which it was questioned whether Van Dyck himself had painted a series of thirteen paintings representing a Savior and twelve apostles (see Document 23). Since that time there has been no systematic attempt to investigate thoroughly the sources in the city archives in Antwerp that refer to Van Dyck's activities in Antwerp. An attempt was, however, made by Margaret Roland in 1984[3] to complete the documents dating from 1660/1662 and to establish a new critical text.

Thus Van den Branden's became the standard version of Van Dyck's biography and was adopted by the literature with little comment until recent times. The aim of the present article is to review and, where possible, to complete the sources summarized by Van den Branden. Relevant documents can be traced back to 1529, the year in which Van Dyck's grandfather was born, after whom Van Dyck himself was named. A number of documents yield information about the elder Anthony's activities. In 1568 he is referred to as "Anthoni Van Dyck, merchant, dealing in and earning his living with silk and small writing materials." In that year he applied to the magistrate in Antwerp to be released from lodging the troops of the duke of Alba on the basis that his house, called Hercules, had insufficient space (Document 2). Eleven years later, in 1579, his situation had, however, improved, as is apparent from the fact that he bought a hereditary lease and purchased the house called Den Berendans in the Marketplace (Grote Markt) in Antwerp.[4] It was in this house that the younger Anthony van Dyck was to be born. From the deed of sale, in which the property is described, Den Berendans appears to be a standard middle-class house, doubtless considerably more spacious than Hercules.

There exists a further document (fig. 1) relating to the profession of the elder Anthony, which has hitherto passed unnoticed. This is an application by a certain Agatha van Yselsteyn, the widow of the late Jan van Ghendrick alias Van Cleve, which was submitted to the governing authorities in Antwerp on 30 September 1563 (Document 1). In her application Van Yselsteyn requests three painters to confirm that they knew her late husband "here in the city twenty and twenty-three years previously as a professional painter and independent master in the guild of painters here." The first painter to be heard as a witness was "Anthony van Dyck,

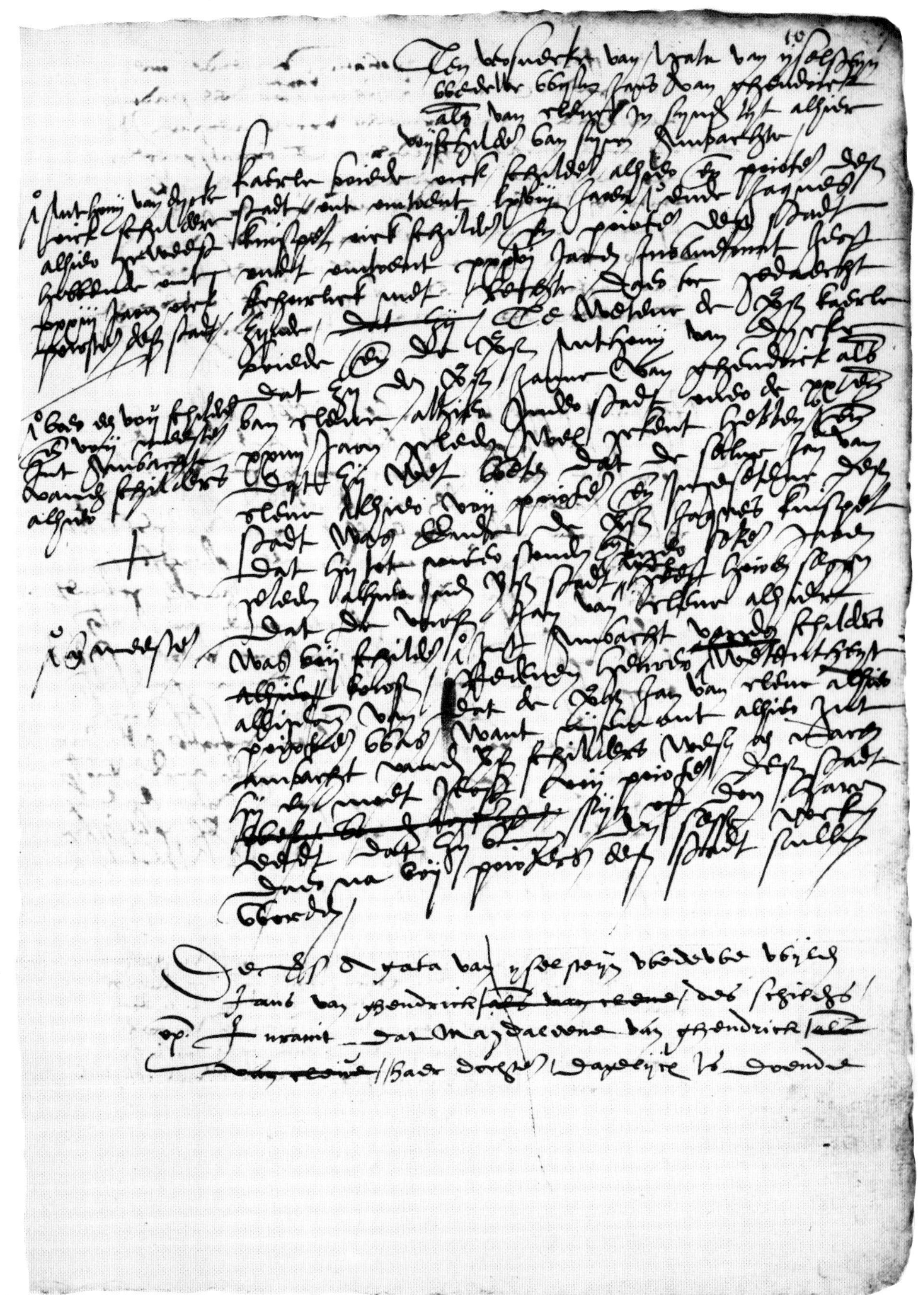

who was also an artist here."[5] Thus Anthony senior had been a painter, and was sufficiently well acquainted with the guild to serve as a witness for the membership of a colleague. Van Dyck's training as an artist is also confirmed by the *Liggeren*, or guild membership book, in which "Tuenken van Dycke, painter, taught by Jan van Cleve (painter)," is recorded under the year 1546.[6]

Thus Anthony the elder gave evidence on behalf of the widow of his former master. At the age of seventeen he was apprenticed to Van Cleve and received the master's title in 1556. Inasmuch as Van Yselsteyn's application dates from 1563, it follows that Anthony practiced as a painter for at most six or seven years. He was possibly a prolific painter at first, and why he became a merchant is not known. There is no reason to believe that he lacked talent, but we do know that his financial situation was problematic (at least in 1568; see Document 2). We may accordingly speculate that it was the unstable political and economic situation shortly before the outbreak of iconoclasm that induced him to pursue an alternative career.[7]

The fact that Van Dyck's father was the son of a master is a valuable piece of information. From an entry in the register of aldermen in Antwerp for the year 1561 one can also conclude that the elder Anthony was a nephew of Hiëronymus or Jerome van Dyck, who was registered in the *Bussenboeck*, or guild mutual insurance fund, in Antwerp in 1549.[8] Thus Van Dyck was not born into a family exclusively composed of merchants. On his father's side his forebears were well acquainted with the profession of painting, and indeed there was enough in his father's background for it to be not altogether surprising that the young Anthony would make painting his career.[9]

In 1569 Anthony the elder gave "a declaration of good character" on behalf of Pieter Pruystinck (Document 3). Here again Anthony is referred to as a merchant, but gives his evidence together with Hans Lambrechts, a painter.[10] Pruystinck was the brother of Anthony's wife Cornelia. Peter van Dyck, one of Anthony's brothers, was married to a Pruystinck, namely Cornelia's sister Elisabeth.[11] Anthony died two years after his purchase of Den Berendans, in 1579. He left three children: Frans, the father of Van Dyck;

Ferdinand; and Catharina (also referred to as Catelyn).[12] On 4 October 1587 Frans married a particularly eligible young woman named Maria Comperis, a daughter of Jan Comperis, land agent of Antwerp.[13] Maria's background was also not entirely unconnected with the artistic milieu, in that her father was a relative of Jacques Comperis, who was registered in the *Liggeren* as an apprentice of Joachim Beuckelaer in 1573.[14] (The painter Canon Comperis, who died in Antwerp in 1713 leaving a large collection of his paintings, was also a member of the same family.[15])

The year 1588 marks the start of the successful trading career of Frans (or Franchois/Franchoys) van Dyck. Together with his mother and brother-in-law Sebastiaen de Smidt[16] he set himself up as a merchant in silk, ribbon, wool, yarn, and other materials. His widowed mother, Cornelia née Pruystinck, contributed six thousand guilders, and he and de Smidt forty-eight hundred guilders each, a major investment for that period. The business flourished, and deliveries are recorded to cities as far away as Amsterdam, Paris, Cologne, and London.[17]

Frans van Dyck had to endure tragedy in his family life. Maria Comperis died in childbirth two years after the marriage, at the birth (28 July 1589) of her first son.[18] The widower remarried the following February. His second wife was Maria Cuypers or Cupers, the daughter of Dierick Cuypers and Catharina Conincx.[19] At the marriage in Antwerp cathedral the land agent Jan Comperis was a witness, which shows the continued good relations between Frans and his former in-laws.[20] Maria Cuypers bore Frans twelve children in the course of seventeen years, the seventh of whom was Van Dyck. Peter Peeters and Johanna de Meester were the witnesses at the baptism of young Anthony on 23 March 1599 (fig. 2). Nothing further is known of them.[21]

The profession of Dierick Cuypers, Maria's father, is not recorded, but the Dierick Cuypers who was apprenticed to Frans Francken the Elder in 1596 and took over the master's position in 1604 is known to have been a relative (possibly a brother) of Maria Cuypers.[22] In 1607 Frans van Dyck defended before the courts the rights of Catharina Ghijsels, "widow of the late Diericx Cuypers," who sold the house called "De dry

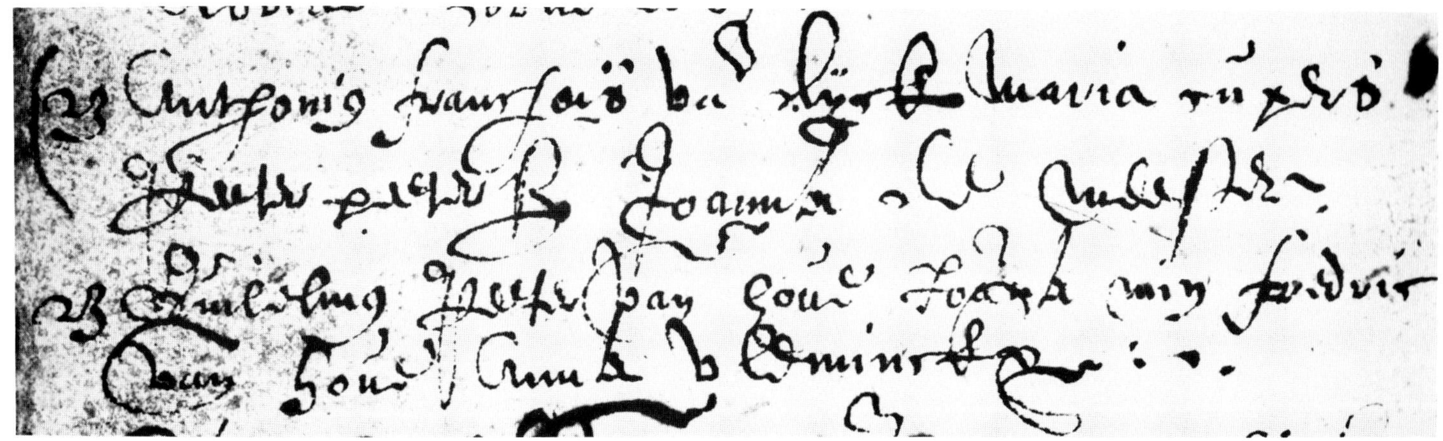

gulden bellen," situated in the "Lange Nieuwstraat" in Antwerp, to the merchant Philippus Bol. On 4 August of the same year "Jouffrouwe Catharina Conincx, widow of the late Diricx Cuypers," sold a lease to Hendrik de Moy, secretary of the city of Antwerp. These two documents make it possible to identify Dierick Cuypers as two different people, maybe even as father and son. From a chronological point of view there is also no difficulty in identifying the younger Dierick Cuypers mentioned here with Francken's apprentice.[23] Maybe Maria Cuypers, Van Dyck's mother, was also a relative of Paulina Cuypers, the wife of Jan Snellinck, as has already been suggested by Monballieu.[24] Furthermore it may be noted that Maria was a niece of Suzanna Cuypers, who married Master Jan Borrekens. When Suzanna died on 9 December 1605 it was Frans van Dyck, Van Dyck's father, who asked for an inventory of the estate of her properties and Ferdinand, Frans' brother, who served as a witness.[25]

It is worthwhile reflecting briefly on these facts because hitherto Van Dyck's artistic talent has always been associated with his mother, Maria Cuypers. The reason for this is a reference in the oldest biographies to the fact that Maria was exceptionally gifted at embroidery. It is even stated that while awaiting the birth of Anthony she embroidered a mantle-cloth with the story of the chaste Susanna.[26] The fact that Maria Cuypers had a relative who was a painter may be more relevant, however, than the fact that she was good at embroidery.[27] Embroidery was a commonplace woman's household activity in the Netherlands in the sixteenth century. It served as a mere *locus*

communis in the biography of Van Dyck, to explain the origins of his artistic talent. Van Dyck's father was a merchant and therefore by definition "unartistic;" hence the need to derive Van Dyck's artistic talent from other sources.

Thus Van Dyck was born into a family that had close associations with painting both on his father's and on his mother's side. His grandfather, whose name he shared, was a trained painter, and his mother, regardless of any talent she may have had for embroidery, had a relative who was a master painter when young Anthony was five years old. The fact that Van Dyck was apprenticed at an early age to Hendrik van Balen confirms his family's approval of his choice of career while he was still very young.

On 17 April 1607, when Van Dyck was eight years old, his mother died. The day before Maria's death the parents of young Anthony had added a codicil to their last will, dated 17 February 1595 (Document 5). A little over a month previously Van Dyck's father had bought a new house in the "Korte Nieuwstraat," which bore the name "Ghendt" or "De Stadt van Ghent" (fig. 3).[28] The house was exceptionally luxurious, with a gallery, a coach entrance, an office, a bathroom, and a garden. Even paintings are mentioned as decoration (Document 4). This home was where Van Dyck was living at the age of ten, when he was apprenticed to Hendrik van Balen, the then dean of the guild of Saint Luke. Van Balen was one of the most outstanding painters of small, decorative cabinet pictures, and the fact that five other apprentices, in addition to Van Dyck, were taken on in 1609 indicates his popularity.

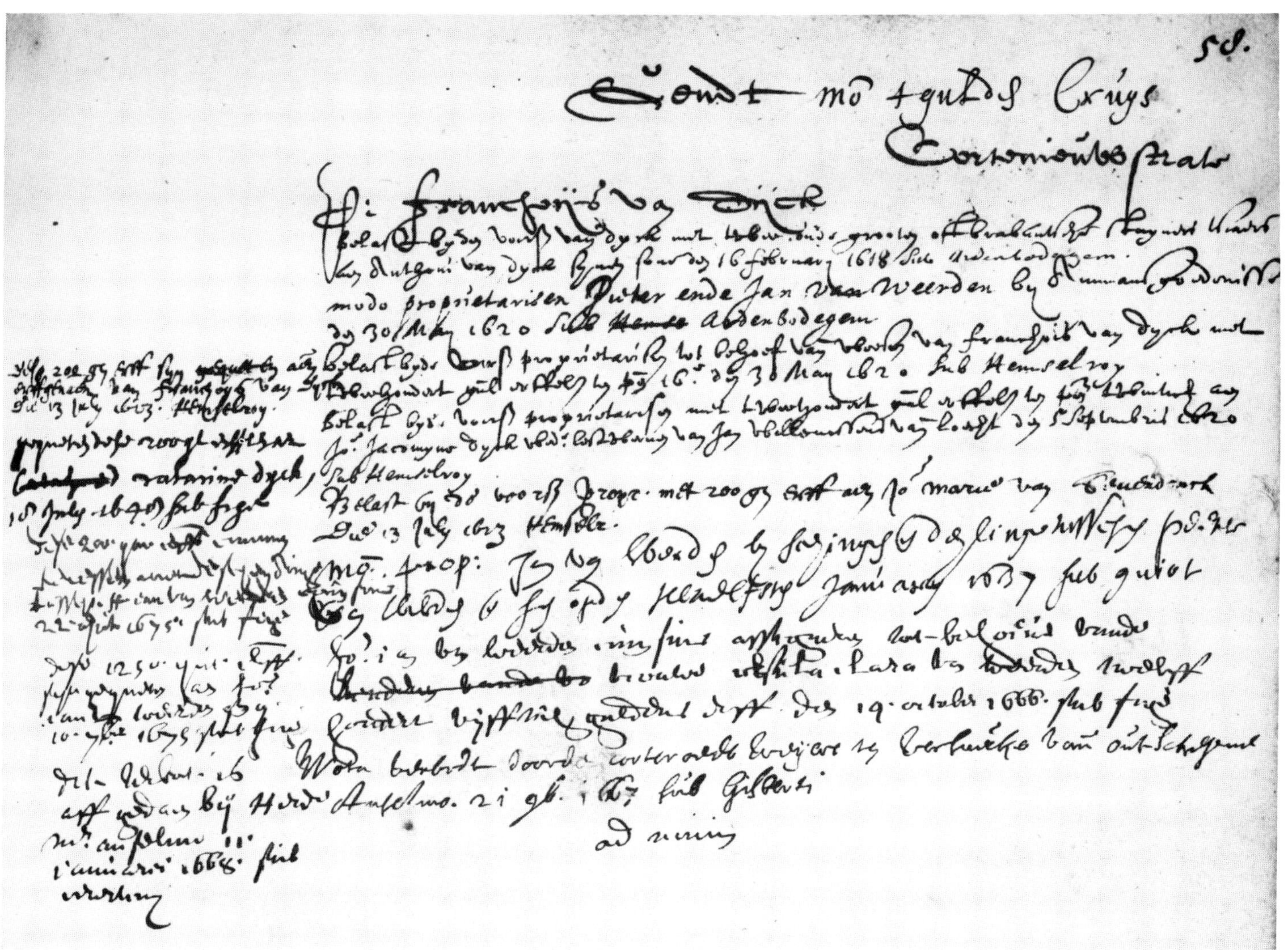

3. Excerpt from the *Wijkboeken*, in which Frans van Dyck is registered as the owner of the houses De Stadt van Ghendt and tGulden Cruys, 1607

City archives, Antwerp

Virtually nothing is known of Van Dyck's apprenticeship to Van Balen. In the eighteenth-century biography of Van Dyck in the Musée du Louvre, which was published by Larsen, it is asserted that starting in 1610 Van Dyck received lessons for two years.[29] On the basis of the usual duration of apprenticeship[30] it might, however, be assumed that he trained under Van Balen for at least three or four years. Be that as it may, it is known that Van Dyck did not remain with Van Balen until 1618, in which year he acquired his master's title. An apprenticeship of nine years to one and the same master would have been exceptionally lengthy, and there are some sources (see Documents 16, 22, 23) that indicate that this was not the case.[31]

The question may well be raised as to why Van Dyck was not apprenticed to Rubens in 1609. There is no doubt that Rubens' reputation even at this early date far exceeded that of Van Balen. Rubens had only just returned from Italy, and it is well known that he wrote to Jacques de Bie on 11 May 1611 that so many would-be apprentices had applied to him that he had had to refuse more than one hundred of them.[32] If the competition was so great, it may well be that Rubens gave preference to slightly older apprentices, who had already received preliminary training. For young Anthony the choice of Van Balen was certainly a good one. Frans van Dyck, who at this stage was still very wealthy, may well have envisaged apprenticing his son to Rubens at a later date. The interesting question is, of course, at what stage Rubens and Van Dyck first came into contact. The date at which Van Dyck did apprentice to Rubens is crucial to the question of whether Van Dyck had a workshop of his own and was active as a painter prior to acquiring his master's title in 1618. The existence of such a workshop in Van Dyck's early youth would have a major impact on the dating of his works. The end of Van Dyck's "first Antwerp period" is always taken to be his departure for Italy on 3 October 1621. The start of this period depends on the date of the establishment of his own workshop in the house called "Den Dom van Ceulen." Our knowledge of the existence of Den Dom van Ceulen is based on the evidence given by Jan Brueghel II on 5 September 1660 in the presence of the notary Van Nos (Document 22). Brueghel declared that he "knew intimately the late famous artist Van Dyck, with whom, being of approximately the same age as he, he was educated." He also confirms that he was always present at times "when the same Van Dyck had some exceptional works in hand, among which he had seen, before the aforesaid departed for Italy and was living in Den Dom van Ceulen near the convent of the Franciscans, that he had in hand the paintings of the twelve apostles and our Saviour" (fig. 4).[33] Less than a year later Brueghel testified again: "that before the aforesaid departed for Italy and was living at the time in Den Dom van Ceulen near the convent of the Franciscans, that he was engaged in painting the twelve apostles and our Saviour."[34] Brueghel does not give a precise date, but such is furnished by the declaration of the seventy-five-year-old Guilliam Verhagen, who testified on 5 September 1660 (Document 23). Verhagen states that he ordered the Apostle series forty-four or forty-five years earlier, "although he could not recall the precise date" (fig. 5).[35] This evidence makes it possible to situate the order for the series around 1615/1616, thus in the hiatus between Van Dyck's apprenticeship to Van Balen and the earliest proof of his collaboration with Rubens.

Brueghel's reference to Den Dom van Ceulen was published by Galesloot in 1868, and Van den Branden hastened to make use of it in 1883. He stated unequivocally that Van Dyck had set himself up independently in the house called Den Dom van Ceulen, and took it upon himself to fix the date as

1615, which he undoubtedly derived from Verhagen's declaration.[36] Thereafter the hypothesis of an early workshop was adopted in the literature on Van Dyck almost unquestioningly, although a number of authors referred to the fact that the date given for the start of Van Dyck's career clashed with the regulations of the guild. It was thought that Margaret Roland had found the solution in 1984.[37] Roland reinterpreted the evidence in the legal case of 1660/1662 and attempted systematically to banish "the myth of the early workshop." Her thesis can be summarized as follows:

1. The basis for the date 1615 is the evidence of the seventy-five-year-old Guilliam Verhagen, who declared in 1660 that the event had taken place forty-four or forty-five years earlier and who stated in 1661 that it had occurred forty-five or forty-six years earlier. Roland holds that the reliability of this evidence must be questioned.[38]

2. The establishment by Van Dyck of a workshop prior to his acquiring the title of "master" is unlikely.

3. Jan Brueghel's evidence is of questionable value. He states merely that he saw Van Dyck at work in Den Dom van Ceulen prior to his departure for Italy. It could be that he had seen him just before his departure on 3 October 1621. Why else did Brueghel not say, for example, that he saw Van Dyck in Den Dom van Ceulen just before Van Dyck departed for England?

4. It was only in March 1621, when Van Dyck returned from England, that he was too experienced to remain a "pupil" of Rubens, but this was not yet the case in 1620, as appears from a letter of July of that year to the earl of Arundel, in which it is stated that Van Dyck nearly always lived in the house of Rubens.[39] Only in 1621, Roland argues, did Van Dyck set up his own workshop in Den Dom van Ceulen.

Thus Roland's conclusion is that Van Dyck's workshop called Den Dom van Ceulen undoubtedly existed, but at a much later stage in his career than had hitherto been believed. The workshop existed for no more than seven months, namely from Van Dyck's return from England in March 1621 until his departure for Italy on 3 October that same year. Although the reasoning behind this argument is well thought out, its con-

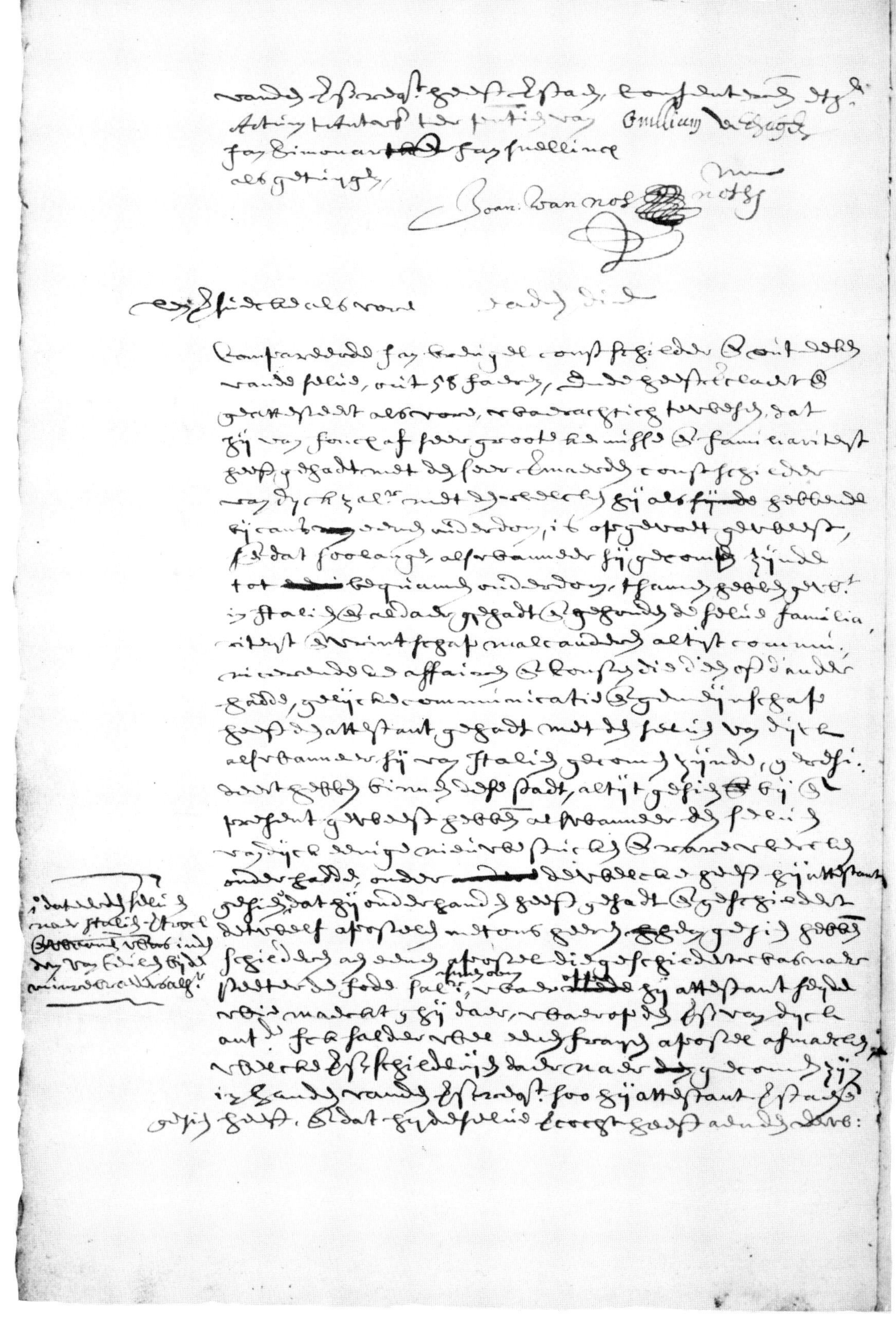

4. Jan Brueghel II testifies
that he knew intimately the
late, famous artist Anthony
van Dyck, who was living in
Den Dom van Ceulen before
he departed for Italy,
5 September 1660
City archives, Antwerp

clusion cannot be correct. The only genuine solution to this problem lies not in reinterpreting the legal documents, but in uncovering sources that offer a new slant on the question. To that end it is worthwhile examining the documentation relating to Den Dom van Ceulen. If Van Dyck ever worked in this house near the convent of the Franciscans, one would expect to find record of his name at some point during the period 1612 to 1621. In the city archives of Antwerp are preserved the so-called *Wijkboeken,* or district books, in which the ownership of each piece of property, rights relating to the property, and mortgages on the property are accurately entered. Curiously enough, no owner by the name of Van Dyck is to be found in the seventeenth century. Thus the house was never owned by the Van Dyck family. If Van Dyck used the house, he rented it, or his father did so for him. From an alderman's deed of 1670 it is known that the house called Den Dom van Ceulen was situated in the street that ran from the "Clapdorp" to the Franciscan convent, and that it had a rear exit into the "Achterstraat." There were several downstairs rooms, a large sitting room, a garden, and a courtyard onto which the house called "De Borsse" also faced.[40] This means that the house was large, with a high rental value.

At what stage would Van Dyck have been able to pay such high rent? His father could have done so only for a short time: contrary to what has been presumed,[41] Frans was in financial difficulty from 1615 on. We know rather well what happened to him and his family during the years 1615–1620, because no fewer than thirteen legal documents relating to the family (Documents 7, 8, 9, 10, 11, 12, 13, 14, 15, 18, 19, 20, 21) have been preserved. From these we learn that during the summer of 1615 Frans had to endure a "disgracie" (see Documents 8, 11), a term of which the exact implications are unknown. Nevertheless, from this time it becomes apparent that he found himself in continual financial difficulties. His two sons-in-law, the notary Adriaen Diericx and the merchant Lancelot Lancelots, tried to save the situation for the children of Frans and the late Maria Cuypers, who were not yet of age. As heirs, Diericx and Lancelots also acted on their own behalf. Fearing the debtors of their

father-in-law, they attempted to protect the inheritance of the late Catharina Conincx and her daughter Maria Cuypers, which altogether amounted to more than sixty-six hundred Flemish pounds, or forty thousand guilders. In July 1615 it looked as if the children "would not be able to recuperate" the inherited goods, and this fact led both sons-in-law to apply to the authorities in Antwerp for permission to sell immediately "nine of the best paintings left by the children's

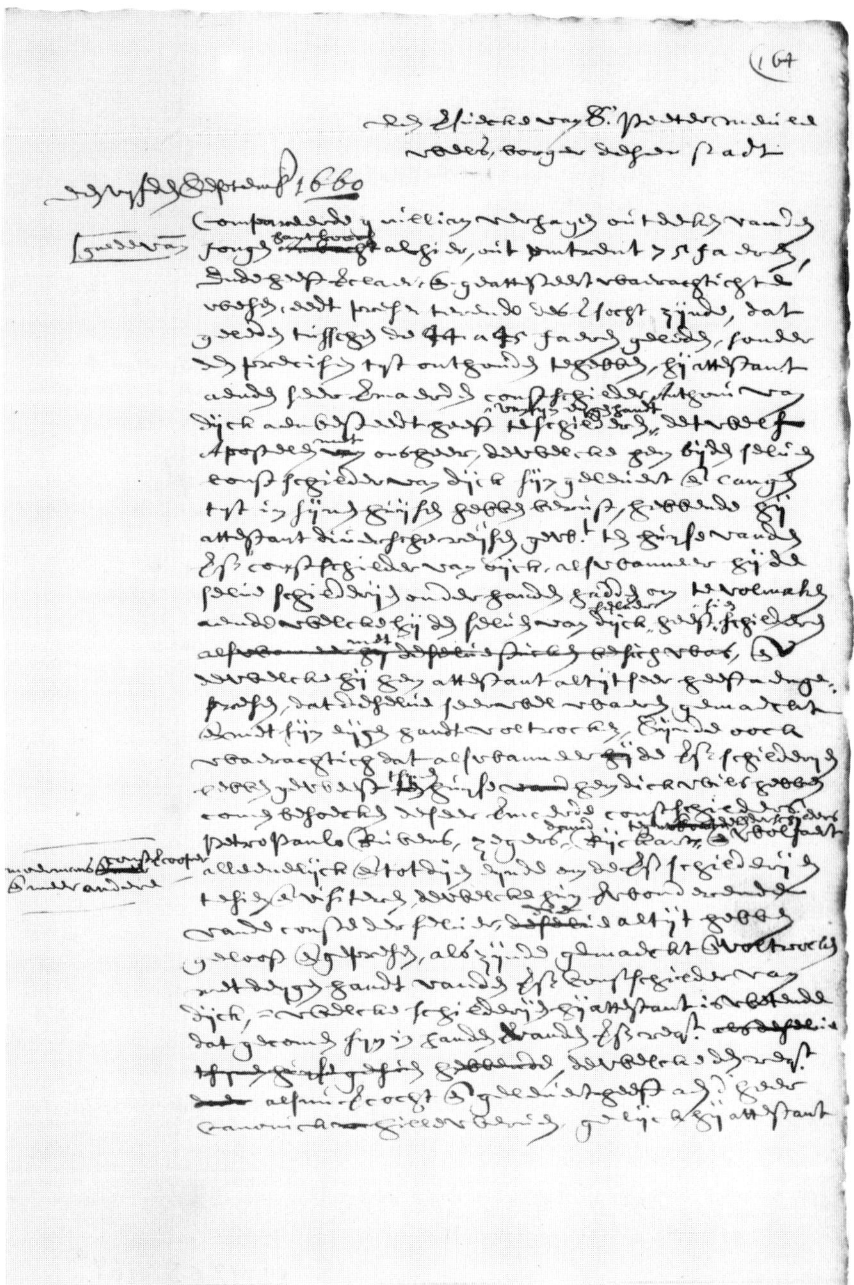

5. Declaration of Guilliam Verhagen that he ordered the Apostle series forty-four or forty-five years earlier, 5 September 1660
City archives, Antwerp

grandmother" (Document 8). This detail is interesting because it shows that Catharina Conincx, Van Dyck's grandmother, apparently had a considerable collection of paintings that was kept in Frans' house. (We learn from a document of 6 June 1615 [Document 7] that Catharina Conincx "lived and died in the same house," that is, De Stadt van Ghendt.)

Anthony van Dyck was of the opinion that his brothers-in-law were intervening excessively in his family's affairs, and for this reason he brought an action against Diericx and Lancelots on 3 December 1616. The document (Document 10) shows that it was not Diericx and Lancelots, but Franchois de Smet and Jacques Knidde who had been appointed executors for those children of Frans who were not of age. In the same document Van Dyck demands that Diericx and Lancelots give an account of their actions in the presence of a commissary, and produce their accounts relevant to the inheritance. Van Dyck also petitioned to be personally present to be able to draw his own conclusions. The accused responded on 8 July 1617 (Document 11) and declared that they had acted entirely in good faith. Reference is again made to the "disgracie" of Frans. Diericx and Lancelots admit that they attempted to recuperate the inheritance of the mother and the grandmother from the public sale of Frans' goods at the Friday market. We also learn that the brothers-in-law on this occasion bought a harpsichord for the children not yet of age ("bought on behalf of the orphans [*sic*] in question a certain beautiful double harpsichord made by Master Ruckers for the sum of one hundred guilders"), and that Diericx purchased "in his own name a certain piece of wall decoration that had also come from and had been in the domicile of the aforesaid Van Dyck." Both of these objects were kept for Franchois van Dyck, Van Dyck's elder brother, free of charge "for starting up the hostelry called De Goublomme." However, as it turned out, Franchois had also gotten into financial difficulties, and creditors had seized all of his household effects including the harpsichord and the "behanxel."

The eighteen-year-old Van Dyck was not yet convinced of the good intentions of his two brothers-in-law, and again brought an action against them in September 1617, this time mainly in order to protect the rights of his younger brothers and sisters, who risked losing all their possessions. Van Dyck requested legal advice, which was granted to him, with the consent of the mayor and the councillors, in the person of the lawyer Bril (Document 12; fig. 6). During the month of February 1618 Van Dyck received the title of master in the guild of Saint Luke in Antwerp, and was declared to be of full age by the law courts on the recommendation of his father. A day later Frans' administrator, Cornelis de Brouwer, awarded Van Dyck an income of a mere two "old big styvers (or styvers from Brabant)," secured on his house, "de stadt van Gendt," in the "Corte Nieuwstrate."[42] On 6 March 1620 Lancelots, a trader by profession, applied to the court for permission to sell the estate of his wife, Maria van Dyck (Van Dyck's sister), and thus claim her inheritance. Maria died intestate (Document 14). In May of that year it appears that the heirs had at last received the 6,620 Flemish pounds they had inherited from their grandmother and mother. The house called De Stadt van Ghendt, which was still Frans' property, having been put up for sale at the Friday market on four consecutive Fridays, was sold to the merchants Jan and Pieter van Weerden, and we must conclude that this sale made the payment of the inheritances possible (Document 15).

Further history of the Van Dyck family's possessions yields insights into the relationships between family members and provides us with information about the day-to-day life of Van Dyck at the start of his career. A document has been preserved from the year 1622, from which it appears that Frans transferred a claim for a debt worth somewhat more than 169 Flemish pounds to his son Franchois (Document 17). Even after Frans' death in December 1622 the court cases brought by the brothers-in-law Diericx and Lancelots did not come to an end. In a document dated 4 December 1623 dealing with the payment of an inherited income from the house called "het Casteel van Ryssel" (Document 18) there is a reference to a painting belonging to the Van Dyck children, but which Cornelis van Wyck thought he could claim. Neither the name of the painter nor the title of the work are mentioned, but it is stated that the painting was "worked on for six years." It is open to question as to whether this may have been a work by the young Anthony van Dyck. Further complaint was made regarding the independent action of the brothers-in-law. According to Cornelis van Wyck they did not have sufficient mandates "particularly in regard to one of the aforementioned children of full years, who was in Italy." In other words, the guardians of the children acted almost certainly without the knowledge of Anthony van Dyck, who at the time was living in Italy. In a lawsuit dated 12 January 1624 Van Dyck's name was also mentioned. On this occasion the brothers-in-law together with Franchois van Dyck and Cornelia van Dyck, a Beguine in Antwerp, protested against the fact that Daniel Lebrun, who was empowered to act for the widow of the late David Moreau, had not acted as agreed by private treaty to make use of the proceeds of a quarter of a debt of 5,000 guilders in favor of the late Frans, which had been collected jointly a year and a half previously (Documents 19, 20). In 1625 the members of the family also had to pay off debts to one another. Franchois van Dyck, who had recovered financially to some extent since the contents of his inn were seized at the beginning of 1617, was able to pay off a debt of 128 guilders on 4 December to his brother-in-law Adriaen Diericx with the aid of a mortgage (Document 21).

On the basis of information derived from the above mentioned documents we can conclude that Van Dyck must have paid the rent on Den Dom van Ceulen himself, if he lived there after about 1615. The question is whether he still needed a workshop and a house from February 1618 on, when he became a master, given his close association with Rubens. Such close cooperation between Rubens and Van Dyck does not necessarily imply that the two artists shared the same house on the "Wapper." It is striking that Rubens' name is nowhere mentioned explicitly in the entire court case of 1660/1662 (except in the passage referring to the valuation of the Apostle series in Verhagen's house).[43] This omission would seem to indicate that there was no direct connection between Van Dyck and Rubens at the time the series was painted.

Up to this point the facts do not contradict Van den Branden's assertion of the existence of an early workshop, but no proof has been adduced either. Attention may be drawn to the fact that Herman Scrvaes, who was one of the witnesses in the lawsuit of 1660/1662, situated Van Dyck's early workshop "during the Twelve Years' Truce."[44] The Truce is known to have ended at the latest in April 1621.[45] Thus there is no explanation for the fact that Servaes did not mention Van Dyck's activities after the end of the "Twelve Years' Truce" if, as proposed by Roland,[46] Van Dyck worked in Den Dom van Ceulen only between March and October 1621. In addi-

6a, b. Anthony van Dyck brings action against Adriaen Diericx and Lancelot Lancelots to protect the rights of his younger brothers and sisters, 13 September 1617
City archives, Antwerp

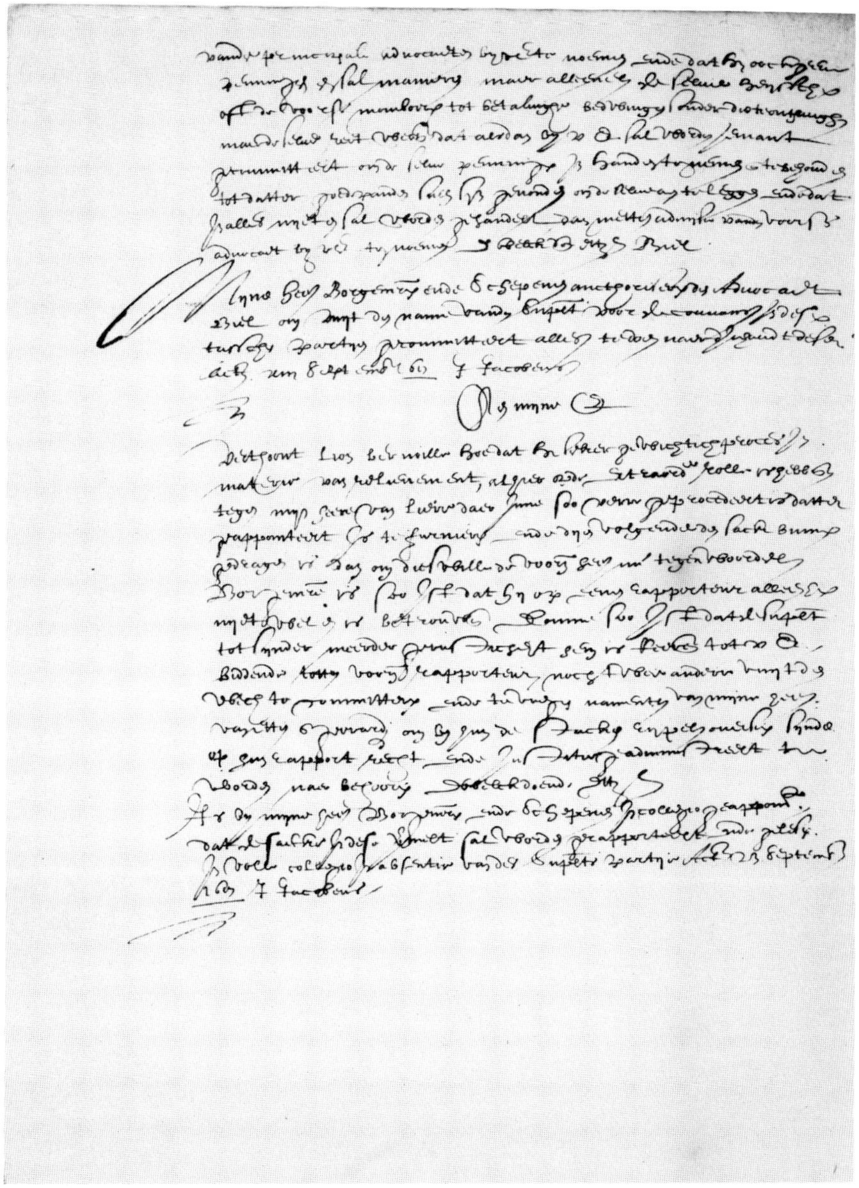

tion, there exists proof that Roland's chronology is incorrect.

In the city archives in Antwerp is preserved a seventeenth-century diary of the Dominican nuns. In this diary the subprioress Sara Derkennis relates in detail how she and several other nuns traveled from Temse to Antwerp, arriving on 19 April 1621 (Document 16). Their first task on arrival was to search for a suitable place to live. Derkennis' account is as follows:

Now to return to the time when the confessor had collected the luggage of the nuns, we rented a house the next day at the request of the prioress, as she too had left with the confessor, which house was located close to the convent of the Franciscans and was called Den Dom van Ceulen, for four hundred and twenty guilders a year, because we had brought with us from our convent some pupils, and we were going to occupy ourselves by setting up school to earn our living and to pay this enormous rent. And at the end of May we moved into the house we had rented and immediately had a wooden altar made in a large room.

This document is particularly interesting because it informs us of two hitherto unknown facts. The subprioress relates first that on 20 April 1621, the day after their arrival in Antwerp, the nuns rented the house called Den Dom van Ceulen and moved in toward the end of May 1621. In other words, Van Dyck left Den Dom van Ceulen at the latest at the end of May 1621 and doubtless somewhat earlier, given that the house was let to the nuns in April. The nuns were familiar with the name of the painter Van Dyck, as is evident from a passage in the diary relating to Van Dyck's crucifixion (Koninklijk Museum voor Schone Kunsten, Antwerp), which was given by Van Dyck to the nuns in memory of his father.[47] The anecdotal character of the diary makes it possible to assert that the painter cannot have lived in the same house as the nuns after May 1621. Sara Derkennis would not have neglected to mention the interesting detail that the nuns did not have to pay all of the rent and that there was a painter occupying part of the house.

The diary of the subprioress also informs us that Den Dom van Ceulen was let at a particularly high rent, which is not surprising, given the spaciousness of the accommodation. Derkennis herself refers to "this enormous rent," and 420 guilders a year was indeed a very considerable sum. The average rental value of the houses of painters in Antwerp throughout the seventeenth century was only 150 guilders a year. The only painter apart from Rubens who lived in a house with a rental value of 450 guilders a year was Jacob Jordaens.[48] The fact that no biographer referred to Den Dom van Ceulen as Van Dyck's splendid residence seems to confirm that he worked there at a time when his professional reputation had not yet been fully established.

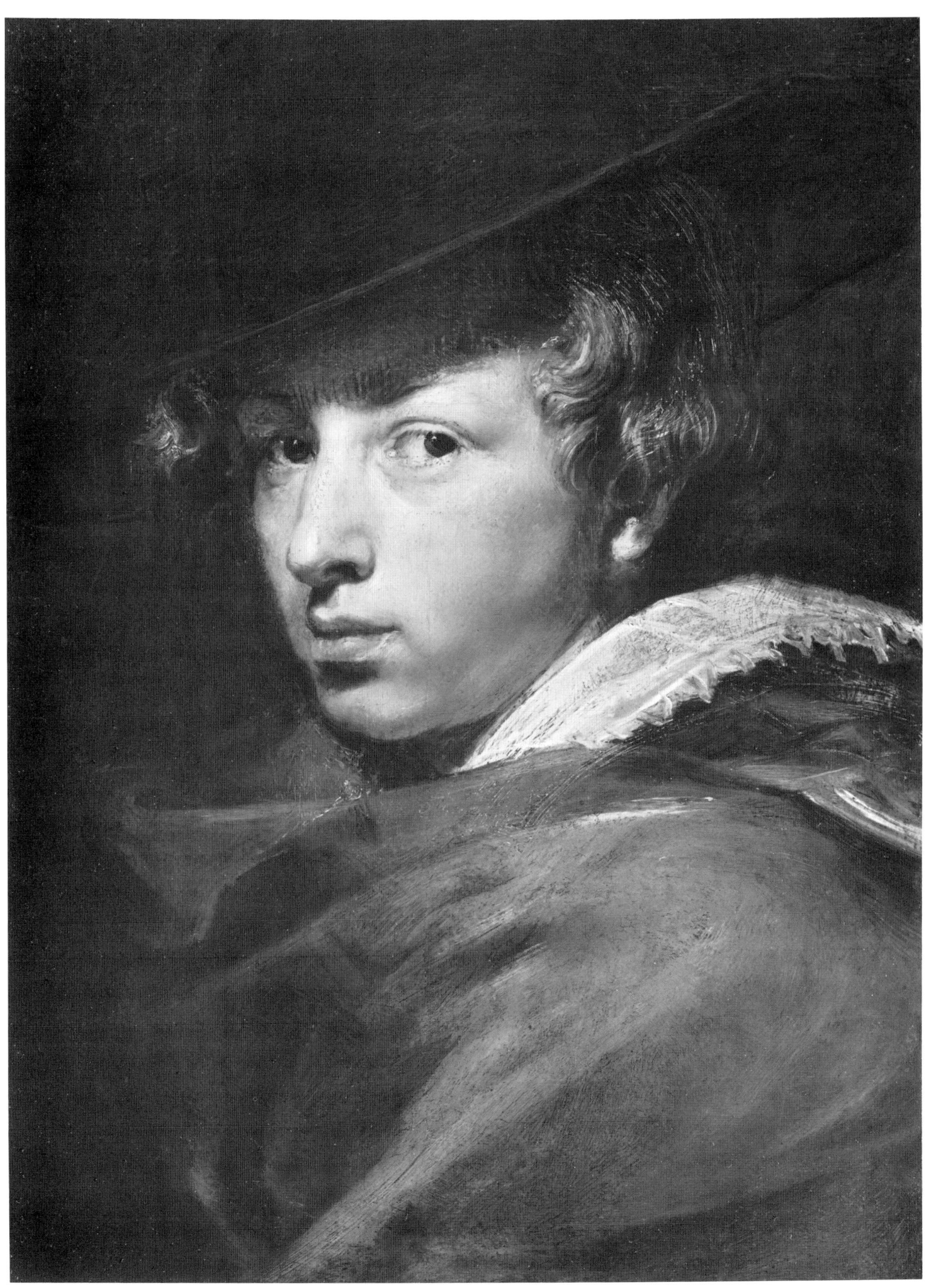

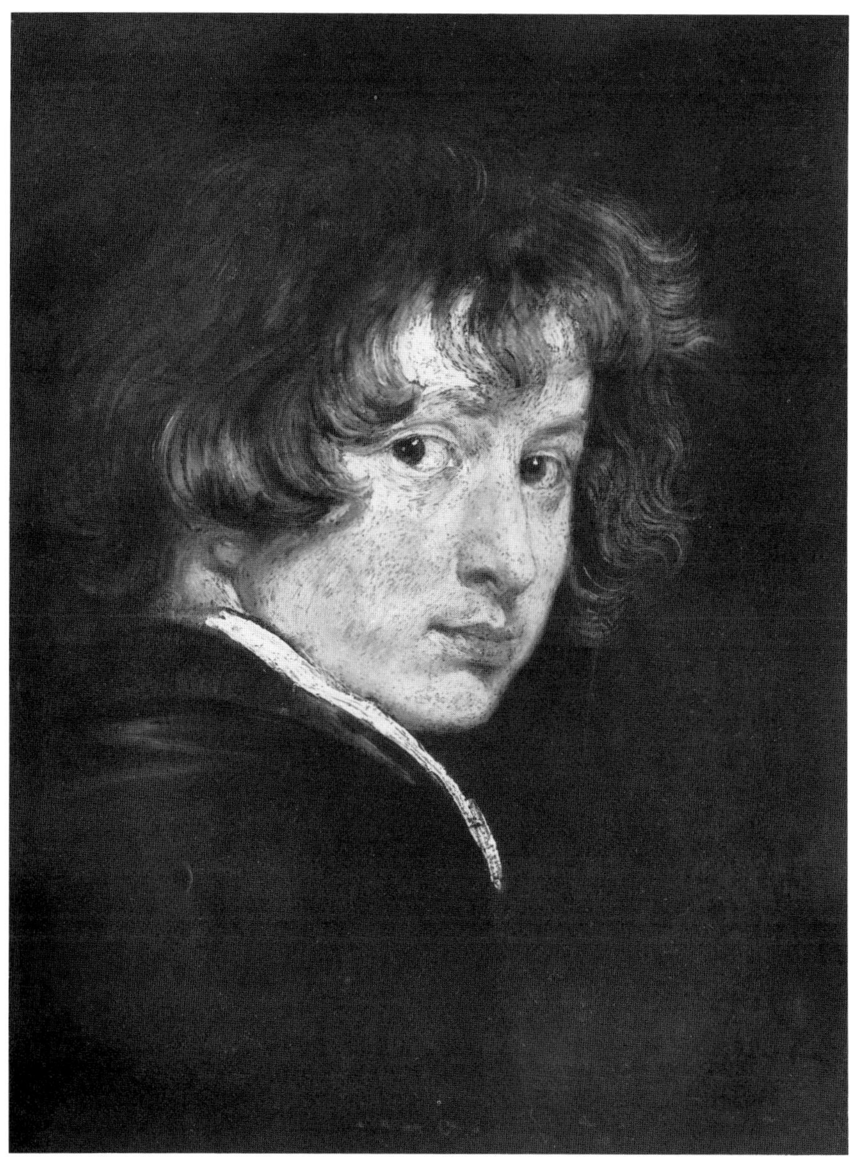

7. Peter Paul Rubens, *Anthony van Dyck as a Youth*, c. 1615, oil on canvas
Kimbell Art Museum, Fort Worth

8. Anthony van Dyck, *Self-Portrait*, c. 1615, oil on canvas
Gemäldegalerie der Akademie der bildenden Künste, Vienna

and could even have received orders such as the Apostle series from Verhagen at a time when he had not yet received his master's title. The only possible solution seems to be that Van Dyck was already under the direct protection of Rubens, who as artist to the court held a position of exceptional influence and could possibly obtain special favors for a few protégés.[49] The earliest written proofs of contacts between Rubens and Van Dyck date from about 1618. For the period prior to this there exist two indications of a relationship. The foremost of these is the portrait of Van Dyck as a youth by Rubens (fig. 7).[50] Rubens is generally considered to be the painter, and the identity of the subject is equally beyond doubt. If we compare the Rubens portrait, for instance, with Van Dyck's *Self-Portrait* in the Akademie der bildenden Künste, Vienna (fig. 8), we can assume that Van Dyck was not older than about fifteen or sixteen when Rubens did his portrait. Thus Rubens' portrait antedates Van Dyck's title of master, which he acquired in February 1618. It is also apparent that Rubens had professional esteem for Van Dyck at that stage, given that Van Dyck was taken on for the Rosary cycle in the church of Saint Paul in Antwerp, which was carried out under the supervision of Rubens. Recent research has shown that the series must date from approximately 1617 (the tender certainly dates from before 1618). The invoices that have been preserved show in turn that Van Dyck—although not yet a master—received for his painting belonging to the series a sum that was as high as that received by Rubens and Jordaens, namely 150 guilders.[51] That this was possible is illustrated by a recent article by Ronald de Jager on apprentices' contracts, which contains a number of facts relating to work that apprentices were entitled to carry out in Holland during the first half of the seventeenth century.[52] There seems little reason to suppose that this situation was different in Flanders.

Thus, in conclusion, it is quite possible that Van Dyck had already established a workshop in Den Dom van Ceulen before receiving his master's title in 1618, and that his artistic production there may have been sufficient for him to support himself from about 1615 or 1616 onward. Guild regulations provide an interpretation of the norm,

The inquiry into the history of Den Dom van Ceulen provides a *terminus ante quem* for Van Dyck's work in his early atelier. This date refutes Roland's hypothesis, since there would have been no more than two or three months (from March to May 1621) during which Van Dyck could have established an independent workshop at this address. The workshop must accordingly have existed prior to Van Dyck's journey to England. The question remains as to whether Verhagen's evidence for the existence of Van Dyck's atelier at Den Dom van Ceulen in 1615 or 1616 can be accepted without reservation.

The greatest problem is to determine how Van Dyck could have been active as a painter

but they do not reflect actual working practices; they can thus be taken only as a starting point for research; reality was, and still is, considerably more sophisticated.

NOTES

I would like to thank H. Vlieghe, Rubenianum, Antwerp, and Catholic University, Louvain; J. S. Held, professor emeritus, Columbia University, New York; and G. Degueldre of the city archives, Antwerp, for their useful comments and references. It is my pleasure to thank Mark Nelissen for his kind help with the transcriptions of the documents, and J. A. J. Dudley for translating the present text from the Dutch.

1. Frans Joseph van den Branden, *Geschiedenis der Antwerpsche schilderschool,* 3 vols. (Antwerp, 1883), 2:210–264.

2. L. Galesloot, "Un Procès pour une vente de tableaux attribués à Antoine van Dyck, 1660–1662," in *Annales de l'Académie d'Archéologie de Belgique* 24 (1868), 561–606.

3. Margaret Roland, "Van Dyck's Early Workshop, the Apostle Series, and the Drunken Silenus," in *Art Bulletin* 66 (June 1984), 211–223.

4. City archives, Antwerp (hereafter SAA), SR 358, fol. 50r. (30 December 1579): Anthony van Dyck bought the house from the merchant Henrick Bertels; it was situated in front of the new city hall ("gestaen ende gelegen opte Yserbrugghe alhier aent nyew stadthuys. . .)."

5. I would like to thank G. Degueldre for drawing my attention to this document. It is my pleasure to thank J. Van Roey and G. Degueldre for permission to publish it.

6. Philip Rombouts and Theodoor van Lerius, *De "liggeren" en andere historische archieven der Antwerpsche Sint-Lucasgilde,* 2 vols. (Antwerp, 1864–1876), 1:157, 198.

7. See Zirka Zaremba Filipczak, *Picturing Art in Antwerp, 1550–1750* (Princeton, 1987), 41–42.

8. SAA, SR 313, fol. 218r., v. The legacy of the late Peter van Dycke, son of Lambrecht and Katelijne van Haecht, had to be divided among his heirs. The children of Hiëronymus—Roberecht, Barbara, Katelijne, and Marie—received together a little more than thirty-seven guilders. Anthony van Dyck the elder, Peter, and Anna van Dyck together came into a fortune of more than 742 guilders. See also Archief der Academie, Antwerp, Bussenboek, fol. 12r.: "Geroen van Dijcke;" in the index his name is written as "Jheroen van Dijcke."

9. See Christopher Brown, *Van Dyck* (Oxford, 1982), 9.

10. Hans Lambrechts was a pupil of Pieter Elisaert (Lisaert) in 1551 and accepted a pupil himself in 1572. See Rombouts and Van Lerius 1872, 1:178, 249, 305.

11. See SAA, SR 360, fol. 70r.

12. See Van den Branden 1883, 2:211. When "Catelyn van Dyck" in January 1579 married Sebastiaen de Smidt (SAA, PR 193, Onze-Lieve-Vrouw [Zuid]), her brother Anthony served as a witness.

13. SAA, PR 193, fol. 875. Frans' brother-in-law Sebastiaen de Smidt served as a witness, and the father of the bride, Jan Comperis, assisted his daughter on this occasion.

14. That they were relatives becomes evident in reading the inventory of the household of the merchant Jehan Comperis, a son of Jan the elder, in which Jacques Comperis is mentioned as "oudoom," a brother of Jehan's grandmother. See SAA, N. 1188 (September 1607).

15. François Donnet, "Un Artiste ecclésiastique: le chanoine Comperis," *Annales de l'Académie Royale d'Archéologie de Belgique* 66 (1914), 185–208; François Donnet, "Une Oeuvre artistique du chanoine Comperis," *Bulletin de l'Académie Royale d'Archéologie de Belgique* (1918), 46–58.

16. See note 12.

17. Van den Branden 1883, 2:211.

18. Van den Branden 1883, 2:212.

19. Van den Branden 1883, 2:212. On 24 December 1616 Adriaen Diericx and Lancelot Lancelots had a claim on Georgio de Wandeler, a merchant living in Milan. This man had to liquidate a debt owed to Catharina Conincx (dating from October 1611), grandmother of Anthony the younger. In this document Catharina Conincx is mentioned as the widow of Theodoro Cuypers and as the mother of Maria Cuypers "estata figlia unica." We know that Dierick Cuypers died before 1607. See SAA, N. 2405, fol. 287 r., v.

20. SAA, PR 195, Onze-Lieve-Vrouw [Zuid], fol. 952 (6 February 1590), with "Jan Comperis Rentmeester deser stadt" and "Meester Jan Boekens" as witnesses.

21. SAA, PR 11, Onze-Lieve-Vrouw, fol. 147.

22. If we believe what is stated in the document cited in note 19, it seems impossible that Maria was a sister of Dierick or Theodoricus Cuypers. However, the document probably only refers to the situation in

1611 or 1616, at which time both persons called Dierick Cuypers were already dead (see note 23).

23. See SAA, SR 467, fol. 146r.; SAA, SR 468, fol. 349 r., v.

24. Adolf Monballieu, "Aantekeningen bij de schilderijeninventaris van het sterfhuis van Jan Snellinck (1549–1638)," *Jaarboek van het Koninklijk Museum voor Schone Kunsten* (1989), 245–268. Maybe it was not mere coincidence that it was Van Dyck who was asked to paint an epitaph for Jan Snellinck and Paulina Cuypers in 1638; see Rombouts and Van Lerius 1864–1876, 1:265. Above the tomb of Andries Snellinck, one of the sons of Jan, in the "Sint-Joriskerk" in Antwerp, there was also installed a portrait of Jan Snellinck painted by Van Dyck. See Katlijne Van der Stighelen, "De (atelier-) bedrijvigheid van Andries Snellinck (1587–1653) en co," *Jaarboek van het Koninklijk Museum voor Schone Kunsten* (1989), 315.

25. Erik Duverger, *Antwerpse kunstinventarissen uit de zeventiende eeuw. 1, 1600–1617, Fontes Historiae Artis Neerlandicae* (Brussels, 1984), 1:120–121.

26. Cornelis de Bic, *Het gulden cabinet vande edel vry schilder const* (Antwerp, 1661), 78, writes:

Sijn Moeder was begaeft met groote wetentheyt, In 't steken mette naeld ghelijck de Faem ons seyt. Sy wist door teeckeningh te stellen heel figuren, En dan met soet coleur der sijden te borduren, Ghelijck sy met vermaeck heeft meesten -deel gedaen, Besonder als sy van, Van Dyck heeft groot gegaen. Soo heeft sy mette naeld' seer aerdich net gesteken, Een schoucleet wonder fray, en vol van cloecke treken, Seer wel gecoloriert en wonder wel ghestelt Dat de Histori van de schoon Susan af belt.

On the basis of this anecdote Van den Branden 1883, 213, refers to Van Dyck's "artistic mother, to whom he owed his talents" ("zijne kunstlievende moeder, door wie hem zijne begaafdheden ingeboren waren").

27. See Christiaan Mees, " 'En seggen wat Van Dyck was voor een edel-man,' Een kritische bijdrage tot de studie van de zeventiende-eeuwse biografieën van Anton Van Dyck," onuitg. licentiaatsverhandeling Catholic University, Louvain (Louvain, 1989), 4–5. G. P. Bellori, *Le vite de'pittori, scultori et architetti moderni* (Rome, 1672), 254: "Qonqueste occasione (la madre s'impiega nel ricamo) Antonio nell' età sua tenera si pose da ses stesso a designare, e la madre, che non era oggimai piu bastante ad ammaestrarlo." In 1609, two years after the death of Van Dyck's mother, a certain Servaes Cuypers, of whom nothing is known, was accepted as an embroiderer in the guild of Saint Luke, Antwerp (Rombouts and Van Lerius 1864–1876, 1:453). About embroidery as a typical seventeenth-century household activity see Katlijne Van der Stighelen, *Anna Maria van Schurman of 'hoe hooge dat een maeght kan in de konsten stijgen,* Symbolae Litterarum et Philosophiae Lovaniensis, series B.4 (Louvain, 1987), 23. Van Schurmans, in her *Dissertatio de ingenii muliebris ad docrinam, et meliores litteras aptitudine* (Leyden, 1641), mentions that it was generally accepted for women to be busy with embroidery.

28. Van den Branden 1883, 2:213. With reference to the houses Van Dyck's parents purchased just before Maria's death see Amand de Lattin, *Evoluties van het Antwerpsche stadsbeeld* (Antwerp, 1943), 3:120–122; see also SAA, Pk 2284, fol. 58r., in which Frans is mentioned as the owner of the house "Gendt met tgulden Cruys, Cortenieuwstrate." At the top of the document is written:

Proprietatris: Franchoijs van Dijck. Belast by den voorseyden Van Dyck met twee oude grooten oft brabantsche stuyvers tsiaers aen Anthoni van Dijck synen sone den 16 februarij 1618 sub Ardenbodegem. Modo proprietarissen Pieter ende Jan van Weerden by ammans goedenisse den 30 May 1620 sub Ardenbodegem. Belast byde voorseyde proprietarissen tot behoef vande weesen van Franchois van Dyck met tweehondert gulden erffelyck ten penninghe 16e den 30 May 1620. Sub Hemselroy. Belast byde voorseyde proprietarissen met tweehondert gulden erffelyck ten penninghe twintich aen Jouffrouwe Jacomyne Dyck weduwe lestwerven van Jan Willemsens vanden Loecht(?) den 5 septembris 1620. Sub Hemselroy.

29. Rombouts and Van Lerius 1864–1876, 1:457, also 456, 506, 524, 531, 565, 618, 645, 646, 661. In 1609 Van Balen received, besides Van Dyck, Heynrick Ingelants, Gilliam Neeffs, Fernande Schuermans, Francoys Denteer, and Johannes Driescheren. One of the pupils was accepted as a master during the same year, and only one other pupil received the master's title before 1618, the year in which Van Dyck became a master. From the *Liggeren* we know that Van Balen did not accept any more new pupils before the year 1614, when he welcomed Hercules Vauseur to his workshop. In 1616/1617 he received two more pupils (Melchior Wouters and J. B. Goyvarts). We may assume that the group of pupils who started to study with Van Balen in 1609 had to be replaced. This argument can be used to presume that Van Dyck left Van Balen's atelier at the latest around 1616, and maybe even earlier. See also Eric Larsen, *La Vie, les ouvrages et les élèves de Van Dyck. Manuscrit inédit des archives du Louvre par un auteur anonyme. Académie Royale de Belgique; Mémoires de la Classe des Beaux-Arts,* 2d ser., vol. 14, 2 (Brussels, 1975), 47: "il [Frans van Dyck] le plaça en 1610 chez Henri van Balen de qui notre jeune homme reçut des leçons pendant deux ans." It is important to mention that Van Balen produced portraits too. We know that his tomb in the "Sint-Jacobskerk" in Antwerp was decorated with a painting executed by him representing the Resurrection and bearing the portraits of himself and his wife (Rombouts and Van Lerius 1864–1876, 2:371).

30. See Ronald de Jager, "Meester, leerjongen, leertijd. Een analyse van zeventiende-eeuwse Noord-Nederlandse leerlingcontracten van kunstschilders, goud- en zilversmeden," *Oud-Holland* 104 (1990), 69–112.

31. In the context of the year 1610 it is interesting to note that in the "Correctieboek," a book concerning punitive measures, of the city of Antwerp there ap-

pears a document revealing that Frans van Dyck had some problems with a woman called Jacobmyne de Cueck, who threatened to kill him and who vilified his name and those of his daughters. The document was mentioned but not published by Van den Branden (Van den Branden 1883, 2:214; see Document 6). The reason for this hostility is not known. Nonetheless, it tells us something about the social hostility aimed at Frans. We can only suppose that some private problems caused such fervent emotions. Van Dyck surely had to know something about the affair; the document relates that windows were broken and that a song of blame was spread about the city. As a motherless boy of about eleven years of age, Van Dyck probably did not experience much happy home life.

32. Max Rooses and Charles Ruelens, *Correspondance de Rubens et documents épistolaires concernant sa vie et ses oeuvres* (Antwerp, 1898), 2:35–36: "want ic van alle canten gheprevenieert ben soo dat noch sommighe voor etlycke jaren by ander meesters haer onderhouden om myn commoditeyt te verwachten. . . . Voorts mach ic segghen met der waerheyt sonder eenich hyperbole dat ic over die hondert hebbe moeten refuseren."

33. Galesloot 1868, 582.

34. Galesloot 1868, 595.

35. Galesloot 1868, 596; see Document 23; compare with Verhagen's declaration, 29 April 1661: "Guilliam Verhagen, huyckmaker . . . daer by bedinght, tuyght ende verclaert dat vyff ofte sessenveertich jaeren geleden, sonder nochtans den preciesen tydt onthouden te hebben, hy, deponent aen den schilder Antoni van Dyck heeft aenbestedt te schilderen de twelff apostelen, ende Ons Heer" (Galesloot 1868, 585–586).

36. Van den Branden 1883, 2:215: "In het afleggen dier zelfder getuigenis, welke Breughel zegt bereid te zijn bij ede te bevestigen, verklaart hij, *ten jare 1615*, eer van Dijck naar Italië trok, dagelijks ten huize te hebben verkeerd van zijnen vriend en kunstmakker Antoon."

37. Roland 1984, 211–223.

38. Roland 1984, 212–213, where some arguments are also given against the reliability of Verhagen.

39. Roland 1984, 216: "He [Van Dyck] returned to Antwerp, where he remained for seven months— from the beginning of March to the beginning of October [1621]. Surely, having entered the services of the King of England, Van Dyck would not return to his role as assistant in the workshop of Rubens. He would set up a studio of his own, the one in the Dom van Ceulen."

40. See SAA, Pk 2266, fol. 192r.; Pk 2259, fol. 224; Pk 2287, fol. 222r.; Pk 2338, fol. 26v., 270v.

41. See, among others, Bellori 1672, 253: "Il padre si esercitava nella mercanzia delle tele, che in Fiandra superano ogn'altre di finezza e di lavaro;" Van den Branden 1883, 2:213; Brown 1982, 9; Zaremba

Filipczak 1987, 91: "Anthony van Dyck began his precocious career with the advantages of wealth and an excellent education."

42. See Document 13.

43. Galesloot 1868, 596: "hem dickwils hebben comen besoecken de seer vermaerde constschilders Petro-Paulo Rubens, Zegers, David Rijckarts, tegenwoordich deken der schilders, Wolfaert, Moermans, constvercooper, ende meer andere, alleenelyck ende tot dyen eynde om de voors(eyde) schilderijen te sien ende visiteren." See also Van den Branden 1883, 2:216; SAA, N.4265, fol. 164r.

44. Roland 1984, 223, appendix 5: "Comparuit Sr. Herman Servaes, constschilder . . . dat hij in den tweelffjarigen treves tusschen sijne Connicklijcke Majesteyt van Spagnien ende de Heeren Staeten van Holland als discipel werckende ende frequenterende de conste ten huyse van den chevallier van Dijck."

45. See Document 16: "Den negentienden april (1621) . . . ons sacken en packen die veel waren ter oorsake den uitganck van den trevis dat iegelyck besich was met vluchten."

46. Roland 1984, 216.

47. See also *Van Dyck tentoonstelling* (Antwerp, 1949), no. 5.

48. Francine van Cauwenberghe-Janssens, "De sociale toestand van de Antwerpse schilders in de 17de eeuw," *Jaarboek Koninklijk Museum voor Schone Kunsten Antwerpen* (1970), 233–240.

49. We can even imagine that Van Dyck could have done so without the special protection of Rubens. We know, for example, that Gonzales Coques completed his so-called "Scholar and His Young Wife" (Staatliche Kunstsammlungen, Gemäldegalerie, Kassel) in 1640, just a year before he obtained his master's title (Rombouts and Van Lerius 1864–1876, 2:115). Another example is Pieter Thys, who accepted the pupil J. C. Hoffman during the year 1643–1644, although he did not become a master before 1644–1645 (Rombouts and Van Lerius 1864–1872, 2:152, 157).

50. Hans Vlieghe, *Rubens' Portraits of Identified Sitters Painted in Antwerp. Corpus Rubenianum Ludwig Burchard*, vol. 19, pt. 2 (London and New York, 1987), 77–78.

51. Marc Robbroeckx, "De vijftien schilderijen van de Sint-Pauluskerk te Antwerpen," onuitg. licentiaatsverhandeling, Rijksuniversiteit, Ghent, 1972, 4–18.

52. De Jager 1990, 86, and, for example, 100, a contract of a pupil of C. J. Delff, painter in Delft, dated 27 March 1621, in which it is stated that the boy has permission to paint for his own profit for five weeks: "voor hem selven ende tot sijnen eijgen prouffijte t'elcken eenich werck sal mogen affmaecken, Int welck hem oock sijn meester behulpich sal wesen, tot sijn discretie." The boy could expect assistance from his master and probably could also sell these paintings. Another example (De Jager 1990, 101) il-

lustrates a contract drawn up in Dordrecht on 12
September 1675. Here the pupil received permission
to work alternately for his master and his mother, so
we can assume that his mother could earn some
money by selling the ("juvenile") paintings made by
her son.

APPENDIX

Document 1

Request by Agatha van Yselsteyn, widow of Jan
van Ghendrick alias Van Cleve, in order to confirm that her late husband was once a member
of the guild of Saint Luke in Antwerp (30 September 1563)

*Ten versuecke van Agata van IJselsteyn we-
duwe wylen Jans van Ghendrick alias van
Cleve in synen tyt alhier vrijschilder van
synen ambachte.*

*Kaerle Briede, oick schilder alhier ende poirter
deser stadt, out omtrent LXVIII jaer,* Anthonij
van Dyck, *oick schildere alhier geweest
hebbende, out XXXIII jaer, oick poirter deser
stadt ende Jacques Knisperen, oick schilder
ende poirter deser stadt, out omtrent XXXVI
jaren, juraverunt ierst behoirlick met rechte
daer toe gedaecht zynde, te wetene de
voorseyde Kaerle Briede ende de voorseyde
Anthony van Dycke dat zy den voorseyde
Janne van Ghendrick alias van Cleve, alhier
inder stadt over de XX ende XXIIII jaren gelden
wel gekent hebben voer een vrij schilder ende
vrij meester int ambachte vanden schilders alhier ende dat zy wel weten dat de selve Jan
van Cleve alhier vrij poirter ende ingesetene
deser stadt was ende de voorseyde Jacques
Knisperen dat hy tot meer stonden ende over
seker jaren geleden alhier in de voorseyde
stadt wel heeft horen seggen dat de voirseyde
Jan van Cleve alhier was vrij schilder ende
meester int ambacht vanden schilders
voirseyd. Redenen heurer wetentheyt al-
ligerende van dat de voirseyde Jan van Cleve
alhier poirter was want nyemant alhier int
ambacht van den voorseyde schilders wesen
ende mach hij en moet ierst vrij poirter deser
stadt syn oft doen haren eedt dat zy binnen
den sesse weken daer na vrij poirters deser
stadt sullen worden.*

SAA, Cert. 19, fol. 10r.

Document 2

Anthony van Dyck the elder requests of the
city council to be relieved from lodging soldiers
in his house called Hercules, situated in the
"Mansstraat" in Antwerp (1568)

Aen myne heren voorseyd

Anthoni van Dycke

*Geeft te kennen in alre reverenten uwe
voorseyde onderdanige dienaer Anthoni van
Dycke creemere, ommegaende ende hem
generende met zyde ende cleyn pennewaer wo-
nende inde Mansstrate inden huyse geheeten
den Hercules, hoe dat de fourners hem
gefournert hebben te decken een bedde nyet
tegenstaende hy hen verclaerde dat hy egeen
plaetse en hadde omme dezelve soldaten te ac-
comoderen, gelyck(?) de huysen binnen tgeheel
straetken gestaen uwen voorseyden kennelyck
wesende, zeer cleyn ende enge zyn ende
geenssins geaccomodeert en zyn omme soldaten te fourneren als tzelve genoch kennelyck
is in Jan van Woonsele uwen voorseyden
medeschepene. Ende want hy suppliant vande
soldaten alduer gefournert wesende nu ter tyt
zeer veroverlast worde voor zyn duere, ende
oyck nyet een huys en is inde geheel straete
daer enich soldaet zoude moegen gefournert
wesen. Bidt daeromme de voorseyde suppliant
dat den zelven uwen voorseyden gelieve te or-
doneren(?) de fourners deser stadt dat zy de
soldaten (gefournert wesende in zyns suppli-
ants huyse) elders in een anders huys
fourneren regard nemende op het groot verlies
welck hy suppliant daer deure zoude mogen
commen te gecrygen, welck doende etc. onderteekent*

SAA, Pk 642, fol. 12r.

Document 3

The merchant Anthony van Dyck the elder and
the painter Hans Lambrechts declare that Peter
Pruystinck is a man of good behavior (18 June
1569)

Ten versuecke van Pieter Pruystinck

*Anthuenis van Dycke, creemere, oudt omtrent
XL jaeren ende Hans Lambrechts, schildere,
oudt omtrent dertich jaeren, oppidani juraverunt et affirmaverunt dat zy wel kennen
ende over langhe wel gekent hebben den
voirseyde Peeter Pruystinck ende dat zy wel
weten ende waerachtig is dat de selve Peeter is
een man van goeden leven, conversatien, name
ende fame ende dat zy den selven altyts van
eenen yegelicken voor sulcx hebben weten
houden, achten ende reputeren sonder contrarie van dien oyt in eniger manieren gehoirt
oft verstaen te hebbene redene van heurlieder
wetentheyt allegerende dat zy comparanten
over badt dan thien jaeren met den voorseyden Peeteren gehandelt, geconverseert, gheten
ende gedroncken hebben.*

Die XVIII Junij a ° 1569

SAA, SR 321, fol. 541r.

Document 4

Franchoys (Frans) van Dyck and Maria Cuypers
buy the house called "Ghendt" or "De stadt
van Ghendt" from Susanna van Surck. It was
situated in the "Korte Nieuwstraat" in
Antwerp (7 March 1607)

*Anthonio van Surck, Anthonissone, coopman,
innegesetene deser stadt inden name ende als
omme tgene nabeschreven te doen specia-
lycken ende onwederroepelicken gemachticht
van jouffrouwe Susanne van Surick, weduwe
wijlen Arnouts Hellemans, woonachtich tot
Hamborch by procuratie, in date den XXVIII
octobris lestleden, ons te desen originelyck
gethoont, in deen partye, ende Franchoys van
Dycke ende jouffrouwe Marie Cuypers zyne
huysvrouwe, in dander partye. Bekenden ende
verlyden onderlinge in beyde partyen dat de
voorseyde Anthonio van Surck inden name
ende gemachticht als vore, gegeven heeft ende
gaf terve ende in erffelycken rechte den
voorseyde Franchoys van Dycke, Jouffrouwe
Marien Cuypers synder huysvrouwe ende
heuren nacomelingen te houdene eeuwelyck
ende erfelyck te besitten ende te gebruyckene,
eerst eene huysinghe vooraen tstrate metter
poorten, plaetse, gaelderyen, borneputte, hove,
packhuysen, coecken, stove, neercamere,*

*schryfstove, baedtstove, keldercoecken,
stallen, diverse kelders, regenbacke, weerdribbe, met allen ende yegelicken den schryn-
wercke van tresooren, cleerschappraeyen, lict
de champs, ende generelyck allen dandere
schrynwercken, ende oock alle ende yegelicke
de schilderyen egeene uutgenomen, ende alle
tgene in de selve huysinghen allomme eertvast
ende nagelvast is, altsamen voor soo vele die
de selven huysingen toebehoorende syn,
gronde ende toebehoorten, gestaen ende gelegen in de Corte Nieuwstrate alhier, tusschen
deser stadts ruye ex una oostwarts ende de
huysinge geheeten tcasteel van Ryssel ende
seker huysinge daer toebehoorende ex altera
westwarts (van welcke huysinge geheeten als
vore tcasteel van Ryssel, de proprietarissen
van desen voorseyde huysinge, ende van dander twee huysen daernaffens als nabeschreven
staet, oostwarts staende, nu synde ende by
tyden wesende, de vensteren in de muer tusschen de huysinge ende de voorseyde huysinge
van tCasteel van Ryssel ter erven waerts van
desen huysinge staende te geene dagen voorder
noch anderssints selen mogen benotsen noch
betimmeren, dan die in tegenwoordelyck
benotst ende betimmert zyn).*

*Commende dese voorseyde huysinghe achter
vuytwarts aen den godshuys vande bogaerden
erve. Item, noch twee huysen voor aen tstrate
metten gronde ende toebehoorten, gestaen
ende gelegen neffens een oock in de voorseyde
Corte Nieuwstrate alhier, tusschen deser
voorseyde stadsruye aen deen syde oostwart
ende de poorte van de voorseyde huysinge
ende de huysinge geheten als vore tCasteel van
Ryssel ende den anderen huysen daertoe be-
hoorende aen dander syde westwarts, commende achter suytwarts aen dese voorseyde
huysinghe ende dit op alsulcke servituten van
waterloopen ende leydingen van de weerdribbe als nu tertyt cours ende loop hebbende
van ende uut de voorseyde huyse genaempt als
vore tCasteel van Ryssel ende twee huysen
daer neffens staende onder deur de plaetse
ende plaveytsel vande kelder van de voorseyde
huysingen met eender grooten ryole naer der-
ser stadtruye toe. Item noch het huys metten
gronde ende toebehoorten daer den schoenmaker inne woont, hier neffens, ende aende
ruye oostwaerts gestaen ende gelegen. Ende
noch de comptoir camer wesende eene stove,
met noch eene groote neercaemer daerneffens
suytwaerts gestaen. Item een poortken ende
selver cleyn vloerken dienende tot den inganck
van de voorseyde comptoircamer. Item eenen
steenen trap. Item selver part vande gaelderye
ende plaetse met oock eene pompe, weer-*

*dribben, kelderen, funde et (?), met oock alle
tgene daerinne op ende omre ertvast ende
nagelvast is, respective altsamen oostwaerts
gestaen ende gelegen vande huysingen
genaemt tCasteel van Ryssele inde voorseyde
Corte Nieuwstrate gestaen, ende dit altsamen
staende neffens een ende by malcanderen tusschen de resterende huysingen ende erve
genaempt het Casteel van Ryssel zuytwest
ende noortwaerts ende oock eenendeels noort
ende oostwaerts. Gelyck ende in alle der
manieren ende met alsulcken actien,
gerechticheden, servituten als de voorseyde.
Jouffrouwe Susanne van Surck constituant alle
de voorseyde huysingen metten appendentien
ende dependentien, gronden ende alle de toebehoorten voorgeruert toecomende ende competerende zyn soo by versterf ende successie
van de voors. wijlen Jaspar van Surck haren
vader, als oock by transport haer(?) by An-
thonise van Surck, haren halven broeder aengaende syn parte ende gedeelte der selver
huysingen opde IX marte anno XVI c ende
vier, gedane. Ende gelyck voorts de voorseyde
Gaspar van Surck de voorseyde eerstgenoemde
huysinge cum funde et p(roprietatis?) predictis
op den lesten februarii anno XVc tsestich jegens Pieter van Surck ende consorten gecregen
ende terve genomen heeft, de welcke Gaspar
tvoorseyde huys daer den schoenmaker inne
woont aende voorseyde ruye voor aentstrate
gestaen, heeft doen bouwen ende opmaken,
Ende gelyck ten leste Anthoni van Surck comparant in desen, als testamentelycke momboir
ende tot behoef vande kinderen ende erfgenamen der voorseyde wylen Gaspar van Surck de
voorseyde lestgenoemde comptoir, camer,
stove, groote neercamer, poortken, cleyn vloerken, steene trap, poort ende gaelderye, plaetse,
gronde ende alle den anderen toebehoorten
voorseyde opten XVden Junij CXVc ende
XCIXsten jegens Jouffrrouw Helena van
Valckenisse gecregen ende terve genomen
heeft, al gront, (rechte?) ende de bescheeden
daeraf synde quas tradidit, Tsiaers erffelyck,
boven de twee hondert carolus guldens erfelyck die de voorseyde erfnemeren den
voorseyde erfgever inde voorseyde qualiteyt in
goeden, ganckbaren ende gepermitteerden
gulden gereet jegens den penninghe XVI
opgeleit(?), betaelt ende afgequeten hebben de
voorseyde penninghen metten laste(?), omme
noch eenhondert vyvenvyftich gelycke carolus-
gulden tot XX schellingen tstuck goed ende
erfbaer prout communiter jaerlyckere ende er-
flyckere renten. Te geldene ende te betalene
van de voorseyde erfnemeren ende van heuren
nacomelingen der voorseyde Jouffrouwe Susanna van Surck ende heure nacomelingen er-*

*flyck ende eeuwelyck durende alle jare te
Kerssavonde. het eerste jaer rente sal verschy-
nen te kerssavonde naestcomende in dese jare
XXVI C ende seven.*

SAA, SR 466, fols. 223r.–225v.

Document 5

Franchois (Frans) van Dyck and Maria Cuypers
draw up a codicil in their own house, De Stadt
van Ghendt, in the presence of the notary
Adriaen de Witte (16 April 1607)

*Inden naem ons Lieffs Heeren Jhesu Cristi ons
salichmakers Amen. By desen tegenwoirdigen
openbaren instrumente, zy condt ende kennelyck eenen yegelyck dat inden jare duesent
ses hondert ende seven up den sestienden dach
der maent van Aprilis, compareerden voer my
Adriaen de Witte, openbaer notaris byden
Rade van Brabant totter exercie van tselve offitie gheadmitteert ende den ghetuyghen
naeghenaempt, d'eersame Sr. Franchoys van
Dycke, coopman, ende Joffrouwe Marie
Cuypers syne wettige huysvrouwe, beyde my
notario wel bekent synde, de voorgenoemde
Sr. Franchoys redelyck wel te passe, gaende,
staende ende de voorgenoemde Joffrouwe
Marie Cuypers sieck te bedde liggende,
nochtans heur vyff sinnen, verstant ende memorie over al wel machtich synde, aenmerck-
ende ende overdenckende de broosheyt ende
crancheyt der mensschelycke natuere als datter niet sekerder en is dan die doot ende niet
onsekerder als die ure derselver, hebben
daeromme sy codicillateuren ghemaect ende
geordineert dese codicille inder manieren naer-
volgend. Ierst lauderende ende approberende
alsulcken testament als sy codicillateuren
opden 17den februari anno 1595 voer my notario voergheseyt in presentie van ghetuijghen
gemaect ende ghepasseert hebben daeraff dat
het inhouden ende de substantie van dien hen
up date deser by my notario is voergehouden
ende verhaelt, willende ende uuteren
begeerende dat tselve in allen synen pointten
sal worden onderhouden ende achtervolcht
daer dat dese henne codicille niet en is con-
trarierende, voorts alsoo sy by hennen
voorseyde testamente hebben gemaect aen
hennen kinderen onder hen allen tsamen de
somme van achthondert ponden vlems ende
nademael dat sy nu meer kinderen syn
hebbende dan sy hadden int maken van hennen voorseyde testamente als hebben nu negen
levende kinderen, soo maecken ende geven sy
codicillateuren nu aen selve henne negen
kinderen inde plaetsse vanden voorseyde acht*

*hondert ponden vlems tsamen onder hen allen
de somme van derthien hondert ponden vlems
eens wesende alsoo voer elck kint een hondert
vyfftich ponden vlems eens om syn aenpert
elck daeraff vvtgereyct te worden ten tyde als
inden voorseyden testamente verclaert staet,
oyck commende den testamenteuren dat des
overledens kint oft kinderen portien sullen versterven opden anderen kinderen hennen hee-
len broeders ende susters totten lesten kinde
toe ende commende het leste kint oyck tover-
lyden aleer tselve tot state oft tot competenten
ouderdomme sonder contrarie dispositie
gecommen ware, dat alsdan de voorseyde
geheele somme van derthien hondert ende
vyfftich ponden vlems sullen versterven ende
succederen opden lancxstlevende van hen
codicillateuren op conditie dat alsdan de selve
lancxstlevende sal schuldich ende gehouden
syn aen allen den naesten vrienden vande
voorseyde kinderen hier bestaende vanden
dooden syde wegen van hen codicillateuren (in
plaetsse van een hondert ponden vlems eens
inden voorseyde testamente gestelt) onder hen
allen te geven tsamen de somme van dryehon-
dert ponden vlems, deselve vrienden indien
ghervalle daermede secluderende uutallen den
goeden ende sterffhuysse vande selve kinderen
by desen. Toen off gebeurde dat de
lancxstlevende van hen codicillateuren hem
begave tot anderen houwelyck, dat deselve
lancxstlevende indien ghevalle gehouden sal
syn te stellen hipoteke voer de voorseyde
somme van derthien hondert vyfftich ponden
vlems eens, vande welcke de lancxtlevende sal
trecken de bladinghe voer het onderhouden
vande selve kinderen gedurende de tyt inden
voorseyde hennen testamente gestelt.*

*Item totten lancxtlevenden van hen codicil-
lateuren soo kiesen sy noch tot momboren
over hennen beyden ombejaerde kinderen d'er-
same her Rombout Huens Rentmeester der
stede van Mechelen des codicillateurs behouden neve ende heer Adriaen de la Rue der
codicillatricen neve, met gelycke macht al off
sy in hennen voorseyde testamente genomi-
neert stonden.*

*Dit verclaerden de voorgenoemde codicilla-
teuren te wesen henne codicille ende uuterste
begeerte wille, willen dat sulcx sal volbracht
worden al off tselve in hennen voorseyde testamente van woerde tot woerde gescreven stont,
van allen dwelck hebben de voorgenoemde
codicillateuren versocht van my notario tgene
voorseyd is wettelyck stipulerende ghemaect
te worden een oft meer openbare instrumenten
inder bester formen, dit is aldus geschiet ten
woonhuysse vande voorgenoemde codicillateuren genaempt Gent, gestaen ende gelegen*

*inde Cortenieuwstrate binnen deser stat van
Antwerpen ten daghe, maent ende jare
voorseyd in presentie ende jegenwordicheyt
van Johannes de Witte, Peter de Bruine ende
Emanuel de Palma, alle poorters ende inge-
seten respective deser voornoemde stat als
ghetuygen totten desen geroepen.
Quod attestor*

Adriaen de Witte, notaris publicus subscripsit

SAA, N. 1181 (16 April 1607)

Document 6

Jacobmyne de Kueck (of Keuck) is accused of
having insulted the name of Franchois (Frans)
van Dyck. Among other things she is reported
to have vilified his name and to have uttered
death threats (15 December 1610)

*Jacobmyne de Kueck, geboren van Honscoten,
overmidts sy haer heeft vernoordert te dichten,
te singen ende te verbreyden seker diffamatoir
lieken tot lasteninge ende blamatie van Franchoijs van Dyck, borger ende coopman deser
stadt, midtsgaders van syne dochtters ende
huysgesien, dat sy oick tot meer reysen by
nachten ende ontyden dessel Franchoys van
Dyck gelaesen heeft vuytgeworpen. Hebbende
voorts noch tegens hem Van Dyck oick
geduerende haere gevanckenisse verscheyden
dreygementen gedaen van hem te vermoorden
ende dyergelycken behalven meer andere gelycke feyten by haer Jacobmyne in andere plaet-
sen gecommitteert boven de correctie op heden
ontfangen, sal porren binnen sonneschyn vuyt
dese stadt ende vryheyt ende binnen den derden daege uut het marckgraefschip van
Antwerpen ende daer vuyt blyven ten
eeuwigen daege opde pene vanden galge, gecor-
rigeert XV December 1610.*

SAA, V 236 ("Correctieboek der Stadt van Antwerpen"), fol. 81r.

Document 7

Adriaen Diericx and Lancelot Lancelots, as
husbands of Catharina and Maria van Dyck and
in their capacity as guardians of the infant children of Franchois (Frans) van Dyck, try to protect the inheritance of the children's late
grandmother Catharina Conincx and their late
mother Maria Cuypers against the claims of
the creditors of their father Franchois (Frans)
van Dyck (6 June 1615)

*Aen myne Eerw.
Verthoont Adriaen Diricx als getrouwt
hebbende Catharina van Dyck oyck als momboir over de kinderen van Franchois van Dyck*

minderjarich, daer moeder aft was Marie Cuypers. Item Lanceloot Lanceloots inden naem van Marie van Dyck zyn huysvrouwe hoe dat zy de supplianten boven de notable meubelen ende huysraet in esse wesende gecommen vuyte successie vander supplianten grootmoeder ten achteren zyn van Francois van Dyck hunnen schoonvader ettelycke duysent ponden vlems gelyck dat by andere requiranten hedent U.E. is verthoont. Ondertusschen, verstaen de supplianten dat eenige van des voornoempde Van Dyck crediteuren seer rigoreuselyck overvallen ende dat erger is pretenderen de meuble goederen zoo dye van henne voorseyde Grootmoeder syn gecommen (dye ten selven huyse gewoont heeft ende overleden is) texecuteren onder ander eenen Jaecques de Cortte dye welcke vuyt crachte van secker vonnis provisioneel in contumacie gegeven ter somme van 80 Liber salvo justo pretendeert deselve goeden te bescryven ende teenen wege te vervueren nae de Vrydachsmerckt totter weesen groot prejudicie dye daer om hier tegens geirne souden willen gehoort zyn boven ende behalvens dat de voornoempde de Cortte der supplianten vader het absoluet woort heeft gegeven van in vierthien daegen tyts nyet te attenteren op hope dat de voornoempde Van Dyck ondertusschen provisie soude mogen crygen dye hy van dage te dage verwacht vuyt Spaignien welcken tyt nochter tyt nyet om en is.

Ende gemerckt dat na recht ende costume toegelaten is sunderlinge weesekinderen hun eygen propre goeden te bescryven ten eynde die ongehoort nyet en moeten gedooghen dat deselve sonder oorsaecke woorden vercocht, soo bidden de supplianten dat U.E. gelieven wille ter syden van dese te consenteren dat zy den voornoempden de Corte selen moghen op dese gemenaceerde executie ende beschryvinghe doen dseghen dit doende

Fiat ut petitur actum in collegie VI Junij 1615
F. Dyck

SAA, Pk 706, fol. 77r.

Document 8

Franchois (Frans) van Dyck's sons-in-law, Adriaen Diericx and Lancelot Lancelots, guardians of his infant children, try to secure Van Dyck's properties against the claims of creditors. For this reason they think it necessary to sell immediately nine among the best paintings from the collection of the children's late grandmother, Catharina Conincx (17 July 1615)

Aen myne Eerw.

Verthoonen Adriaen Diericx ende Lanseloot Lanceloots soo voor hun selven als getrouwt hebbende de twee oudtste dochters van Franchois van Dyck. Item als momboiren testamentari van hunne swageren ende swagerinnen hoe dat sy vuyt redenen van de disgracie *Franchois van Dyck hunnen schoonvader overcommen alle mogelycke devoir hebben gedaen omme te salveren der kinderen moederlycke ende grootmoederlycke goederen vele duysent ponden bedragende, hebbende tot dyen eynde vuyt crachte van vonnis alle desselffs goederen gebrocht subhastatie deur doffitie myns heeren des amptmans. Item ist soo dat de supplianten raedtsaem vinden ja nootelyck met eenen te laeten vercoopen negen der beste schilderyen by der kinderen grootmoeder achtergelaeten op conditie dat de selve tot behoeve van negen der voornoempde Van Dyck kinderen in specie souden volgen op keuse na rade van der kinderen ouderdom ende van gelyckinge van den prys der voornoempde schilderyen als deselve kinderen gecommen sullen syn tot den ouderdom van XXV jaeren nyet alleenelyck ende dat deselve van grooten importantien syn, maer oyck omdat de weeskinderen op vele naer huysmoederlycke ende grootmoederlycke goet nyet en sullen connen verhalen.*

Bidden daeromme dat U.E. gelieven in margine te verleenen consent om te doen als voren, dwelck doende

Is van myne heeren Borgemeesteren ende schepenen gecommiteert Mr Pauwels van Liere, schepene om hem op de gelegentheyt deser zaecke te informeren om tselve gedaen ende desselffs rapport gehoort
Voorsts zy(?) actum XVII Julij 1615.

SAA, Pk 706, fol. 113r., v.

Document 9

Franchois (Frans) van Dyck is brought to court by his sons-in-law, guardians of his infant children. They want to recuperate the inheritance of the children's grandmother and mother, which is estimated at about sixty-six hundred Flemish pounds (24 July 1615)

Aen myne Eerw.

Verthoonen Adriaen Diericx ende Lanceloot Lanceloots hoe dat sy lieden supplianten soo wel als getrouwt hebbende de twee outste dochters van Franchois van Dyck als inde qualiteyt van testamentelycke momboiren over henne minderjarige swagers ende swagerinnen, hebben te rechte betrocken Fran-

chois van Dyck hunnen schoonvader by con-
sent van U.E. tot conservatie van hunne moed-
erlycke ende grootmoederlycke goederen badt
als 6600 Liber vlems importerende soo byden
cleiren staet ende respective testamenten is
blyckende inder vueghen dat sylieden suppli-
anten dyenvolgende hebben geobstineert von-
nis ende vuyt crachte van dyen alle desselffs
goederen laeten inventarieren ende by doffitie
myns heeren des amptmans vercoopen. Item
ist zoo dat onder andere crediteuren eenen
Jacques de Cortte van gelycken schynt von-
nisse te hebben ter somme van 80 Liber salvo
justo, dye welcke by de supplianten voor date
van de vacantien gedaecht synde in cas van
preferentie heeft connen antwoorden by on-
tkennen als ignorerende sulcx dat naer alle
waerschynlyckheyt de sake niet een verbael
oft tween soude wordden gedecideert(?) ten
waere dat hun supplianten de tegenwoordighe
vacantien obstrueerden(?), keeren hun
daeromme tot U.E. Collegie biddende om con-
sent merginaelyck daertoe dienende geconsid-
ereert dat dese zaecke weesen aengaet ende
dat de procureur Santvliet van de tegenpartye
daerin by onderteeckeninge van dese consen-
teert.

Dit doende Gilliam de Hertoghe

Fiat ut petitur Actum XXIIIJ Julij 1615
J. Jacobens

SAA, Pk 706, fol. 120r.

Document 10

Anthony van Dyck brings his brothers-in-law
Adriaen Diericx and Lancelot Lancelots to
court for illegally governing the properties of
the infant children of Franchois (Frans) van
Dyck and the late Maria Cuypers (3 December
1616)

Aen mynen heeren
Geeft te kennen Anthonij van Dyck oudt on-
trent 18 jaeren hoe dat deur d'afflyvicheyt van
syn grootmoeder op hem syn verstorven ver-
scheyden goederen daer over hoewel byden
testamente vande selve syne grootmoeder
waeren gestelt executeurs ende testamentely-
cke momboirs Franchois de Smet ende Jacques
Knidde, soo bevindt hy dat nu tertyt deselve
goeden administreren ende eenige tyt gead-
ministreert hebben Meester Adriaen Dierixen
ende Lancelot Lancelots, sonder dat hy weet
oft kan weten vuyt wat chrachte ende sonder
dat de selve hem eenige openinge daer van
willen doen waerdeur ende dat hy oock ver-
staet dat sy in henne administratie nyet veel
en quyten. Soo versueckt de suppliant dat u. E.
gelieve te ordonneren den voorseyden Die-

ricxen ende Lancelots dat sy sullen schuldich
syn aen eenen commissaris by u. E. te depu-
teren over te geven ende te doene rekeninge,
bewys ende reliqua ende hem suppliant te auc-
thoriseren om met assistentie van yemant van
syne goede vrinden te mogen present wesen
ende mede overhooren de selve rekeninge,
alsoo by de medegaende attestatien blykt van
syn goet comportement ende dat hy de selve
rekeninge gesien voor de selve commissaris sal
mogen nemen alsulcke conclusien als hy te
raede sal vinden dwelcke ende etc. by myne
heren Burgemeesters ende Schepenen gecom-
mitteert Jonker Pauwels van Halmale sche-
pene, ende Meester Jan Jacobens greffier deser
stadtvan etc. Actum III decembris 1616
J. Jacobens

SAA, Pk 708, fol. 165r, v.

Document 11

The accused Adriaen Diericx and Lancelot
Lancelots declare that they have acted entirely
in good faith. Reference is made to the "disgrace" of Franchois (Frans) van Dyck. Diericx
and Lancelots admit to having attempted to recuperate the inheritance of Van Dyck's grandmother and mother from the sale of all Frans'
goods, which were sold in public at the Friday
market. Van Dyck's older brother has also gotten into financial difficulties and creditors have
seized all his household effects, including a
harpsichord made by Master Ruckers and a red
wall decoration that once had been in the
domicile of Franchois (Frans) van Dyck (8 and
15 July 1617)

Aen myne Eerw.

Verthoonen Adriaen Diericx notaris ende
Lancelot Lanceloots testamentelycke mom-
boiren over donbejaerde kinderen van Fran-
chois van Dyck daer moeder aff was Joffrouwe
Marie Cuypers ende grootmoeder Joffrouwe
Catharina Conincx, hoedat midts de disgrace
Franchois van Dyck der weese vader overcommen, *sy lieden supplianten hebben gepro-*
cedeert op alle syne goeden omme daeraen te
verhaelen de moederlycke ende grootmoeder-
lycke gerechticheyt, synde de selve publique-
lyck ter vrydaechs merckt al vercocht ende tot
gelde gemaeckt onder andere soo hebben de
supplianten ten behoeve van de voornoemde.
weesen ingecocht sekere schoon dobbel
clavesingel gemaeckt door Meester N. Ruckers
ter somme van hondert guldens als blyckt by
dextract getrocken vuyten generaelen vercoop-
boeck over dander syde heeft Adriaen Dierix
in synen eygen naemen ingecocht seker root
behancxel oock gecommen ende geweest

Document 12

Van Dyck brings an action against Adriaen
Diericx and Lancelot Lancelots in order to protect the rights of his younger brothers and sisters, who in his view might lose all their possessions owing to the behavior of their
brothers-in-law (13 September 1617)

SAA, Pk 709, fol. 227r., v.

Document 13

Cornelis de Brouwer, administrator of Franchois (Frans) van Dyck, awarded an income of a
mere two "old big styvers" (or styvers from
Brabant) to Anthony van Dyck. This income
was secured on his house De Stadt van Ghendt
in the Korte Nieuwstraat in Antwerp (16 February 1618)

Veneris decima sexta februarÿ 1618
(. . .)
Cornelis de Brouwere als procuratie hebbende
van Francois van Dycke, gepasseert voir borge-
meesteren ende schepenen deser stadt den 15
deser heeft geemancipeert met alle solem-
niteyten van rechte ter(?) deser vierschaere,
Anthoni van Dyck synen sone, hem be-
wysende twee oude grooten oft brabantsche
stuyvers op syn huys genaempt de stadt van
Gendt gestaen inde Corte Nieuwstrate alhier.

SAA, V 154, fol. 142v.

Document 14

The merchant Lancelot Lancelots applies to
the court for permission to sell the estate of
Maria van Dyck, Van Dyck's sister, and thus
claim her inheritance. She died intestate
(6 March 1620)

Aen myne Eerw.

Verthoont reverentelyck Lanceloot Lanceloots,
coopman, poorter ende ingesetene der selver
stadt, hoe dat hy suppliant geerne soude liq-
uideren het sterffhuys van wylen Joffrouwe
Marie van Dyck syne huysvrouwe was, tegens
heure erffgenamen ab intestato mitsgaders aen
hun doende rekeninge van dadministratie die
hy over hunne gemeyne goeden gehadt heeft
eensaementelyck tegens hun contenderende
ten eynde dat middelertyt hem sal wesen
gepermitteert van syne huysen ende gronden
vanden erve te disponeren. Ende want dierge-
lycke saecken besundere tusschen soo naer
vrinden ende maeschap aldergevueghelycxste
connen ende behooren beslist te worden voor
commissarissen, te meer dat het apparent is
dat tusschen hun diversche debatten vallen
selen. Soo bidt ootmoedelyck dat u.E. gelieve
tot dien eynde vuyt hun collegie eenen oft
meer commissarissen te committeren met au-
thorisatie in forma dwelck doende etc.

Myne Heren Borgemeesters ende schepenen
hebben gecommitteert soo zy committeren
mits desen Joncker Robrecht Tucher schepene
ende meester Ambroisius Roose, secretaris
deser stadt omme te doen ende te besongneren
naer inhout van desen. Actum den 6den dach
van meerte a° 1620 onderteekent J. Brandt.

Saa, Pk 713, fol. 198r.

Document 15

Adriaen Diericx and Lancelot Lancelots, sons-
in-law of Franchois (Frans) van Dyck and
guardians of the infant children of Frans and
the late Maria Cuypers, proceed against Frans

and force him to pay the sum of about 6,620
Flemish pounds. His house, De Stadt van
Ghendt, is put up for sale on four consecutive
Fridays at the Friday market. It is sold to the
merchants Jan and Pieter van Weerden (30 May
1620)

H. Jan van Stembok
Jan Roose

De voorseyde stadthouder de Merre bekend
ende verclaerde alsoo Adriaen Diericx als
getrout hebbende Jouffrouwe Catharina van
Joffrouwe Marie van Dijck, de selve Adriaen
Dierix ende Lanceloot Lanceloots tsamen als
testamentelycke momboiren over de minder-
jarige kinderen van Franchoys van Dijck daer
moeder aff was Joffrouwe Marie Cuypers ende
indyer qualiteyt comparerende voor myne
heeren Amptmannen, Borgemeesters ende
schepenen deser stadt in rechte betrocken had-
den Franchoys van Dyck hennen vader
voorseyt ende jegens denselven geconcludeert
tot betaelen ende by provisie tot u amptesaem
vande somme van sesse duysent sesse hondert
ende tseventich ponden twelff schellingen
negen grooten vlems salvo justo, behoudelyck
affcorting van alle deuchdelyck bewys van be-
taelen maeckende heysch van costen, schaden
ende interesten in welcke conclusie de
voorseyde verweerder(?) is gecondempneert
volgens dat actum van vonnese daeraff synde
in date den sesten Junij XVIc vyfthiene
geteekent F. Dyck gelyck oock de sommatie
daernae is gevolcht ende dexecutie versocht
ende geconsenteert den XI Junij alsdoen lestle-
den geteeckent C. de Wyse loco dominj ampt-
manni dat den voorseyden heeren amptman
vuyt crachte van synre voorseyde offitie exe-
cuterende tvoorseyde vonnis, heeft ten ver-
suecke ende vervolge laste ende pericule van-
den voorseyde comparanten tot vele ende
diverse vrydagen ter vryer vrydaechs merct
deser stadt by Hans van Heynsberch als sub-
stituyt van Jacques Verschriecke, gesworen
oudecleercoper myns heeren des amptmans
doen vuytroepen ende veyl te coopen eenen
yegelyck en nae, eene huysinge mette poorten,
plaetse, gaelderye, borneputte, packhuyse,
cueckene, stove, neercamer, schryffstoven,
baetstove, keldercoecken, stalle, diverse
kelders, regenbacke, weerdribbe met allen
ende yegelyck alle dander schrynwerck ende
oock alle ende yegelyck de schilderyen egeene
vuytgenomen ende oock alle tgene inde selve
huysinge allomme eertvast ende nagelvast is
altesamen voor soo vele die der selve huysinge
toebehorend syn vuyten twee fournaise gron-
den ende toebehoren gestaen ende gelegen
inde corte Niewstraet alhier, tusschen deser

Document 16

Relevant excerpts from the diary entitled
"Gestoriboek van ons clooster van Sinte Caterina van Sene in Antwerpen" written by Sara
Derkennis, subprioress of the cloister
(1621–1629)

*Desen boek sullen wy noemen gestoriboek van
ons clooster van Sinte Caterina van Sene in
Antwerpen aangetekent door raet vanden
eerweerdigen Meester pater Johannis Bouquet
van welcken hier naer voor de tweede reyse
wederom proventiael geworden was. . . .*

*Op de schilderye van onsen autaer geschildert
door den Beroemden Schilder Antonius Van*

Dijck staen dese naervolgende woorden: "Ne Patris sui Manibus, Ferra gravis esset, hoc Saxum, Cruci advocebat et huic loco donabat, Antonius Van Dijck," gevolgd door de woorden "Siet blad 71 van desen boek."

Den negentienden April (1621) syn wy int sibiet gesonden tot Antwerpen van de eerweerde suster Caterina Brys doen wesende moeder priorinne van ons clooster gelegen in Vlanderen int Landt van Waes tot Themssche en was onder de gehorsaemheydt van den bisschop van Gent sonder dat wy weinich uren van te vooren van wiste, soo dat wy niet verwacht en werden van gestelyck oft van werlyckheydt van vrinden oft van wremden, wy en wisten oock niet waer wy souden ghaen logeeren want wy waren wel 15 oft 16 int getal sonder ons sacken en packen die veel waren ter oorsake den uitganck van den trevis, dat iegelyck besicht was met vluchten, door Godts gratie vonden wy logist ten huysen van eenen degelycken borger by name Jaqus(sic) Forminos die voor syn huysvrou getrout haddle myne suster Cristina Derkennis dewelcke ons seer dienstelyck waren. . . .

Nu om wederom te comen tot het voorghhande daer den bichtvader de reliseusen sacken ende packen halden, soo hebben wy sanderdach een huys gehuert met den last van de priorinne want sy ock met den bichtvader vertrocken was, welck huys gelegen was by de minnenbroeders genoemt den dom van Ceulen voor vier hondert en twintich guldens tsaers end gelyck wy uut ons clooster eenige scholdochters mede gebrocht hadde in de vluchtinge, soo ginnen wy ons geneeren met schoel te houwen om den cost te winnen en dese groote huyshuer te vervallen ende in eynde lieten terstont eenen autaer van hout in eene groote camer timmeren ende wy lenden tot de eerwerde paters de predicheeren doer een seeker goede dochter by naem Elisabet Cocx, een suster vanden derden regel, die ons al met groete liefden aenhalden. . . .

Int jaer dusent ses hondert negen en twintich soo wert ons kercken hooger geresen ter oorsaken van een seer schoon kunstich autaer stuck wesende een Cruys daer onder stondt onsen heyligen vader Dominequs ende anen de gebendedyden voeten vant cruys knielden onse heylige Moeder Sinte Caterina van Seenen, onder den cruys was een graf gemaekt met eenen engel daer by sittende en was ons vereert van den vermaerden constigen schilder men heer Antonius van Dyck om seeker vrinschappen ende getrouwicheden die wy gedaen hadden in syne absensie aen synen vader Sr Franscisi van Dyck ende in syne doodt bedde dat voor ons aen synen soon begeert hadden

godt wilt hennen loen weesen inder eeuwicheydt want wy wel grootelycx daer mede vereert en vervlydt waren want veel personen comen om de werdicheydt van de kunst te sien soo wy met epprientie ondervindende syn soo hebbe ick diet oek tot danckbaerheydt in desen boek gescreven.

SAA, K 559 (introduction without pagination), fols. 1r., 7r., 71r.

Document 17

Franchois (Frans) van Dyck transfers a claim for a debt worth somewhat more than 169 Flemish pounds to his son Franchois van Dyck (12 March 1622)

den XIIe meert 1622

D'eersame Franchois van Dijck den ouden my notario bekendt synde, bekende dat hy mits de weerde tsynen contentement gehadt ende ontfanghen van Franchois van Dyck de jonge synen sone, den selve Franchois van Dyck syne sone overgegeven, gecedeert ende getransporteert heeft, gaff overich(?) de een hondert negenentsestich ponden Vlems eens die Hans van Coster hem comparant schuldich is ter saecken van twee cassen indigo aenden selven vercocht ende gelevert den XIIIJn January a° 1609 ende war innne de selve van costen ende vonnisse van heeren Guldedekens ende Oudermans vande lakengulde deser stadt den XXVIJn January 1620 gecondempneert is wegens de acte daervan synde ondertekent N. Gillis die daervan comparant mede overgaff mette rechten, costen daerover gedaen ende alle anders recht oft actie die hy comparant daerinne hadde ende houdende was ende bekende dat hy geen recht meer daerover en behielt, makende den voorseyden synen sone daeraff vry meester ende proprieatris ende hem constituerende procureur in syn eygen sake omme de voorseyde somme ende costen te heysschen ende ontfangen quitantie daervan te geven ende disponeren als van syne eygene ende propre goeden, behoudelyck nochtans altyts cortinge aende voorseyde schult van alle tgene de voorseyde van costen deuchdelyck sal connen(?) bethoenen opde selve betaelt te hebben. Sonder argelist, Actum ante(?) ten woonhuyse der voorseyden comparants aende Minnebroeders alhier gestaen, presentibus Edwaert van Beveren(?), oick notaris ende Jan de Cnodder als getuygen.

Franchoys van Dyck doude

SAA, N. 2411, fol. 58v.

Document 18

Request by Adriaen Diericx and Lancelot Lancelots, as guardians of the infant children of Franchois (Frans) van Dyck, to recuperate the proceeds of a hereditary lease of fifty guilders from the house called "tCasteel van Ryssel." There is also reference to a painting belonging to the Van Dyck children, which Cornelis van Wyck claims (4 December 1623)

Ten versuecke van Adriaen Diericx notaris als momboir vande kinderen van wylen Franchois van Dijck, hebbe ick Guillam le Rousseau, openbaer notaris t'Antwerpen residerende, my getransporteert ten huyse ende neffens den persoon van Cornelis van Wyck coopman ende den selven afgevraecht oft hij van sinnen was te tellen de capitale penninghen van eene rente van vyftich guldenen erffelyck die de voirseyde kinderen op synen huyse genaempt het Casteel van Ryssel waren heffende per reste van eene rente van hondert ende vyftich guldenen erffelyck mits tsyne behoeve passerende schepene quitantie met behoorlycke authorisatie opden voet ende inder manieren gelyck hy de voorseyde een hondert guldenen erffelyck hadde gequeten. In welcken gevalle soude de voorseyde schepene quitantie op morge worden gepasseert, van gelycken hebbe hem afgevraecht oft hy van sinne was te betalen de twee jaren verloops der voorseyde vyftich gulden erffelyck alreede vervallen mits hem gevende quitantie vande selve byden voorseyden Diericx ende synen medemomboir der voorseyde kinderen Lanceloot Lansloots ondertekent ende dat oick de schilderije die hy vande voorseyde kinderen was pretenderende onder handen was ende in corten dagen deselve soude thuijs hebben.

Ende dat daerop de voorseyde Cornelis van Wyck heeft geantwoirdt dat de voorseyde authorisatie nyet genoech en was besondere in regarde van een der voorseyde kinderen meerderjarich ende in Italien sijnde ende voorts dat hy verstondt opde voorseyde capitale penninghen arrest te doen om daerane te verhalen de schade die hy soude commen te lyden aengaende sekeren waterloop daeromme hy in processe was tegens Peeter ende Jan van Weerden, welck proces alle daghe stondt om gewesen te worden. Ende aengaende de verloope seyde de voorseyde van Wyck dat hy tevreden was deselve te betalen mits dat hy werde gelevert de schilderye die den voorseyden Diericx van wegen de voorseyde kinderen hem gehouden was te leveren ende dat het wel ses jaren hadde geduert dat de voorseyde

schilderye onder handen hadde geweest. Adm.(?) den vierden december anno XVIc ende dryentwintich.

G. le Rousseau, notaris

SAA, N. 2412, fol. 228v.

Document 19

Franchois van Dyck, Cornelia van Dyck, Adriaen Diericx, and Lancelot Lancelots conclude a contract with Daniel le Bruyn (Lebrun), living in Cologne, in order to recuperate the sum of five thousand guilders owed by Adriaen van Ede to the late Franchois (Frans) van Dyck. A quarter of the debt is destined for the widow of David Moreau, who once was the "creditrice" (creditor) of Franchois van Dyck (12 January 1624)

den XIIn Januarij 1624

Franchois van Dijck Franchoissone wijlen, Jouffrouwe Cornelia van Dyck syne sustere, beghijne op het beghijnhoff alhier, Adriaen Diericx, notaris ende Lansloot Lansloots als in houwelyck gehadt hebbende respective Jouffrouwen Catharina ende Maria van Dijck, oick des voorseyde Franchois susteren waren elck voor syn selven ende voorts de voorseyde Adriaen Diericx ende Lansloot Lansloots als testementelycke momboirs over d'onbejaerde kinderen vande voorseyde wylen Franchois van Dyck, daer moeder aff was Jouffrouwe Maria Cuypers de welcke sy hier inne vervingen ende geloefden te vervane hun daer vore sterckmakende ende in desen gebruyckende het consent ende approbatie by mijne heeren Borgermeesteren ende Schepenen deser stadt verleent by hunne appostille in date den XXVIIen Junij anno XVIc dryentwintich, onderteekent J. de(?) Pape, ter deser originelyck gethoont ende in dyer qualiteyt constituerunt Daniel le Bruijn coopman, woonende tot Ceulen, omme vuytten name ende ten wegen der voorseyde constituanten metter minnen oft metter rechte te heysschen manen opbeuren ende ontfanghen vande goeden ende erfgenamen van wijlen Adriaen van Ede, Sr de Lespierre ende alle andere daertoe verobligeert zijnde alsulcke somme van vyff duysent gulden capitaels als de voorseyde Sr de Lespierre bekendt heeft by voluntaire condempnatie voorden hooghen rade tot Mechelen op den XIXe January XVIc derthienen schuldich te sijn aende voorseyden wylen Franchois van Dijck, ende daer van geloeft te betalen oft te constitueren twee duysent vierhondert guldens eens tot een erffelycke rente van hondert ende vyftich gulden tsiaers den

*penninck XVI ende cours te hebben den
voorseyden XIXe January XVIc derthien ende
de reste te betalen in gelde van eerste penningen dije procederen souden van verloopen van
grammene ende van tiende van God pen-
ninghen(?) alles in conformiteyt vande brieven
daeraff zynde, ende dat metten verloopen
daeraf verschenen ende te verschijnen totte
volle betalinge toe, welcke schuldt hen constituanten is competerende by transporte ende
goedenisse daervan geschiet by het officie
myns heeren des amptmans den XXIIIe decembris lestleden Quitandum Item omme
metten voorseyden erfgenamen ende alle andere dyen tselve aengaen mach dyenaen-
gaende te accorderen ende transigeren ende
hoedanighe compositien, transactien ende
minnelycke appointementen te maken ende
aen te gaen met alsulcke conditien ende voor-
waerden geloeften renuntiatien ende verbin-
tenissen als het den voorseyden gemechtich-
den goetduncken sal, Et si opus fuerit etc. litis
etc. domicione(?) etc. iurandum arrestandum
sententias ex (?) mandandum et appellandum
cum potestate substituendi; ende voorts etc.
alwaert etc. gelovende etc. sub obligatione etc.
salvo computu behoudens dat de voorseyde
Lebrun van wegen de weduwe van David
Moreau creditrice vande voorseyden wylen
Franchois van Dyck sal mogen innehouden
tgerechte vierdepaert van tgene ter saecken
voorseyd ontfangen ende geproffiteert sal worden volgens den accorde daervan tusschen partyen gemaeckt ende ondertekent in Antwerpen
op den XXVIIen Junij anno voorseyd, Actum
Antwerpiae presentibus P. le Rousseau ende
Jan de Cnodder als getuijgen.*

*A. Diericx
Franchois Vandyck
Cornelia van Dijck
Lansloot Lanceloots
G. le Rousseau*

SAA, N. 2413, fol. 6r., v.

Document 20

Adriaen Diericx, Lancelot Lancelots, and Franchois and Cornelia van Dyck break the contract concerning the recovery of a debt of five
thousand guilders with Daniel Lebrun (see
Document 19) because Lebrun did not succeed
in recuperating the money of the late Franchois
(Frans) van Dyck. From this moment on the in-
heritors of the late Franchois (Frans) van Dyck
will try to arrange the affair by themselves.

Den negensten Julij 1625

*Compareerden Franchois van Dijck, Fran-
choissone wijlen, Joffrouwe Cornelia van Dijck
sijne sustere, begijne opten begijnhove alhier,
Adriaen Diericx, notaris voor hem selven als
in houwelyck gehadt hebbende Joffrouwe
Catharina van Dijck oock des voorseyde Franchois sustere ende voorts deselve Diericx
inden name ende als testamentelyck momboir
vande ombejaerde kinderen des voornoemden
wijlen Franchois van Dijck, daer moeder aff
was Joffrouwe Marie Cuypers, die hij hier inne
vervane ende geloefde te vervane hem daer
vore sterck makende, de voorseyde Adriaen
Diericx alnoch inden name ende hem sterckmakende voor Lancelot Lanceloots in houwelyck gehadt hebbende Joffrouwe Maria van
Dijck oock hune suster was ende als medemomboir van voorseyde ombejaerde kinderen,*

*Ende verclaerden also sy comparanten met-
ten voorseyde Lansloot Lansloots inder
voorseyde qualiteyten opden XXVIIen Junij A°
XVI c dryentwintich, met Daniël Lebrun als
volmachticht vande weduwe wylen David
Moreau gemaeckt ende aengegaen hebben
seker manuel contract, daerby geseyt is onder
andere dat de voorseyde comparanten op de
voornoemden Lebrun procuratie souden
passeren omme metter minnen oft metter
rechte in te voorderen ende ontfangen alsulcke
actie den voorseyden wylen Franchois van
Dijck toebehort hebbende als de voorseyde
Daniël Lebrun den comparanten soude de-
signeren, gelijck oick dijenvolghende deselve
comparanten aenden voorseyden Daniël Lebrun voor my notario ende getuygen procu-
reren.*

*In amplissima forma hebben verleent den
XIIen Januarij XVIc ende vierentwintich, ten
eynde ende omme te innen ende recouvreren
alsulcken sommen van penningen als wylen
Adriaen van Ede, Sr Delespiere den voorseyden
wylen Franchois van Dijcke schuldich was,
met conditien daerinne ondersproken dat de
voorseyde Lebrun van wegen de voorseyde weduwe David Moreau creditrice van voorseyden
Franchois van Dijck soude mogen inhouden
gerechte vierde paert van tgene ter saecken
voorseyd ontfangen ende geproffiteert soude
worden. Ende want tvoorseyde accort, alsoo
geschiet ende de voorseyde procuratie daerop
gegeven is met sulcken meyninghe ende ver-
stande dat de voorseyde Lebrun deselve van
stonden ane int werck soude leggen ende de
comparanten de vrucht daer van metten
eersten doen genyeten, ende dit ter contrarie
van dijen de voorseyde Lebrun tsedert den
date der voorseyde procuratie wesende, tot nu
toe ander halff jaer nyet met allen inde
voorseyde saecken en heeft vuytgerecht
dwelck naermaels tot groote achterdeele vanden comparanten soude mogen strecken. Soo*

ist dat de voorseyde comparanten hebben ge-
protesteert ende protesteren mits desen wel ex-
presselyck van nulliteyt van voorseyde con-
tract metten voorseyden Le Brun als voren
aengegaen den XXVIIen Junij 1623 ende vande
procuratie dyenvolgende hem gegeven op den
XIIen Januarij XVIc vierentwintich, deselve
procuratie mits desen revocerende ende
casserende ende de sake naer hun nemende
om daer inne te doen soo hunnen raedt sal
gedragen. Ende opdat de voorseyde Daniël Le-
brun daervan geen ignorantie en souden pre-
tenderen, hebben de voorseyde comparanten
versocht alle notarissen ende andere publicque
pesoonen van desen proteste ende revocatie
aenden voorseyden Lebrun wete ende insinu-
atie te doen ende daer van mitsgaders van
syne antwoirde den comparanten te verleenen
acte behoorlycke forme, Actum Antwerpiae
ten comptoir myns notaris presentibus Jan de
Cnodder ende Jacobus le Rousseau incolis
testibus.

Cornelie van Dijck
Susanna Van Dijck
A. Diericx
G. le Rousseau notarius

SAA, N.2414, fol. 177r., v.

Document 21

Franchois van Dyck confirms that he is going
to pay off a debt of 128 guilders to his brother-
in-law Adriaen Diericx with the aid of a mortgage (4 December 1625)

Den vierden decembris a° 1625

Compareerde Franchois van Dijcke, Franchois-
sone wijlen, my notario bekendt, ende be-
kende dat hy in betalinghe van de hondert
achentwintich gulden eens die hy comparant
schuldich is aen Adriaen Diericx notaris, syn
swager, den selven overgegeven, gecedeert
ende getransporteert heeft, gaff cedeerde ende
transporteerde mits desen het sevenste deel
ende alle syn recht paert ende actie was eene
rente van vyftich guldens erffelyck gecon-
stitueert den penninck XIIe mette verloopen
daeraf verschenen ende onbetaelt staende die
hij comparant ende zyne broeders ende susters
heffende sijn opde Staten van Brabant int
quartier deser stadt. Bekennende hy com-
parant daer ane geen recht oft actie meer te
hebben noch te behouden, constituerende
voorts onwederroepelyck tsamen ende elcken
besondere omme tvoorseyde transport voer
hoedanighe heeren, hoven ende gerechten daer
sulcx van noode wesen sal te vernieuwen ende
onderwerven te passeren gelovende, Actum

Antverpiae ten comptoire myns notaris presen-
tibus Franchois vanden Steene de jonge ende
Jan de Cnodder als getuyghen,

Franchois van Dyck
G. le Rousseau notaris

SAA, N. 2414, fol. 359r., v.

Document 22

Jan Breughel II declares that he knew intimately the late famous artist Anthony van
Dyck, with whom he was educated. He also
confirms that he was present at times when
Van Dyck had some exceptional works in
hand, among which he had seen—before the
aforesaid departed for Italy and was living in
Den Dom van Ceulen near the convent of the
Franciscans—the head of an apostle, to which
his uncle Peter de Jode served as model (5 September 1660)

Ten (ver)suecke als vore
eadem die

Compareerde Jan Breugel constschilder ende
outdeken vande selve, out 58 jaeren, ende
heeft verclaert ende geattesteert als vore, waer-
achtich te wesen, dat hij van joncx af seer
groote kennisse ende familiariteyt heeft gehadt
met den seer vermaerden constschilder van
Dyck alhier met dewelcke hij als hebbende bi-
jcans eenen ouderdom, is opgevoet geweest,
ende dat soolange, als wanneer hij gecomen zi-
jnde tot bequamen ouderdom, tsamen hebben
gew(ees)t in Italien ende aldaer gehadt ende
gehouden de selve familiatiteyt ende
vrintschap malcanderen altyt commu-
nicerende de affairen ende consten die deen oft
d'ander hadde, gelijcke communicatie ende
gemeijnschap heeft de attestant gehadt met
den selven van Dyck alswanneer hij van Ital-
ien gecomen zijnde, geresideert hebben binnen
dese stadt, altijt gesien bij ende present ge-
weest hebbende als wanneer den selven van
Dijck eenige nieuwe stucken ende rare wer-
cken onder hadde, onder die welcke heeft hij
attestant gesien dat eer den selven naer Italien
vertrock ende woonende was inden Dom van
Ceulen bij de minrebroeders alhier dat hij
onder handen heeft gehadt ende geschildert de
tweelf apostelen met ons heeren hem gesien
hebbende schilderen aen eenen apostel die
geschildert was naer Peeter de Jode saliger
mynen oom waer oppe hij attestant seyde wie
maeckt ghij daer, waerop de voorseyde van
Dyck antwoordde ick sal der wel eenen frayen
apostel afmaecken welcke voorseyde schilder-
ije daer naer gecomen zijn in handen vanden
voorseyden requirant soo hij attestant ver-

*staen ende gesien heeft, ende dat hy deselve
vercocht heeft aenden eerweerden heere
canoninck Hillewerven. Welcke voorseyden
stucken, hy attestant, is houdende ende ken-
nende dat de selve syn geschildert met d'eygen
hant van den voorseyden constschilder Van
Dyck. Consenterende hier van oock dese acte
geexpedieert te worden. Actum ter presentien
van de voorseyde getuygen ende heeft den attestant de minute onderteeekent.*

*Quod attestor Ende was ondertheekent,
Joannes van Nos, Notaris publicus.*

SAA, N. 4265, fol. 165r.
Published (with small variations) by Galesloot 1868,
594–595.

Document 23

Guilliam Verhagen declares that he had ordered the Apostle series from the painter Anthony van Dyck forty-four or forty-five years
earlier (5 September 1660)

*Ten versuecke van Sr. Peeter Michiels Wils,
borger deser stadt*

den vyfden september 1660

*Compareerde Guilliam Verhagen outdeken
vanden gulde vanden jongen hantbooch alhier,
out omtrent 75 jaeren, ende heeft verclaert
ende geattesteert waerachtich te wesen, eedt
presenterende als versocht zijnde, dat geleden
tusschen de 44 a 45 jaeren geleden, sonder den
precisen tyt onthouden te hebben, hij attestant
aenden seer vermaerden constschilder Anthoni
van Dijck aenbesteedt heeft van syn eygen
handt te schilderen, de twelf apostelen met
ons Heer, dewelcke hem bijden selven constschilder van Dijck sijn geschildert ende lange*

*tyt in sijnen huijsen hebben berust. Hebbende
hij attestant diverse reijsen geweest ten
huyse vanden voorseyde constschilder van
Dijck, als wanneer hij de selve schilderijen
onder handen hadden om te volmaken aende
welcke hij den selven van Dijck selver heeft
sien schilderen ende dewelcke hij hem attestant altijt seer heeft aengepresen, dat deselve
seer wel waeren gemaeckt ende met sijn eijgen
handt voltrocken. Sijnde oock waerachtich dat
als wanneer de voorseyde schilderyen hebben
geweest tsynen huyse hem dickwils hebben
comen besoecken de seer vermaerde constschilders Petro Paulo Rubens, Zegers, David
Rijckarts tegenwoordich deken der schilders,
Wolfaert, Moermans, constvercooper ende
meer andere, alleenelijck ende tot dijen eynde
omme de voorseyde schilderijen te sien ende
visiteren, dwelcke hun verwonderende vande
conste der selver die altijt hebben gelooft ende
gepresen, als zijnde gemaeckt ende voltrocken
met deygen handt vanden voorseyden constschilder van Dijck, welcke schilderijen hij attestant is wetande dat gecomen syn in handen
vanden voorseyde requirant, dwelck den requirant alsnu vercocht ende gelevert heeft aen
dheer canonick Hillewerven, gelijck hij attestant, van den voorschreven requirant heeft verstaen. Consenterende van dese acte geexpedieert te worden. Aldus gedaen ende gepassert
t'Antwerpen ter presentien van Jan Simonart
ende Jan Sneleinck, als getuygen, ende heeft
den attestant de minute onderteekent.*

SAA, N. 4265, fol. 164r., v.
Published (with small variations) by Galesloot 1868,
597–598.

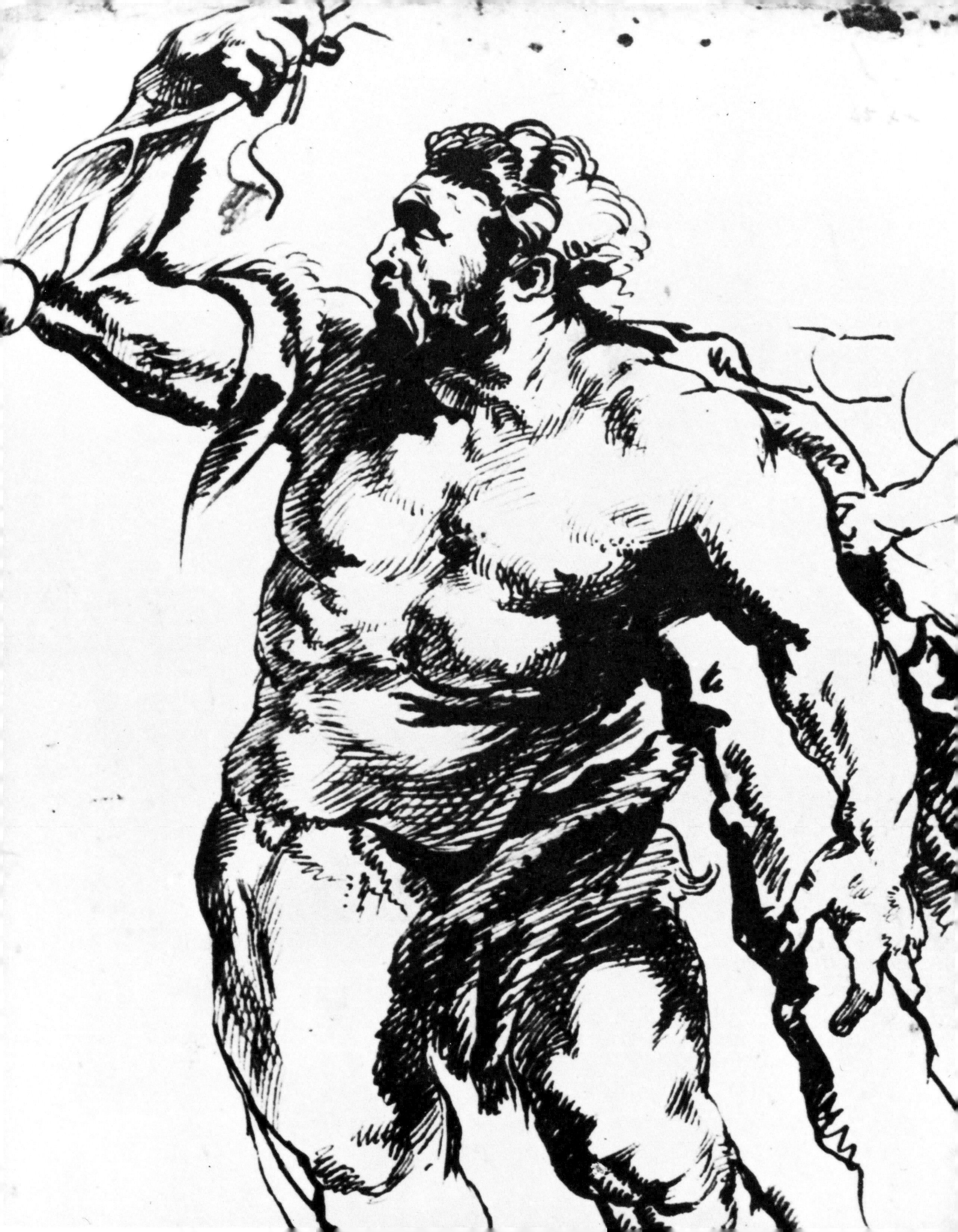

JUSTUS MÜLLER HOFSTEDE
Kunsthistorisches Institut der Universität Bonn

Van Dyck's Authorship Excluded: The Sketchbook at Chatsworth

An octavo sketchbook with pen drawings and manuscript notes[1] belonging to the Devonshire collection, presenting the work of a Flemish artist active in the sphere of Peter Paul Rubens, raises a number of paramount questions with regard to Anthony van Dyck's authorship and his early development. The traditional attribution of the booklet to Van Dyck was rejected by Lionel Cust in 1900; Horst Vey dismissed the attribution again in 1962. Since their publication in two sumptuous volumes by Michael Jaffé[2] in 1966 as *Van Dyck's Antwerp Sketchbook*, dated between 1615 and 1620, the drawings and notes have presumed to occupy a very important position within the fascinating field of the artist's precocious beginnings. There was, however, no immediate affirmative answer to Jaffé's publication, as one would have expected; no review was written, no article on the young Van Dyck took inspiration from the publication of the sketchbook. Two important exhibitions dealing mainly with the achievements of Van Dyck's early activities, *Van Dyck as Religious Artist* of 1979, organized by John Rupert Martin and Gail Feigenbaum at the Art Museum, Princeton University,[3] and *The Young Van Dyck* of 1980, arranged by Alan McNairn for the National Gallery of Canada, Ottawa,[4] did not even mention the sketchbook.

The acceptance of the sketchbook came hesitantly and recently.[5] Sir Oliver Millar wrote some approving lines in 1960, shortly after Jaffé's first announcement that he

would publish the sketchbook in full. In the same year the first important exhibition since 1945 of Van Dyck's drawings, *Antoon van Dyck: Tekeningen en Olieverfschetsen*, was held in Antwerp, without including the sketchbook; in the catalogue, Roger A. d'Hulst and Horst Vey rejected the attribution of the sketchbook to Van Dyck. Christopher White stated rather cautiously in his review that a number of works could have been better studied, compared, and discussed had they been shown in Antwerp, ". . . especially the Chatsworth Sketchbook and the landscapes in body-colour, which are, in my opinion, entirely genuine." Evidently this assertion of genuineness was related only to the mentioned group of landscapes,[6] which are mainly in the British Museum, where Christopher White was active for many years as a keeper at the department of prints and drawings. Julius Held[7] made a short reference to the sketchbook in 1986, apparently accepting Van Dyck's authorship as a fait accompli. Egbert Haverkamp-Begemann appeared to be inclined, in an oral communication in 1987, to accept the attribution, and Arnout Balis assumed a similar attitude in the same year. The present writer published in 1988 the first results of his reexamination of the sketchbook with a number of facts advanced against Van Dyck's authorship.[8] The discussion was again revived in 1991, when the sketchbook was lent to the splendid exhibition *The Drawings by Anthony van Dyck* organized by Christopher Brown for the Pierpont Morgan Library.[9] Brown's arguments supporting the attribution to Van Dyck, and his reservations, will be considered within the framework of the following comments.

Michael Jaffé's publication of 1966 was in many respects an example of excellent scholarship. He located the draftsman convincingly in the immediate sphere of Rubens; he was able to reconstruct important sections of a lost sketchbook by Rubens, copied by the artist of the Chatsworth Sketchbook; and he identified the models of many drawings with accuracy and diligence. The attribution to Van Dyck, however, imparts to the Chatsworth Sketchbook an additional degree of historical significance and artistic importance: if it could be proved that Van Dyck produced these drawings and notes between about 1615 and 1620, we would in fact possess outstanding testimony to the artist's early orientation toward models and formulas of the antique and the Italian High Renaissance, and be confronted with rich evidence of his very first activity and style as a draftsman. It is the aim of the present contribution to exclude the Chatsworth Sketchbook from this role.

I

Our analysis first presents four observations concerning factual, intrinsic parts of the sketchbook. In this way we can distinguish the material of the sketchbook itself, which forms one strong body of evidence against Van Dyck's authorship, from the inconsistencies that characterize Jaffé's argument. These methodological shortcomings will be discussed later.

An observation of crucial importance is that the drawings of *Hercules in the Garden of the Hesperides*, on folio 47 recto with the upper parts of the figure (fig. 1) and folio 46 recto with the legs (fig. 2), are evidently copies after a late painting by Rubens (fig. 3), executed c. 1636–1639, formerly in the collection of Marchese Stefano Cattaneo, today in the Galleria Sabauda in Turin.[10] Jaffé related the drawings to an oil sketch on paper in the Cabinet des Dessins, Musée du Louvre, which shows the same *Hercules*, traditionally attributed to Rubens but most probably only a later Flemish copy.[11] Based on his attribu-

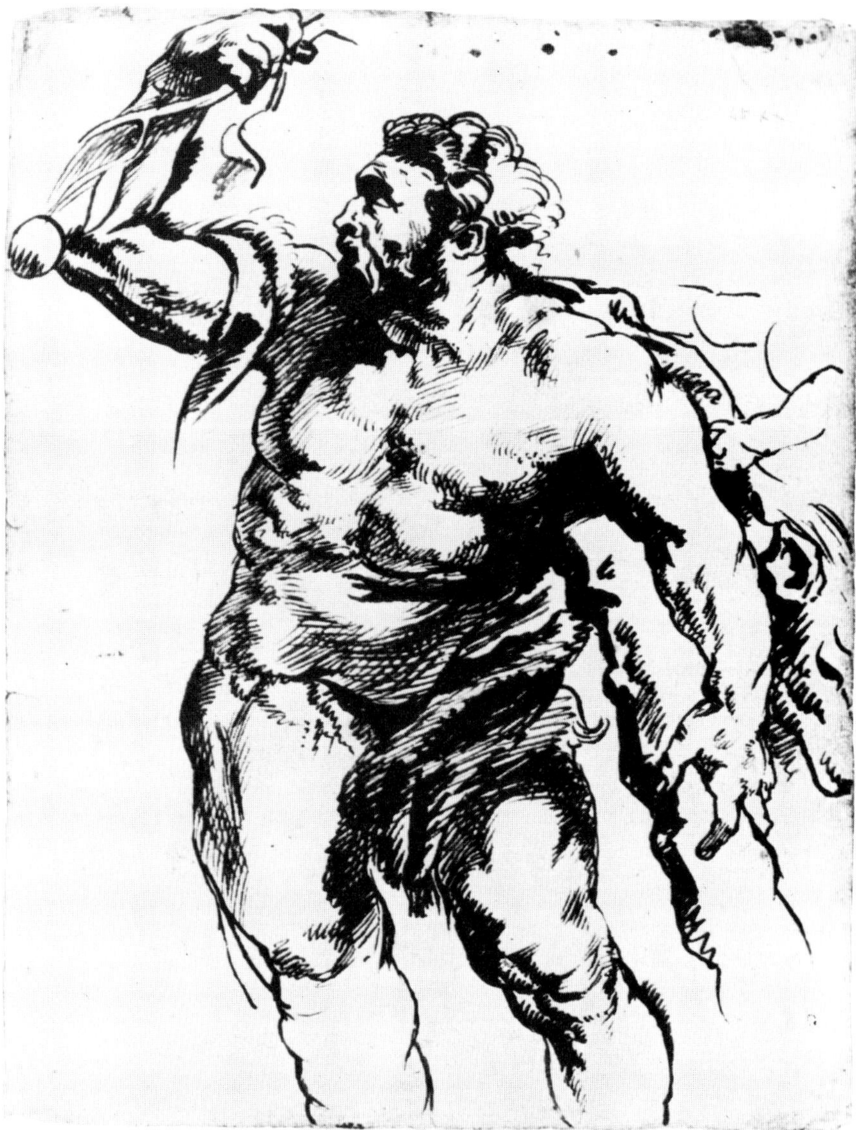

1. Anonymous Flemish artist after Peter Paul Rubens, *Hercules in the Garden of the Hesperides*, c. 1636–1639, pen and ink, Chatsworth Sketchbook, fol. 47r. Chatsworth Settlement

tion of the Chatsworth Sketchbook to the young Van Dyck, Jaffé dated the oil sketch in the Louvre between 1615 and 1620. As early as 1956 Ludwig Burchard and Roger A. d'Hulst had considered the *Hercules* composition in Turin a very late work by Rubens;[12] Julius Held (1980) followed this opinion.[13] In his comprehensive volume *Rubens: Opera Completa* (1990), Jaffé illustrated and discussed the *Hercules* in Turin,[14] dating the picture c. 1638 without mentioning the copy in the Chatsworth Sketchbook and his own earlier dating of the oil sketch in the Louvre. Finally, Christopher Brown stated: "the Sabauda painting must date from the 1630s."[15] If we were to express the problem in terms of a detective story, we would say that a gentle-

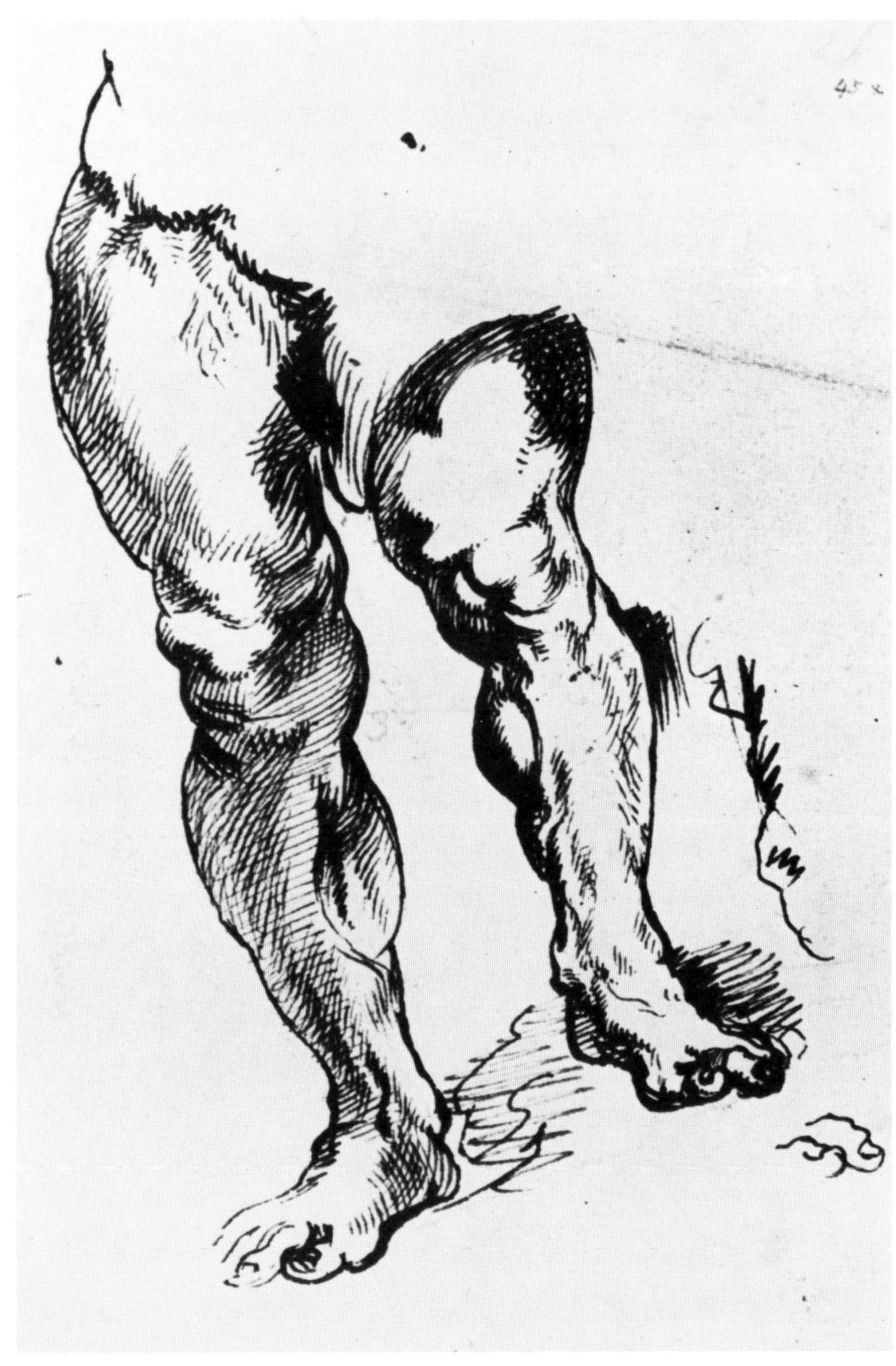

man born about 1638 could not have been murdered in about 1618. Also, the companion piece to Rubens' *Hercules, Deianeira Listening to the Fama Loquax* (fig. 4),[16] also in the Galleria Sabauda, points clearly and irrefutably to a late dating,[17] c. 1637–1638. The Chatsworth copyist must have been active around that time in Rubens' workshop, because he had access to a lost sketchbook of the master.

During a short colloquium at the Pierpont Morgan Library, New York, in 1991 on the problems of the sketchbook, initiated by Anne Marie Logan and involving Arnout Balis, Kristin Belkin, Christopher Brown, Egbert Haverkamp Begemann, Michael Jaffé, Justus Müller Hofstede, Katlijne Van der Stighelen, Carl Van de Velde, and Hans Vlieghe. The sketchbook was kindly made accessible by Peter Dreyer. The question was raised whether folio 46 and folio 47, which are loose pages tipped in, should be considered original or as later additions to the sketchbook. Subsequently, at the request of Christopher Brown, an examination of folios 46 and 47 was undertaken in November 1991 by Eric Harding and June Wallis from the conservation department of the National Gallery in London to study the relationship of the folios to other such sheets in the Chatsworth Sketchbook. The results of this examination were kindly communicated to the present writer by Christopher Brown. Beta-radiographs were made of folios 46 and 47. Radiographs were also made of folios 60 and 61, based on the supposition that these sheets originally formed undivided pairs with folios 46 and 47. In a representative sampling from the sketchbook, beta-radiographs were also made of folios 16, 24, 37, and 81. Folio 37 was chosen because Jaffé had identified it as being slightly different from the other leaves. The radiographs were viewed on a light-table, and a visual count was taken of the chain and laid line structure of the papers. It was possible to make the following observations:

i. Folio 37—but not folios 46 and 47—appeared to be of quite different paper from the other leaves within this sample;
ii. Folios 46 and 47 appeared to be very similar to folios 60 and 61, and to the other folios taken as a random sample.

Eric Harding and June Wallis summarized their results as follows:

Using the criteria of paper type alone and based on a very small sampling test described above, Folios 46 and 47 would appear to have been part of the sketchbook in its original form. The differences noted in the appearance of Folio 37 confirm the presence of at least one other type of paper.

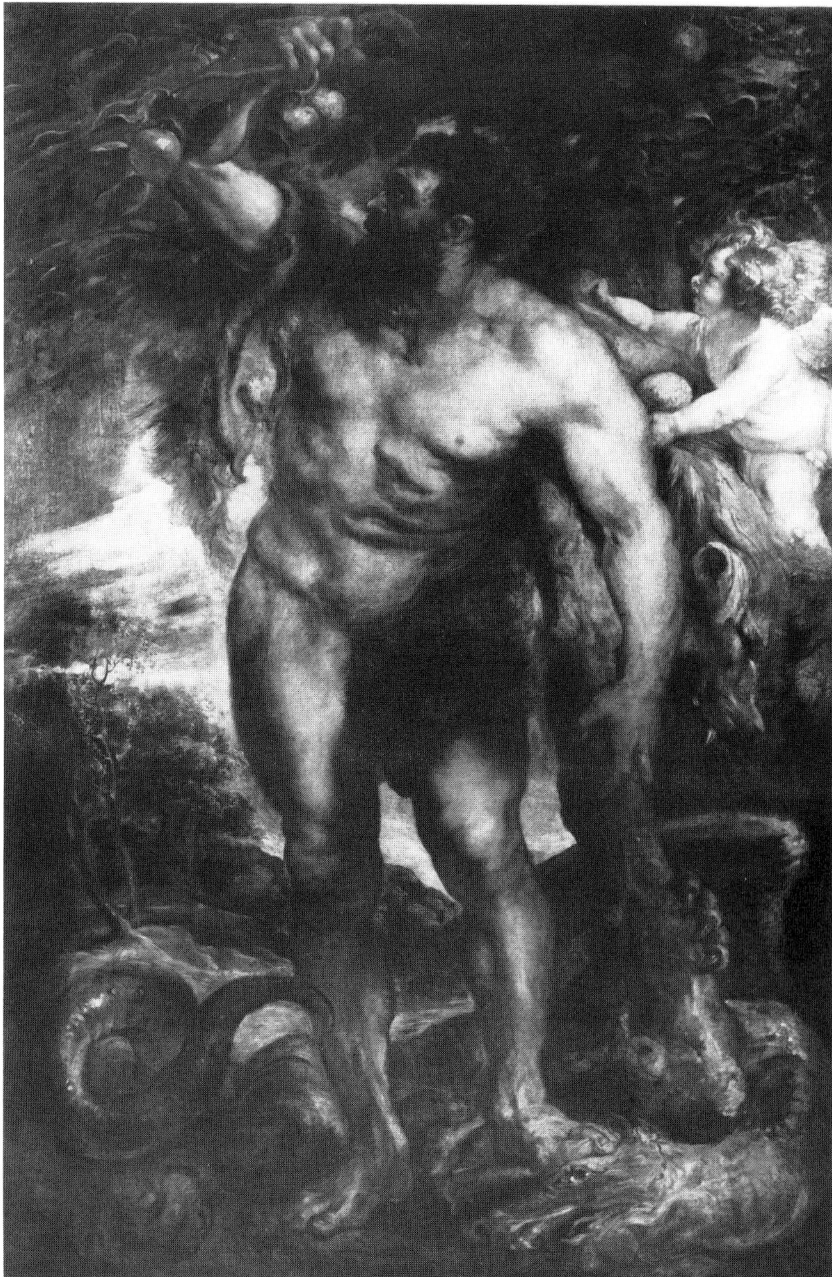

3. Peter Paul Rubens, *Hercules in the Garden of the Hesperides*, c. 1636–1639, oil on canvas Galleria Sabauda, Turin

Similar results were obtained by the computer-enhanced analysis of the laid line structure of several folios of the sketchbook, undertaken by David Saunders and Nicos Dessipris of the scientific department of the National Gallery in London. In order to determine the probability that the same type of paper was used in folios 16, 24, 37, 46, 47, 60, and 61, beta-radiographs of these pages were digitized and analyzed by image processing techniques. A second analysis was carried out only on the beta-radiographs of folios 46,

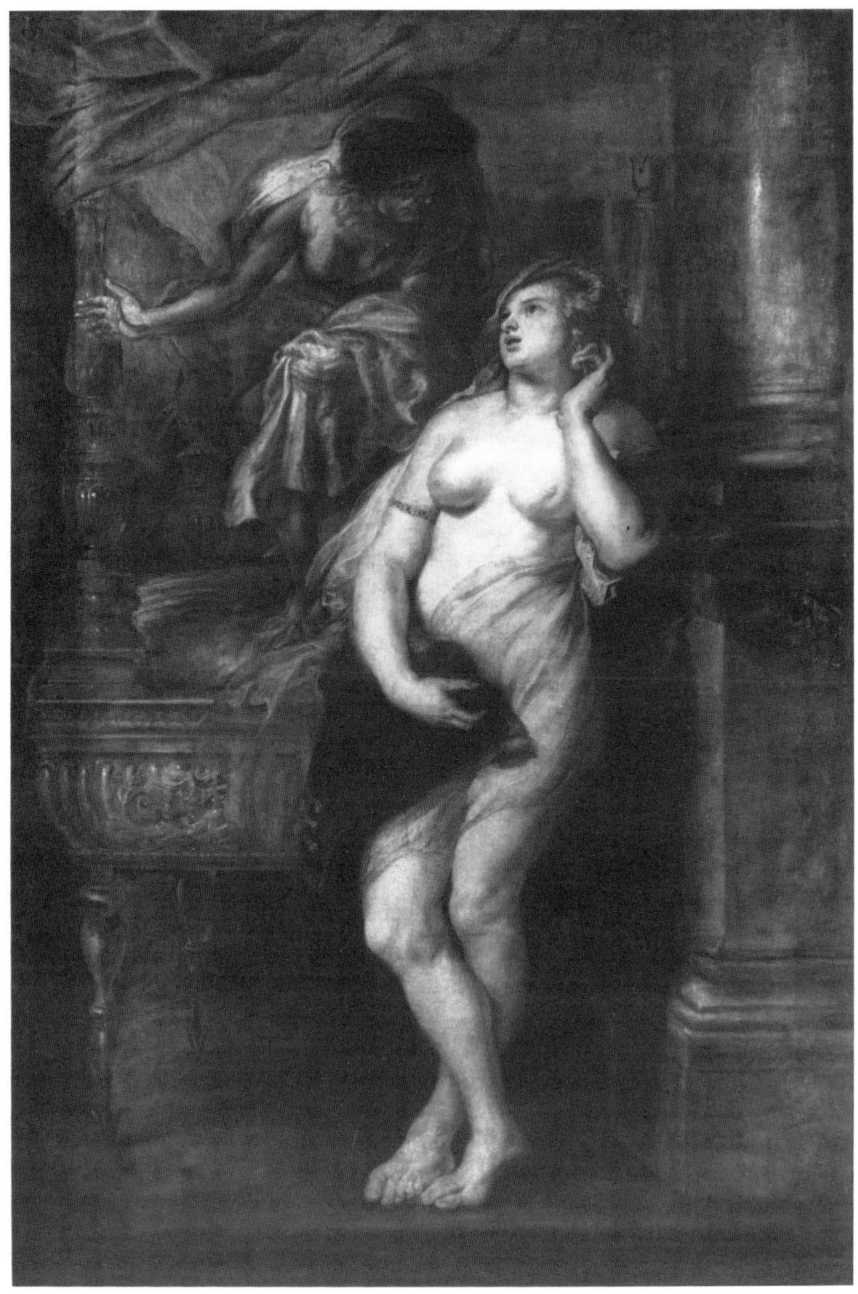

4. Peter Paul Rubens,
*Deianeira Listening to the
Fama Loquax*, c. 1636–1639,
oil on canvas
Galleria Sabauda, Turin

47, 60, and 61. On this occasion the original images were reduced by a factor of six before a sample area of the same size was extracted from each image. Thus a greater number of horizontal lines could be included in the count. The outcome of this second examination was summarized by Saunders as follows: "It can be speculated that since the four Folios above present similar high frequency patterns of horizontal lines, it is probable that they come from the same source." Therefore we have good reason to state that

folios 46 and 47, the drawings after Rubens' *Hercules*, are not a *corpus alienum* within a sketchbook otherwise produced by the young Van Dyck; they belong to the original corpus of the sketchbook. As Brown noted, "in style they are perfectly consistent with it,"[18] and they prove that the young Van Dyck has to be ruled out as the artist of the whole sketchbook. Also, the idea that Van Dyck was copying in Antwerp an earlier composition by Rubens, which Rubens later reworked, has to be rejected. Folios 46 and 47 closely follow the muscular and gigantean figure of Rubens' late *Hercules* (fig. 3).

A second observation concerns a drawing of *A Prisoner Led to Execution* (fig. 5), folio 17 verso of the Chatsworth Sketchbook. Surprisingly, the very same group, with slight modifications, particularly with the omission of one of the soldiers, was drawn by Van Dyck in black chalk in Italy after 1621. It was reworked in pen by a later hand on folio 19 verso of his Italian Sketchbook in the British Museum (fig. 6). Up to now it has not been possible to point out the model of both these drawings. Brown[19] took the repetition in the Italian Sketchbook as proof that Van Dyck also produced the Chatsworth Sketchbook. This argument, however, does not seem very convincing. Why should Van Dyck have repeated a composition that he had already recorded in the earlier sketchbook? Sketchbooks were used by young artists to gather copies, ideas, and inventions, but were not for duplications. There is not a single case in the oeuvre of the draftsman Van Dyck in which a composition or a motif recorded after a model was repeated. The artist's rich imagination, coupled with an extraordinary narrative inventiveness, excludes his authorship for the group in the Chatsworth Sketchbook; the drawing in the Italian Sketchbook was certainly a first.

The arguments against the attribution to Van Dyck of the Chatsworth Sketchbook have to be extended to the entire range of drawings in the book. They differ, in all that we understand by the concept of "style," from examples of Van Dyck's masterly, sensitive draftsmanship. If we consider the soft, delicate, swinging handwriting, the *ductus* of Van Dyck's drawings in the Italian Sketchbook,[20] whose earliest examples were probably executed soon after December 1621, then

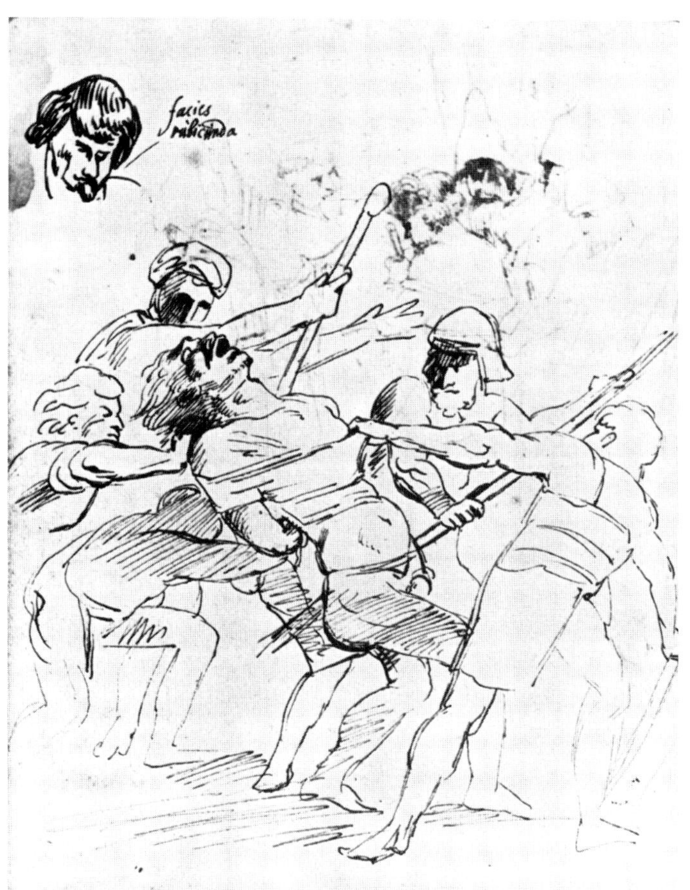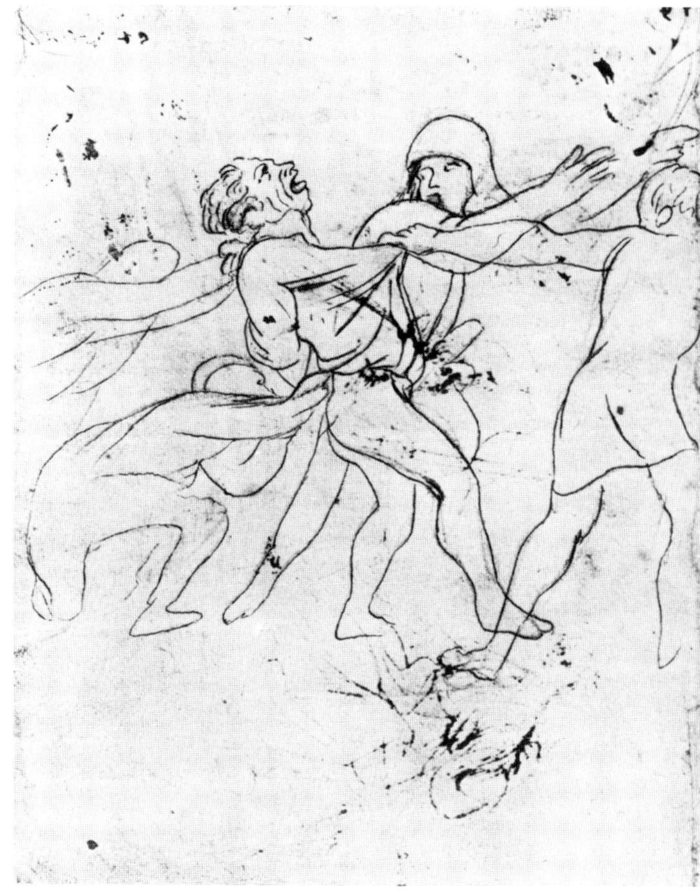

no bridge backward to the Chatsworth drawings is imaginable. Within the narrow confines of this paper only a few examples can be discussed. Folio 18 recto of the Chatsworth Sketchbook (fig. 7) and folio 20 recto of Van Dyck's Italian Sketchbook (fig. 8) show a somewhat similar composition. The Chatsworth sheet is a copy after *Prisoners Brought before the Pope* from Raphael's *Battle of Ostia;* the Van Dyck example is of a group of horsemen and a prisoner kneeling before his execution. The sharp difference in style between these two drawings cannot be explained by the development of a young artist between about 1617 and about 1621– 1622. In the Chatsworth sheet a broader, thicker pen is at work, distinguishable throughout the sketchbook. The outlines are drawn hesitantly, often reinforced or repeated; the hatchings have no function; and the formulation of the figures is awkward and clumsy. In the Italian Sketchbook Van Dyck uses a pointed, thin pen and records his

figures with fluent, nervous, swinging lines. He does not try to suggest much plasticity; his long figures are imbued with movement. The heavy and rude language of the pen described above in folio 18 recto of the Chatsworth Sketchbook is again to be found on folio 13 verso (fig. 9), a copy after Giorgio Ghisi's engraving of Giulio Romano's *Triumph of Scipio Africanus.* Folio 24 recto, a drawing of *A Drunken Priest Supported by Two Young Men, Followed by a Torch Bearer* (fig. 10) after an engraving by Marcantonio Raimondi, shows an obvious search for plasticity, ponderously achieved by sharply stressed hatchings and washes. This approach is quite alien to Van Dyck's artistic conceptions.

Michael Jaffé had to admit that "what Van Dyck has left us in the sketchbook is often inelegant, sometimes downright ugly."[21] These traits of the Chatsworth drawings, however, testify against Van Dyck's authorship. Already the young artist was gifted as a draftsman with the elegance and assurance that is

5. Anonymous Flemish artist, *A Prisoner Led to Execution,* c. 1636–1639, pen and ink, Chatsworth Sketchbook, fol. 17v. Chatsworth Settlement

6. Anthony van Dyck, *A Prisoner Led to Execution,* c. 1622–1623, pen and ink, Italian Sketchbook, fol. 19v. British Museum, London

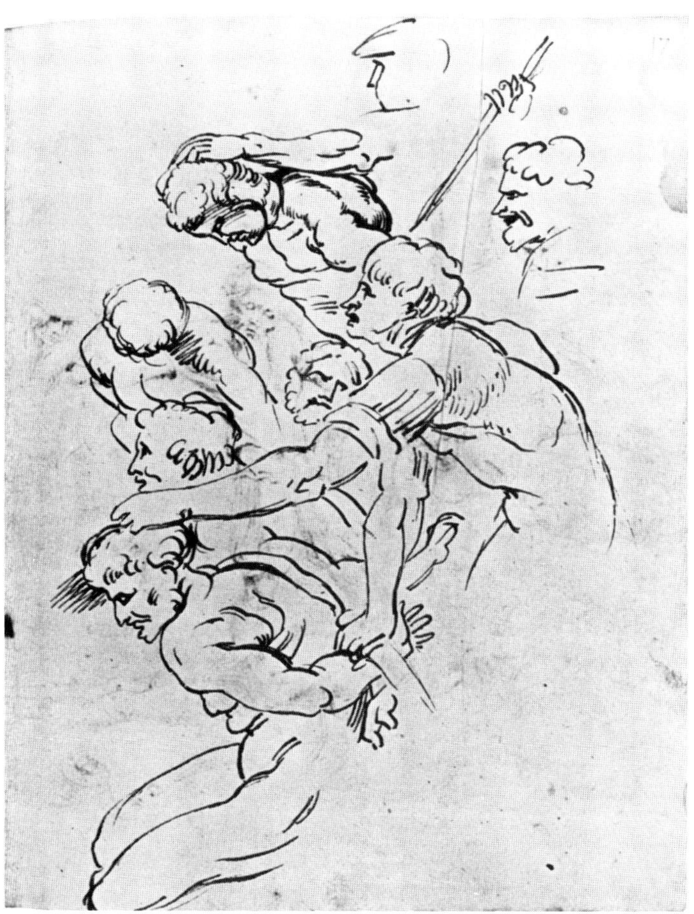

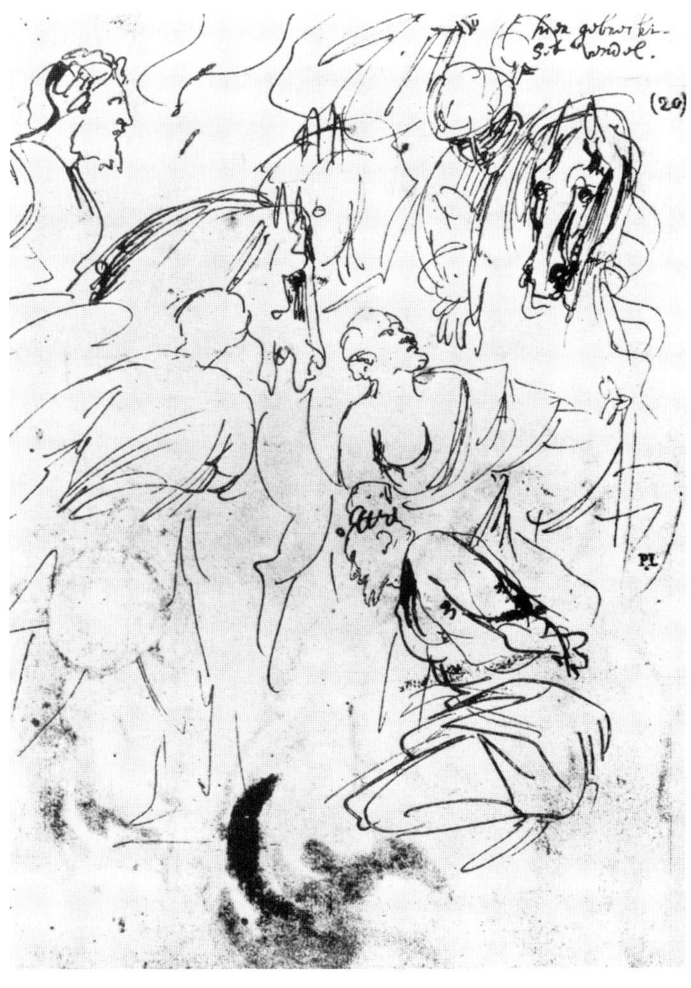

7. Anonymous Flemish artist after Raphael, *Prisoners Brought before the Pope after the Battle of Ostia,* c. 1636–1639, pen and ink, Chatsworth Sketchbook, fol. 18r.
Chatsworth Settlement

8. Anthony van Dyck, *A Group of Horsemen and a Kneeling Prisoner,* c. 1622–1623, pen and ink, Italian Sketchbook, fol. 20r.
British Museum, London

to be found in his marvelous early oil sketch of an *Armed Soldier on Horseback* (Christ Church, Oxford), c. 1615–1616, essentially a drawing done with the brush in oils.[22] Folios 18 verso, 19 recto, 20 verso, 24 verso, 25 recto, 28 verso, 29 recto, 31 verso, 39 recto, 39 verso, 40 recto, 45 recto, 45 verso, 48 recto and verso, 49 recto and verso—to give only some particularly conspicuous examples—speak a quite different, clumsy, and dull language that separates the Chatsworth volume from the Italian Sketchbook. This gap cannot be bridged by introducing a presumed evolution from a juvenile awkwardness to maturity and mastery of draftsmanship; two different artists were at work. Jaffé dated the Chatsworth drawings into Van Dyck's formative years, between 1615 and 1620;[23] the style of the sketchbook does not show the slightest change or development. An artist producing drawings of this uncouth manner about 1620 cannot be identical

with the artist who began the Italian Sketchbook about 1622.

A fourth observation is that the script of the notes of the Chatsworth Sketchbook is not congruous with the early examples of Van Dyck's handwriting. There are three types of script in the sketchbook:

i. First, there are the technical and pharmaceutical notes on folio 2 recto through folio 7 recto, which are written in Flemish (fig. 11). A similar note in Flemish, "hier gebreckt het vendel," written by Van Dyck on folio 20 recto of his Italian Sketchbook (fig. 12),[24] shows a distinctly different handwriting.

ii. On several pages of the Chatsworth Sketchbook, beginning on folio 7 recto and 7 verso (fig. 13), there is a kind of starchy secretarial script used for Flemish notes. It appears also on folio 14 recto (fig. 14) with some remarks on

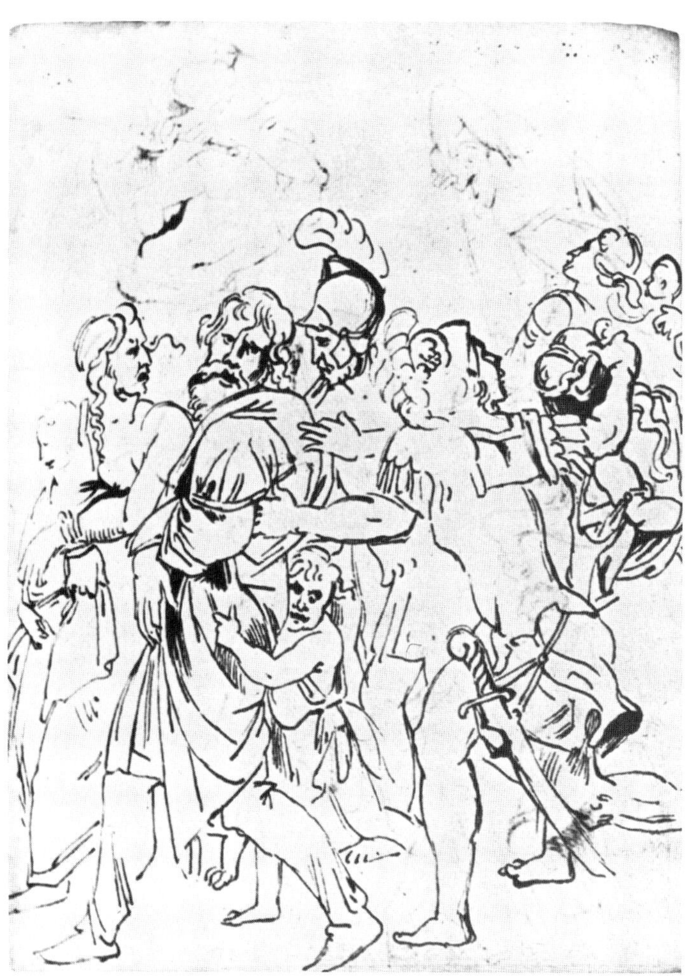

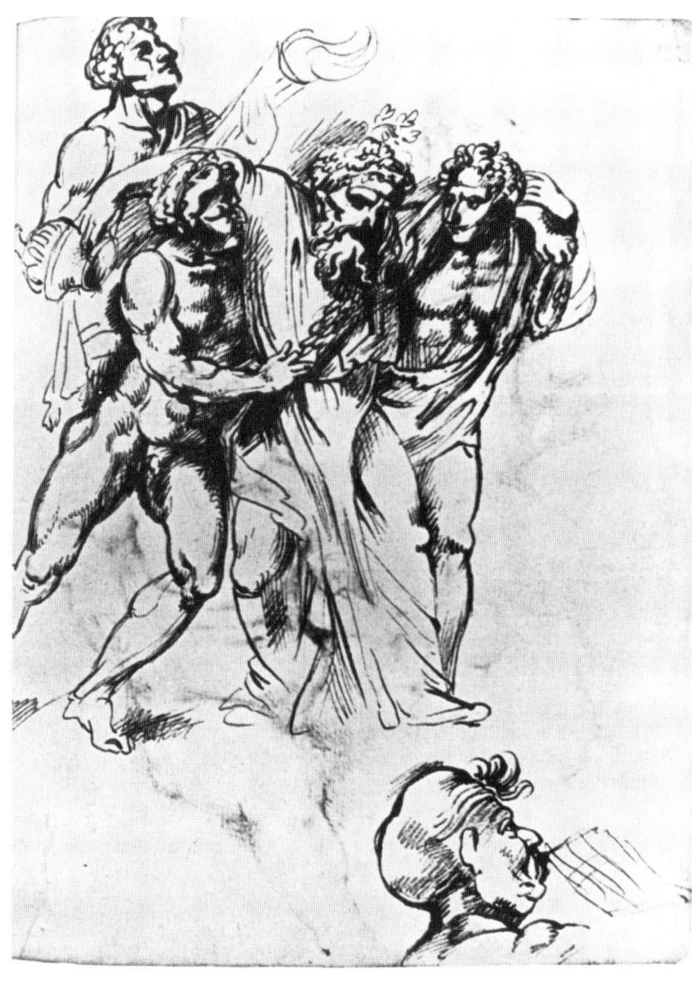

portraiture. This type of script is rather calligraphic and marked by constraint and pedestrian meaning. A corresponding secretarial, calligraphic type of script from among the early handwritten notes by Van Dyck can be seen on folio 2 recto (fig. 15) of his Italian Sketchbook, where the artist records the addresses of the painter Andrea Vicentino in Venice and the name of the physician Don Fabrizio Valguarnera. This script is completely different from the stiff, vertical letters of the Chatsworth volume. It is not necessary to dwell on Van Dyck's swinging signature on this page, for the names and addresses sufficiently demonstrate the way in which the young artist uses this type of script. They prove that the notes in the Chatsworth Sketchbook were written by a different author.

iii. A third type of script in the Chatsworth Sketchbook, for instance the notes on the *Columna Toscana* on folio 76 recto (fig. 16), has a pronouncedly ceremonial character. The notes suggest a comparison with the last page of Van Dyck's Italian Sketchbook, particularly with the addresses in the lower part of the page (fig. 17). Although superficially similar and apparently comparable with the Chatsworth script, Van Dyck's letters reveal themselves not as stiff, but as much more free and dynamic.

II

In this second, shorter section the inconsistencies and omissions in the scholarly presentation of the Chatsworth Sketchbook will be discussed.

9. Anonymous Flemish artist after Giorgio Ghisi and Giulio Romano, *Prisoners from the "Triumph of Scipio Africanus,"* c. 1636–1639, pen and ink, Chatsworth Sketchbook, fol. 13v. Chatsworth Settlement

10. Anonymous Flemish artist after Marcantonio Raimondi, *A Drunken Priest Supported by Two Younger Men, Followed by a Torch Bearer,* c. 1636–1639, pen and ink, Chatsworth Sketchbook, fol. 24r. Chatsworth Settlement

11. Anonymous Flemish artist, Monogram *A V D* or *D V A* and pharmaceutical notes, c. 1636–1639, pen and ink, Chatsworth Sketchbook, fol. 2r.
Chatsworth Settlement

12. Anthony van Dyck, "hier gebreckt het vendel," c. 1622–1623, pen and ink, Italian Sketchbook, fol. 20r.
British Museum, London

13. Anonymous Flemish artist, technical notes, c. 1636–1639, pen and ink, Chatsworth Sketchbook, fol. 7v.
Chatsworth Settlement

A special problem is the monogram on folio 2 recto (fig. 11), evidently not a testimony of masterly draftsmanship. The artist was not sure how to connect the A with the D in a striking way. The V is convincingly inserted into the D, but the initial A is not satisfactorily adapted to the monogram. Jaffé read the monogram as A D V; it could also be read as D V A.

The invention of a monogram with an interlaced pattern is equivalent to the invention of a printer's mark, intended to be durable and to be used again, particularly if it appears in a somewhat ceremonial way at the opening of a sketchbook. It speaks against Jaffé's assumption that this monogram was never used in one of Van Dyck's generally accepted works. The monogram (A V D), which Van Dyck employed for his *Portrait of an Elderly Man* (Musées Royaux des Beaux-Arts, Brussels) of 1613, is very different. The combination of three clear-cut *antiqua* capital letters[25] is united with an inscription that indicates proudly that the painting was executed in Van Dyck's fourteenth year. It is regrettable that this very important early monogram was not mentioned in Jaffé's presentation of the Chatsworth monogram. Another interlaced monogram (A V D) appears on the bottom of the drinker's jug in Van Dyck's *Drunken Silenus* (Gemäldegalerie Alte Meister, Dresden), of c. 1618.[26] Compared with these two authentic signatures by the young artist, the monogram in the Chatsworth Sketchbook cannot be regarded as genuine.

Another problem is presented by Jaffé's suggestion of a provenance of the Chatsworth Sketchbook from the artist's widow. Jaffé supposed that both volumes, Van Dyck's Italian Sketchbook and the booklet at Chatsworth, belonged to Sir Peter Lely (1618–1680). He assumed that Lely had acquired both of them directly from the painter's widow, Mary Ruthven, shortly after Van Dyck's death (9 December 1641). This provenance would indeed be an excellent proof of Van Dyck's authorship, but only the Italian Sketchbook bears the collector's marks of Peter Lely. No Lely stamp is to be found in the Chatsworth volume. Jaffé explained this significant deficiency by conjecturing that Lely's executor, Roger North, had intentionally not put Lely's collector's stamp in the Chatsworth Sketchbook because he saw it as less important. Thus Jaffé favored the improbable and complicated solution over the probable and simple one—that did not, of course, confirm Van Dyck's authorship. Folio 35 verso of the Chatsworth Sketchbook shows the stamp of the Flemish painter and collector Prosper Henry Lankrink (1628–1692). Lankrink was born in Antwerp and was largely patronized by the wealthy Antwerp merchant and collector Antoon van Leyen, to whom Cornelis de Bie dedicated his *Het gulden cabinet vande edel vry schilder const* in 1661. It is quite pos-

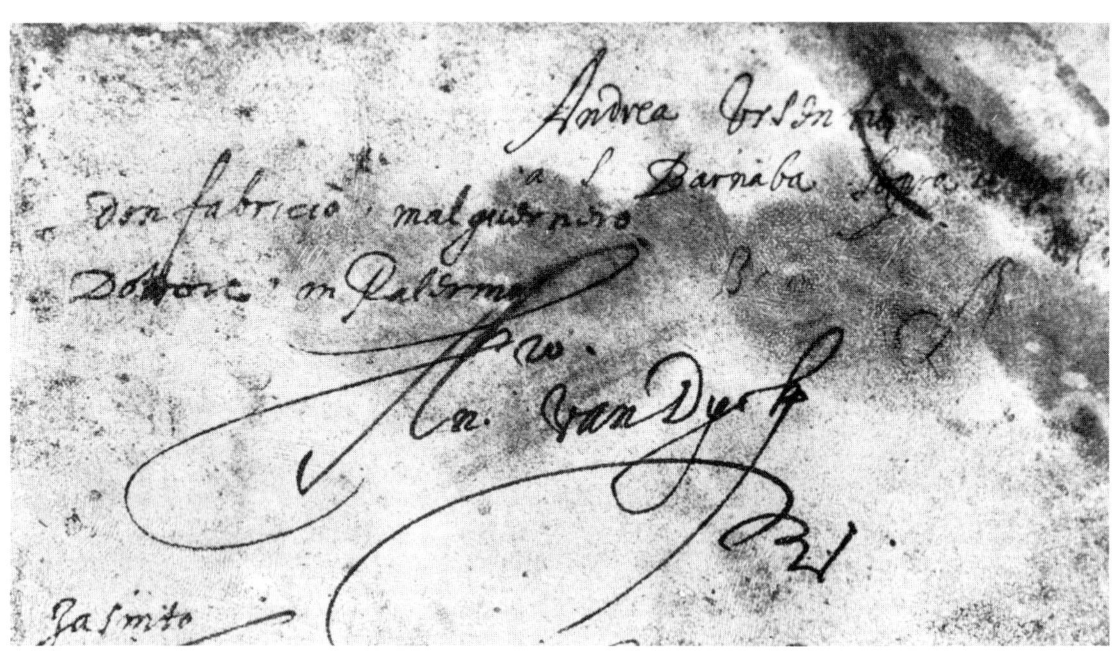

14. Anonymous Flemish artist, notes on portraiture, c. 1636–1639, pen and ink, Chatsworth Sketchbook, fol. 14r.
Chatsworth Settlement

15. Anthony van Dyck, notes with addresses and names, c. 1622–1623, pen and ink, Italian Sketchbook, fol. 2r.
British Museum, London

16. Anonymous Flemish artist, notes on the *Columna Toscana*, c. 1636–1639, pen and ink, Chatsworth Sketchbook, fol. 76r.
Chatsworth Settlement

17. Anthony van Dyck, notes of addresses and sketch for a *Penitent Magdalen*, c. 1624–1625, pen and ink, Italian Sketchbook, fol. 121v.
British Museum, London

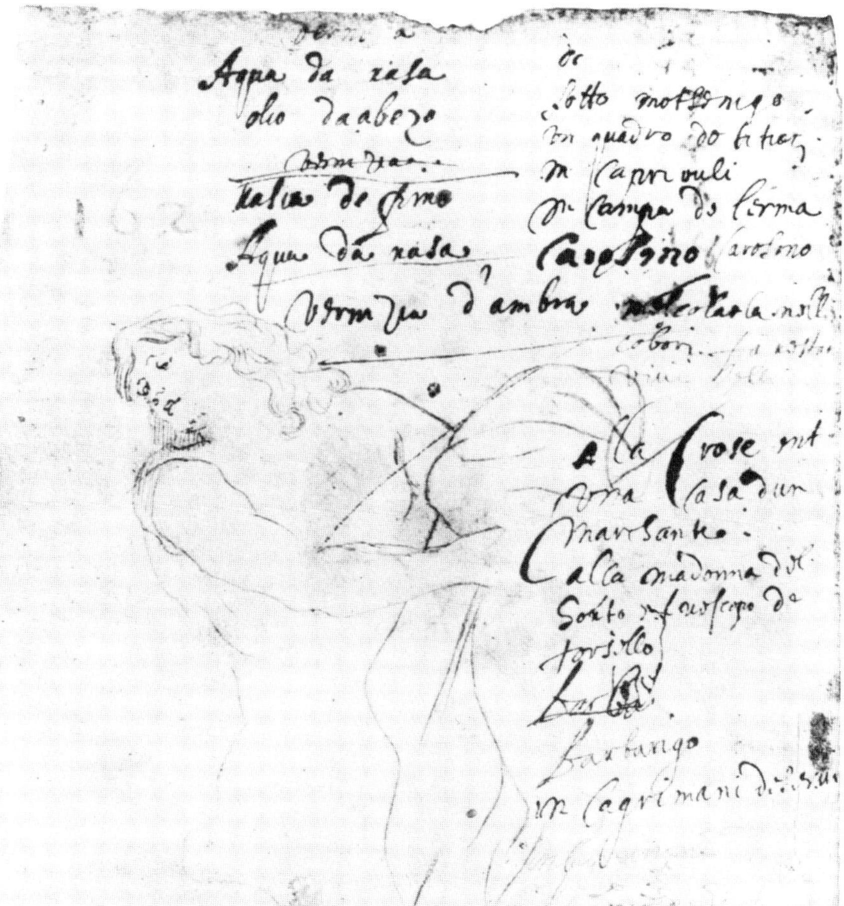

sible that Lankrink acquired the Chatsworth drawings in Antwerp, a long time after Van Dyck's death, before he went to London. Lankrink was rich and a passionate collector. A direct trace of the Chatsworth volume to Van Dyck's estate cannot be maintained.

A further objection to Jaffé's attribution concerns the issue of iconography, which Jaffé did not address in his publication of 1966. One might argue that the entire contents of the Chatsworth manuscript consist of the ordinary, regular exercises of a young Flemish artist in the first half of the seventeenth century. However, this is by no means the case. There are several distinct and special iconographical areas that were evidently consciously chosen by the artist of the sketchbook from among the sources and models that were available. These personal artistic preferences do not point to the young Van Dyck. Ten pages of the sketchbook are devoted to the theme of Hercules, the prototype of the *vir robustus*, and to his physical appearance; another ten pages have drawings relating to physiognomical theory based on comparisons between man and animal. No indications of these two iconographical areas can be detected in Van Dyck's oeuvre. Also, there are hardly any traces in the artist's paintings from c. 1615–1620 or thereafter of a later working up of the sketchbook drawings.

The rediscovery and publication of the Chatsworth Sketchbook was clearly an excellent achievement. It should be explored with regard to the theory and practice of a young Flemish artist active about 1636–1639 under the influence of Rubens. The Van Dyck attribution, however, has to be abandoned.

NOTES

1. Pen and brown ink with brown washes. The sketchbook contains eighty-seven leaves plus eight additional pages or inserted fragments. The size of the original pages is c. 21 x 16 cm. For the provenance of the sketchbook see Michael Jaffé, *Van Dyck's Antwerp Sketchbook*, 2 vols. (London, 1966), 1:47–58. The scholarly literature on the sketchbook since 1966 and a recent discussion of its authorship are presented by Christopher Brown, *The Drawings of Anthony van Dyck* [exh. cat., Pierpont Morgan Library] (New York, 1991), 38–47.

2. Jaffé 1966.

3. John Rupert Martin and Gail Feigenbaum, *Van Dyck as Religious Artist* [exh. cat., Art Museum, Princeton University] (Princeton, 1979).

4. Alan McNairn, *The Young Van Dyck* [exh. cat., National Gallery of Canada] (Ottawa, 1980). McNairn rejected the attribution of the sketchbook to Van Dyck (74).

5. For the quoted literature see New York 1991, 38–42.

6. As pointed out to me by Christopher White in London, 1967, during a conversation about the problems of the sketchbook.

7. For the following quotations see New York 1991, 38–42.

8. Justus Müller Hofstede, "Neue Beiträge zum Oeuvre Anton van Dycks," *Wallraf-Richartz-Jahrbuch* 48–49 (1987–1988), 125–131. My rejection of Van Dyck's authorship is based on a first examination of the sketchbook in 1967, granted by T. S. Wragg, keeper of the Devonshire collection, and of a second examination in 1984, kindly made possible by Christopher Brown, deputy keeper of the National Gallery, London.

9. New York 1991, 38–47.

10. 246 x 168.5 cm. A recent discussion of this painting is by Giuliano Frabetti, *Rubens e Genova* [exh. cat., Palazzo Ducale] (Genoa, 1977–1978), no. 4, with incorrect dating about 1606.

11. Frits Lugt, *Musée du Louvre: Inventaire général des dessins des écoles du nord. Ecole Flamande*, 2 vols. (Paris, 1949), vol. 2, no. 1013, oil on paper, 43.9 x 25.2 cm, as early work by Rubens.

12. Ludwig Burchard and Roger A. d'Hulst, *Tekeningen van P. P. Rubens* [exh. cat., Museum Rubenshuis] (Antwerp, 1956), no. 140.

13. Julius S. Held, *The Oil Sketches of Peter Paul Rubens: A Critical Catalogue*, 2 vols. (Princeton, 1980), 1:323, 647.

14. Michael Jaffé, *Rubens: Catalogo completo* (Milan, 1989), no. 1362, dated c. 1638.

15. New York 1991, 46.

16. The subject of the painting was identified by Held 1980, 1:323.

17. A color plate of the *Deianeira*, which demonstrates the late date of this painting and the *Hercules*, its companion piece, is to be found in Rosalba Tardito Amerio, *La Galleria Sabauda* (Turin, 1984), plate 22.

18. New York 1991, 46.

19. New York 1991, 38–39.

20. Gert Adriani, *Anton van Dyck: Italienisches Skizzenbuch* (Vienna, 1940). This sketchbook belongs now to the British Museum, department of prints and drawings. A new facsimile edition is being prepared by Christopher Brown.

21. Jaffé 1966, 1:67.

22. Arthur K. Wheelock, Jr., et al., *Anthony van Dyck* [exh. cat., National Gallery of Art] (Washington, 1990), no. 88, with color plate.

23. Jaffe 1966, 1:48, 49.

24. Adriani 1940, fol. 20r. All further quotations of the Italian Sketchbook refer to Adriani 1940.

25. Washington 1990, no. 1, with color plate.

26. Washington 1990, no. 12, with color plate.

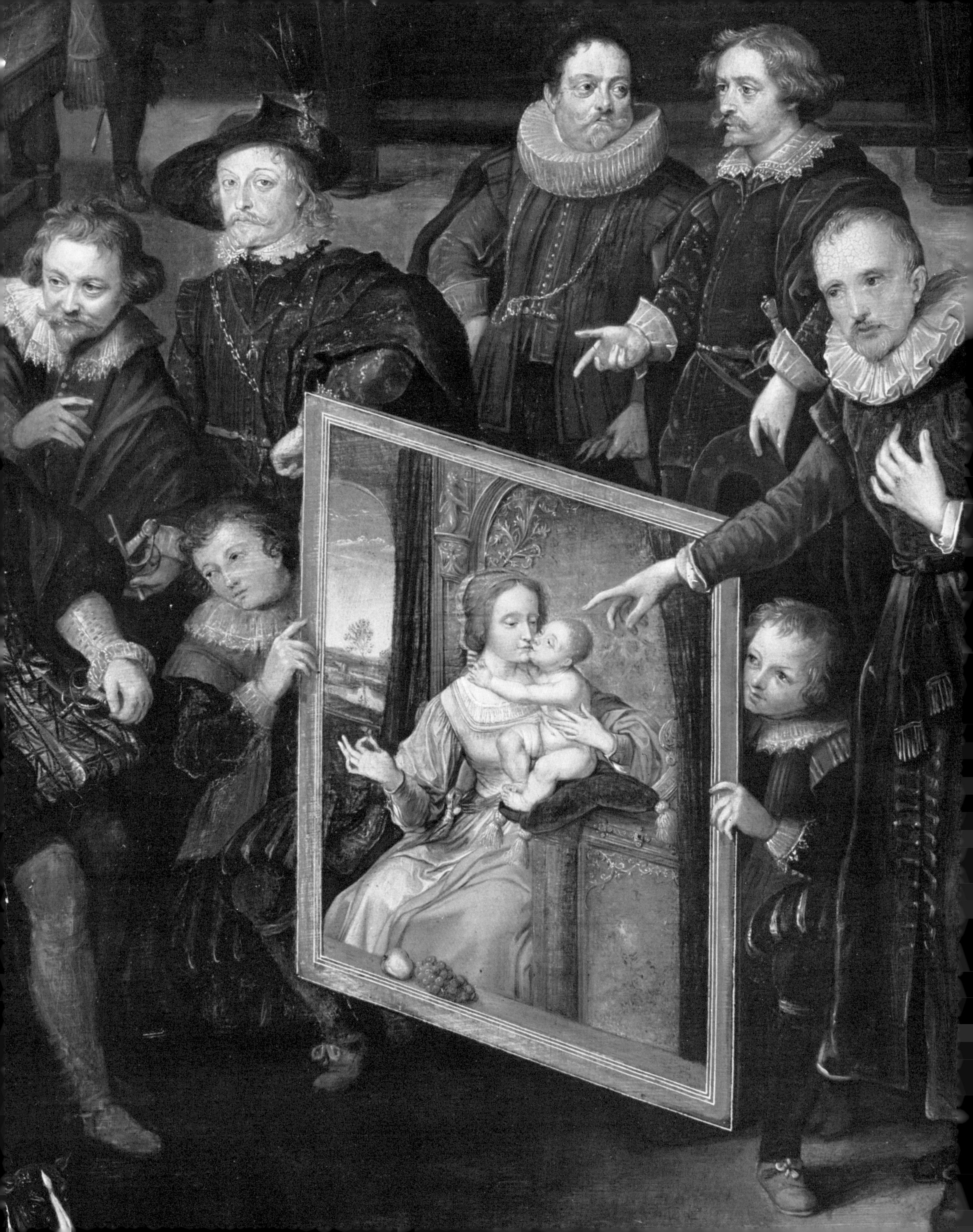

JULIUS S. HELD
Barnard College, Columbia University (emeritus)

Van Dyck's Relationship to Rubens

The close pairing of two names such that the mention of one almost immediately brings to mind the other is familiar in the history of literature, the arts, and even science: there are Horace and Virgil, Petrarch and Boccaccio, Ariosto and Tasso, Goethe and Schiller (who with joined hands recently graced a German thirty-pfennig postage stamp); in art there are Leonardo and Michelangelo, Dürer and Grünewald, Bernini and Borromini, Picasso and Matisse; in science Galileo and Kepler. The most famous pairs may well be the apostles Peter and Paul (both combined in Rubens' name) and Plato and Aristotle, who in Raphael's *School of Athens* (fig. 1) dominate a glittering assembly of scientists and philosophers. Whether or not they were contemporaries, these poets, artists, or scientists owe their historical eminence to the powerful originality and individuality of their work. Occasionally they may have been veritable antipodes, as were Dürer and Grünewald, or founders of very different philosophical schools, as were Plato and Aristotle.

Pairing Rubens and Van Dyck, as has often and justifiably been done, creates a "unit" of a very different kind. There are surprising biographical similarities, though we must keep in mind that Van Dyck was twenty-two years younger than Rubens. His biographical clock ran at an accelerated pace, since he died only a year and a half after Rubens. Both artists came from upper middle-class families, long established in Antwerp; both were first trained by competent Antwerp painters, and both went to Italy in their early twenties—Rubens at twenty-three, Van Dyck at twenty-two years of age. Both stayed there several years, Rubens eight, Van Dyck six. They both had stunning successes, Rubens with large religious paintings, Van Dyck with portraits. Both established conspicuous professional contacts with the most powerful courts of Europe, Rubens with those of France, England, and Spain, Van Dyck chiefly with England, though on a truly exceptional level of intimacy. And not only were both of them international celebrities, but their lifestyles at the height of their careers were equally grand, as befits men knighted by the same English king, and known to be not only wealthy but also surrounded by the visible symbols of their wealth, in the form of splendid private collections of works of art.

These parallels in their careers and lifestyles lose some of their mystery if we remember that for many years the younger artist had been in close contact with the older one. In fact, even in some of the earliest documents we have about Van Dyck's life and activity, he is referred to as Rubens' pupil, a statement to which I shall return. The aura of being (or having been) the pupil of Rubens surely smoothed the way for the younger artist, even though it obviously would not have helped if his art had not done honor to that parentage. Nor can there be any doubt that in living the life of a cavalier and engaging in conspicuous consumption as he

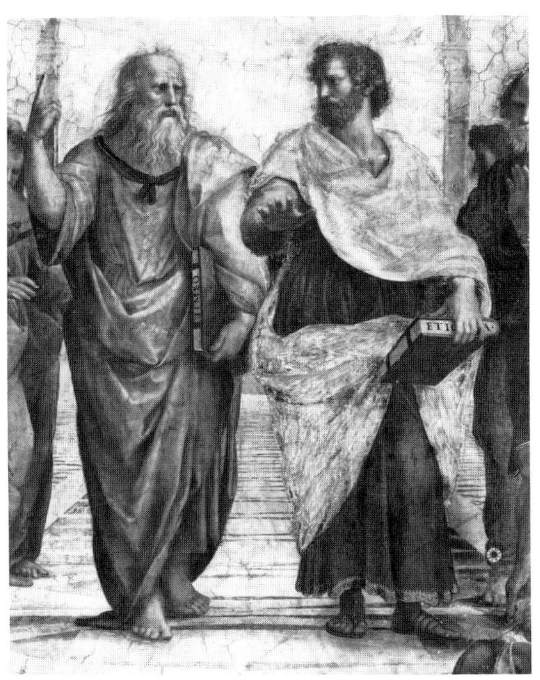

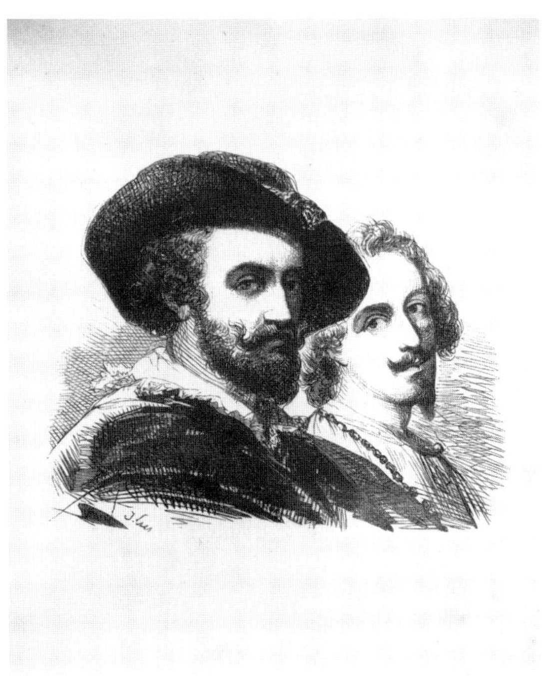

1. Raphael, *School of Athens* (detail of Plato and Aristotle), 1510–1511, fresco
Vatican, Rome; photograph: Anderson

2. J. Lies, *Anthony van Dyck and Peter Paul Rubens*, lithograph, from William Hookham Carpenter, *Mémoires et documents inédits sur Antoine Van Dyck, Rubens et autres contemporains . . .* (Antwerp, 1845)

did, Van Dyck adopted a style he had observed, and surely admired, with Rubens. (His frequently mentioned sexual appetite was his personal icing on that cake.) All these biographical comparabilities would not suffice to establish the close linkage generally accepted, if in their art the two masters did not show extraordinary affinities. These are so obvious and seem to be so self-evident that they are rarely spelled out; the burden of much of the Van Dyck literature, in fact, has been the proof that there are, after all, considerable differences between the work of the two men. And not only between their work. They really were very different personalities, an aspect that has fascinated many writers, especially since the middle of the nineteenth century.

As the frontispiece for the French edition of William Hookham Carpenter's book of unpublished documents on Van Dyck, Rubens, and other Flemish artists (Antwerp, 1845) there appears a lithograph by J. Lies, rendering Rubens and Van Dyck side by side (fig. 2). It does not take much acumen to read the characterization intended by the illustrator. He modeled Rubens' likeness on a celebrated self-portrait in Windsor Castle. Under his grandly curving hat, Rubens fixes the beholder with a glance of firm and proud self-assurance. Van Dyck, with longer hair, is shown bareheaded, inclining his head sideways. The graphic artist surely wanted to make him appear weaker, more pliable, and willing to submit to Rubens' dominance. I might say that the nineteenth-century lithographer, in the language of a less egalitarian age than ours, wanted to stress Van Dyck as a feminine type. Thirty years later, in 1875, this characterization was spelled out with great eloquence in Eugène Fromentin's *Les Maîtres d'autrefois*. This still highly readable book, published in 1963 in an English translation with a brilliant introduction by Meyer Schapiro, compares the two artists, using the analogy of father and son: "all sons, like Van Dyck, have a feminine quality [un trait féminin] added to the qualities of the father." Fromentin continues linking the presumed feminine nature of Van Dyck to the perceived effeminacy of the personages in Van Dyck's portraits. This kind of character reading comes close to what has often been termed the psychological fallacy, but I cannot deny that Van Dyck's self-portraits make this kind of character reading understandable. The earliest, in Vienna, shows him as a tender youth, surely no older than fourteen or fifteen, but already an accomplished painter; in the next one, in Munich, he seems to be quite pleased with his reflection in the mirror, while the one in New York shows

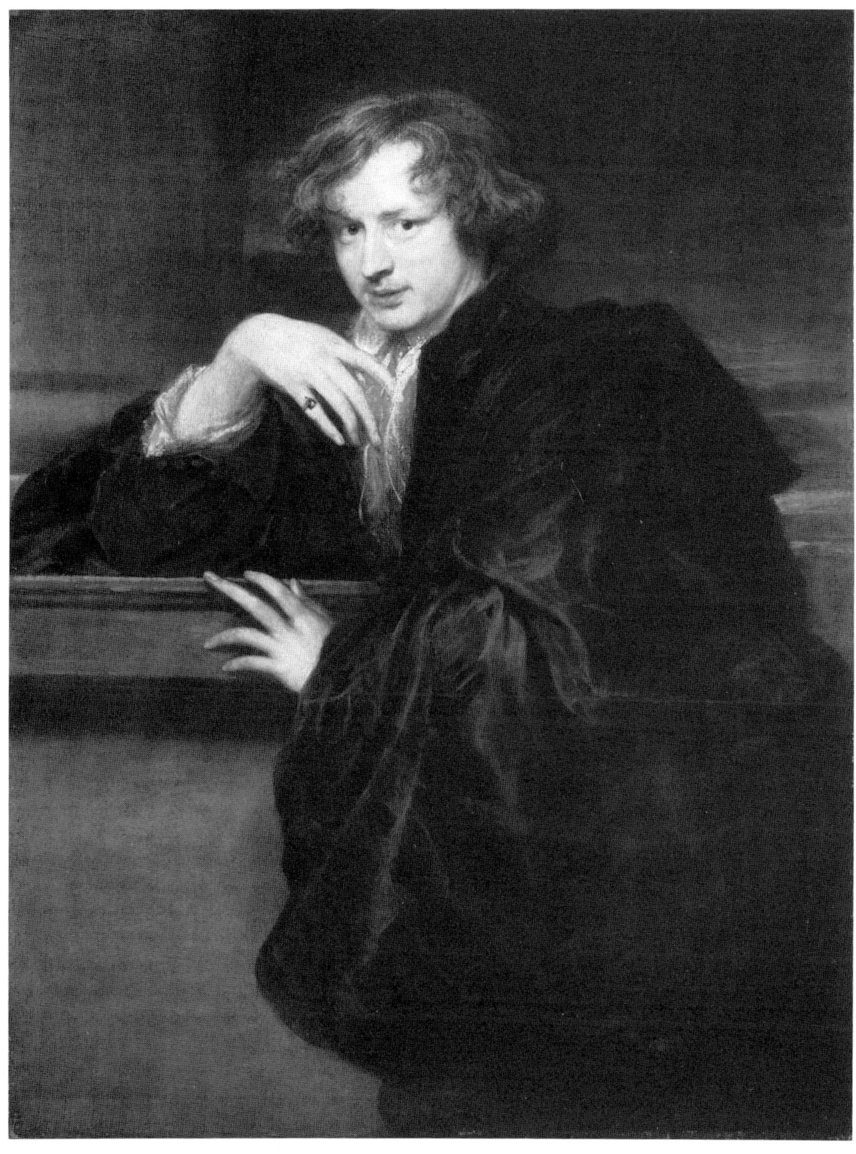

3. Anthony van Dyck, *Self-Portrait*, c. 1619–1620, oil on canvas
Metropolitan Museum of Art, New York

arranged so that the word *eques* ("knight") appears in exactly the same way above each head, a reminder that both had been knighted by Charles I. Yet the contemporary beholder could not fail to notice that both portrayals were derived from prints based on Van Dyck's drawings, which he had made for the so-called Iconography, a collection of portraits of fellow artists but also of various kinds of dignitaries and scholars. The portrait of Rubens is copied from a small grisaille that in the Iconography was actually replaced by a different one. Van Dyck's likeness is derived from a print by Lucas Vorsterman that *does* figure in that collection of portraits. Since both images are based on models by Van Dyck, the print depicting both masters is hence more of a glorification of Van Dyck than of Rubens; in fact, Van Dyck's elegantly turned pose clearly draws our attention more to him than to Rubens, and a not insignificant detail makes it rather likely that the print was intentionally slanted in favor of Van Dyck. Both artists wear a gold chain, a symbol of high honor that came with the knighthood, but only a few links of that chain can be seen in the Rubens portrait. Pontius made one seemingly minor change when he copied the Vorsterman print: he replaced the white collar of his model with a simpler one, so that the chain could be displayed more fully as it circles the neck.

It is not quite clear for whom or for what purpose Pontius' print was made. There is reason to think that it was planned as part of, or at least to arouse interest in, the Iconography, but this question apparently has not yet been properly investigated.

There is another and still earlier pictorial document that, if not actually pairing Rubens and Van Dyck, clearly gives them equal standing. In a painting of the gallery of Cornelis van der Geest, one of the foremost art patrons of Antwerp in the first half of the seventeenth century, the artist Willem van Haecht depicted (quite unhistorically) a true historical event, the visit of Archduke Albert and his spouse Isabella Clara Eugenia at the home of Van der Geest. Seated at the left and surrounded by members of the court, the archduke and duchess look at a painting by Quentin Massys which Van der Geest is showing them (fig. 5). The aim of the artist

him with a most elegant posing of his hands (fig. 3).

The image formulated by Fromentin has been reflected in countless biographies and it has only been in recent times that efforts have been made to correct it. Early critics had never thought of Van Dyck as a delicate flower grown in Rubens' garden. Between 1641 and 1645, thus shortly after the death of both Rubens and Van Dyck, an Antwerp publisher issued an engraving by Paulus Pontius in honor of both artists (fig. 4). The design, furnished by Erasmus Quellinus, one of Rubens' followers, clearly aims at honoring the two artists equally. That equality is marked almost obtrusively in the inscriptions framing their portraits, which are

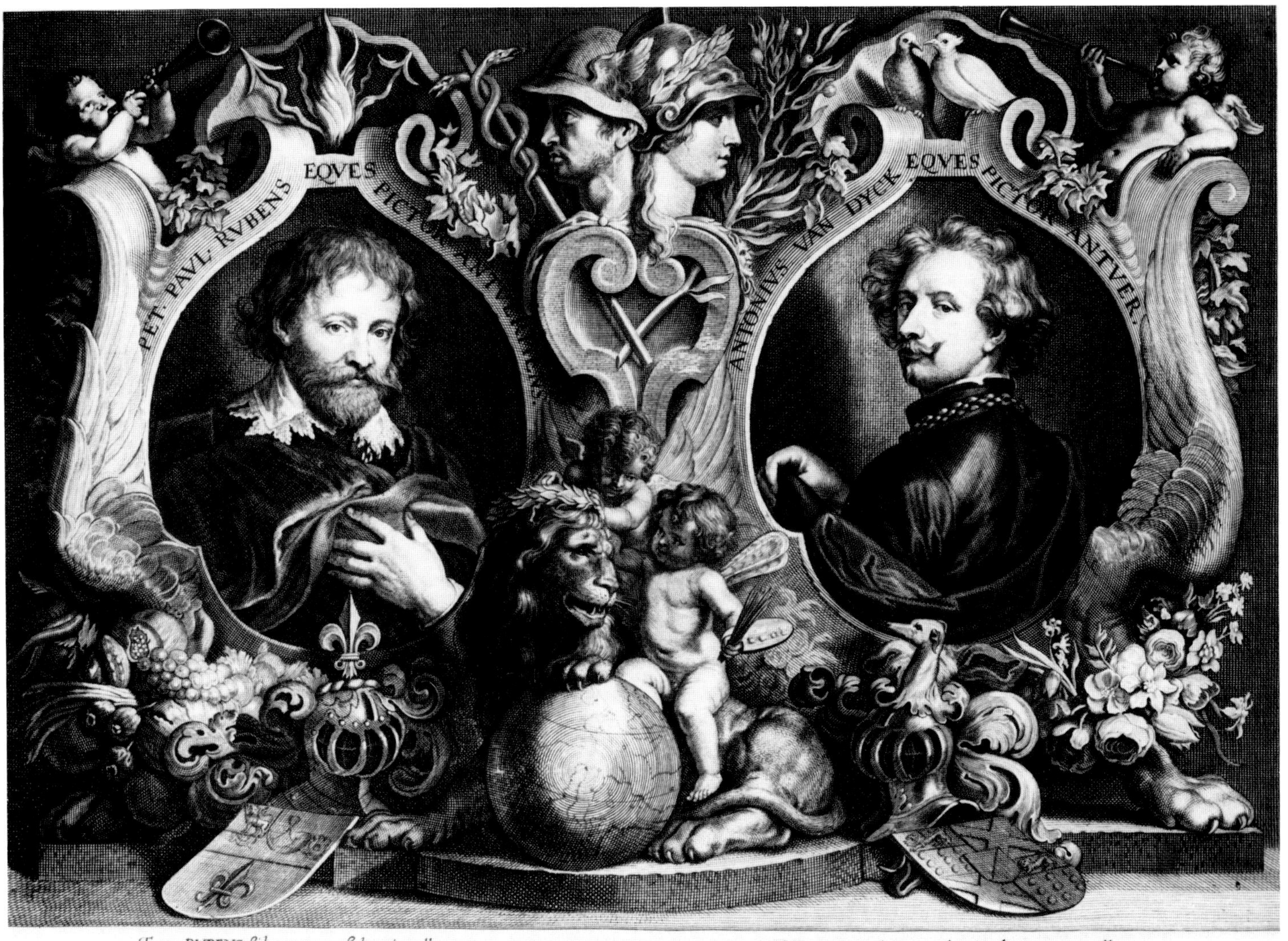

4. Paulus Pontius after Erasmus Quellinus, *Peter Paul Rubens and Anthony van Dyck*, engraving
Rubenshuis, Antwerp

was less to depict that event than to extol Antwerp's tradition as a city of art. Many of the people assembled can be identified as artists or collectors of art. Four people are prominently placed near the picture by Massys: the one with a big hat is Wladislas Sigismund, king of Poland; the stout fellow next to him is Jan van Montfort, Master of the Mint (or, as we would say, secretary of the treasury). Then there are Rubens, who seems to explain something to the archduke, and Van Dyck next to Van Montfort, whose likeness was taken from a portrait by Van Dyck. In fact several of the personages attending this "pictorial" event can be identified *only* because of the portraits, some drawn, some painted, that Van Dyck had made of them.

Distinct from the other Antwerp artists depicted, Rubens and Van Dyck are shown not only of equal rank, but also as men equally privileged to associate with the highest layers of contemporary society.

The earliest written piece of evidence attesting to Van Dyck's eminence, particularly vis-à-vis Rubens, is found in an often-cited letter sent from Antwerp on 17 July 1620 by Francesco Vercellini, secretary to the earl of Arundel. After describing how Rubens had gone about painting the portrait of the earl's wife, Aletheia Talbot, he ends by saying, "Van Dyck is still with Rubens and his works are coming to be scarcely less highly esteemed than those of his master." Although Vercellini fears that it would be diffi-

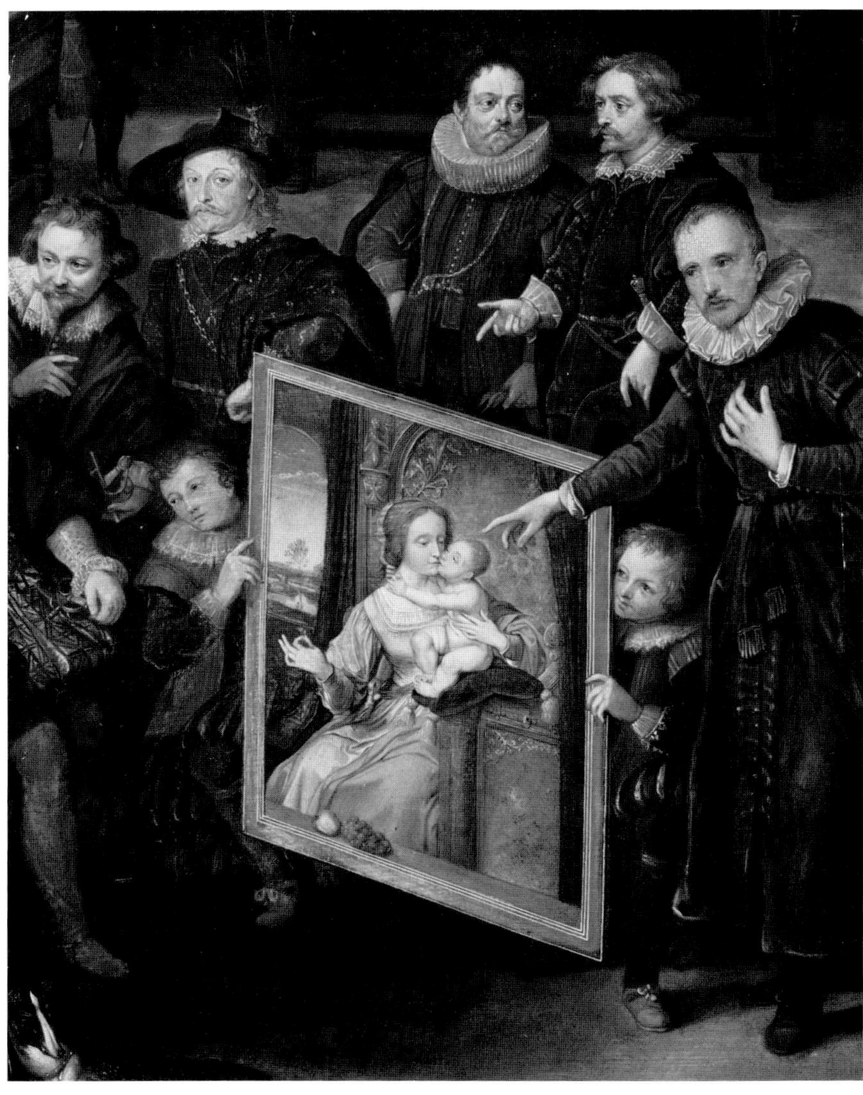

5. Willem van Haecht, *The Cabinet of Cornelis van der Geest* (detail), 1628, oil on panel
Rubenshuis, Antwerp

ing, "He will do a better job than anyone else." Van Dyck turned down the honor but declared himself willing to paint one of the subjects in a picture of his own composition. That, too, however, never materialized.

A pupil of Rubens: that evidently is how contemporaries thought of Van Dyck, even as late as 1640, when Van Dyck had become a celebrated master (and himself had only one more year to live). Yet in the strictly technical sense, Van Dyck was the pupil of Hendrik van Balen, to whom he was apprenticed in 1609, when ten years old. (Such early training was not unusual: the brothers Wierix made unbelievably skillful engravings at ages twelve and fourteen). Nine years later (11 February 1618) Van Dyck made a payment of a little over twenty-three guilders, the price of admission to the Antwerp artists guild as an independent master. On 28 April of the same year Rubens wrote the famous letter to Sir Dudley Carleton, English ambassador at The Hague, offering him a number of paintings for a collection of ancient marbles. One of them is described as "Achilles dressed as a woman, done by the best of my disciples and entirely retouched by my hand;" Rubens added that it was a highly desirable picture, full of the most beautiful girls. (Despite this calculated sales talk, Carleton did not buy it.) Although Van Dyck's name is not mentioned and Rubens could conceivably have referred to another of his pupils, there is general agreement that the reference was indeed to Van Dyck. It so happens that the painting in question still exists; it is in the Museo del Prado in Madrid. To the best of my knowledge no one has tried, let alone succeeded, in discovering a hand different from that of Rubens in the work. It is solidly anchored in Rubens' canon.

It should be obvious that "pupil" (disciple), as used here, has a broader significance than is normally thought. If pupils could begin major paintings, even though Rubens would again retouch them and make them "his own," such pupils must have had a level of competence that permitted them to work independently. The fact that we have no lists, as we have for other masters, of pupils registered as such with the guild is generally explained by the *Privilege* that exempted Rubens from guild regulations. Yet since from the moment Rubens had returned from Italy he aimed at, and received, large-scale

cult to persuade Van Dyck to quit Antwerp for England, something Arundel apparently had in mind, we read in a letter dated 25 November 1620 by Toby Matthew, a freewheeling English exile active also as an agent in purchasing art, that "Van Dike his [Rubens'] famous Allievo is gone into England and the King gave him a Pension of £100 a year."

When, twenty years later at Rubens' death, several of Rubens' paintings, commissioned by King Philip of Spain, were found to be unfinished, the king's brother Ferdinand, who as governor of the Netherlands resided at Brussels, wrote to Philip that he had heard Van Dyck was coming to Antwerp (from London). "And since he is such a great painter and moreover a pupil of Rubens," he writes, he should be the first painter to be asked to finish these works. He ends by say-

commissions, it seems to be almost a matter of course that he avoided cluttering his working space with young boys who had to learn the painter's craft from scratch. His pupils, hence, were probably young artists, trained elsewhere, whose "pupilship" consisted of the privilege of assisting Rubens in his huge undertakings. Van Dyck, by virtue of his extraordinary talent, surely occupied a special place in the organization of Rubens' workplace.

There is one prominent group of works that has played a major role in the discussions of Van Dyck's work in Rubens' studio: the cycle of Decius Mus, consisting of eight canvases of different size, now in the Liechtenstein collections in Vaduz. They were painted to serve as cartoons for a set of tapestries to be woven in Brussels. Six of the canvases depict the story of the Roman consul Decius Mus, who sought death in battle when the soothsayer told him, after having inspected the liver of a sacrificial bull, that only his death would ensure the victory of the Romans in their war against the Latins. No one doubts that Rubens is the author of the compositions, all of which he prepared in sketches or more elaborate *modelli.* The contract for the tapestries was signed in November 1616, with the stipulation that the tapestries should be delivered one year later. As so often in Rubens' career, it was a rush job. The large canvases in Vaduz must have been painted in the first few months of 1617. In fact, Rubens referred to them in his correspondence with Sir Dudley Carleton of 12 May 1618, when apparently the Brussels *manufacture* was still working on the tapestries; with pride he says that only recently he has made some very grand cartoons for tapestries ("ho fatto alcuni cartoni molto superbi"), a reference that can hardly be to anything other than the pictures in Vaduz, since the word "cartoni" must be understood functionally rather than materially. The same set of pictures is mentioned several times during the second half of the seventeenth century and always as having been painted by Van Dyck! Trusting, I fear, the literary tradition rather than their eyes, several scholars, among them the venerable Gustav Glück, have stated unequivocally that they are indeed the works of Van Dyck.

What we surely will have to accept is that Van Dyck must have been involved to some degree in the production of the large canvases, as other collaborators may have been. Any examination of the paintings in Vaduz should indeed make clear that there is a good deal of stylistic variation between them. The last one, *The Obsequies of Decius Mus,* seems to be largely done by assistants and lacks so much in spirit and life that neither Rubens nor Van Dyck could have had much part in it. But in all the other narrative pictures major passages are done with a power, boldness, and economy in placing the accents that they are without parallel in the early work of Van Dyck. Indeed, it seems to me to be an odd, not to say bizarre, idea to think that Rubens could have turned over the final responsibility for the cartoons of his first and most prestigious commission for tapestries, monumental in size and grand in action, to a barely eighteen-year-old, no matter how gifted, without reserving for himself the right to give them the decisive touches that would make them his own.

How, then, are we to understand the repeated assertions in seventeenth-century sources that the cartoons of the Decius Mus cycle were painted by Van Dyck? We must, I believe, remain conscious of the enormous esteem in which the artist was held throughout the seventeenth century. It was above all his portraiture that had met with well-deserved admiration and fame. His social and financial success (though he was probably less thrifty than was Rubens) increased his reputation. Sandrart could not resist mentioning three times how much money Van Dyck had made with his art. No one doubted that artistically he had been Rubens' equal, and in the opinion of some, his superior. This admiration carried over into the eighteenth century, as we learn from a passage in Arnold Houbraken that at an exhibition of some paintings by Van Dyck the public swarmed around the pictures like flies around a light, and that one painting was sold for the fabulous sum of 12,050 guilders. Should we be astonished to find that once it was known that Van Dyck had taken some part in the execution of the cartoons for the Decius Mus tapestries, the degree of his participation was magnified (possibly even for commercial reasons) and then passed about until it became an *opinio communis*?

What would we not give for any first-hand information about the actual working arrangements in the years of Van Dyck's activity as Rubens' disciple and assistant. We are not even sure when the association began or how long it lasted. Was it five, six, or, as one author guessed, nearly ten years? Were the two masters linked, as later historians wrote, by bonds of a warm personal friendship? We may be sure of one thing: early on, Rubens must have realized the amazing talent of this youth and his usefulness in the organization of a busy workshop.

No less than nine paintings by Van Dyck were in Rubens' estate, all from the period before Van Dyck left Antwerp, first for England and then for Italy. It would be interesting to know how Rubens acquired them: by gift? by exchange? or did he pay for them? (The last is not very likely, considering Rubens' well-known healthy respect for money.) Rubens surely provided Van Dyck with recommendations, chiefly to Genoese noble families, when Van Dyck left for Italy. And there is certainly no truth in an old, malicious story that Rubens steered Van Dyck into portrait painting to keep him from large-scale narrative pictures, supposedly to protect his own turf. We can easily imagine that the two artists must have had conversations about technical matters, narrative patterns, and the use of iconographic traditions.

If the attribution of a sketchbook at Chatsworth to the young Van Dyck is correct (and it seems to be generally accepted), Rubens must have given Van Dyck access to some of his own theoretical studies; and since these studies are lost, Van Dyck's copies in that sketchbook may help us to reconstruct them to some extent.

I have trouble, however, associating Van Dyck with other aspects of Rubens' life. Rubens was much more than a painter and head of a large studio. Did Van Dyck have access to that other part of Rubens' life, too?

In 1637 Franciscus Junius, librarian in the service of the earl of Arundel, published a book, *De pictura veterum* ("On the Painting of the Ancients"), which later came out also in English and Dutch. Both Rubens and Van Dyck received copies (Rubens directly from the author) and both acknowledged receipt. In his letter of 1 August 1637 Rubens begins with an apology because the book has reached him only after a delay, and then another two weeks have gone by, since he has not wanted to write before he has read the book. Having now done so, he applauds the author's erudition as well as the manner of presentation, adding the hope that he (Junius) might now proceed to write a book on the Italian masters, "whose works are still before our eyes," while those of the ancients are seen only indistinctly in our imagination. And anyone, he continues, who would try to reconstruct them from the descriptions by Pliny or other ancient authors would produce only an inferior wine compared to the superior quality of the original vintage.

Van Dyck begins his letter to Junius (fig. 6) by saying that Lord Conway (a high official in the English government), who had sent him the book, had praised it as a meritorious and very learned work, and he has heard the same thing from another and equally erudite person who considers it one of the profoundest studies he has ever known; therefore he, Van Dyck, expects that the book will add to the appreciation of the arts, as well as augment the reputation (he uses the word glory) of its author. Using the opportunity, he asks Junius for a motto to go with an engraved portrait of Sir Kenelm Digby, whom he had recently portrayed. (Junius suggested two words—*impavidum ferient*—from a famous ode by Horace.) In contrast to Rubens—and the frilly character of Van Dyck's script makes an interesting comparison with the spare and extremely regular hand seen in many of Rubens' letters (fig. 7)—Van Dyck evidently had not read the book, nor did he say that he planned to do so. Was he too busy or—perish the thought—was his Latin not good enough? His flattering compliments were clearly based on the opinion of others. (His letter is of 14 August 1637—erroneously dated 1636.) Not knowing Latin is hardly a serious handicap today, but in the seventeenth century most educated people had a workable command of the language. This was particularly true of Rubens, whose art is intricately linked to and affected by his literary and antiquarian interests. He consorted and corresponded with scholars and made sure that his sons would get a first-rate humanist education. Shortly before Van Dyck entered in contact with him, he had painted the celebrated picture in which he stands modestly, as a marginal fourth, in the company of three learned Latinists: Justus Lipsius, Jan Woverius, and his own brother Philip, sitting beneath the bust of the Roman playwright Seneca (or what was then believed to be Seneca's likeness). That painting symbolizes beautifully a world that largely determined Rubens' life—the world of books and of men of classical education. Was there possibly a place in that learned world for a man who portrayed himself coyly as the shepherd Paris, holding the golden apple ready to give it to any available Aphrodite? Rubens had of course many other interests, for instance the political affairs of his time, in which he was destined to play an active role. That, too, was an area of no concern to Van Dyck.

As we try to visualize the working conditions in Rubens' studio, we have the help of the travel record of a young Danish physician, Otto Sperling, who visited Rubens' house in 1621. He and his companions were first ushered into Rubens' studio, where they found the master at work while listening to readings from Tacitus; there was also a secretary to whom Rubens dictated letters; yet he was willing to converse with his visitors while still continuing to paint. What we learn from this is, first, that Rubens worked in a room by himself—something that should not surprise us, but somehow has never been given the attention it deserves. Indeed, when these visitors had thanked him for the friendly reception, he had them taken around the house (most likely by a servant), where they were shown a large room filled with pupils working on grand canvases from drawings on which Rubens had indicated the composition and choice of colors. We can take it as certain that Rubens did not change his solitary way of painting during the time Van Dyck was around. Nor would Van Dyck have appreciated working in a room where he would have had to listen to readings from Tacitus or any other ancient author. Whatever Van Dyck painted in close association with Rubens was probably done in spaces occupied by other assistants. Yet according to Jan Brueghel II, who was his friend, Van Dyck had painted independently since about 1615, his studio being in a house called "Den Dom van Ceulen" ("the cathedral of Cologne"). His early business affairs, result-

ing in an oeuvre of considerable size, could never have been conducted out of Rubens' house, and not only because space there was not unlimited. And he certainly never lived with Rubens, as has been said (first by Max Rooses). When Vercellini wrote to Arundel in 1620, "Van Deick sta tuttavia con il Sigr. Rubens," he surely meant only that Van Dyck was still closely associated with the master.

Let us now examine briefly the well-known contract for the thirty-nine paintings to adorn the ceilings of the side aisles and galleries of the new Jesuit church at Antwerp. Signed 29 March 1620 between Rubens and Father Tirinus, prefect of the Professed House of the Antwerp Jesuits, it stipulated that Rubens furnish the sketches, but that Van Dyck and other students were to paint the compositions in the appropriate larger format. Rubens promised "by his

6. Letter from Anthony van Dyck to Franciscus Junius, 14 August 1636 (erroneous for 1637)

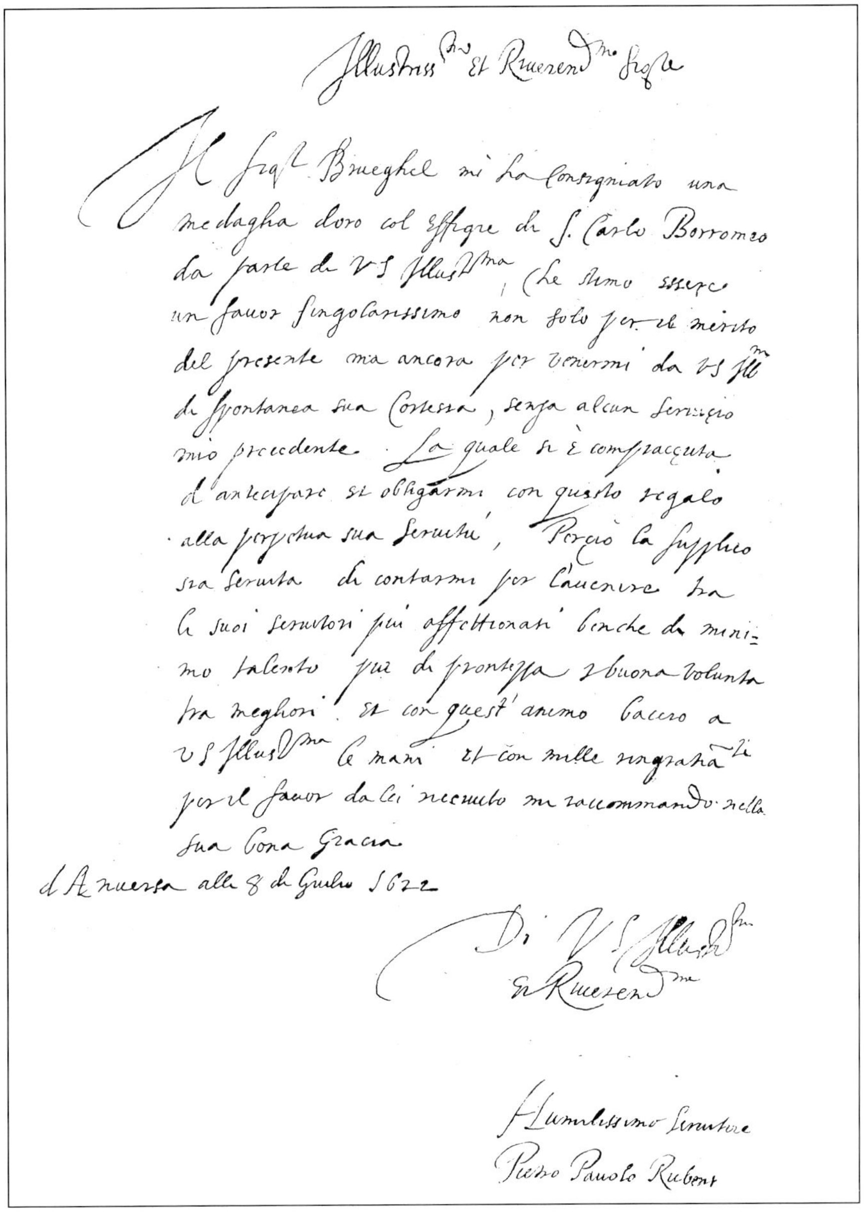

7. Letter from Peter Paul
Rubens to Federico
Borromeo, 8 July 1622

its equivalent of the thirty-nine sketches) was fixed at 7000 guilders. The church, however, already owed Rubens 3000 guilders for two large altarpieces. If we calculate—modestly—the price for the sketches Rubens was to do (or their equivalent, the painting for one side altar) at 1000 florins, the thirty-nine larger canvases would cost 6000 florins, or about 150 guilders each. This, I am sure, is considerably less than Rubens would have charged if he had painted all thirty-nine himself. Knowing how strapped the church was for funds, and being very busy with other commissions, Rubens probably persuaded the church authorities that Van Dyck and other pupils would do just as good a job and for considerably less. Unfortunately, we can no longer examine these works. They were all destroyed in a fire in 1718.

From Toby Matthew's letter of 25 November 1620 it emerges that despite Van Dyck's growing fame there was still, at this time, a sizeable difference between the prices for pictures by Rubens and those for works by Van Dyck. Matthew had apparently negotiated with Rubens for a hunting scene, but was unsuccessful in getting its price reduced. Van Dyck, as Matthew says, had just gone to England and, provided he had a drawing of the composition with him, Matthew was willing to bet his hand against a pair of gloves that Van Dyck would make a much better picture than Rubens(!) and do it for half the price! This price differential between works of Rubens and his "best disciple" did not continue for very long. Nor did Matthew lose his hand.

After five months in England Van Dyck returned to Antwerp, but in the fall of 1621 he left for Italy. Twice more he returned to Antwerp, first in 1627, staying for more than four years, and again in 1634 for a shorter period. For those who assume that he and Rubens had developed a warm personal relationship during the years of Van Dyck's pupilship with the master, there is an awkward fact: with one exception our sources are completely silent about any later contact between the two artists. The one exception is a letter written by the earl of Carlisle, newly appointed English ambassador to Savoy, who passed through Antwerp on 17 May 1628. Carlisle had called on Rubens but had been told that the artist was away. "The day fol-

honor and conscience" to finish these canvases so that nothing would be missing. In addition, Rubens agreed to paint with his own hand an altarpiece for one of the four side altars; if he failed to do so, he was to turn over to the church the thirty-nine sketches he had made for the ceiling paintings. With a polite bow to Van Dyck, Father Tirinus promised that at a convenient time ("ter bequame tide") he would commission him to paint a major painting for one of the four side altars. Nothing came of this rather vague promise.

The price for the thirty-nine paintings for the ceiling plus the additional altarpiece (or

8. Anthony van Dyck,
Samson and Delilah,
1619–1620
Dulwich Picture Gallery, London

lowing after dinner," says Carlisle, "taking occasion to see some curiosities at Monsr Van-digs, I met Monsr Rubin there, newly returned from Bruxelles." Should we understand this as pure coincidence, that Rubens, just returned from Brussels, had immediately gone to see his former student and there found, by sheer accident, the English diplomat? Or is it not much more likely that on coming home from his trip, Rubens had been informed of Carlisle's visit at his house and had found out—Antwerp not being a large town—where the Englishman had gone (if Carlisle had not actually left a message about his plans). Since this was exactly the time when Rubens was deeply involved in diplomatic matters, eventually leading to a peace treaty between England and Spain, he must have had good reasons to meet the English diplomat, surely a more important task than having a chat with Van Dyck. (Had he gone to Brussels to get instructions, since he may well have had advance notice that Carlisle might come to Antwerp? A similar reading of the incident has been given independently by Jeffrey Muller.)

This meeting at Van Dyck's house is the single event that documents a personal contact between the two artists who many years before had lived so close to each other. We have no reason to suspect that they were estranged or that tensions had developed be-

tween them. Yet there is clearly no evidence that any bonds of real friendship existed between them, and I am also inclined to think that this coolness should warn us not to read too much into the earlier phase in their lives, when Rubens was the teacher and Van Dyck his pupil and collaborator.

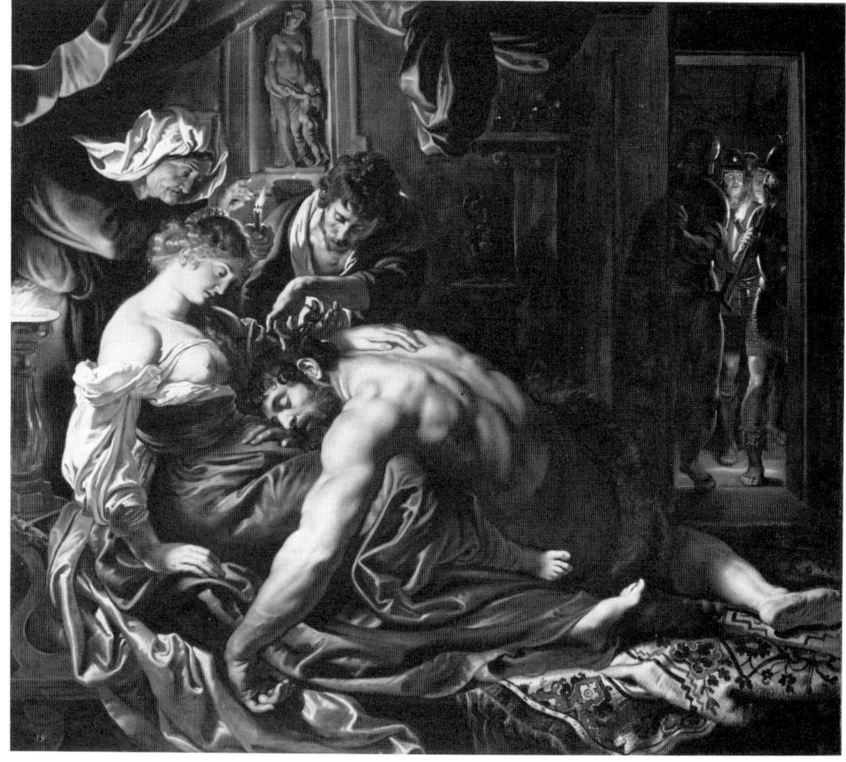

9. Peter Paul Rubens,
Samson and Delilah, 1609
National Gallery, London

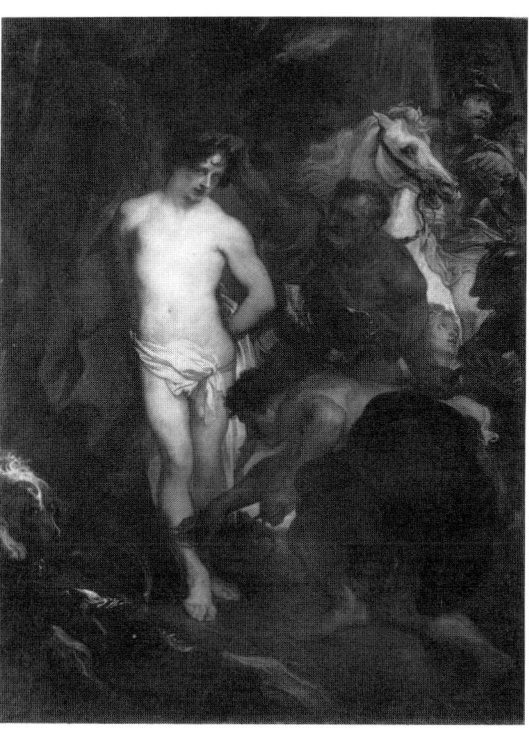

10. Anthony van Dyck,
The Martyrdom of Saint Sebastian, c. 1619–1620
Alte Pinakothek, Munich

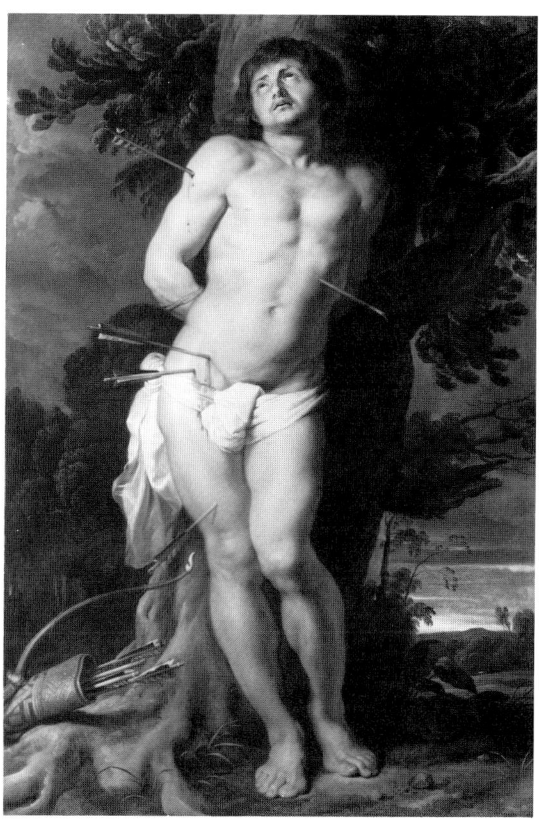

11. Peter Paul Rubens,
Saint Sebastian, c. 1615
Gemäldegalerie, Berlin

In a discussion principally concerned with the personal contacts between Rubens and Van Dyck, the central problem of the relationship of Van Dyck's art to that of his master evidently has to be left out. Yet it seems to me, as a historian of art, to be almost callous not to say a word about the activity that alone justifies the interest we take in the lives of these men. That Van Dyck owed much to his close association with Rubens is self-evident; that he managed early to stake out his own artistic domain has often been demonstrated and could well be seen in the Van Dyck exhibition at the National Gallery of Art (November 1990–February 1991). Van Dyck himself provided the material that permits us to judge his work under both aspects, since there is a surprising number of paintings in which he dealt with the same subject that Rubens had previously formulated in major works. Only a few years lie between his version of the story of Samson and Delilah in Dulwich (fig. 8) and Rubens' painting of the same subject, now in the National Gallery in London (fig. 9). Van Dyck knew Rubens' picture well; it had been done for Nicholas Rockox, burgomaster of Antwerp, whose portrait (Hermitage, St. Petersburg) Van Dyck painted in 1621. The moment chosen and the cast of actors are nearly the same, but whereas in Rubens' painting the conspiratorial and furtive character of the action has been stressed, Van Dyck interpreted the fatal haircut as an almost melodramatic event, in which the Philistine, approaching with the scissors at the ready, dominates the scene with his menacing presence. It is not unusual in these early years for Van Dyck's compositions to appear to be more "Rubensian" than Rubens' own, which makes good psychological sense. A more Vandyckian Van Dyck can be seen in his several versions of the *Martyrdom of Saint Sebastian*, in which the graceful, lissome youth seems to pay no heed to the machinations preceding his ordeal (fig. 10). Rubens' *Saint Sebastian* (fig. 11), by contrast, is a muscular, heroic figure, whose shape and pose still echo the ancient marbles the master had studied in Italy.

Finally I want to touch briefly on a question that still crops up every now and then; it was of particular concern to me in the years when I prepared a book on Rubens' drawings. There were a number of drawings that in the previous literature had been moved back and forth, from a Rubens attribution to one to Van Dyck, to Rubens again. And there is still no unanimity in all cases even today. In the same year in which I acclaimed a drawing for an Assumption of the Virgin as an important work of Rubens (fig. 12), Otto Benesch, a highly respected Viennese scholar, discussed it at length as a drawing by Van Dyck. What made this particularly embarrassing for me is the fact that Benesch was the curator of the Albertina in Vienna, which owned the drawing. (I believe it is now safely in the Rubens column.) I might also mention the drawing of a lost allegorical composition by Titian (fig. 13), which I believe to be a work of Rubens, but which my friend and colleague Anne-Marie Logan, who is preparing a complete catalogue of Rubens' drawings, wants to place in Van Dyck's oeuvre. Finally, there is a striking painting of the *Four Studies of the Head of a Negro* (who may have been a servant or a dock-worker in Antwerp) in Brussels (fig. 14). It is a famous and popular picture that at one time decorated a Belgian five-hundred franc note. In the eighteenth century it was called Van Dyck. In Brussels, ever since it was acquired in 1857, it has been exhibited as a work of Rubens. Yet some of the foremost contemporary scholars (Glück, Burchard, Millar, and Jaffé) have reverted to the Van Dyck attribution. In 1980 I came out for Rubens and have had some support since then, but I am prepared for the continuation of the disagreement.

There should be no doubt in regard to a panel at the Getty Museum that shows four sketches of the same head differently and not very imaginatively arranged (fig. 15). Exhibited in London in 1818 and twice listed by John Smith as an excellent study by Rubens, it was given to Van Dyck by L. Cust and was sold as such in 1971. Yet on entering the Getty Museum it was given back to Rubens. (I understand that label has now been retired.) A distinguished British scholar has thrown a third name into the ring: he attributes it to Jacob Jordaens. With three candidates vying for our vote I prefer the "solution" we are familiar with in the field of politics: "none of the above." The greatly

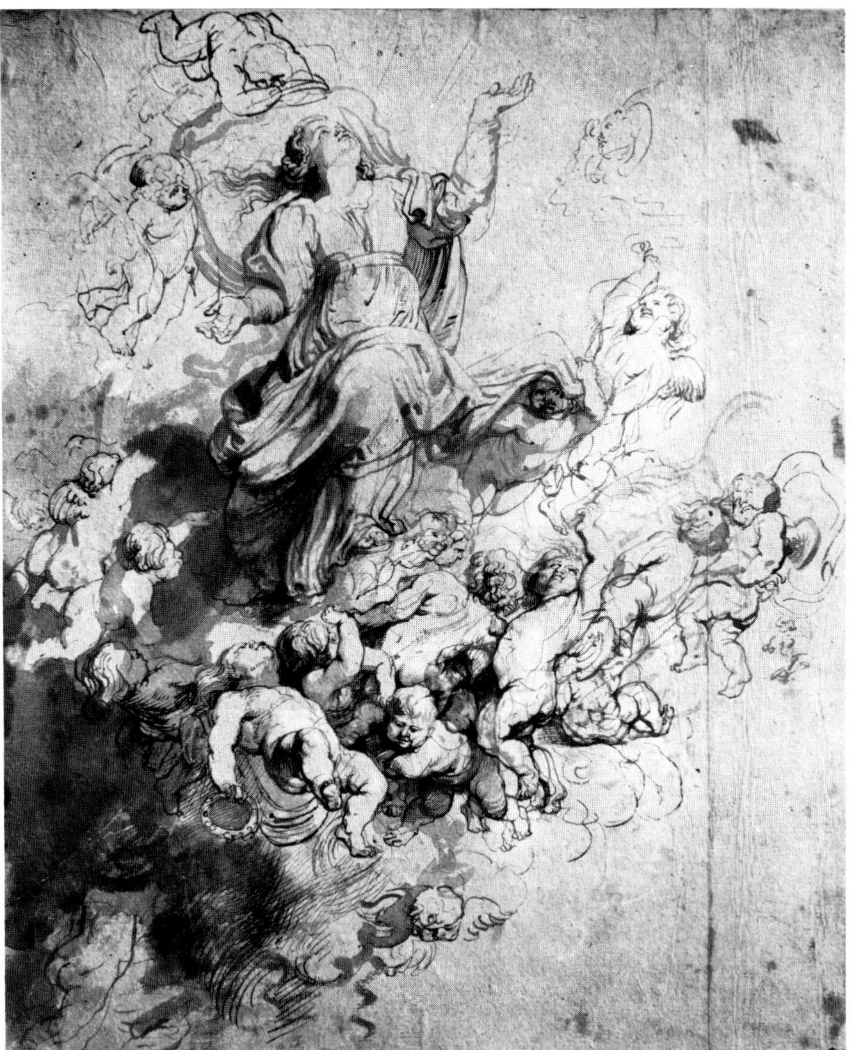

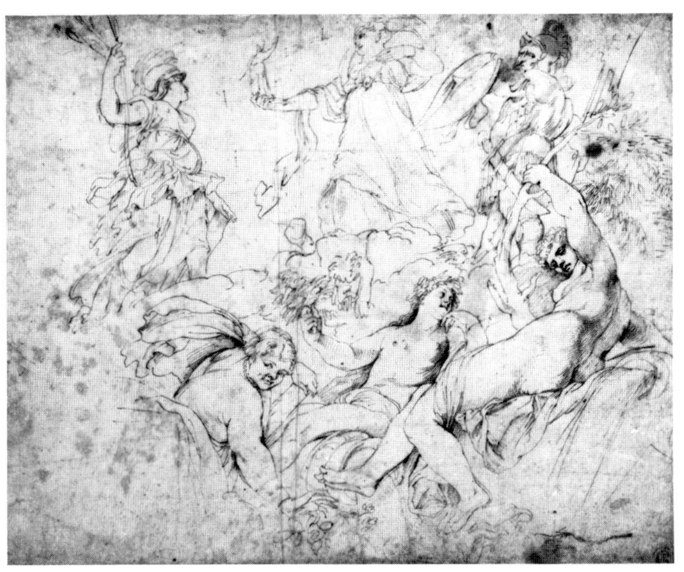

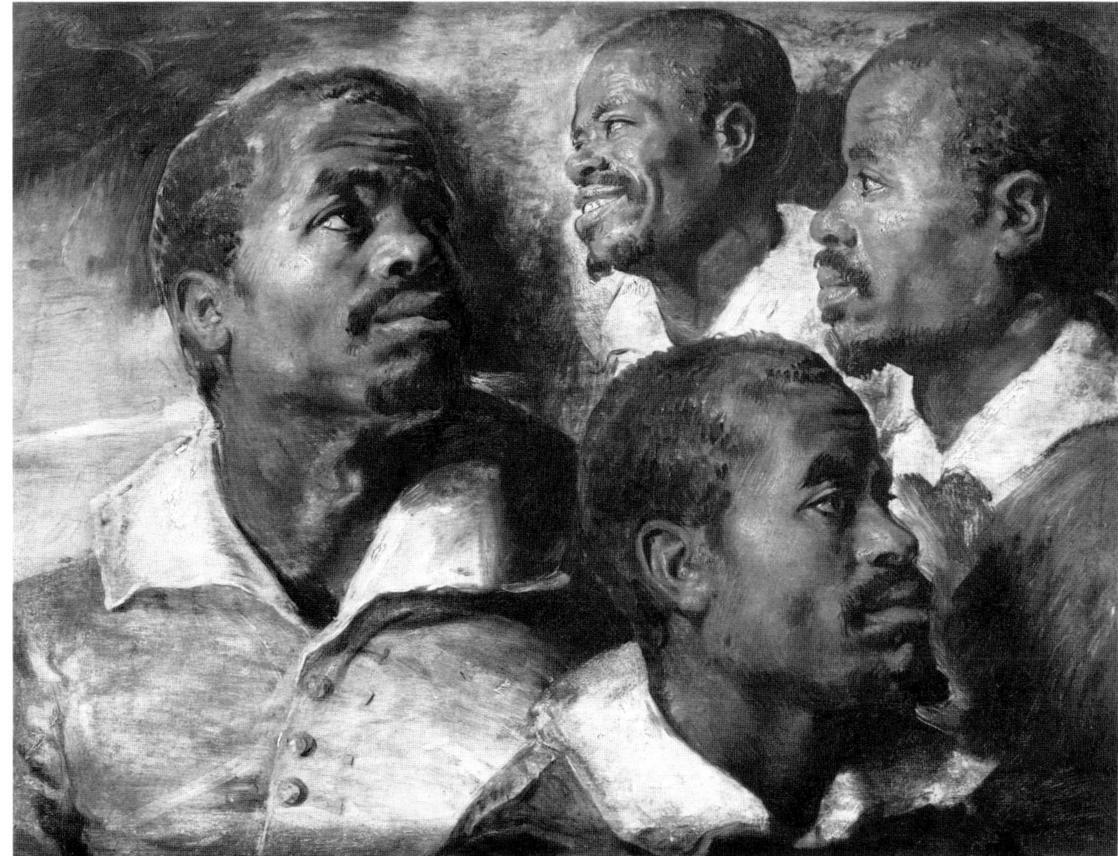

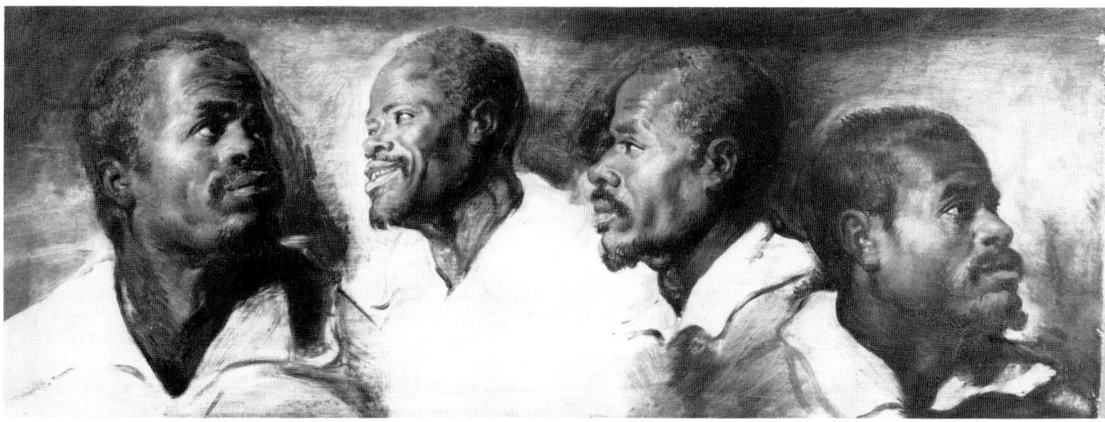

overrated picture is probably a later copy.

To close with a personal anecdote: I recall that in 1968 the National Gallery of Art in Washington published an illustrated catalogue of European paintings and sculpture. It reproduced the portrait of Isabella Brant (fig. 16), which had been in the collection since 1937 and had ever since been displayed as the work of Rubens. Around 1970 I gave a lecture on Rubens at the Gallery and in the course of it showed the portrait, with the re-

mark that it really was by Van Dyck, as many specialists long before had agreed. The next morning a curator asked to see me, and told me that a report had come from a guard (who attended my talk) that a visiting lecturer had claimed that a painting exhibited at the museum as by Rubens was really by someone else. I pleaded guilty, but also pointed out that in the *Fachliteratur* the painting had many times been published as by Van Dyck (a view that today no one

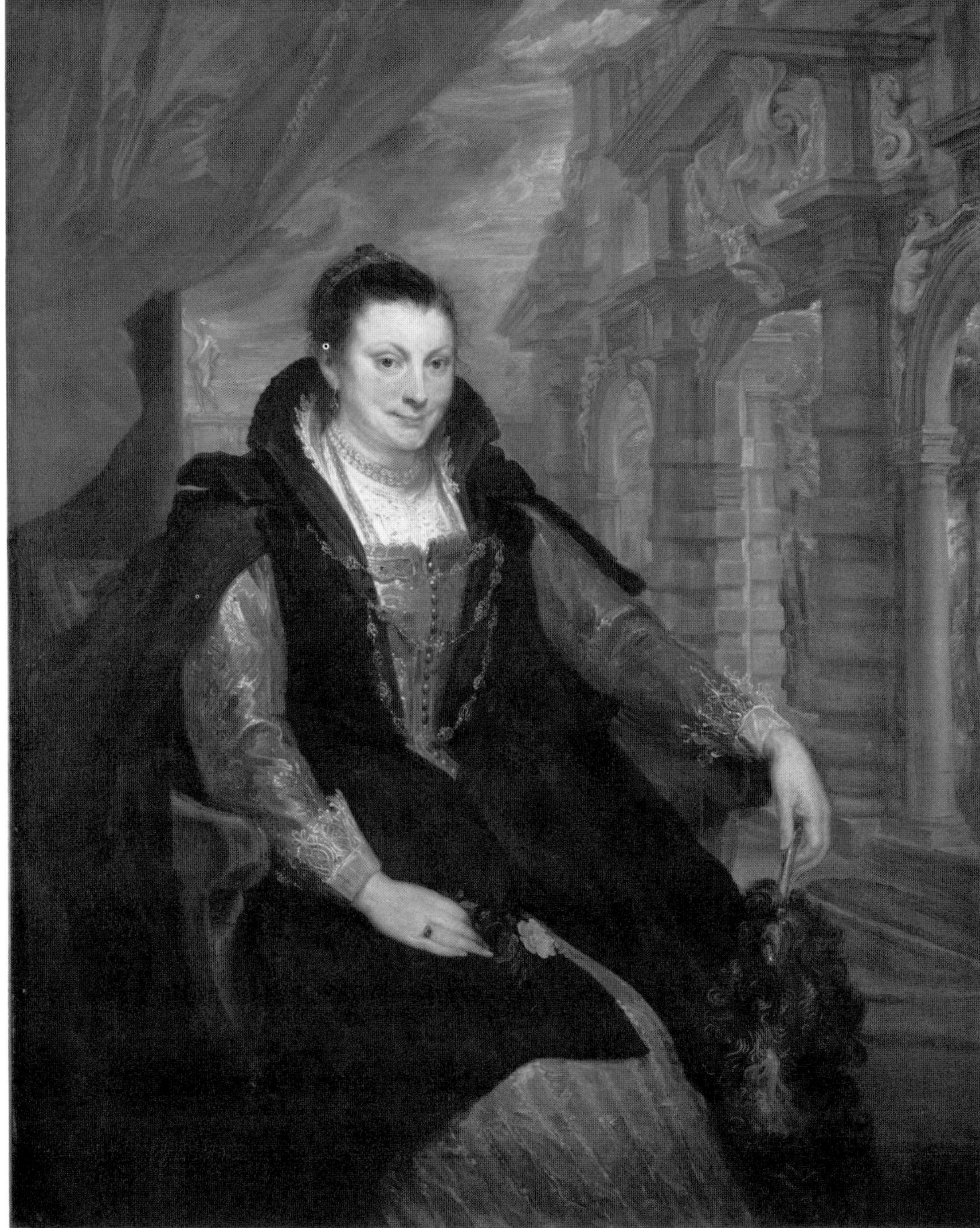

would seriously question). At any rate, soon after this incident the Rubens label was exchanged for one of Van Dyck (credit for which goes to Arthur Wheelock). Yet there is still a small mystery attached to this picture. The seventeenth-century art critic André Félibien stated that before leaving for Italy, Van Dyck painted a portrait of Rubens' wife and gave it to the master as a sign of his gratitude and affection. Christopher Brown has characterized this as an attractive romantic notion, though without historical foundation. Jeffrey Muller has gone even further, since in his studies he has not found any evidence that Rubens ever actually owned the picture. Brave skepticism! But as an old romantic, I am very fond of legends that might even be true. And if not, I hold with the nice Italian saying: *se non è vero, è ben trovato.*

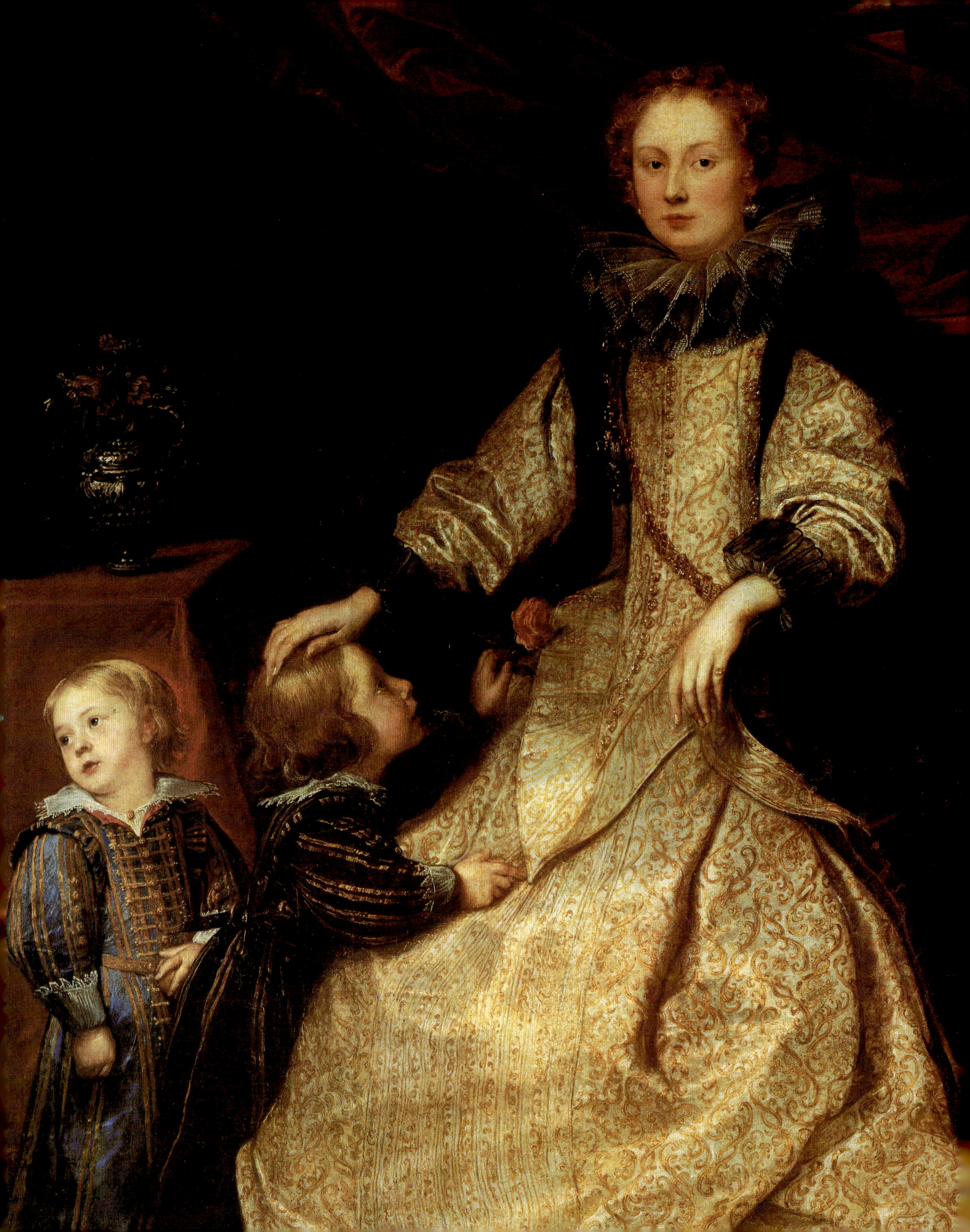

PIERO BOCCARDO
Galleria di Palazzo Rosso, Genova

Ritratti di Genovesi di Rubens e di Van Dyck: Contesto ed identificazioni

I ritratti di Rubens e di Van Dyck eseguiti per committenti genovesi hanno una particolarità comune: degli effigiati una parte non è più riconosciuta, e di un'altra si può facilmente dubitare dell'identificazione tradizionale. La ragione di questo fatto è indubbiamente riconducibile alle peculiarità che caratterizzarono la classe di governo dell'antica Repubblica di Genova, alla quale quei personaggi appartennero, e alle sue vicende storiche.

Va subito specificato che si è usata volutamente l'espressione "classe di governo" e non i termini più consueti e pur sempre corretti di "patriziato" o "aristocrazia" perché delle circa trecento famiglie che la costituivano nella prima metà del Seicento,[1] solo una parte si poteva allora fregiare di titoli nobiliari, e un numero più ridotto da antica data. Si trattava in realtà di un'aristocrazia essenzialmente di censo, dedita al commercio in campo internazionale—in particolare del denaro—e le cui fortune erano legate strettamente all'andamento dell'economia.[2]

Le origini, l'attività mercantile, e l'appartenenza di questa classe ad uno stato repubblicano, ancorché oligarchico, comportarono forme di celebrazione più personale che dinastica, e comunque quasi sempre limitate agli spazi privati, mentre nel contempo il verificarsi di *boom* e di rovesci finanziari determinò di tempo in tempo l'*exploit* di alcune famiglie e il ridimensionamento di altre.[3] In questo senso è utile menzionare, fra i vari tipi di fazioni politico-sociali presenti in campo, la contrapposizione fra "nobili vecchi" e "nobili nuovi," in quanto a quest'ultimo raggruppamento appartenne un gruppo di famiglie—i Balbi, i Brignole, i Durazzo . . .—decisamente emergente nel corso del primo quarto del Seicento.[4]

Si deve poi ricordare che altre casate—in particolare gli Spinola, i Doria e i Lomellini—erano articolate in decine di rami genealogici paralleli, sicché accadeva che portassero lo stesso cognome personaggi con patrimoni e interessi culturali assai differenti: in questo senso ogni forma di generalizzazione a riguardo risulta inopportuna, laddove lo stesso termine "famiglia" può apparire oggi inadeguato in considerazione del numero di componenti della stessa e dei vincoli di parentela non sempre stretti fra i suoi vari rami.[5]

Doti, successioni ereditarie, estinzioni e vendite interessarono continuativamente i consistenti patrimoni dei membri più eminenti di questa oligarchia nel corso di più di due secoli, con la conseguenza che le nobili residenze cittadine appartennero nel tempo a più d'una di queste casate, cambiando o aggiungendo via via i nomi, mentre le quadrerie in esse contenute potevano essere, di volta in volta, lasciate a loro posto, o spostate nella nuova dimora del loro proprietario, o, ancora, vendute all'asta, divise fra gli eredi o accorpate ad altre collezioni.[6]

Vicende di questo genere—per venire direttamente al tema di questo contributo—hanno fatto sì che già nel 1658, cioè solo

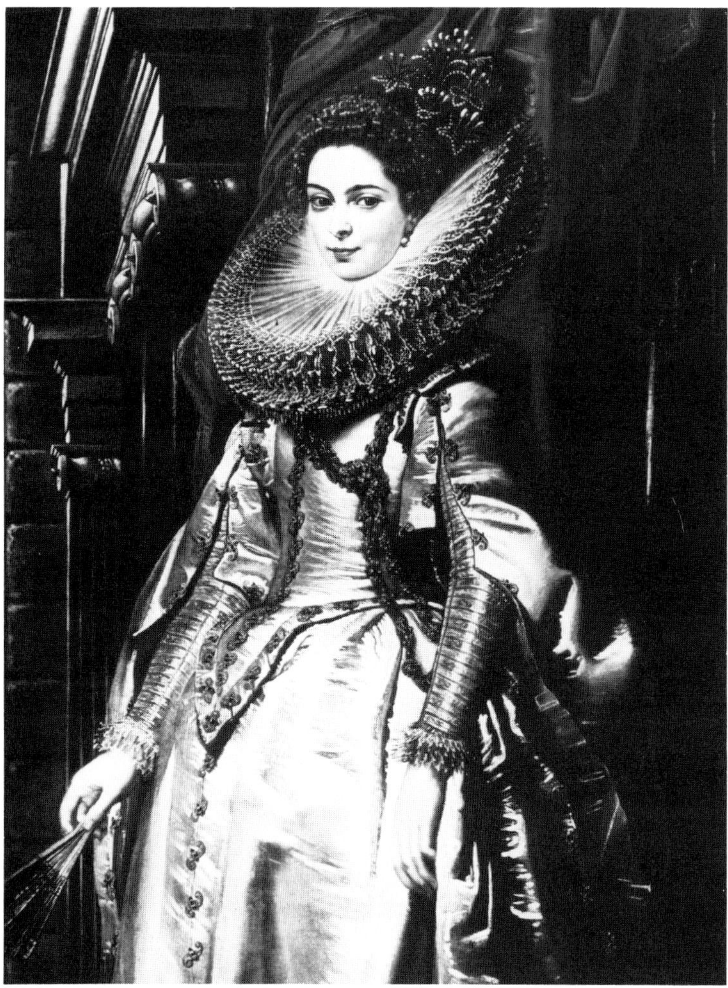

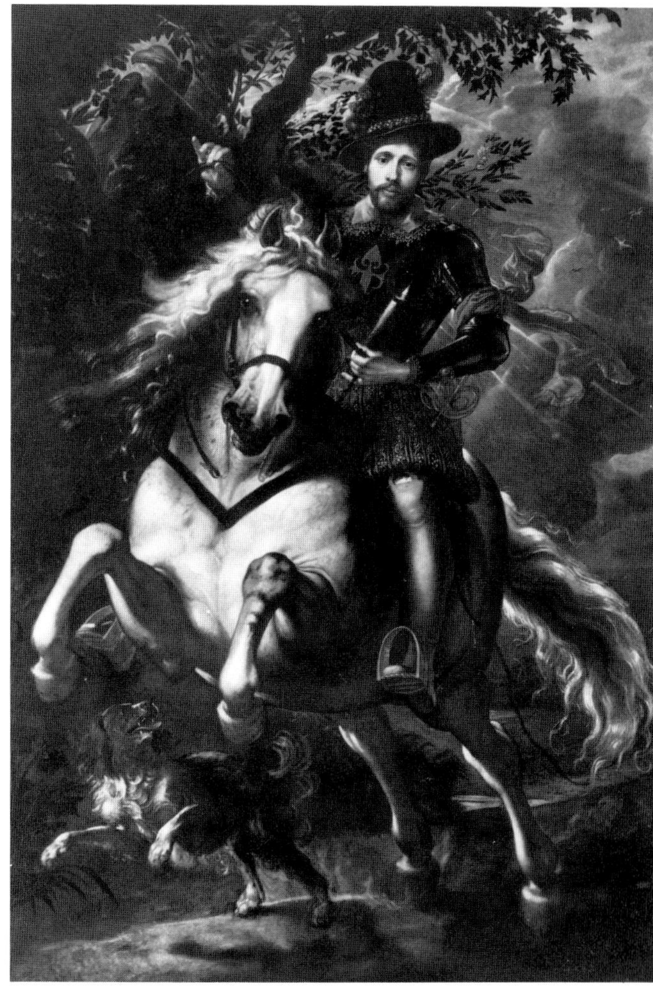

trent'anni dopo la partenza di Van Dyck, un suo ritratto virile potesse aver già perso l'identità;[7] mentre quando nel 1780 lo storiografo locale Carlo Giuseppe Ratti pubblicò la seconda edizione della sua guida[8]—certamente la più completa descrizione del patrimonio artistico genovese pubblico e privato prima della caduta della Repubblica—solo per una decina dei più di ottanta ritratti complessivamente riferiti a Rubens o a Van Dyck era ancora in grado di fornire le generalità, in alcuni casi, per altro, rivelatesi errate.[9]

La fine del regime oligarchico nel 1797, le guerre napoleoniche, e la crisi economica susseguente, in concomitanza con la forte richiesta del mercato artistico inglese, presto determinarono uno stillicidio di vendite, per cui un gran numero di capolavori—e fra questi molti ritratti—lasciò definitivamente Genova. Presso i mercanti e nelle nuove collezioni di destinazione presero a radicarsi in quel momento fittizie identificazioni dei personaggi effigiati, le quali in realtà spesso traevano origine semplicemente dal casato dell'ultimo proprietario genovese.

In questa situazione complessiva, risulta evidente come sia stato quasi inevitabile che fino a tempi assai recenti i contributi sui ritratti del periodo genovese dei due artisti in questione, relativamente ai soggetti rappresentati, si siano limitati a riportare le indicazioni tradizionali, mentre quelli specificamente dedicati al problema delle identificazioni, per la generalmente superficiale conoscenza del contesto di provenienza e la scarsa attenzione dedicata ad eventuali riscontri storici ed archivistici, risultino scarsamente attendibili e, nel caso di opere dubbie, meramente finalizzati ad accreditare l'improbabile attribuzione.

Adesso che le indagini sulla committenza e sul collezionismo a Genova cominciano a

1. Peter Paul Rubens, *Marchesa Brigida Spinola Doria*, 1606, olio su tela
National Gallery of Art, Washington

2. Peter Paul Rubens, *Gian Carlo Doria a cavallo*, c. 1606, olio su tela
Galleria Nazionale di Palazzo Spinola, Genova

fornire dati oggettivi ed importanti sull'ambiente culturale ed artistico cittadino fra Cinque e Settecento, la ricerca e il riscontro documentario a proposito dell'identità dei magnifici personaggi rappresentati da Rubens e da Van Dyck perdono ogni connotazione di mera curiosità erudita e vengono a costituire parte integrante di quelle stesse indagini, permettendo spesso di fornire utili indicazioni, quando non precisi elementi circostanziali, sulla data d'esecuzione di quelle opere.

In questo senso, è esemplare quanto si è potuto ricavare—anche a proposito della tematica più generale della fortuna del ritratto a Genova—studiando la famiglia di Agostino Doria (1534–1607), doge della Repubblica per il biennio 1601–1603.[10] Dell'intero suo nucleo famigliare esiste, anche se ne è ignota l'ubicazione, una "miniatura di ritratto naturale di Agostino Doria quando era Duce (= doge) e dei suoi figli" che gli inventari attribuivano a Rubens, e si conosce a livello documentario un *Ritratto* a mezza figura in veste di senatore (o di procuratore perpetuo), sempre opera del pittore fiammingo; dei membri della sua ristretta cerchia famigliare sono poi tuttora conservati, dello stesso artista, il ritratto della nuora, *Brigida Spinola Doria*—moglie allora del figlio primogenito Giacomo Massimiliano[11]—che è alla National Gallery of Art di Washington, e quello equestre del figlio terzogenito, *Gian Carlo Doria*, presso la Galleria Nazionale di Palazzo Spinola a Genova (figg. 1, 2).

Pur dovendo segnalare che il riscontro documentario esclude, almeno per ora, l'esistenza di un ritratto rubensiano della moglie di quest'ultimo[12]—cioè di quella Veronica Spinola finora ipoteticamente riconosciuta nei dipinti della Staatliche Kunsthalle di Karlsruhe e nella collezione Faringdon a Buscot Park[13]—le altre opere citate attestano un intento di esaltazione attraverso l'effigie dipinta da un artista di gran fama che, indagando, è risultato caratterizzare più generazioni di questo ramo dei Doria, del quale è necessario, per chiarezza d'esposizione, presentare un estratto dell'albero genealogico in forma schematica.

Prendendo a riferimento i rapporti di parentela evidenziati con questa genealogia non si potrà ritenere un dato casuale quanto è emerso dalla collazione delle fonti e dalla ricerca d'archivio, e cioè il fatto che di Giacomo Doria, qui designato come stipite del ramo, e del figlio maggiore di questi, Nicolò, siano noti i *Ritratti* ad opera di Tiziano (figg. 3, 4)—il secondo dei quali datato 1545—e che apparentemente costituiscono vere e proprie eccezioni per Genova.[14] Dell'altro figlio, il già ricordato Agostino, oltre alle effigi rubensiane, esisteva anche un *Ritratto* del pittore genovese Gian Battista Paggi. Del primo figlio di Agostino, Giacomo Massimiliano, si sono potuti documentare un *Ritratto* di Tin-

---

Giacomo
∞ Battina de Marini

  Nicolò (1525 c.–1592)
  ∞ Aurelia Grimaldi { *

  Agostino (1534–1608)
  ∞ Eliana Spinola

    Giacomo M. (1571 c.–1613)
    ∞ Brigida Spinola { *

    Marcantonio (1572–1651)
    ∞ Isabella della Tolfa {
      *
      Vittoria (1600–?)
      ∞ Agostino Spinola   Luca / Giacomo / Violante / Marcantonio

    Gian Carlo (1576–1625)
    ∞ Veronica Spinola {
      Agostino (1615–1640)

    Gian Luca (1585–1626?)
    ∞ Paola Spinola { *

* ulteriore discendenza

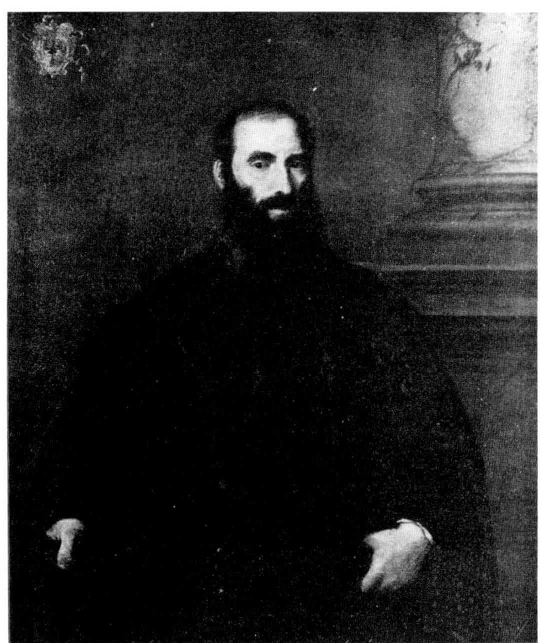

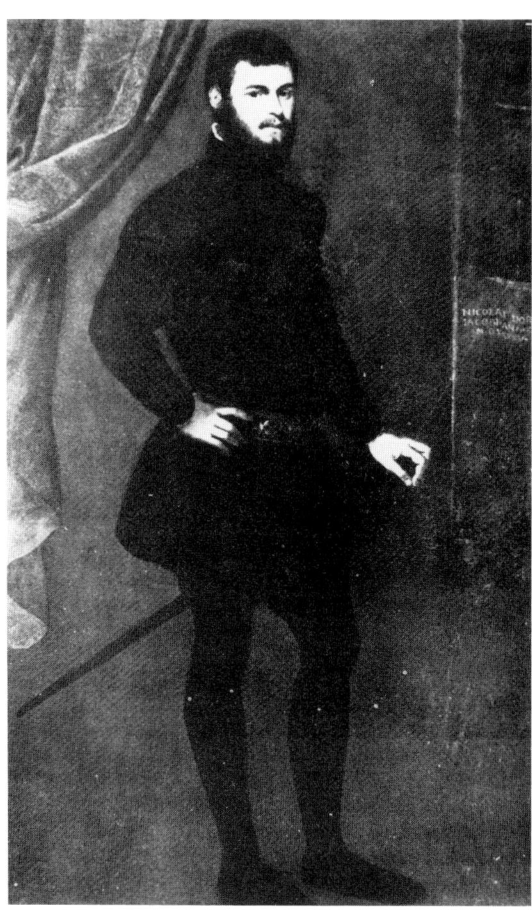

toretto, uno del genovese Luciano Borzone, ed un altro, di Giulio Cesare Procaccini, in cui era raffigurato insieme al fratello Gian Carlo, del quale, oltre al citato *Ritratto equestre*, esiste quello ad opera di Simon Vouet, ora al Louvre. Solo le fonti settecentesche ricordano poi del più giovane Gian Luca un dipinto di Van Dyck che lo ritraeva "in armi," ed uno—della stessa mano—del più anziano Marcantonio con i figli.[15] Di quest'ultimo, secondogenito di Agostino, sono dispersi il *Ritratto* opera ancora del Paggi, quello di Bernardo Azzolino e quello di Battistello Caracciolo, ma è noto quello più tardo di Justus Sustermans.[16] Si è infine accertato che nipoti di Marcantonio erano i tre bimbi raffigurati da Van Dyck nel dipinto della collezione Durazzo-Pallavicini (fig. 5), in quanto l'arma araldica sulla sinistra attesta trattarsi dei figli di Agostino Spinola e Vittoria Doria. E di conseguenza si può pensare—pur mancando, almeno per ora, ogni supporto documentario—che lo stesso artista abbia eseguito anche i ritratti dei genitori di quei fanciulli.[17]

Ad ogni modo, una simile "concentrazione" di ritratti di grandi maestri nell'ambito di un'unica famiglia non può non lasciare sbalorditi e non trova riscontro, per quanto si sa, non solo in Genova ma addirittura—a parità di livello sociale—nemmeno in Europa; considerando poi l'interesse che quelle tele dovevano suscitare—credibilmente insieme alle quadrerie di cui facevano parte—si possono presumere rapporti fra committenti e artisti estremamente proficui per entrambe le parti.

In questo senso, per quanto attiene Rubens, all'intrinsichezza con i membri di questo ramo dei Doria documentata dai ritratti citati, è lecito aggiungere l'ipotesi che il pittore, arrivato a Genova al seguito del duca di Mantova, sia stato ospitato nella magnifica villa di Sampierdarena di proprietà della famiglia, analogamente a quanto poi sarebbe avvenuto per Vouet.[18]

Per ciò che riguarda Van Dyck, prove più concrete dimostrano ad un tempo la frequentazione e le opportunità che la stessa offriva ad un artista: alla carta 104r del "Taccuino italiano" il maestro fiammingo ha infatti sommariamente copiato un ritratto di Tiziano—che non è quello di Giacomo Doria—indicando nel contempo di averlo visto "in casa di Gio. Carlo Doria."[19] Il disegno in questione, quindi, non solo docu-

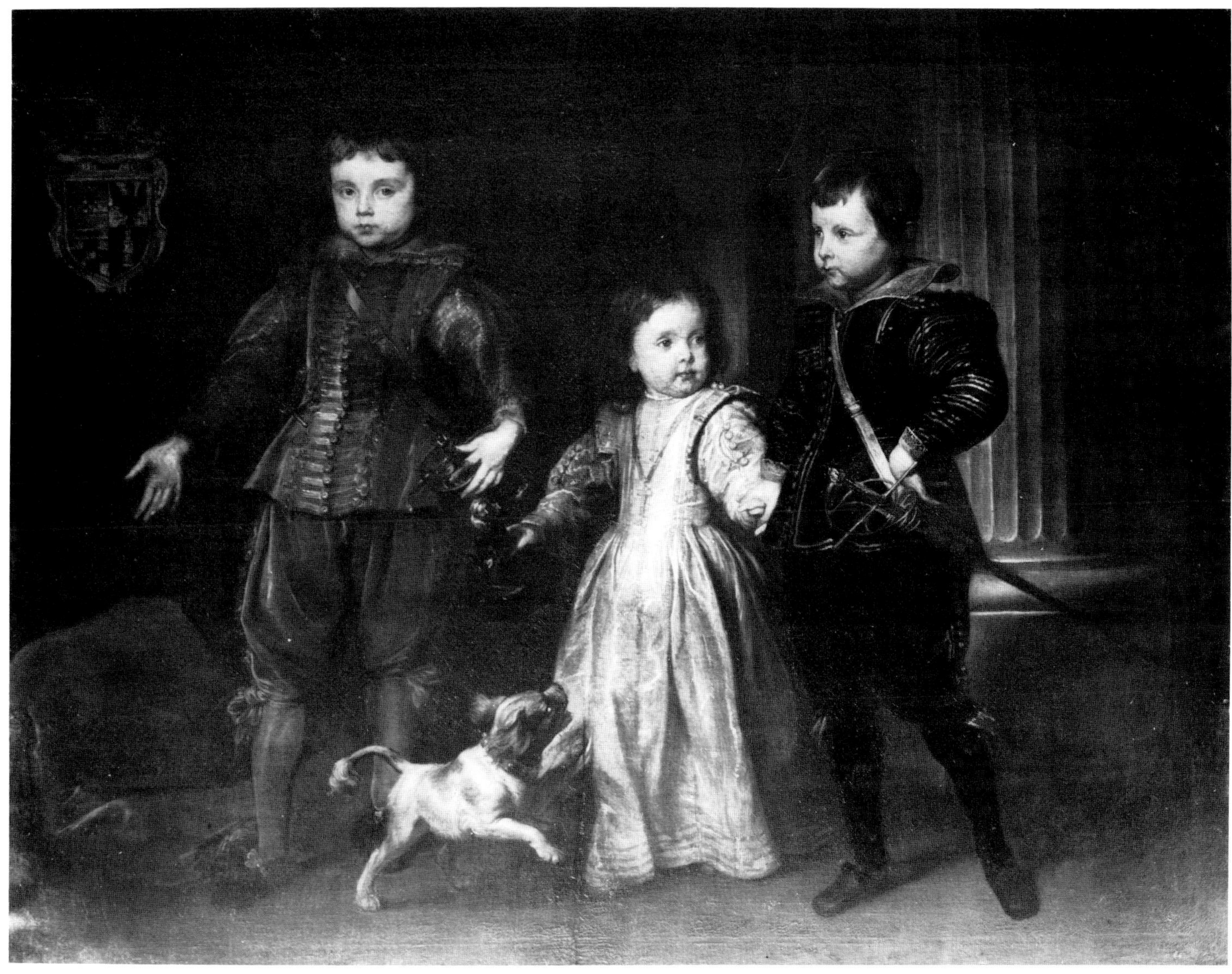

5. Anton van Dyck,
*Luca, Marc'Antonio, and
Violante di Agostino
Spinola*, c. 1625–1627,
oil on canvas
Palazzo Durazzo-Pallavicini, Genoa

menta nell'ambito delle collezioni dei Doria un'altra opera del maestro cadorino, ma anche l'attività di studio di Van Dyck in quello stesso contesto. In questo caso, perciò, la ricerca e l'identificazione dei dipinti con quella provenienza può contribuire in maniera determinante all'individuazione precisa di fonti figurative della ritrattistica vandyckiana.

È ancora da aggiungere in proposito che la disponibilità e l'atteggiamento mecenatistico di Gian Carlo Doria nei confronti dell'artista fiammingo trovano riscontro in ciò che le fonti ci hanno tramandato del gentiluomo: risulta infatti che fu promotore, patrono e ospite di quella pur effimera "Accademia del nudo" nell'ambito della quale si formò un gran numero di artisti genovesi di primo Seicento.[20]

La riscoperta della committenza e del ruolo avuto nelle vicende artistiche non solo genovesi da parte di questa famiglia—la memoria della quale era stata oscurata anche in conseguenza di morti premature, di divisioni patrimoniali e di vendite di opere—oltre all'interesse intrinseco, fornisce lo spunto per ridimensionare l'affermazione che contrappone Rubens, ritrattista dei "nobili vecchi," a Van Dyck, che lo sarebbe stato di quelli "nuovi."

Facevano parte dei "vecchi," infatti, oltre ai Doria, anche famiglie come i Cattaneo, i

Grimaldi e i Pallavicino, membri delle quali sono stati riconosciuti con sicurezza fra i personaggi effigiati dal pittore anversano.[21] E a questa stessa fazione doveva appartenere anche Placidia—o più credibilmente Luigia—Cattaneo Gentile, che un fortunato ritrovamento documentario può permettere di identificare nella dama ritratta da Van Dyck nel dipinto oggi a Strasburgo (fig. 6), e che finora si è ritenuto, per via della provenienza, rappresentasse una dama della famiglia Durazzo.[22]

L'individuazione è basata sulla testimonianza di un erudito genovese della seconda metà del secolo scorso, Marcello Staglieno, che ha lasciato una memoria di questo tenore:

La Marchesa Elena Remedi vedova Durazzo, abitante in via Roma n. 3, il 3 luglio 1890 vendeva al Signor Back Borgomastro di Strasburgo, per la pinacoteca di quella città, un ritratto di dama del Wandik [sic!] pel prezzo di £. 30/mila. Questo ritratto era quello della Signora Placidia Gentile Cattaneo che stava in casa Gentile, detta dei Gentile di San Pietro in Banchi ed è accennato nella Guida di Genova del Ratti, a pagina 120 e 129. Lo stesso rappresenta una signora vestita di nero, ed era pervenuto nella Marchesa Durazzo in eredità, per esser discendente dei Gentile. Una copia di esso esiste presso il marchese Lorenzo Centurione che l'ebbe da sua moglie Isabella de Marini, la quale a sua volta lo ereditava da sua madre Teresa Gentile.[23]

Nonostante il fatto che la descrizione sia più che sommaria, la precisa indicazione relativa alla destinazione dell'opera ha permesso un'immediata identificazione, confortata dal fatto che il dato corrisponde con quanto già si sapeva della provenienza del quadro del museo francese.

Deponendo la natura della memoria a favore dell'attendibilità delle affermazioni del suo autore, viene provato che il casato al quale fino ad oggi si è ritenuto appartenesse la dama è invece quello del marito—il marchese Gerolamo Durazzo—dell'ultima proprietaria genovese dell'opera, e soprattutto che la stessa ha invece un'altra provenienza. A questo proposito va detto che rispondente al vero è risultata la discendenza per via femminile di Elena Remedi dai Gentile, e precisamente da quel Filippo Gentile che ai primi dell'Ottocento è risultato aver ereditato la parte più consistente della quadreria di famiglia, specificamente descritta dal Ratti nel 1780.[24]

Tuttavia la questione non è ancora pienamente risolta, poiché il nome di Placidia Cattaneo Gentile indicato per la prima volta proprio dallo storiografo settecentesco, non appare—alla verifica—del tutto attendibile. Infatti non è stato possibile trovare negli alberi genealogici delle due famiglie in questione alcuna Placidia Cattaneo sposata ad un Gentile, e nemmeno una Placidia Gentile sposata ad un Cattaneo! Si è però appurata, in compenso, l'esistenza di tal Luigia Cattaneo che, sposata prima dell'anno 1600 ad Ambrogio Gentile, gli aveva dato diversi figli fra i quali una femmina cui era stato dato il nome di Placidia. La tradizione sembra quindi avere un minimo fondamento, anche se ha equivocato fra madre e figlia; in ragione degli elementi cronologici che si sono potuti ricavare a riguardo e dell'età non più giovanile dimostrata dal personaggio ritratto, si può proporre di identificarlo con Luigia Cattaneo Gentile, già vedova all'epoca del soggiorno di Van Dyck a Genova.

Conseguenze opposte rispetto al ritrovamento della nota manoscritta dello Staglieno ha avuto l'individuazione di un'incisione raffigurante—come attesta la dicitura—Filippo Spinola (fig. 7), il condottiero che come il padre, il più celebre Ambrogio, militò nell'esercito spagnolo. Infatti attraverso questa immagine si è potuta dare un'identità ad un ritratto—nel passato erroneamente attribuito a Van Dyck[25]—che faceva parte della dispersa collezione Balbi (fig. 8), ma nel contempo si è documentatamente smentita la tradizione che riconosceva questo personaggio in ben due dipinti la cui autografia vandyckiana è indubbia: quello della Queensland Art Gallery di Brisbane e quello della Alte Pinakothek di Monaco di Baviera.[26] Questo disconoscimento comporta parallelamente anche quello di due ritratti di dama, sempre della stessa mano, ritenuti entrambi raffigurare la moglie di Filippo Spinola, Geronima Doria. Infatti per il primo di essi, conservato alla Gemäldegalerie di Berlin-Dahlem, l'inconsistente identificazione era stata proposta ritenendolo *pendant* del *Ritratto di armato* di Brisbane, mentre per il secondo, al Louvre, era stata dedotta dalla supposta somiglianza col primo![27]

Nonostante il fatto che, allo stato attuale delle ricerche, ridimensionata appaia la committenza Spinola nei confronti di Van Dyck,[28] il numero di famiglie "vecchie" documentate in relazione con l'artista anversano è sufficiente a controbilanciare i "nobili nuovi" che, come si è detto, sono stati ritenuti spesso i suoi clienti più assidui.

In realtà un rapporto preferenziale può essere evidenziato per ora solo nei confronti dei Balbi, o meglio, di due rami di quella casata—poi confluiti in uno—e cioè quelli che facevano capo a Gerolamo e a Bar-

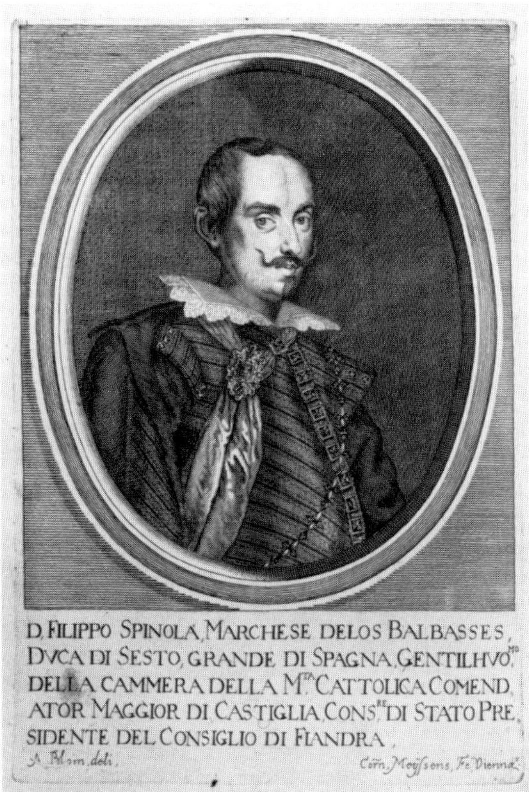

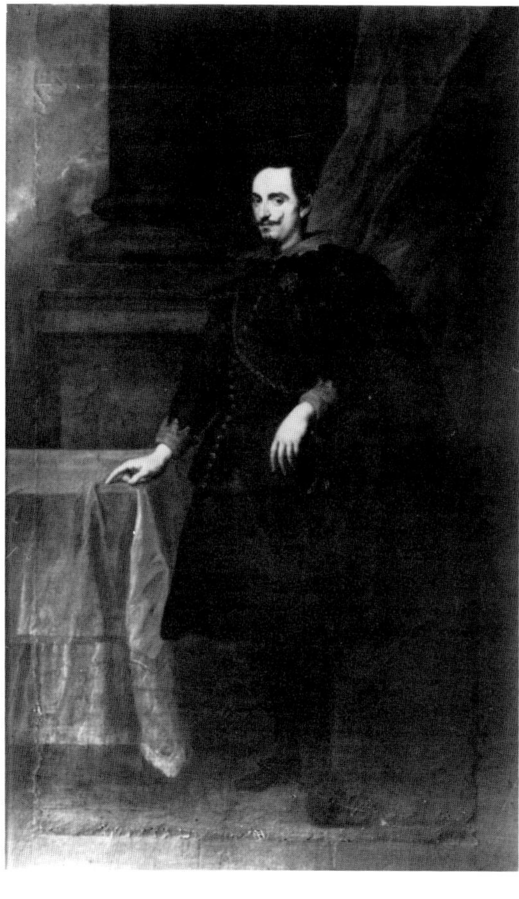

7. Cornelis Meyssens,
Filippo Spinola, 1674,
incisione
Galeazzo Gualdo Priorato, *Vite et azzioni di personaggi militari e politici* (Wien, 1674)

8. Adriaen van Bloemen(?),
Filippo Spinola,
c. 1640, olio su tela
Già Collezione Balbi-Senarega, Genova

tolomeo, due dei cinque figli maschi di Nicolò. Ma anche in questo caso, prima di esporre la documentazione sui rapporti dei Balbi con Anversa e soprattutto la prova documentaria definitiva dell'attività di Van Dyck come ritrattista per almeno un membro di questa famiglia anteriormente al suo viaggio in Italia, è necessario presentare uno stralcio della relativa genealogia.[29]

Riprendendo e integrando quanto è già

	Battina ∞	(1) Giovanni Durazzo (m. 1622) (2) Ippolito Invrea	Giacomo (n. 1620) Carlo Emanuele (n. 1622)
Gerolamo ∞ Geronima Giustiniani	Caterina ∞ Marcello Durazzo		Silvestro (n. 1624) Marcello (n. 1625) *
	Bartolomeo ∞ *Ottavia*		*
	Gian Paolo		
	Francesca ∞ Gian Battista De Franchi		
	Ottaviano		
Bartolomeo ∞ Lucrezia van Santvoort	Gian Agostino ∞ ? (m. 1621)		*Ottavia* Maria

* ulteriore discendenza

stato reso noto a proposito della presenza di questi due rami della famiglia Balbi ad Anversa, va ricordato che Gerolamo risulta console della "Nazione genovese" nella città belga dal 1585 al 1591, mentre Bartolomeo sposò l'anversana Lucrezia van Santvoort; uno dei due figli nati da questo matrimonio, Gian Agostino, fu a sua volta console nel biennio 1610–1611, e nel 1615 fondò, sempre nella stessa città, il convento di San Francesco da Paola.[30] A questi dati va aggiunto che le prime fortune dei Balbi—come per altre famiglie "nuove" con loro imparentate: i Brignole, i Durazzo . . . —furono legate alla produzione e al commercio della seta,[31] sicché si può presumere che già ruoli ufficiali e attività economica possano aver favorito relazioni col padre dell'artista, Frans van Dyck, di professione mercante anch'egli di seta.

Ma è poi l' "Inventario de Quadri spettanti all'heredità del quondam Signor Gerolamo Balbi" steso dal figlio Bartolomeo a fornire l'argomentazione risolutiva per dimostrare il contatto già ad Anversa tra Anton van Dyck e almeno Gian Agostino Balbi. Nel documento—sulla cui attendibilità non vi è da dubitare in considerazione della diretta conoscenza dei fatti da parte dell'estensore—accanto ad un gran numero di quadri che risultano, come i due ritratti di Gerolamo con un cane "fatti in Anversa," sono infatti elencati "il ritratto mio a cavallo del Vandich," "il ritratto di N. a cavallo del detto, levato di casa per essere indegno di starci" e "il ritratto del quondam Gio. Agostino Balbi del detto Vandich."[32]

Al di là della considerazione per questa consistente serie di dipinti, due dei quali—di cui si dirà più avanti—di grande prestigio trattandosi di ritratti equestri, l'elemento determinante è costituito dal fatto che Gian Agostino, effigiato nell'ultimo dei soggetti citati, risulta sia morto nel settembre 1621,[33] e quindi prima dell'arrivo di Van Dyck in Italia!

Il dipinto in questione, sebbene da tempo disperso,[34] si pone dunque come uno dei ritratti giovanili dell'artista anversano, in quanto Gian Agostino Balbi, di cui non si conosce purtroppo l'anno di nascita, deve essere definitivamente rientrato a Genova da Anversa fra 1618 e 1620, cioè entro il periodo durante il quale si protrassero i lavori di

costruzione della sua maestosa dimora—allora certo uno degli edifici privati più imponenti della città[35]—che lo poneva di fatto fra i genovesi più eminenti.

Quindi, sebbene Genova si trovasse sulla rotta che dalle Fiandre portava in Italia, ed allora vi avessero preso dimora i fratelli de Wael, quanto finora esposto prova in maniera circostanziata le ipotesi avanzate relativamente al fatto che il capoluogo ligure sia stato la prima e la più frequentata tappa nel corso del soggiorno italiano di Van Dyck.[36] Da un lato infatti i documentati rapporti dell'artista con i figli di Agostino Doria—il mecenatismo dei quali doveva essere ben noto—fanno ritenere che i contatti con questa famiglia fossero stati favoriti da Rubens; dall'altro si può essere pressoché certi che già prima di partire Van Dyck si fosse assicurato l'appoggio dei Balbi, credibilmente proprio di Gian Agostino, la notizia della cui recente scomparsa deve averlo colto solo al suo arrivo a Genova.

Ritornando agli altri due ritratti vandyckiani citati nell'inventario—dato che nulla si può per ora dire sulla reale identità del *Ritratto d'uomo a cavallo* del Koninklijk Museum voor Schone Kunsten di Anversa (fig. 9), che comunque per ragioni di prestigio sociale oltreché fisionomiche[37] non è Cornelis de Wael, e che piacerebbe riconoscere in Bartolomeo Balbi, cugino ed erede del patrimonio di Gian Agostino attraverso il matrimonio con la figlia naturale di questi, Ottavia—solo uno è attualmente noto: quello di cui nel documento si tace il nome. Si tratta del *Ritratto di Gian Paolo Balbi* (fig. 10)—cioè del fratello minore di Bartolomeo—che ora è conservato alla Fondazione Magnani-Rocca a Corte di Mamiano in provincia di Parma. L'effigiato, protagonista di una congiura contro le istituzioni della Repubblica di Genova nel 1648, non è nominato nell'inventario perché aveva subito una sorta di *damnatio memoriae* da parte della sua stessa famiglia, che riuscì in questo modo ad evitare il sequestro dei beni e l'esilio allora normalmente prescritti anche per i parenti dei colpevoli del reato di alto tradimento. Dopo la metà del secolo il ritratto in questione passò ad un cugino, Francesco Maria Balbi, che ne fece ridipingere il volto con la sua effigie dal pittore francese Simon de Bois.[38]

Non è invece menzionato nel documento in questione un ritratto di Ottavia Balbi: la lacuna rende molto improbabile la possibilità di riconoscerla, così come è stato fatto,[39] nella cosiddetta "Marchesa Balbi" della National Gallery di Washington. A proposito di quest'ultimo dipinto va tuttavia osservato innanzitutto che il titolo nobiliare unito al cognome è del tutto immotivato, in quanto ottenuto solo da altri rami della famiglia; e secondariamente che non chiare sono le notizie sulla sua provenienza. Secondo quanto tramandato, infatti, il ritratto venne venduto al barone J. B. Heath nei primi decenni dell'Ottocento dal marchese Giacomo Balbi-Senarega, che abitava nel palazzo di via Balbi 4:[40] ma un'opera siffatta non figura negli inventari e nelle descrizioni della quadreria allora colà conservata; inoltre, sarebbe stato poi direttamente trasferito a Londra, ma risulta esistere una litografia ottocentesca—ne è autore il francese Pierre Vogt—tratta da questo soggetto e la cui didascalia recita "M.me la Marquise Balbi de Gênes. L'original appartient à Monsieur Auguste de Sivry à Venise."[41]

All'impossibilità di riconoscere, almeno per ora, la giovane gentildonna di Washington compensa l'identificazione per via documentaria di due delle tre sorelle di Bartolomeo e Gian Paolo Balbi—Battina e Caterina—in altrettanti dipinti che, sebbene pagati dalle famiglie dei rispettivi sposi,[42] completano il quadro dei rapporti fra Van Dyck e i Balbi.

L'identificazione di Battina Balbi—moglie in prime nozze di Giovanni Durazzo, ed in seconde di Ippolito Invrea—con la cosiddetta "Dama d'oro" della collezione Durazzo-Pallavicini (fig. 11), è confortata dai dati relativi all'ingresso in quest'ultima raccolta. Giacomo Filippo II Durazzo l'acquistò infatti nel 1720 da Ippolito Settimio Invrea impegnandosi a farne eseguire una copia per il venditore: la clausola appare indizio sufficiente a ritenere che la dama ritratta fosse un'antenata—specificamente la nonna paterna—dell'Invrea.[43] Che quest'ultima fosse stata effigiata da Van Dyck sembra provarlo anche un altro riferimento documentario, e cioè la citazione in un inventario di metà Settecento del "ritratto di testa della signore Battinetta

Balbi Durazzo del Vandich fatto per studio, di palmi 1,8 e 1,4 esclusa aggionta,"[44] opera avvicinabile a quella della Galleria Palatina di Firenze (fig. 12).[45] Ma ulteriori indagini biografiche inducono a precisare l'epoca di esecuzione del triplo ritratto.

Dal matrimonio di Battina Balbi con Gio-

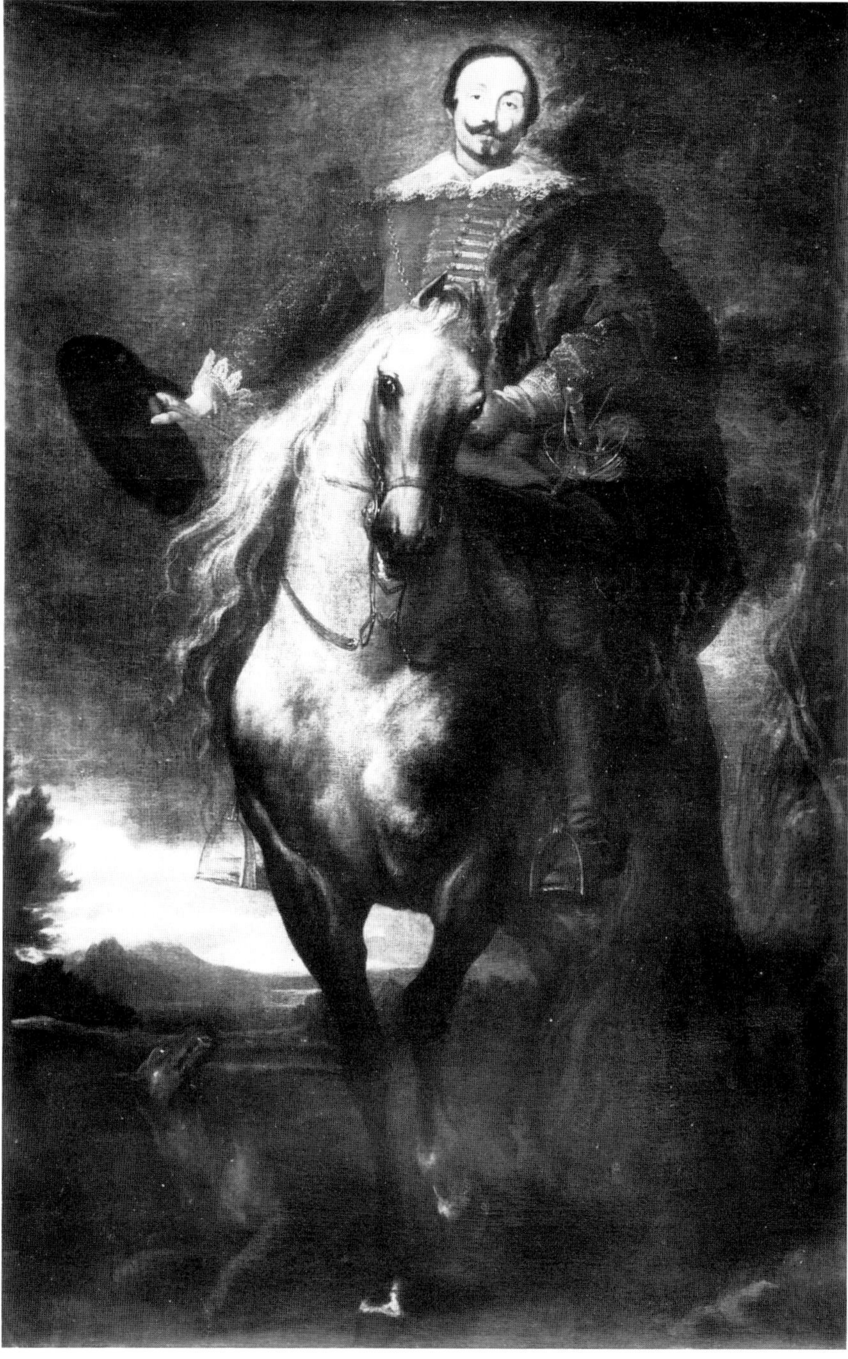

9. Anton van Dyck, *Gentiluomo genovese(?) a cavallo*, c. 1622, olio su tela Koninklijk Museum voor Schone Kunsten, Antwerpen

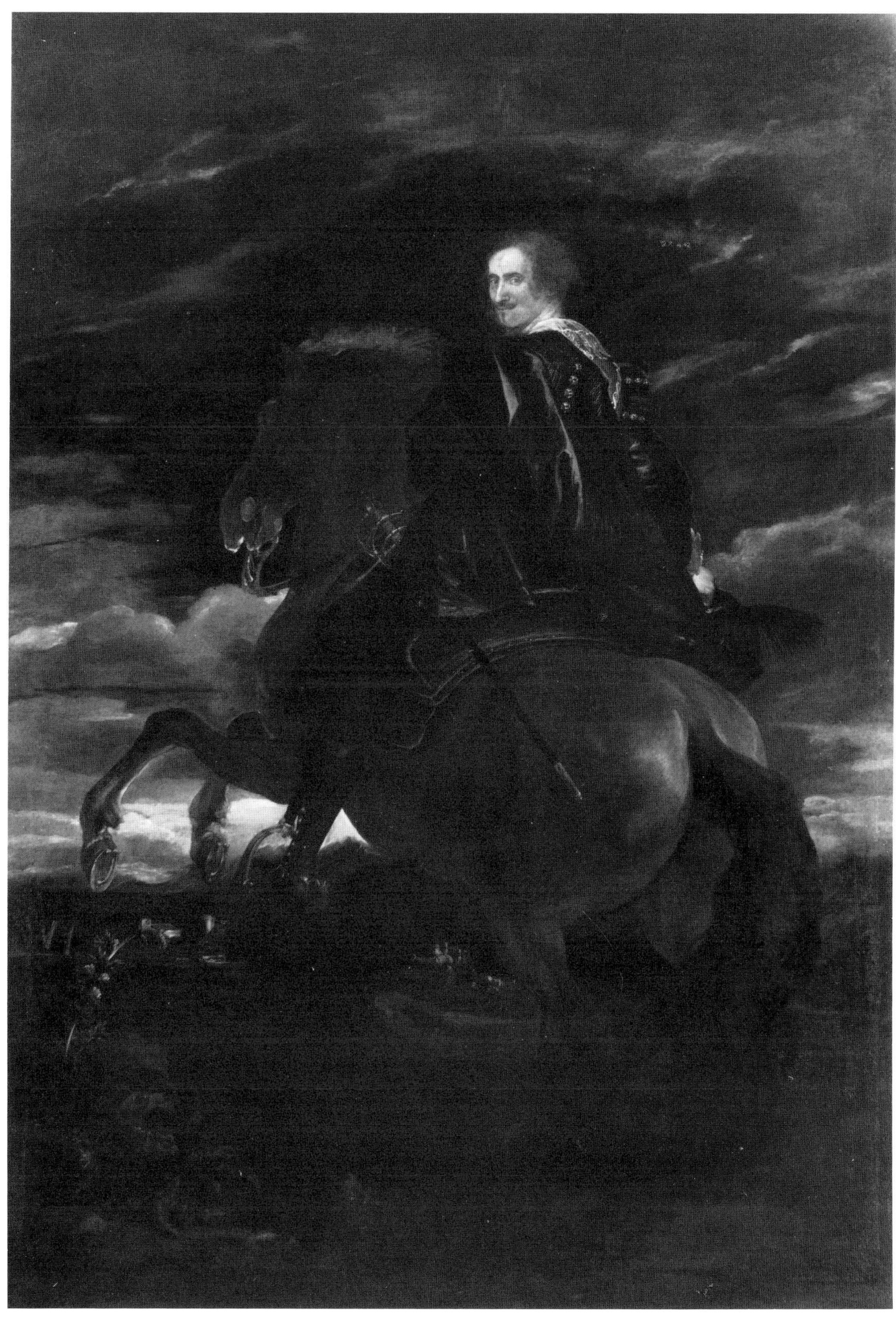

10. Anton van Dyck, *Gian Paolo Balbi a cavallo*, c. 1622, olio su tela
Fondazione Magnani Rocca, Corte di Mamiano, Parma

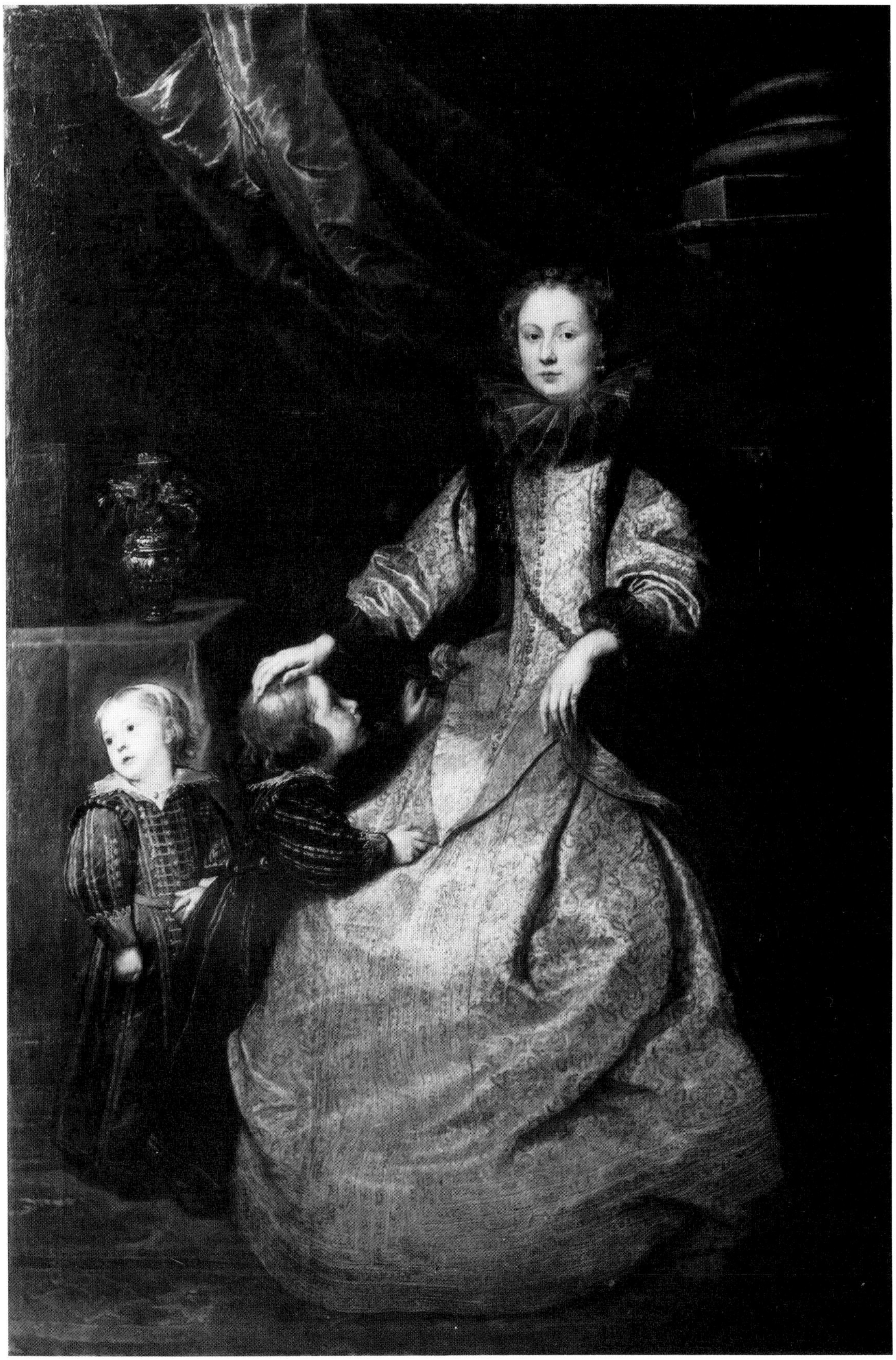

11. Anton van Dyck, *Battina Balbi Durazzo Invrea*, 1627, olio su tela
Palazzo Durazzo-Pallavicini, Genova

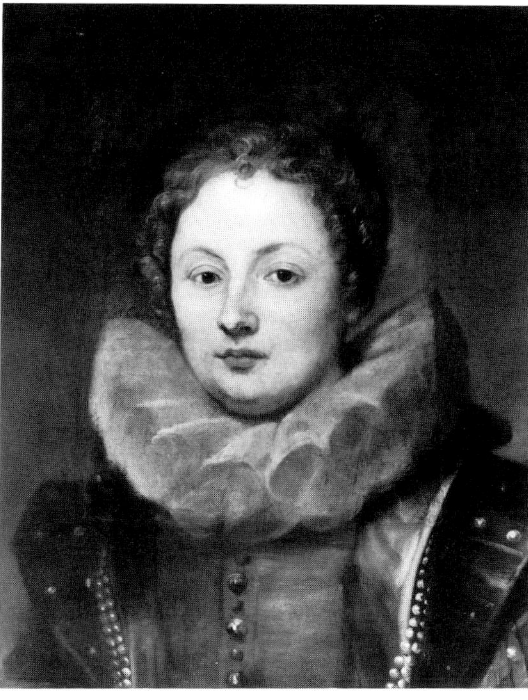

vanni Durazzo nacquero, fra 1620 e 1622, tre figli, dei quali solo due sopravvissero, Giacomo e Carlo Emanuele II Durazzo, che si potrebbero presumere effigiati con lei nel dipinto, riferendolo al 1624 circa. Considerando tuttavia che pochi mesi dopo il battesimo dell'ultimo nato Giovanni morì, e la pur opinabile età dimostrata dal più piccolo dei due bimbi ritratti, si può escludere che Van Dyck abbia eseguito l'opera mentre Giovanni era in vita. Brevissimo, per altro, deve essere stato il periodo di vedovanza di Battina, che già nel corso del 1624 partoriva il primo figlio dal secondo marito, Ippolito Invrea. A questo punto, non sembrando verosimile che Battina si sia fatta ritrarre quand'era ormai moglie di Ippolito con i figli di primo letto, si ritiene di poter identificare i due bimbi nei primi due figli di secondo letto, Marcello e Silvestro Invrea, nati rispettivamente nel 1624 e nel 1625, e di poter riferire il ritratto al 1626–1627, cioè ad un'epoca assai prossima a quella dei ritratti di Geronima Sale Brignole con la figlia Aurelia, di Anton Giulio Brignole-Sale e di Paolina Adorno Brignole-Sale, pagati nel 1627 da Gian Francesco Brignole 747 lire.[46]

Nel caso di Caterina Balbi, invece, accertando l'identità della dama che la tradizione,

non lontana dal vero, ci ha tramandato col nome di Caterina Durazzo,[47] era in realtà quella appunto di Caterina Balbi maritata ad un Durazzo, è stato anche possibile individuare il ritratto del marito, Marcello Durazzo di Agostino (figg. 13, 14). Il primo dato riguardante questi due dipinti è quello relativo al pagamento: nei libri di conti di Agostino Durazzo risulta infatti registrata al 31 dicembre 1624 la cospicua cifra di 373 lire "per costo de doi retrati di Marcello e Catterina con li tellari di noce,"[48] senza tuttavia indicazione dell'autore. Il prezzo pagato e l'elencazione dieci anni più tardi di "due ritratti d'Antonio Vandich del quondam Signor Marcello e della Signora Caterina" nell'inventario dei beni dello stesso Marcello,[49] morto poco tempo prima, conforta l'identificazione della spesa. Successivamente—secondo gli accordi conclusi fra gli interessati nel 1658—i due dipinti, insieme ad altri beni, vennero assegnati in usufrutto a Caterina, per tornare alla sua morte agli eredi del marito, cioè i nipoti Marcello e Giuseppe Maria, figli di Giacomo Filippo I, e l'altro fratello, Gerolamo.[50] Gli inventari delle collezioni di Marcello e Giuseppe Maria[51] permettono di escludere che alla morte di Caterina i due ritratti siano toccati ad uno di loro. Della discendenza di Gerolamo non si conoscono per ora inventari, ma sono in compenso note le residenze via via occupate a Genova: la prima è l'attuale Palazzo Reale in cui ancora si trova per l'appunto il ritratto detto Caterina Durazzo; la seconda, acquisita dopo la vendita della precedente ai Savoia, è il palazzo già Brignole di piazza della Meridiana dove, negli ultimi anni dell'Ottocento, venne acquistato il ritratto ora alla Ca' d'Oro di Venezia,[52] da identificare dunque con Marcello Durazzo. Conforta questo riconoscimento anche la corrispondenza dei tratti fisionomici con quelli della statua a lui dedicata nel 1632 per ricordare il lascito in favore dell'antico ospedale genovese di Pammatone (fig. 15).[53]

Relativamente al *Ritratto di Caterina Balbi Durazzo* merita soffermarsi un momento sull'iconografia dell'opera. Per quanto si sa questo è l'unico soggetto del periodo genovese che presenti il motivo della dama presso una fontana, ripreso poi dallo stesso artista in alcuni altri ritratti di gentildonne

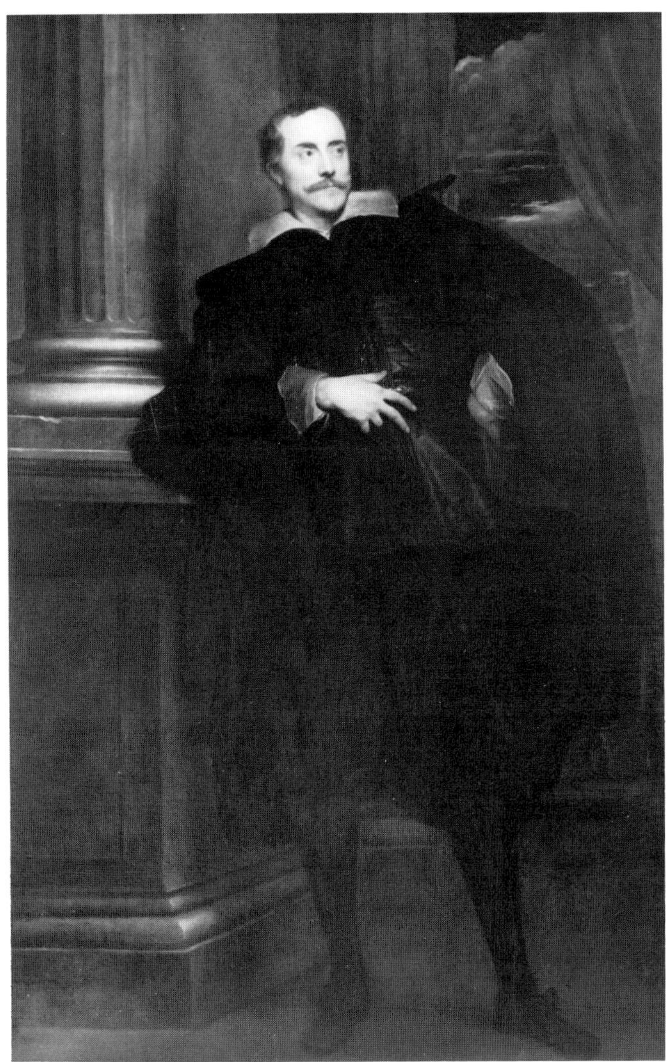

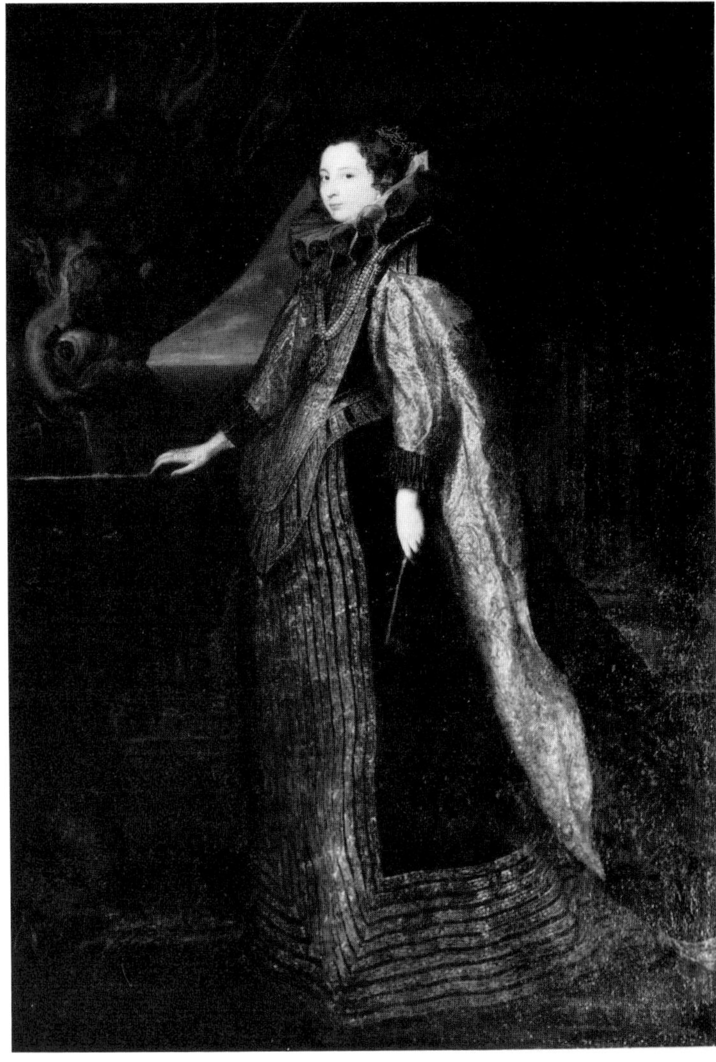

inglesi.[54] Non è stato però notato finora che nell'ambito di questa tipologia e tra le più dirette fonti iconografiche si deve annoverare il *Ritratto di dama*, oggi identificabile in Giovanna Spinola Pavese, di Rubens del Museo Nazionale d'Arte di Bucarest (fig. 16),[55] trattandosi di un dipinto di sicura provenienza genovese. Autografia e identità sono infatti precisamente espressi nell'inventario del 1660 della collezione di Gian Filippo Spinola che elenca in successione "un quadro ritratto di M. Pallavicina di Rubens figura intera alto p. 10 e largo sei (= cm 247,5 x 148,5) senza cornice" e "un quadro di detto Rubens ritratto di Donna Giovanna Pavese di misura in tutto come sopra, con una fontana appresso, e fiori sopra la testa a modo d'arco." Quest'ultima indicazione iconografica non era stata notata da nessun autore, ma è talmente specifica da togliere ogni dubbio in proposito.[56] In margine a questo e in considerazione del soggetto di questo contributo, si coglie l'occasione per notificare che il primo dei due dipinti descritti va identificato con la rubensiana *Dama in bianco* della collezione Bankes di Kingston Lacy (fig. 17)[57]—non solo le misure corrispondono perfettamente, ma anche l'indicazione dell'identità si concilia con l'arma araldica dello sfondo—che dunque rappresenta Maria Serra Pallavicino, sorella del cardinale Giacomo Serra, protettore e committente di Rubens a Roma, e moglie di Nicolò Pallavicino, patrono della cappella della chiesa del Gesù di Genova per la quale lo stesso artista realizzò la pala dei *Miracoli di sant'Ignazio*.

13. Anton van Dyck, *Marcello Durazzo*, 1623, olio su tela
Ca' d'Oro, Venezia

14. Anton van Dyck, *Caterina Balbi Durazzo*, 1623, olio su tela
Galleria di Palazzo Reale, Genova

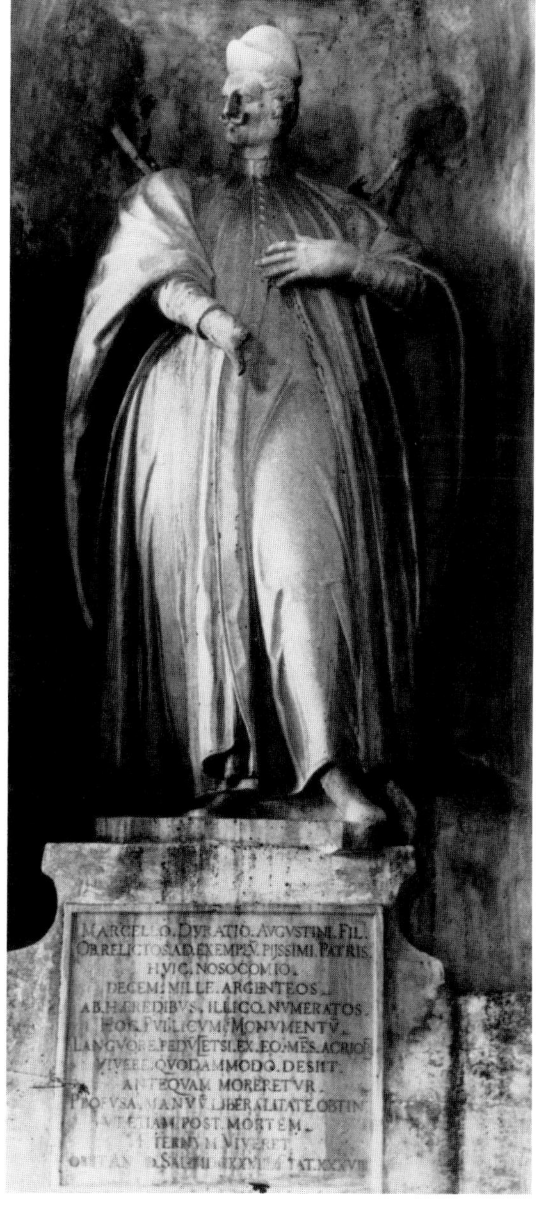

15. Martino Rezzi, *Marcello Durazzo*, 1632, marmo
Ospedale di San Martino, Genova

16. Peter Paul Rubens, *Giovanna Spinola Pavese*, c. 1608, olio su tela
Muzeul de Arte al Republicii Romania, Bucarest

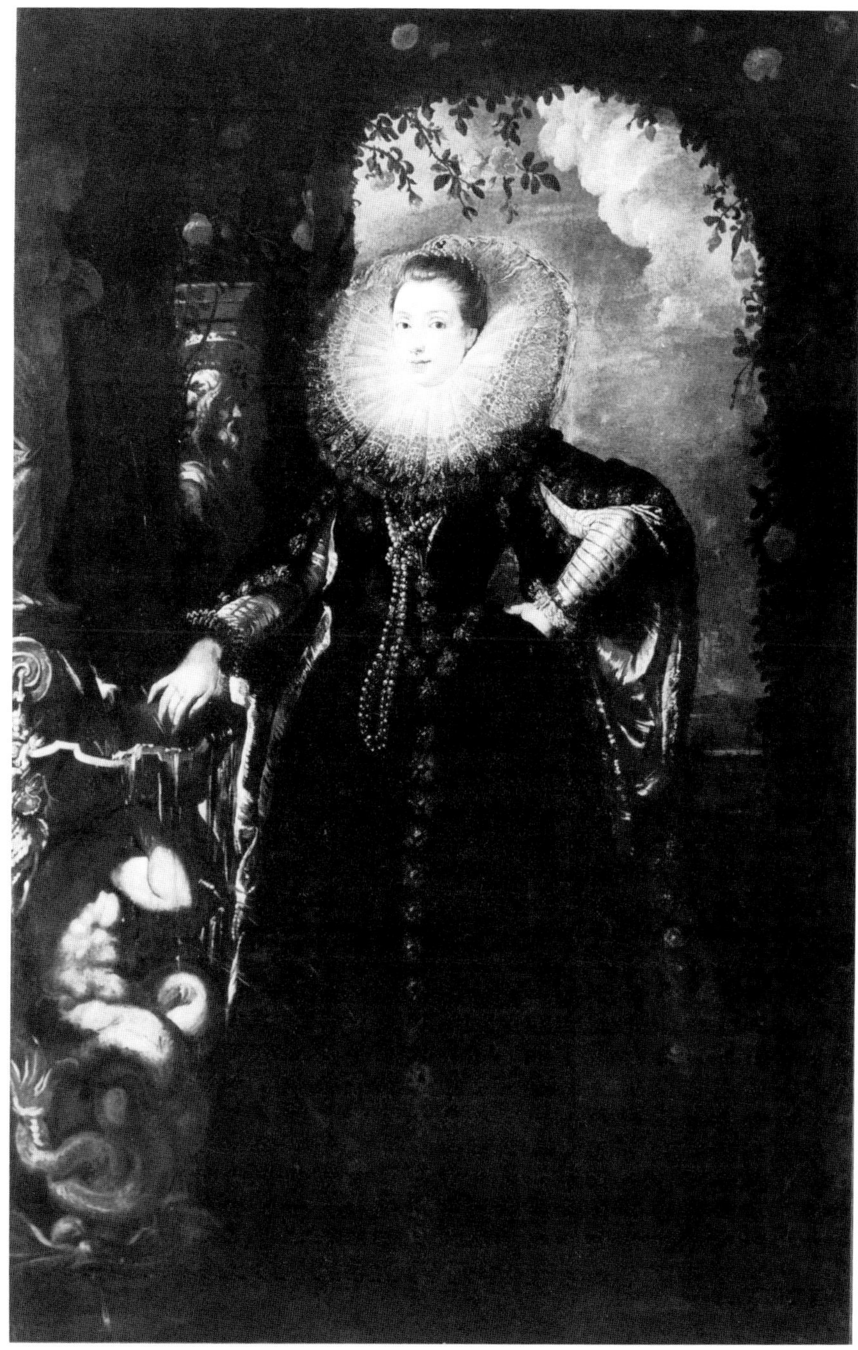

Ritornando alla ritrattistica vandyckiana, c'è ancora da osservare che l'impressionante intreccio di vincoli di sangue esistenti fra il ristretto novero delle casate "nuove" fin qui nominate,[58] e le implicazioni di prestigio sociale ad essi collegati consentono di ipotizzare, da ultimo, che anche altri fra i loro membri possano essere stati effigiati da Van Dyck. Fra i tanti personaggi "possibili" merita segnalare Maddalena Brignole Du- razzo—sorella di Anton Giulio e cognata di Marcello e Caterina Durazzo—in quanto i libri di conti del suocero—l'Agostino Durazzo già citato in precedenza—documentano nel 1623 la spesa di 128 lire per il suo ritratto, senza tuttavia dar conto dell'autore.[59] Facendo il paragone con le cifre dei pochi pagamenti a Van Dyck già noti e ricordati in questo contributo, la somma indicata dovrebbe aver corrisposto più o meno ad un

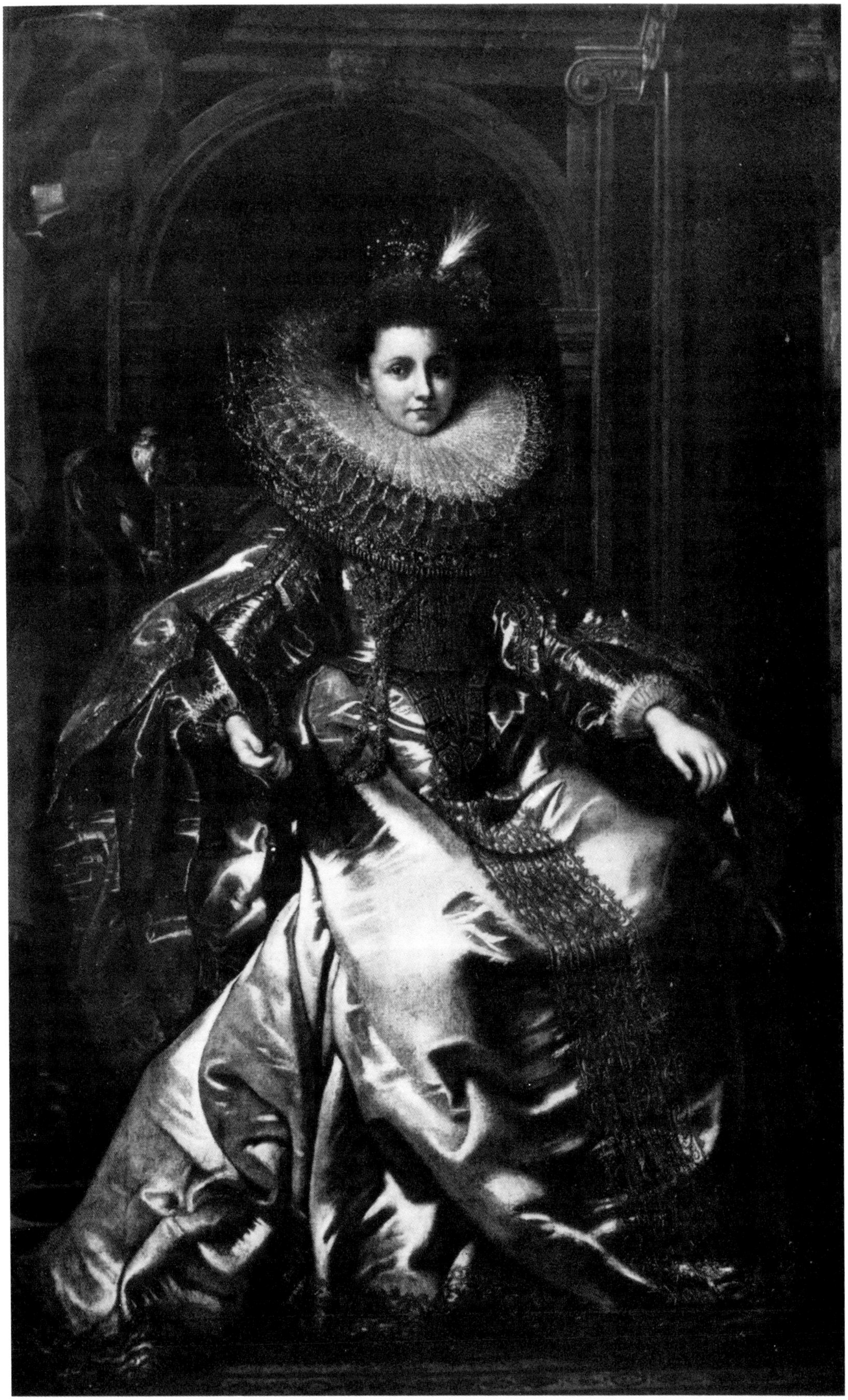

17. Peter Paul Rubens, *Maria Serra Pallavicino*, c. 1606, olio su tela
Collezione Bankes, Kingston Lacy

ritratto a tre quarti di figura, ma il fatto che
l'artista non sia nominato induce per ora a
molta prudenza nella sua identificazione e,
nel contempo, stimola a nuove ricerche
d'archivio.

NOTE

Rispetto alla relazione presentata in sede di convegno
questo testo presenta non poche varianti: infatti,
avendo potuto disporre, nel frattempo, dell'encomia-
bile lavoro di Susan J. Barnes, "Van Dyck in Italy:
1621–1628," tesi dottorale (New York University,
1986), ove per la prima volta si affronta in maniera
oggettiva il problema dell'identità dei personaggi ritratti a Genova da Van Dyck, si sono soppresse tutte
le parti che sarebbero state ripetitive rispetto a quello
studio. In compenso i riferimenti ivi contenuti al
contesto genovese, e i risultati delle ricerche e degli
approfondimenti effettuati hanno indotto ad allargare
il discorso anche su alcuni ritratti di genovesi di
Rubens. Si dà qui conto quindi dei risultati relativi ai
due artisti fiamminghi di diverse indagini condotte
in questi anni ed aventi per comune denominatore la
committenza e il collezionismo a Genova nel Seicento. In questo senso molte sono le persone con le
quali, pur per motivi diversi, sono in debito di ri-
conoscenza: innanzitutto Susan J. Barnes che mi ha
offerto la possibilità di partecipare al convegno; poi
Marzia Cataldi Gallo e Rodolfo Savelli che hanno
sempre confortato le mie ricerche delle loro speci-
fiche conoscenze; ed ancora Roberto Bilotti, Clario
Di Fabio, Peter Fuhring, Ezia Gavazza, Lauro Magnani, Laura Malfatto, Giovanna Rotondi Terminiello, Liana Saginati e Laura Tagliaferro.

1. Il dato numerico è ricavato per approssimazione
dalle testimonianze dell'epoca riportate da Carlo
Bitossi, *Il governo dei Magnifici. Patriziato e politica
a Genova fra Cinque e Seicento* (Genova, 1990), 87.

2. In proposito vedi Giorgio Doria, "Un pittore fiammingo nel 'Secolo dei Genovesi,'" in *Rubens e Genova* [cat. mostra, Palazzo Ducale] (Genova, 1977),
13–29; Rodolfo Savelli, *La Repubblica oligarchica.
Legislazione, istituzioni e ceti a Genova nel Cinquecento* (Milano, 1981); Giorgio Doria, "Conoscenza
del mercato e sistema informativo: il know-how dei
mercanti-finanzieri genovesi nei secoli XVI e XVII,"
in *La Repubblica internazionale del denaro*, a cura
di Aldo De Maddalena e Hermann Kellenbenz
(Bologna, 1986), 57–121.

3. Bitossi 1990, 120–123.

4. Bitossi 1990, 127–132.

5. Genealogie, discendenza, rapporti di parentela e
dati biografici sono stati ricostruiti attraverso i
seguenti testi a stampa: Natale Battilana, *Genealogie
delle famiglie nobili di Genova* (Genova, 1828–1833);
Guelfo Guelfi Camajani, *Il "Liber Nobilitatis Ge-
nuensis" e il governo della Repubblica di Genova
fino all'anno 1797* (Firenze, 1965); Carlo Sertorio, *Il

patriziato genovese: discendenza degli ascritti al
Libro d'Oro nel 1797* (Genova, 1967); e i volumi
manoscritti della Civica Biblioteca Berio di Genova:
Anton Maria Buonarroti, "Alberi genealogici di diverse famiglie nobili" (m.r.VIII, 2, 30–32); Agostino
Della Cella, "Famiglie di Genova antiche e moderne,
estinte e viventi, nobili e popolari, delle quali si trova
memoria nelli annalisti, storici o notarj . . ." (m.r.X,
2, 167–169).

6. Esemplari in questo senso le vicende che hanno in-
teressato la collezione della Galleria Nazionale di
Palazzo Spinola, per la quale vedi Piero Boccardo,
"Per la storia della quadreria di Palazzo Spinola," in
"Palazzo Spinola a Pellicceria. Due musei in una
dimora storica," *Quaderni della Galleria Nazionale
di Palazzo Spinola* 10 (1987), 60–86.

7. È quanto risulta nell'inventario della collezione di
Gian Battista Balbi pubblicato in Piero Boccardo e
Lauro Magnani, "La committenza [della famiglia
Balbi]," in *Il Palazzo dell'Università di Genova. Il
Collegio dei Gesuiti nella strada dei Balbi* (Savona,
1987), 81–82.

8. Carlo Giuseppe Ratti, *Instruzione di quanto può
vedersi di più bello in Genova in pittura, scultura ed
architettura* (Genova, 1780). Di quest'opera esiste
una prima edizione, pubblicata sempre a Genova nel
1766, che, sebbene risulti nel complesso meno det-
tagliata, in qualche caso fornisce dati che non si
ritrovano nel testo di quattordici anni dopo.

9. Vedi Appendice. Per altri dati sui problemi di riconoscimento e identificazione dei dipinti si veda
anche Barnes 1986, 65–69.

10. Salvo diversa indicazione, per tutte le notizie
sulle vicende, i personaggi e i dipinti menzionati nel
testo in riferimento alla famiglia di Agostino Doria si
rimanda a Piero Boccardo, "Materiali per una storia
del collezionismo artistico a Genova nel XVII secolo," tesi dottorale (Milano, Università degli Studi,
1989), 8–52.

11. Dopo la morte di Giacomo Doria, da collocarsi
nel 1613, Brigida Spinola si risposò infatti con Gian
Vincenzo Imperiale. Si coglie l'occasione per precisare che il suo *Ritratto* dipinto da Rubens venne lasciato dal primo marito al fratello terzogenito Gian
Carlo, e solo dopo la morte di questi, nel 1625, passò
in casa Imperiale. È sempre questo dipinto, per altro,
e non la creduta *Caterina Grimaldi con un nano* di
Kingston Lacy, come ha proposto Justus Müller Hofstede, ad essere menzionato nell'inventario dei dipinti di Gian Vincenzo Imperiale del 1661. A

riguardo si veda Renato Martinoni, *Gian Vincenzo Imperiale, politico, letterato e collezionista genovese del Seicento* (Padova, 1983), 305.

12. Oltre al fatto che da un passo del testamento di Veronica Spinola Doria si desume che prima delle sue nozze, avvenute nel 1608, ella aveva risieduto in Spagna e quindi non avrebbe potuto essere ritratta da Rubens, va sottolineato che del dipinto non si trova alcuna menzione in nessuno degli inventari noti delle quadrerie dei vari membri della famiglia.

13. Pubblicati da Ludwig Burchard, "Genuesische Frauenbildnisse von Rubens," *Jahrbuch der preussischen Kunstsammlungen* 50 (1929), 336–337 e 348–349, come ritratti di Brigida Spinola Doria, sono stati riferiti a Veronica Spinola Doria da Justus Müller Hofstede, "Bildnisse aus Rubens' Italienjahren," *Jahrbuch der Staatlichen Kunstsammlungen in Baden-Württemberg* 2 (1965), 89–92 e 96. In realtà quanto si legge dell'arma araldica raffigurata sullo stendardo o tenda di sfondo porta a riconoscere nella dama un membro della famiglia Serra, ipoteticamente individuabile in una sorella o una cognata del cardinal Giacomo Serra (relativamente alle relazioni fra Rubens e i Serra si veda più avanti).

14. Non risultano esistere infatti altri ritratti di Tiziano di personaggi genovesi.

15. Vedi Ratti 1780, 311 e 332; e l'Appendice a questo contributo.

16. Riprodotto in *Collezioni del principe don Marcantonio Doria d'Angri* [cat. vendita, Galleria Ciardiello] (Napoli, 1940), n. 49, tav. 14.

17. L'ipotesi ha il suo limite nel fatto che i documenti d'archivio dimostrano che allora, in generale, si attribuiva maggior valore al ritratto in quanto immagine della persona piuttosto che in considerazione del suo autore, per cui quando un'individuo possedeva già una sua effige non necessariamente ricorreva—presentandosi l'occasione—ad un artista più noto o qualificato.

18. È significativo in questo senso quanto Simon Vouet scrisse al Cavalier dal Pozzo il 4 settembre 1621: "questi signori Doria . . . m'hanno condotto in S. Pier d'Arena in un bellissimo luogo, dove vanno a villegiare, e là m'hanno pregato a far qualche loro ritratto, cio che infin ora non avevo voluto fare in conto alcuno, ma le loro cortesie appresso di me hanno operato, che non ho potuto dir di no." Questa lettera, attualmente dispersa, è stata pubblicata da Stefano Bottari, *Roccolta di lettere sulla pittura, scultura ed architettura*, 7 voll. (Roma, 1754–1783), 1:333.

19. Segnalato per la prima volta da Maurice Vaes, "Le séjour de Van Dyck en Italie (mi-novembre 1621–automne 1627)," *Bulletin de l'Institut historique belge de Rome* 4 (1924), 200; si veda poi Gert Adriani, *Anton van Dyck. Italienisches Skizzenbuch* (Wien, 1940), 65.

20. Scarsissime notizie sono state reperite finora su questo cenacolo artistico: i pochi dati noti derivano da Raffaello Soprani, *Le vite de' pittori, scoltori ed architetti genovesi e de' forastieri che in Genova*

operarono (Genova, 1674), 129, 168, 180, 237, 312, 315; inoltre si veda Boccardo 1989, 16.

21. Si veda, da ultimo, Susan J. Barnes, "Filippo Cattaneo, Clelia Cattaneo," "Elena Grimaldi," "Agostino Pallavicini," in *Anthony van Dyck*, a cura di Arthur K. Wheelock, Jr., et al. [cat. mostra, National Gallery of Art] (Washington, 1990), 170–171, 174–176, 147–148.

22. Si veda Alain Roy, "Portrait d'une dame génoise de la famille Durazzo," in *Le siècle de Rubens dans les collections publiques françaises* [cat. mostra, Grand Palais] (Paris, 1977); e Barnes 1986, 302–303, che non accoglie l'identificazione tradizionale.

23. Marcello Staglieno, "Note storico artistiche," carte rilegate in un volume manoscritto composito, Genova, Civica Biblioteca Berio, m.r.VIII, 3, 6, carta 53 recto.

24. Vedi Ratti 1780, 129–132; e *Descrizione della città di Genova da un anonimo del 1818*, a cura di Ennio e Fiorella Poleggi (Genova, 1969), 82–83.

25. Vedi *100 opere di van Dyck* [cat. mostra, Palazzo dell'Accademia] (Genova, 1955), 45 scheda 97.

26. L'identificazione tradizionale, ancora riportata da Erik Larsen, *The Paintings of Anthony van Dyck*, 2 voll. (Freren, 1988), 2:168, non è stata accettata già da Barnes 1986, 288–289 e 275–276.

27. Analogamente vedi Larsen 1988, 168; e Barnes 1986, 311–312 e 315–316.

28. Privo di fondamenti documentari è infatti il contributo di Giorgio F. Costa, "Antonio van Dyck e la famiglia Spinola," *Genova* (luglio 1939), 26–28, incentrato sulle identificazioni tradizionali dei ritratti.

29. Sull'intera famiglia vedi Boccardo e Magnani 1987, 47–88.

30. Oltre al testo indicato alla nota precedente, si veda Barnes in Washington 1990, 24–25; le indicazioni relative agli incarichi diplomatici sono state ricavate da Vito Vitale, "Diplomatici e consoli della Repubblica di Genova," in *Atti della Società Ligure di Storia Patria* 63 (1934), 304.

31. Interessi economici di questo tipo sono documentati da consistente materiale d'archivio; un riscontro viene comunque da Bitossi 1990, 127.

32. Vedi Boccardo e Magnani 1987, 78–79, nota 11.

33. Il dato si ricava dall'atto di ammissione degli eredi al fedecommesso disposto con le sue ultime volontà da Gian Agostino Balbi: nel documento, steso dal notaio Ambrogio Rapallo il 27 settembre 1621, e conservato presso l'Archivio di Stato di Genova, si specifica che lo stesso è morto nei giorni precedenti.

34. Il ritratto, documentato dapprima nell'inventario dei dipinti dello stesso Gian Agostino Balbi da lui vincolati in fedecommesso (vedi Boccardo e Magnani 1987, 79, nota 14), risulta poi pur sempre nel palazzo di Gian Agostino quando questo, attraverso il matrimonio della figlia di quest'ultimo col cugino Bartolomeo Balbi, passa in proprietà degli eredi di Gero-

lamo Balbi (vedi nota 32). Notizie sulla quadreria di questi ultimi, e sugli spostamenti subiti in ambito cittadino, si ricavano poi da Ratti 1780, 116, e da Federico Alizeri, *Guida per la città di Genova*, 3 voll. (Genova, 1846–1847), 3:1349–1351, ma senza che il dipinto in questione venga più nominato.

35. Il palazzo, tuttora esistente in via Balbi 1, è significativamente documentato in *I Palazzi di Genova* (Anversa, 1626?), figg. 19–21; notizie sulla costruzione e bibliografia in Boccardo e Magnani 1987, 48.

36. Si veda a riguardo Barnes 1986, 4–5.

37. Quanto sappiamo sui ceti e gli *status symbol* dell'epoca porta ad escludere che un artista come Cornelis de Wael potesse avere un ritratto dell'importanza di quelli di esponenti certo molto in vista—anche dal punto di vista patrimoniale—dell'aristocrazia genovese, mentre per ciò che riguarda la corrispondenza fisionomica si rinvia a quanto detto da David Freedberg nel corso della conferenza del 10 febbraio 1991 presso l'auditorium della National Gallery of Art di Washington. Barnes 1986, 378, però, non considera il ritratto autografo di Van Dyck.

38. Vedi Barnes 1986, 197–198; Boccardo e Magnani 1987, 56 e figg. 27 e 50. Il ritratto è stato riportato al suo aspetto originale dall'ultimo proprietario dopo il 1974; Larsen 1988, 133 e 429 non ha riconosciuto trattarsi dello stesso dipinto prima e dopo il restauro. L'insolita vicenda del ritratto ha "contaminato" anche un'altro ritratto equestre già pertinente la collezione Balbi, quello di *Filippo IV* che si è supposto nascondesse un'altra effigie di Gian Paolo Balbi ridipinta in questo caso addirittura da Velasquez! La tradizione è priva di ogni fondamento, e l'opera del tutto originale è ora attribuita a Pietro Novelli (vedi Piero Boccardo, "Le 'rotte mediterranee' del collezionismo genovese," *Bollettino dei Musei Civici Genovesi* 10 [1988], n. 28–30, 100).

39. Si veda Boccardo e Magnani 1987, 79, nota 13; e, per i primi rimarchi in proposito, Barnes in Washington 1990, 146.

40. Barnes in Washington 1990, 146, forse sulla scorta di Giorgio Balbi, "Fatti e misfatti di un palazzo Balbi," *Genova* (agosto 1958), 25 e 29, nota 7, identifica il "marchese Giacomo Balbi" che risulta aver venduto il dipinto al barone Heath, con il figlio del doge Costantino Balbi, membri entrambi del ramo cadetto della famiglia, e proprietari in successione del palazzo sito in via Balbi 6. Ma il "Ritratto di donna con mano al petto del Vandich" che è descritto nella raccolta colà conservata fino agli inizi del secolo scorso misurava cm 85 x 55 circa (vedi Boccardo e Magnani 1987, 86, nota 8) e va identificato, con buon margine di sicurezza, col dipinto della Galleria Nazionale di Palazzo Spinola, inv. n. 43. Inoltre, sebbene non si conosca l'anno di morte di Giacomo Balbi di Costantino, lo stesso è da collocarsi presumibilmente prima della fine del Settecento. Il "marchese Giacomo Balbi" in questione deve essere credibilmente Giacomo Balbi-Senarega (1759–1832) del ramo primogenito della famiglia, che abitava il palazzo di via Balbi 4. La precisazione, tuttavia, non

risolve il problema della provenienza esposto da Barnes in Washington 1990, 146, in quanto nemmeno nelle descrizioni di questo secondo edificio si trova notizia del ritratto.

41. A riguardo si veda Balbi 1958, 29, nota 7, che dà conto della litografia ma non la riproduce.

42. La documentazione disponibile dimostra ampiamente che il ritratto di una donna sposata veniva sempre addebitato all' "azienda" della famiglia dello sposo, intestata al maschio più anziano, e come tale rientrava poi nei beni ereditari di quest'ultimo: si veda in proposito la vicenda più avanti documentata del ritratto vandyckiano di Caterina Balbi Durazzo che, morti suocero e marito, le viene lasciato "in uso" vita natural durante.

43. Il pagamento è stato pubblicato da Dino Puncuh, "Collezionismo e commercio di quadri nella Genova sei-settecentesca. Note archivistiche dai registri contabili dei Durazzo," in *Rassegna degli Archivi di Stato* 44 (1984), I, 189 n. 76 e 190 n. 83; ed è stato interpretato in termini analoghi, salvo un particolare di cui si dirà tra poco, da Barnes 1986, 193–196; e Barnes in Washington 1990, 144–146.

44. Archivio Storico del Comune di Genova, Archivio Brignole-Sale, carte in corso di riordino. L'inventario da cui si è estrapolata la citazione riguarda la dimora di Carlo Emanuele e Francesco Maria Durazzo.

45. La documentata presenza di quest'ultimo soggetto nelle collezioni medicee già agli inizi del Settecento esclude che possa trattarsi della stessa opera; dello studio della Galleria Palatina si conoscono per altro almeno due copie: si veda Didier Bodart, "Studio per il ritratto detto di Caterina Durazzo Adorno," in *Rubens e la pittura fiamminga del Seicento nelle collezioni pubbliche fiorentine* [cat. mostra, Palazzo Pitti] (Firenze, 1977), 116–118; e Barnes 1986, 191–192.

46. Per la datazione della *Battina Balbi* al 1623 circa e per il pagamento Brignole vedi Barnes 1986, 195 e 205; Barnes in Washington 1990, 144–146.

47. Con questo nome figura già in Ratti 1780, 211.

48. Vedi Puncuh 1984, 180, n. 21.

49. Dell'inventario in questione si è reperita una trascrizione allegata al documento citato alla nota successiva.

50. Vedi Archivio di Stato di Genova, Notaio Gian Luca Rossi, filza 6, 1657–1659, 23 ottobre 1658.

51. Vedi Puncuh 1984, 183–185 e 203–207.

52. Vedi Mario Menotti, "Ritratto di Antonio van Dyck," *L'Arte* 2 (1899), 254.

53. Già nell'antico ospedale genovese di Pammatone, è stata trasferita dopo l'ultima guerra nei viali dell'ospedale di San Martino. Si veda in proposito Marzia Cataldi Gallo, "Ritratto e costume: status symbol nella Genova del Seicento," *Bollettino Ligustico per la storia e la cultura regionale*, nuova serie 1 (1989), 88–89, ove sono ripresi anche alcuni dei dati citati in precedenza.

54. Vedi Zirka Zaremba Filipczak, "Reflections on Motifs in Van Dyck's Portraits," in Washington 1990, 60–61.

55. L'identificazione era già stata ipotizzata da Giuliana Biavati, "Il recupero conoscitivo dei Rubens 'genovesi,'" in Genova 1977, 153, sulla base di un inventario seicentesco (si veda più avanti) pubblicato in estratto, con molte imprecisioni e data erronea da Venanzio Belloni, *Penne, pennelli e quadrerie. Cultura e pittura genovese del Seicento* (Genova, 1973), 54–55. Non verificando il testo sul documento originale, alla studiosa sono venuti a mancare due elementi determinanti—iconografia e dimensioni—che le avrebbero permesso di rendere l'ipotesi una certezza. La proposta è comunque sfuggita a Maria Matache, autrice della relativa scheda in *Capolavori europei dalla Romania* [cat. mostra, Palazzo Ducale] (Venezia, 1991), 76–79, che per altro segnala la provenienza del dipinto dalla collezione del barone Felix Bamberg. Il dato non è di poco conto dato che del barone sono documentati altri acquisti di opere d'arte a Genova nella seconda metà dell'Ottocento.

56. In proposito si veda quanto detto sulla ricca collezione d'arte di Gian Filippo Spinola in Boccardo 1989, 70–83.

57. In precedenza identificata come Brigida Spinola Doria da Gustav Friedrich Waagen, *Galleries and Cabinets of Art in Great Britain* (London, 1857), 375; e più recentemente come Caterina Grimaldi da Michael Jaffé in *The Treasure Houses of Britain: Five Hundred Years of Private Patronage and Art Collecting* [cat. mostra, National Gallery of Art] (Washington, 1985), 558–559.

58. Si vedano in proposito le tavole pubblicate da Bitossi 1990, 128–131 e 133. Ivi fra le famiglie più nominate risultano anche De Franchi, Giustiniani e Saluzzo: per i primi si ricorda che riconoscibili come membri di quella famiglia sono i *Tre bimbi* della National Gallery di Londra (vedi Boccardo 1987, 85, nota 42); ai Giustiniani o ai Saluzzo dovrebbero invece aver appartenuto i due anziani personaggi dei ritratti in *pendant* della Gemäldegalerie di Berlin-Dahlem (vedi Barnes in Washington 1990, 150–151).

59. Vedi Puncuh 1984, 180, n. 19: "Per costo del ritratto de Maria Maddalena Lire 128." Lo studioso riferisce il nome alla sorella di Agostino Durazzo, quando è più logico pensare si tratti dell'omonima moglie del figlio primogenito di questi, cioè la nuora Maddalena Brignole. Secondo quanto si è detto in precedenza, infatti, un'eventuale ritratto della sorella di Agostino sarebbe stato pagato dalla famiglia del marito, Federico de Franchi.

APPENDICE

Le tavole che seguono elencano i ritratti che risultano attribuiti a Van Dyck nella guida dello storiografo settecentesco Carlo Giuseppe Ratti, *Instruzione di quanto può vedersi di più bello in Genova in pittura, scultura ed architettura* (Genova, 1780). Questo testo costituisce la fonte a stampa più attendibile e completa per la conoscenza del patrimonio artistico genovese, pubblico e privato, nel Settecento. Per quel che riguarda le collezioni d'arte cittadine è importante il fatto che presenti la situazione prima delle grandi dispersioni ottocentesche. Sebbene le ricerche abbiano permesso in qualche caso di integrare il testo con notizie desunte da altre guide locali, indicate in nota, va considerato che è quanto meno probabile che altri ritratti, in collezioni per qualche motivo meno accessibili, siano stati completamente ignorati.

Nella prima colonna sono indicati i nomi dei proprietari dei palazzi in cui risultavano conservati i ritratti attribuiti a Van Dyck; seguono l'indicazione della pagina nel testo settecentesco, e il soggetto dell'opera reso in forma moderna; l'asterisco (*) contrassegna quelle la cui assegnazione al maestro fiammingo non può essere più accolta. Nell'ultima colonna è l'attuale ubicazione dei ritratti laddove è conosciuta; se l'indicazione è tra parentesi si tratta di un'identificazione dubbia. Alcune note, infine, integrano questi dati.

Proprietà	Pagina	Soggetto	Ubicazione
Gian Battista Cattaneo	106	alcuni ritratti[1]	
	106	Dama a figura intera con un moro che tiene un parasole[2]	Washington, National Gallery of Art
Gian Luca Giustiniani	109	Alessandro Giustiniani in veste di senatore	
Pietro Gentile	120	Dama di casa Gentile	
Giacomo Gentile	129	Placidia Cattaneo Gentile[3]	Strasbourg, Musée des Beaux-Arts
	130	Fanciullo in abito da caccia con cani[4]	
	130	Testa di giovane donna	
	131	Giovane uomo a mezza figura[5]	
	131	Dama a figura intera	
	131	Ritratto d'uomo in armatura a figura intera	Edinburgh, National Gallery of Scotland
	131	Ritratto d'uomo in armatura a figura intera	
	132	Donna morta in letto[6]	Genova, Collezione Gentile
Pier Francesco Grimaldi	134	Quattro ritratti a figura intera[7]	
		Dama con un bimbo per mano[8]	(Washington, National Gallery of Art)
		Dama con un bimbo per mano	
		Uomo in armatura	South Brisbane, Queensland Art Gallery
		Fanciullo che carezza un cane[9]	Collezione privata
Gian Battista Grimaldi	136	Uomo (sovraporta)	
	136	Dama a figura intera	
	137	Fanciullo a figura intera	
Paolo Spinola	139	Fanciullo a figura intera	Genova, Galleria Nazionale di Palazzo Spinola
	140	Andrea Spinola in veste di doge[10]	Malibu, J. Paul Getty Museum
	140	Due ritratti di dama a tre quarti di figura[11]	
	142	Testa[12]	
Vincenzo Lomellini	161	Tre ritratti a mezzo busto	
	161	Tre ritratti a figura intera	
	161	Quattro ritratti a mezza figura	
Agostino Lomellini	162	Dama	
	162	Gruppo di famiglia[13]	Edinburgh, National Gallery of Scotland
Marcello Durazzo	181	Ritratto in tondo[14]	Genova, Collezione Durazzo-Pallavicini
	183	Dama con due bimbi[15]	Genova, Collezione Durazzo-Pallavicini
	183	Fanciullo in veste di Tobia	Genova, Collezione Durazzo-Pallavicini
	183	Fanciullo vestito di bianco	Genova, Collezione Durazzo-Pallavicini
	183	Tre fanciulli con un cane[16]	Genova, Collezione Durazzo-Pallavicini
Francesco Maria Balbi	185	Signore della famiglia Balbi a cavallo[17]	Corte di Mamiano, Fondazione Magnani
	187	Dama seduta a figura intera	Roma, principi Odescalchi
	190	Uomo a figura intera *[18]	
	192	Dama con fanciullo in braccio[19]	London, National Gallery

Proprietà	Pagina	Soggetto	Ubicazione
	192	Figura vestita alla spagnola	Cincinnati Museum of Art
	193	Generale in armatura	
Giacomo Balbi	195	Tre fanciulli a figura intera[20]	London, National Gallery
	195	Uomo in armatura	
	195	Uomo con mano al petto	
	195	Testa	
	195	Senatore seduto[21]	Berlin, Gemäldegalerie
	195	Dama anziana seduta	Berlin, Gemäldegalerie
	195	Dama con mano al petto	(Genova, Galleria di Palazzo Spinola?)
Marcello Durazzo	205	Uomo vestito alla spagnola *[22]	Genova, Galleria di Palazzo Reale
	210	Dama a mezza figura vestita alla spagnola	Genova, Galleria di Palazzo Reale
	211	Caterina Durazzo[23]	Genova, Galleria di Palazzo Reale
Giulio Raggi	232	Tommaso Raggi a cavallo *[24]	
	235	Dama a mezza figura	
Anton Giulio Brignole	252	Il principe d'Orange *[25]	Genova, Galleria di Palazzo Rosso
	252	Padre e figlio a mezze figure[26]	Genova, Galleria di Palazzo Rosso
	253	Anton Giulio Brignole-Sale a cavallo	Genova, Galleria di Palazzo Rosso
	253	Paola Adorno Brignole-Sale	Genova, Galleria di Palazzo Rosso
	258	Geronima Sale Brignole con la figlia Aurelia	Genova, Galleria di Palazzo Rosso
	258	Figura intera[27]	Genova, Galleria di Palazzo Rosso
	259	Ritratto di una balia *	Genova, Galleria di Palazzo Rosso
Gaetano Cambiaso	269	Testa di donna	
Maria Margherita Carion de Nisas Spinola	274	Uomo a cavallo	
	275	Testa	
Giacomo Filippo Carrega	281	Prelato	
	281	Ritratto (sopraporta)	
Agostino Imperiale Lercari	284	Dama a figura intera	
Benedetto Spinola	289	Dama con un bambino[28]	
Gian Francesco Centurione della Rovere	291	alcuni ritratti[29]	
	293	Dama	
Giuseppe Doria	311	Gian Luca Doria in armi	
Ambrogio Doria	313	Uomo con due fanciulli[30]	County Tyrone, Barons Court
Stefano Franzone	325	Il cardinale Rivarola[31]	(Des Moines?)
Gian Francesco e Gian Carlo Pallavicini	331	Gruppo di famiglia *[32]	Genova, Collezione Durazzo-Pallavicini
Marcantonio Doria	332	Ritratto a mezza figura	
	332	Marcantonio Doria con alcuni fanciulli[33]	

1. La genericità dell'indicazione non permette di accertare quanti e quali ritratti si trovassero a quella data nel palazzo di Gian Battista Cattaneo, dal quale per altro risulta provengano—a seguito della vendita del 1907—i seguenti:

Ottaviano Canevari	Frick Collection, New York
"Giovanna Cattaneo"	Frick Collection, New York
"Gian Battista Cattaneo"	National Gallery, Londra
"Marchesa Cattaneo"	National Gallery, Londra
Filippo Cattaneo	National Gallery of Art, Washington
Clelia Cattaneo	National Gallery of Art, Washington
"Marchesa Lomellini coi figli"	Museo de Arte, Sao Paolo

oltre a quello di *Elena Grimaldi Cattaneo con un negro* citato di seguito.

2. Riconosciuta da tempo come *Elena Grimaldi Cattaneo*, vedi Barnes in Washington 1990, 174–177.

3. Per l'identificazione si rimanda al testo di questo contributo.

4. Lo storiografo settecentesco precisa che il soggetto era creduto il "ritratto di uno dei Filippi re di Spagna."

5. Nella *Descrizione della città di Genova da un anonimo del 1818*, a cura di Ennio e Fiorella Poleggi (Genova, 1969), 83, è precisato "con colletto rivolto e berretta."

6. Questo è l'unico dipinto di questo nucleo che nel 1818 (vedi nota precedente) non risulta nella quadreria di Filippo Gentile, allora temporaneamente sistemata nel palazzo Balbi-Senarega, e successivamente divisa. Sembra quindi di poter dedurre che fosse passata in eredità a suo fratello Gian Antonio, e dovrebbe essere rimasto, almeno fino al 1947 in proprietà dei discendenti di quest'ultimo. Vedi *Mostra della pittura del '600 e '700 in Liguria*, a cura di Antonio Morassi [cat. mostra, Palazzo Reale] (Genova, 1947), 36.

7. Di seguito alla generica indicazione del Ratti vengono riportati i soggetti così come si sono ricavati dal testo della *Description des beautés de Gênes et de ses environs* (Genova, 1773), 49. Va segnalato che di questa quadreria Grimaldi si conosce un inventario del 1684 ove non figura alcun ritratto attribuito a Van Dyck: si dovrebbe quindi desumere che questi siano entrati a farne parte in data successiva.

8. La specifica indicazione del gesto dei due personaggi ritratti—del tutto eccezionale nelle opere genovesi di Van Dyck—porterebbe ad identificare uno dei due dipinti qui citati con il corrispondente soggetto della National Gallery of Art di Washington (vedi Washington 1990, 193–195), ma questo non sembra conciliabile con le notizie sulla provenienza di quell'opera. In termini del tutto ipotetici si può proporre di identificare con uno di questi due ritratti

quello del Museum of Art di Cleveland, nel quale, però, il gesto è solo accennato (vedi Washington 1990, 178–179).

9. Vedi Barnes 1986, 324. Oltre alla corrispondenza iconografica, confermano l'identificazione le notizie sulla provenienza: risulta infatti essere stato venduto dal conte Landi, uno dei quattro eredi di questo ramo dei Grimaldi.

10. Si tratta in realtà di Agostino Pallavicino: vedi Barnes in Washington 1990, 147–149.

11. Credibilmente venduti ad Andrew Wilson nel 1841, come il precedente.

12. Definita dallo storiografo "sullo stile del Rembrandt."

13. Oltre alla tradizionale identificazione come *Famiglia Lomellini*, va ricordata anche quella più antica di Giustiniani: vedi Barnes 1986, 337–339, che fa riferimento alla copia otto-novecentesca di un elenco di dipinti il cui originale di metà Settecento è stato possibile rintracciare presso l'Archivio Storico del Comune di Genova.

14. Attribuzione non condivisa da Barnes 1986, 379.

15. Da identificare come *Battina Balbi Durazzo Invrea con i figli Ippolito e Silvestro*: in proposito si veda il testo di questo contributo.

16. Da identificare come *Luca, Giacomo e Violante Spinola*.

17. In realtà *Gian Paolo Balbi*, ma con il volto ridipinto: in proposito si veda il testo di questo contributo.

18. Già erroneamente attribuito a Van Dyck, si tratta di Filippo Spinola: si veda il testo di questo contributo.

19. Tradizionalmente identificato anche come *"La moglie di van Dyck."*

20. Da riconoscere come *Tre fanciulli De Franchi*: vedi in proposito nota 58 di questo contributo.

21. Vedi nota 58 di questo contributo.

22. Se si tratta del *Ritratto di Filippo II* tuttora *in situ* è da escludere l'autografia vandyckiana.

23. Vedi il testo di questo contributo.

24. Nel testo del Ratti del 1780 l'opera è menzionata senza indicazione dell'autore per un mero errore tipografico: che lo storiografo settecentesco l'attribuisse a Van Dyck lo si ricava dalla precedente edizione della sua guida. Dati cronologici e documenti d'archivio, comunque, consentono di espungere questo ritratto dal catalogo dell'artista fiammingo.

25. Più credibilmente riferibile all'attività della bottega di Van Dyck.

26. Identificato già nel Settecento come *L'orefice Puccio col figlio*; l'attribuzione è rifiutata da Barnes 1986, 379.

27. Si tratta del *Ritratto di giovane gentiluomo* più

volte riferito in anni recenti a Peter Paul Rubens: da
ultimo vedi Barnes 1986, 106.

28. Numerosi sono i ritratti di *Dama col figlio* che si
sono ritenuti identificabili con questo: quello del
Cleveland Museum of Art (vedi nota 8), e quello dei
Musées Royaux des Beaux-Arts di Bruxelles, entrambi a figura intera, e quello oggi alla Galleria
Nazionale di Palazzo Spinola a Genova, a mezza
figura.

29. Alizeri 1846–1847, 1:551, cita più specificamente
"due stupendi guerrieri."

30. Vedi Barnes 1986, 375–376, che dubita dell'attribuzione.

31. Vedi Barnes 1986, 355–357, che discute l'attribuzione.

32. Il dipinto, il cui soggetto risulta variamente identificato, è stato riferito a Vincent Malò (vedi Piero
Torriti, *La Galleria del Palazzo Durazzo-Pallavicini
a Genova* [Genova, 1967], 249); è passato all'attuale
proprietà per via ereditaria.

33. In proposito vedi Barnes 1986, 376, nota 1.

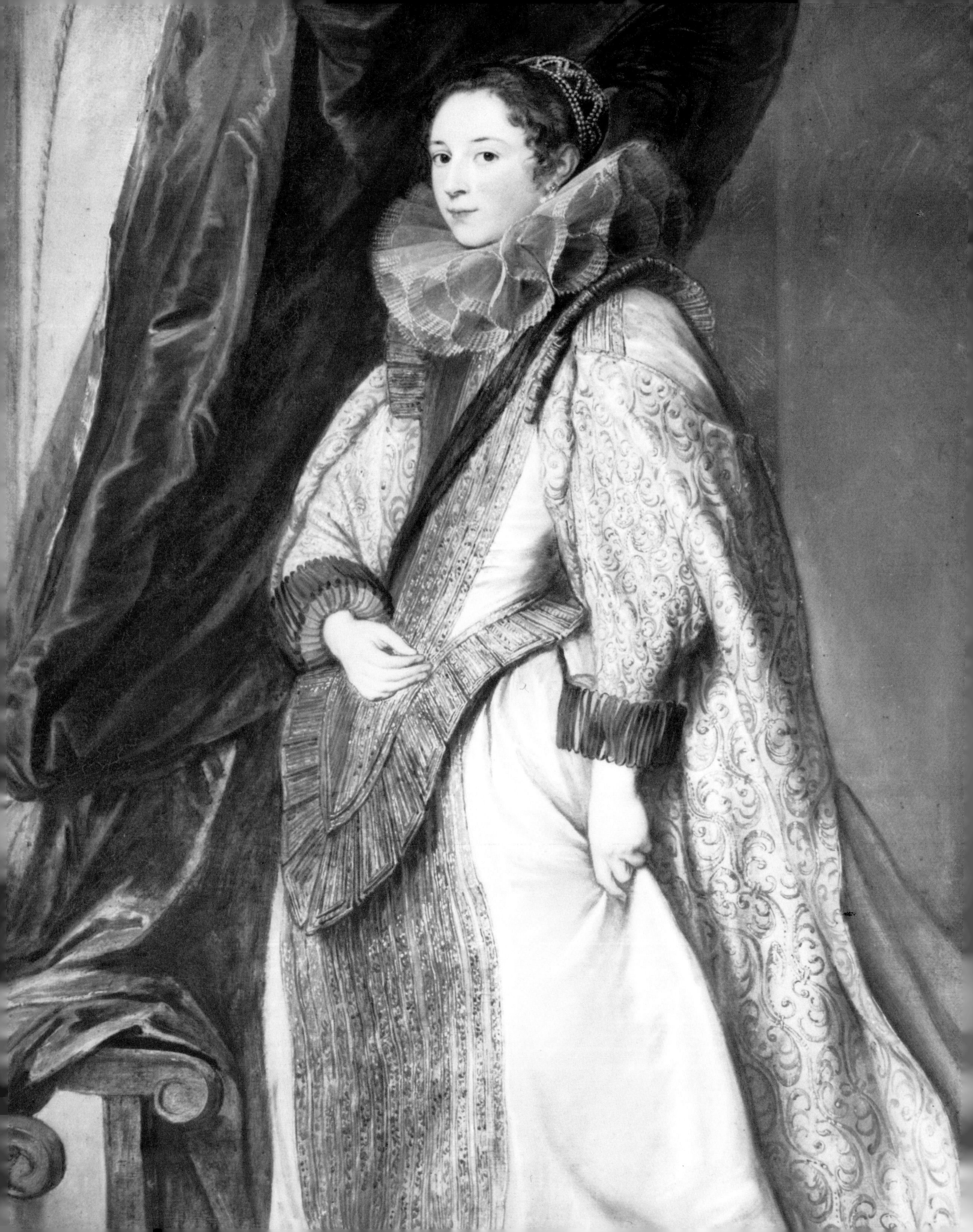

MARZIA CATALDI GALLO
Soprintendenza per i Beni Artistici e Storici, Genova

Per una storia del costume genovese nel primo quarto del Seicento

L'indagine sull'abbigliamento degli aristocratici genovesi nel primo quarto del Seicento è purtroppo irrimediabilmente limitata, almeno allo stato attuale delle conoscenze, dalla mancata conservazione di abiti di quel periodo. Questa gravissima lacuna, che di fatto impedisce di acquisire "certezze" sulle fogge in uso, è parzialmente colmata dai numerosi ritratti di genovesi—in particolare per gli anni 1621–1627, periodo della permanenza a Genova di Van Dyck—e dalla possibilità di attingere notizie da fondi archivistici pubblici e privati. Le leggi suntuarie[1] e le polemiche contro il lusso sostenute in numerose opere letterarie, infine, favoriscono la nostra comprensione dell'ambiente e del clima culturale, fornendo dati meno concreti ma più vivi di quelli ricavati dall'esame di libri di conti ed inventari.

L'influsso della moda spagnola e la sua persistenza

Alla morte di Carlo V, nel 1558, la Spagna era all'apice della sua potenza e poiché la moda è stata, ed è ancora, intimamente legata al potere,[2] ben presto la moda spagnola sopraffece le fogge originate da altre nazioni, come le Fiandre, la Francia, l'Italia, prima più seguite. Come ha rilevato Janet Arnold la sua diffusione fu molto rapida, poiché la moda spagnola fu adottata sia dagli Asburgo in Austria sia da gran parte dell'aristocrazia in Italia;[3] a Genova, in particolare, l'influsso spagnolo fu seguito con un rigore che non trova riscontro nelle altre città d'Italia.[4]

L'incontro fra Spagna e Italia (fig. 1), incisione che compare in un manoscritto intitolato *Dialogo per lode della casa di Spagna* databile intorno al 1588, illustrato dal pittore genovese Cesare Corte,[5] esemplifica gli stretti legami che si erano instaurati fra la moda spagnola e quella italiana. Non è azzardato supporre che la foggia dell'abito indossato dalla figura femminile che impersona l'Italia rispecchi la moda allora in uso a Genova; il dialogo infatti, illustrato da un pittore nato e attivo per lunghi periodi a Genova, è svolto da due personaggi genovesi: un marchese, col quale si vuol alludere forse a Giovanni Andrea Doria, ed un vescovo, forse Antonio Sauli. Gli abiti delle due donne che personificano la Spagna e l'Italia sono praticamente uguali nella struttura: il busto scende a punta sotto la vita e accompagna la linea del collo terminando sotto il mento, incorniciato da un collare a lattuga; la parte inferiore dell'abito è sostenuta da un'armatura interna (verdugale) che la distende. La diversa potenza delle due nazioni, anche se l'abito è uguale, è espressa con altri simboli: l'Italia ha due chiavi d'oro nella mano destra e due scettri nella sinistra "ma con poca coda" (allusione allo strascico della veste), la Spagna—come spiega il vescovo al marchese—"si fece innanzi con la veste in dosso di un color solo lavorata di preziose gemme, strassinandosi dietro una gran coda, ed havea un scettro solo ma grande in mano, e la real

corona in capo." "La gran coda di Spagna si-
gnifica la dipendenza di tanti suoi regni, e
stati che la seguono, et ubediscono" aggiunge
il vescovo, attribuendo un preciso significato
simbolico allo strascico—che compare in
molti dei ritratti di dame genovesi eseguiti
da Van Dyck—come emblema del potere
("questa foggia delle code dietro è cosa da
gentildonne e non da par mie" afferma la pettegola serva Agnese nella commedia tardo
cinquecentesca *Il Barro* del genovese Paolo
Foglietta).[6] Il disegno in esame offre lo
spunto per mettere in luce un aspetto di
grande importanza nella valutazione dei
meccanismi della moda fra la fine del Cinque
e gli inizi del Seicento: la durata di una foggia. Infatti confrontando gli abiti raffigurati
nel manoscritto, o molti altri ritratti tardo
cinquecenteschi come ad esempio quello
dell'*Infanta Isabella Clara Eugenia* (Madrid,
Prado) eseguito da Felipe De Llano nel 1584,
con i ritratti di dame eseguiti da Van Dyck
nel periodo della sua permanenza a Genova
(1621–1627), si nota come la linea dell'abito
sia sostanzialmente immutata: il busto scende
a punta sotto la vita ed accompagna rigidamente la linea del collo, addolcita dai leg-
giadri collari a lattuga; le maniche, attaccate
alle spalle e pendenti, sono molto ampie e si
aprono su quelle che aderiscono al braccio.
Nell'arco dei quarant'anni trascorsi le variazioni nell'abito sono state minime. Infatti già
nel Settecento il gesuita padre Roberti, nel
criticare la durata "solo" triennale di un
abito ai suoi tempi, indicava come un esempio edificante il primo Seicento, quando un
abito veniva usato per quarant'anni.[7] Eppure
proprio su questo argomento verte gran parte
della polemica contro il lusso del periodo di
cui ci si occupa: "alle donne prudenti conviene conservar la robba che mette in casa il
marito, e voi fate il contrario, chè lo pelate [=
lo riducete in miseria] *cangiando ogni giorno
nuovi abiti e nuove foggie*, ch'è un argomento della vostra pazzia" dice il vecchio
Demetrio alla moglie in un dialogo della
commedia *Il Barro*.[8] Evidentemente quelle
che ai nostri occhi sembrano variazioni minime, ad esempio nelle guarnizioni e nei diversi tipi di collare, all'epoca venivano con-
siderate "nuove foggie."

D'altra parte è bene tenere a mente che il
tono delle polemiche contro il lusso del vestire e del modo di vivere sembra cristalliz-
zato su alcuni temi fissi, e con tali caratteri
si ripropone nelle diverse epoche, cosicché in
ogni tempo si esaltano le virtù e l'austerità
delle epoche precedenti. È nondimeno evidente che nella Genova tardo cinquecentesca
l'aumento delle ricchezze produsse effettiva-
mente un notevole mutamento nello stile di
vita. L'abbigliamento è solo un aspetto del
più alto tenore di vita adottato dai ricchi
mercanti e banchieri genovesi, che—come
osservava Paschetti nel 1583—"non fab-
bricherebbero tanti palagi, né così superbi se
non abbondassero di molti denari."[9]

È quindi naturale che i "censori," colpiti
da tanta magnificenza, ne condannassero gli
eccessi. Un osservatore non genovese, il romano Gian Battista Confalonieri, di passag-
gio a Genova nel corso di un viaggio da Roma
a Madrid nel 1592, osservava: "Hanno introdotto grandissimo lusso in casa, molti agi e
mense laute con argenti et oro, cosa che
prima non usavano. Lascio stare le sete,
drappi, recami, letti e cose simili, perchè non
vi è gentiluomo che non ne sia fornitis-
simo."[10]

Per quanto riguarda il lusso dell'abbigliamento, di cui ci danno ampia testimonianza
anche i confronti fra ritratti di dame genovesi
con quelli di nobildonne di altre nazioni, può
essere interessante considerare la consi-
stenza del guardaroba maschile e femminile,
per quanto si è potuto ricavare da alcuni documenti che si ritengono significativi.[11] L'inventario steso nel 1613 alla morte di Giacomo Doria riporta l'elenco delle vesti sue e
della moglie Brigida Spinola, la cui effigie ci è
nota dal ritratto di Rubens del 1606.

Le vesti di Brigida comprendono 36
"robbe,"[12] 2 ungaresche, 2 "camisette" ("di
veluto bianco e turchino" e "di teletta argentina, e argentata"),[13] 5 faldette, 2 sot-
tane, 1 corpetto, 3 mantelline, 1 "Penna
d'Armellini" (pelliccia d'ermellino) oltre a
vari capi di biancheria.[14] Ancora sul "fronte"
femminile, il conto di "mastro Bolero"—
sarto *à la page* da cui si serviva anche Geronima Brignole[15]—ci dà un'idea della consis-
tenza del guardaroba di Livia Balbi, moglie di
Gian Francesco Pallavicino,[16] esponente
come il Doria della più alta e più ricca aristocrazia "vecchia"; vi sono elencate 15 "ongaresca, faldete e maniche" e relativamente
ad altre 5 è precisato "ò in dubio se egli le
habia fate," 4 "faldete e busto e maniche," 2

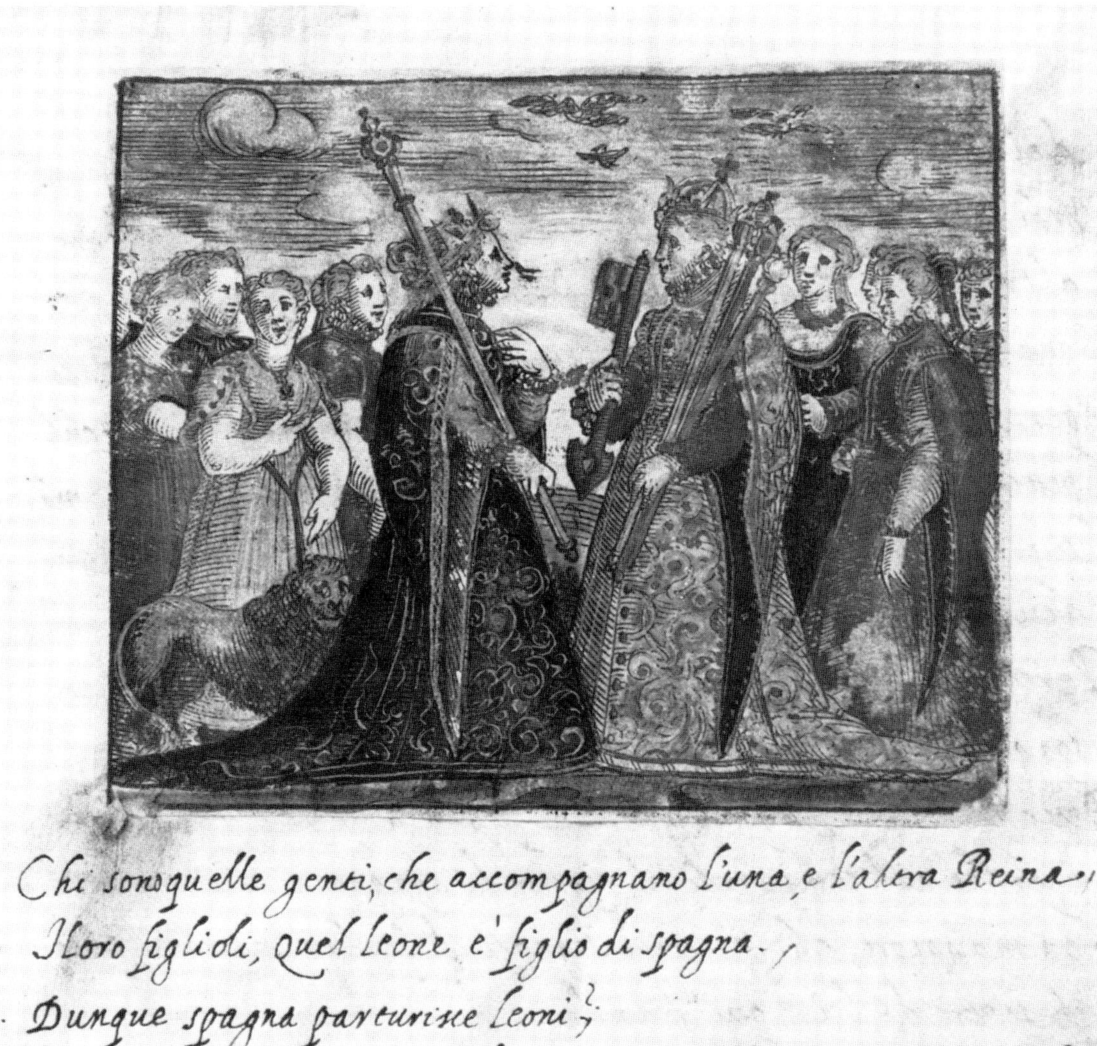

robe e 1 "robeta da letto," 1 "camiseta," 2
corpetti, 3 manti. Se si considera la ricchezza
dei tessuti e delle guarnizioni usate (velluti,
in un caso con fodera di ermellino, taffetà e
damaschi per lo più "guarniti d'oro"), si comprende facilmente l'importanza di questi
corredi. Risulta altrettanto ricco l'elenco
delle "Robbe da Huomo" compreso nel citato
inventario di Giacomo Doria del 1613: vi

sono indicati 42 "calzoni e casaca," 8 cappe,
24 ferraioli, 35 giupponi, 3 coletti (uno di tela
d'oro, uno d'ambra, uno in pelle di Spagna),
calze di raso ed altri indumenti.

Le "spese del vestire"

I dati relativi agli acquisti di capi di vestiario
registrati nei libri di conti della famiglia Bri-

gnole—che si può considerare esempio rappresentativo dello stile di vita dei nobili "nuovi" emergenti—fra il 1602 e il 1627, consentono di verificare i costi ed evidenziare l'andamento delle spese effettuate per l'abbigliamento. È stato possibile rilevare come esse registrino forti impennate in date corrispondenti a particolari occasioni: nel 1620 vengono effettuate spese attorno alle 1500 lire genovesi per gli abiti di Geronima e di sua figlia Maria Maddalena[17] per il matrimonio di quest'ultima con Giacomo Filippo I Durazzo (figlio di Agostino e fratello del Marcello ritratto da Van Dyck); nel 1621 per l'ambasceria a Roma Gian Francesco, accompagnato dal figlio Anton Giulio, spende circa 2400 lire per il suo guardaroba, 2200 lire per quello di suo figlio ed altro ancora per le livree. Le cifre diventano ancor più rilevanti negli anni 1625–1626 in occasione del matrimonio di Anton Giulio con Paolina Adorno, quando le "spese per la sposa" ammontano, limitatamente a quanto concerne l'abbigliamento, addirittura a circa 6000 lire nel solo 1626. Per scendere nel particolare i vestiti di Anton Giulio e Paolina, molto probabilmente gli stessi che indossavano quando vennero ritratti da Van Dyck, costarono rispettivamente all'incirca 1000 e 2000 lire (figg. 2, 3).

Anche lo spoglio dei libri di conti (già esaminati in altra sede)[18] della famiglia Durazzo e di Agostino Pallavicino—ritratto da Van Dyck con il robbone di damasco rosso in occasione della sua "ambasceria" a Roma presso la Santa Sede del 1621 (condotta fra gli altri insieme a Gian Francesco Brignole)—ha rivelato lo stesso andamento: le spese più ingenti venivano effettuate in occasioni particolari quali matrimoni, assunzioni di incarichi politici o per viaggi all'estero legati allo svolgimento di missioni diplomatiche. L'abbigliamento aveva quindi un preciso ruolo nella vita sociale del tempo, esistendo uno stretto legame fra l'atto e l'abito indossato per compierlo.

Per cogliere meglio l'entità delle spese per l'abbigliamento è forse opportuno considerarle in rapporto al potere di acquisto della lira genovese e a quanto si spendeva, ad esempio, in generi di prima necessità (olio, vino e grano), per i salari della servitù, per gli "arnesi di casa" (sotto questa voce nei libri di conti si registrano le spese effettuate per l'acquisto di mobili, dipinti, arazzi ed arredi in generale). È opportuno sottolineare che la maggior parte dei dati qui considerati riguarda famiglie di nobiltà vecchia e nuova, aventi in comune fortune economiche considerevoli anche in rapporto al resto dell'aristocrazia cittadina: così Giacomo Doria, Gian Francesco Pallavicino, Agostino Pallavicino fra i "vecchi"; Agostino Durazzo, Gerolamo Balbi e Gian Francesco Brignole emergenti fra i "nuovi" per ricchezze e prestigio.[19]

Il potere d'acquisto della lira genovese nel decennio 1620–1630 si può rilevare dai seguenti esempi:

1500 lire corrispondevano a 8 anni e mezzo di salario di un muratore, a un veliero di 45 tonnellate, a 4 ettari di terreno, a 15 buoi, a due alloggi popolari di circa 80–85 metri quadrati l'uno.

2000 lire corrispondevano a 11 anni e mezzo di salario di un muratore, a un veliero di 60 tonnellate, 5,3 ettari di terreno, 20 buoi, 3 alloggi.

6000 lire corrispondevano a 34 anni di salario di un muratore, a un veliero di 135 tonnellate, 16 ettari di terreno, 60 buoi, 8 appartamenti.[20]

Gian Francesco Brignole fra le "spese del vivere" registra ogni anno le spese effettuate per l'acquisto di vino, olio, grano—i cui prezzi sono indicati come esempio dell'aumento del costo della vita a Genova nel tardo Cinquecento da Barro, protagonista della omonima commedia il cui nome indica la sua arte di ingannare per mestiere[21]—e salari della servitù: esse ammontano mediamente dalle 900, 200, 800, 1500 lire (rispettivamente) del 1612 alle 900 (vino), 1100 (grano), 2200 (salari) del 1618.[22]

Come si è già visto nel caso di Paolina Adorno Brignole Sale, le spese per gli abiti delle giovani spose che entravano in famiglia venivano sostenute dal capo della famiglia del marito (in questo caso Gian Francesco Brignole). È quindi abbastanza naturale pensare, anche in ragione del loro costo elevato, che essi fossero ritenuti parte del patrimonio familiare e come tali considerati anche in caso di divisioni ereditarie. È quanto sembra di capire dalla vendita degli abiti di Caterina Balbi Durazzo effettuata nel 1633 e 1634, quindi un anno dopo la morte di suo marito Marcello Durazzo. Le vendite, registrate nei libri contabili tenuti da Giacomo Filippo I e Gerolamo (il padre Agostino era morto nel 1630), sono realizzate per mezzo di due mediatrici e consentono di ricavare una cifra considerevole (complessivamente circa 1800 lire genovesi), anche se, evidentemente, gli abiti erano usati. Va tenuto presente che la vendita di abiti era prassi molto seguita anche in ambienti aristocratici e veniva effettuata per mezzo di intermediari o, più comunemente, tramite le vendite all'asta (a Genova chiamate "Calleghe").23

La veste più importante fra quelle di Caterina vendute nel 1633, cioè "ungaresca, faldette, giupone e maniche di veluto orseletta e nero guarnite d'oro," venne pagata 412 lire genovesi; per avere un termine di paragone si consideri che nel 1624 i due ritratti a figura intera di Caterina (Genova, Palazzo Reale) e Marcello (Venezia, Ca' d'Oro) (si veda Boccardo in questo volume, figg. 13, 14) eseguiti da Anton van Dyck erano stati pagati 373 lire genovesi e nel 1630 "uno buffetto . . . et uno scrittorio d'ebano lavorato d'avorio" 245 lire.24 La struttura rigidamente formale della società in quel periodo imponeva, con regole più rigorose dell'attuale concetto di moda, questo tipo di abbigliamento formale e costoso alle classi sociali più alte, e a quelle che aspiravano a raggiungerle. In questo contesto sociale anche il ritratto—costituendo praticamente l'unico mezzo a disposizione delle persone per lasciare una testimonianza visiva di sè—assumeva un ruolo celebrativo di primaria importanza. Per questo ci si faceva immortalare indossando la veste ufficiale propria della carica ricoperta, quando si trattava di sottolineare l'importanza dell'incarico—e questo si riscontra più frequentemente nei ritratti maschili—o la veste più ricca, come si nota soprattutto nei ritratti femminili. È esempio emblematico di questa mentalità il caso di Agostino Pallavicino che nel giro di pochi anni si fece ritrarre tre volte, sempre con gli abiti relativi all'incarico assolto. La prima volta nel 1621 in occasione della sua ambasceria presso la Santa Sede (il ritratto di Anton van Dyck è a Malibu, J. Paul Getty Museum), la seconda nel 1629 per il suo viaggio presso il re di Francia (il ritratto di Agostino con il figlio Ansaldo è a Genova,

Galleria di Palazzo Spinola), la terza nel 1637 in occasione della sua incoronazione a Doge (di Domenico Fiasella si trova a Palazzo Spinola).25

È significativo anche il caso di Anton Giulio Brignole Sale e di sua moglie Paolina Adorno. Le nozze fra i due vennero celebrate il 9 dicembre 1625; il 1 aprile 1626 sono registrate nei libri contabili, fra le altre, le spese relative a due abiti che, con buona probabilità, sono quelli che indossarono per farsi ritrarre da Van Dyck, pagato per questo lavoro nel 1627. Data l'uniformità dei colori nell'abbigliamento maschile, è difficile stabilire con certezza l'identità del vestito (termine che definisce l'insieme di calzoni e casacca) indossato da Anton Giulio nel ritratto (fig. 2) con quello pagato 1033 lire genovesi a Cosimo Paoli nell'aprile 1626, ma si può avanzare questa ipotesi in quanto esso è il più importante acquistato in quegli anni.26 Più sicura grazie al colore dell'abito nel ritratto di Paolina (fig. 3), la sua identificazione con le parti componenti la veste verde, indicate, accanto ad altre di diversi colori, nel registro.27

Moda e letteratura

Prima di affrontare la descrizione dei vari capi di abbigliamento il cui uso è testimoniato da ritratti e documenti, si cercherà, attraverso le parole dei contemporanei, di rendere più vive le immagini che siamo abituati ad ammirare nei ritratti, cercando di ricreare gli atteggiamenti ed il modo di muoversi delle dame genovesi, definite dal Vecellio "le più affabili, e piacevoli donne nel conversare di tutta Italia."28

Il *Ragionamento di sei nobili fanciulle genovesi* (Lavinia, Fiammetta, Claudia, Cassandra, Laura, Virginia), che dopo aver ascoltato la Messa domenicale si radunano a casa di Lavinia, scritto da Cristoforo Zabata nel 1583,29 rende con fresca immediatezza i pensieri delle ragazze su vari aspetti della loro vita (la virtù, il matrimonio, le lamentele contro la severità delle madri, la condanna nei confronti delle donne che giocano a carte o frequentano le veglie in Quaresima). Per quanto riguarda la moda le "ciancie [= chiacchiere] delle figlie" sono molto vivaci e ricche di informazioni di carattere generale e particolare. Sembrano tutte d'accordo sulla

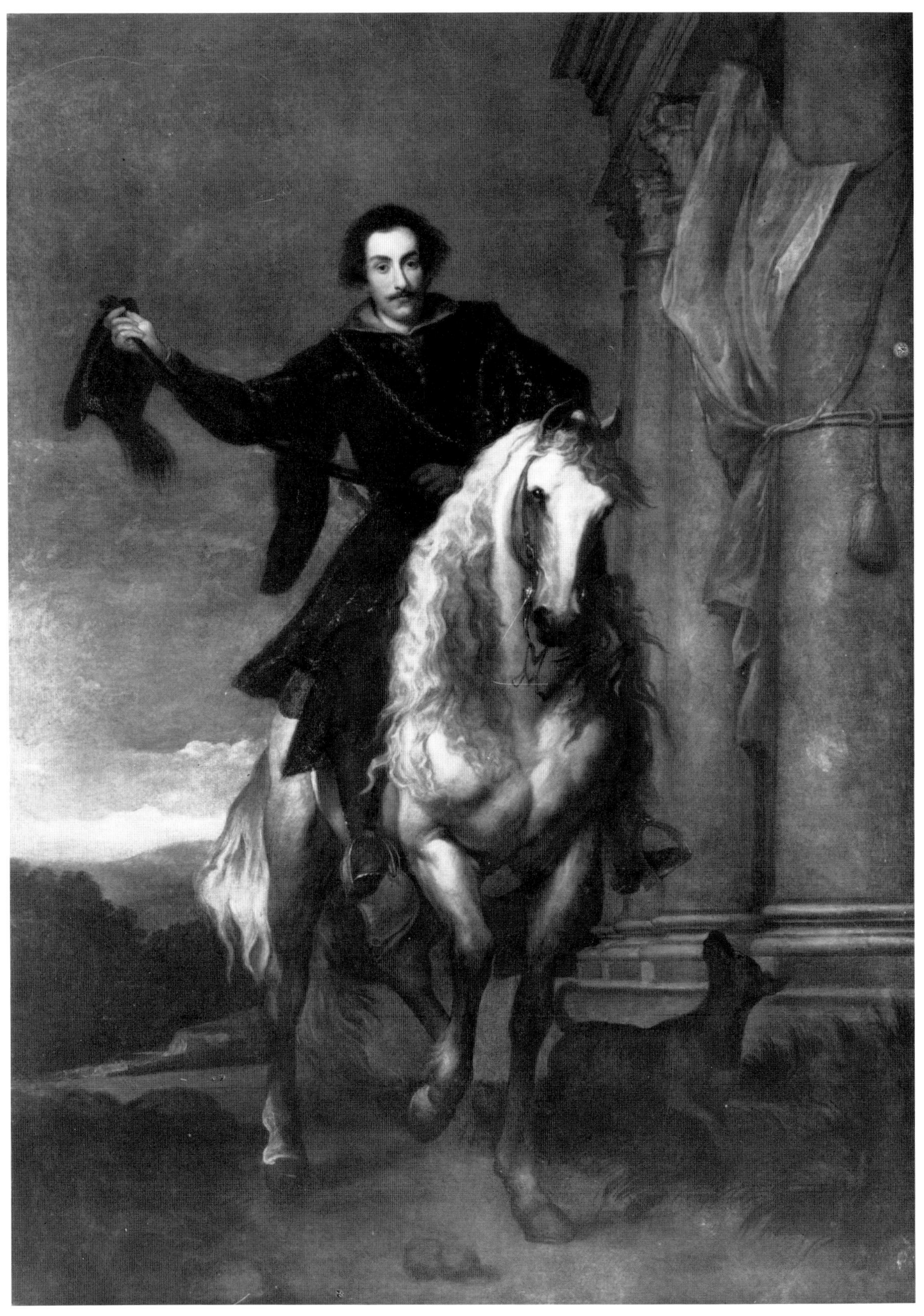

2. Anton van Dyck, *Anton Giulio Brignole Sale*, 1626–1627, olio su tela
Galleria di Palazzo Rosso, Genova

3. Anton van Dyck, *Paolina Brignole Sale*, 1626–1627, olio su tela
Galleria di Palazzo Rosso, Genova

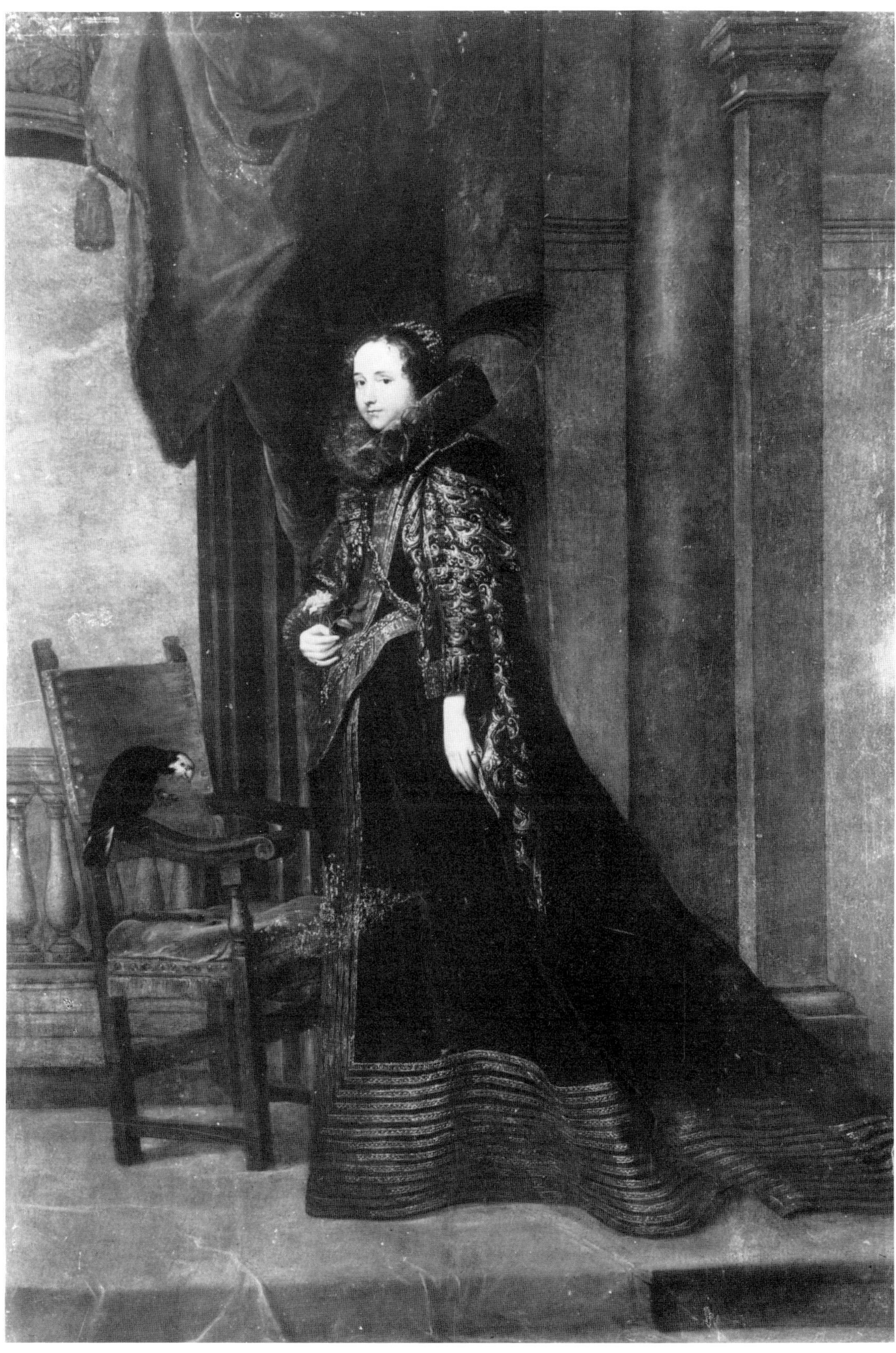

necessità di seguire la moda, come precisa Fiammetta: "parendomi che l'usanza in quanto alla forma si debba interamente osservare, ma non in quanto alla politezza e leggiadria, come saria à dire se i busti longhi si costumano non voglio che si faccino curti, e se le vesti curte s'usano, non è bene farle con la coda [= strascico], e se aperte dinanti non staranno bene, che s'aprino di dietro, e questo non perchè stia male, ma perchè l'usanza il prohibisce, & in tal forma del vestire essendo sottoposta alla consuetudine o bona o rea che la sia, bisogna seguitarla, perchè contrafacendo non solo sarebbe vitio, ma un presumer di voler dar leggi à gli altri, oltre che tali vesti non approvate dall'uso comune non sogliono piacere."

Spaventata all'idea di soffrire nel matrimonio Virginia asserisce che preferisce farsi monaca ed abbandonare le preoccupazioni legate all'estetica: "à me basterà un solo semplice velo, & una vil tonicella, senza quel cruccio di ogni mattina polirmi, & ornarmi i capelli, & con grande affanno, & arte pingermi la faccia di bianco, & vermiglio colore, per conservarmi ilesa la delicata pelle dà rabiosi venti, & da cocenti raggi del Sole impiastrarmi hor di bigio, hor di giallo, & hor di verde." Il tempo speso per vestirsi e per imbellettarsi era uno degli argomenti ricorrenti nelle polemiche contro le cattive abitudini delle donne: "So che prima ch'una di voi sia imbellettata, e vestita di tutto ponto, s'armeria una galea" [si isserebbero le vele su una imbarcazione].[30]

"Politezza e leggiadria," "grazia e misura," rispetto della "consuetudine" sono le qualità che, secondo le fanciulle del *Ragionamento*, si addicono ad una nobildonna, secondo una concezione che ricalca la donna ideale—elegante, moderata e graziosa—già tratteggiata nel trattato del *Cortegiano*, di cui Baldassar Castiglione agli inizi del Cinquecento propone il modello ideale. L'abbigliamento di gusto spagnolo usato a Genova si adatta molto bene all'espressione di queste qualità, infatti la maestosità della veste e gli alti collari a lattuga conferiscono quella grazia un po' altera e distaccata, che ben si riconosce nei ritratti vandyckiani.

Io rimiro le donne oggi far mostra
di sua persona avvolte in gonne tali,
che stancano la man di cento sarti.
Men ricamato stassi fra le nubi

l'arcobaleno. Io tacerò dell'oro:
oro il giubbone, or le faldiglie, ed oro,
sparso di belle gemme, i crini attorti. . . .
Or sì fatta donzella è non contenta
di sua statura; ma levata in alto
su tre palmi di zoccoli, gioisce
di torreggiare, e per non dare un crollo,
e non gire a baciar la madre antica,
se ne va da man destra e da man manca,
appuntellata su due servi, ed alza
il piede, andando, come se 'l traesse
fuor d'una fossa; onde movendo il passo,
è costretta a contorcer la persona,
ed a ben dimenar tutto il codrizzo.

Questa immagine femminile tratteggiata dai versi di Chiabrera,[31] ci restituisce, anche se un po' caricato dal tono satirico, l'immagine delle austere dame che, immote e distanti nei ritratti di parata, si muovono con difficoltà con abiti che certamente non erano concepiti per una vita attiva. La polemica contro l'uso degli zoccoli (nel Sermone di Chiabrera alti tre palmi cioè circa 73 centimetri) è un *topos* ricorrente nelle polemiche contro il lusso donnesco, ma non si hanno riscontri precisi riguardo alla loro utilizzazione.[32]

"Le Robbe da donna" e "da huomo"

"Robba" era il termine usato sia in senso generico per definire gli abiti nel loro insieme sia in modo specifico, ma ancora senza un significato ben definito, come attualmente il termine abito. In documenti tardo cinquecenteschi e di pieno Seicento si è infatti trovato il termine variamente usato per indicare "ongaresca," "faldette e Samara" ed ancora "falde, busto con avaniglie et ongaresca."[33]

L'ungaresca è forse il capo di abbigliamento che compare più spesso negli inventari e nei libri di conti fra la fine del Cinquecento ed il primo quarto del Seicento. Questo tipo di sopraveste—della stessa tipologia ma meno usata è la "samara" (zimarra)—lunga ed aperta davanti è allacciata con alamari, cioè "ornamenti di cordoncini sull'abbotonatura,"[34] elemento decorativo/funzionale di origine turca. Questa tipologia di veste "da sopra" era diffusa nel corso del Cinquecento in molte zone orientali e fu assunta in Italia con il termine ungaresca, con un evidente riferimento alla nazione di origine di questa foggia. L'esotismo del vestiario di turchi,

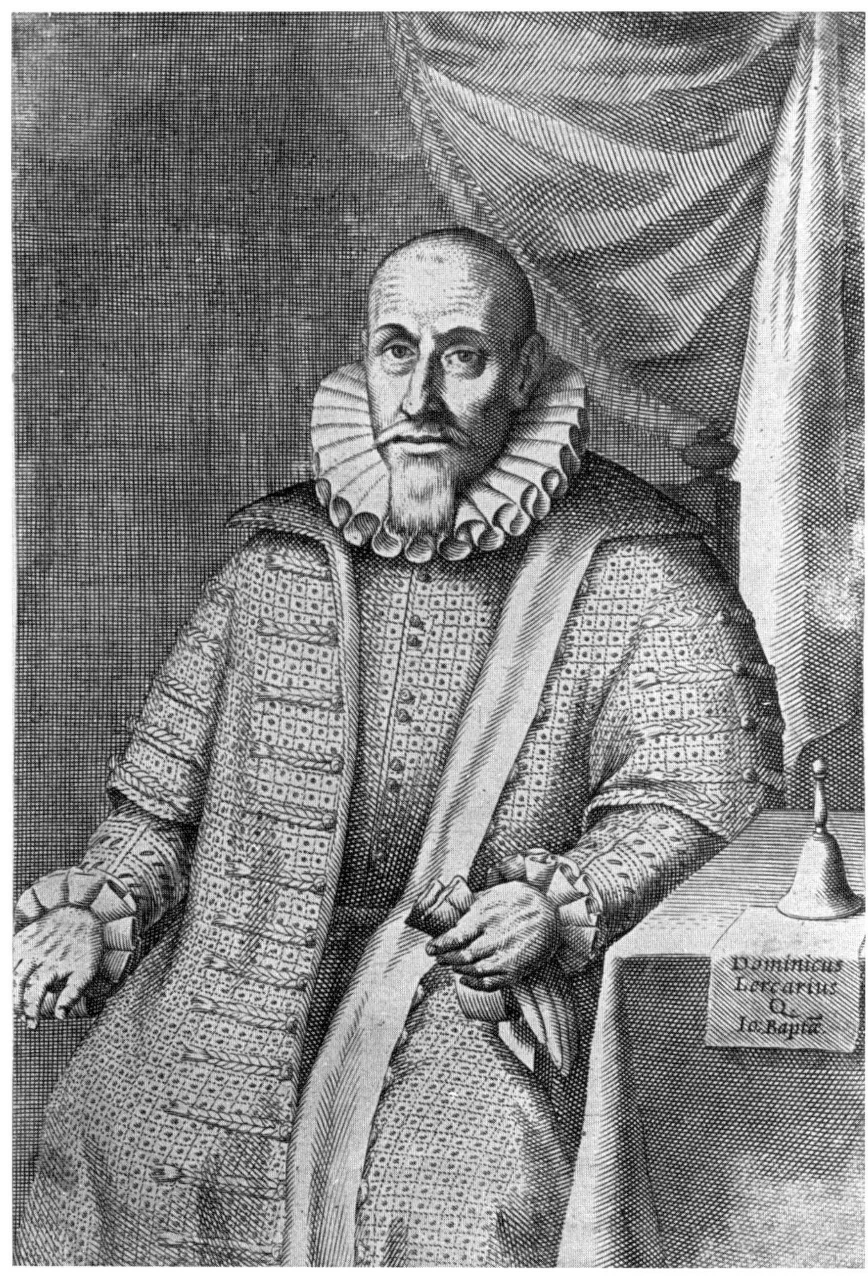

4. *Domenico Lercari quondam Gian Battista*, 1644, incisione
Collezione privata, Genova

menti rievocanti le zone di confine più lontane (nel 1526 l'imperatore diviene re di Ungheria).[35] Le ungaresche fino al tardo Cinquecento sono diffuse nell'abbigliamento maschile (fig. 4) e femminile, ma con il procedere del Seicento diminuiscono nelle liste di corredi maschili mentre risultano molto usate dalle dame. Ciononostante esse si riscontrano raramente nei ritratti femminili, ci si riferisce in particolare ai ritratti di genovesi (perché destinata all'uso in esterno o, forse, perché avrebbe nascosto la preziosità delle vesti?), mentre si conoscono numerosi ritratti di bambini in "ongarina,"[36] valga per tutti l'esempio del bambino accanto alla madre Battina Balbi Invrea dipinto da Van Dyck (Genova, Collezione Durazzo-Pallavicini) (fig. 5). Di origine turca[37] è anche l'uso di indossare le maniche—spesso nei secoli punto focale delle variazioni delle mode—pendenti dalle spalle, cui erano applicate per mezzo di lacci. L'allacciatura era coperta da un'aletta,[38] talvolta ornata da bottoni in oro, di cui i ritratti vandyckiani forniscono ampia documentazione. Questo modo di vestire inizialmente nato per soddisfare l'esigenza di facilitare i movimenti, fu poi adottato nell'abbigliamento maschile e femminile di rappresentanza come elemento puramente elegante e formale. Le leggi suntuarie emanate nel 1571 forniscono interessanti informazioni riguardo alle maniche differenziate fra "quelle, che non si investeno [= indossano], che non possono essere di maggior larghezza di palmi duoi, e mezzo in giro [cioè cm 61 circa]" e che "non possino essere fodrate al più, che di taffetà, & che non si possan mettere pomelli, né gassette se non all'apertura della manica dinanzi." D'altra parte "Le maniche che s'investino, possano essere di raso, o damasco d'ogni colore, però non misto, o di taffetà di tutti li colori concessi di sopra senza guarnitione se non l'orlo di veluto sopra, o siano raponti dritti, o traversi, però senza riccamo alcuno."[39] Le maniche aderenti al braccio, a quanto risulta dalla documentazione consultata, potevano essere un elemento indipendente o, come si legge in più di una descrizione, la parte visibile del giuppone, capo di abbigliamento in origine maschile la cui definizione deriva dallo spagnolo *jubon*. Le due maniche erano differenziate in alcuni casi per l'uso di tessuti diversi (si pensi al ritratto di Brigida Spinola

ungheresi, albanesi esercitò una speciale attrazione sugli europei del Cinque e poi del Seicento. L'adozione di fogge o dettagli di origine orientale, mediata dalla moda spagnola e imperiale, è forse da ricondurre inizialmente alla volontà di Carlo V di formulare un linguaggio europeo ed imperiale di vasto respiro, da mettere in relazione con la sua grandiosa visione politica. Egli, anche attraverso la diffusione della moda, voleva ribadire il suo potere sull'Europa, in certo modo simboleggiato con più forza da ele-

Doria di Rubens del 1606) o, come nei ritratti di Van Dyck, per i diversi motivi decorativi, simili ma di maggiori dimensioni sulla fodera delle maniche pendenti (ad esempio *Ritratto di dama in bianco,* New York, Frick Collection) (fig. 6). Per quanto riguarda la forma, le maniche aderenti al braccio hanno una certa ampiezza all'altezza del gomito e si stringono verso il polso, mentre le maniche pendenti sono di due tipi: corte e chiuse al polso, con un'apertura anteriore ed una in corrispondenza del gomito (fra i ritratti vandyckiani si confronti ad esempio *Ritratto di "Giovanna Cattaneo,"* New York, Frick Collection) (fig. 7), oppure lunghe, terminanti a punta, e aperte in modo da far vedere la fodera preziosa.

L'abito da parata che conosciamo attraverso i ritratti, stando ai documenti consultati, era composto, oltre alle maniche e al giuppone, da "faldette e busto." Il busto, che veniva indossato sopra la camicia e sopra un corpetto (termine usato nel Seicento anche come equivalente di busto), probabilmente reso rigido con stecche di balena, era dello stesso colore, e talvolta dello stesso tessuto, delle "faldette" e della parte esterna delle maniche pendenti. La sua forma mostra una certa evoluzione dagli inizi del Seicento, quando aveva una punta molto stretta orlata da una baschina corta (si considerino i ritratti "genovesi" di Rubens databili intorno agli anni 1606–1608), agli anni venti quando la punta risulta più larga ed è orlata da baschina alta composta da linguette di tessuto rettangolari profilate da gallone (ad esempio il citato *Ritratto di "Giovanna Cattaneo"*) (fig. 7).[40] La guarnizione, solitamente costituita da liste di galloni, in velluto o in oro, applicati sul petto in righe verticali più o meno estese, richiedeva l'impiego di grandi quantità di materiali, nel 1626 si spendono 129.0.9 lire per 200 palmi (= m 49) di "lavor d'oro" per un corpetto di Paolina Adorno Brignole Sale. Si può pensare che una quantità così alta servisse per un tipo di busto molto ricco, come ad esempio quello indossato nel *Ritratto di Caterina Balbi Durazzo* del 1624 (Genova, Galleria di Palazzo Reale) (si veda Boccardo, fig. 14), tutto decorato con galloni dorati sul petto, lungo gli orli della baschina, e all'attaccatura delle maniche.

La parte inferiore della veste era chiamata falde o faldette, termine derivante dallo spa-

gnolo *faldiglia,* definita nel vocabolario del Franciosini, stampato nel 1620,[41] "una sottana di tela, cerchiata d'alcune funicelle, che la tengono intirizzata, e l'usano le donne, perchè tenga lor le veste sospese, e non impediscan loro il cammino."

La linea conica della parte inferiore delle vesti femminili usate dalle dame genovesi prova che esse facevano uso di faldiglie, che nel tardo Cinquecento erano chiamate "verdugale." Su questa moda di origine spagnola[42] Fiammetta, una delle fanciulle del

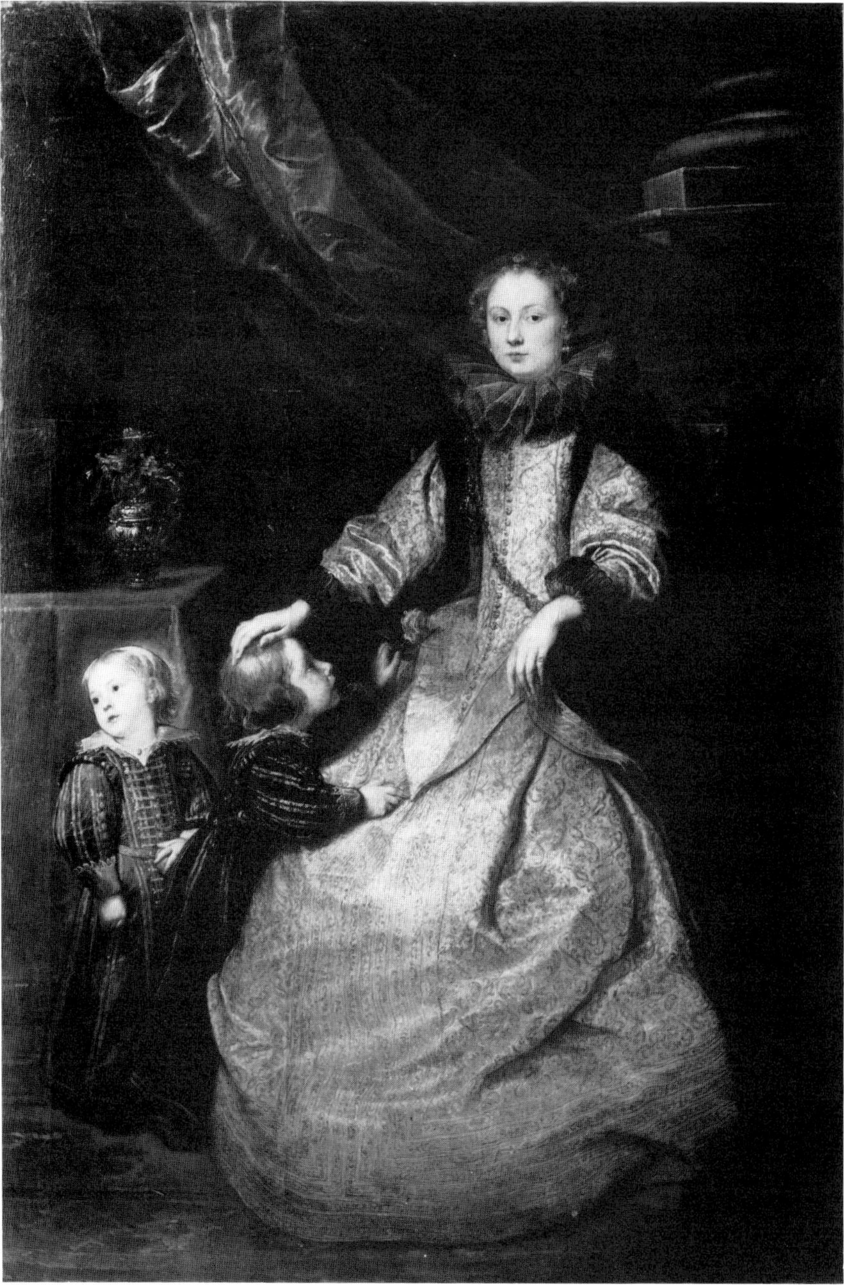

5. Anton van Dyck, *Battina Balbi Invrea,* c. 1626, olio su tela
Palazzo Durazzo-Pallavicini, Genova

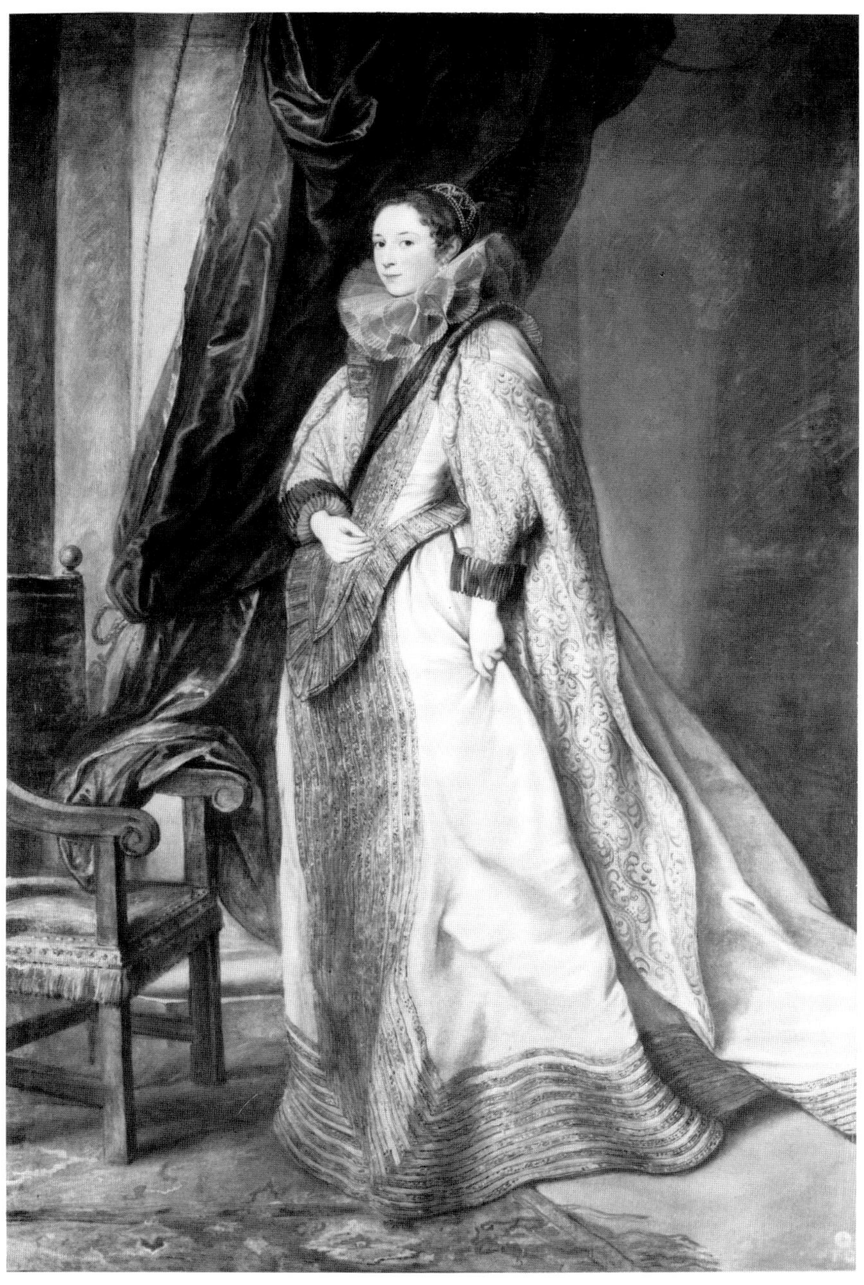

6. Anton van Dyck, *Ritratto di dama in bianco,* 1621–1627, olio su tela
Frick Collection, New York

antonomasia la parte inferiore della veste, quindi non solo l'intelaiatura ma anche il tessuto che la copriva. Dalle numerosissime citazioni di faldette negli inventari—in cui erano elencate come componenti di una "robba" o singolarmente[44]—risulta che erano eseguite in svariati tessuti e colori. Da una citazione del 1626, relativa all'acquisto di 24 palmi (circa) di "ermesino porcelletta [= turchino] per faldette" si arguisce che erano necessari alla manifattura di questo capo circa 5 metri e 80 centimetri.[45] Naturalmente questo dato è indicativo solo per quanto riguarda gli anni intorno al 1625, in mancanza di dati analoghi relativamente agli anni precedenti; bisogna inoltre considerare che la quantità di tessuto era subordinata, anche, dalla presenza e dalla lunghezza della già menzionata "coda," ossia strascico.[46] Nei ritratti eseguiti da Van Dyck sembra infatti di notarne di diverse dimensioni, apparendo più lungo ad esempio quello della veste di Paolina Adorno Brignole Sale di quello della suocera Geronima (entrambi Genova, Galleria di Palazzo Rosso).

Per quanto riguarda i tessuti si segnala l'uso di un tessuto nero decorato con tagli disposti simmetricamente in vari ritratti vandyckiani, e segnatamente quello di Geronima Brignole (se ne pubblica una fotografia non recente in cui l'abbigliamento risulta più leggibile) (fig. 8) e quello della *Dama con il figlio* della National Gallery of Art di Washington, datato da Susan Barnes al 1626 circa,[47] quindi praticamente contemporaneo a quello di Geronima. L'usanza di praticare tagli nei tessuti è nata nella prima metà del Cinquecento fra i militari tedeschi, per favorire i movimenti di braccia e gambe, e si è diffusa attraverso i mercenari tedeschi che allora combattevano praticamente su tutti i campi di battaglia d'Europa. Secondo una tendenza riscontrabile di frequente, l'usanza, in origine legata all'abbigliamento militare, è poi passata a quello civile, sia maschile—si confrontino ad esempio il *Ritratto di Agostino Durazzo* eseguito da Domenico Tintoretto nel 1610 (Genova, Collezione Durazzo-Pallavicino) e quello di *Cornelio e Luca de Wael* di Van Dyck (Roma, Musei Capitolini)—sia femminile, come puro elemento di decoro. Prima vietati e poi concessi (nel 1594) dalle leggi suntuarie, i tagli sono oggetto delle critiche di Paolo

Ragionamento del 1583, esprime le sue perplessità con queste parole: "Et i verdogali ancora non mi quadrano, massime certi grandi che se ne veggono, che paiono la campana grossa di San Lorenzo, & se ben dicono che sono di gran comodità nel caminare, . . . né tanpoco gli ho mai voluti portare, tanto gli abbhorisco nell'altre: molte de' quali ho già vedute, che duravano fatica ad entrare in una porta."[43] I termini "verdogale" e "falde" o "faldette," nell'arco di tempo considerato, cioè fra la fine del Cinquecento ed il primo quarto del Seicento, sembrano designare per

Foglietta nella sua poesia in lode della toga, la cui moda era ormai tramontata, perché impedivano la riutilizzazione dei tessuti.[48] La Du Mortrier, a proposito dell'abbigliamento nelle Fiandre, fa risalire la ripresa della moda dei tagli ad un editto emanato in Francia nel 1625 che, proibendo di indossare indumenti ricamati o con galloni, favorì la diffusione alla corte francese di tessuti piani decorati con tagli; difficile dire se gli esempi "genovesi" citati siano da ricondurre all'influsso francese, ma si può considerare l'ipotesi.[49]

Forse del resto, considerando la moda degli anni venti, si può ipotizzare un influsso francese anche per quanto riguarda la struttura che sostiene la parte inferiore della veste; infatti osservando la linea degli abiti delle dame si può notare una minor rigidità nella linea conica della gonna—si confrontino ad esempio il *Ritratto di dama* del Van Deynen del 1610 (Genova, Galleria di Palazzo Bianco) (fig. 9) con i ritratti vandyckiani di dame genovesi ritratte in piedi—che, in quegli anni, appare più ricca e sostenuta attorno al giro della vita. Il suo aspetto, così morbido e arrotondato, fa pensare al probabile uso di un supporto del tipo detto "alla francese," consistente in un imbottitura a rotolo posta attorno alla vita, recentemente descritto da Janet Arnold.[50] Il ricorso a imbottiture "con il bambagio [= cotone], e con il canevazzo [= tela di cotone] piegato in mille doppie" era un artificio già usato dalle dame genovesi come si evince dalla descrizione dell'usanza di imbottire le spalle criticata da Fiammetta nel *Ragionamento* del 1583.[51]

Le "faldette" erano solitamente ornate da file di galloni, più o meno ampie a seconda dei periodi, che correvano lungo l'orlo inferiore e salivano verso la vita sulla parte anteriore. La prammatica emanata nel 1582 e stampata nel 1594 sancisce: "Ne possino le dette vesti hauere altro ornamento, o guarnitione, saluo d'un orlo a torno di veluto piano, o di raso, o taffetale, o di una punta di raso, il qual orlo, o punta possi essere accompagnata da due pipinelle,[52] pur che tutti insieme non eccedano di larghezza la duodecima parte d'un palmo [= cm 2 circa], o in luogo di dett'orlo se li possi mettere un velutino, o sia trenino della larghezza sodetta, la quale guarnitione sia dell'istesso colore della veste."[53] Nel 1605 si concede un'ampiezza di 6 cen-

timetri—già ammessa nella *Riforma fatta l'anno 1594*—e che il "lavoro non si possa fare, saluo di seta, e di margaritini, o sia canutigli di vetro, come si sogliono usare."[54]

Una ulteriore precisazione è fornita dalla *Legge fatta intorno alle Pompe* del 1613[55]— ultima emanata fino alla successiva del 1635—in cui si mantiene la misura di 6 centimetri e si concede per il "dinanzi [= davanti], & alle maniche doue le guarnitioni vanno doppie" che le guarnizioni non eccedano "giuntamente" [= insieme] mezzo palmo, cioè poco più di 12 centimetri. I ritratti del periodo dimostrano in modo evidente quanto poco fossero osservate le leggi suntuarie; si nota comunque un notevole vive aumento fra la larghezza delle guarni-

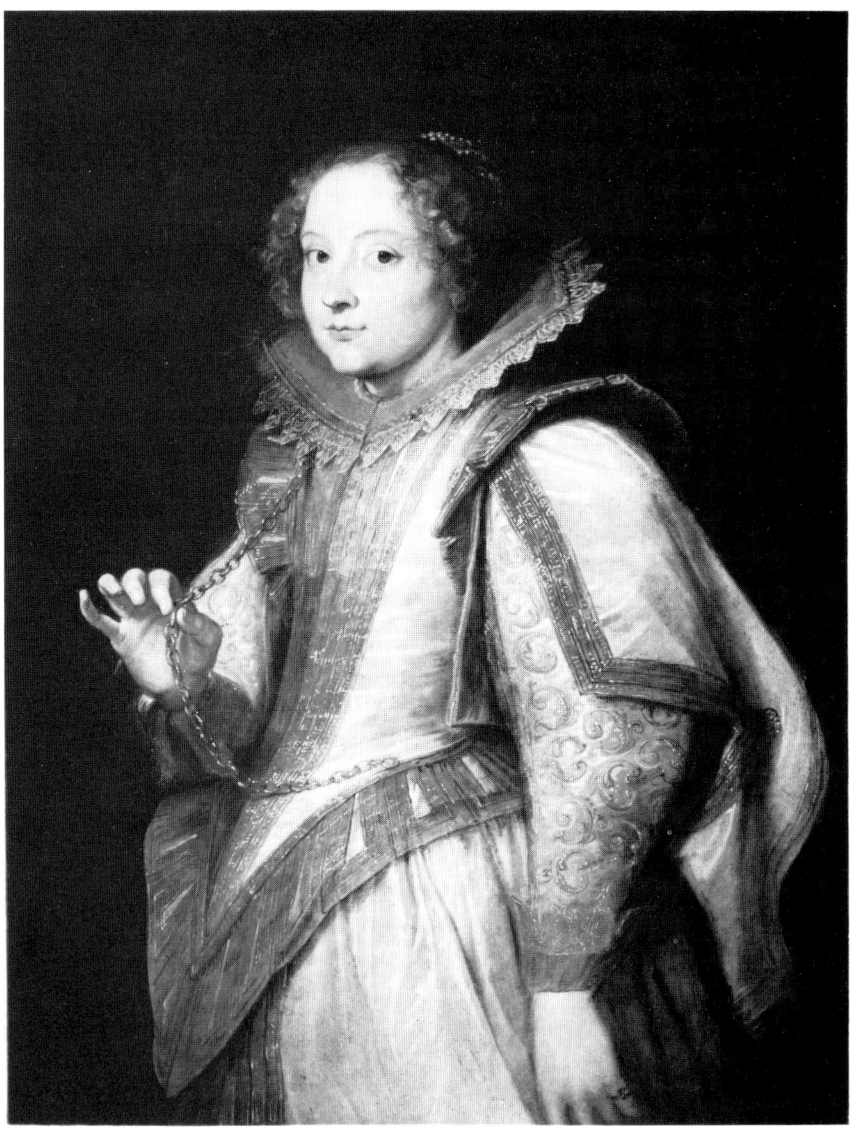

7. Anton van Dyck, *Ritratto di "Giovanna Cattaneo,"* 1621–1627, olio su tela
Frick Collection, New York

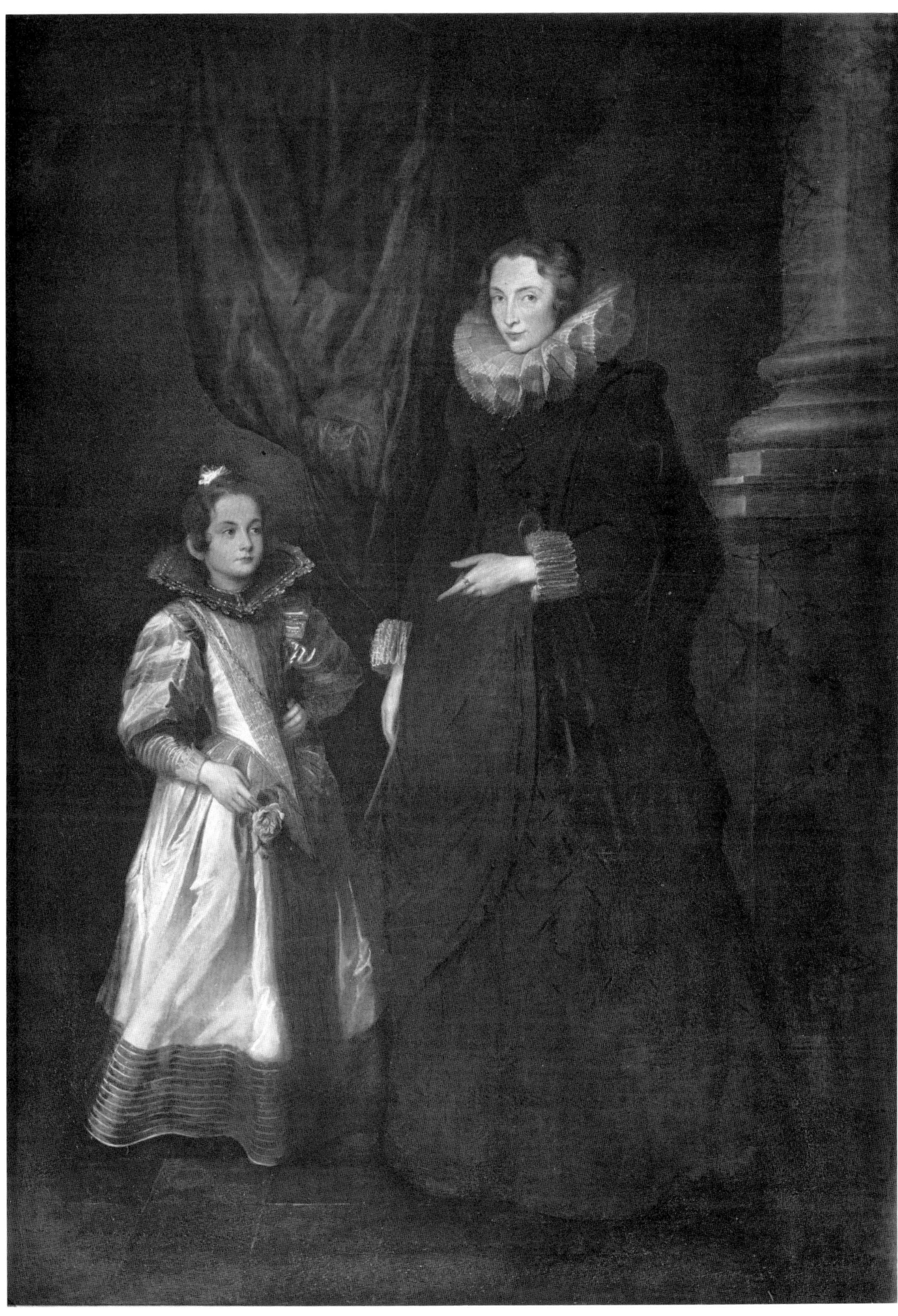

8. Anton van Dyck, *Ritratto di Geronima Brignole con la figlia Aurelia*, 1626–1627, olio su tela
Galleria di Palazzo Rosso, Genova

zioni fra i primi e gli anni Venti del Seicento. Avendo precedentemente considerato i costi dell'abbigliamento è opportuno rilevare che le guarnizioni in oro (vermigli, canuttiglia, pimpinelle . . .) erano la parte più costosa del vestito, maschile e femminile, bastino come esempi la spesa di 687.12 lire effettuata nel 1621 per "oro filato, vermigli, et altro per un abito di Anton Giulio"[56] e quella di 1155.12 lire spese nel 1626 per la guarnizione "d'oro di vermigli" della veste verde di sua moglie Paolina, che conosciamo attraverso il ritratto eseguito da Van Dyck conservato a Palazzo Rosso (fig. 3).

Due ritratti muliebri di Van Dyck, quello di Elena Grimaldi alla National Gallery di Washington, databile al 1623, e quello detto di Geronima Spinola alla Gemäldegalerie di Berlin-Dahlem,[57] forniscono un esempio di abbigliamento inusuale e curioso, che si ritiene utile sottoporre all'attenzione per stimolare ulteriori ricerche. Le due dame, infatti, sollevano intenzionalmente la veste nera (busto nero abbottonato davanti e faldette nere) e lasciano intravvedere l'orlo, ornato di galloni dorati, di una gonna sottostante. L'identico abbigliamento delle due dame presenta anche altre caratteristiche inconsuete: i manichini attorno ai polsi, solitamente bianchi, sono rossi ed entrambe tengono un fiore nella mano destra. Il fiore d'arancio, più precisamente identificato come arancio doppio nel caso di Elena Grimaldi, è tradizionalmente considerato simbolo del matrimonio.[58]

Si fa presente inoltre come possibile spunto per ulteriori approfondimenti quanto Tommaso Rinuccini afferma a proposito dell'abbigliamento delle donne fiorentine del Seicento: le spose si vestivano in bianco "ma per l'altre donne non s'aveva riguardo nessuno né al colore né al concerto dell'abito. . . . Le donne di tempo, se erano maritate, portavano la zimarra nera; ma la sottana, o veste, di colore."[59]

Oltre agli abiti da parata raffigurati nei ritratti, le dame indossavano abiti di diversa fattura di cui è difficile per noi immaginare la foggia, senza il supporto di documentazione iconografica. Di alcune tipologie ci danno testimonianza i documenti, come nel caso della "camisetta" (talvolta "camixia"). Nonostante l'affinità del termine con "camicia," infatti, i materiali con cui erano eseguite le "camisette" (velluto, tela d'argento ed altri) e la quantità necessaria per confezionarle inducono a ritenere che esse fossero un tipo di veste forse informale, e non camicia da sotto.[60]

Le fonti scritte testimoniano l'uso di una varietà di colori ben più ampia di quanto si potrebbe pensare sulla base dei ritratti, che per lo più raffigurano dame in nero, bianco,

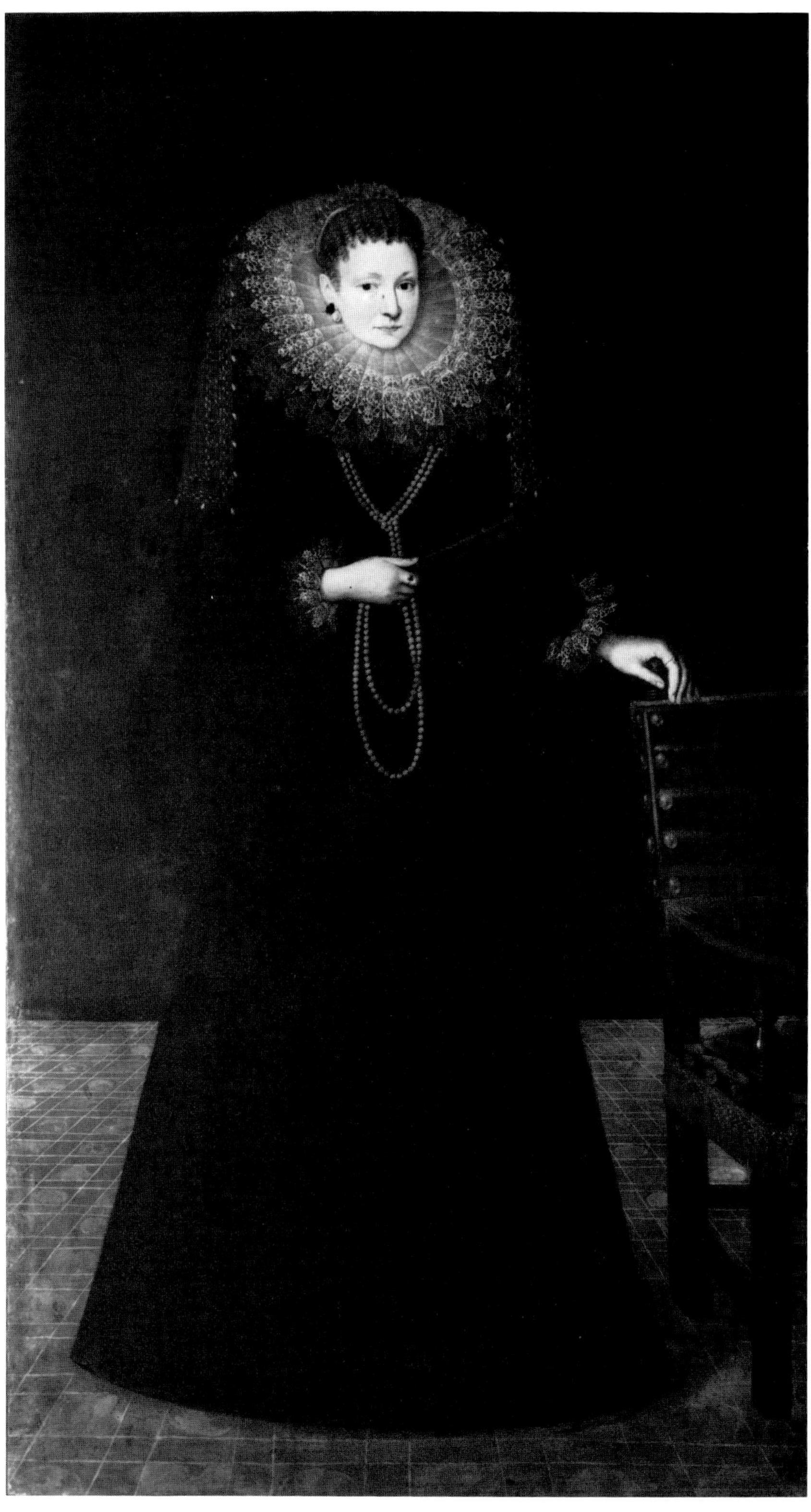

9. Guglielmo van Deynen, *Ritratto di dama*, 1610, olio su tela
Galleria di Palazzo Bianco, Genova

rosso o verde. Stando alle "chiacchere" di Fiammetta i colori si sceglievano in base al colore dei capelli e della carnagione (solo bianco e nero per le pallide, mentre "una, che sia di color bianco, & vivo, & fresca, potrà comodamente vestire tutti li colori, & quantunque il bianco, & nero anche in queste compirà per eccellenza, il turchino chiaro, che noi chiamiamo porcelletta, & l'incarnattino [= rosso] ancora le suole apportare molta vaghezza") ed anche a seconda del clima. Infatti "certi colori, che in mirarli pare che apportino fresco, harebbono del disconvenevole nella fredda stagione del verno, & per lo contrario di state disdicono quelli che hanno del caldo, & quando piove anche se si sa molto bene, che non si deve mettere una bella veste bianca se non vuoi che il fango te la ricami d'altro, che di lavori o trenini alla Milanese."[61]

La legge suntuaria emanata nel 1582 proibisce alle donne di indossare abiti di seta tranne: "teletta nera, raso piano di color nero, bianco, giallo, verde, turchino, carmesile, morello, o leonato, semplice però, e non misti, damasco e taffetale degli istessi colori." Comunque le donne "così maritate come vedove" devono vestire di sopra—probabilmente riferito alle sopravesti—in nero dal 15 ottobre al 15 maggio di ogni anno, escludendo le vesti di taffetà che possono essere dei colori concessi ed i giorni in cui sono invitate a nozze.[62] I manti—elementi caratteristici dell'abbigliamento delle dame genovesi (si consideri quello indossato da Geronima Brignole nel ritratto vandyckiano) (fig. 8)—possono essere solo di panno di lana o di buratto, cioè velo di seta, piani e neri.[63] È di particolare interesse visti i numerosi ritratti di dame in bianco, si pensi in particolare al ritratto di Brigida Spinola Doria eseguito da Rubens nel 1606, la seguente norma dedicata alle spose: "che per un mese dal giorno, che vanno a marito, o che escono fuori in abito di spose possino portare le solite brille in capo, e vestire di sopra una veste di damasco, raso, o taffetale di color bianco, con la guarnitione però regolata come sopra; e per altri tre mesi susseguenti possino vestire delli colori nella presente riforma concessi." Si precisa inoltre che le norme devono essere osservate in città e nelle ville. Nel 1594 vengono fatte alcune concessioni, in particolare, riguardo all'uso del velluto, fino ad allora tassativamente

proibito, a patto però che non fosse tessuto con più di un colore, mentre le vesti di altri tessuti potevano essere oltre ai colori consentiti anche "incarnato e porcelletta [cioè turchino]," ed anche di due colori (bianco e diversi tipi di rosso, e bianco e giallo).

Per quanto riguarda il lutto, non mi sembra chiara, allo stato attuale delle ricerche, la definizione della durata del periodo durante il quale la vedova vestiva di nero. Alla festa descritta nel *Capriccio poetico* del 1640 si parla di una bella vedova "ammantata di neri panni,"[64] ma ci si può domandare per quanto tempo ci si vestiva in nero, e quali segni erano adottati, dopo l'abbandono del lutto stretto, per significare lo stato vedovile. A mio parere si potrebbero considerare in quest'ottica alcuni particolari, che si sono notati in ritratti di Van Dyck, come ad esempio la fodera nera delle maniche di *Battina Balbi Invrea* (fig. 5) (da pochi anni rimasta vedova di Giovanni Durazzo; si veda Boccardo in questo volume) e, forse, anche la banda nera che attraversa il petto della *Dama in bianco* della Frick Collection (fig. 6), difficilmente spiegabili in altra maniera.

I collari a lattuga, a Genova definiti "collari" e "sciorette," registrano nell'arco di anni qui considerato una progressiva semplificazione. Nella legge suntuaria del 1571—utile per l'accurata descrizione di fogge e materiali—per i collaretti è concesso usare "tela di lino di ogni sorte, compreso bruges [sic], & anco di rete di filo di lino fatti al tellaro, con raponti, & pizzetti semplici alle bosse dinanzi," potendosi anche indossare attorno al collo "un mandilletto di taffetà, che si dice taffetaletto al collo," "una tovagliola, osia tovaglioletta di ogni tela di lino," "un mandillo [= fazzoletto] al collo di tela d'ogni sorte." Ci possiamo fare un'idea di questo complicato apparato attraverso il *Ritratto di dama* di Van Deynen (fig. 9), in cui il collare di grandi dimensioni, ornato da un alto pizzo, è arricchito da un leggero velo, orlato di perline, che ricade sulle spalle. I collari ritratti nel periodo trascorso a Genova da Van Dyck sono ancora di grandi dimensioni, ma assai più semplici nel decoro: la parte esterna è infatti per lo più ornata da semplici motivi geometrici (losanghe). I collari a lattuga richiedevano il consumo di altissime quantità di tessuto ed erano molto costosi; nel 1620 è registrato nel libro contabile di Gian

Francesco Brignole l'acquisto di 46 palmi, cioè più di 11 metri, di "lavor ponentino" (denominazione locale di un tipo non identificato di pizzo che si è riscontrata con molta frequenza) per 290.12 lire genovesi e poco meno (268.4 lire) si spende "per un collaro di ponentino per Anton Giulio" nel 1621.[65] Sempre attraverso i ritratti è possibile identificare un altro tipo di collare, apparentemente usato con una certa frequenza dalle dame negli anni venti: si tratta di un colletto piatto, con le punte squadrate orlate da trine, rialzato dietro la testa per mezzo di un supporto in tessuto (chiaramente visibile nel *Ritratto di dama genovese con la figlia* di Bruxelles) (Musées Royaux des Beaux-Arts). Questa tipologia deriva, probabilmente, dal *col rotonde* francese,[66] caratterizzato dall'essere assai rialzato dietro il capo. Lo stesso tipo di collare piatto e con punte squadrate, ma non rialzato dietro, si riscontra nella maggior parte dei ritratti maschili vandyckiani, attraverso i quali si può seguire il progressivo tramonto dei collari a lattuga, il cui uso è testimoniato praticamente solo nei ritratti in abbigliamento ufficiale (da ambasciatore, senatore o Doge). Si può presumere che questo cambiamento nella moda sia in qualche modo collegato ai *Capitulos de Reformación* emanati nel 1623 a Madrid da Filippo IV per limitare il lusso dell'abbigliamento. Il collare a lattuga era divenuto un simbolo di notevole spreco, era fatto dei lini più fini e spesso orlato con pizzi preziosi, inoltre, doveva essere spesso lavato e inamidato e quindi si usurava molto velocemente. Per questo l'11 febbraio 1623 Filippo IV ordinò agli uomini di ogni stato o grado di indossare *valonas. Valona,* termine riferito al luogo d'origine nelle zone francesi delle Fiandre, è un tipo di collare semplice e senza pizzi, che si indossava su un supporto rigido (cartone o strati di fogli di carta, talvolta rivestiti di tessuto)[67] chiamato *Golilla,* da cui successivamente prese il nome questo colletto, usato alla corte di Spagna fino al tardo Settecento.

Uno dei sermoni di Gabriello Chiabrera testimonia la diffusione di questa foggia a Genova (si considerino ad esempio il *Ritratto di Marcello Durazzo* [si veda Boccardo, fig. 13] e quello di *Anton Giulio Brignole Sale* [fig. 2]) con una descrizione così accurata che ci permette di cogliere anche alcune sot-tigliezze, come l'usanza di indossare colli tinti con polveri blu, espressamente proibita in Spagna.

Chi potrà dir de' collarini bianchi
più che neve di monte, ovvero azzurri
più che l'azzurro d'ogni ciel sereno?
Ed acconci per via, che non s'asconde
il groppo della gola, anzi s'espone
alle dame l'avorio del bel collo.

Il disagio degli uomini a mostrare il collo, prima mascherato dal collo a lattuga, era sentito anche dagli spagnoli come testimonia una poesia di Quevedo.[68] Contemporaneamente era in uso un tipo di colletto senza il supporto rigido della golilla, chiamato in Spagna *valona,* talvolta impreziosito da pizzi (in vari ritratti maschili di adulti e bambini), che era forse usato per occasioni informali. Questo collo deriva dal costume militare; nel Vecellio (1590) è indossato nell'incisione che raffigura un "Soldato disarmato."[69] In base alla documentazione esaminata si avanza l'ipotesi che i colli piatti a Genova fossero chiamati "revertiche," termine che si è riscontrato con frequenza nel Seicento per designare un tipo di colletto distinto dal "collare."[70]

L'abbigliamento maschile, cui fino ad ora si è fatto cenno relativamente ad alcuni elementi di costume come le maniche pendenti e i collari, assume fin dai primi anni del Seicento una configurazione abbastanza stabile, sia dal punto di vista formale che da quello lessicale, e si struttura nell'uso di casacca e calzoni. La loro foggia, che non è possibile esaminare nei dettagli in questa occasione, è descritta con toni un po' caricati, ma molto vivaci nel Sermone 20 di Gabriello Chiabrera, dedicato a Iacopo Gaddi, letterato fiorentino, in cui il poeta ironizza su "la leggiadria dell'italica gente," contrapponendola alle solide e rigide abitudini militaresche di tedeschi, olandesi, francesi e spagnoli.

. . . . E dove
calzar potrassi una gentil scarpetta,
un calcagnetto si polito? Arroge [aggiungi]
i bei fiocchi del nastro onde s'allaccia,
che di Mercurio sembrano i talari.
Io taccio il feltro de' capelli tinto
oltre misura a negro; e taccio i fregi
sul giubbon di ricchissimi vermigli.
Chi potrà dir de' collarini bianchi
più che neve di monte, ovvero azzurri
più che l'azzurro d'ogni ciel sereno?

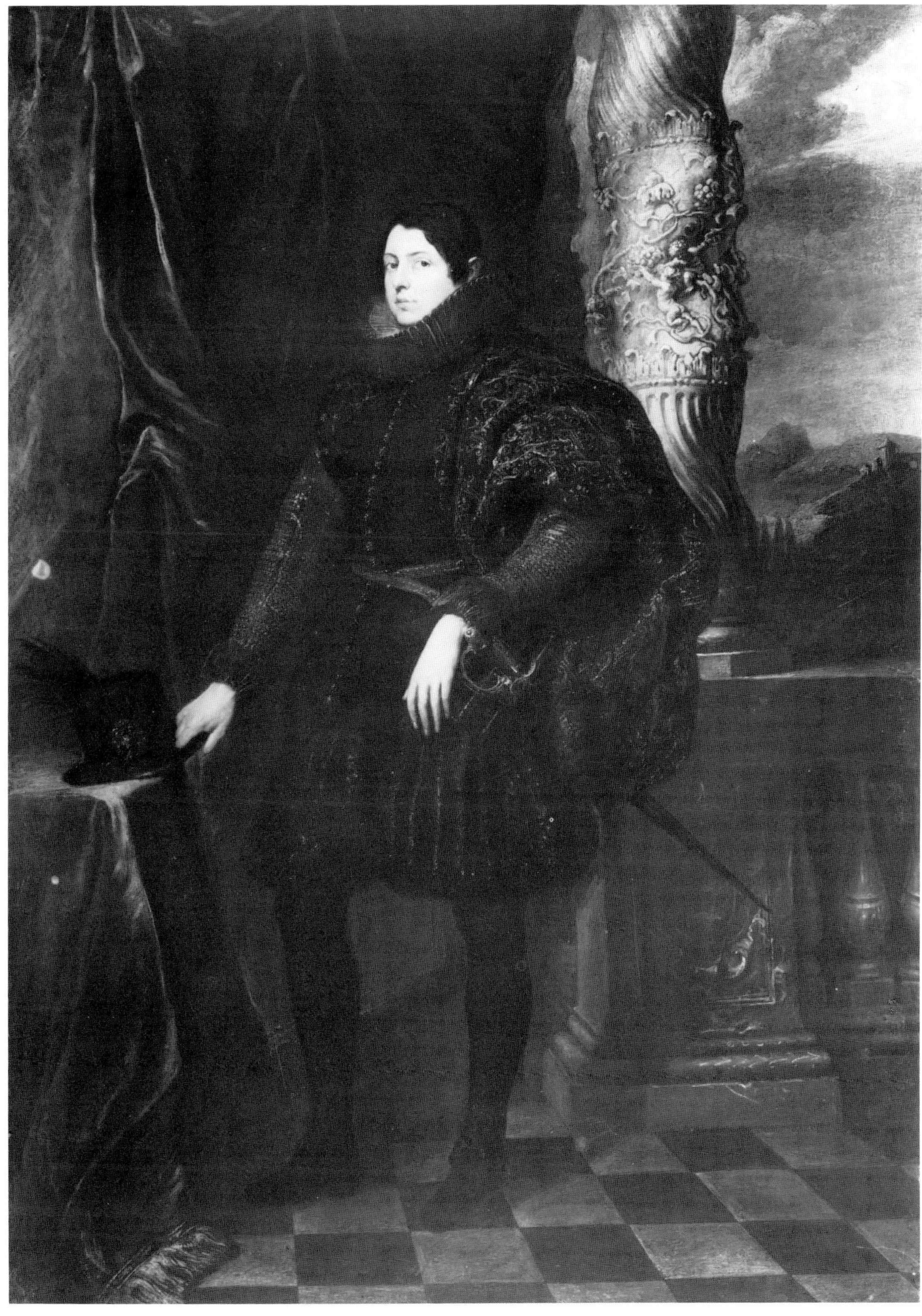

10. Peter Paul Rubens(?),
Ritratto di giovane,
1610–1618, olio su tela
Galleria di Palazzo Rosso, Genova

*Ed acconci per via, che non s'asconde
il groppo della gola, anzi s'espone
alle dame l'avorio del bel collo.*

*Lungo fora a narrar come son gai
per trapunto i calzoni, e come ornate,
per entro la casacca, in varie guise*

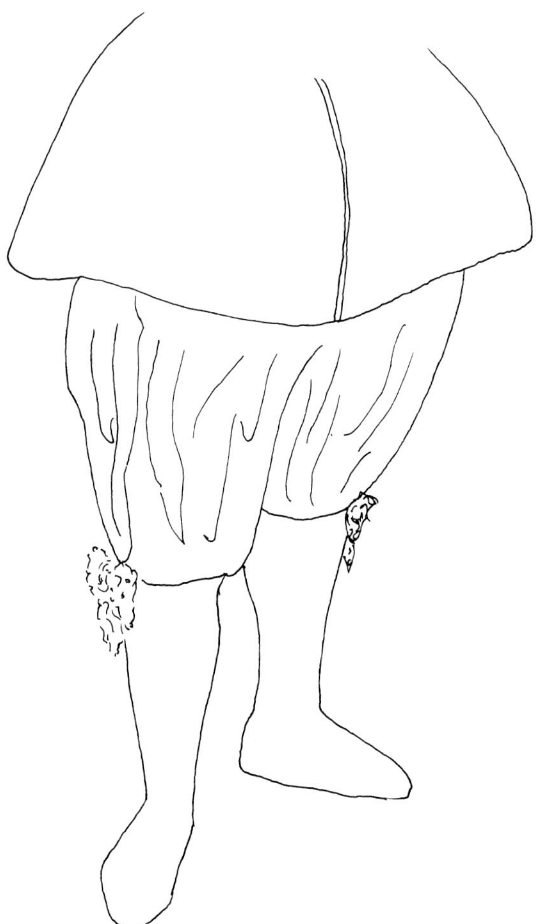

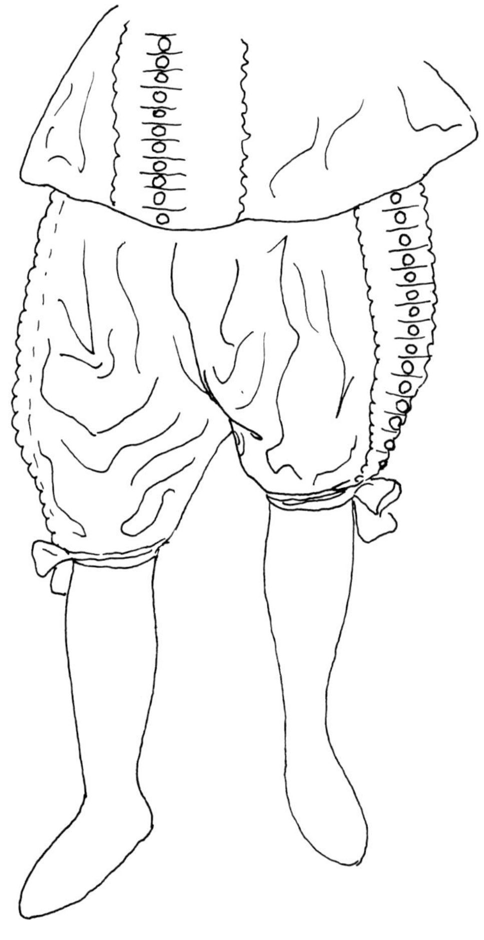

serpeggiando sen van bottonature.
Splendono soppannati i ferraiuoli
bizzarramente; e sulla coscia manca,
tutto d'argento arabescati e d'oro,
ridono gli elsi della bella spada.
Or prendasi a pensar qual è mirarsi,
fra si fatti ricami, in tale pompa,
una bionda increspata zazzeretta,
per diligente man di buon barbiere
con suoi fuochi e suoi ferri; e per qual modo
vi sfavilli la guancia si vermiglia,
che può vermiglia anco parer per arte;
e chi sa? forse forse . . . .

La polemica del poeta è rivolta contro i giovani nobili imbelli, oggetto anche degli strali di Ansaldo Cebà ed Andrea Spinola e, negli anni successivi, di Anton Giulio Brignole Sale.[71] Negli eccessi del lusso dei giovani "zerbinotti" si vedeva una minaccia per la salute morale della Repubblica, il cui cittadino ideale doveva perseguire uno stile di vita ispirato a un certo rigore morale, che doveva essere riflesso anche da un tipo di ab-

bigliamento adeguato, anche se non certo dimesso. Lussuoso e costoso—secondo il costume del tempo—me senza eccessi, era l'abbigliamento di Anton Giulio e degli altri aristocratici ritratti da Van Dyck. I loro abiti, in particolare quello di Marcello Durazzo (si veda Boccardo, fig. 13) e Filippo Spinola (si veda Boccardo, fig. 8),[72] riflettono la piena adesione alla moda spagnola nell'uso del nero, nei calzoni stretti al ginocchio e nella casacca, tagliata in vita con baschina piuttosto alta e, nel ritratto di Spinola, ornata di bottoni in oro anche sulle alette delle maniche ("in varie guise serpeggiando sen van bottonature"). File di bottoncini sui lati esterni dei calzoni sono elemento frequentemente ricorrente nell'abbigliamento maschile di adulti e bambini; sono presenti nel ritratto datato al 1623 di Filippo Cattaneo (Washington, National Gallery of Art) e in quello del 1629 di Agostino Pallavicino attribuito a Domenico Fiasella (Galleria di Palazzo Spinola), denotando la continuità di una foggia testimoniata anche da un abito del

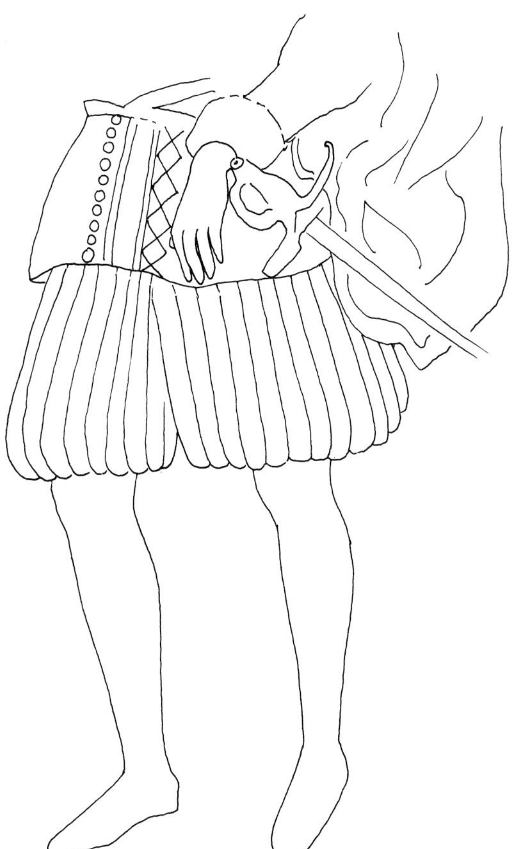

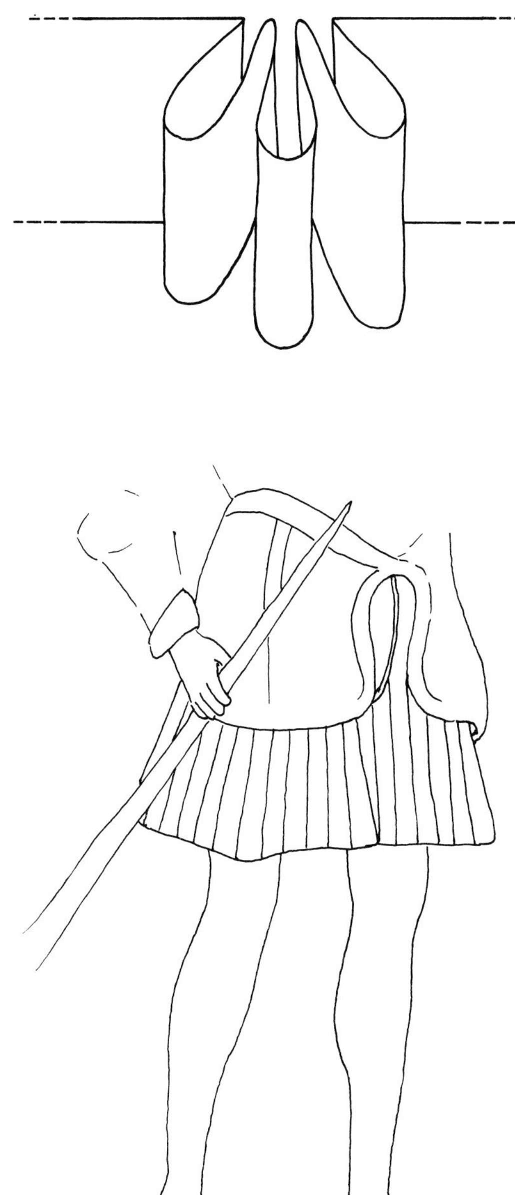

13. Rilievo grafico dei calzoni indossati in Anton van Dyck(?), *Ritratto di giovane*, Galleria di Palazzo Rosso, Genova
Disegno: Daria Vinco

14. Schema delle pieghe (fig. 13)
Disegno: Daria Vinco

15. Rilievo grafico dei calzoni indossati dalla figura maschile a sinistra in Anton van Dyck, *Ritratto della famiglia Lomellini*, National Gallery of Scotland, Edimburgo
Disegno: Daria Vinco

1627 del re di Svezia Gustavo Adolfo (Stoccolma, Royal Armory).[73] Alcuni dei fanciulli ritratti da Van Dyck[74] ed il cosiddetto Cornelis de Wael a cavallo di Anversa (Koninklijk Museum voor Schone Kunsten) indossano casacche rosse chiuse da alamari, allacciatura di origine orientale di cui si è già parlato. L'unico riferimento fino ad ora rinvenuto a casacche chiuse da alamari è relativo a 14 "vestiti per paggio di veluto negro ed alamari rossi," indicati in una parte dell'inventario di Gian Vincenzo Imperiale del 1648;[75] forse ulteriori ricerche permetteranno di comprendere se questo particolare abbigliamento era legato a qualche specifico ruolo nell'ambito militare, cerimoniale o sociale.

Le informazioni variamente ricavabili da ritratti e documenti ci trasmettono un'immagine dell'abbigliamento maschile negli anni venti sostanzialmente uniforme. Si discosta da questo quadro abbastanza omogeneo l'abbigliamento del *Giovane uomo* conservato a Palazzo Rosso (fig. 10), di cui l'attribuzione a Van Dyck e la datazione sono controverse; alcuni studiosi, infatti, lo ritengono opera del periodo italiano di Rubens (1606–1608).[76] La storia del costume può fornire qualche indicazione che possa favorire la collocazione cronologica del dipinto, anche se è bene precisare che le ricerche, in questo campo, a Genova sono agli inizi e, come si è visto in questo breve *excursus*, restano ancora da chiarire molti aspetti problematici. Il *Giovane uomo*, il cui volto è incorniciato da un alto collare a lattuga (poco usato nell'abbigliamento non ufficiale negli anni Venti), indossa un vestito (casacca e calzoni) di un tessuto marrone scuro (per quanto il mediocre stato di conservazione del dipinto consente di cogliere) riccamente decorato in oro in ogni sua parte, compreso il ferraiolo e la sua fodera. In particolare la foggia dei calzoni è diversa da quella dei calzoni definiti "alla spagnola" (figg. 11, 12), prevalentemente riscontrata intorno agli anni venti essi infatti sono molto larghi ed il tessuto forma pieghe "a soffietto" (figg. 13, 14), che si stringono sopra il ginocchio. Una tipologia simile si riscontra in numerose incisioni relative all'abbigliamento dei giovani veneziani nel Vecellio (1590), mentre per quanto riguarda il Seicento si sono riscontrate fogge analoghe, con particolare riferimento alle pieghe "a soffietto," in ritratti di nobiluomini inglesi datati intorno agli anni 1610–1618,[77] quindi in un periodo precedente la produzione genovese di Van Dyck. Al momento sfugge il circuito di circolazione di questa foggia, fra Venezia, l'Inghilterra e Genova. L'influsso inglese sulla moda maschile era molto sentito, ed è docu-

mentabile, a Genova nella seconda metà del Seicento,[78] ma non si hanno notizie relativamente ai primi decenni del secolo. Comunque la foggia di questi calzoni non va confusa con quella dei calzoni a liste di cuoio, spesso impreziositi da decori in oro e pietre preziose, solitamente indossati con la corazza (si confrontino il *Ritratto di Gian Carlo Doria* di Rubens, 1606, Palazzo Spinola) ed il gentiluomo in armatura nella *Famiglia Lomellini* di Van Dyck, c. 1626 (Edimburgo, National Gallery of Scotland) (fig. 15), che sono stati identificati da Boucher[79] con quelli definiti "alla vallona" nei documenti.

Dai dati emersi in questa rapida analisi si può concludere confermando l'assunto iniziale secondo cui la moda genovese era rigorosamente fedele a quella spagnola, pur rilevando—con qualche analogia con quanto stava succedendo negli ambienti della politica e della diplomazia?—i primi influssi di quella moda francese, che da lì a poco sarebbe divenuta l'incontestata regina in quel settore.

Dedicato all'amico Mauro De André. Il ricordo sempre vivo della sua simpatia e dei suoi consigli intelligenti è stimolo a cercare di dare il meglio. Oltre alle persone menzionate nelle note desidero esprimere la mia gratitudine agli amici e colleghi Franco Boggero e Farida Simonetti Ruffini, a Daria Vinco che ha eseguito i rilievi grafici ed inoltre a Giovanna Rotondi Terminiello, soprintendente per i beni artistici e storici della Liguria.

1. Le leggi suntuarie, finalizzate a regolare l'ostentazione del lusso nell'abbigliamento e nello stile di vita, forniscono preziose indicazioni sull'abbigliamento anche se erano costantemente disattese. Lo dimostrano la ricchezza degli abiti in cui gli aristocratici si facevano ritrarre, gli inventari dei loro beni, le denunce dei censori contro i cittadini che contravvenivano alle norme stabilite e le numerose domande di esenzione dall'osservanza delle stesse che venivano inoltrate al Magistrato competente. Date queste premesse si comprende che l'interesse per questo tipo di documentazione si incentra sui termini usati, sulla descrizione delle fogge consentite, dei tessuti, dei colori e su quanto si può comprendere relativamente a certe usanze quali ad esempio il matrimonio o la vedovanza. Per riferimenti bibliografici, anche relativi al tardo Seicento, si rimanda alla recente ed esauriente ricerca di Carla Campodonico, "Normative suntuarie e pratiche sociali nella Genova moderna: le dinamiche della moda del vestire e dell'abitare," in *Miscellanea storica ligure* 18, 1 (1986), 105–132.

2. Marzia Cataldi Gallo, *Abbigliamento e potere—La corte come centro di diffusione della moda*, in un Seminario sulla storia del costume tenuto presso l'Istituto di Storia dell'Arte dell'Università di Urbino nel 1990, in corso di stampa.

3. Janet Arnold, *Queen Elisabeth's Wardrobe Unlock'd* (Leeds, 1988), 123.

4. Rosita Levi Pisetzky, *Storia del costume in Italia*, 4 voll. (Milano, 1966–1967), 3:351.

5. In Archivio di Stato di Genova (A.S.G.), Ms. 280, c. 41, per cui si rimanda a Rosa Lopez Torrijos, "Imagenes de Cesare Corte para ilustrar un elogio a Espana," *Studi di Storia delle Arti* 4 (1983), 55–86, e Franco Boggero, "Per la pittura genovese tra Cinque e Seicento: il percorso dell'eretico Cesare Corte," *Arte Cristiana* 78, 741 (1990), 417–434. Il manoscritto, in riferimento alla storia del costume, è citato in Cataldi Gallo in corso di stampa.

6. Michele Rosi, "Il Barro di Paolo Foglietta commedia del secolo XVI," *Atti della Società Ligura di Storia Patria* 25,2 (Genova, 1892), 419–535. Atto secondo, scena quinta: la pettegola serva Agnese nel lamentarsi degli uomini che la importunano per la strada, ne cita uno particolarmente insistente che arriva a prometterle "una veste con coda dietro, come s'usa. Io allora me le volto con un mal volto, e gli dico: va in mal punto che questa foggia delle code dietro è cosa da gentildonne e non da par mie, alle quali per essere spedite conviene andar in veste corta

e tonda." La commedia fu scritta ante 1589, l'azione dovrebbe svolgersi a Genova intorno al 1550, vi si parla infatti di Andrea Doria (1466–1560) come vivo e attivo.

7. Giovanni Battista Roberti, "Lettera critica sulle qualità del lusso presente in Italia," in *Opuscoli quattro sopra il lusso* (Bassano, 1785), 238–240, citato in Levi Pisetzky 1967, 4:29.

8. Rosi 1892, 419–535, Atto secondo, scena ottava.

9. Bartolomeo Paschetti, *Dialogo delle Bellezze di Genova* (Genova, 1583), 52.

10. *Genova nel 1592 da una memoria di Gio Battista Confalonieri Romano* (Genova, 1911), 26. Si citano altri esempi: nella commedia *Il Barro*, Atto secondo, scena settima, Isabetta la gentildonna si lamenta del lusso introdotto in città: "in questi [tempi] ognun tiene paggi e schiere de servitori, e le donne diverse serventi e cameriere, né più si degnano andar con i loro piedi che si fanno portar in sedia, o, se pur vanno a piedi, portano i *zoccoli* tanto alti che per non cadere si fanno regger da' servitori. . . . I nostri antichi insomma dormivano in letti di panno e broccatello, e noi nel broccato e nella seta ornata d'oro, perchè la pompa adesso è in colmo." Paschetti 1583, 53: "[I palazzi di Genova] Son ricchi e superbi non solo per quel che si vede di fuori, ma etiandio per le cose che han dentro, essendo addobbati in maniera, che porgono meraviglia a Principi, . . . le case di mediocre fortuna abbondano di più argenti, che non fanno le principali di Lombardia."

11. Per quanto concerne la società parigina l'argomento è trattato in modo sistematico ed esaustivo da Daniel Roche, *La culture des apparences* (Paris, 1989), in particolare cap. 6, "Le contenu des armoires de l'age classique à la Révolution," 119–148.

12. Vedi oltre.

13. Per la definizione di questa foggia si veda più avanti.

14. Inventario dei beni del quondam Giacomo Doria di Agostino, 1613, gentilmente segnalatomi da Piero Boccardo, cui sono grata anche per le lunghe utili conversazioni e soprattutto per aver stimolato il mio interesse per il ricco patrimonio degli archivi genovesi. Si ritiene utile riportarne il testo integrale per quanto di interesse in questo contesto:

Robbe da Donna
Ungarcesca e faldette di veluto verde e vinato con vermiglij
Robbe di veluto bianco e gialdo 2
Robbe di veluto bianco e nero 2
Camisetta di veluto bianco e turchino
Camisetta di teletta argentina, e argentata
Robbe di veluto verde 2
Robbe di veluto turchino guarnite d'oro 2
Robbe di teletta velutata di tre collori 2
Faldette de veluto cremesi lam.[inat]o 2
Faldette de teletta veluta gialdo e verde

Robbe di veluto rizzo sopra rizzo de Milano nero 2
Robbe di veluto nero fondo raso de Milano 2
Robbe di teletta veluta nera, vecchie 2
Penna d'Armellini con fodra di teletta veluta
Robbe di Damasco bianco e turchino guarnite d'oro 2
Robbe di Damasco argentino guarnite d'argento 2
Robbe di Tabino porcelletta 2
Faldette di Damasco bianco e zizola
Faldette di tabino bianco e gialdo
Robbe di Taf.[fet]ta nero lav.te al tellaro 2
Robbe di Taf.ta nero guarn.te de margher.ni
Robbe di Taf.ta nero tagliate a pocette 2
Robbe di Taf.ta bianco e nero lav.te 2
Robbe di Taf.ta de tre collori
Robbe di Taf.ta verde e nero guarnite d'oro 2
Robbe di Taf.ta bianco e giallo lav.to 2
Sottana di Taf.ta bianco e verde
Sottana de tre collori
Corpetto di taf.ta cremesile ed oro
Ungaresca de boretta con margher.[iti]ni
Robbe de canevazetto nero 2
Mantellina di veluto nero fodrata di felpa ineavinata
Mantellina di veluto cremesile per battezare
Mantellina di teletta veluta argentina, fodrata de
    felpa

Biancherie
Lenzuoli d'olanda para 2
Scionie de ponentino p.e 2, de ponto reale p.e 3
Camise da giorno de cartina n.2
Camisa bianca e rossa n.1
Camise de ponentino n.2
Camisa de ponto Buso n.1
Camisa de cartina bianca e nera n.1
Camise da notte bianco e nero n.2
Camise de ponentino n.2
Camisia bianca, nera, e rossa n.1
Camisa di ponto buso n.1
Revertega tempestata n.1
Tovagliole de rense [rensa] da testa n.1
Tovagliola nera da testa n.1
Tovagiole per tauletta n.6
Tovagliola Tempestata n.1
Tovagliola de più collori n.1
Cuffie di ponto buso n.2
Cuffia tempestata n.1
Cuffie ordinarie n.2
Cuffie di rense(?) n.1
Tovaglia lav.[ora]ta d'oro 1
Mandilli de ponentino e sfilatino n.6
Mandillo de ponto reale n.1
Mandillo de ponto buso n.1
Mandilli lav.ti di nero n.4
Mandillo de cadeniglia n.1
Tovagliola per battezare n.1
Facciolo lav.to di nero n.1
Cuffietta
Lenzuoletto per la cuba n.1
facciolo bianco 1

Robbe da Huomo
Calzoni e casaca de Taf.a nero, e morello senza
    maniche
Calzoni e casaca di veluto rizzo zanetto guarnito
    d'argento
Cappa simile fodrata di felpa

Calzoni e casaca di veluto a opera zanetto e verde
Calzoni e cas.[ac]a d'Arbasetto argentato guarniti de
    bindellino
Calzoni e cas.a de teletta fior di lino guarniti d'oro
Cappa simile fodrata di Teriglia
Calzoni e casaca di Teletta velutata zanetto e nero
Calzoni e casaca di veluto nero lavorato al Telaro
Calzoni e casaca da veluto guarnito da guarnitioni
    asole mopresso(?) e Tagli
Calzoni e cas.a de veluto nero guarnito a portigiole
Calzoni e cas.a de veluto nero a opera
Calzoni e cas.a de veluto rizzo guarnito de
    guarnitioni
Calzoni e cas.a de Taf.a argent.[i]no e argen.[tat]o
Ferraiolo d'Arbasetto per detto vestito
Calzoni e cas.a di Teletta veluta vinata e nera
Ferauolo de rosetta mischia
Calzoni e cas.a di Taf.a nero guarniti de guarnitioni a
    Taglio
Calzoni e casaca de Taf.ta nero lavorati al tellaro
Feraulo de pano fodrato di teletta veluta vinata e nero
Calzoni e cas.a di raso ed guarnitioni
Calzoni e casacca di Teletta veluta zanetto e nero
Calzoni e casacca di taf.a argentato
Calzoni e cas.a de taf.a nero a Trappella lavorato al
    Telaro
Calzoni e cas.a di Taf.a nero con guarnitioni lavorato
    al Telaro
Cappa per d.[ett]o vestito
Calzoni e cas.a de tabino ondato nero
Ferauolo simile fodrato di taf.a lavorato
Calzoni e Giup.[on]e di pelle lavo.[ra]ti d'oro
Casaca de veluto nero rizzo
Calzoni e casaca di pano fratesco
Ferauolo dell'istesso
Calzoni e cas.a de sagobia verdoia
Ferauolo dell'istesso
Calzoni e cas.a di pano fratesco
Ferauolo dell'istesso
Calzoni e cas.a d'Arbasetto argentato
Ferauolo dell'istesso
Ferauolo di teletta nera fodrato de taffeta lauorato
Cappa de veluto rizzo nero fodrata de veluto lauorato
Ferauolo de teletta nera fodrato di teletta velutata
Ferauolo de lustrino di seta nero
Cappa de rasetta nera co' liste 2 di raso
Ferauolo de rasetta nera fodrato di teletta velutata
Ferauolo de pano nero
Ferauolo de sagobia fod.[ra]to de baietta
Ferauolo di lanetta fodrato di taf.a ed guarnit.[ion]e
    d'argento
Cappa de caneuazetto di Milano fodrato di taf.ta
Casacone de rasetto di Milano fodrato de taf.a giallo e
    porcelletta
Giup.[on]e di taf.a fiordelino lau.to d'oro
Giup.e di tela lau.to de vermiglii fodrato di taffetta
    vinato
Giup.e di tela lau.to d'oro e argento fodrato de taf.ta
    argentato
Giup.e de tela luorato d'oro al telaro fodrato di tela
Giup.e di tela lau.to d'oro, fodrato di taf.ta zanetto
Giup.e di raso vinato guarnito di cadenetta d'oro
Giup.e di tela d'oro
Giup.e di taf.a biancho
Giup.e de taf.a color di mare e vinato

Giup.e di tela de seta gialda vinata e argentina
Giup.e di tela di seta morella e verde
Giup.e di seta vinata e nero
Giup.e di taf.a con trappella argen.ta e argen.o
Giup.e di taf.a nero imbotito
Giup.e de fustagno con cadeneta d'argento
Giup.e de taf.a nero alla spagnola
Giup.e di taf.a nero lau.to al telaro
Giup.e di taf.ta lau.to de ponto reale
Giup.e di raso lau.to di cordetta
Giup.e de raso stampato guarnito de trenini
Giup.e di taf.a piano
Giup.e de canevazetto lau.to a scorgionetti
Giup.e de taf.ta guarnito di cadenetta
Giup.e de taf.a lau.to a scorgionetti
Casacca de raso stampato guarnita de guarnitioni
Calze e colletto di raso ed color d'oro e nero
Calze de raso stampato con gli taglii de guarnitioni
Ferauolo de pano de collore, con bacrano zanetto
Cappa de rasetta di collore fodrata di teletta veluta
    vinata e nera
Ferauolo de saia de Milano mischia fodrato di taf.a
    gialdo e turchino
Colletto d'ambra guarnito de guarnitione
Colletto di pelle de spagna guarn.[i]to de
    guarn.[itio]ni
Robbetta di pano fodrata de baietta
Robbetta de Damasco vinato e nero
Robbetta de damasco guarnita d'oro
Ferauolo de sagobia nera
Casaca de sagobia nera
Ferauolo de pano nero
Calzoni e cas.a de raso nero lauorato al telaro
Calzoni e cas.a de taf.a argent.no piano
Calzoni e cas.a de saia di Milano argenta e argentino
Calzoni e cas.a di taf.a argento piano
Calzoni e cas.a de taf.ta turchino e nero
Calzoni e cas.a de saia argentata con trina d'argento
Calzoni e cas.a di veluto nero di Milano
Calzoni e cas.a di rasiglio nero
Calzoni e cas.a de taf.ta nero di Milano
Calzoni e cas.a de burato nero de Fiandra
Calzoni di taf.ta nero lengieri
Calzoni e cas.a d'Arbasetto nero
Calzoni e cas.a di burato nero
Calzoni e cas.a de ferrandina nera
Calzoni de baietta per 3 casa.e 2
Cas.ce di burato de Spagna per desmuto
Casaca de burato nero
cas.a de burato de Fiandra
Giup.e di taf.a bianco verdetto
Giup.e de fustagno argentato
Giup.e di tela d'oro e collori
Giup.e di tela lau.to d'oro e vinato
Giupponi di cirvetto duoi
Giupponi di ferrandina duoi
Giup.e di burato di leone uno
Giup.e di taf.a a opera son dua
Giup.e di tela argentata uno
Giup.e di taffetta bianco uno
Giup.e de taf.a rigato bianc'e nero uno
Camisolle de baietta due
Camisola de seta verde una
Ferauolo d'Arbasetto
Ferauolo de burato de Napoli

Cappa de burato de Napoli
Ferauoli de burato leon
Ferauolo de ferrandina
Ferauolo de baietta uno di seta
Ferauolo d'Arbasetto verde
Ballandrano di pani vecchio
Ferauoli, calzoni e casache de pano per lauorare n.
    quattro
Calze con fondo de raso, casache e cappotti de veluto
    per . . . . (?) n.8
Calze con fondo raso, casache e cappe de pano liste di
    veluto per laurare n.6
Berrette di veluto per laurare n.4
Berrette di veluto rizzo 3
Banda di tela d'argento 1
Banda di taf.ta cremesile lauorata d'oro 1
Pettinere di più sorti 3
Pettinatore di taf.ta verde 1
Mezaro di taf.ta vinato 1
Meizaro di taf.ta cremesile ed oro 1
Suonia di taf.ta gialdo 1
Scuopette con manicho d'argento

15. Archivio Storico Comune di Genova (A.S.C.G.), *Libri diversi*, 1599 in 1650, n. 44, *Cartulare di Gio Francesco Brignole*, 1599 in 1611, c. 98, "spese del vestire," 7 novembre 1609: "spese e manifatture di Geronima da Mastro Giorgio Bolero da che si saldi per il sposalitio in qua L.308 e dopo L.55.17." Il matrimonio è forse quello dello stesso Gian Francesco con Geronima Sale celebrato nel 1603. Negli anni successivi il sarto preferito di Geronima, e della figlia Maria Maddalena, sembra essere Bartolomeo Oneto (il cui nome compare frequentemente nei libri di conti). Egli compare nell'elenco degli artigiani compilato nel 1628 per la riscossione della tassa per costruire le nuove mura fra i *Sartores*, si veda A.S.G., ed è tassato per 13366 lire.

16. Archivio Durazzo Giustiniani Genova (A.D.G.G.), Fondo Pallavicino in corso di riordino, databile ai primi anni del Seicento. I due si sposarono nel 1600, Gian Francesco morì prima del 1627, Livia, figlia di Pantaleo Balbi, nel 1656. Devo queste informazioni al dott. Bologna, che ringrazio.

17. Si riportano notizie riguardanti la famiglia di Gian Francesco Brignole manoscritte all'inizio del *Cartulare* dello stesso (A.S.C.G., *Libri diversi*, 1599 in 1650, n. 44, Gian Francesco Brignole, *Cartulare*, 1599 in 1611):

25 luglio 1603 matrimonio con Geronima figlia di
    Giulio Sale
28 giugno 1604 nasce Maria Maddalena
5 marzo 1605 muore Antonio Brignole
26 giugno 1605 nasce Anton Giulio
1607 muoiono Giulio Sale e Aurelia Sale
3 figli morti infanti
24 aprile 1610 nasce Aurelia

18. Marzia Cataldi Gallo, "Ritratto e costume: *Status symbol* nella Genova del Seicento," *Bollettino Ligustico*, n.s. 1 (1989), 82–103. Per le spese di Agostino per l'ambasceria a Roma ed il dogato, 86.

19. Indicativo a proposito il titolo del terzo capitolo del recente volume di Carlo Bitossi, *Il Governo dei*

Magnifici Patriziato e politica fra Cinque e Seicento (Genova, 1990), 79: "Pochi tra i pochi. Patriziato e cariche di governo, 1576–1657." Si rimanda a questo testo per i legami fra le varie famiglie e per i rilievi riguardo ai loro patrimoni, in particolare, oltre al capitolo terzo, 117–137 ed oltre 210–217.

20. Questi dati mi sono stati indicati da Giorgio Doria, che ringrazio di cuore per la sua disponibilità. Fonti: relativamente al costo degli alloggi Luciano Grossi Bianchi e Ennio Poleggi, *Una città portuale del Medioevo—Genova nei secoli X–XVI* (Genova, 1979), 267 e 303. Relativamente a terreni e bovini: Giorgio Doria, *Uomini e terre di un borgo collinare dal XVI al XVIII secolo* (Milano, 1968), 399–401, 404. Relativamente ai velieri: Giuseppe Felloni, "Una fonte inesplorata per la storia dell'economia marittima in età moderna: i calcoli di avaria," in *Wirtschaftskräfte und Wirtschaftswege*, vol. 2 (Nürnberg, 1978), 37–57. Per i salari dei muratori: Giulio Giacchero, *Il Seicento e le Compere di San Giorgio* (Genova, 1979), 683.

21. Rosi 1892, Atto primo, scena seconda: "non solo il grano che vien di fuora è qui sempre carissimo, ma l'olio ancora, che, se bene la Natura madre benigna e pietosa produce tant'olio in questo paese d'abondar quattro Genove non ch'una sola, egli non solamente si vende a pretii altissimi, ma spesso gli huomini non nen trovano per danari a comprar tanto da farsi un'insalata né da farsi lume, talché molti hora vanno a tentone. Né manco caro dell'olio è il vino, le legna, l'erbe, i frutti, e ogni cosa insomma che produce la liguria costa un occhio d'huomo in questa terra, dove abita e regna la carestia, né mai v'entra l'abbondantia; siché chi non ha borsa ben ferrata travaglia a vivere a Genova, ch'è città da ricchi e non da un povero par mio."

22. A.S.C.G., *Libri diversi*, 1599 in 1650, n. 44, Gian Francesco Brignole, *Cartulare*, 1599 in 1611, c. 125, *spese del vivere* 1610: vino l.683.16.6—salari 975.9—olio l.229.10; A.S.C.G., Gian Francesco e Gian Battista Brignole, 1612 in 1620, *Cartulare*, n. 45: c. 28, *Spese del vivere* 1612: vino l.915.14—salari della servitu e maestro l.1474.19—olio l.195.11—grano l.816; c. 52, 1614: olio l.203.5—salarii l.1615.6; c. 73 1616: olio 202.10—vino 804.16.8—grani 732; c. 120, *spese del vivere* 1618: salari l.2170.4.8—grano l.1068.l.8—vino l.933.7.

23. Per una ricerca specifica su questo argomento Marzia Cataldi Gallo, "Il mercato degli abiti usati a Genova nel XVII secolo," in *La moda pronta— Ricerche e problemi di storia della confezione*, Atti del V Convegno Internazionale del Centro Italiano per lo Studio della Storia del Tessuto (Milano, 1990 [1991]).

24. Per l'identificazione dei due ritratti si rimanda al contributo di Piero Boccardo in questo stesso volume e figg. 13, 14. In riferimento al rapporto fra ritratto e costume l'argomento è stato trattato anche in Cataldi Gallo 1989, 89 e 92. I dati relativi agli arredi sono tratti dal *Cartulare* di Agostino Durazzo, 1629–1636 (A.D.G.G., n. 494), *sub voce* "arnesi di casa."

25. Piero Boccardo, "Per la storia della quadreria di Palazzo Spinola," in *Quaderni della Galleria Nazionale di Palazzo Spinola* 10 (1987), 63–86, 68–70 e Cataldi Gallo 1989, 83–86.

26. A.S.C.G., Gian Francesco Brignole I, 1620 in 1627, n. 48 *Cartulare*, "spese per la sposa," c. 300:

l.200 vestito di velluto riccio bordato
l.30 maniche di tabi nero bord.[at]e
l.68 lav.[ora]re p.[al]mi 228 lista di v.[elu]to riccio per ferr.[aio]lo
l.600 bord.[datu]ra di vestito, maniche di giub[on]e, e fodra di fer.[raio]lo di veluto piano con marg.[ariti]ni non compreso ambra.
l.135 p.mi 298 guar.[nitio]ne per detto vestito e p.mi 431 x fer.[raio]lo.

È bene tener presente che Cosimo De Paoli compariva nell'elenco degli artigiani tassati nel 1630 (A.S.G., Camera n. 2605) fra i *recamatores* (tassato L.30), quindi è probabile che a questa somma vadano aggiunte le spese per il tessuto e la manifattura, difficili da rintracciare perché indicate in modo generico.

27. A.S.C.G., Gian Francesco Brignole I, 1620 in 1627, n. 48 *Cartulare*, c. 312, *Spese per la sposa*: 1 aprile 1626 "e per quanto si nota quanto è in debito Cosimo de Paoli per le robe di sotto . . . l.2564.8 (le parti componenti la veste verde sono indicate con • •):

l.86 p.[al]mi 260 guar.[nitio]ne d'orlo di v.[elu]to chermesi
l.775.16 p.mi 1274 guar.ni cioè 600 chermesi, 528 verde• •, e 524 incarnato e nero s.9 l'una per l'altra
l.220 bord.[atu]ra di fodra di man.[ich]e cher.[mes]i, e maniche da br.[acci]o per roba grande(• •?)
l.44 lavorare giub.[on]e di raso verde• •
l.1155.12 p.mi 537.0/2 compreso li Garibi(?) di guar.ne d'oro di vermigli per roba verde a s.43 il p.mo• •
l.303 lav.ro di giubone e maniche verde di v.to • •.

Anche in questo caso si tenga presente quanto rilevato alla nota precedente.

28. Cesare Vecellio, *Habiti antichi et moderni di Diverse Parti del Mondo* (Venezia, 1590), edizione consultata a cura di Gillo Dorfles (Bologna, 1982), 88.

29. Cristoforo Zabata, *Ragionamento di sei nobili fanciulle genovesi* (Pavia, 1583), in *Rime diverse in lingua genovese* (Pavia, 1583); le citazioni sono rispettivamente 54 e 24–25.

30. Rosi 1892, Atto secondo, scena ottava: colloquio fra il vecchio Demetrio e la moglie Despina.

31. *Sermone XV*, "Al Signor Francesco Gavotti," un nobile savonese, in Gabriello Chiabrera, *Opere e lirici del classicismo barocco*, a cura di Mario Turchi (Torino, 1984). Chiabrera cominciò a scrivere i Sermoni nel 1624.

32. Si rimanda alla nota 10 e Emilia Biga, "Una polemica antifemminista del '600," *Quaderno dell'Aprosiana* 4 (Ventimiglia, 1989). Nell'incisione raffigurante una nobile genovese pubblicata da Vecellio 1590 si riscontra l'uso di una pianella con tacco relativamente alto.

33. Nell'ordine in A.S.G., Miscellanea Senato, Sala Bartolomeo Senarega, *Denunce del 1598* (si tratta di denunce sporte contro le persone che vestivano in modo diverso da quanto sancito dalle leggi suntuarie); A.S.G., Notaio Lorenzo Paravagna, scansia 442 filza 4, Inventario dei beni di Gian Agostino Caroccio, 5 aprile 1584; l'ultimo riferimento è in un inventario del 1658, precisamente dei beni di Gaspare Carroccio, nipote del sucitato Agostino (A.S.G., notaio Giuseppe Celesia, scansia 1040 filza 1, 24 aprile), in cui si legge: "robba di ciamelotto nero di Levante usata, con tagli cioè falde, busto con avaniglie et ongaresca." Nello stesso inventario compare la definizione "veste intiera . . . cioè falde, busto, manice et ongaresca" e "veste . . . cioè falde, ongaresca e busto." Si rimanda alle pagine seguenti per l'analisi delle varie tipologie. Il termine "avaniglie" forse designa quella che noi oggi chiamiamo la baschina del busto, composta da linguette di tessuto rettangolari profilate da gallone, ad esempio Anton Van Dyck, *Ritratto di "Giovanna Cattaneo"* (fig. 7). Lorenzo Franciosini, *Vocabulario Espanol e Italiano*, 3ª ed., 2 voll. (Roma, 1638), vol. 1, riporta: *auanillo* = ventaglio strumento da far vento e cacciar le mosche.

34. Gian Luigi Beccaria, *Spagnolo e spagnoli in Italia—Riflessi ispanici sulla lingua italiana del Cinque e del Seicento* (Torino, 1968), 95: *alamaro* "ornamento di cordoncini sull'abbotonatura" da spagnolo alamar e da arabo maghrebino al-amara.

35. Si confrontino le vesti di ungheresi e polacchi pubblicate fra le incisioni di Vecellio (1590). L'influsso orientale sulla moda europea è stato trattato da Fritz Saxl, *Costumi e feste della nobiltà milanese negli anni della dominazione spagnola*, in *Il libro del Sarto della Collezione Querini Stampalia di Venezia* (Modena, 1988), 31–55; Carmen Bernis, *Indumentaria española en tiempos de Carlos V* (Madrid, 1962); Cataldi Gallo, in corso di stampa; e nel recente articolo di Grazietta Butazzi (che mi ha consigliato con la consueta gentilezza e competenza), "Oriente e Moda nel Rinascimento: una proposta di ricerca," *Arte Tessile* 2 (1991), 3–8.

36. Grazietta Butazzi, "Indicazioni sull'abbigliamento infantile dalle liste della Guardaroba Granducale tra la fine del secolo XVI e il Seicento," in *I principi Bambini, abbigliamento e infanzia nel Seicento* [cat. mostra] (Firenze, 1985), 25–32.

37. Bernis 1962, 29.

38. In Franciosini 1638, vol. 2, *sub voce* "pistagna": "quel pezzetto di panno in forma di scacco, che sopravanza dove comincia la manica, cioè sopra e attorno all'omero."

39. *Capitoli di nuovo formati nel vestire tanto per le Donne quanto huomini . . .* (Genova, 1571), in A.S.G., Sala Bartolomeo Senarega, n. 1069. Si fa spesso riferimento a questo testo in quanto le descrizioni sono molto accurate, anche se le norme sono in gran parte annullate dalle successive leggi. Tuttavia è lecito pensare che le norme, non espressamente mutate in altre leggi, rimanessero in vigore. L'ultima frase è probabilmente riferita al decoro che poteva essere eseguito con applicazioni di galloni o di ricami a punto posato (il filo è disteso sul tessuto e fissato con punti di fermatura in seta, senza passare all'interno del tessuto).

40. Si veda nota 33.

41. Franciosini 1638, vol. 2, *sub voce*. Anche Beccaria 1968, 100–102.

42. Carmen Bernis, *Trajes y modas en la España de los reyes católicos* (Madrid, 1978), 1:38.

43. Si veda p. 58. Segue l'elenco dei problemi dati dall'uso di verdugali nell'atto di sedersi e di montare a cavallo.

44. Nota 32: "faldette e samarra." Nella callega [= vendita all'asta] dei beni di Raffaele De Turri quondam Gian Maria (A.S.G., Notaio Lorenzo Pallavagna, scansia 442 filza 3) del 23 dicembre 1580 si legge: "Faldette con le maniche di camucato gialdo con lista di veluto per [= vendute a] Giacomo Vignolo L.15.13" e "verdugale camocato gialdo con maniche in Giacomo Vignolo L.18." Lo stesso acquirente acquista per 18 lire "faldette di damasco morello [= rosso scuro]." Nell'inventario dei beni di Gian Agostino Carroccio venduti in callega il 5 aprile 1584 (A.S.G., Notaio Lorenzo Pallavagna, scansia 442 filza 4) compaiono "faldette razo gialdo (L.25); ongarescha telletta et faldette taffeta incarnatto (l.53); faldette bambagina bianca (L.3); faldette paro di dobletto bianco (l.3.10); faldette paro . . . gialdo (L.2); faldette ciamelotto rosso (L.6); faldette paro taffetà turchino (L.3.10); faldette paro di damasco verde con rebusto [= tipo di busto] et mamole [?] (L.14)." Un "paro di faldette di damasco argentato" è citato fra i beni di Gian Battista Roche nel 1590 (negli atti dello stesso notaio).

45. A.S.C.G., Gian Francesco Brignole I, 1620 in 1627, n. 48, *Cartulare*, c. 327, "Spese per Paola," 18 settembre 1626; si riporta le nota delle spese da pagare a Camillo Serravalle "per diverse spese di anno" 853.7 lire:

l.33.11 p.mi 25 raso nero per guar.[nitio]ne per roba simile
l.207.7 p.mi 78.0/4 tabi incar.[nati]no
l.47.6.8 p.mi 23.8/3 er.[mesi]no porcelletta per faldette
l.83.13.9 p.mi 47.8/4 er.no giallo per ongaresca e faldette
l.16.9 p.mi 7 er.no crem.[esi]le per ombrello
l.83.17 p.mi 39 er.no capelli e camisetta
l.31.10 p.mi 14 er.no verde e p.mi 7 nero per faldette lav.te
l.118.16 p.mi 36 teletta verde velutata a 5.66
l.230.14.7 diverse altre per fodra di dette robe et altro.

Camillo Serravalle, che risulta in più occasioni fornitore di manufatti per i Brignole, era un "seatero," tassato per 51250 lire nel 1628. I seateri potevano vendere e in qualsiasi modo commerciare panni di seta all'ingrosso, non al minuto in quanto questa era competenza dei merciai; Cataldi Gallo 1991, 95–106.

46. Per il calcolo del materiale richiesto per la confezione di capi di abbigliamento si rimanda a Juan De Alcega, *Tailor's Pattern Book 1589* (Carlton Bedford,

1979), in particolare 22–60. Si confronti inoltre Janet Arnold, *Patterns of Fashion: The Cut and Construction of Clothes for Men and Women c. 1560–1620* (London, 1985), con particolare riferimento ai diagrammi degli abiti esaminati.

47. *Antony van Dyck*, a cura di Arthur K. Wheelock, Jr., et al. [cat. mostra, National Gallery of Art] (Washington, 1990), 193–195.

48. Paolo Foglietta, *Rime diverse in Lingua Genovese* (Pavia, 1583):

E se l'homo a ra fin pu ra frustava
Mille cose da puossa fa ne poeiva,
Come vesti suoe figi se o ne haveiva,
Perché ra toga noe se tagiucava.
Ma demo aura a' re robe mille tagi,
Si costa chi u' dra toga, e duran men,
E a mettesere, e tra chi u' breiga ghemo
E como fruste un poco este robe hemo,
Ne fazemo a i oxelli spaventaggi,
Che atro fa no poemo noi Citten.

Traduzione libera: "E se l'uomo alla fine la usurava/ Ne poteva fare mille cose/ Come vestire i suoi figlioli se ne aveva/ perché la Toga non si tagliuzzava/ ma ora diamo alle vesti mille tagli/ così costano più della toga e durano meno/ e appena abbiamo usurato un po' le vesti/ ne facciamo spaventapasseri per gli uccelli/ perché noi Cittadini non ne possiamo fare nient'altro." Sull'uso di praticare tagli decorativi ai tessuti Arnold 1988, 185–189.

49. Bianca Du Mortier, "Costume in Frans Hals," in *Frans Hals* [cat. mostra, Royal Academy of Arts] (London, 1989), 45–60, 55.

50. Arnold 1988, 199–200, fig. 282.

51. Zabata 1583, 55, "già si costumavano li busti tanto larghi che cadevano fin a meza braccia per mostrare maggior ampiezza nelle spalle, il che non solo era cosa mostruosa, & brutta a vedere il far delle braccia spalle, ma grandissimo impedimento ci apportava alla persona senza gratia, né vaghezza alcuna . . ." ed ancora, 56, "ho voluto dar questo essempio per quello che già si costumava fare tra le nostre donne, le quali pensavano con il bambagio, e con il canevazzo piegato in mille doppie coprire l'artificio loro." Anche la Arnold (1988, 197) fa riferimento all'uso di imbottire le spalle.

52. In altri documenti "pimpinelle," tipi di passamani sottili in filati metallici.

53. L'abbigliamento maschile fu regolato con la *Riforma circa lo vestir de gli Huomini fatta l'Anno 1582*, in Biblioteca Universitaria Genova, *Liber Decretorum* (1576–1590), Ms.C.VI.2; quello femminile con *Pramatica intorno al vestito, et ornato delle donne, fatta detto anno 1582*, in A.S.G., Miscellanea Senato, Sala B. Senarega, n. 1069, diffusa in grida pubblica nel febbraio 1583.

Le due normative sono state riproposte insieme nel 1594: *Riforma fatta circa le Pompe*, in A.S.G., Miscellanea Senato, Sala B. Senarega, n. 1069. Coloro che facevano passamanerie erano congregati nella corporazione dei "Treninieri," che, secondo un documento

(A.S.G., Artium, Busta 178, n. 25) relativo alla corporazione, nel 1614 contava 300 iscritti. Nel 1630 in occasione della tassazione per le nuove mura (A.S.G., Camera 2605) erano 135.

54. *Capitoli delle Pompe* (Genova, 1605) in A.S.G., Miscellanea Senato, Sala B. Senarega, n. 1069. I margaritini sono una delle guarnizioni che si riscontra più spesso nei documenti (ad esempio l'inventario delle vesti di Brigida Spinola Doria [nota 14] e la descrizione dell'abito di Anton Giulio Brignole Sale nel 1626, nota 26); sembra di capire che si trattasse di piccoli cannelli di vetro forati. La moda durò a lungo: nel 1640 il vestito di Cesare Gentile è "ricamato a canutigli neri": Claudio Filippi, *Capriccio poetico* (Milano, 1640), recentemente pubblicato in *Domenico Fiasella*, a cura di Franco Vazzoler [cat. mostra, Palazzo Reale] (Genova, 1990), 259–274, 272. Il termine canutiglia (Beccaria 1968, 95–96) deriva dallo spagnolo *can(n)ut(t)iglia, cannutiglio, canotiglia*: striscioline d'argento battuto e d'oro, un poco attorcigliate, che si usano per ricami. La voce deriva dallo spagnolo *canutillo* o *canutillo* = cannello. Si ritiene più probabile questa derivazione per i margaritini in vetro. Lo spagnolismo comincia a diffondersi dai primi del 500.

55. (Genova, 1613) in A.S.G., Miscellanea Senato, Sala B. Senarega, n. 1069.

56. A.S.C.G., Gian Francesco Brignole I, 1620 in 1627, n. 48, *Cartulare*, c. 88, "Spese del vestire." Si confrontino anche i costi della guarnizione "d'oro di vermigli per roba verde" di Paolina che ammontavano a 1155.12 lire nel 1626 (nota 27).

57. La dama ritratta è stata tradizionalmente identificata con Geronima Doria di Paolo sposata con Filippo Spinola, Susan J. Barnes, "Van Dyck in Italy: 1621–1628," tesi dottorale (New York, 1986), 311–312.

58. Mirella Levi D'Ancona, *The Garden of the Renaissance* (Firenze, 1977), 272–277.

59. Tommaso Rinuccini, *Le usanze fiorentine del secolo XVII*, a cura di Pietro Fanfani (Firenze, 1863), 18.

60. Nella legge suntuaria del 1571 (*Capitoli di nuovo formati nel vestire tanto per le donne quanto huomini . . .* [Genova, 1571]) si parla di "Giacchette, camisette & Ungaresche"; nel citato inventario di Gaspare Carroccio del 1658 si parla di una "camicietta d'ormesino giallo cioè falde, busto e maniche guarnite d'argento." Per una "camisetta" di Paolina Adorna Brignole Sale si acquistano nel 1626 (A.S.C.G., Gian Francesco Brignole I, 1620 in 1627, n. 48, *Cartulare*, c. 327) 529 palmi (129,60 metri!) di "lavori d'argento," difficile pensare che servissero per l'ornamento di una camicia da sotto. Del resto per confezionare una "camisietta" di Geronima Brignole si acquistano 31 palmi di ormesino nero nel 1608 e 32 di damasco nero e tanè [= marrone chiaro] per una zimarra, che—come è noto—era una sopraveste.

61. Zabata 1583, 61. L'ultima frase dimostra in quale onore fossero tenute le manifatture milanesi.

62. Non mi è chiaro se sia riferita a questo passo la

seguente frase, scritta in fondo al paragrafo concernente le vesti nella *Riforma fatta l'anno 1594*: "con potersi portare li detti colori da ogni stagione, non ostante le limitazioni de' detti Capitoli."

63. Il manto si drappeggiava attorno al corpo ed era trattenuto su una spalla o sul petto da un nodo o una fibbia (come nel caso di Geronima). Vecellio 1590, a proposito delle dame genovesi, osserva: "Di sopra alle vesti poi si annodano con qualche brochetta d'oro alcuni manti, o sbernie di diverso colore delle vesti, ma di seta colorata, quale lasciano pendere fino alla lunghezza delle vesti." Sull'origine e la diffusione di questo capo di abbigliamento si rimanda a Carmen Bernis, "La 'Sbernia' y la 'Berne' en Italia y Francia," *Waffen und Kostümkunde,* parte 1 (1960), 27–40; François Boucher, "La Berne en Europe," *Waffen und Kostümkunde,* parte 2 (1961), 108–113; Janet Arnold, "Jane Lambarde's Mantle," *Costume* 14 (1980), 56–72.

64. Si veda nota 52.

65. Si veda A.S.C.G., Gian Francesco Brignole I, 1620 in 1627, n. 48, *Cartulare,* "spese per il matrimonio di Maria Maddalena," c. 55 e "spese del vestire," c. 88. Sulla tipologia dei pizzi più diffusi nel periodo considerato si veda Santina M. Levey, *Lace* (London, 1983), 11–20.

66. Ruth M. Anderson, "The Golilla: A Spanish Collar of the 17th Century," *Waffen und Kostümkunde* 1 (1969), 1–19, 3–5.

67. Anderson 1969, 1.

68. Francisco Gomez de Quevedo Villegas, *Acusanse de sus culpas los cuellos cuando se introdujeron las valonas,* citata da Anderson 1969, 5, cui si rimanda per le notizie relative all'uso della golilla in Spagna.

69. Maria Teresa Binaghi Olivari, "I pizzi nell'abbigliamento," in *I Pizzi: Moda e Simbolo* [cat. mostra, Museo Poldi Pezzoli] (Milano, 1977), 7-21. 15. Per il colletto del tipo "à la confusion" indossato dal *Bambino* ritratto da Van Dyck di Palazzo Spinola, Cataldi Gallo 1989, 85. Si confronti inoltre il *Ritratto di Gian Carlo Doria* dipinto da Simon Vouet (Museo del Louvre, Parigi) databile intorno al 1621.

70. Nell'inventario dei beni di Marieta Valle, moglie di Gian Battista Rebeccho del 1618 (A.S.G., Notaio Gian Francesco Valdetaro, scansia 382 filza n. 158 o 159) sono indicati: "colari due con le sciorete di Cambrè" e "revertiche e corpi di colari n.18."

Nell'inventario dei beni di Oriettina Fieschi (figlia del quondam Alessandro) in A.D.G.G., Fondo Pallavicino, filza n. 45, n. 18, 1627, si legge: "7 rivertiche con sua trappella [= golilla?] e quattro senza; 8 corpi per collaro; 2 riverticche con ponte piccole di Fiandra." Anche in quello di Gaspare Carroccio (A.S.G., Notaio Giuseppe Celesia, scansia 1040 filza 1) del 1658 troviamo: "colli osia riverticche n.14 . . . et uno pezzo di retino giallo per far collari." Nel libri contabili delle "Brignoline," le fanciulle ospitate nel Conservatorio di Nostra Signora del Rifugio, fondato da Emanuele Brignole nel 1641 (*Maggiore Protettori del Rifugio,* 1641–1664), si riscontrano moltissime voci relative alla confezione di "riverticche." In Giacomo Casaccia, *Dizionario Genovese—Italiano* (Genova, 1876; edizione consultata Cosenza, 1964) alla voce "revertega" si legge: "collarino: striscia di tela azzurra che si porta al collare de' preti."

71. Per un approfondimento si rimanda a Claudio Costantini et al., *Dibattito politico e problemi di governo a Genova nella prima metà del Seicento* (Firenze, 1975). Ringrazio in particolare Chicca Gallo Tomasinelli e Franco Vazzoler, che mi ha gentilmente indicato i testi letterari di maggiore interesse nell'ottica di questa ricerca.

72. Per l'attuale identificazione dei personaggi ritratti si rimanda a Boccardo, in questo stesso volume.

73. Il monarca lo indossò in una battaglia presso Danzica nel 1627, in *Sweden: A Royal Treasury* [cat. mostra, National Gallery of Art, Washington] (Princeton, 1988), 30.

74. Uno dei *Tre fanciulli,* Genova, Collezione Durazzo-Pallavicini e dei *Fanciulli Balbi,* Londra, National Gallery of Art; *Fanciullo con cane,* Dublino, National Gallery of Ireland.

75. A.S.G., Notaio Giacomo Lanata, scansia 792 filza 4, "Nel guardarobba sotto la terazza coperta ci sono le infrascritte robbe."

76. Barnes 1986, 106.

77. Arnold 1985, 28–29.

78. In quel periodo lavoravano a Genova molti artigiani inglesi, fra cui il sarto Tomaso Radcliff; vedi Marzia Cataldi Gallo, "Anglomania," in *L'uniforme borghese* (Milano, 1991).

79. François Boucher, *Histoire du costume en France,* 2ª ed. (Paris, 1983), 278.

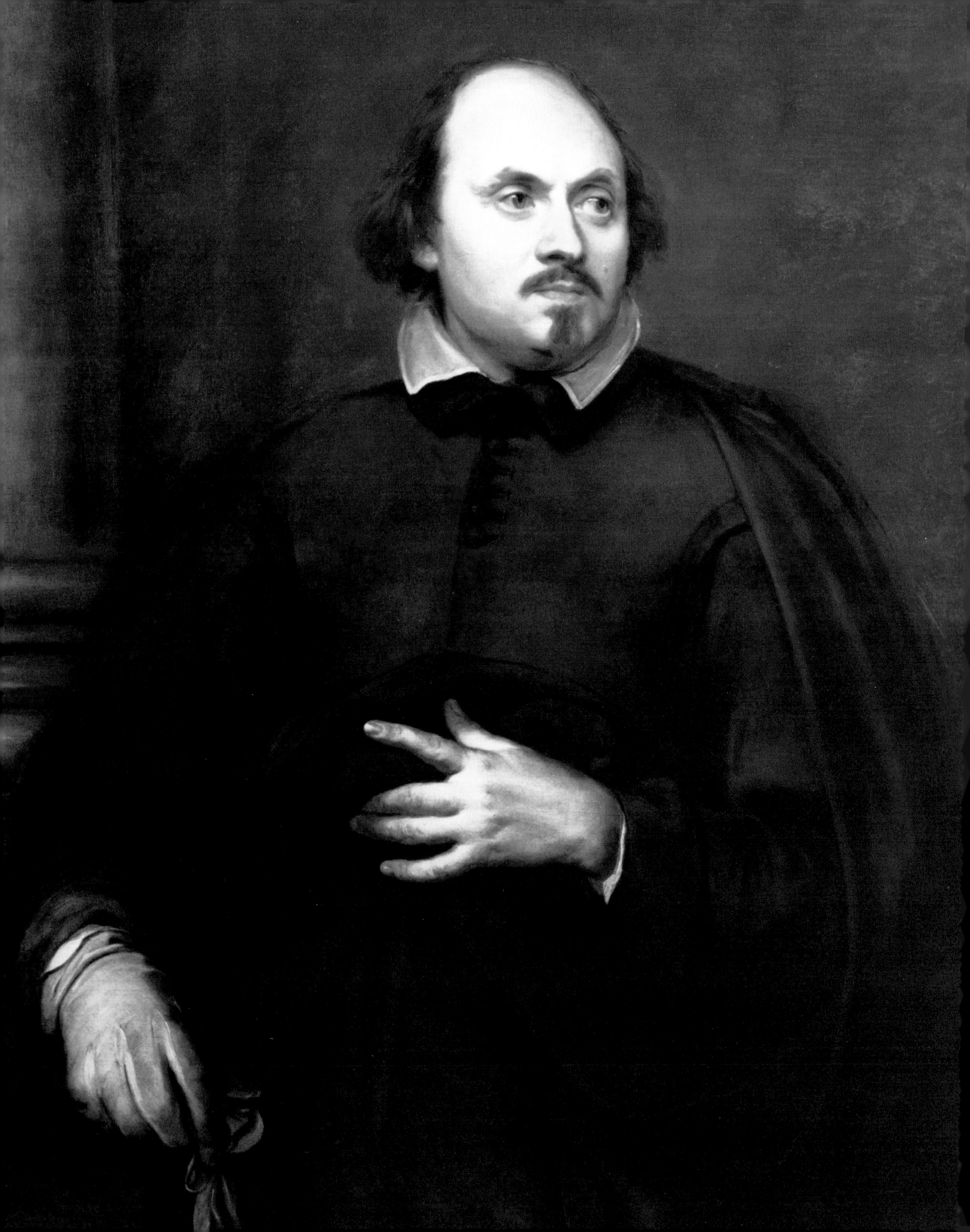

MICHAEL JAFFÉ
Fitzwilliam Museum, Cambridge (emeritus)

On Some Portraits Painted by Van Dyck in Italy, Mainly in Genoa

Van Dyck's *Self-Portrait* in St. Petersburg (fig. 1) is dated by Susan Barnes about 1623.[1] She sensibly associates the brushwork with that of the portrait identifiable as that of *Filippo Cattaneo* (National Gallery of Art, Washington), aged four years and seven months, which is dated that very year. In reviewing the Van Dyck exhibition at the National Gallery of Art for the February 1991 issue of the *Burlington Magazine*, I remarked the significance of the broken column depicted beside the painter, on which he rests his right arm with conscious Raphaelite grace. This stump, which to Susan Barnes "suggests antique architecture" and "gives further evidence for placing the work about or just after Van Dyck's Roman visits in 1622 and 1623," suggests to me something more precise and more poignant: mourning for his father who died in Antwerp on 1 December 1622.

News of the death of Frans van Dyck would have reached Italy within weeks. The self-scrutiny by the bereaved son, in the worldly sense the new head of his family, is likely to have been painted in January or at the latest February 1623. Whether or not it was dispatched by Van Dyck to his brothers and sisters sheltered in Antwerp, it appears as an immediate expression of private grief; and we find the same appropriate imagery in the portrait of the brothers-in-law *Killigrew and Crofts* (fig. 2), which Van Dyck signed and dated fifteen years later in England. Within a year of his return from Italy Van Dyck was to paint as a public memorial, in

pious fulfillment of a promise made on his behalf by his father to the Dominican nuns, the altarpiece of the *Crucifixion with Saints Dominic and Catherine of Siena*.[2] The only other self-portrait to be dated with even greater confidence in the painter's Italian years is the one manifestly incomplete, but which autoradiography has revealed upside down beneath the *Santa Rosalia Interceding for the Plague-Stricken of Palermo* belonging to the Metropolitan Museum of Art, New York. The latter work must have been painted in Palermo in the summer of 1624.[3]

In more than one way the Hermitage *Self-Portrait* stands out in Van Dyck's Italian period. It is highly personal, and the identification of the person is indubitable. It is exceptionally well preserved, and it is closely datable by style and circumstance. There are indeed few portraits of men painted by Van Dyck south of the Alps of which one can say as much: the *Agostino Pallavicini* (J. Paul Getty Museum, Malibu), robed as an ambassador to the Holy See, painted shortly after Pallavicini's return from Rome and during Van Dyck's first stay in Genoa between late November 1621 and February 1622; the *Sir Robert Shirley* (National Trust, Petworth House), painted during the Shirleys' passage through Rome between 22 July and 29 August 1622; the *Emmanuel Philiberto of Savoy* (Dulwich Picture Gallery, London), painted in Palermo between spring and the end of June 1624; and, despite its poor state, the *Cardinal Guido Bentivoglio* (Pitti Palace,

Florence), probably painted on Van Dyck's second visit to Rome between March and October/November 1623. Two brilliant portraits of *Lucas van Uffel* have generally been considered to have been painted between August and October 1622 when Van Dyck was in Venice, on the assumption that the merchant remained static in the Serenissima. This is by no means certain. Stylistically the portrait in the Metropolitan Museum of Art consorts with the *Bentivoglio* and might have been painted in Rome. The mountainous coast viewed through the casement in the Herzog Anton Ulrich-Museum portrait in Braunschweig is more reminiscent of Liguria than of the northern Adriatic. According to the anonymous manuscript biography of Van Dyck in the Musée du Louvre, the double portrait of *Cornelis and Lucas de Wael* (Pinacoteca Capitolina, Rome) was a parting present by the artist to those brothers who had been his hosts in Genoa.

When did Van Dyck decide to quit Italy? Susan Barnes prudently dates the Pinacoteca Capitolina double portrait, which owes something to Lotto, something to Raphael, about 1626. The lack of finish, most obvious in the hands but also visible in the drapery, suggests that it was painted in 1627, on the very eve, as it were, of departure. Was the standing figure of the Genoese *Cardinal Rivarola* (Iowa State Education Association, Des Moines), who died in 1626, painted by Van Dyck in Rome rather than in Genoa? Probably. Van Dyck seems to have painted in Rome, more likely in 1622 than 1623, the group portrait of George Gage being offered a piece of statuary (National Gallery, London); and he painted the pale *Roman Cleric* (Hermitage, St. Petersburg), seated so conversationally in an armchair, in 1623 rather than 1622, for that portrait is painted over an adumbration of the *Bentivoglio*. All those other portraits of men, as well as of women—with the signal exception of *Teresia, Lady Shirley* (National Trust, Petworth House)—that are claimed with justification to have been painted by Van Dyck in Italy are assumed to have been painted in Genoa of members of the local patriciate. Whereas the provenance of several portraits from particular palaces may be distinct, an embarrassing number of portraits are now recognized to have been dubbed with the names of families, or, de-

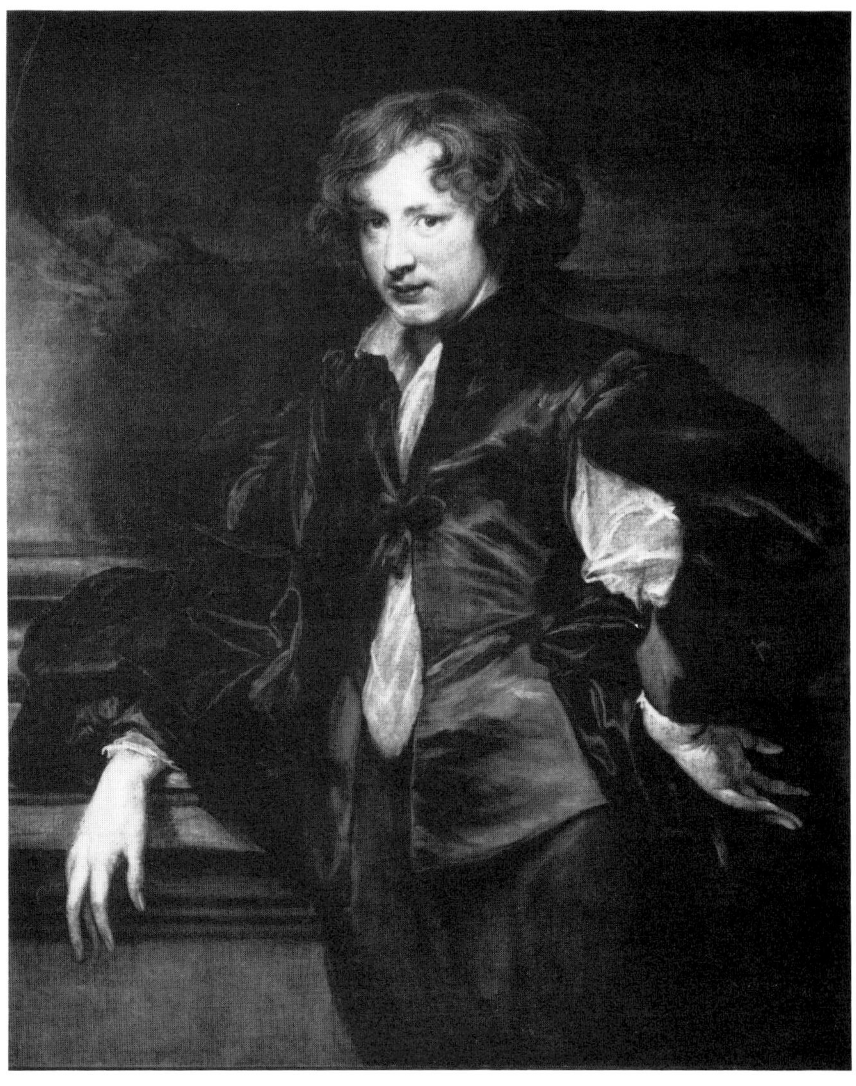

1. Anthony van Dyck, *Self-Portrait,* 1623, oil on canvas
Hermitage, St. Petersburg

spite changes of ownership, with the names of those palaces from which agents such as Buchanan, Irving, Wallis, or Wilson acquired them: Balbi, Brignole Sale, Cattaneo, Doria, Grimaldi, Imperiale, Lomellini, Pallavicini, Spinola. Unlike at least one early eighteenth-century member of the newer nobility in Genoa (to whom I shall return), clients abroad during the period from about 1820 to 1920 were not in the market for portraits by Van Dyck unless they had social éclat. Household tradition was invoked or a plausible guess made to supply patronymic or even baptismal names.

More genealogical and heraldic delving has to be done, as well as research into letters, diaries, account books, inventories, and guides, in order to support arguments based on stylistic development. In these pursuits two men

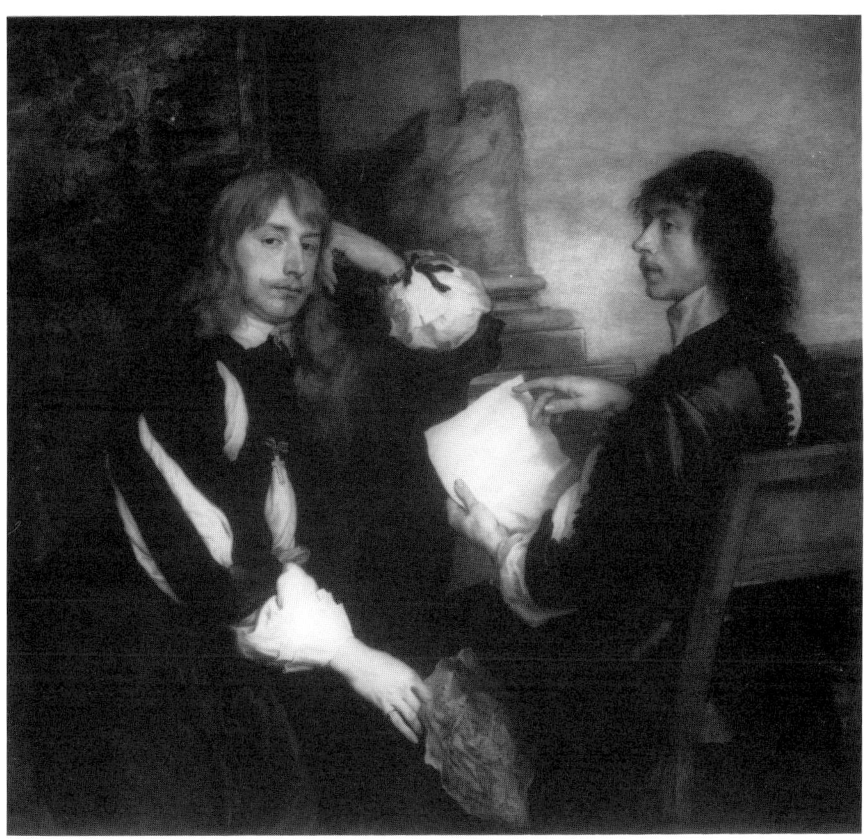

2. Anthony van Dyck,
*Thomas Killigrew and
William, Lord Crofts*, 1638,
oil on canvas
Her Majesty Queen Elizabeth II

living in Genoa have been notably success-ful: Dino Puncuh, an archivist who has put in order the Durazzo archive at the Palazzo Durazzo-Pallavicini,[4] and Piero Boccardo, historian of Genoese families and of the works of art they commissioned. I wish to pay tribute to these scholars in presenting material from my own observation and searches.

A part of the difficulty in discussing Van Dyck's Genoese portraits is the very varied state of their preservation. Gustav Waagen in 1854 reported at Hopetoun House, outside Edinburgh, a full-length of the man identified as *Filippo, Son of Ambrogio Spinola* (fig. 3),[5] which had been bought in 1827 by Andrew Wilson from a Marchesa Grimaldi for the earl of Hopetoun. It is now in Brisbane. According to Emil Schaeffer in 1909 the companion picture (fig. 4) of Geronima, Filippo Spinola's wife, the daughter of Paolo Doria, which was acquired by the Kaiser Friedrich-Museum in Berlin from Adolf Thiem in San Remo, came from the Palazzo De' Fornari in Genoa.[6] When I recommended the acquisition of the man's portrait to the new Queensland Art Gallery in 1981, I was provided by

Lord Hopetoun from his family archives at Hopetoun with a letter written to his ancestor by Andrew Wilson. It explains why the wife's portrait was left in Spinola possession.

1827. October 30. Andrew Wilson, Genoa, to the Earl of Hopetoun, Hopetoun House.
My Lord,

I beg to inform your Lordship that I have succeeded in purchasing one of the whole length portraits by Vandyke which I had taken the liberty of proposing to your Lordship through Sir Alexr.Hope as suitable acquisitions for the collection at Hopetoun House.

I came here under the idea of finding both the pictures nearly of equal merit but on examination I found that I could only fully approve that of the Gentleman in Armour; the portrait of the lady is also a good picture but has suffered more from time and Vandyke's genius seems not to have been much excited in the execution; in regard to the portrait of the Gentleman he has made more of it than a mere portrait, it is rich in composition and colouring and is in every respect one of the finest works of the Master.

The picture I have purchased for your Lordship is the resemblance of a person apparently under Forty dressed in armour fine manly figure hansome countenance, the head uncovered, his helmet lying at his left foot, on the right of the figure a rich crimson curtain on the left part of a Column beyond which is the head of a white horse held by a servant.

I have experienced great difficulty in purchasing the one picture without its companion but I am so well acquainted with the collection at Hopetoun House I could not even although I could have obtained the two on still more reasonable terms think of encumbring the collection with a single picture merely as a companion to the other unless it was of a quality to enrich it as a whole.

I have during my residence here examined every collection and I have seen many Vandykes that I have reason to believe will be sold, there is a family picture in the Lomalini Palace [fig. 5], and a half-length of a Lady most excellent pictures; therefore I think I could do better at a future time than at present for Hopetoun House meantime your Lordship will be able to judge from the picture at present to be sent off, of the propriety of my making any further acquisitions during my stay in Italy.

I do not attempt anything like a particular discription of the picture I have purchased, it must be seen, but the head is quite perfect and

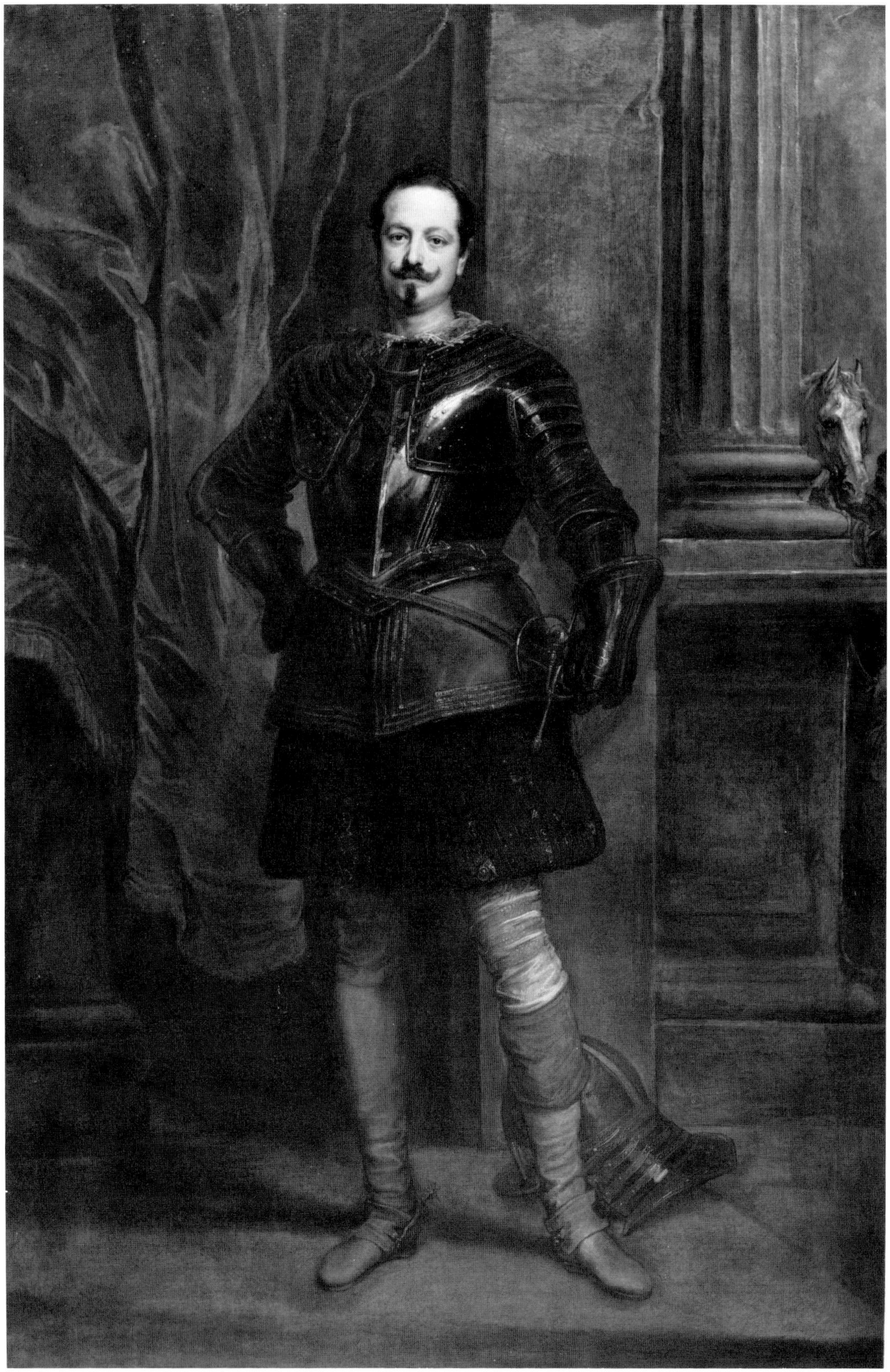

3. Anthony van Dyck,
Filippo di Ambrogio Spinola,
c. 1623, oil on canvas
Queensland Art Gallery, Brisbane

4. Anthony van Dyck,
*Geronima Doria, Wife of
Filippo Spinola*, c. 1623,
oil on canvas
Gemäldegalerie, Berlin

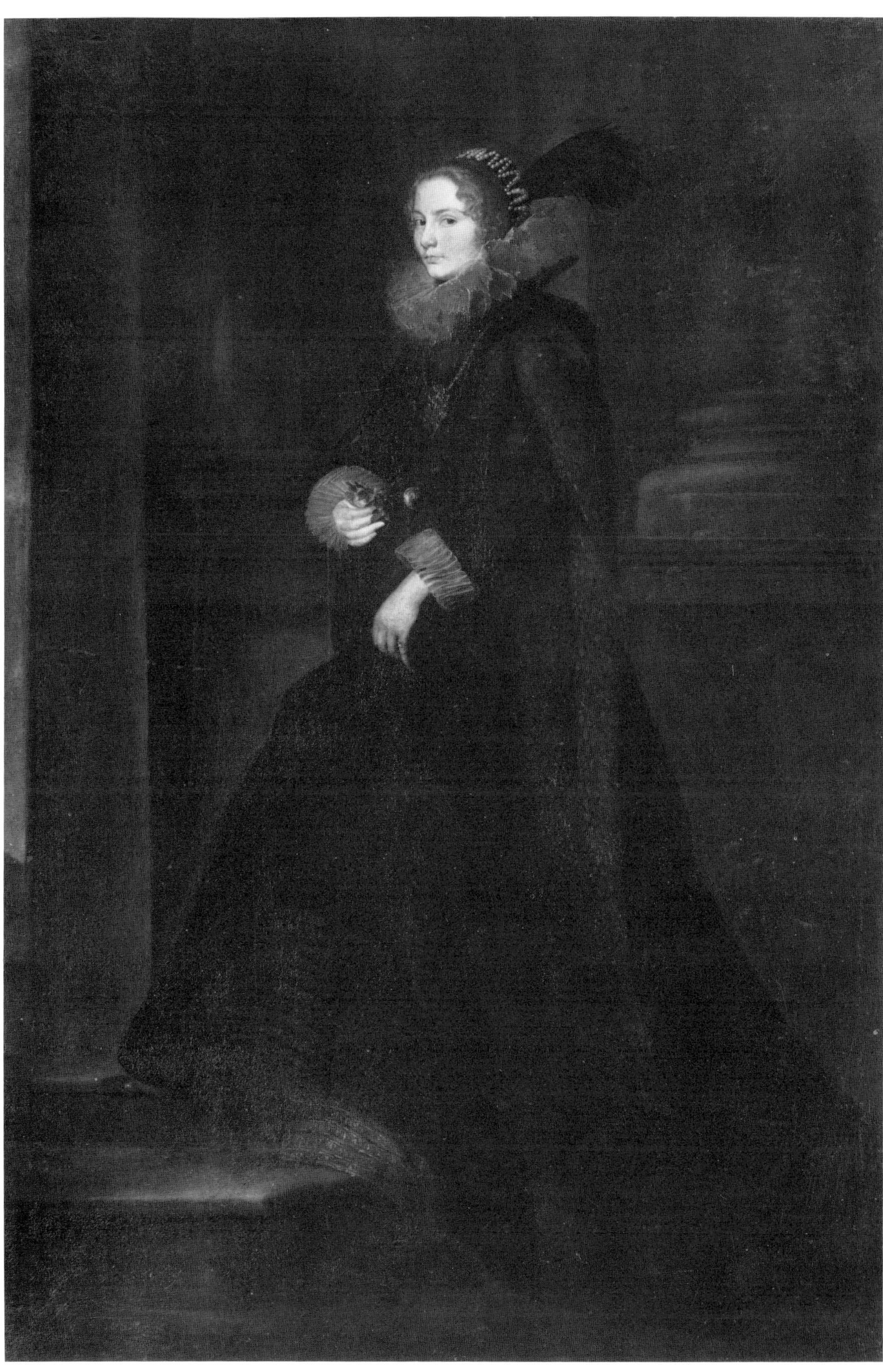

equal in point of preservation to that of any picture in existance by Vandyke. The picture will require to be varnished on its arrival at Leith. I have had it new lined for fear of accidents on the voyage as all pictures here are in too tender a condition to travel also a new stretching frame; I intend forwarding it by a vessel which is to sail immediately for Liverpool which I think the most secure mode as the case will not be opened before it arrives at Leith; at the Customs-house in London they do not allow cases to be reshipped without their being opened.

I mentioned to Sir Alexr.Hope that the pictures were of the Grimaldi family this was a mistake into which I was led by Mr William Wilkie; they belonged to a Spinola who is married to a Sr. Grimaldi and the picture I have bought is supposed to be of the Son of the Celebrated General Spinola who commanded in the Netherlands under I think Phillip the 2nd.

The Picture costs your Lordship here one hundred and ninety Five pounds Stg including Brokerage, new lining, packing case and twenty per cent duty I have therefore drawn on your Lordship for the above sum at fifteen days sight to the order of Messrs. Couts and Co. London.

In regard the price of the picture it is under the estimate price of similar picture in any other of the palaces here; immediately the picture is shipped I shall transmit to your Lordship the Bill of Lading. My Draft is under the date of yesterday the 29th Inst.

I have the honour to be

My Lord with the greatest respect

Your Lordships

most Obedient Servt.

Wilson's account of the respective states of preservation of this pair, as each appeared to him over a century and a half ago, seems just today. Less just seems the reason apparently given by the Metropolitan Museum of Art for discarding, not quite a decade ago, another full-length of a Genoese man (fig. 6), which had been published by Gustav Glück[7] when it was in the collection of William R. Timken in New York. It came to the Metropolitan Museum in 1951 from Timken's widow. To my knowledge it was never exhibited at the museum, but only in Tokyo and Kyoto between August and November 1972 in an exhibition entitled *Treasured Masterpieces of the Metropolitan Museum of Art*. It was said to be in a ruinous state, and

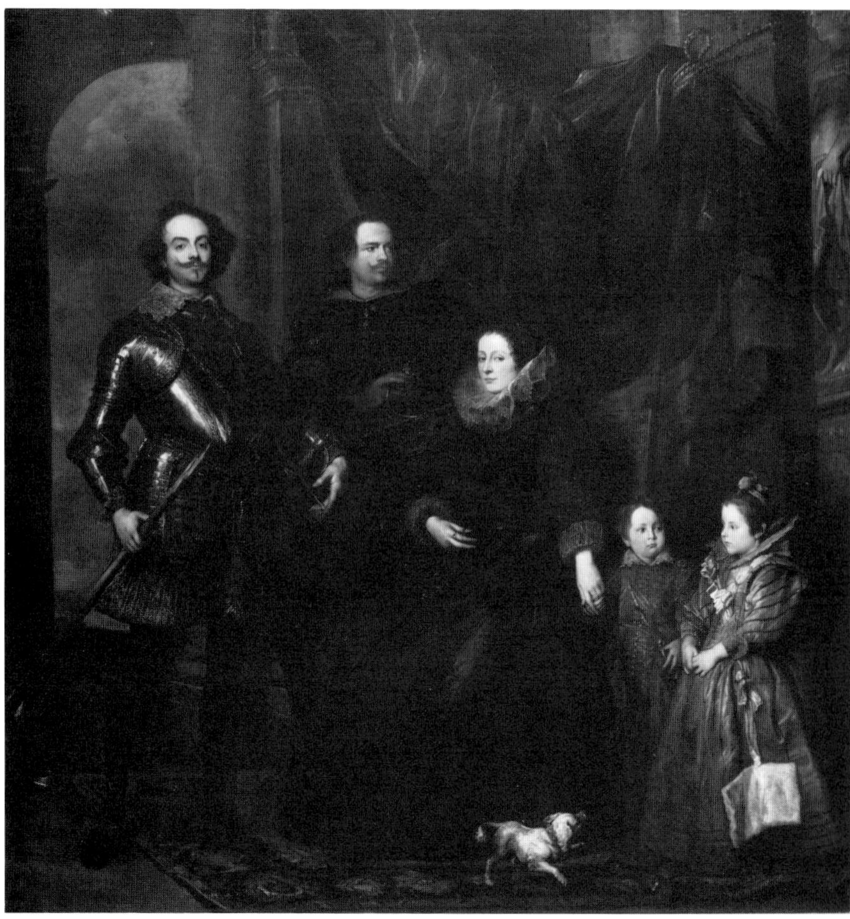

5. Anthony van Dyck, *The Family of Niccolò Lomellini,* c. 1623, oil on canvas
National Gallery of Scotland, Edinburgh

the museum allowed it to be sold. It was offered on 7 June 1984 by Sotheby's, New York, among "Property of Various Owners" as "studio of Anthony Van Dyck."[8] There is, of course, no evidence that Van Dyck employed painting assistants in Italy. The painting previously at the Metropolitan Museum is by Van Dyck himself, not by any Genoese imitator; and it has been recognized as such at least since it was acquired by Wilhelm von Bode on behalf of Oscar Huldschinsky in Berlin before 1907. In its stripped state it could be seen to have suffered in no vital respect. The black shoes and their bows, the stockinged legs exposed below the slashed breeches are particulars to have excited Velázquez on one or other of his passages through Genoa. The fashion of the breeches puffed out and slashed, *en suite* with the jacket and ending above the knee, had evidently not given way wholly as yet to the severer style of breeches extending below knee to be fastened above the calf, such as we find in the full-length portrait of a mem-

6. Here reattributed to
Anthony van Dyck,
*Unidentified Genoese
Patrician*, c. 1623,
oil on canvas
Private collection

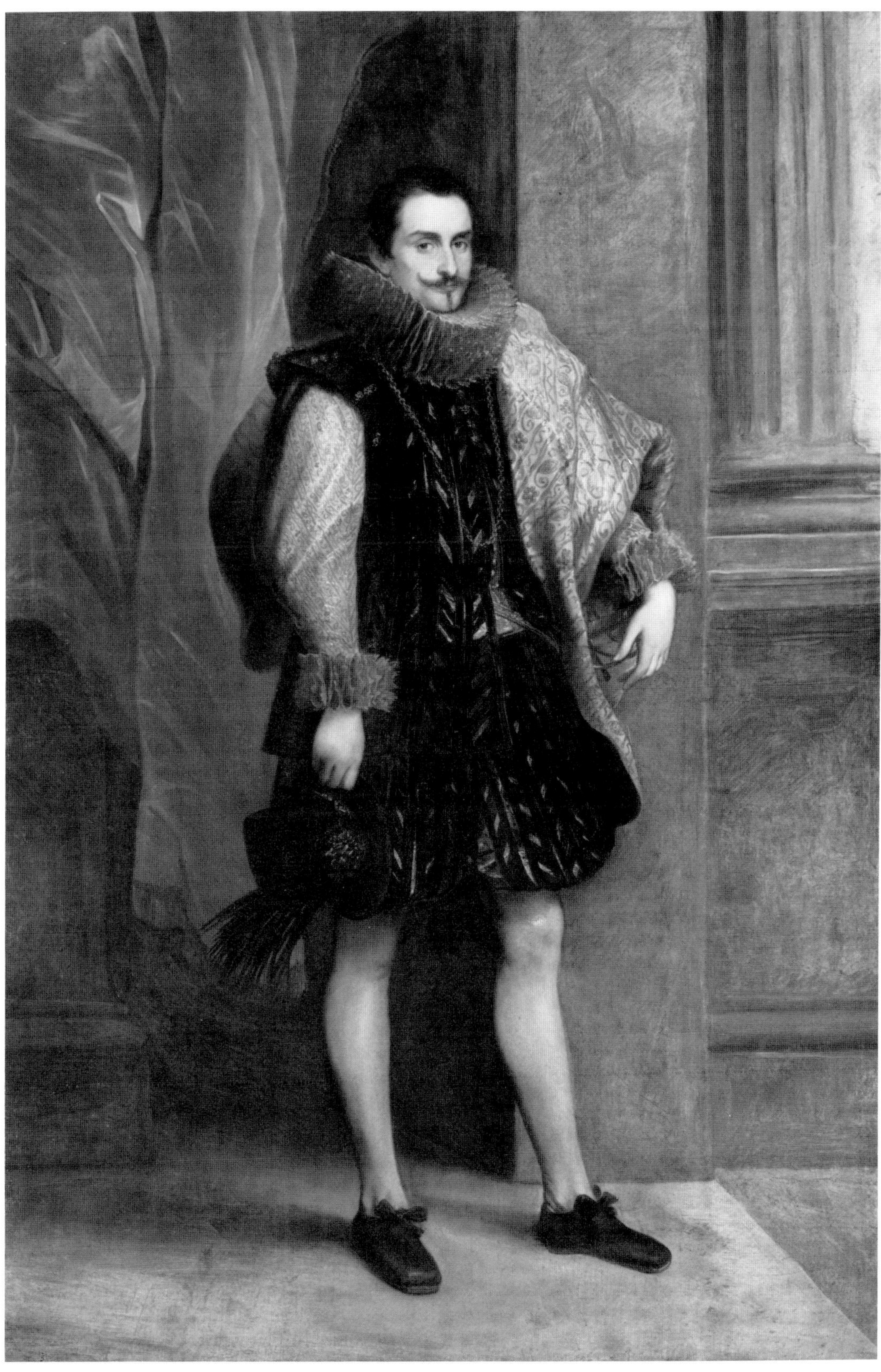

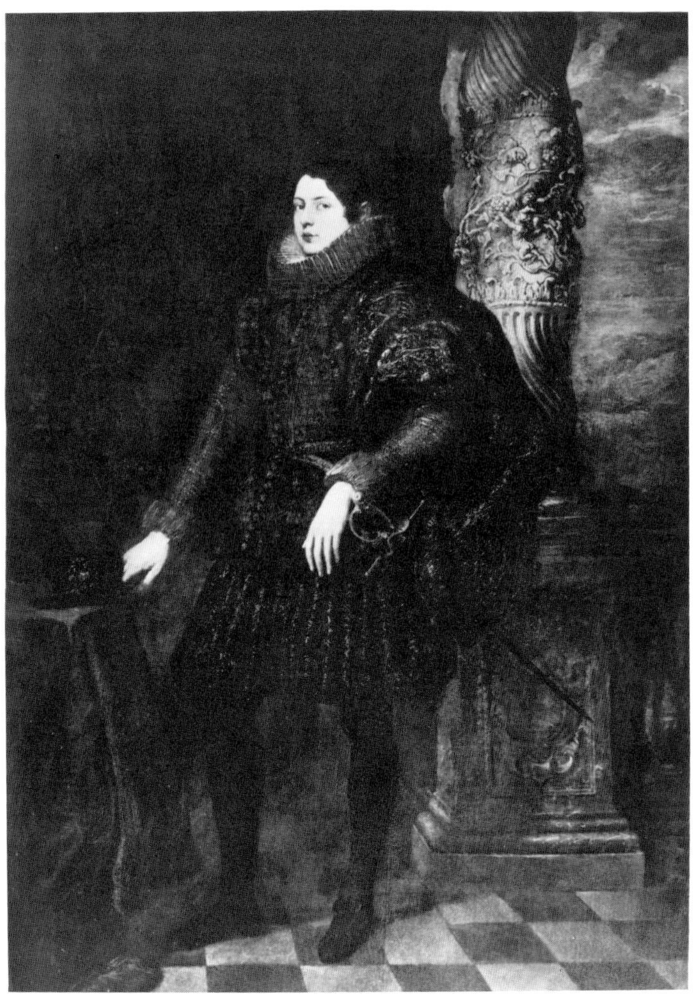

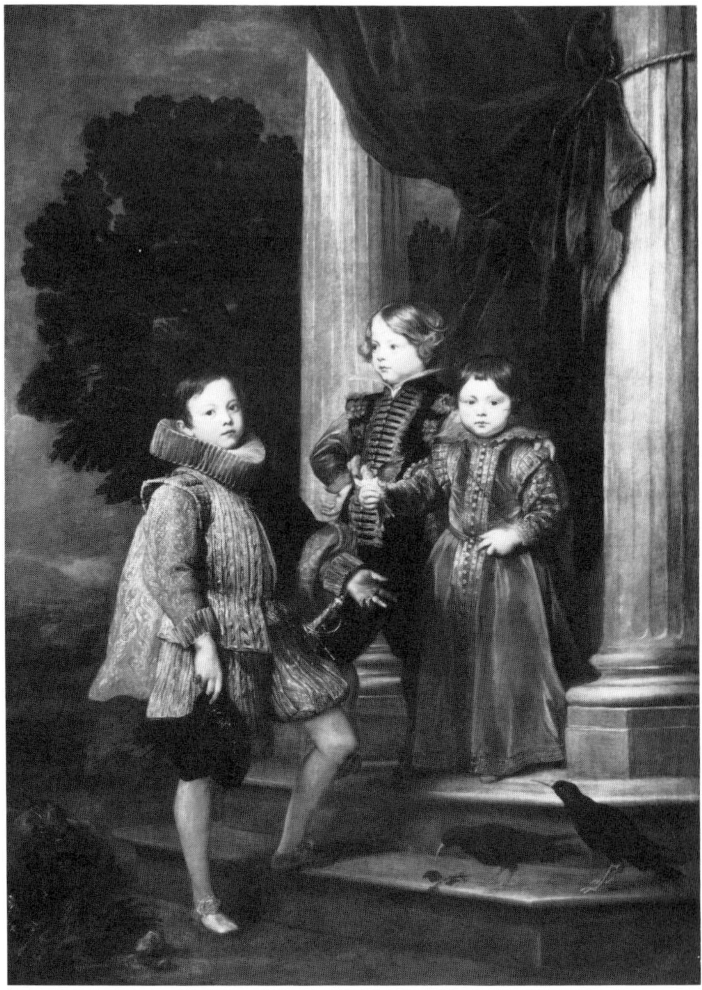

ber of the Brignole family (Galleria della Ca d'Oro, Venice). The earlier fashion is shown also by Van Dyck in another full-length of an unidentified young nobleman, which is owned by the Comune di Genova at the Palazzo Bianco (fig. 7); and it persisted as an accepted feature of military dress for men in half-armor, for example in the *Family of Niccolò Lomellini* in Edinburgh and in the *Filippo Spinola* in Brisbane. The crucial test, however, of high fashion in dress is the garb chosen for the children of the rich. In the *"Balbi Children"* (fig. 8) in the National Gallery, London, which Piero Boccardo has identified more plausibly as a portrait of the sons of Girolamo de' Franchi,[9] the eldest child, Cesare, wears the longer established dress of a ruff and breeches that are puffed and slashed, while the second son, Giovanni Benedetto, wears a *golilla* (a stiff, plain collar) and the newer Spanish style. About 1625 to 1626 it is evident that these fashions coex-

isted in fashion-conscious Genoa.

Van Dyck's portrait of Filippo Spinola is likely to have been painted on the soldier's return from the wars in 1626. The portrait of an unidentified younger, and presumably less important man (fig. 6), for whom Van Dyck did not invent a fresh setting, is likely to have been painted soon after. Indeed the stagings in these two pictures, both in the fall of drapery and in the elements of architecture, are remarkably similar except for the omission in the second work of the horse's head held by the groom. We are reminded of the exact similarities of background provided by Van Dyck for *Lady Clanbrassil* (Frick Collection, New York) and for the *Marquess of Hamilton* (Collections of the Prince of Liechtenstein, Vaduz Castle), and, as Oliver Millar has pointed out,[10] of the poses as well as the backgrounds for *Anne Kirke* (Huntington Library, San Marino, California) and for *Isabella, Lady de la Warr* (Museum of Fine

7. Anthony van Dyck, *Unidentified Genoese Patrician*, c. 1623, oil on canvas
Palazzo Bianco, Genoa

8. Anthony van Dyck, *The Three Sons of Girolamo de' Franchi ("Balbi Children")*, c. 1625, oil on canvas
National Gallery, London

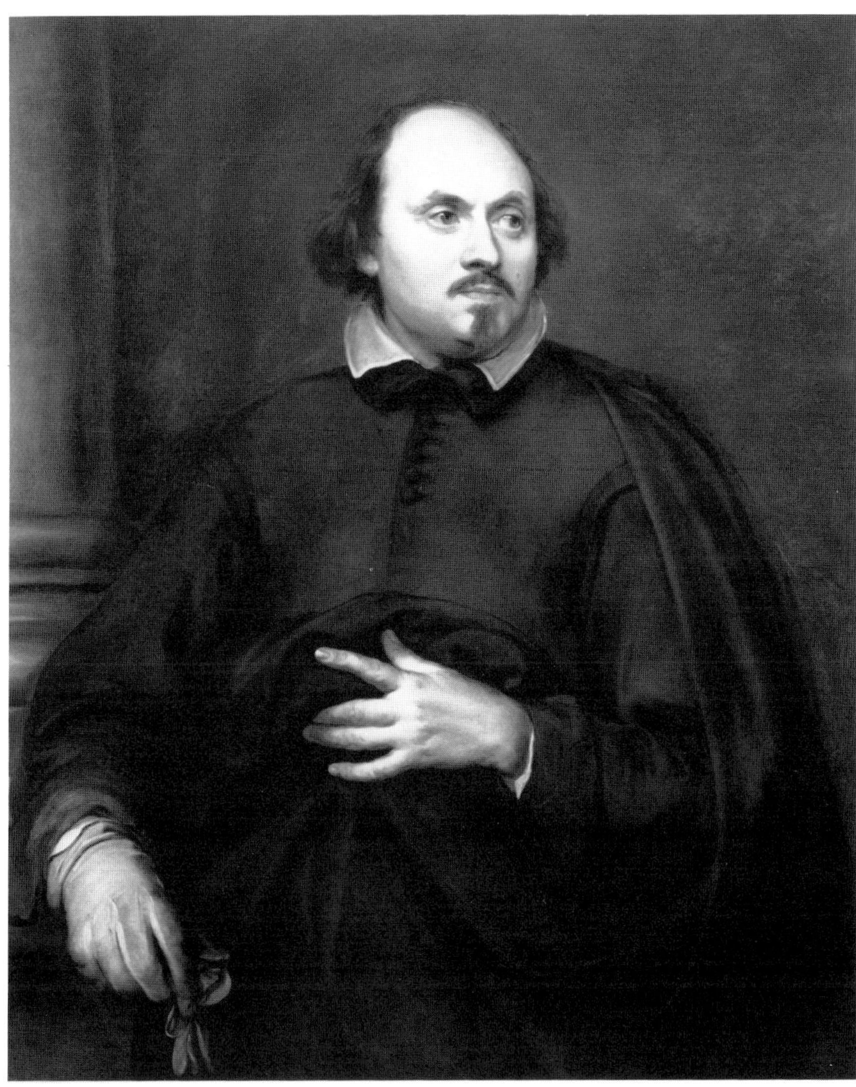

9. Here attributed to Anthony van Dyck, *Unidentified Gentleman,* c. 1623, oil on canvas
Private collection

stroke to model the jowl, as well as an iridescence in the piercing glance of the brown eyes (the left one is slightly misshapen) and an unexpended energy in the exposed right hand contrasted with the more languorous left. I would propose a date early in 1627, close to the *Cornelis and Lucas de Wael* which was painted in Genoa, and anticipating the *Peeter Stevens* (Koninklijk Kabinet van Schilderijen "Mauritshuis," The Hague), which Van Dyck signed and dated 1627 in Antwerp. Was there a pendant by Van Dyck of this man's wife? Almost our only chance of identifying the sitter, who, if he were armigerous, displays no armorials, is through an engraving or conceivably a medal or bust. However, since he appears unmilitary, there is in Genoa no readily accessible engraved reference to consult. Unlike the portrait of the brothers De Wael that was to be engraved by Wenceslaus Hollar, this man's portrait was probably still south of the Alps when Van Dyck was planning his Iconography.

Soon after Van Dyck's arrival in Genoa in 1621 we may assume that his compatriots introduced him in the palaces to the splendors of the portraits painted by Rubens fifteen years earlier: the 1606 portrait of *Brigida Spinola Doria,* posed as though standing on her terrace; the *Gian Carlo Doria* of 1606–1607, the rider who bounds toward us in his newly authorized habit as a Cavaliere di San Giacomo; and the portraits of the two Grimaldi ladies enthroned, which were bought from the Grimaldi palace in Genoa by Ralph Bankes for Kingston Lacy in Dorset. Nothing of Rubens' later work, which Van Dyck could have seen in Antwerp, would have prepared his eyes for such grandiloquence; and the lasting impact on his conception of portraiture is well known, as also are its reverberations in Genoese painting and on Velázquez passing between Spain and Italy. Yet there were no Rubens portraits to be seen of Genoese children. It was left to Van Dyck to follow the example of Titian in 1542; not only in the three-quarter-length of *Ranuccio Farnese* (National Gallery of Art, Washington), a princeling, but also in the socially daring—one could almost say revolutionary—full-length devoted to a single child not of royal birth, the two-year-old *Clarice Strozzi* (Gemäldegalerie, Berlin) fondling her pet spaniel. Titian both licensed and inspired Van

Arts, Boston).

Where should we place a recently discovered half-length, a vivid image projected by Van Dyck in Italy (fig. 9)?[11] We may guess that this sallow gentleman, a powerful personality in middle life, was indeed an Italian, affluent and distinguished in his profession but not of noble birth, quite possibly but not certainly Genoese. In his gloved right hand he holds a key on a ribbon, suggesting that he might be a treasurer or a chamberlain. His portrait was acquired about 1829 for Kinturk Castle in Westmeath, Scotland (renamed Castle Pollard after the rebuilding that followed a marriage between an Urquhart of Kinturk and a Pollard heiress). No traditional identification of the sitter has come down to us. There is a characteristic use of umber in a single dab under the chin and in a single

Dyck in a new series of portraiture of children without their parents, which he began with the *Filippo* and the *Clelia Cattaneo* (National Gallery of Art, Washington) of 1623, and which he continued until he left Italy.

Son of a Noble Genoese House (fig. 10), the portrait of a boy standing on a terrace, belonging to the National Gallery of Ireland, is painted almost as freely and economically as is the boy who stands by his mother's armchair holding her hand in the National Gallery of Art's portrait, *Genoese Noblewoman and Her Son.* Susan Barnes dates the latter about 1626. I would not dissent. The leaping dog, a domesticated and diminutive rephrasing of the curvetting hound that Van Dyck used twice compositionally in his treatments before Italy of the Venus and Adonis theme,[12] is an animating device shared by the portraits in Dublin and Washington, as is the engagement of balustraded parapets and columns. Of the provenance of the Dublin picture, which might lead to its identification, we know only that it is part of the Hugh Lane Bequest.

In cataloguing the Flemish paintings for a new book about the Galleria del Palazzo Durazzo-Pallavicini,[13] I have come to a few conclusions about the splendid group of full-lengths by Van Dyck that still adorn the *salotto primo a ponente,* having been bought for the purpose—as Dino Puncuh has elicited from the Durazzo archive[14]—by Giacomo Filippo II Durazzo. Of this group the most renowned is *"La Dama d'Oro"* (fig. 11), seated with two of her infants, undoubtedly boys not yet of an age to be breeched. The elder child, seemingly aged about five, has a manly dagger at his hip; the younger, turning away from his mother toward an invisible pendant (presumably portraying his father) and clutching an orange, seems aged three to four. The flowers in the silver vase on the red tablecloth would have offered a brilliant suggestion to Velázquez, visiting Genoa in 1629 and 1649, for his portrait painted about 1652 of the *Infanta Margherita in Pink* (this portrait, in the Kunsthistorisches Museum in Vienna, displays the only known still life in the work of Velázquez as a portraitist). Giacomo Filippo bought the Van Dyck as a Van Dyck from a member of the older nobility, Ippolito Settimio Invrea; an entry in his ledger for 11 August 1721, without identify-

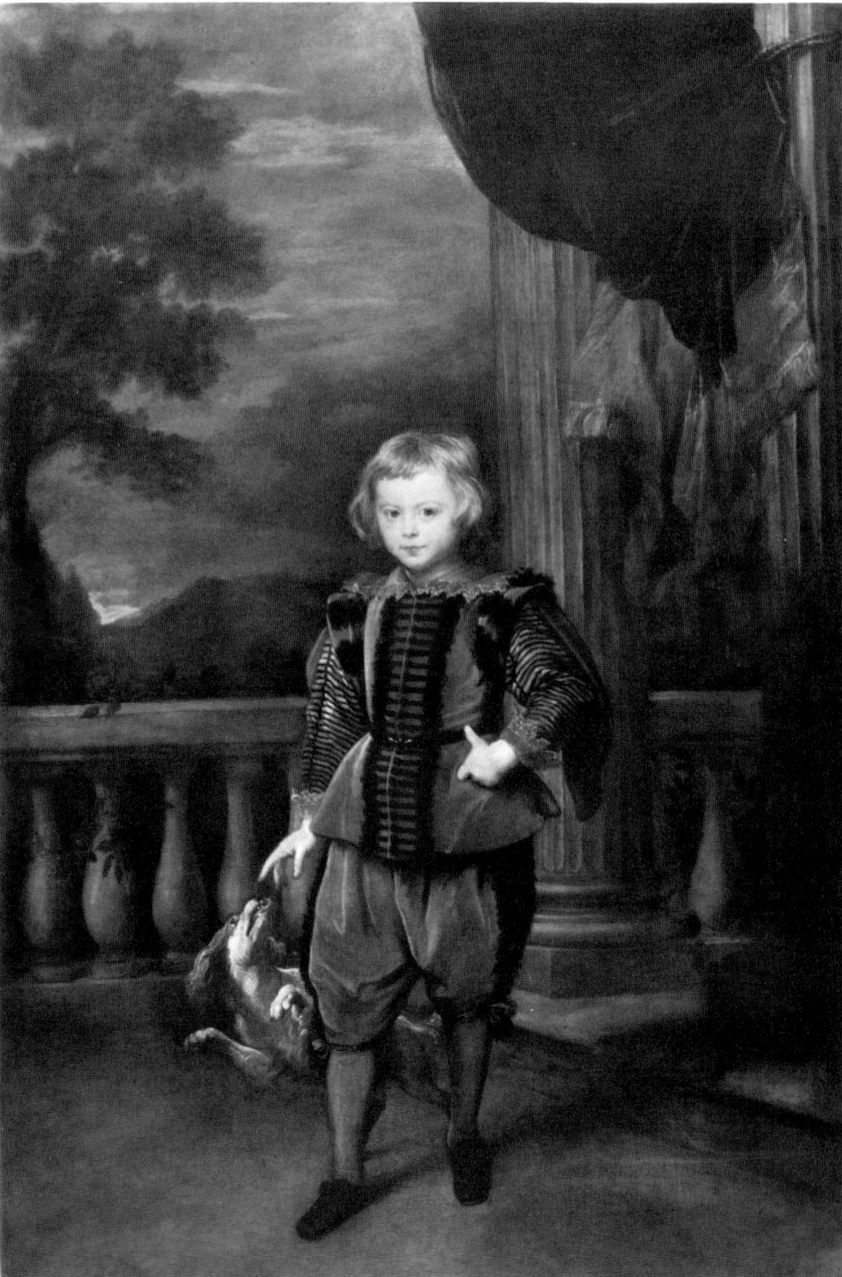

10. Anthony van Dyck, *The Son of a Noble Genoese House,* 1625–1627, oil on canvas
National Gallery of Ireland, Dublin

ing the persons represented, shows that as part of his bargain the purchaser paid 220 lire to Giovanni Andrea della Piane for replacing with a copy the empty space on the vendor's wall.[15] Piero Boccardo found in Genoa, and communicated at a 1991 symposium at the University of Maryland, an eighteenth-century inventory that enables him to be sure whose wife is thus portrayed by Van Dyck about 1626: it is Battina Balbi Durazzo Invrea with Marcello and Silvestro, her sons by an earlier Ippolito Invrea.

I turn to another image that at a glance

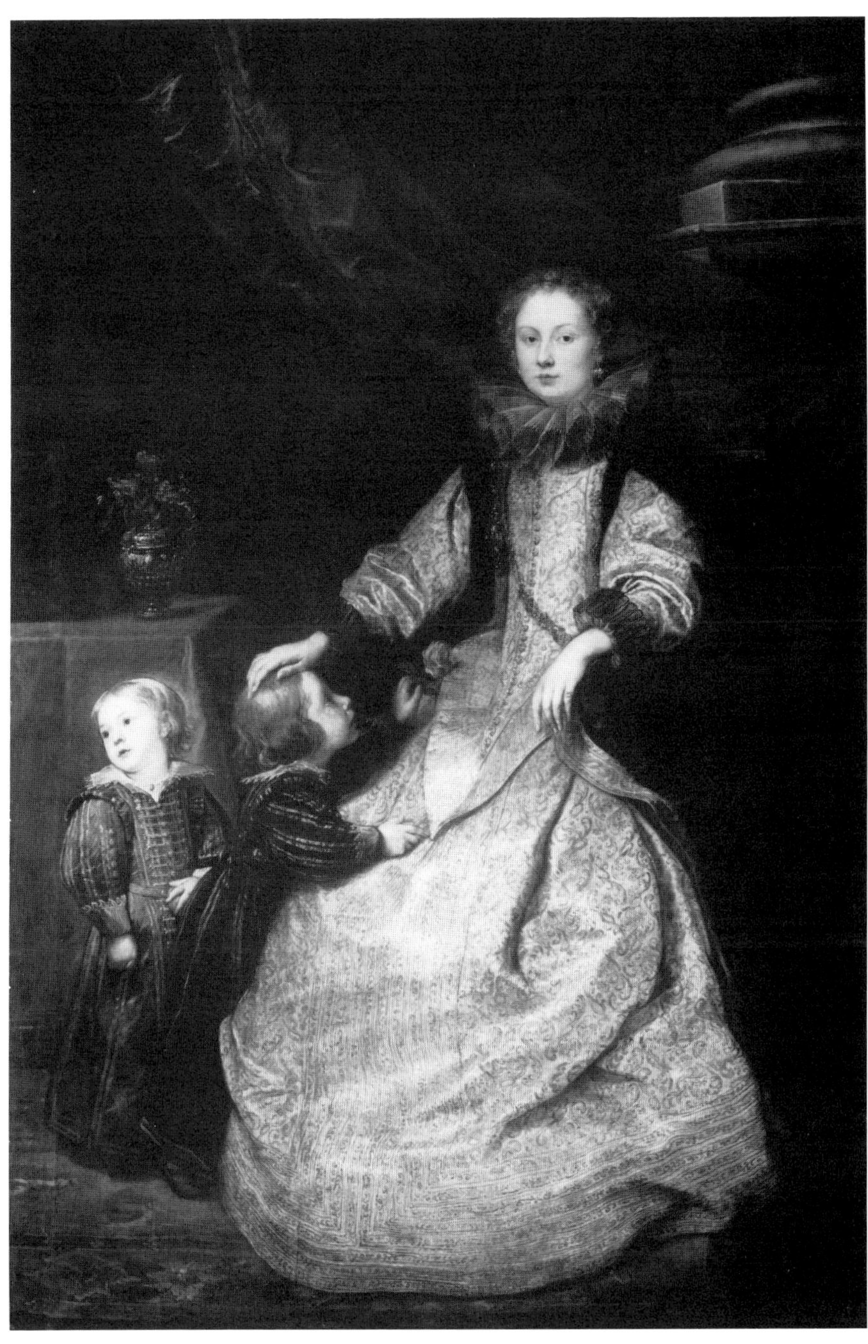

11. Anthony van Dyck, *The Marchesa Battina Balbi Durazzo Invrea with Her Sons Marcello and Silvestro* ("*La Dama d'Oro*"), 1625–1627, oil on canvas
Palazzo Durazzo-Pallavicini, Genoa

ness of the sky, the coldness of the whites, and the brushwork point firmly in that direction. In the original (fig. 13) the still life of fruit—fruit not flowers—was introduced by Van Dyck's fellow countryman, Filippo Roos, then fashionable in Genoa. But the parrot and the monkey are surely by Van Dyck himself, even though monkeys and a parrot are among the creatures charmed by the viol of Orpheus in a painting wholly by Roos, now in a Genoese private collection. Roos was a capable *animalier* as well as a painter of vegetable life, but he was no Snyders. Van Dyck would hardly have hesitated to manage without him. The copy of *"Putto Vestito di bianco"* came to Rossie Priory in Scotland about 1840 as a gift to George, 9th lord Kinnaird, from an unnamed "Dutch gentleman" in gratitude for some service. The hope to trace the family for whom it was commissioned in order to replace the original is slender. The original of 1625–1626 was bought by Giacomo Filippo not through an agent such as Nicolo Tassorello, from whom he was to buy the *"Dama d'Oro,"* but in a block purchase from Frederico Miconi and his brothers, regular dealers established near the via Balbi who, if they knew of the provenance of the paintings, would have been discreet.

A more or less contemporary portrait of another Genoese child belonging to a different private collection (fig. 14) is likewise of unknown provenance and identity.[18] When I was shown the picture twenty years ago the frame (not, alas, its first frame) bore an old label "une Princesse de Gênes," although the rather truculent infant is patently an unbreeched boy wearing a chain baldrick from which only the dagger is missing. If hardly an Adonis, he was evidently apprenticed early to the chase. Van Dyck painted the child and the hound he fondles. Only in the dead game should we suspect the hand of Filippo Roos.

Turning to the other two Van Dyck portraits bought from the Miconi by Giacomo Filippo Durazzo on 1 April 1721: the ostensible subject of the *"Tobiolo e l'Arcangelo Raffaelle"* (fig. 15)[19] cannot be in doubt. It appears to be the second of Van Dyck's disguised or allegorical portraits, preceded only by the Buckinghams as Venus and Adonis and to be followed, again in England, by a variety: the posthumous *Venetia Stanley, Lady Digby, as Prudence* (National Portrait

looks familiar (fig. 12); but it is not the *"Putto Vestito di bianco di Vandich con fiori del Rosa"*[16] that was one of fifteen paintings, including two other portraits of Genoese children by Van Dyck, acquired by Giacomo Filippo four months before the *"Dama d'Oro,"* to be hung (after adjustments to their dimensions) in the same *salotto* of his palace at the eastern end of the via Balbi. It is a late seventeenth- or early eighteenth-century copy by G. B. Gaulli or by an able Genoese in his following.[17] The particular blue-

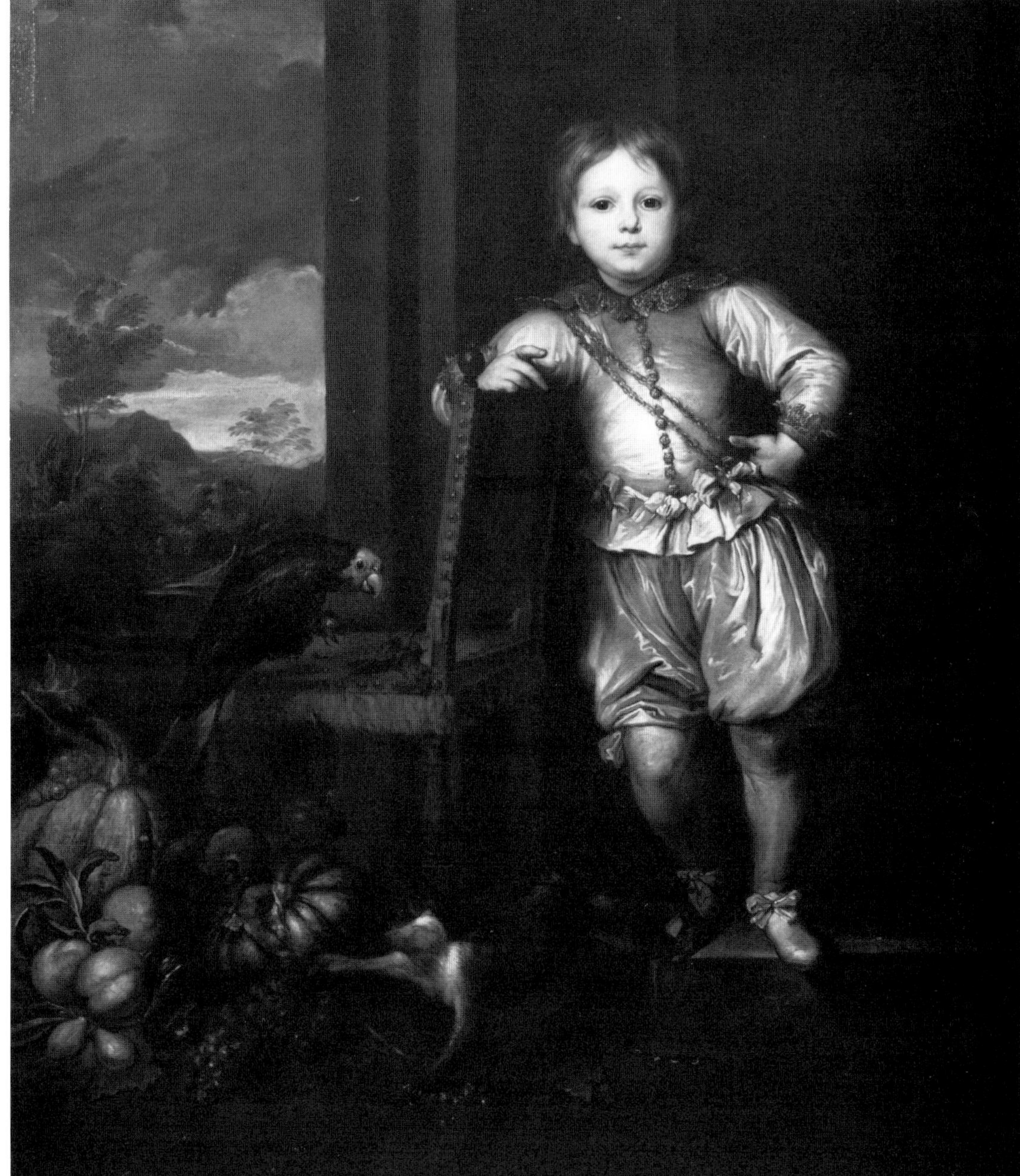

Gallery, London); the lively *Lord Arran as Cupid, Accompanying Lady Mary Villiers*, a Venus in modern dress (North Carolina Museum of Art, Raleigh); *Mary Villiers, Duchess of Lennox as St. Agnes* (Windsor Castle); the unidentified *Young Woman as Erminia* (Blenheim Palace); and *Rachel de Ruvigny, Countess of Southampton* (Fitzwilliam Museum, Cambridge), cloudborne and triumphant over death. But unlike the posthumous tributes to Lady Digby and Lady Southampton, both probably devised by Sir

Kenelm Digby, the "*Tobiolo*," a rare subject south of the Alps, is of simple interpretation. The boy thus portrayed was surely called Tobia, a name conspicuously favored by the Pallavicini, but one scarcely used by any other leading Genoese family. At a reasonable guess he is aged ten. Again the style is of about 1626. Only one Tobia Pallavicino fits the mold, a direct descendant of the immensely wealthy Tobia who died in 1483, the grandfather of the Tobia who married Battina Spinola. That second Tobia's son,

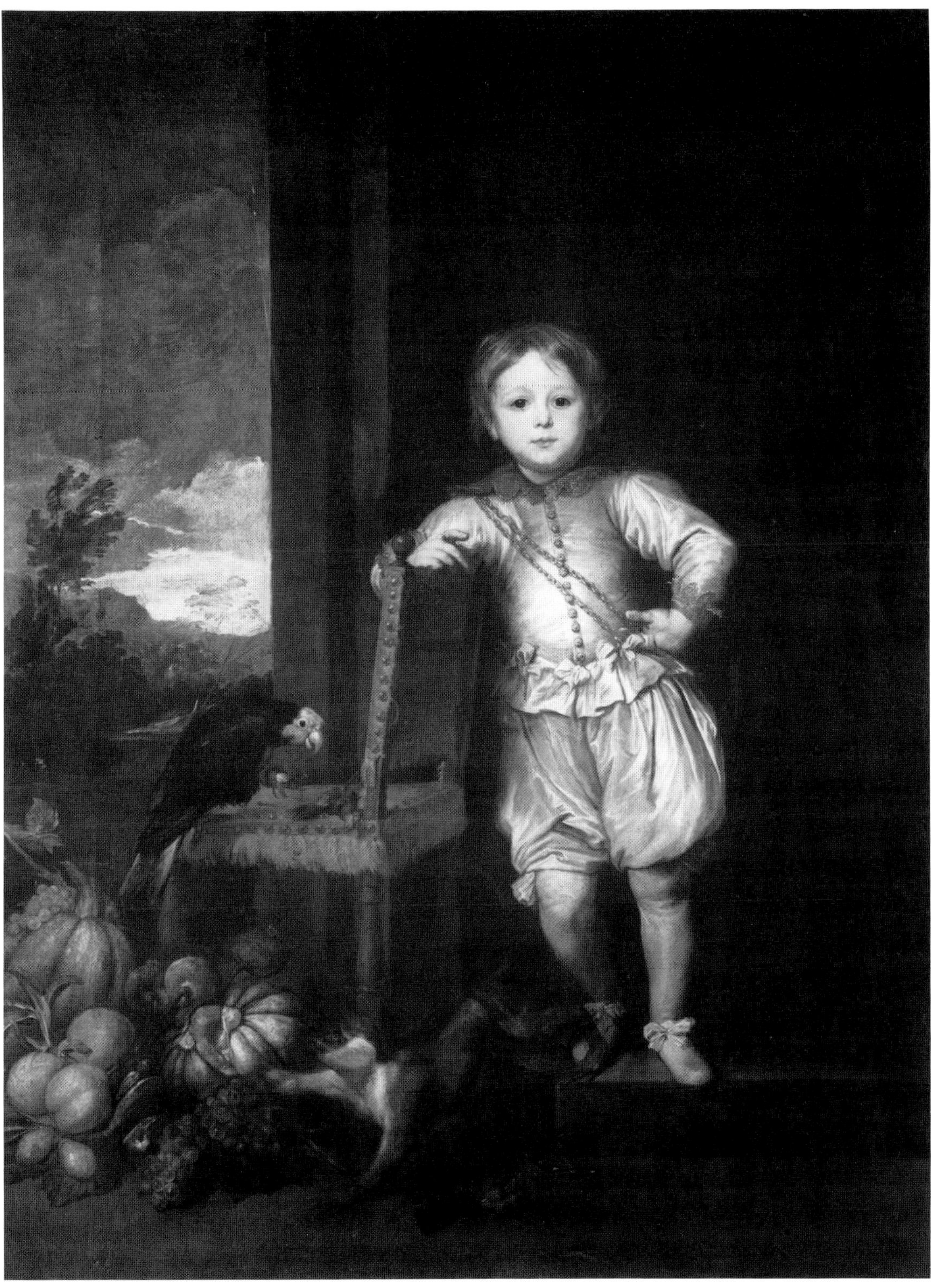

13. Anthony van Dyck,
"Putto Vestito di bianco,"
c. 1623–1625, oil on canvas
Palazzo Durazzo-Pallavicini, Genoa

Gian Andrea, married Dorotea Negroni. The eldest of their large issue, born in 1595, was named Francesco Tobia. He died in 1612, as did one of his younger brothers, Francesco. Gian Andrea and Dorotea's ninth child and seventh son was called, this time as a first name, Tobia, for his grandfather and great-great-grandfather. His birth year is unknown, but apparently he was born after his brother Camillo (1614–1658), most likely by not more than a year or two. So he could have been eight or nine when he sat to Van Dyck. He died in 1656. His father Gian Andrea was a first cousin of Nicolò Pallavicino, whom Rubens had painted in Genoa early in 1604 (on loan to the Fitzwilliam Museum, Cambridge). Tobia Pallavicino, unlike his contemporaries in portraits by Van Dyck, is not dressed *alla spagnuola*, but in sporting costume of exotic fancy. The archangel with the golden brown hair, the gray of his drapery faintly broken with lilac, anticipates the style in Genoa of Gaulli.

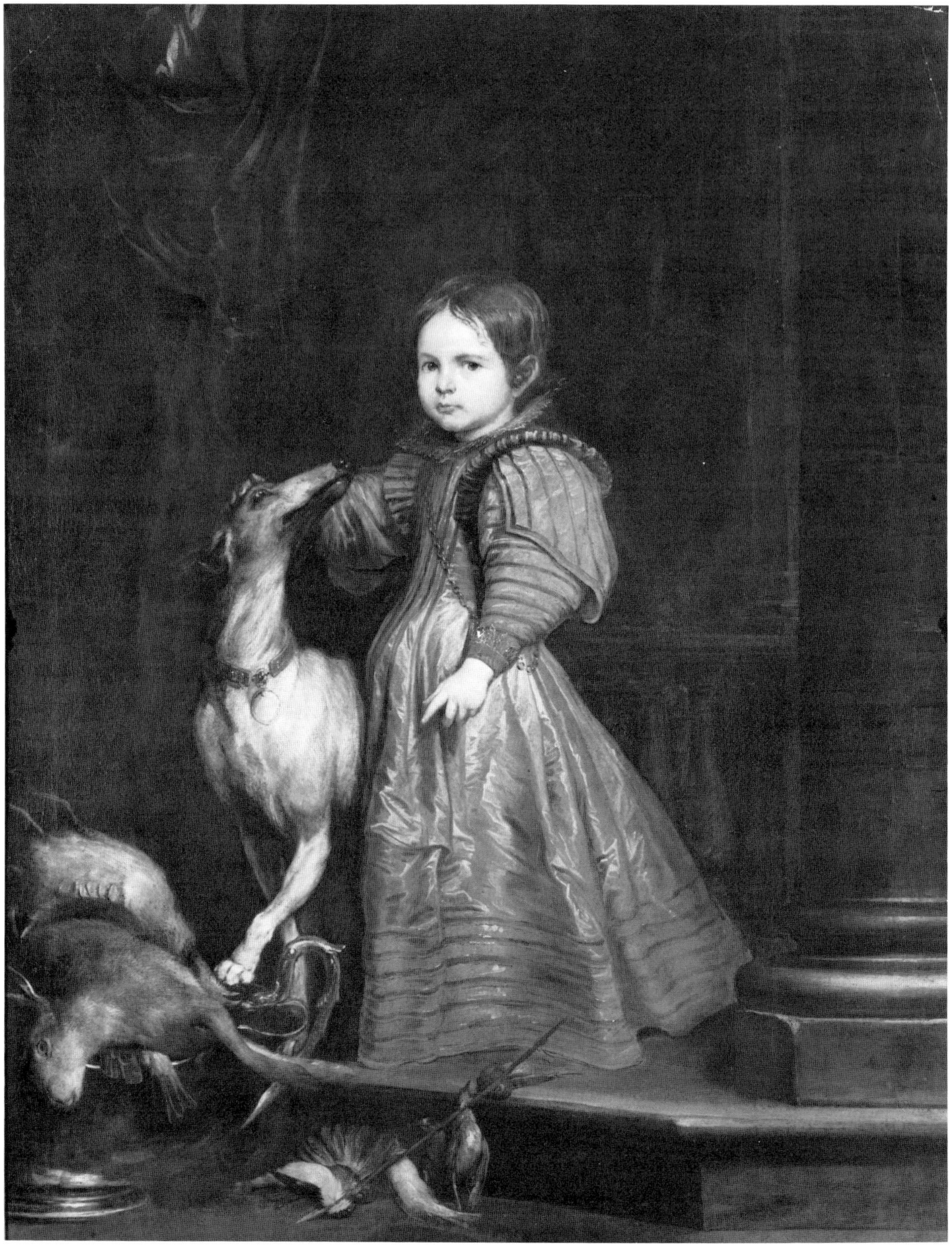

The identity of the third portrait of chil-

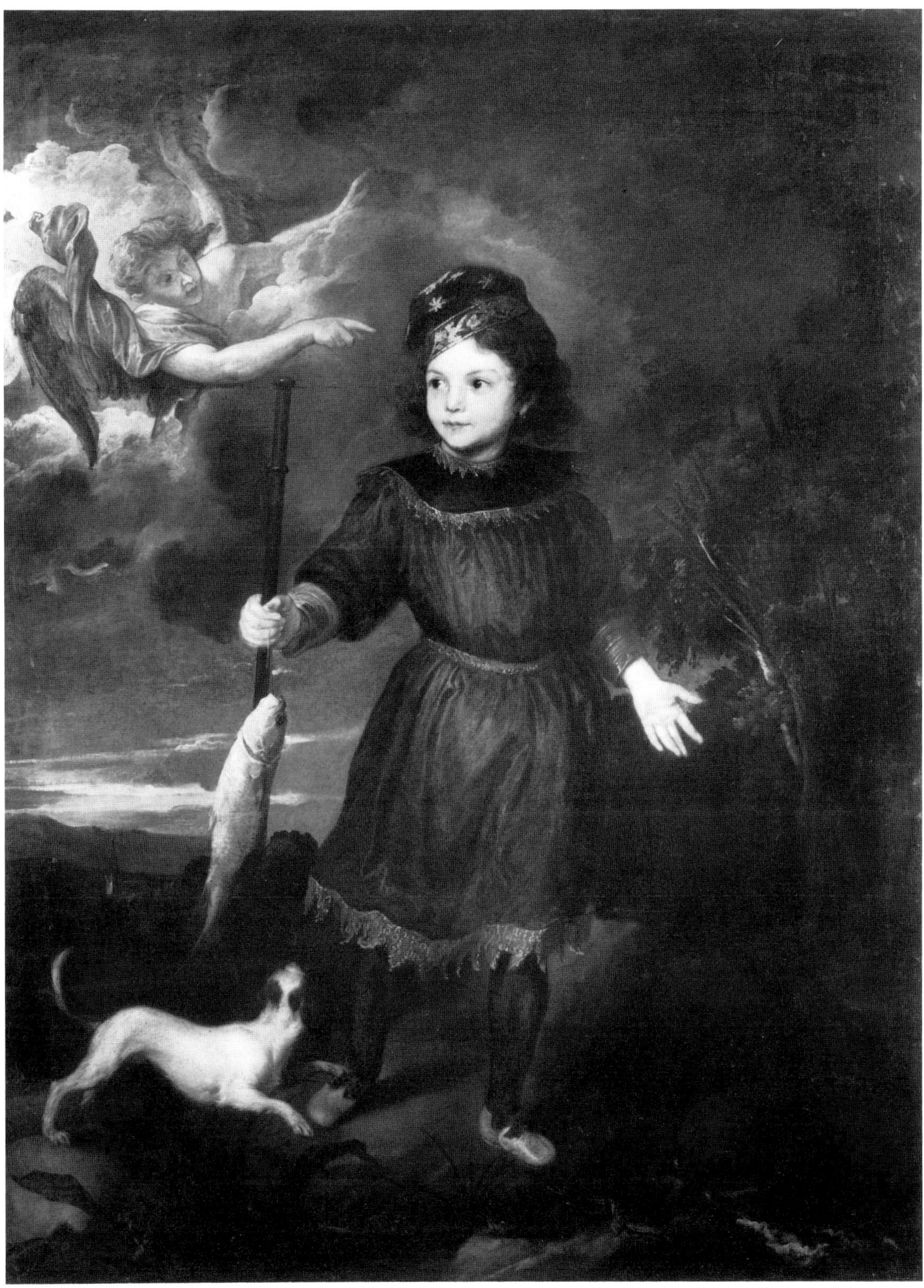

dren acquired by Giacomo Filippo Durazzo on 1 April 1721, the *"Tre Putti, del Vandich"* (fig. 16), is no less evident.[20] Heraldry, not genealogy alone, provides the clue. The ar-

morials of a marchese, upper left, are too stiff and tame to have been painted by Van Dyck, but, to judge from the style and the age of the paint, they were added within the children's

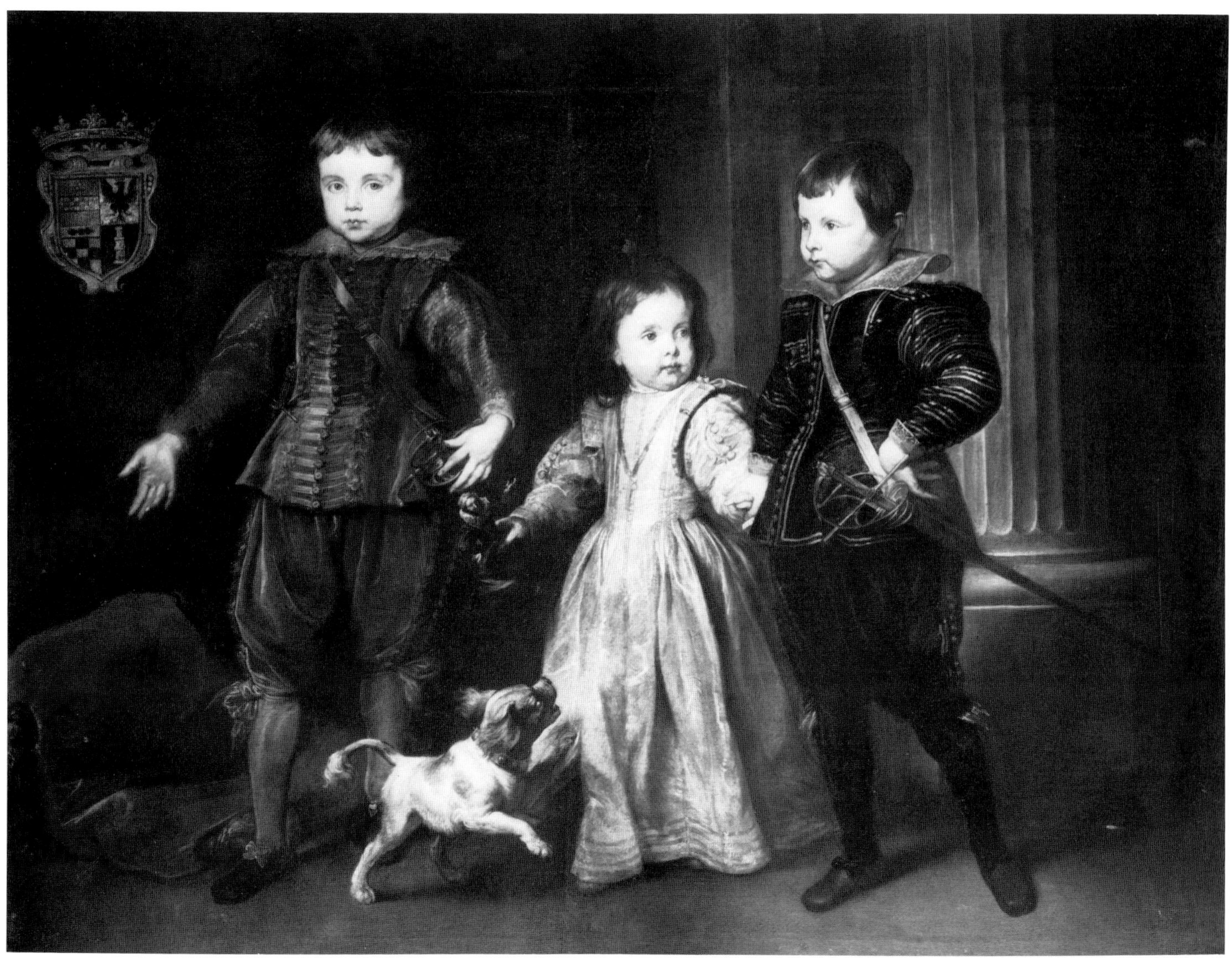

generation, presumably by a local painter available in Genoa. There is no reason not to trust their evidence. Read correctly, as they have not been hitherto, they show Spinola over Pallavicini quartered with Doria over della Tolfa. They can only refer to the second marriage in 1619 of Agostino, son of G. Luca Spinola, marchese de Lerma, and Violante, daughter of Agostino Pallavicino, with Vittoria, daughter of the senator Marcantonio Doria, and Isabella, daughter of a Neapolitan nobleman, Carlo della Tolfa, conte di san Valentino. Marcantonio Doria was, like the subject of Rubens' equestrian portrait *Giancarlo Doria* (Palazzo Vecchio, Florence), a son of Doge Agostino Doria and Eliana Spinola. Their chestnut-haired grandchildren, having also descent both from the Pallavicini

and the Spinola di San Luca, were of the highest breeding in their city. The eldest, Luca, was born in 1619, so he would have been eight years old in 1627, the probable year of the painting; his brother, Marc'Antonio, was born in 1620 and would have been aged seven; their sister, Violante, who clutches in her right hand a no less fashionably dressed female doll, was born in 1623, and so would have been aged four. Their appearances fit these ages. In Genoa, together with the so-called *"Balbi Children"*—according to Piero Boccardo the De' Franchi children—this was Van Dyck's most ambitious essay in his special genre of rendering a group of children without their parents. It has long been recognized as a foretaste of the very charming but much staider grouping of *The*

16. Anthony van Dyck, *Luca, Marc'Antonio, and Violante di Agostino Spinola*, c. 1625–1627, oil on canvas
Palazzo Durazzo-Pallavicini, Genoa

Children of Charles I with Their Spaniel (Windsor Castle), devised during the 1630s when the artist was employed by the Stuart court. It marks a high point in Van Dyck's admiration of Titian and his passion to rival Titian as a brilliant and sympathetic portrayer of a family group of children with their pet dog. It is peculiarly fitting that the *Vendramin Family* (National Gallery, London) is one of the masterpieces by Titian that Van Dyck himself was to own.

That the *"Dama d'Oro,"* the *"Boy in White,"* the *Tobia,* and the three children with a dog were identified as commissioned neither by nor for Giacomo Filippo Durazzo, and not indeed until these last ten years as bought for his descendants, is a revealing feature of the history of taste in Genoa. By 1720, in at least one important house, Van Dyck's luxurious vision was prized more for its unsurpassed art and aura than for its evocation of the ties of consanguinity and lineage. Van Dyck's inexhaustible vanity would have been soothed by that.

NOTES

1. Arthur K. Wheelock, Jr., et al., *Anthony van Dyck* [exh. cat., National Gallery of Art] (Washington, 1990), no. 33.

2. Washington 1990, 69, fig. 1.

3. Walter A. Liedtke, *Flemish Paintings in the Metropolitan Museum of Art*, 2 vols. (New York, 1984), 1:43, following M. Ainsworth, J. Brealey, E. Haverkamp Begemann, *Art and Autoradiography: Insights into the Genesis of Paintings by Rembrandt, Van Dyck, and Vermeer* (New York, 1982), 12–18.

4. *L'archivio dei Durazzo Marchesi di Gabiano* in *Atti delle Società Ligure di Storia Patri* (Genoa, 1981).

5. Gustav Waagen, *Galleries and Cabinets of Art in Great Britain* (London, 1857).

6. Emil Schaeffer, *Van Dyck. Des Meisters Gemälde*, Klassiker der Kunst, vol. 13 (Stuttgart and Leipzig, 1909), 189.

7. Gustav Glück, *Van Dyck. Des Meisters Gemälde*, Klassiker der Kunst, vol. 13, 2d ed. (Berlin and Stuttgart, 1931), 192.

8. Lot 101, oil on canvas, 203 x 134.5 cm, acquired for an English private collection. Provenance: Oscar Huldschinsky, Berlin (sale, Charles Sedelmeyer, Paris, 3–5 June 1907, repro., as by Van Dyck); French private collection; (Benedict & Co., Berlin, 1926); (Van Diemen, Lilienfeld Galleries, New York, 1926); P. Jackson Higgs, 1927.

Exhibitions: *Trésor de l'art belge au XVII siècle*, Brussels and Paris, 1912, vol. 1 (Tableaux); *8th Loan Exhibition of Old Master Paintings by Anthony Van Dyck*, Detroit Institute of Art, 1929, 3–20, no. 23, repro., as by Van Dyck; *Masterpieces of Art*, New York World Fair, May–October 1949, 77, repro.

Literature: *Art News* 35 (30 April 1927), 1, repro., as by Van Dyck; Eric Larsen, *L'opera completa di Van Dyck*, 2 vols. (Milan, 1980), 2: A.65, as "follower of Van Dyck." I am grateful to the present owner for permission to reproduce and discuss this portrait.

9. Piero Boccardo, "Per la storia della quadreria di Palazzo Spinola" in *Palazzo Spinola a Pelliceria*. *Quaderna della Galleria Nazionale di Palazzo Spinola* (Genoa, 1982), 77–78, nn. 41, 42.

10. Oliver Millar, *Tudor, Stuart and Early Georgian Pictures in the Collection of Her Majesty the Queen* (Cambridge, 1963), no. 180.

11. 103 x 81.5 cm. Sale, Christie's, London, 17 June 1988, as "follower of Sir Anthony Van Dyck." I am grateful to the present owner for permission to publish this portrait.

12. For instance in *Sir George Villiers and Lady Katherine Manners as Adonis and Venus* (Harari & Johns Ltd., London).

13. Piero Torriti, *La Galleria del Palazzo Durazzo Pallavicini a Genova* (Genoa, 1967), is the current publication. See also comments in Otto Mündler, *Travel Diaries*, ed. Carol Togneri Dowd, *Walpole Society* 51 (1985), 133 (5 and 6 October 1856).

14. Dino Puncuh; see *L'archivio dei Durazzo 1981*.

15. Dino Puncuh, "Collezionismo e commercio di quadri nella Genova sei-settecentesca," in *Rassegna degli Archivi di Stato* 44 (1984), no. 1, 189 (76), 190 (83).

16. 149 x 100 cm. Torriti 1967, 75, fig. 55; Puncuh 1984, 189 (79.5), 198 (50).

17. 112.5 x 110 cm. Formerly at Rossie Priory, Scotland, and known as "Prince Rupert by Van Dyck." I am grateful to the present owner for permission to publish this painting.

18. 147.3 x 111.7 cm. Provenance: Landi, Genoa; Nathaniel Rothschild, Vienna; (Rosenberg and Stiebel, New York). I am grateful to the present owner for permission to publish this painting.

19. 151 x 110 cm. Torriti 1967, 73, fig. 53/54; Puncuh 1984, 190 (79.10), 198 (49).

20. 135 x 170 cm. Torriti 1967, 70, fig. 50/51; Puncuh 1984, 189, (79.8), 198 (51). I am grateful to Principe Alerame Pallavicino for expert help with the della Tolfa quartering and family connection, and generally to the late Marchesa Carlotta Cattaneo Adorno for her encouragement of my researches.

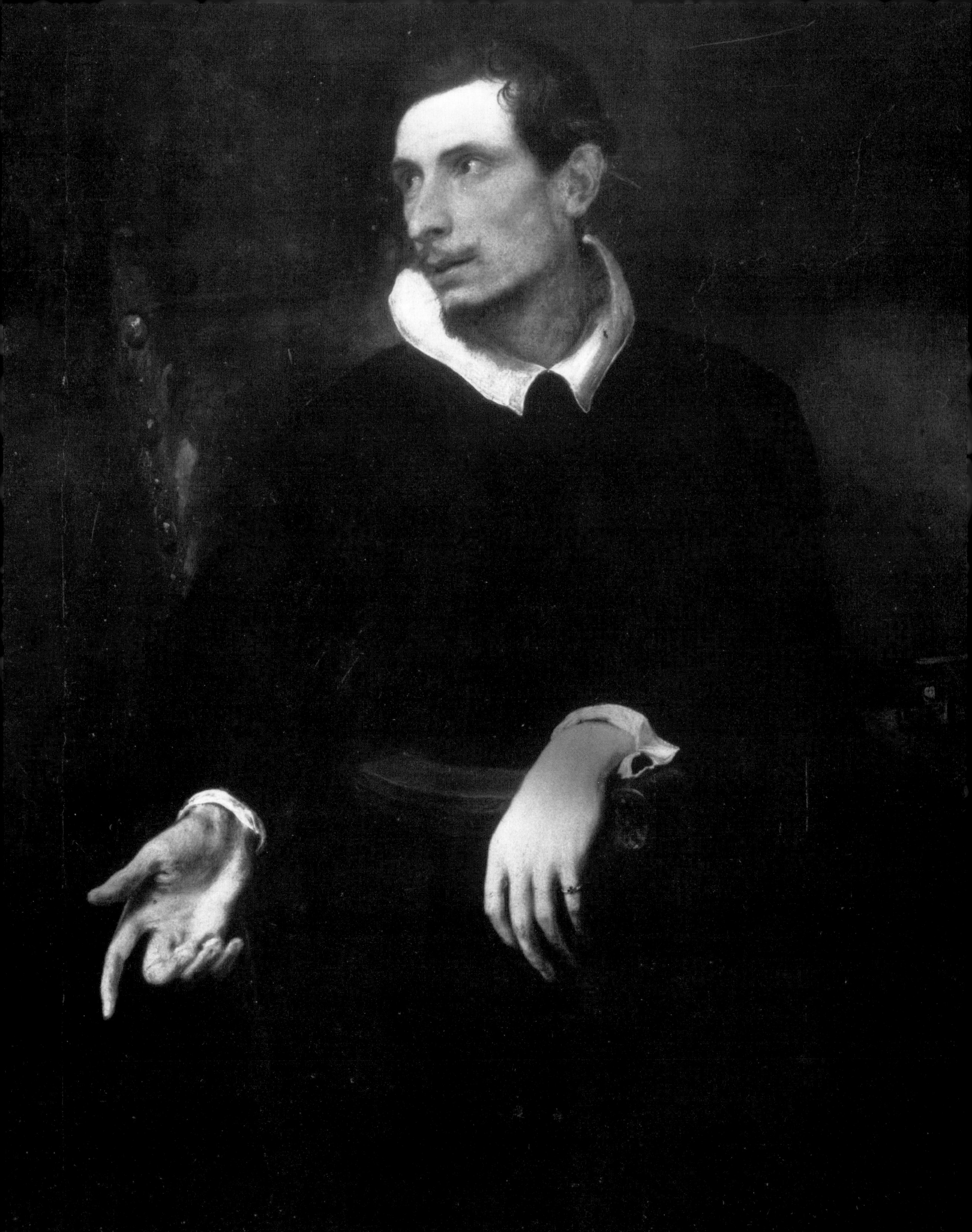

DAVID FREEDBERG
Columbia University

Van Dyck and Virginio Cesarini: A Contribution to the Study of Van Dyck's Roman Sojourns

Van Dyck was in Rome between February and August 1622,[1] and again between March and October or November 1623.[2] A small group of half- or near three-quarter-length portraits, each one tinged with melancholy and each representing someone Van Dyck probably knew intimately, has been assigned to one or the other of these sojourns. The portraits are painted in a restricted, almost monochromatic range of colors that seems at complete odds with the great coloristic performances of the first Roman stay, namely the incomparable, shimmering portraits of Sir Robert (fig. 1) and Teresia Lady Shirley,[3] and the wistful, searching splendor of the picture of Cardinal Guido Bentivoglio (fig. 8).[4]

Like the self-portrait that has justly been dated to the Roman years (fig. 2),[5] the half- and three-quarter-lengths are pictures in which elegance is accompanied by a certain neurasthenic refinement. They include the portraits of Dudley Carleton's agent, George Gage (which I believe can only date from the first Roman stay; fig. 3),[6] the German sculptor Georg Petel (fig. 4),[7] and the underestimated painting said to be of the French painter and engraver Jean Leclerc (fig. 5).[8] The portraits of the art dealer Lucas van Uffel in Braunschweig and New York (fig. 6) were certainly done in 1622–1623, but whether they were painted in Genoa, Venice, or Rome has not yet been established with certainty.[9] It has recently been suggested that the Brussels portrait of a sculptor (fig. 7) is neither of François Duquesnoy, as it has

traditionally been said to be (following the inscription of the 1751 engraving by Pieter van Bleek), nor a work of the Roman years, as has always seemed plausible.[10] But whatever the identity of the sitter, Duquesnoy is the one sculptor, as we shall see, with whom Van Dyck is likely to have enjoyed a particularly close association from his earliest days in Rome.[11] Finally, there is the picture (fig. 9) that is perhaps the quietest and most compelling in this whole group, but which has so far eluded identification.[12] It has always been called a portrait of a Roman cleric, someone perhaps only a few years older than Van Dyck; and it is painted in such a way—to speak generally and impressionistically—as to seem to reflect a peculiar sympathy between the sitter and the painter.

The formats of this picture and the Hermitage self-portrait of Van Dyck are unusually close. Both sitters have a similarly casual coif, and both have their hands disposed so as to suggest a combination of languor, elegance, and significance, as if some telling part of the character of each were invested in the gesture of the hand that is not simply allowed to fall over chair or pedestal. I believe that the young man, once erroneously said to be an Antwerp doctor known as "Lazarus Maharkyzus" (on the basis of the inscription on a late seventeenth-century engraving by Sebastian Barras),[13] can now be identified, and that the new identification casts considerable light on the range of Van Dyck's friends, associates, and patrons during his Roman period.

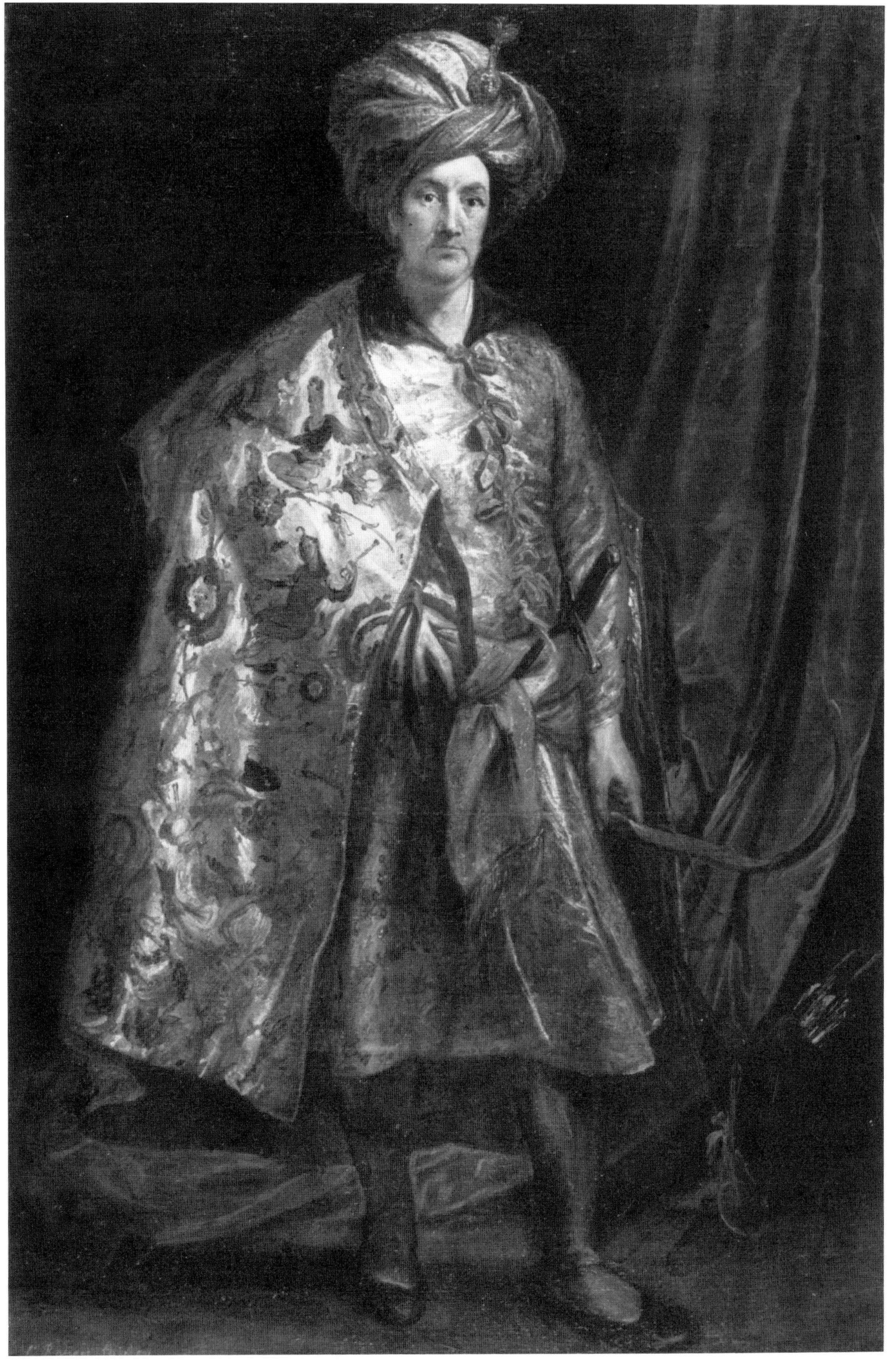

1. Anthony van Dyck,
Sir Robert Shirley, 1622,
oil on canvas
Petworth House

2. Anthony van Dyck,
Self-Portrait, c. 1623,
oil on canvas
Hermitage, St. Petersburg

3. Anthony van Dyck,
George Gage with Two Men,
1622/1623, oil on canvas
National Gallery, London

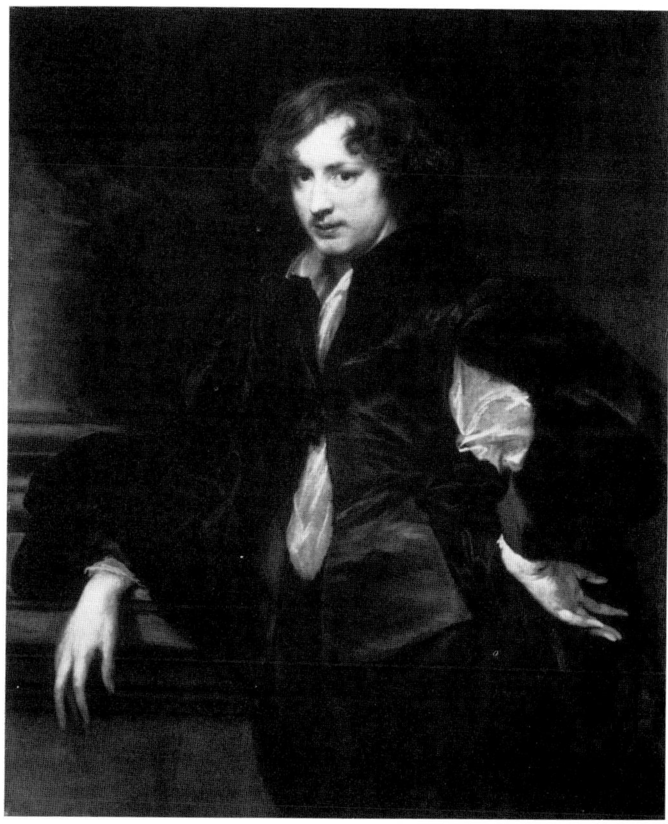

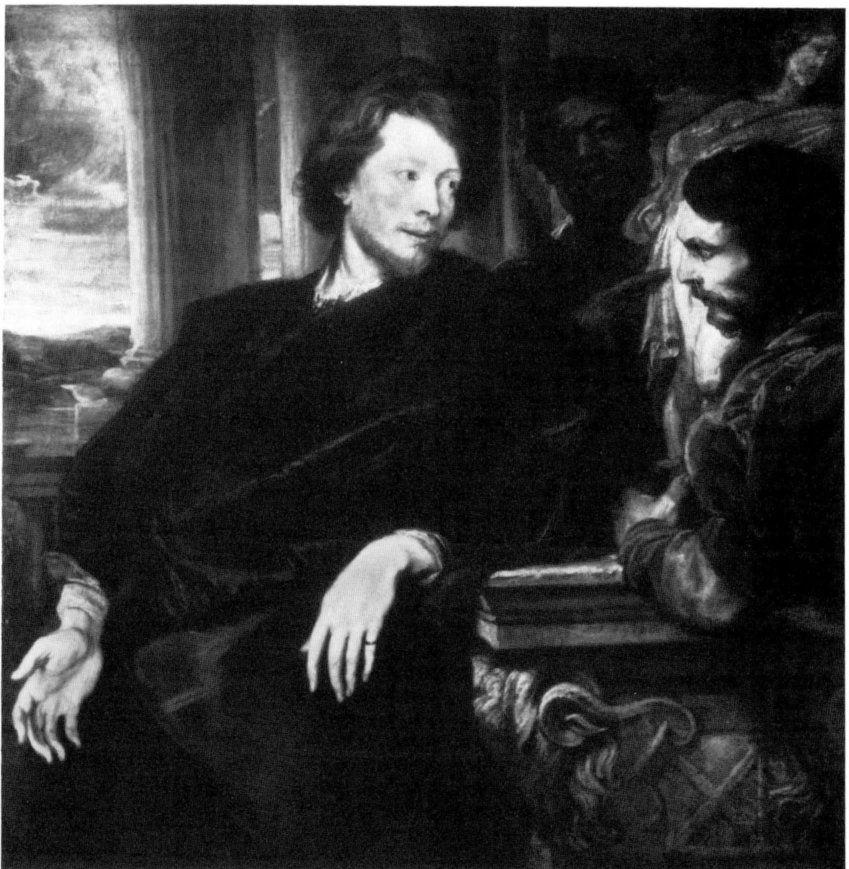

A certain amount has long been known (or plausibly surmised) about the circles in which Van Dyck mixed in Rome. Given the closeness of Van Dyck's association with his Genoese hosts and friends Lucas and Cornelis de Wael (particularly Cornelis), we can be fairly sure that it was through them that he had an introduction to the group of Flemish artists who gathered round the Flemish hospice of San Giuliano dei Fiamminghi.[14] Most significant in this group was the young and promising sculptor François Duquesnoy, whom Passeri recalls having seen in the company of his Flemish compatriots at the hospice.[15] Passeri also notes that Duquesnoy's earliest protector in Rome was the rich Flemish merchant Pietro Pescatore,[16] treasurer of the hospice of San Giuliano in the very years Van Dyck was in Rome,[17] and the chief Roman patron of another ex-student of Hendrik van Balen's, Cornelis Schut,[18] whom Van Dyck later portrayed for the series of portrait engravings known as the Iconography.[19] Pescatore would remain a consistent patron of Duquesnoy from the time he commissioned Duquesnoy's first major work, the *Venus Nourishing Amor*.[20] All in all there is no reason to doubt the report of Van Dyck's friendship with Duquesnoy given in the eighteenth-century manuscript life of Van Dyck now preserved in the Musée du Louvre.[21] The evidence for this friendship, and for many others, would also, presumably, emerge from the regrettably lost correspondence between Cornelis de Wael and the Antwerp dealer resident in Venice, Lucas van Uffel.[22]

Through Duquesnoy and his roommate and early supporter, the sculptor Claude Lorrain,[23] Van Dyck could not have failed to meet the members of the French colony in Rome.[24] Indeed, if he had stayed in Rome just a few more months after the autumn of 1623, he might have encountered Nicholas Poussin, the young French painter who would soon become Duquesnoy's close friend, roommate, and neighbor, who arrived in Rome in March 1624.[25] Very shortly after this date Duquesnoy is known to have begun receiving commissions from the Barberini family—from both Urban VIII, elected in August 1623, and his nephew Cardinal Francesco—and their circle, including the famous collector, scientist, and antiquarian Cassiano dal Pozzo.[26] It is not surprising,

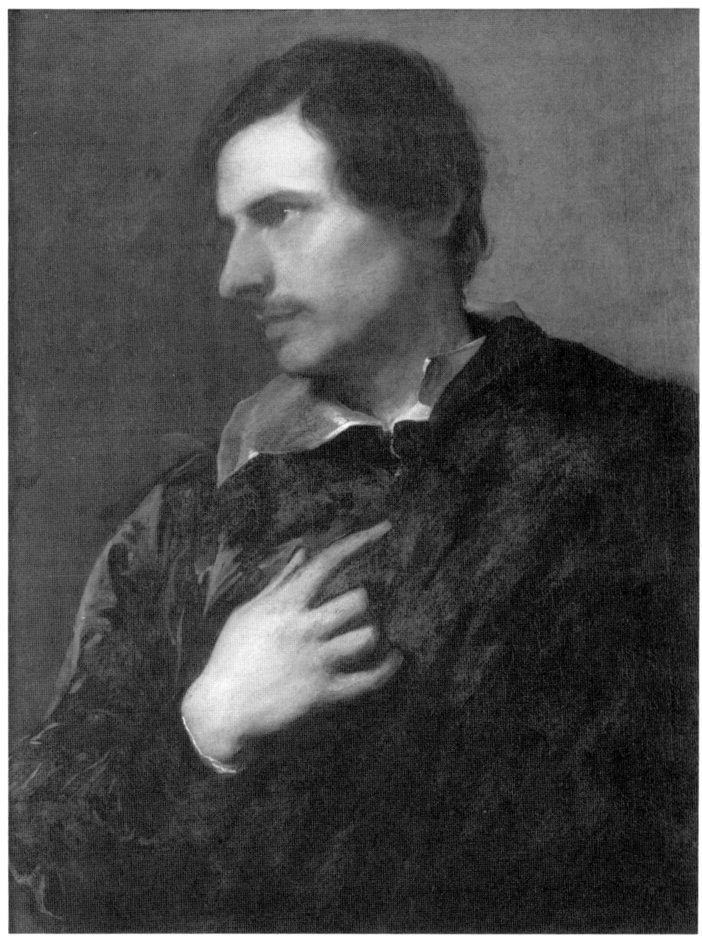

both in light of circles such as these and from what we can only guess of the character of the young painter from the almost overly refined self-portraits, that Van Dyck shunned the company of the well-known rougher elements of the Flemish colony in Rome, and that they shunned him.[27]

But how much did Van Dyck have to do with the richer Flemings of Rome and its environs, such as the merchants who gathered round the more prestigious church of Santa Maria dell'Anima? It was through Pietro Pescatore that Duquesnoy received the orders for some of his most moving creations, the funeral monuments for the Northern merchants Adriaen Vrijburch (1628–1629) and Ferdinand van der Eynden (1633–1640);[28] but at the time Van Dyck was in Rome he seems to have had very little to do with them or their circle. The reason was probably that he was too busy with the portraits of his friends or of friends of friends, and of some of the most distinguished Romans of his day. Chief of these would have been the two por-

traits recorded in the eighteenth-century biography in the Musée du Louvre.[29] No trace, unfortunately, remains of the portrait Van Dyck is supposed to have painted of Maffeo Barberini, but we do at least have the great painting, now in the Pitti Palace, of Cardinal Guido Bentivoglio (fig. 8). Even more than several other of Van Dyck's Roman sitters, Bentivoglio, who was elevated to the cardinalate in 1621, had significant connections with Flanders. His portrait by Van Dyck is one of the greatest essays in reds and scarlets ever painted, even more so than Philippe de Champaigne's *Omer Talon*, 1649 (National Gallery of Art, Washington). In the Bentivoglio portrait the high forehead, keen and searching gaze, and delicate features are all testimony to a refinement and honesty of spirit that emerge with great clarity in the literary works of the cardinal, above all in his *Memorie*,[30] in the letters and *Relationi* he wrote at the time of his nunciature in Brussels from 1607 to 1615,[31] and in his great history of the Revolt of the Netherlands, the

4. Anthony van Dyck,
Georg Petel, 1622–1623,
oil on canvas
Alte Pinakothek, Munich

5. Anthony van Dyck,
"Jean Le Clerc," 1622–1623,
oil on canvas
Private collection

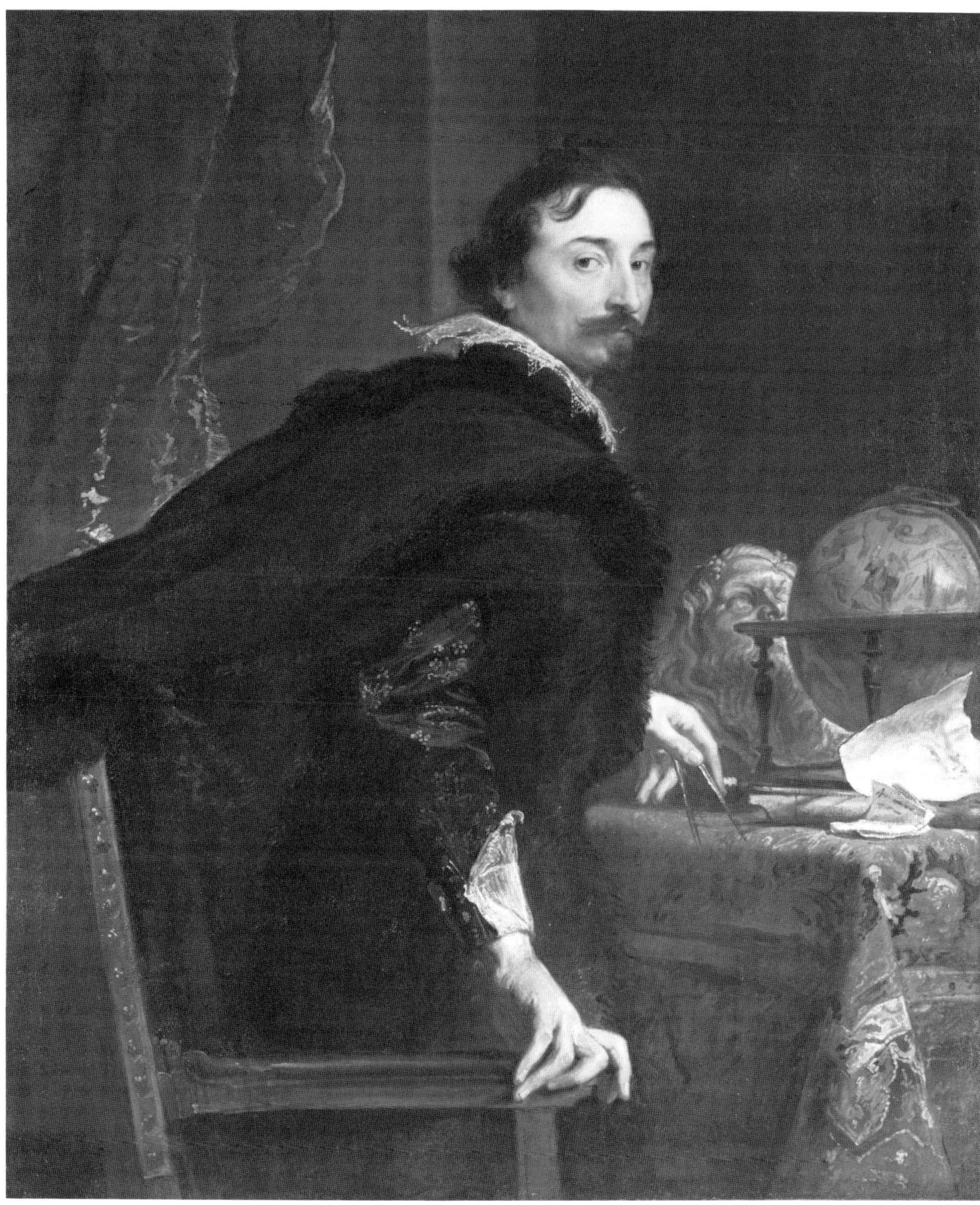

Della Guerra di Fiandra, first published in 1632.[32] Bentivoglio knew the regents of the Netherlands, Albert and Isabella, well; in short, no Roman prelate knew Flanders better. He had also known Galileo ever since his student days at Padua, when Galileo had instructed him in the use of the sphere.[33]

Even if Bentivoglio had not met the already promising Flemish painter at the time of his Flemish missions, what could have been more natural than that this great lover and historian of Flanders—"amorevole della nazione fiamminga" says Bellori[34]—should have commissioned his portrait from the promising young Flemish painter, albeit only twenty-three or twenty-four years old, newly arrived in Rome? After all, Van Dyck had already proved his mettle in the Genoese portraits. There was a fine (though in comparison wholly staid) precedent in the portrait of

Agostino Pallavicini (J. Paul Getty Museum, Malibu);[35] but nothing Van Dyck did in Rome ever matched the brilliance of the Bentivoglio picture, or that of the pendant portraits of the Shirleys, fresh from the East, perhaps introduced to Van Dyck by George Gage or through one or other of his English connections.[36]

Apart from these, Van Dyck seems to have concentrated all his attention on the more sober group of half- or three-quarter-length pictures. If there is one among them that matches—possibly even outstrips—the Bentivoglio in terms of the penetrating and searching gaze of the sitter, it is the portrait of the unknown young man in clerical garb (fig. 9). If we imagine this portrait and the Bentivoglio together, the two sitters seem almost to respond to each other, not by word but by the very manner of their gaze. Indeed, the young man's gaze seems even more intense, even more visionary than that of the calmer and more self-contained Bentivoglio. Bentivoglio gives the impression of someone at peace with himself, the young man of someone still restless, anxious, and striving. But who is the young man? Unlike the sitters shown in a state of repose, such as Bentivoglio or Lucas van Uffel, he is someone who seems both visionary and almost morbidly afflicted. His is an elegant but febrile personality, a man with sunken cheeks, wan complexion, and a gaze that for all its intensity seems abstract and distant, as if he were lost in some world beyond this one, or exhausted by labor and illness.

In the Sala dei Capitani in the Capitoline Museum there is the tomb and funerary bust, long attributed to François Duquesnoy, of Virginio Cesarini, one of the most distinguished and talented young Romans of his day (figs. 10, 11).[37] Van Dyck's portrait is of the same young man. Cesarini was only four years older than Van Dyck, and would thus have been twenty-seven or twenty-eight when Van Dyck painted him. Even if one takes into account the fact that physiognomic similarities are not always easy to detect across such different media, still one may discern in the sculpture several of the same emotional and physical characteristics as are in the sitter in the painting. In both works the flesh is drawn tightly over sunken cheeks. The two men have the same mustache, hairstyle, and fragile, incipient beard

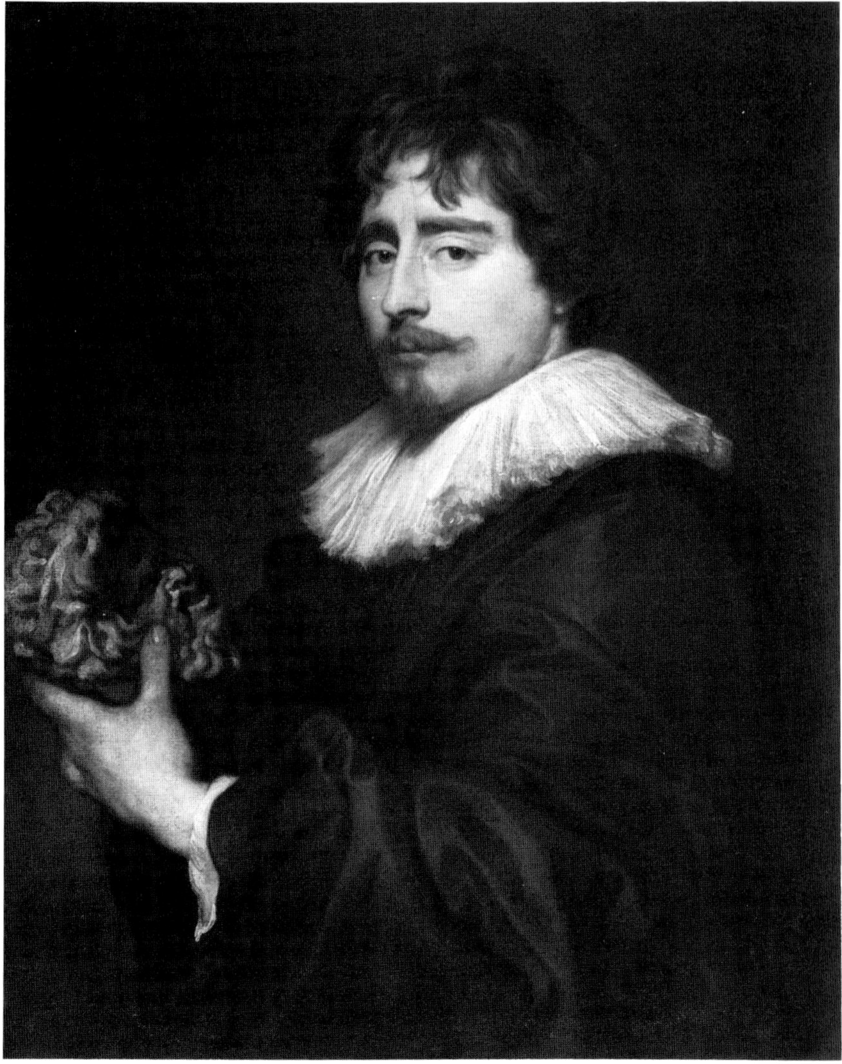

7. Anthony van Dyck,
François Duquesnoy?,
1622–1623, oil on canvas
Musées Royaux des Beaux-Arts,
Brussels

(even though it is a little fuller in the sculpture). Even the part in the hair is the same. One instantly recognizes the large and distinguished nose, a feature still more evident in the engravings made for Cesarini's funeral eulogy and for the posthumous publication of his literary remains (figs. 12, 13). The bust on the tomb also has slightly fleshy lips, large ears (more clearly visible when viewed from the side, in the corner of the Sala dei Capitani), and clearly swollen eyes. And beneath the great swath of fur that seems to protect the sitter are exactly the same garments as in the painting: the long, buttoned clerical robe known as the *zimarra*, and the open-necked white collar that protrudes from it. (Although often lost in reproduction, the buttons are clearly visible in the picture itself.) Above all, however, it is the drawn expression, visionary but evidently very sick, that both portraits share, and that points to exactly what we know about Virginio Cesarini in these years. That none of these similarities is coincidental or haphazard emerges when one compares Van Dyck's picture with other tomb busts by the sculptor of the monument in the Capitoline, such as those of Bernardo Guglielmi in San Lorenzo fuori le Mura (fig. 16), 1627/1628; John Barclay in Sant'Onofrio, 1627/1628; and George Conn in San Lorenzo in Damaso, 1640.[38]

It was in the very years that Van Dyck was in Rome that the still very young Cesarini (he was born on 23 October 1595)[39] occupied a pivotal position in the cultural, scientific, and political life of the city. He was the editor and defender of Galileo, and the favorite of Maffeo Barberini. Related on his mother's side to the Orsini family, he had close connections with several of the most powerful and interesting Roman families of his day, ranging from the troubled Cesi family to the Farnese and the Aldobrandini. He was loved by many, from the great Cardinal Bellarmine to a host of other intellectuals and literati; and his friendships were just as wide. He was noted for his severe morality, but in his heart he found space for a number of the best-known freethinkers and libertines of his day.

Cesarini died on 1 April 1624, at age twenty-eight. For eight years he had been tormented by a terrible pleuritic illness, quite probably tuberculosis. Despite the pain, he worked stoically, unremittingly, and wholly devotedly on his poetry, philosophy, and science.[40] Such was his fame in all of these areas, from boyhood on, that no one could have been surprised when in 1618 he was asked to join the first modern scientific academy, the Accademia dei Lincei, founded in 1603 by that other great prodigy of the age, the eighteen-year-old Federico Cesi. Galileo was the academy's sixth member, having been elected in 1611.[41] Soon Cesarini was befriended by the man who would go on to become one of the most renowned virtuosi and patrons of the arts and sciences in Rome, Cassiano dal Pozzo.[42] Together with Cassiano, Cesarini's own best friend Giovanni Ciampoli,[43] and Rubens' old friend and doctor, Johannes Faber (all members of the Accademia dei Lincei themselves), Cesarini encouraged Galileo to reply to his Jesuit critics and helped in the preparation of Galileo's epoch-making response to his opponents.

This was the heroic work known as the *Saggiatore*, published in the very year in which Van Dyck probably painted Cesarini.[44] In fact, the *Saggiatore* took the form of a letter to Cesarini himself, as the title page (fig. 14) makes clear. The title also shows the insignia of the Accademia dei Lincei, the sharp-eyed astute lynx itself, and reveals that the work was still produced under the patronage of the Barberini, who before the decade was out would turn their backs on Galileo.

For the whole period in which Cesarini worked on the publication of the *Saggiatore* (together, above all, with Cassiano), he continued to suffer. His illness was described by many of his contemporaries,[45] but perhaps never with such dolor as in the funeral oration delivered for him by his Jesuit friend Alessandro Gottifredi (fig. 15):

You would see the wretched relic of a man in the flower of his youth and manhood, bloodless and emaciated, deprived of all his strength, cast down and obviously oppressed by the sheer burden of his pain, a living cadaver, the shadow of a man, without blood, or juice, or color. You'd say he was simply the guest of calamity. And yet he never, in such great distress, felt sorry for himself, or lost his spirit; but with constant expression and clear eyes looked upon his own wreckage, unsinkable despite the waves that battered him, an immobile rock [of Marpessa] *in the face of adversity.*[46]

The illness affected both Cesarini's chest and throat. From his own letters and from his friends Ciampoli and Cesi we know of the constant torment of his catarrh and *flussioni*.[47] There are also several letters from Cesarini to Cassiano, in which Cesarini describes some of his distress about his illness and his anxiousness to go to Bologna to meet the famous French doctor Pierre Potier, who had already sent him—via Cassiano—a number of herbal remedies.[48] Indeed, the correspondence with Cassiano is full of references, characteristically, to experimentation with cures and simples.[49] Cesarini worries constantly about the weather, since the cold was evidently very bad for him. Thus on 19 January 1620 he writes from Nettuno that:

until now the rain and the warm winds have confined me to my house. The change of air particularly in these torrid times has given me a chill. Since then my throat has become in-

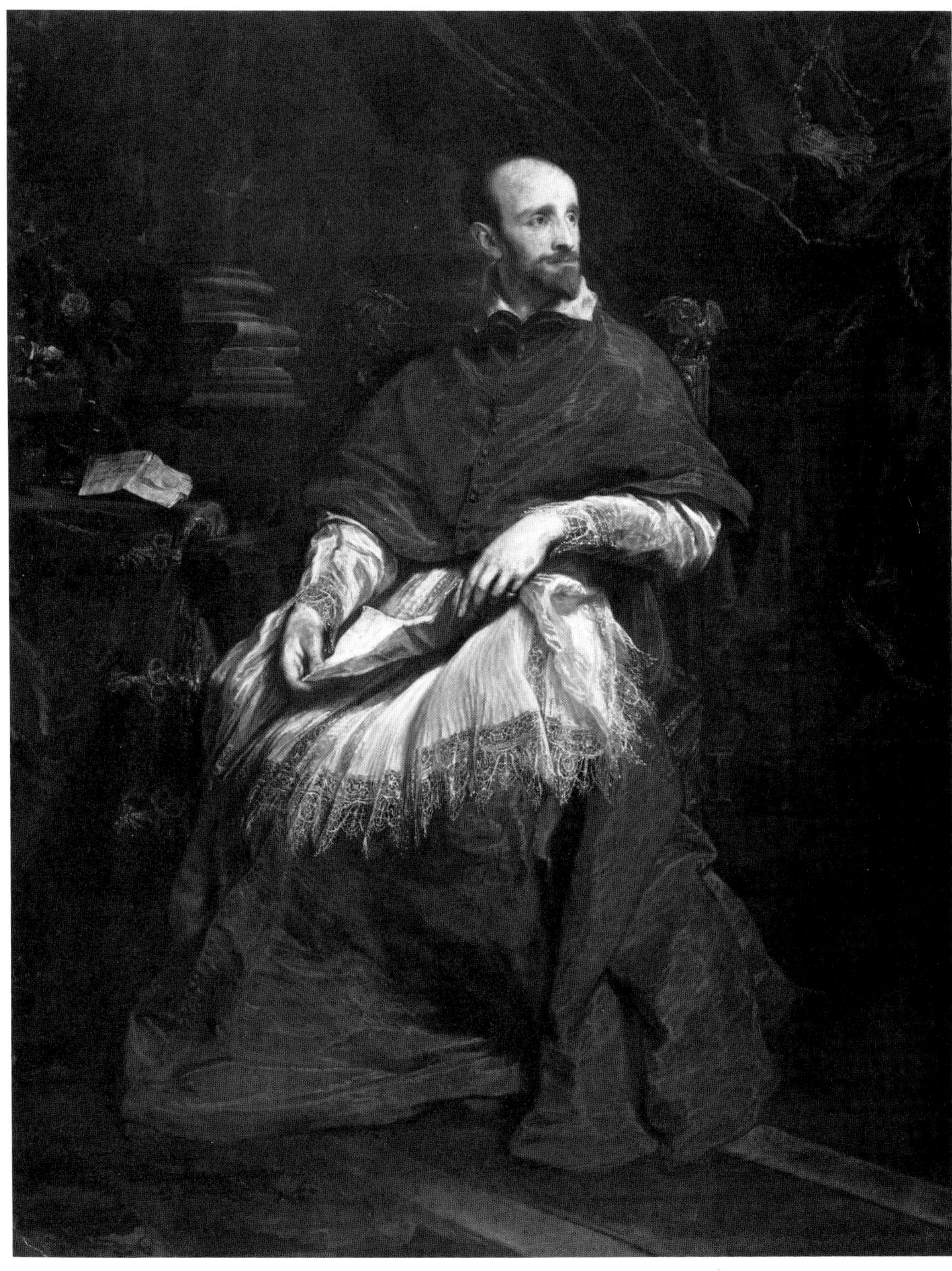

*flamed with the usual catarrh, which seems to
want to accompany me all the time. But still I
have some confidence in Sr Potier. . . .*[50]

Five days later things are looking up, and he
writes that for two days he has felt much less
weak and out of breath, and is waiting hope-
fully for better weather.[51] No wonder the
sculptor who portrayed him in the Capitoline showed him swathed in a fur wrap.

Cesarini's literary work, too, is full of references to his illness.[52] He suffered constantly, and we are left with the image of a
wasted visionary, a new Pico, as he was

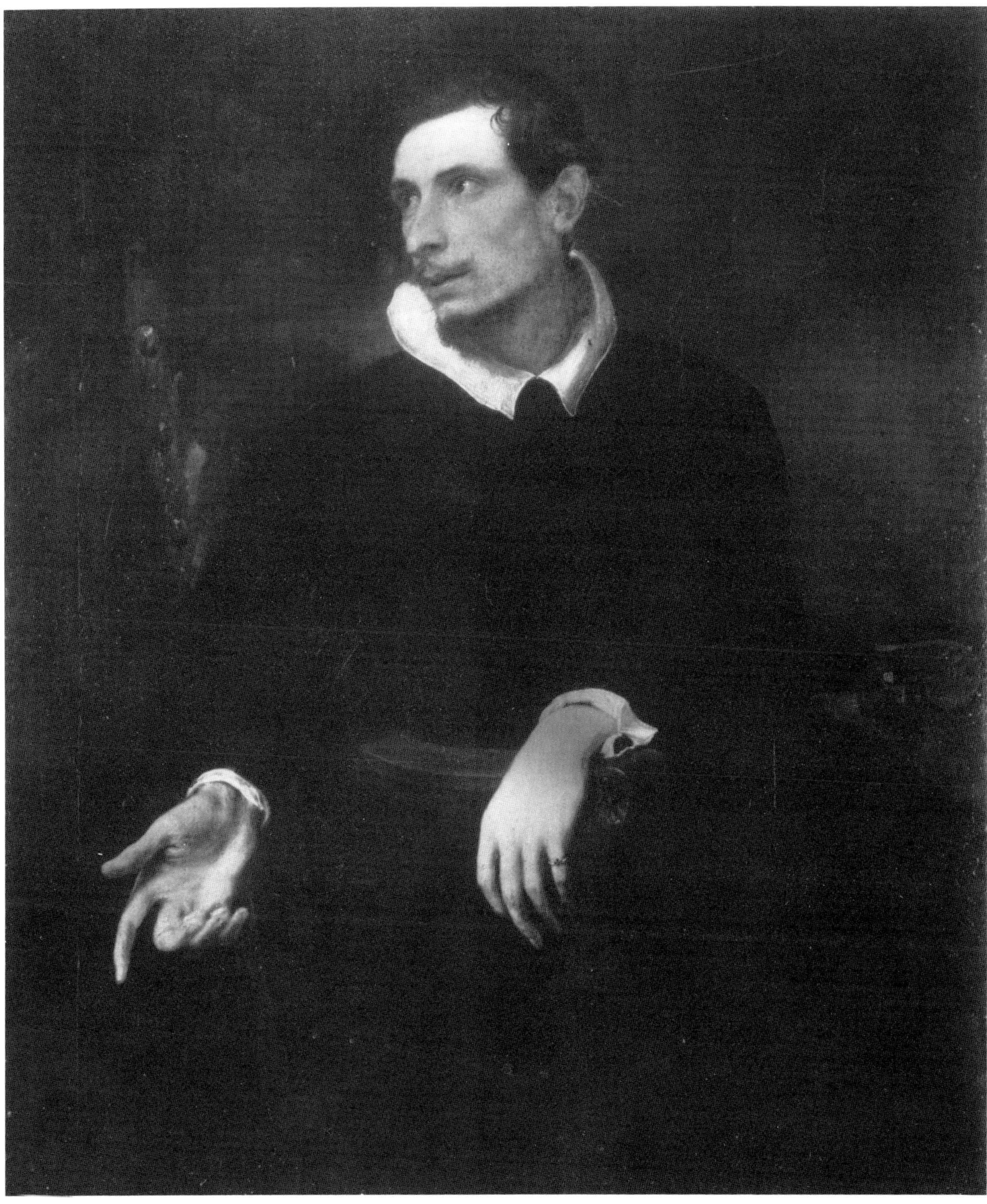

9. Anthony van Dyck,
"A Roman Cleric,"
here identified as Virginio
Cesarini, 1623, oil on canvas
Hermitage, St. Petersburg

called by all his eulogists, including Gottifredi (see fig. 15),[53] Robert Bellarmine,[54]
and the still too little-known canon from
Ghent, Justus Riquius, perhaps the most important Fleming in the Lincean circles in
these years.[55] Riquius corresponded with almost everyone in the republic of letters in
these years, from Cassiano to Cesi, from Gaspar Scioppius to Rubens,[56] and barely let slip
an opportunity to refer to the brilliant young
man in their midst who was tormented by an

inexorable illness. It is from Riquius' eulogy
that we may glean still further details of Cesarini's illness and his legendary fortitude in
bearing it.[57]

When Antonia Nava Cellini published the
tomb of Cesarini as by Duquesnoy, she commented on "gli occhi perduti in una strana
fissità, che seguono un interno pensiero o si
dilatino per il terrore della morte sempre presente."[58] These are words that apply even
more precisely to Van Dyck's portrait. So,

too, does Nava Cellini's further description of the way in which the sculpture shows the elevated humanity of Cesarini reflected in the drawn face: "che la origine di così spirituale estenuazione si vorrebbe vedere in una malinconia del tutto poetica; invece un morbo procurato forse da studi logoranti, poi scongiurato invano e continuamente temuto; morbo di cui conosciamo le fasi."[59] In one of the many lines of his poetry alluding to his illness Cesarini writes: "Me dolor adsiduus vicino funere terret."[60] From his biographers and eulogists, and from his poems both in Latin and the vernacular, we know about the phases of his malady.[61] He periodically lost his voice; his eyes were in constant pain; and his breathing, impeded by increasingly severe catarrh, grew more and more difficult. Death was ever near.

There can be little doubt that the sculptor of the Cesarini tomb was the young François Duquesnoy, as Nava Cellini claimed in 1955,[62] and not, as Ann Harris recently suggested, the young Bernini.[63] First of all the style, as Nava Cellini convincingly showed, is perfectly consistent with Duquesnoy's work. It may indeed be more refined than portraits such as those of Bernardo Guglielmi of 1627–1628 (fig. 16) or of George Conn of 1640;[64] but its elegiac tone points forward to the beautiful tombs of Adriaen Vrijburch and Ferdinand van der Eynde in the grander Flemish and German church of Santa Maria dell'Anima. Indeed, the great swath of fur that protects Cesarini from the cold seems to have provided the idea for the tooling on the extraordinary texture of the swath behind the putti in the Vrijburch monument (fig. 17) of a few years later.

As we have seen, Duquesnoy was the leading Flemish artist in the circle that gathered around San Giuliano dei Fiamminghi. By April 1624 he had entered the orbit of Cassiano, who lived a few steps away in the via dei Chiavari. Along the street in the other direction was the Cesarini palace. Duquesnoy would soon begin to work (if he had not already begun to do so) for the two most prominent members of the Barberini family, Maffeo and Francesco. Cesarini was Cassiano's closest friend at the time, and the absolute favorite of Maffeo Barberini, created Pope Urban VIII eight months before Cesarini's death. Surely the Cesarini bust is the work with which Duquesnoy showed his mettle to

the new pope and the pope's artistically inclined nephew, Francesco. For it was immediately after the execution of the Cesarini tomb that Duquesnoy began working for them in earnest, from the ivory crucifix and the Saint Sebastian (whereabouts unknown) done for Urban VIII[65] to the funerary busts of John Barclay in Sant'Onofrio and Bernardo Guglielmi in San Lorenzo fuori le Mura (fig. 16), paid for by Francesco Barberini in 1628.[66] Duquesnoy would then work on Bernini's great Baldacchino and the soon famous statue of Saint Andrew in Saint Peter's.[67]

If the similarities between the painting and sculpture of Cesarini still give rise to skepti-

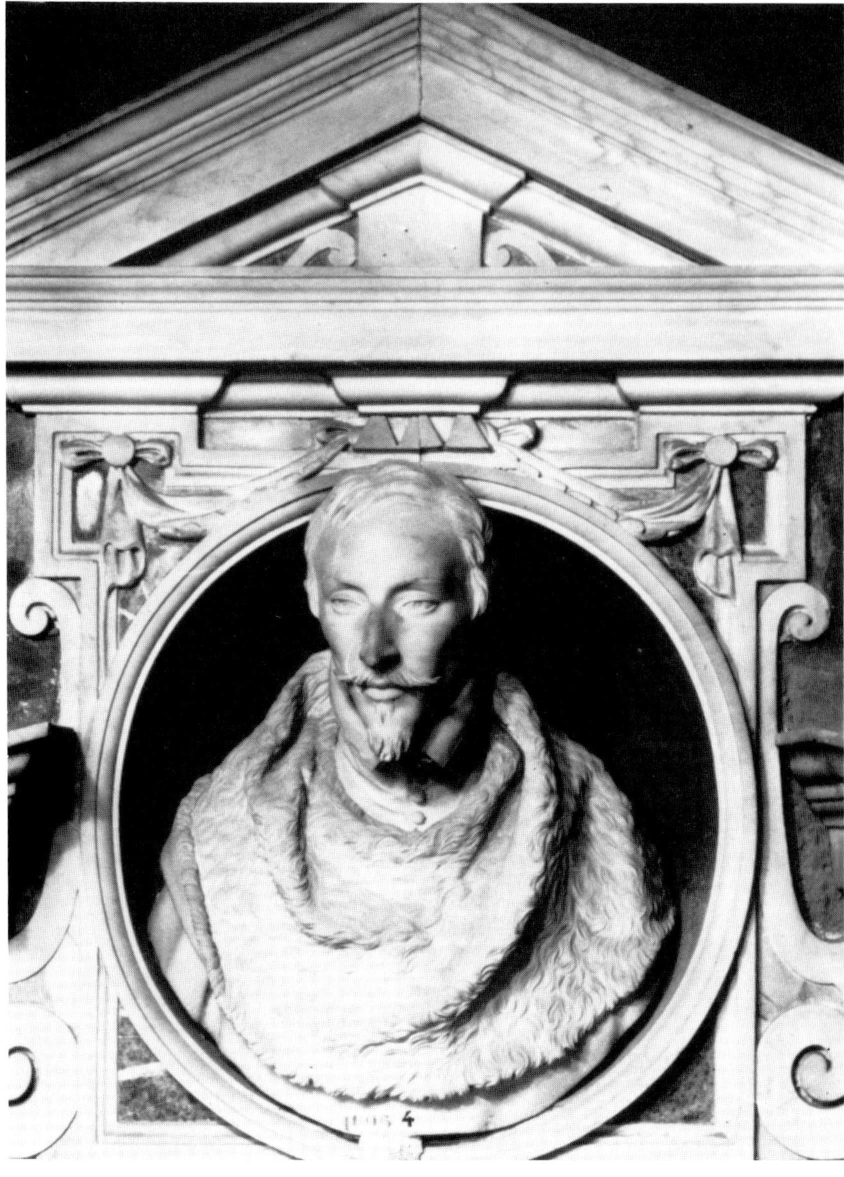

10. François Duquesnoy, Upper Portion of Tomb of Virginio Cesarini, 1624, marble
Musei Capitolini, Rome

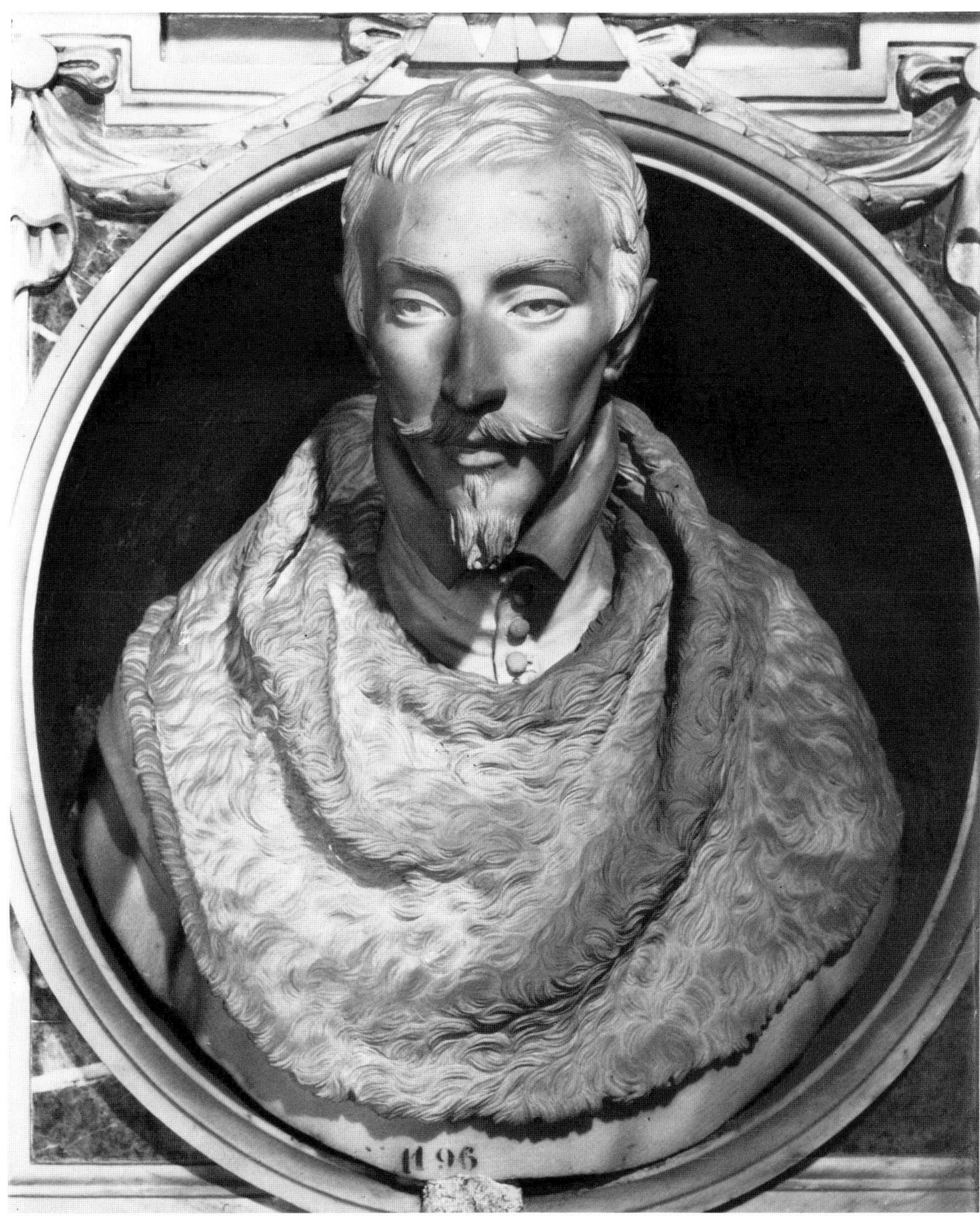

cism, and it is thought that features such as the hairstyle, the beard, and the part are all common enough in seventeenth-century portrait busts, one has only to compare the painting with the other sculptures by Duquesnoy, say that of George Conn, the Scotsman so beloved by Urban, his nephew Francesco, and Cassiano, but so hated by all good Englishmen for his later proselytizing of a num-ber of ladies from the circle of Henrietta Maria, including the wife of Endymion Porter.[68] To make this sort of comparison, whether with secure works by Duquesnoy or by anyone else, is to be even more certain of the identity between the bust of Cesarini on the Capitoline and the painting by Van Dyck.

The eighteenth-century manuscript biog-

raphy of Van Dyck records that in addition to
the portrait of Bentivoglio, Van Dyck also
painted a portrait of Maffeo Barberini, which
"lui attira les plus grands applaudisse-
ments."[69] Whether or not this is the case—
prima facie, perfectly plausible—it is worth
remembering that the elevation of Maffeo to
the papacy in August 1623 occurred while
Van Dyck was still in Rome. Maffeo, too, had
been a friend of Galileo; and he, too, was a
deeply talented Latin poet. He was the uncle
of Cassiano's good friend and patron,
Francesco Barberini, who was also patron of
several promising young artists from the
North. Furthermore, Maffeo was close to
Bentivoglio, whose portrait has survived, and
the bonds between the two men are mov-
ingly recorded by Bentivoglio himself, in his
memoirs. In fact, Bentivoglio refers to Maffeo
in the same breath as he names the third
member of their trio:

. . .incontro egli [Bentivoglio] *specialmente una
somma felicità in partecipare i suoi studij con
due rarissimi ingegni di somma riputatione in
materia di lettere; e questi furono il Cardinale
Maffeo Barberino, regnante hora Papa Urbano
VIII, e Don Virginio Cesarini. . . .*[70]

This is the nexus to remember when one
considers the sketch that survives beneath
the portrait of the man here identified as Cesarini. Even now one can see that there must
have been another picture beneath the unusually thickly painted surface; and the X-
rays taken in 1955 unequivocally reveal that
beneath the picture we now see was a preliminary oil sketch for the great Bentivoglio
portrait (figs. 18–20; compare fig. 9).[71] It is
impossible not to recall that the very first
thing Bellori notes about Van Dyck's move
to Rome is that "fu trattenuto in corte del
Card. Bentivogli amorevole della nazione fiamminga, per essere egli dimorato in Fiandra
e per avere scritto quella istoria che vive im-
mortale."[72]

In addition, we know that Cesarini was the
closest favorite of Maffeo, that he was made
Maffeo's *Maestro di Camera* on Maffeo's elevation to the papacy, and that he would have
been made a cardinal himself had a premature death not snatched him away. Urban
loved and appreciated him so much that he
ordered a funeral for him on the Capitoline,
and had his tomb placed in the most prestigious room of all there, the Sala dei Capi-

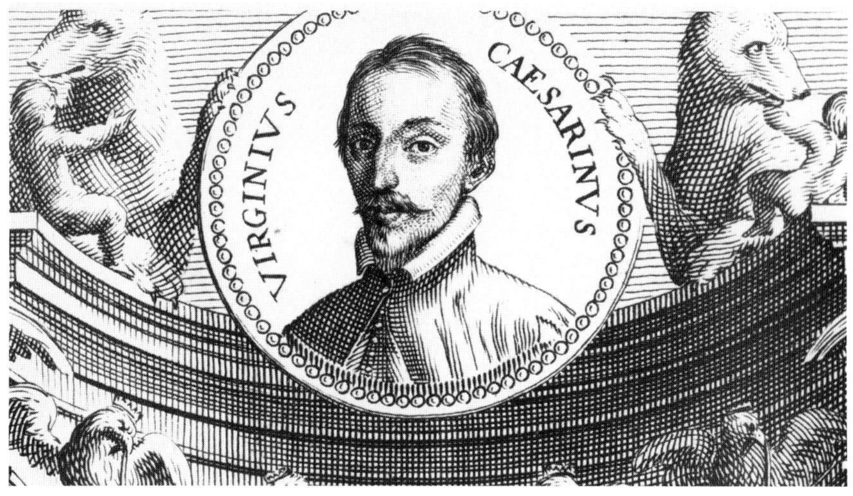

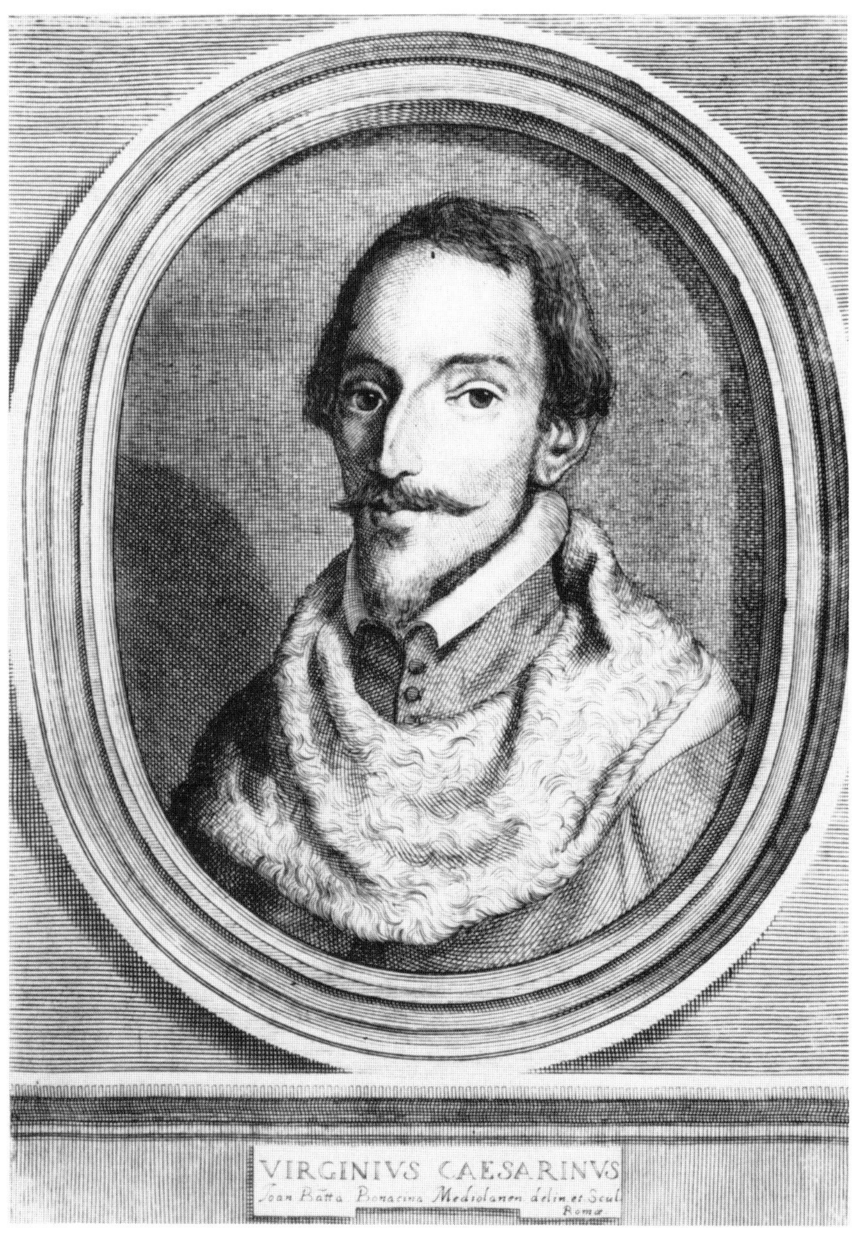

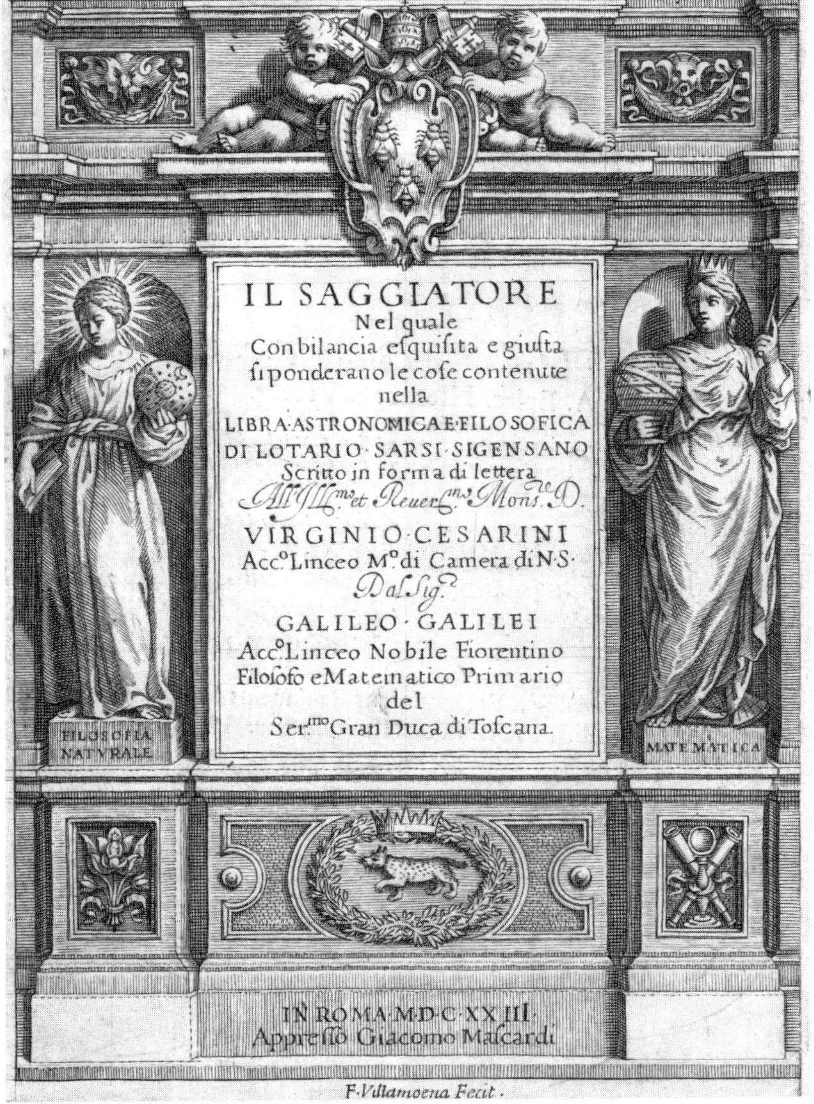

12. Claude Mellan after Pomarancio, engraved frontispiece (detail of head of Virginio Cesarini)
From A. Gottifredi, *In funere V. Cesarini Oratio* (Rome, 1624)

13. Giovanni Battista Bonacina, engraved portrait of Virginio Cesarini
From V. Cesarini, *Carmina* (Rome, 1658)

14. Francesco Villamena, engraved frontispiece
From Galileo Galilei, *Il Saggiatore* (Rome, 1623)

and sensitive of the Flemish painters then clustering around the church hard by his palace?

There remains the question of Cesarini's "clerical" garb. It is not, strictly speaking, clerical. It is the garb of a Jesuit. Why should the young prince be wearing this? It would appear that as his illness became worse, Cesarini grew ever closer to the Jesuits in Rome. The irony of his affection for the order could escape no one, for in the very years in which he was encouraging Galileo to respond to his Jesuit critics, most notably the talented member of the Collegio Romano Orazio Grassi, the mathematician, astronomer, and designer of Sant'Ignazio, Cesarini was applying to join the order.[75] He had many Jesuit friends, in particular Tarquinio Galluzzi, well-known professor of Greek, and Famiano Strada, professor of rhetoric at the Collegio Romano and the author of the other great history of the revolt of the Netherlands, the *De Bello Belgico*.[76] Cesarini was also close to the man who was to deliver the funerary eulogy on the Capitoline in 1624 (fig. 15), Alessandro Gottifredi, who later became the general of the Jesuit order. It is from Gottifredi that we learn of Cesarini's affection for the order and of his wish to be buried in full Jesuit garb.[77] This is a wish that the young man had already expressed in 1620, at the age of twenty-five, when he drew up his will and testament at the house of his friend Federico Cesi in Acquasparta:

I wish to be buried in the habit of a religious of the Order of Jesus, in recognition of the fact that the Father General of the Order has already graciously accepted me into the said Order at my request. Therefore I wish to have my body honoured by the said habit . . . and if I die in Rome I wish to be buried in the Church of the Gesù in the same tomb where my mother the duchess is buried; and if I die elsewhere I wish to be buried in a church of the Order.[78]

Only part of this request could be fulfilled, as we now know. Cesarini was interred in the habit we see him wear in Van Dyck's picture; but his great protector, by then Urban VIII, wanted him buried in civic splendor in the great room adorned by the statues of members of his own and other illustrious Roman families, such as the Farnese. Fittingly, the most restrained monument in this splendid room, which adjoins the stupendous

tani.[73] What could have been more appropriate than that Van Dyck should have been commissioned to do a portrait of Cesarini at the same time as he undertook the portraits of Maffeo Barberini and Guido Bentivoglio? Or at the time of one of those meetings so affectionately remembered by Bentivoglio? Perhaps first it was through Cesarini that Van Dyck was introduced into these elevated circles. This could be the case, since there is one other piece of evidence that strongly supports the identification proposed here. The Flemish church and hospice of San Giuliano, being so close to the Cesarini palace, was generally known in those days as San Giuliano *ai Cesarini*.[74] What more natural than for the sensitive young poet and scientist to have himself portrayed by the most talented

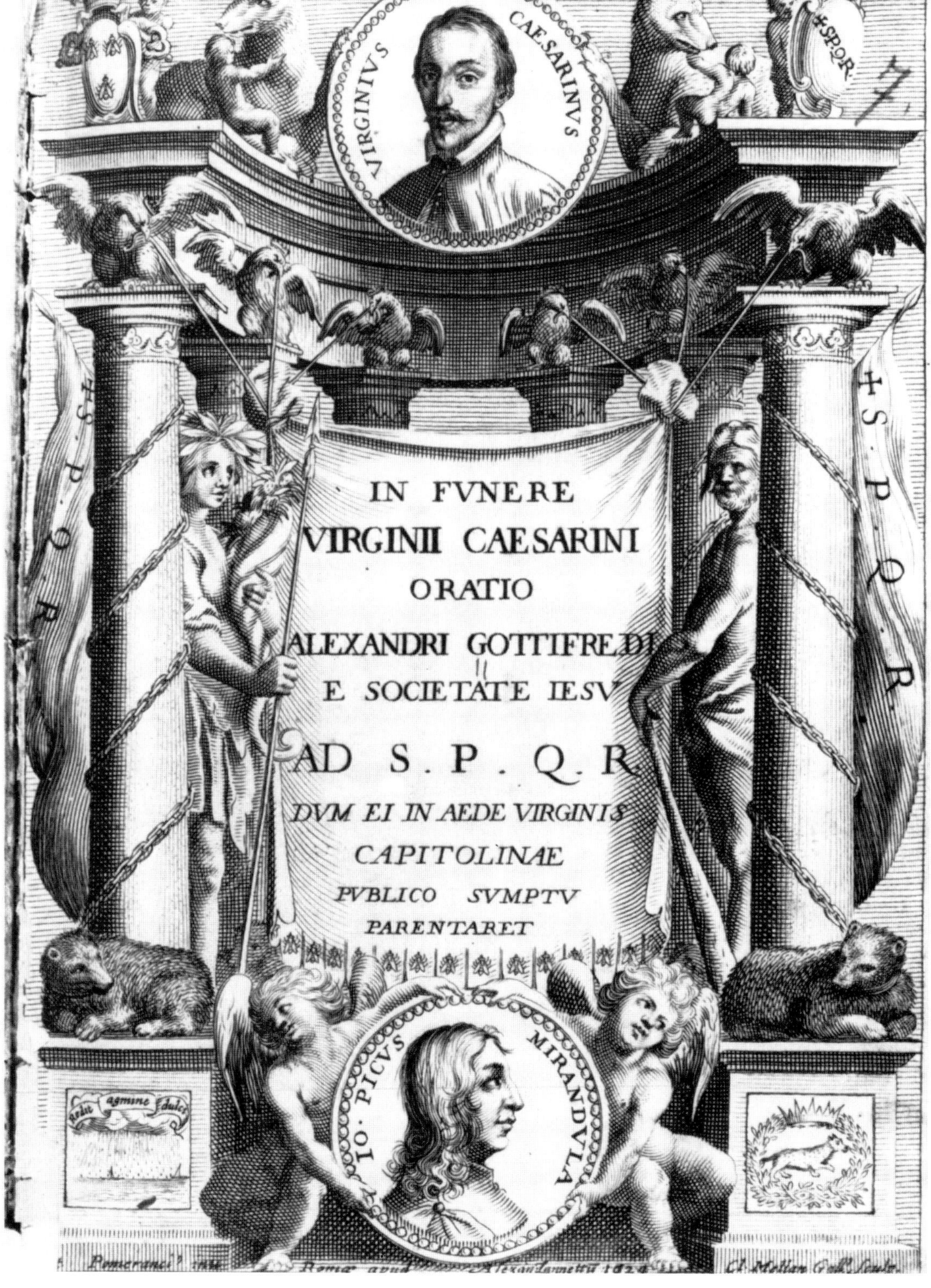

15. Claude Mellan after Pomarancio, engraved frontispiece
From Gottifredi 1624

room with the great statues by Bernini and Algardi of Urban himself and of his successor Innocent X, is that of Virginio Cesarini. The monument is in the far corner, a modest bust atop a flat wall tomb with a long eulogistic inscription composed by Giovanni Ciampoli.[79] This was indeed an honor for the young man, but an appropriate one for the close friend and defender of Galileo, to whom the great Florentine scientist dedicated one of the

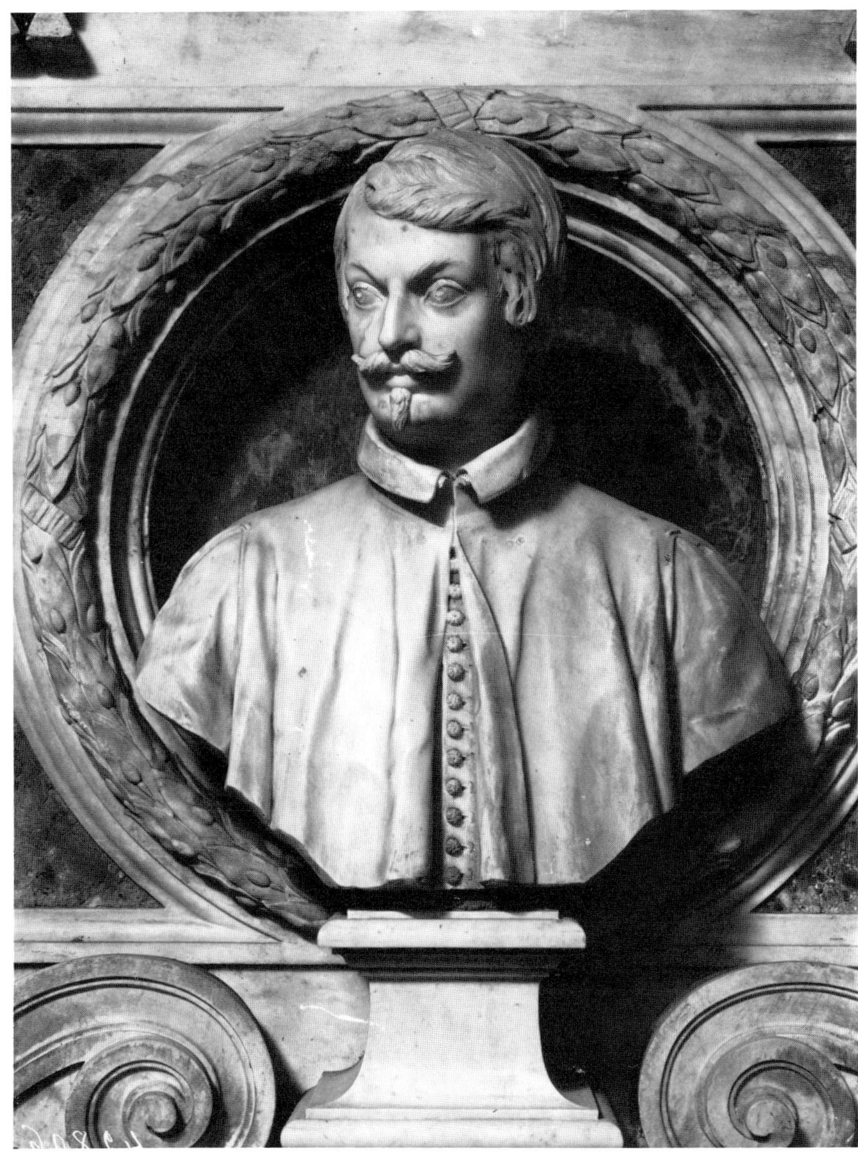

16. François Duquesnoy,
Funerary Bust of Bernardo
Guglielmi, 1627/1628,
marble
San Lorenzo fuori le Mura, Rome

cided that Galileo's reply to his critics was to be dedicated to Cesarini. Why? Because, as Pietro Redondi has plausibly pointed out,[81] with his extraordinary range of friends and protectors, from Maffeo Barberini to the great cardinal protectors of the Jesuits themselves, Robert Bellarmine and Ludovico Ludovisi, Cesarini offered the best cover for this audacious effort, the effort that would establish once and for all the heliocentric system of the universe.

Throughout 1622 Cesarini was working on the text of Galileo's so-called "letter" to him. Assisting him in this task were two other men: his constant friend Ciampoli, and above all Cassiano dal Pozzo, who united in his person love of art and love of science and already then was in correspondence with everyone who was anybody in the learned society of his time. This was the trio that brought the crusade against Lotario Sarsi (as Orazio Grassi called himself) to its conclusion. By the time Van Dyck returned to Rome in March the three men had already made arrangements with the printer, the manuscript had been submitted, very swiftly, to the censor, and Rubens' old friend Johannes Faber was working on the feverish final preparation of the manuscript. By May or June 1623 the *Saggiatore* was already being printed.[82] By the end of the first week of August Maffeo Barberini was pope. Was it during this period that Van Dyck painted the brilliant and much-loved young man who had been at the center of the efforts to encourage Galileo and prepare his great work for publication? He is shown here (fig. 9) worn out by all his labors, his eyes swollen and red-rimmed, as everyone commented, by his incessant nocturnal lucubrations, his cheeks sunken as a result of wasting disease, his thin hair unusually disheveled even for a sitter to Van Dyck. But in the gesture of his left hand one detects something assured, almost assertive, a sense of decisiveness that reminds one, yet again, of the effectiveness with which Van Dyck so regularly combined the elegant and the demonstrative. The gesture is elegant enough; but there is no hesitancy here, just as there is none in the gesture of the hand placed against the hip in the self-portrait (fig. 2) of these years.[83] In the picture of Cesarini the eyes, though tired, gaze into the distance, heavenward. They seem to be scanning the heavens for the

most famous of all his works committed to proving that the sun and the planets did not revolve round the earth.

Such is the extraordinary milieu on whose periphery we must now set Van Dyck. Whether the artist painted Cesarini in 1622 or 1623—and I incline to the latter date—these were the very years in which Cesarini was ruining his health still further, but remained tireless in his work on behalf of what he knew to be the truth.

It was on the occasion that Cesarini drew up his last will and testament at the Cesi Palace in Acquasparta in July 1620 that he, Cesi, and Ciampoli (himself a close friend of Bentivoglio and much favored by him)[80] de-

truth, but they also carry in them the signs of imminent death. Perhaps they imply the presence of some interlocutor, if not Bentivoglio or Maffeo Barberini, then perhaps Cesarini's beloved Giovanni Ciampoli. The picture is all the more poignant for the fact that the sitter was evidently so young, only twenty-eight at the most, when the picture was painted, less than a year before he died.

Something still more moving emerges when one turns again to the Van Dyck self-portrait (fig. 2). The artist is little more than a boy—indeed, no more than twenty-four at this time—and yet the pictures he produced are testimony to an insight into the soul that one can only imagine coming from some graver and more experienced being. This stripling was capable of the supreme subtleties of gesture and gaze that characterize all his portraits, and above all the deceptively subdued yet infinitely artful ones of his Roman years.

Era egli ancor giovine, spuntando di poco la barba, ma la giovinezza sua veniva accompagnata da grave modestia di animo e da nobiltà di aspetto, ancorchè piccolo di persona. Erano le sue maniere signorili piú tosto che di uomo privato. . . .

says Bellori.[84] No wonder that the young painter was so swiftly taken up by the great cardinals Bentivoglio and Barberini. What maturity was it, though, that made Van Dyck capable of investing even his more modest pictures, even those of his friends, with the signs of their deepest character and their most profound emotions? The question cannot, of course, be answered in a scholarly paper, for, as the ancients said of the very best portraits: it is the works themselves that speak.

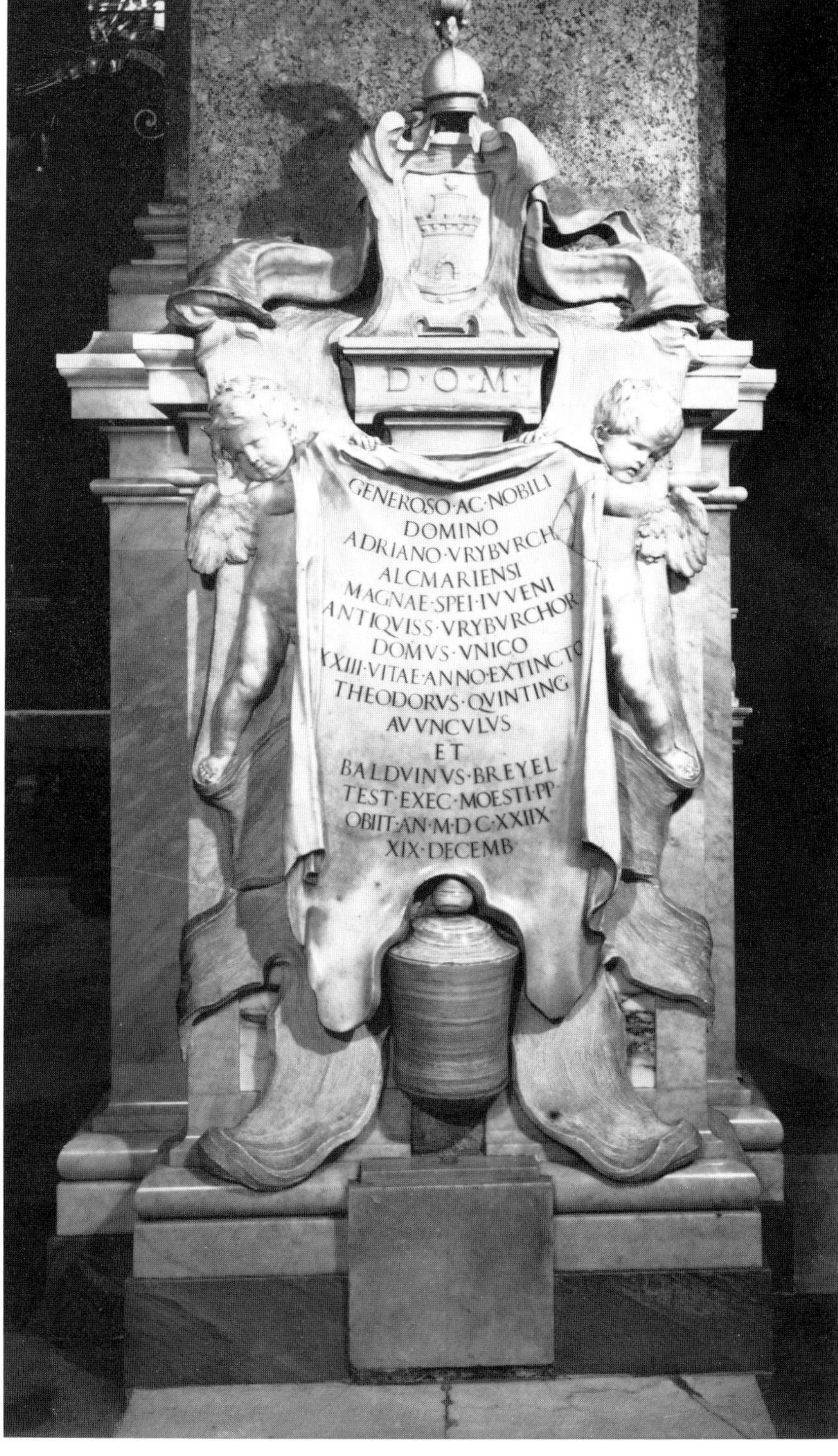

17. François Duquesnoy,
Tomb of Adriaen Vrijburch,
1633–1640, marble
Santa Maria dell'Anima, Rome

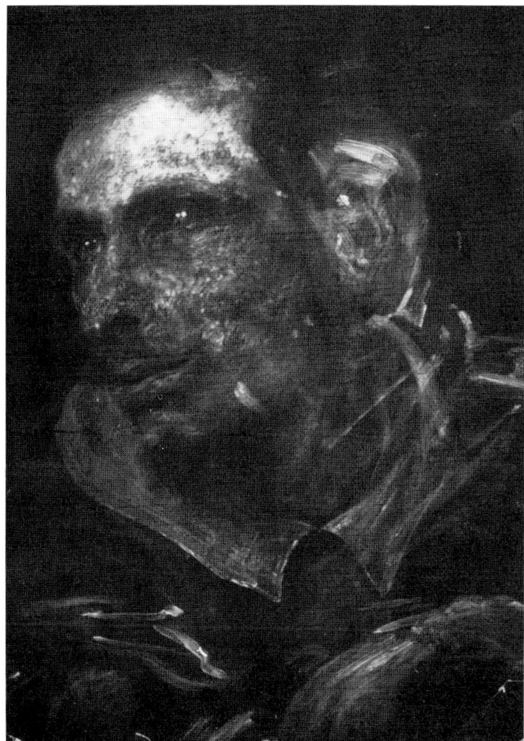
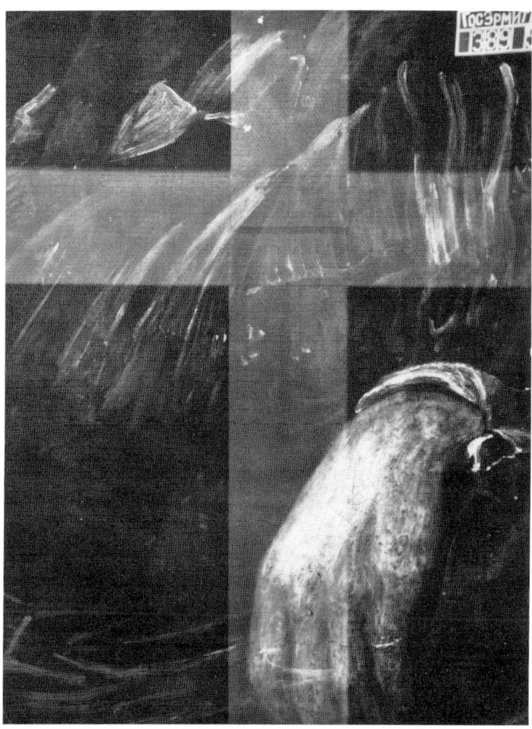

18. X-radiograph of *"A Roman Cleric,"* here identified as Virginio Cesarini (detail)
Hermitage, St. Petersburg

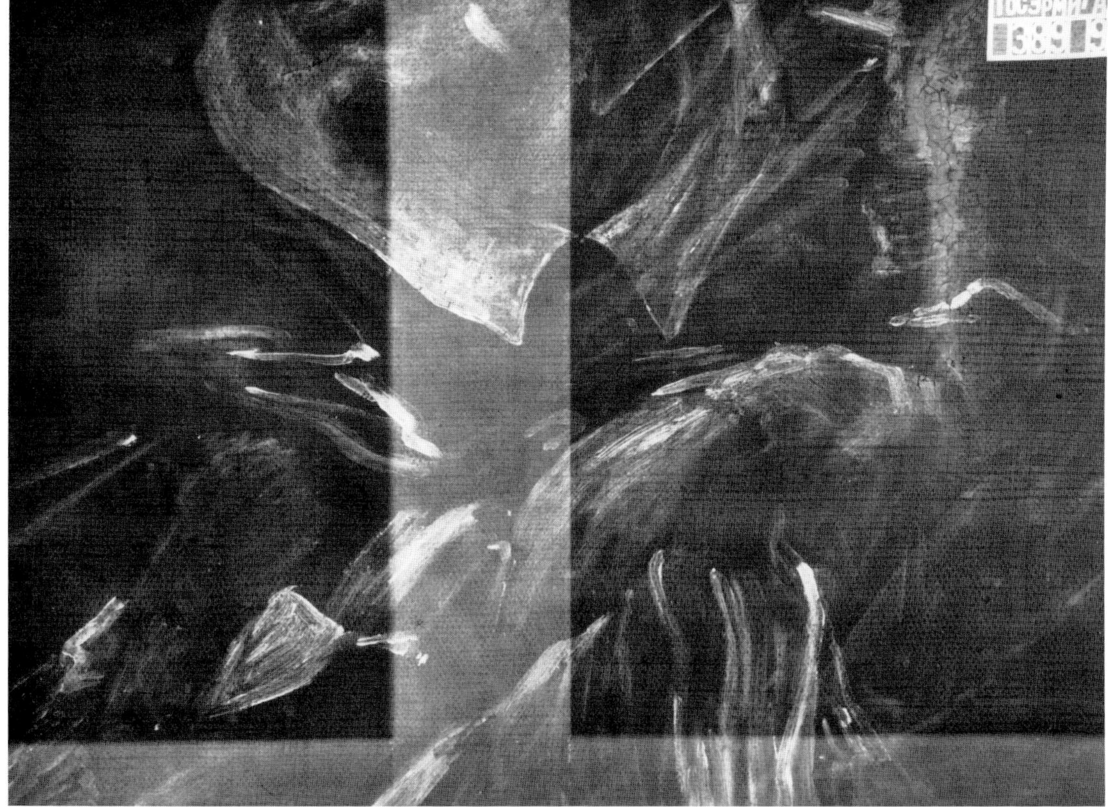

19. X-radiograph of *"A Roman Cleric,"* here identified as Virginio Cesarini (detail)
Hermitage, St. Petersburg

20. X-radiograph of *"A Roman Cleric,"* here identified as Virginio Cesarini (detail)
Hermitage, St. Petersburg

NOTES

1. For the evidence see Maurice Vaes, "Corneille de Wael (1592–1667)," *Bulletin de l'Institut Historique Belge de Rome* 5 (1924), 201–205, 224–225; Erik Larsen, ed., *La Vie, les ouvrages et les élèves de Van Dyck. Manuscrit inédit des Archives du Louvre par un auteur anonyme. Académie Royale de Belgique. Mémoires de la classe des beaux-arts*, 2d ser., vol. 14, fasc. 2 (Brussels, 1975), fols. 38–43.

2. Vaes 1924, 211, 214.

3. Gustav Glück, *Van Dyck. Des Meisters Gemälde*, Klassiker der Kunst, vol. 13, 2d ed. (Berlin and Stuttgart, 1931), 510, 511; Arthur K. Wheelock, Jr., et al., *Anthony van Dyck* [exh. cat., National Gallery of Art] (Washington, 1990), nos. 28, 29.

4. Glück 1931, 180. Although the dating of this work has sometimes wavered between 1622 and 1623, I see no reason to doubt the evidence of Jean Morin's 1644 engraving, which bore the inscription "Ant. van Dyck pinxit anno 1623," a date corroborated both by Smith's statement that the picture itself was signed and dated 1623 (John Smith, *A Catalogue Raisonné of the Works of the Most Eminent Dutch, Flemish and French Painters*, vol. 3 [London, 1831], 70, no. 158), and by the picture's stylistic and documentary affinities with other works that were presumably painted in the second Roman stay. *La Vie* 1975, fol. 41, also suggests that the picture was painted in 1623. Although this information could simply be taken from Morin's engraving, we are reminded of the need to take the Louvre manuscript seriously as a source for the life of Van Dyck.

5. Glück 1931, 122; Washington 1990, no. 33. The arguments in favor of a Roman dating are well summarized by Susan Barnes in Washington 1990, 167–168.

6. Glück 1931, 129; Washington 1990, no. 30. For arguments in favor of the Roman date see Susan Barnes in Washington 1990, 158–160. Compare also Maurice Vaes, "Le Séjour de Van Dyck en Italie (mi-Novembre 1621–Automne 1627)," *Bulletin de l'Institut Historique Belge de Rome* 4 (1924), 203.

7. Glück 1931, 158.

8. Private collection; sold Sotheby's, New York, 17 January 1985, no. 116. Glück 1931, 159. For the tenuous basis for the identification of the sitter simply on the grounds of a drawing owned by Lord Palmerston inscribed "Leclerc the painter" see Susan J. Barnes, "Van Dyck in Italy: 1621–1628," 2 vols. (Ph.D. diss., Institute of Fine Arts, New York University, 1986), 1:228, no. 31. If the painting is indeed of Jean Le Clerc, then it would be one of the earliest Van Dyck painted in Rome, since Le Clerc is recorded as being back in Nancy on 22 April 1622 (see *Claude Lorrain e i pittori lorenesi in Italia nel XVII secolo* [exh. cat., Accademia di Francia a Roma] [Rome, 1982], 77).

9. Glück 1931, 126, 127, respectively; Washington 1990, no. 31 (Braunschweig only).

10. Glück 1931, 158. See Nora de Poorter, "Antoon van Dyck. Portret van Frans du Quesnoy (?)," *Openbaar Kunstbezit in Vlaanderen* 7 (1969), 17a–b. I believe that De Poorter is too hasty in dismissing the possible resemblance between the painting by Van Dyck and the engraved portrait in J. von Sandrart, *L'academia tedesca della architectura scultura et pictura: Oder teutsche Academie der Edlen Bau- Bild- und Mahlerey-Künste . . .*, 1675, ed. A. R. Peltzer (Munich, 1925), 201. Nor am I convinced that the portrait is to be dated to the beginning of the second Antwerp period, as De Poorter suggests.

11. See, for example, *La Vie* 1975, fol. 38; Vaes 1924, 202–203; Emile Dony, "François Duquesnoy (1594–1643)," *Bulletin de l'Institut Historique Belge de Rome* 2 (1922), 95, for the meager documentary but very substantial circumstantial evidence, as well as for the evidence presented in the course of the present article.

12. Glück 1931, 281; Washington 1990, no. 32.

13. Since "Maharkyzus" can only have been painted in Antwerp, the picture was traditionally assigned to the years immediately following the return from Rome; but as soon as the X-radiographs revealed the underlying sketch of Cardinal Bentivoglio (see O. I. Panifilowa, "Eskis Van-Dijka k portretu Kardinala Bentivoglio," *Bulletin du Musée de l'Hermitage* 8 [1955], 36–37) it became clear that the picture could only date from the Roman years, as first noted by V. F. Lewinsohn Lessing in *Meisterwerke der Hermitage* (Leningrad, 1962).

14. See Maurice Vaes, "Les Fondations hospitalières flamandes à Rome du XVe au XVIIIe siècle," *Bulletin de l'Institut Historique Belge de Rome* 1 (1919), 205–210; Vaes 1924, 182–183; see also *Die Künstlerbiographien von Giovanni Battista Passeri. Nach den Handschriften des Autors Herausgegeben und mit Anmerkungen versehen von Jacob Hess* (Leipzig and Vienna, 1934), 104. (Quoted in note 15.)

15. "[Duquesnoy] si godeva spesso la ricreazione delli Fiammeng[h]i suoi compatrioti dentro l'ospizio di quella Nazione alla chiesa di San Giuliano alli Cesarini, ed io che abitavo incontro, benchè fossi assai giovinetto, ce lo vedevo ivi spesse volte a banchettare con molti;" *Passeri* 1934, 104.

16. *Passeri* 1934, 103–104; Vaes 1919, 286–287; Vaes 1925, 287–290; Dony 1922, 98; Mariette Fransolet, "François du Quesnoy sculpteur d'Urbain VIII 1597–1643," *Mémoires de l'Académie Royale de Belgique. Classe des beaux-arts*, 4th ser., 9 (1941), 41–42; Noelle de la Blanchardière and Didier Bodart, "Pietro Pescatore e gli affreschi di Cornelis Schut e di Timan Craft al Casino Pescatore di Frascati," *Arte Illustrata* 7 (1974), 179–190.

17. G. J. Hoogewerff, *Bescheiden in Italië omtrent Nederlandsche kunstenaars en geleerden (Rijks Geschiedkundige Publicationen. Kleine serie, 12)*, vol. 2 (The Hague, 1913), 144–145, 150.

18. On Pescatore and Schut see de la Blanchardière and Bodart 1974, 179–190; I. G. Wilmers, "The Paintings of Cornelis Schut the Elder 1597–1655" (Ph.D. diss., Columbia University, 1990), 29–30, 130–134. For the most thorough and up-to-date biography of

Schut see Wilmers 1990, 20–49.

19. Marie Mauquoy-Hendrickx, *L'Iconographie d'Antoine van Dyck* (Brussels, 1956), no. 91.

20. *Passeri* 1934, 103–104; Giovan Pietro Bellori, *Le vite de'pittori, scultori e architetti moderni* (Rome, 1672), 270; Dony 1922, 97–98; Fransolet 1941, 41–42, 179.

21. *La Vie* 1975, fol. 38; Vaes 1924, 201.

22. On this correspondence and on De Wael's relations with Van Uffel see Vaes 1924, 182–183, 201–203; Vaes 1925, 161–164.

23. As Bellori called him. He is not to be confused with the painter Claude Lorrain, to whom Duquesnoy was later to be close. On the sculptor whom Passeri simply called "Lorenese" and Bellori "Claudio Lorenese" see *Passeri* 1934, 103; Bellori 1672, 270. Of course the possibility must remain that knowing of Duquesnoy's later friendship with the painter, Bellori simply mistakenly gave the name of Claude to the *intagliatore* from Lorraine who initially helped Duquesnoy in Rome.

24. In addition to the possibility of an acquaintanceship with Jean Le Clerc and the sculptor Claude, one has also to remember that painters ranging from Vouet to Jean Lemaire, Charles Mellin, and Claude Mellan (see also note 52) were all in Rome at this time. For a summary see Jacques Bousquet, "Les Relations de Poussin avec le milieu romain," in A. Chastel, ed., *Actes du colloque Poussin* (Paris, 1960), 1:2–3.

25. For the relations between Duquesnoy and Poussin see, among others, *Passeri* 1934, 105–106; Bellori 1672, 411–412. See also Bousquet 1960, 2–3.

26. On Duquesnoy's early commissions for the Barberini see Fransolet 1941, 164–165, 176, 179; *Passeri* 1934, 104–106; Bellori 1672, 271–272. Karl Noehles, "Francesco Duquesnoy: Un busto ignoto e la cronologia delle sue opere," *Arte Antica e Moderna* (1964), 88, raises, albeit very tentatively, the possibility that Francesco Barberini may already have been thinking of Duquesnoy as the possible sculptor of the tomb monument of William Barclay (d. 1621) in Sant'Onofrio as early as 1623 (even though the monument was only executed in 1627–1628). On Cassiano himself see note 42. See also Francis Haskell, *Patrons and Painters* (London and New York, 1963), 104: "The sculptor who really appealed to Cassiano's tastes and whose wax and terracotta *modelli* he collected was Bernini's Flemish rival, François Duquesnoy" (compare also *Passeri* 1934, 107).

27. Bellori 1672, 256.

28. *Passeri* 1934, 111–112; Bellori 1672, 276; Fransolet 1941, 118–120, 183–184. For good color illustrations see also Antonia Nava Cellini, *Duquesnoy* [*I Maestri della Scultura*, 83], (Milan, 1966), pls. VIII, XII, XIII.

29. *La Vie* 1975, fol. 41; Bellori 1672, 255 (on Bentivoglio portrait only). On the close friendship between Bentivoglio and Barberini see text and note 70.

30. Guido Bentivoglio, *Memorie del Cardinale Bentivoglio, con le quali descrive la sua vita, e non solo le cose a lui successe nel corso di essa, ma insieme le più notabili ancora occorse nella città di Roma, in Italia, & altrove* (Venice, 1648). In the previous year there were two editions, in Venice and in Amsterdam.

31. Guido Bentivoglio, *Raccolta di lettere scritte in tempo delle sue nuntiature di Fiandra, e di Francia* (Cologne [?], 1631), and many subsequent editions (Paris, 1635; Venice, 1636; Paris, 1642). The *Relationi* were, if anything, still more popular, first appearing in 1629 (Guido Bentivoglio, *Relationi fatte in tempo delle sue nuntiature di Fiandra e di Francia. Date in luce da Erycio Puteano* [Anversa [sic?], 1629; Colonia [sic?], 1629]). Imprints are recorded in Cologne in 1630, Paris in 1631, Brussels in 1632, Venice in 1633, Liège in 1635, and Venice in 1636. The *Lettere* and the *Relationi* were also published together, often also with the *Guerra di Fiandra* (see note 32). These books may be said to have been the best-sellers of the 1630s.

32. Guido Bentivoglio, *Della guerra di Fiandra* (Cologne [?], 1632); subsequent editions: in Cologne (or with Cologne as place of publication), 1633, 1634, 1633–1639, 1635 (Leiden?); in Venice: 1637, 1640, 1645; Spanish editions, from 1643 on; French ones, from 1634; English, from 1652; Dutch, from 1674. The work appeared together with the letters and the *Relationi* in the several editions of the *Opere* published in Paris in the second half of the 1640s. Compare note 75 for the rival work on more or less exactly the same topic, Famiano Strada's *De Bello Belgico*, which enjoyed a similar vogue in more or less the same years.

33. In addition to the previously cited literary material see also the useful article by A. Merola in *Dizionario biografico degli Italiani* (Rome, 1980), 24:634–638.

34. Bellori 1672, 255.

35. Glück 1931, 204; Washington 1990, no. 25.

36. The importance of the visit of the Shirleys for circles close to Van Dyck should not be underestimated. In addition to his probable relations with agents such as George Gage, with Sir Kenelm Digby, English resident in Rome, and possibly with Lucas van Uffel (all of whom Van Dyck knew well), Robert Shirley may well have provided a number of members of the Accademia dei Lincei—including the soon-to-be-elected Cassiano dal Pozzo—with valuable information about the East. In this respect, and in many others, there is a remarkable parallel with that other intrepid traveler to the East, Pietro della Valle, who also married the daughter of an oriental nobleman (in this case a Mesopotamian) and returned to Rome in 1626, having just been invited to become a Linceo himself (compare Giuseppe Gabrieli *Contributi alla Storia della Accademia dei Lincei*, 2 vols. [Rome, 1989], 1:467). Robert Shirley died in 1628, but his wife stayed on in Rome, living among the nuns of Santa Maria della Scala in Trastevere until her death almost forty years later. On the Shirleys (both this pair and Robert's al-

most equally enterprising and adventurous brother)
see the useful bibliographic references in Washington
1990, 154–155.

37. On the tomb see Nava Cellini 1966; Ann Suther-
land Harris, "Bernini and Virginio Cesarini," *Burlington Magazine* 131 (1989), 17–23. On Cesarini himself
see also note 39.

38. See notes 66, 68. In this context one might also
compare the bust of a cardinal attributed to Duquesnoy by Steffi and Herwarth Röttgen (*Connoisseur*
167 [1968], 94–99) and proposed by them to be none
other than Guido Bentivoglio himself.

39. The date is given in Justus Riquius, *De vita viri
praestantissimi Virginii Caesarini Lyncei, Juliani
Civitatis Novae Ducis Baronis romani f. Liber. Auc-
tore Justo Riquio Belga Canonico Gandavensi Cive
romano*, Patavii Antenoris: Johannes Thuillius, 3, as
"diem X ex ante Kal. Nov., horam diei XV 1595."
The basic biographical material on Cesarini is to be
found in the typically rich and indispensable articles
by Gabrieli, "Due prelate lincei in Roma alla corte di
Urbano VIII: Virginio Cesarini e Giovanni Ciampoli"
and "Virginio Cesarini e Giovanni Ciampoli con
documenti inediti," now usefully brought together in
Gabrieli 1989, 763–818. Besides N. Conigliani, *Virginio Cesarini* (Piacenza, 1928), there is also the article by C. Mutini in the *Dizionario biografico degli
Italiani*, vol. 8 (Rome, 1980), 199–201. These are nevertheless to be supplemented by the much too sel-
dom consulted seventeenth-century eulogies and biographies, such as those by Gottifredi and Riquius,
and the slightly later biography by Riquius' editor
Agostino Favoriti, given in *Virgini Cesarini Carmina*
(Rome, 1658).

40. Aside from the references in all the biographical
works to his fortitude and renunciation of frivolous
pleasures in pursuit of literature and science, his
abstinence and stoicism emerges even from his in-
tensely moralizing vernacular poetry, as in the
poems headed "L'infermità del corpo esser deside-
rabile," "Che i lussi, e le delitie fanno la vita infe-
lice," "L'avversità esser desiderabili," and "I piaceri
del sesso esser noiosi" (Virginio Cesarini, *Poesie
liriche toscane* [Rome, 1664], 66, 131, 136, 141,
respectively).

41. See Giuseppe Gabrieli, "Galileo in Acquasparta,"
"La prima Accademia dei Lincei (1603–1630) nella
luce della recente documentazione," "Il carteggio
scientifico ed accademico tra i primi Lincei," and
"Verbali delle adunanze e cronaca della prima
Accademia Lincea (1603–1630)" in Gabrieli 1989,
1:195–224, 225–242, 399–478, 497–550, respectively.
See also Gabrieli's edition of the correspondence be-
tween Galileo, Cesi, and the other early Lincei, "Il
carteggio Linceo della vecchia accademia di Federico
Cesi (1603–1630)," *Memorie dell'Accademia dei
Lincei, classe di scienze morali, storiche e filo-
logiche*, 6th–7th ser., 7 (1938–1942), 1–1446. For
Galileo himself the basic reference work is Galileo
Galilei, *Le Opere di Galileo Galilei*, 20 vols. in 21
(Florence, 1929–1939). For a useful summary of perti-
nent material see also Ada Alessandrini, *Documenti*

Lincei e Cimeli Galileiani [exh. cat., Accademia
Nazionale dei Lincei] (Rome, 1965) [*Accademia
Nazionale dei Lincei. Indici e Sussidi Bibliografici
della Biblioteca, 4*].

42. Cassiano's activities as an artistic Maecenas and
collector of drawings after the antique are well
known (see, for example, Haskell 1963, 98–114; Cornelis C. Vermeule, "The dal Pozzo-Albani Drawings
of Classical Antiquities. Notes on Their Contents
and Arrangement," *Art Bulletin* 38 [1956], 31–46;
Cornelis C. Vermeule, "The dal Pozzo-Albani Drawings of Classical Antiquities in the Royal Library at
Windsor Castle," *Transactions and Proceedings of
the American Philosophical Society*, n.s., 56, pt. 2
[1966]. It has only been in the last few years that
Cassiano's scientific activities and patronage have
come to the fore again, although they were perfectly
obvious from the many references to his activities in
works such as the great book known as the *Tesoro
Messicano* and from the way in which, for example,
he was referred to when he was first proposed (by Cesarini) as a prospective Linceo in 1621: "hic industria
chymica sua iam multis principibus et viris doctis
notissimus est, et in corrodendis [?] plurimis rerum
naturalium secretis magnas impensas fecit" (cited by
Giuseppe Gabrieli, "Verbali delle adunanze e cronaca
della prima Accademia Lincea [1603–1630]," in
Gabrieli 1989, 1:540; for a summary see David Freedberg, "Cassiano, Natural Historian," *Quaderni
Puteani* 1 [1989], 10–16).

43. Much evidence for the friendship is brought together in "Due Prelati" and "Cesarini and
Ciampoli," in Gabrieli 1989; C. Mutini in *Dizionario
biografico*, 199–200; see also Bentivoglio 1648, 96;
Riquius, 10, in which Cesarini's other friends are
also listed. But in some ways the best evidence
comes from Ciampoli himself, in the letter in which
he describes to Galileo how he went to stay with Cesarini in 1616: "Venni per alloggiar dal signor don
Virginio due giorni e la cortesia di questo Signore
non mi vuol lasciar partire;" he continues to describe
at some length the personal gifts of Cesarini in the
closest and most affectionate terms. Ciampoli recalls
how he was received "con sì affettuosa insistenza
che non mi par lecito il ricusarla, anzi al genio mio è
desiderabilissima, particolarmente seguendo ciò
senza una minima diminutione della mia solita lib-
ertà" (Galilei 1929–1939, 12:300, cited by Mutini in
Dizionario biografico, 199).

44. For Cesarini's role and the extraordinary events
surrounding the preparation and editing of the manuscript see Pietro Redondi, *Galileo Eretico* (Turin,
1983), especially 53–60; see also Galilei 1929–1939,
20: *Indice dei nomi* (125) and *Indice biografico* (416),
for the references (including the earlier ones) to
Cesarini in Galileo's correspondence. For the relationship between Galileo and Ciampoli see also
"Due Prelati," in Gabrieli 1989, 769–773.

45. As, for example, in Riquius, 12–14, 18; but see
also the letters by Ciampoli and to Cesi, Maffeo Barberini, and Cassiano dal Pozzo cited in notes 47–51.

46. "Vidisses ex illo aetatis ac formae flore miseras reliquias, exanguem atque emaciatum, viribus defectissimum, demersum, ac plane oppressum dolorum mole, spirans cadaver, hominis simulacrum, sine succo, sine sanguine, sine colore, hospitium plane dixisses calamitatis. Neque tamen in tanta doloris materia indoluit, ipse unquam, aut animum deiicit humiliter; sed stante vultu & siccis oculis sua spectans naufragia adversis rerum immersabilis undis, Marpesia veluti cautes stetit immobilis" (Alessandro Gottifredi, *In funere Virginii Cesarini Oratio ad S.P.Q.R. dum ei in aede Virginis Capitolinae publico sumptu parentaret* [Rome, 1624], 25). Gabrieli's description (Gabrieli 1989, 1:788) of Gottifredi's work as "poco piu di una chiaccherata" seems unduly harsh, not only in light of the useful information Gottifredi provides, but above all in the context of passages such as the one cited above.

47. See, for example, the letter from Cesarini to Maffeo Barberini, 24 March 1619, in which he explains "Non ho potuto sfuggire gli assalti del male in coteste parti perchè è troppo difficile il riparo dai nemici interni. . . ." And he goes on to describe a number of remedies, such as essences of citrons, lemons, and jasmine (Biblioteca Apostolica Vaticana, Vatican City [hereinafter BAV], MS Barb. Lat. 6461, fols. 125–125v). Compare the letter from Ciampoli to Cesi, 24 May 1618: "Il Sr Virginio non ha goduto mai intera sanità in quest'estate; e se bene egli studia tutta via più che ordinariamente, pure rispetto all sua consuetudine si e temperato pur assai. . . ." (Biblioteca dell'Accademia Nazionale dei Lincei e Corsiniana, Rome [hereinafter BLC], Archivio Linceo, MS 12, fols. 338–339) and the letters from Cesarini to Cassiano cited in the present text and in notes 49 and 50. See also the autograph manuscript written by Cesi himself immediately after Cesarini's death, BLC, Archivio Linceo, MS 4, fols. 310–312, reproduced in Gabrieli 1989, 1:783–785.

48. For example BLC, Archivio dal Pozzo, MS XII (10), fols. 546–563; MS XXXVI (33), as well as the passages from several letters between Cesarini and Cassiano cited in Gabrieli 1989, 1:802–804. On Potier see Gabrieli 1989, 1:803, n. 5.

49. As, for example, the "oglio dai fiori di naranti e con li semi di pere" mentioned in BLC, Archivio dal Pozzo, MS XII (10), fol. 555. Compare the extract of citrons described at great length in BAV, MS Barb. Lat. 6461, fol. 125, and cited in Gabrieli 1989, 1:800.

50. "Fino a qui la pioggia, e gli scirocchi mi hanno confinato in casa. La mutatione dell'aria fatta particolarmente in tempi torbidi mi ha fatto infreddare: di poi mi tiene infiammata la gola con le solite flussioni, che mi vogliano accompagnar per tutto. Mi resta non poco di confidenza nel Sr Potier; e sono quasi risoluto, che a nuovo tempo o egli venga a Roma, o io vada a trovarlo a Bologna;" BLC, Archivio dal Pozzo, MS XII (10), fol. 561.

51. "Scrivo a lungo a P. Potier, dandoli distinta relatione della mia infirmità. . . . da due giorni in quà mi sento meno affannato: però sto à gloria aspettando il tempo buono" (24 January 1620); BLC, Archivio dal Pozzo, MS XII (10), fol. 550.

52. As in note 61.

53. Gottifredi 1624, 20, 29. See also the frontispiece to this work by Mellan after Pomarancio, in which the medallion showing Pico della Mirandola at bottom center of the page balances that of Cesarini at the top; and the pair of profile medallions in *Carmina* 1658, in the biography edited by Agostini Favoriti (see note 55).

54. See, for example, Gottifredi 1624, 20; Janus Nicius Erythraeus, *Pinacotheca* (Cologne, 1645), 59, noting that it was none other than the renownedly severe Robert Bellarmine who called Cesarini a modern Pico.

55. See Riquius, 10–11. The parallel is also drawn in the biography of Cesarini by Agostino Favoriti, the editor of the posthumous edition of Cesarini's literary remains (*Carmina* 1658; *Poesie* 1664). See also the pair of engraved medallions showing the idealized profiles of the two young philosophers facing each other in *Carmina* 1658, n.p. On Riquius see Giuseppe Gabrieli, "Giusto Ricchio Belga: I suoi scritti editi ed inediti," *Atti dell' Accademia Nazionale dei Lincei. Rendiconti della classe di scienze morali,* 6th ser., 9 (1933), 142–185, reprinted in Gabrieli 1989, 1:1133–1164; "Ancora di Josse Rycke [Giusto Ricchio] Panegirista o Encomiatore Ufficiale dei Lincei Defunti nella Prima Accademia," *Bulletin de l'Institut Historique Belge de Rome* 21 (1941), 71–83, reprinted in Gabrieli 1989, 1:1165–1175.

56. A useful list of Riquius' correspondents is given in Gabrieli 1989, 1:1146–1162, on the basis of the letters published in the extremely rare *Primitiae Epistolicae* (Cologne, 1610), the *Epistolarum selectarum centuria altera* (Louvain, 1615), and the "Epistolarum selectarum tertia," ed. R. van den Berghe, in R. van den Berghe, "Justus Riquius," *Messager des sciences historiques* (1881), 166–185, 457–477.

57. For example Riquius, 12–14, 18, where he refers to the last year of Cesarini's life "adeo consumptus fuerat [in the winter of 1623–1624], ut ἀδύνατον quivis crederet, in tam imbecilli corpusculo aliquid vitalis spritius deinceps posse residere. Sic tamen convaluerat e periculosissimo & atrocissimo morbo, ut ad vitae officia, ac studiorum labores subinde & intervallo rediret."

58. Antonia Nava Cellini "Aggiunte alla ritrattistica Berniniana e Algardiana," *Paragone* 6 (1955), 27.

59. Nava Cellini 1955, 27.

60. *Carmina* 1658, 58, in the poem dedicated to Fulvio Testi (see also note 61, with further references).

61. Besides the many details in Gottifredi and Riquius (see note 57). In the Latin poetry see, for example, the poem to Fulvio Testi, "Queritur se loquendi usum morbo amisisse," (*Carmina* 1658, 56), the long lament to Ciampoli, "Morbo recrudescente" (*Carmina* 1658, 81), and the whole of the affectionate, plaintive ode to Famiano Strada (*Carmina* 1658, 64).

62. Nava Cellini 1955, 27–28. The attribution is also

supported by Claudia Freytag, "Neuentdeckte Werke des François du Quesnoy," *Pantheon* 34 (1976), 199.

63. Harris 1989, 17–23.

64. On the Guglielmi tomb in San Lorenzo fuori le Mura see Karl Noehles, "Francesco Duquesnoy: Un busto ignoto e la cronologia delle sue opere," *Arte Antica e Moderna* (1964), 86–96; on that of George Conn in San Lorenzo in Damaso see Freytag 1976, 207–209.

65. A *terminus ante quem* for the ivory crucifix and the Saint Sebastian is provided by the papal chirograph of 4 April 1626 first published by A. Bertolotti, *Giunte agli artisti belgi e olandesi in Roma nei secoli XVI e XVII* (Rome, 1885), 30.

66. For the documents regarding the payments by Francesco Barberini for these tombs in 1628 see Noehles 1964. Although the tombs of Barclay (d. 1621) and Guglielmi (d. 1623) were only paid for in 1628 (Noehles 1964, 96), it is not impossible, as Noehles himself implies (87–88), that Duquesnoy was chosen as their sculptor several years earlier—perhaps just after the evident success of the Cesarini tomb? It is worth noting that in the very year of his death Barclay was proposed to become a member of the Accademia dei Lincei by none other than Virginio Cesarini (Gabrieli 1989, 1:459).

67. The many documents on all these papal commissions are summarized in Fransolet 1941, 164–165, 176–179. Compare also Oskar Pollak, *Die Kunsttätigkeit unter Urban VIII.*, 2 vols. (Vienna, 1931), 2:93, 355–359, 429–436, 451. For the other works done for the Barberini see also Bellori 1672, 271–272; Freytag 1976, 199–207; Irving and Marilyn Lavin, "Duquesnoy's 'Nano di Créqui' and Two Busts by Francesco Mochi," *Art Bulletin* 52 (1970), 132–149.

68. On Conn and the Conn tomb (commissioned by Francesco Barberini and dated 1640) see Freytag 1976, 207–211.

69. "Earned him the greatest applause," *La Vie* 1975, fol. 41.

70. "In particular he [Bentivoglio] derived the greatest pleasure in sharing his studies with two of the rarest talents of the highest repute in the field of letters; and these were Cardinal Maffeo Barberini, now Pope Urban VIII, and Don Virginio Cesarini." Bentivoglio 1648, 95–96.

71. See also Panifilowa 1955, 36–37.

72. "He was entertained in the house of Cardinal Bentivoglio, who was a lover of the Flemish nation, as a result of having lived in Flanders and having written that history [of the Flemish Wars] which will live forever." Bellori 1672, 255.

73. In addition to Bentivoglio 1648, 95–96, and the *Epistola Dedicatoria* to Urban in Gottifredi 1624, 3–5, see also the description of Urban's affection for Cesarini in Riquius, 16 (on the Capitoline funeral see also 23–24).

74. Compare *Passeri* 1934, 104: "si godeva spesso la ricreazione delli fiammeng[h]i suoi Compatrioti den-

tro l'Ospizio di quella Nazione nella Chiesa di San Giuliano alli Cesarini. . . ."

75. In addition to the evidence of his own testament (cited in note 78) see also Gottifredi 1624, 29; Riquius, 16. Redondi 1983, 49–60, has an important discussion of the role of Grassi in these years, as well as the relationship with Cesarini.

76. Famianus Strada, *De Bello Belgico Decas Prima ab excessu Caroli V Imp. usque ad initia Praefecturae Alexandri Farnesii* (Antwerp, 1635; Rome, 1637); the *Decas Secunda (ab initio praefecturae Alexandri Farnesii . . . an. MDLXXXVIII usque ad an. MDXC* was published by the heirs of Francesco Corbelletti in Rome, 1647. Further editions of the first decade appeared in Rome in 1640 and in Leyden in 1643, while both decades appeared together in Frankfurt in 1651 (preceded by Scheus' combined imprint of 1638–1649 of the Italian translation). I do not mention the several later editions of this work, whose publication history is, if anything, even more complicated than that of Bentivoglio's *Della guerra di Fiandra* (see note 32). While it does not seem to have been quite as popular as Bentivoglio's history, it was certainly an important competitor, and provides further indication of the extraordinary interest in the Revolt of the Netherlands in Rome during the 1630s, 1640s, and 1650s. An important list of Cesarini's friends is given in Riquius, 15 (including both Strada and Galluzzi); see also the revealing poem about Cesarini's illness addressed to Strada in the *Poesie* 1664, 64–66.

77. Gottifredi 1624, 29; see also Riquius, 16, as well as note 78.

78. "Lascio di essere portato a seppellire con l'habito di religioso della Compagnia di Gesù havendomi il R.mo P.dre Generale fatta grazia di accettarmi in detta religione conforme alla istanza fattagliene da me. Però supplico S.P. R.ma a fare honorare il corpo mio del detto habito, et ad aiutare la anima mia con li suffraggi soliti farsi per morte di alcuni Padri. Morendo in Roma, lascio di essere sepolto nella chiesa del Gesù in quella sepoltura ove è sepolta la signora Duchessa mia Madre, e se morisse altrove ove sieno i Padri de detta Compagnia, lascio di essere sepolto nella chiesa loro;" Archivio Notarile del Comune, Acquasparta, *Rogiti* del Notaio Cesarini (1624), 12–13; reprinted in Gabrieli 1989, 1:804–805.

79. The full inscription is given in the unpaginated biography of Cesarini by Favoriti in *Carmina* 1658.

80. See Bentivoglio 1648, 96–97.

81. Redondi 1983, 53.

82. Redondi 1983, 54–55.

83. See note 5.

84. "He was still young, with his beard just beginning to show, but his youth was accompanied by a grave modesty in his soul and by a nobility of aspect that belied his small size. His manners were those of an aristocrat rather than of a private person. . . ." Bellori 1672, 255.

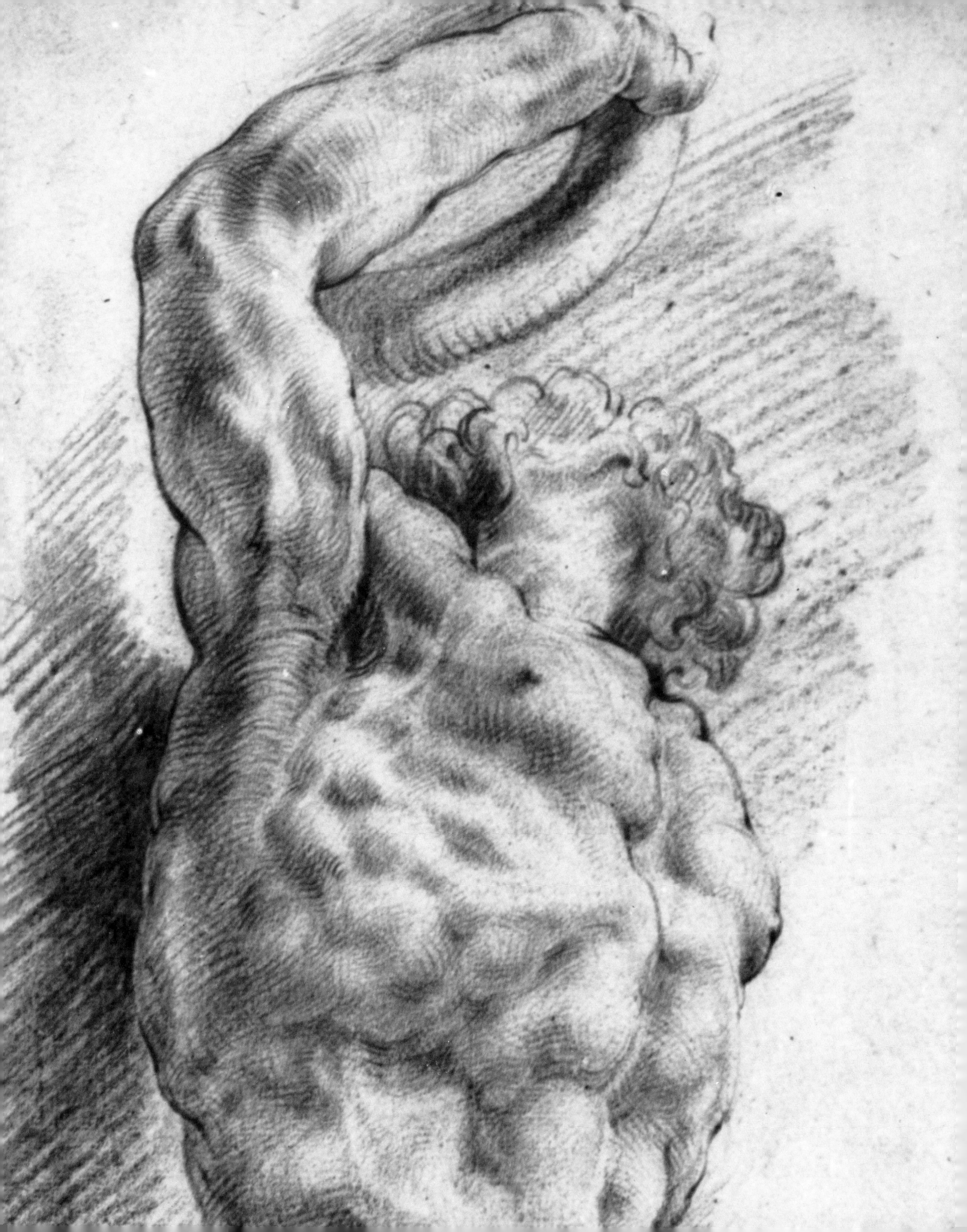

ARNOUT BALIS
National Centrum voor de Plastische Kunsten
van de 16de en 17de Eeuw

Van Dyck: Some Problems of Attribution

The value of an attribution, given the methodology involved, does not lie solely in its correctness (which is, in any case, very difficult to establish), but also in its capacity to trigger a critical response. Statements about attribution invite confrontation, elicit comparisons and closer scrutiny, and thus bring about unforeseeable critical activity that is more likely than not to yield new observations. It might thus be argued that any attribution, however unsound, may serve a useful purpose, and this much should, I think, be granted; but the context in which such an attribution is presented and the style in which it is enunciated are relevant to its value as a contribution to the critical process. At its worst, an unsound attribution can obfuscate rather than illuminate, and litter the critical field. Given the peculiar nature of the arguments involved in this debate—as far as they are properly set forth, anyway—it is very difficult to assess the value of an attribution unless one can fall back on one's own expertise in the area concerned. This might sound as if we witness only a clash of opinions. The healthiness of any particular field of art history, I submit, depends on the kind of infrastructure that allows more constructive critical work to run its course. When it comes to attribution, we need a hierarchy of authority (even when we want to contest it in particulars) and full documentation on the objects to be evaluated. Van Dyck scholarship is rather disappointing in both respects.

One would expect that for an artist of the importance of Van Dyck, well studied since the eighteenth century (witness the so-called Louvre Manuscript), there would be, by now, a reliable catalogue. Indeed, in recent years two publications have claimed to fill this gap. One is a cheaply produced photographic inventory of all Van Dyck's paintings, the other an expensive two-volume catalogue raisonné of Van Dyck's production as a painter. Both are by Erik Larsen.[1] Unfortunately, perusal of these works teaches us that we should not alter our habit of reaching for the over sixty-year-old Klassiker der Kunst volume prepared by Gustav Glück;[2] but we are thus left rather at a loss when we would like full documentation on these paintings, or when confronted with specific questions as to the status of works not recorded by Glück. Hundreds of paintings that orbit our artist (with attributions launched by a mixed group, consisting of art dealers as well as academic art historians) still have to be properly mapped. There are versions or copies of known Van Dyck compositions and independent compositions. A few of these may indeed be by the master, but a large number most certainly are not. There is still much pruning to be done. This article can do no more than signal the problem and suggest ways of remedying it.

My first case is a panel in the Musée J. P. Pescatore in Luxembourg representing *The Arrest of Samson* (fig. 1).[3] It is an extremely faithful but reduced reproduction in grisaille of that wonderful painting by Van Dyck in

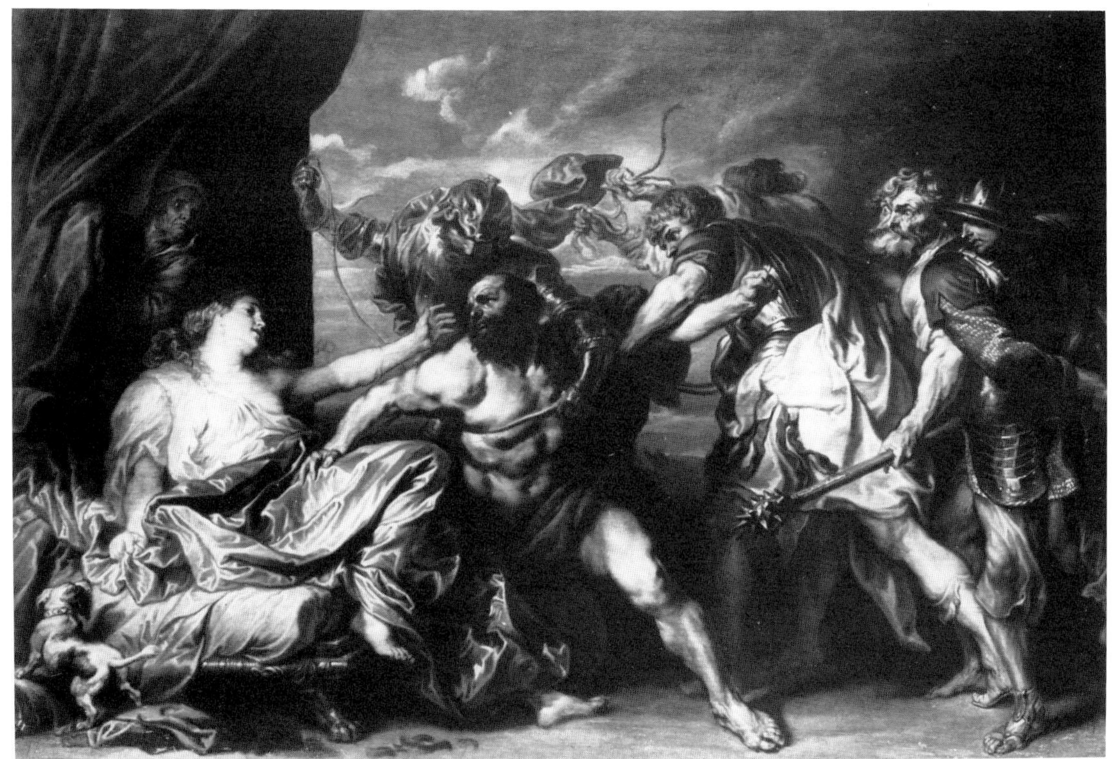

1. Abraham van Diepenbeeck, *The Arrest of Samson*, c. 1642, oil on panel
Musée J. P. Pescatore, Luxembourg

2. Anthony van Dyck, *The Arrest of Samson*, 1628–1630, oil on canvas
Kunsthistorisches Museum, Vienna

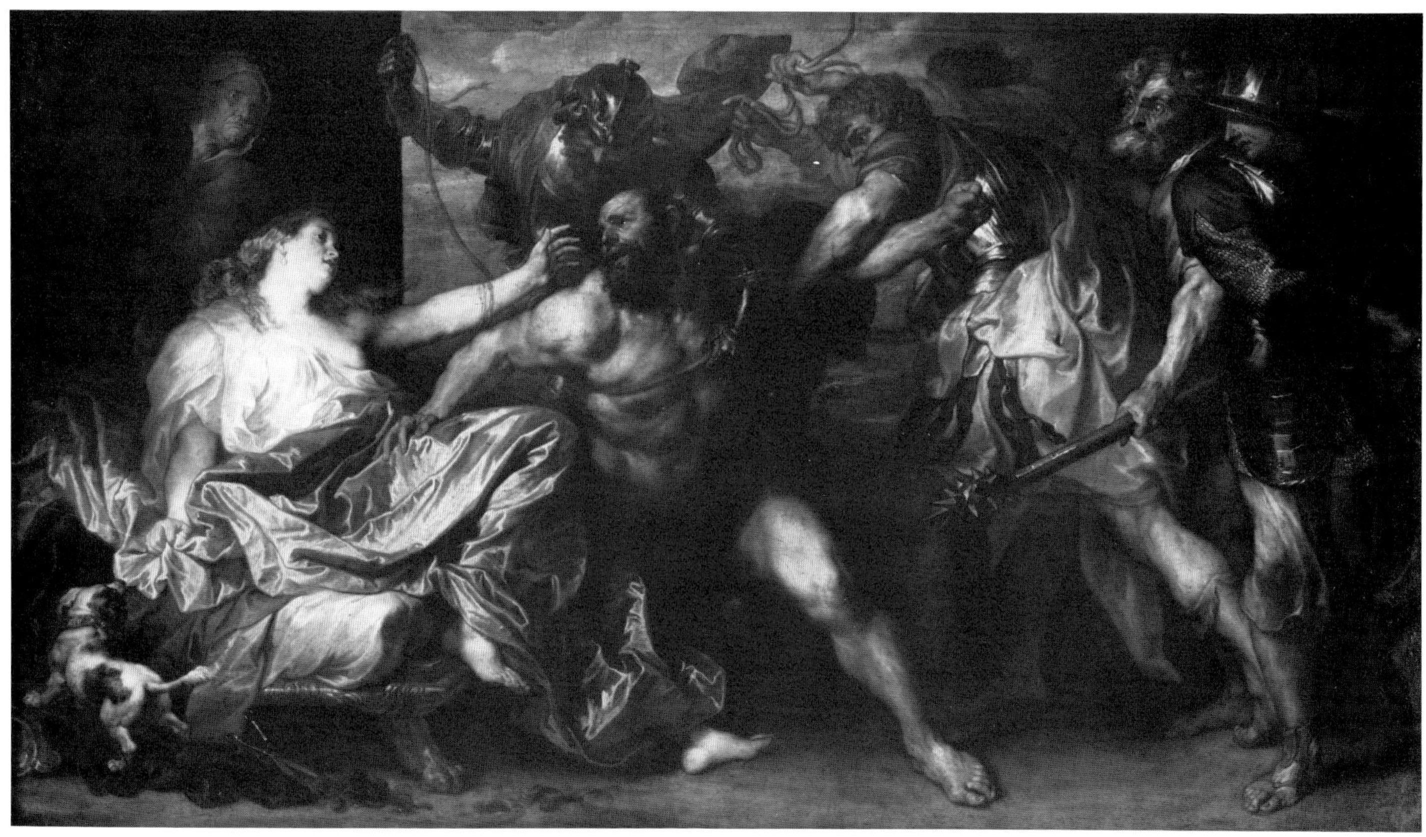

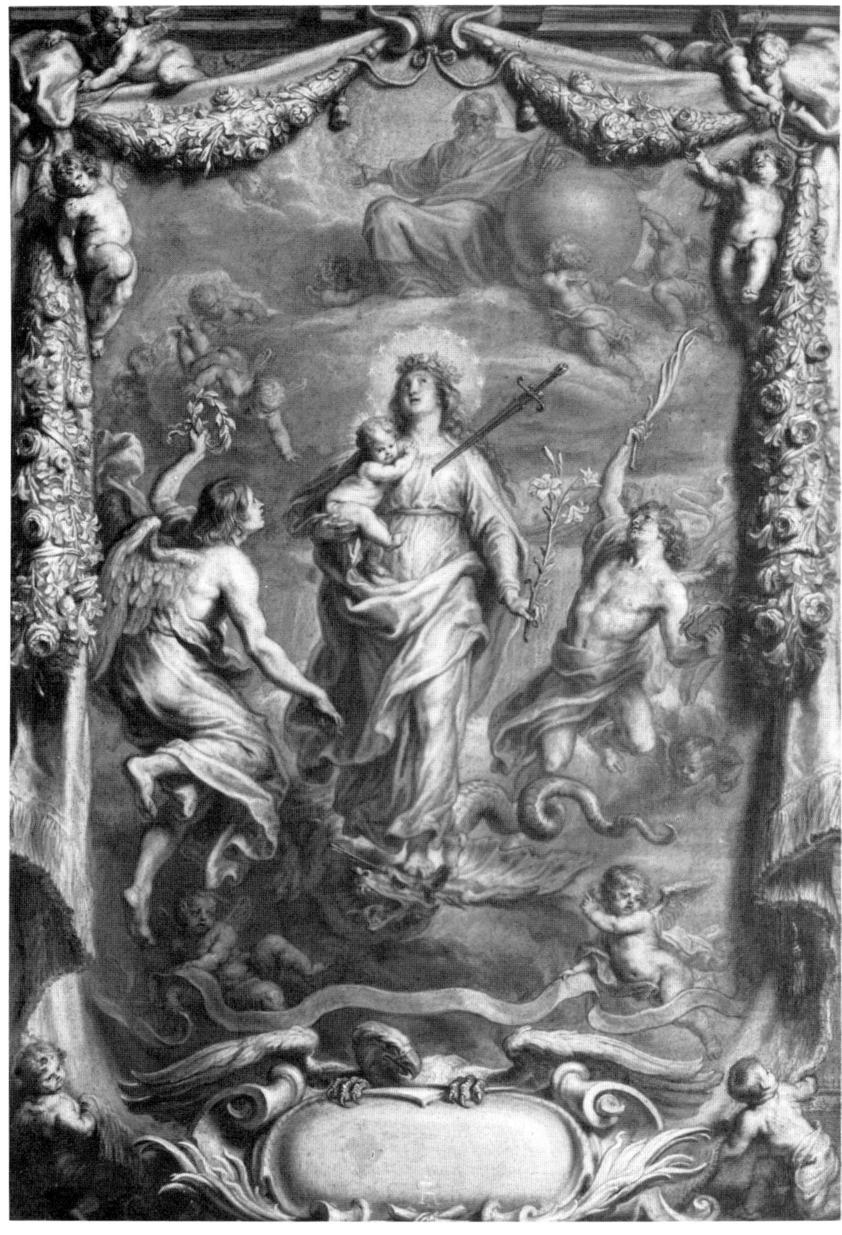

3. Abraham van
Diepenbeeck, *Our Lady of
the Apocalypse*, oil on panel
Galleria degli Uffizi, Florence

painted very accurate *modelli* of his compositions in preparation for engravings.[5] Nor is the panel in Luxembourg of inferior quality; on the contrary, it is a virtuoso performance. It has been attributed to Van Dyck himself by Michel Lefèbvre in a small booklet of 1980, and this attribution was repeated in the most recent catalogue of the Pescatore museum collection.[6]

The technical qualities of the Luxembourg panel notwithstanding, there is reason to doubt Van Dyck's authorship of it. Instead of the lively treatment of highlights found in Van Dyck's *modelli*, we find here a slick and rather monotonous surface in which all the elements seem to be wrought from the same rubberlike material.

The Luxembourg panel apparently served as the model for an engraving by Hendrik Snyers, which has the same measurements and shows the composition in reverse—including the addition at the top.[7] This observation may lead us to the name of the artist who actually executed the Luxembourg panel. The print in question was published by Abraham van Diepenbeeck (1596–1675). It is known that on 3 September 1642 Van Diepenbeeck engaged Hendrik Snyers to engrave the copies he himself had made over the last few years of "artful and remarquable paintings."[8] He also obtained a privilege on these prints for twelve years, which protected his rights against imitators. Van Diepenbeeck seems to have selected, in particular, works by Rubens and Van Dyck. A grisaille painting similar in style to the one under discussion, a rendering of Rubens' *The Real Presence in the Holy Sacrament* in Saint Paul's church in Antwerp, turned up recently. This composition was also engraved by Snyers and published by Van Diepenbeeck.[9] The attribution of these *modelli* to Van Diepenbeeck can be substantiated by comparing them with other grisaille paintings by this artist, such as *Our Lady of the Apocalypse* (fig. 3) or *The Crucifixion* (Fitzwilliam Museum, Cambridge).[10] Here also we find a strong grasp of the general form combined with an accurate rendering of the minutest detail, but the painterly surface is somewhat monotonous and dull.[11]

That Van Diepenbeeck studied Van Dyck's *Samson* closely appears from the fact that he reused a head from it—that of the elderly

Vienna (fig. 2), one of his most rhythmical compositions.[4] The only difference of importance between the two is that the Luxembourg panel allows for more space at the top. The Vienna canvas dates from Van Dyck's second Antwerp period and must have been executed around 1628–1630. By 1659 it belonged to Leopold Wilhelm, the former governor of the southern Netherlands, who had taken it with him to Vienna. Faithfulness to the painting in Vienna need not necessarily be held against the Luxembourg panel. Van Dyck himself seems occasionally to have

Philistine on the right—in one of his own compositions. I am referring to a tapestry cartoon with a wolf hunt in the Hermitage (fig. 4), a work that can be given securely to Diepenbeeck on documentary basis.[12]

A case such as that presented by the Luxembourg grisaille (fig. 1)—in which neither figural style nor compositional structure is a help in determining authorship, for which we can only rely on less easily grasped characteristics such as brushwork—would seem to make heavy demands on the inconclusive discipline of connoisseurship. We are lucky to have had some circumstantial evidence that suggests a particular solution. One would expect more certainty in the case of original compositions, but in fact much work still needs to be done here, too. I shall make a few proposals in this respect.

A painting depicting *The Martyrdom of an Unknown Saint in the Presence of Saint Anthony* in a private collection in Brussels (figs. 5, 6) has attracted little attention.[13] This canvas was offered for sale in Brussels in 1925 as by Van Dyck. When it was exhibited in 1988 in Tokyo, the attribution was toned down to "studio of Van Dyck." "Follower" would have been more appropriate, since Pieter Thys (1624–1677), who I think is the author of this altarpiece, apparently never worked with Van Dyck, although he closely modeled his style on Van Dyck's.[14] The ecstatic head of the martyr (fig. 6) makes this dependence abundantly clear. The sentimental expression and sfumato treatment make the initial attribution of this canvas to Van Dyck himself somewhat understandable, but Thys' drawing in other parts is rather heavy, and the modeling unwieldy. Typical motifs we encounter in other works by Thys are the leftmost angel in the sky, who reappears in his *Saint Adrian* (Saint Peter's church, Ghent),[15] and the executioner, who plays a similar role in his *Crucifixion of Saint Peter* (fig. 7).[16] The general conception of the composition may be compared to Thys' *Martyrdom of Saint Benedict* (fig. 8)—Saint Benedict the martyr, not the monk—a canvas with similar dimensions in the Musées Royaux des Beaux-Arts, Brussels.[17] Here also we find the anachronistic combination of an early Christian martyr and a saint of the order of Saint Francis. Given the similarity in iconography as well as in composition and

size, one might be tempted to suppose that both paintings belong together, but apparently this was not the case: the *Martyrdom of Saint Benedict* can be traced to the Brussels Capucin church, and the detailed eighteenth-century descriptions of that church do not refer to a painting like the one here under scrutiny.[18]

The two paintings I have commented on have never been included in any general publication on Van Dyck,[19] and can now be removed from the fringe of Van Dyck to more congenial surroundings. By contrast, the next two canvases I want to discuss have gained a firmer foothold within the Van Dyck literature. They both belong to the Pinacoteca Vaticana and represent *Saint Ignatius of Loy-*

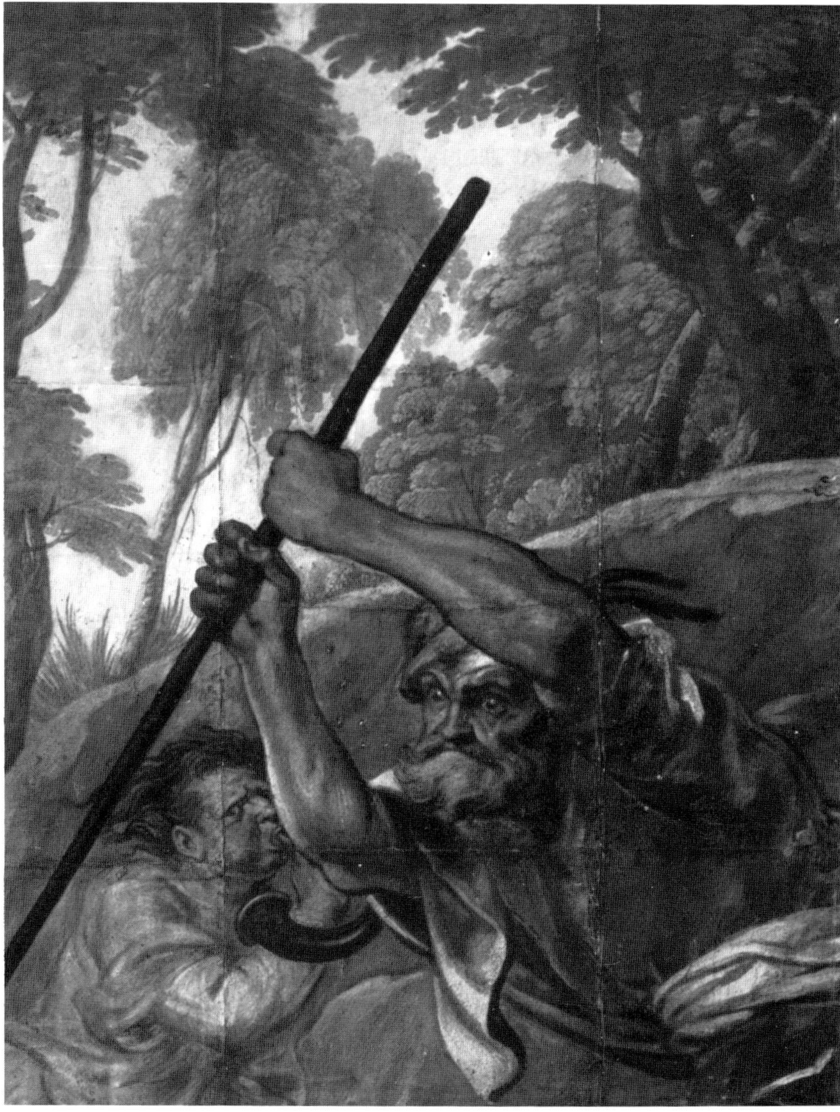

4. Abraham van Diepenbeeck, *Wolf Hunt*, (detail), c. 1665–1670, gouache on paper Hermitage, St. Petersburg

ola (fig. 9) and *Saint Francis Xavier* (fig. 10).[20] Their provenance seems to be Il Gesù in Rome. They were first published in 1936 by Redig de Campos, who attributed them to Van Dyck, referring to a description of the Roman churches of 1674 in which they figure as by that master.[21] Redig de Campos argued that Van Dyck must have painted them during his second stay in Rome in 1623, shortly after the canonization of both saints on 12 March 1622. This attribution was accepted by Vaes and Antonio Muñoz,[22] but rejected by Van den Wijngaert in 1943.[23] Subsequent attributions to Rubens (by Van Puyvelde) or to one of the Gimigniani (by Pecchiai) did not carry any conviction.[24] More recently two authors, Ursula König-Nordhoff and Eric Larsen, have again argued for an attribution to Van Dyck.[25]

I would first like to point out that these paintings cannot possibly have been executed in Rome in 1623, since the landscape in both is clearly painted by Jan Wildens, who lived in Antwerp at that time.[26] But it is more important to find out who might have painted the figures. The physiognomic types are of no great help here, since the artist clearly followed recognized prototypes that were then widely circulated in prints.[27] More important than the types are the characteristics of the execution, and here we encounter quite the opposite from Van Dyck's sensuality: the features are hard and sharply drawn. The hands, for instance those of Xavier, are muscular without the nervous tension we expect from Van Dyck. Similar characteristics are found in the work of Gerard Seghers (1591–1651).[28] Especially revealing are the putti hovering above both saints. Here the painter did not have to conform to any standards but his own, and he accordingly felt free to use his personal types, as is clear from a comparison with a putto from Seghers' *Saint Yves* (fig. 11).[29]

Reverting once again to the compositions as a whole, it is clear that the awkwardness of the stance of *Saint Ignatius* is totally unacceptable for Van Dyck, whereas it is not for Seghers, in whose oeuvre we come across more instances of this particular weakness. This should not be construed to mean that the rather elegant pose of *Saint Francis Xavier* argues against an attribution to Seghers. The latter's *Flagellation of Christ*

(Saint Michael, Ghent), for instance, proves that such elegance was also part of his vocabulary.[30]

Both paintings, the *Saint Ignatius* and the *Saint Francis Xavier*, may thus be given to Gerard Seghers and must date from his mature period, after he had given up his initial Caravaggesque style to adopt a more Rubensian idiom. That he would have been commissioned by the Jesuits in Rome to execute these two important altarpieces is not so surprising in view of the fact that he had been working quite intensively for that order, with commissions for their churches in Antwerp and Ghent as well as Cologne and Landshut.[31]

My last example may be the most interesting one. It is a painting in the Musées Royaux des Beaux-Arts, Brussels, of *Saint Sebastian Assisted by Three Angels* (fig. 12).[32] It entered the museum in 1919 and was catalogued as by a "follower of Van Dyck," tentatively ascribed to Erasmus Quellinus. In later catalogues it figures as "school of Van Dyck." Recently Larsen ascribed it to Van Dyck himself, dating it around 1630–1632 and commenting that "it shows an unaccustomed approach by the artist, one that incorporates concepts echoing the earlier years, when Van Dyck worked in company with Jordaens." He compared it with another version of the same theme, which is totally different in approach, concluding that:

both paintings . . . show us the opposites which Van Dyck could attain in the picturing of basically the same subject matter. Extreme realism versus an almost Manneristic delicacy and nervousness: two almost opposite conceptions—yet still both are representative of the same period in Anthony's career. It is as if Van Dyck had attempted to vary his spiritual approach, demonstrating how a basically tragic circumstance could be interpreted visually in different ways.[33]

I must admit that I personally fail to grasp which features in the present work may have suggested this particular attribution. At the most it could be said that this strange mixture of mannerism and virility somewhat reminds one of the early Van Dyck, with his penchant for violent and exaggerated forms, but the Brussels *Saint Sebastian* is certainly not by his hand. The paint texture is rather poor, the modeling unimaginative, and the

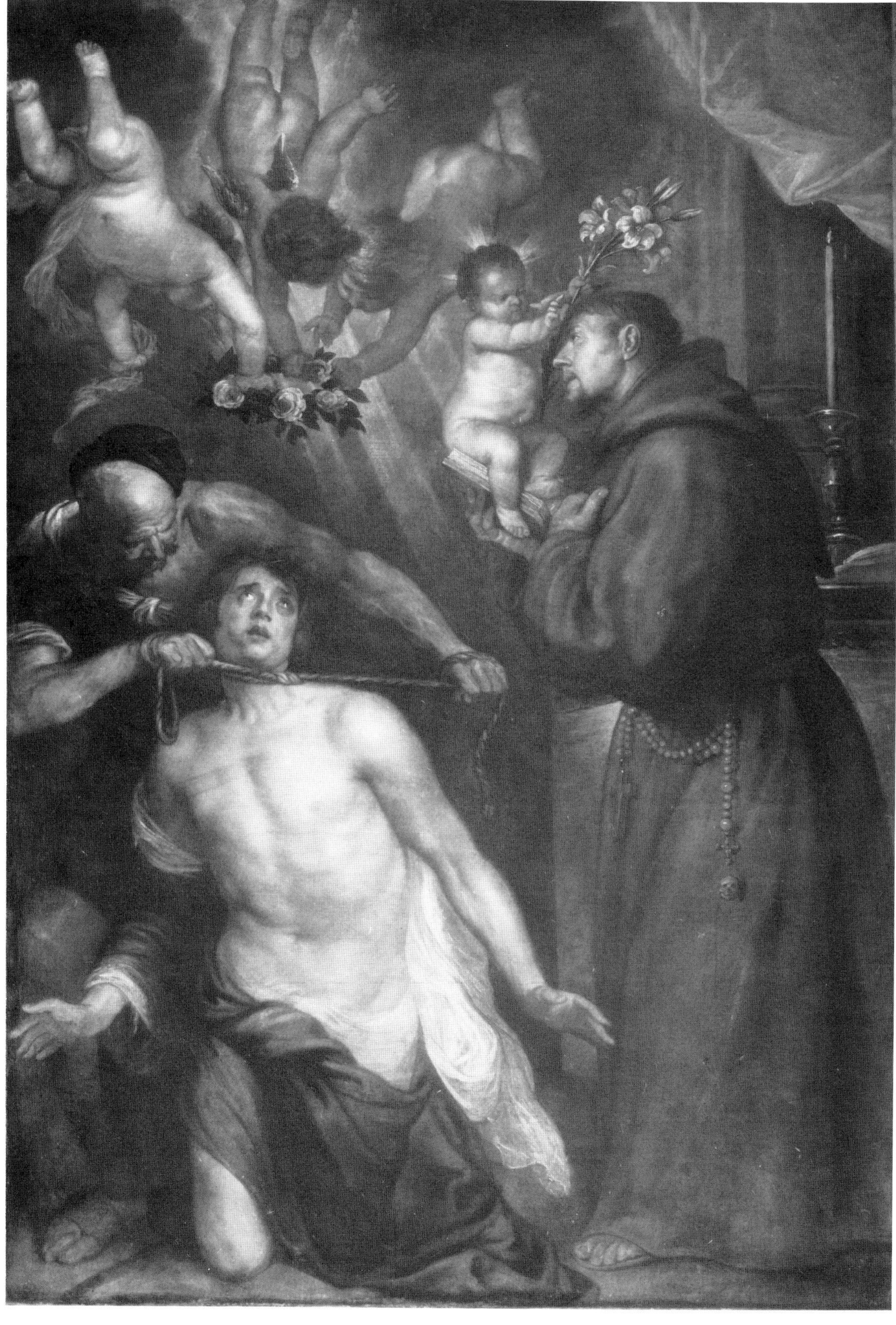

5. Pieter Thys, *The Martyrdom of an Unknown Saint in the Presence of Saint Anthony*, oil on canvas
Fondation Coppée, Brussels

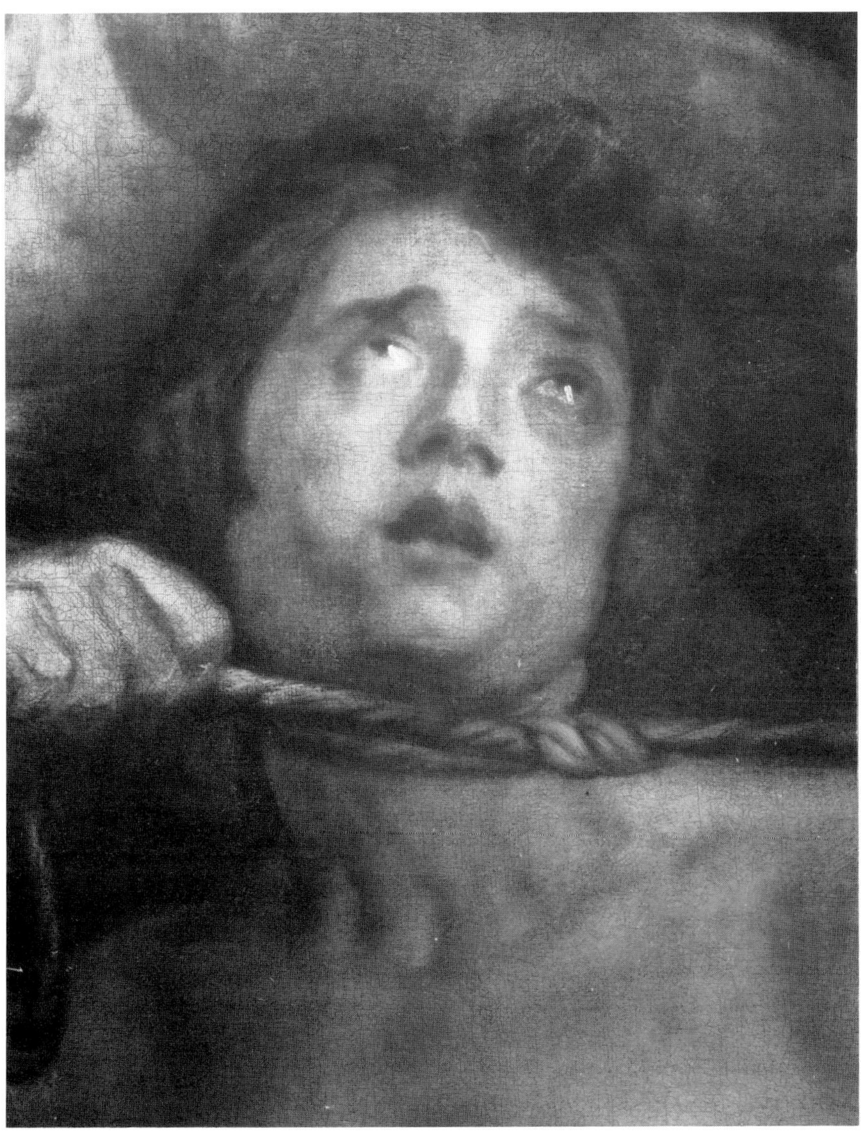

6. Detail of fig. 5

7. Pieter Thys, *Crucifixion of Saint Peter*, oil on canvas
Saint Peter's church, Berlaar

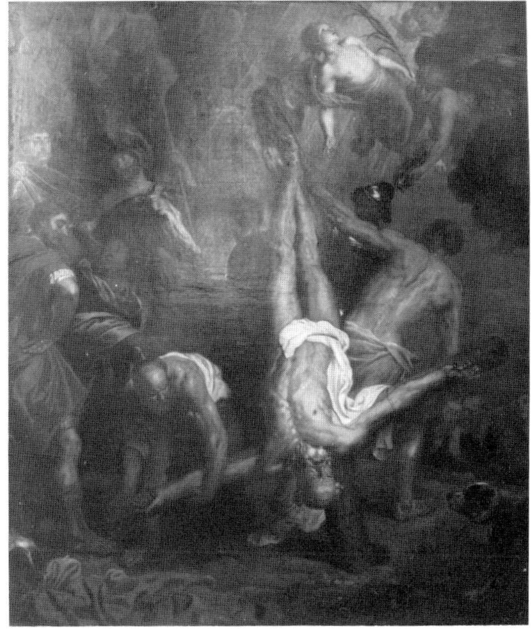

color scheme dull. This painting is, however, clearly the product of the Rubens school: witness the muscular anatomy, the heroic poses, the care with which the carnations are rendered, and generally the figural types. The work strikes me as a caricature of a Rubens composition, but who, of Rubens' pupils or followers, may be responsible for it? I would venture an attribution to Willem Panneels. I am fully aware that this may seem somewhat adventurous, since no securely documented painting by that master has yet come to light.[34] Let me, then, set out the reasons for this attribution at some length.

What is known about this artist, Panneels, amounts to no more than the following few facts:[35] he was born in or around 1600, presumably in Aachen. He was accepted as a master in the guild in Antwerp in 1627–1628,[36] after having been employed in Rubens' studio for several years. On 1 June 1630 Rubens made a declaration before the city fathers, testifying to the artistic competence of his former apprentice and mentioning that he proved a reliable housekeeper during the time Rubens was abroad on his diplomatic missions to Spain and England, from 1628 to 1630.[37] Shortly afterward Panneels himself left the country: we can follow his itinerary from Cologne (still in 1630) through Frankfurt, Baden, and Mainz (in 1631), to Strasbourg (1632). He died in Baden-Baden on 1 July 1634.[38]

The months Panneels was in charge of Rubens' house during the master's absence were apparently not spent in idleness. It has convincingly been argued that the bulk of the drawings after Rubens that are kept in the royal print room in Copenhagen and are known as the "Rubens Cantoor" are in fact by him.[39] He must have been very busy in those months copying—possibly without Rubens' consent—everything he could lay his hands on, finished paintings as well as

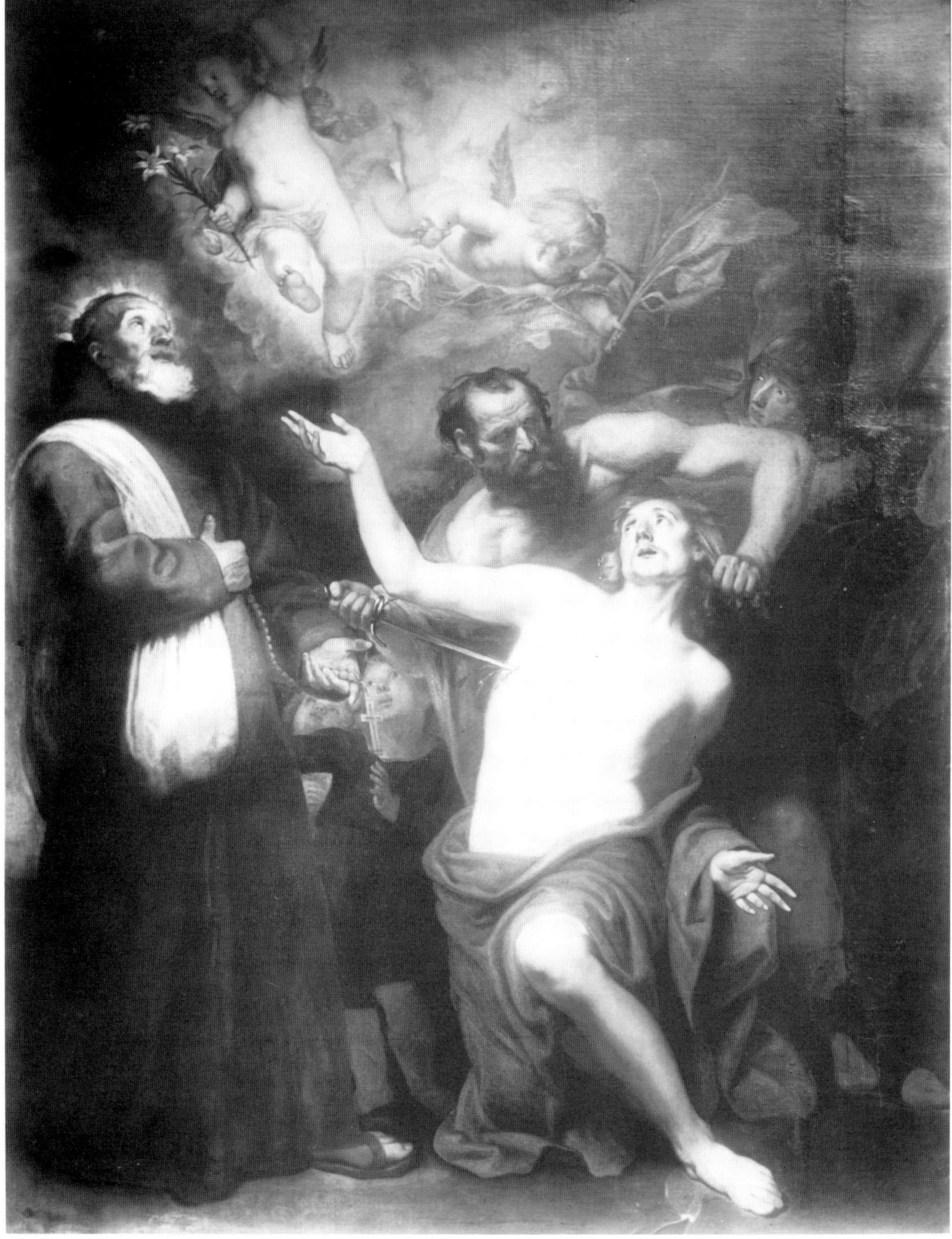

8. Pieter Thys, *Martyrdom of Saint Benedict*, oil on canvas
Musées Royaux des Beaux-Arts,
Brussels

preparatory material and study drawings that Rubens kept in his study, the "Cantoor" Panneels refers to in his inscriptions on his copies.[40] In their recent catalogue of that collection, Jan Garff and Eva de la Fuente Pedersen attribute some 250 of these sheets to Willem Panneels.[41]

Apart from these drawings, Panneels is best remembered as an etcher. Some thirty-five prints by him are known, and almost invariably his signature is accompanied by the statement that he used to be Rubens' apprentice: *Excelentissimi Pictoris P.P. Rubeni olim Discipulus*.[42] These prints render paintings by Rubens as well as some original designs by Panneels himself.[43] The latter allow us to form some idea of this artist's own style. It is striking how closely he sticks to the lessons of Rubens even in his own compositions. Often he literally borrows motifs from his master's compositions, and even when he at times makes an attempt at a more personal invention, as in his etching of *Jupiter and Anthiope* (fig. 13),[44] his heroic figure types betray their provenance. Typical for this artist seems to be the exaggerated anatomy rendered by bulging but forceless outlines: the envelope of these human bodies would seem to be stuffed with some material other than flesh or bones.[45] The ankles, wrists, and generally the joints seem too weak to enable the system to work adequately, which results in the same strange mixture of brutality and mannerism I had occasion to point out in the case of the Brussels *Saint Sebastian* (fig. 12). Panneels' etching of the same subject (fig. 14)[46] certainly offers the most suggestive parallel to the painting: the pose is similar—although not identical—and similar also is the mannered heroism of the nude, endowed with a rather inept motoric system in both cases.

Reviewing Panneels' Copenhagen drawings, one is often struck by a close correspondence to the painting in Brussels (fig. 12). Or, to put it another way, one can easily imagine Panneels using this precious visual documentation to build up the composition at hand. This applies to the anatomy of individual limbs (a leg for instance; fig. 15)[47] as well as to poses, such as the upward-lifted arms of the saint, which seem to reflect a study after the *Laocoön* (fig. 16)[48] or another of the Copenhagen drawings representing *Marsyas* (fig. 17).[49]

For the heads, too, we find parallels in the "Rubens Cantoor," the most striking of which is no doubt a head in profile to the left (fig. 18), which Panneels copied after a Saint John in an altarpiece by Rubens (Schlossmuseum, Weimar), somewhat exaggerating the sharpness of the profile.[50] This head he used for the angel to the right in the painting in Brussels. My argument for attributing the painting of *Saint Sebastian* to Panneels rests, then, mainly on the present drawing and on the etching depicting the same saint. It is a hypothesis I have been entertaining for some years now, and I think the moment has come to invite my colleagues, in their turn, to test it out. It is clear that, since Panneels is as yet almost a blank as an artistic personality in his own right, future research will determine how this hypothesis fares.

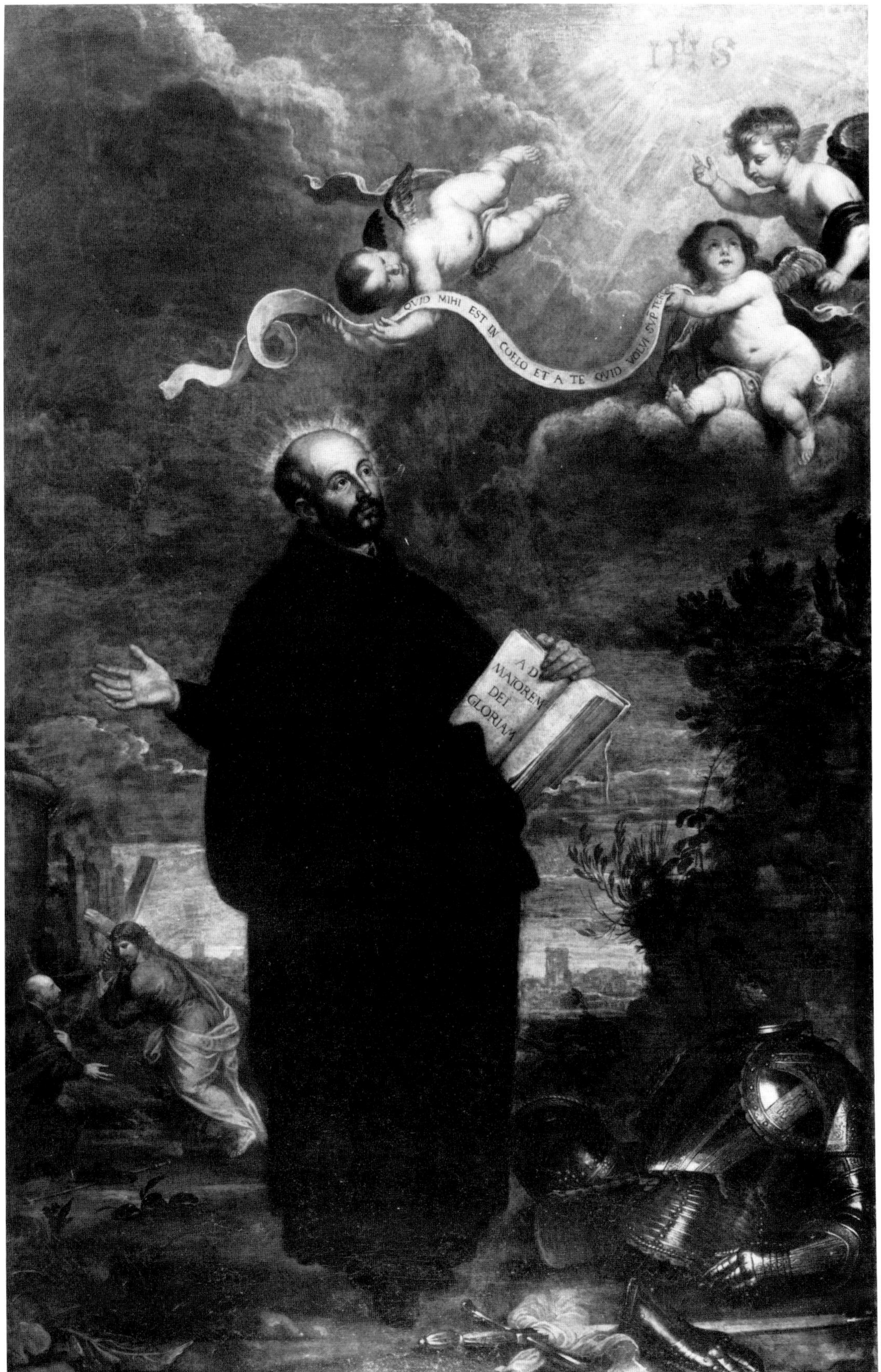

9. Gerard Seghers, *Saint Ignatius of Loyola*, oil on canvas
Pinacoteca Vaticana, Vatican City

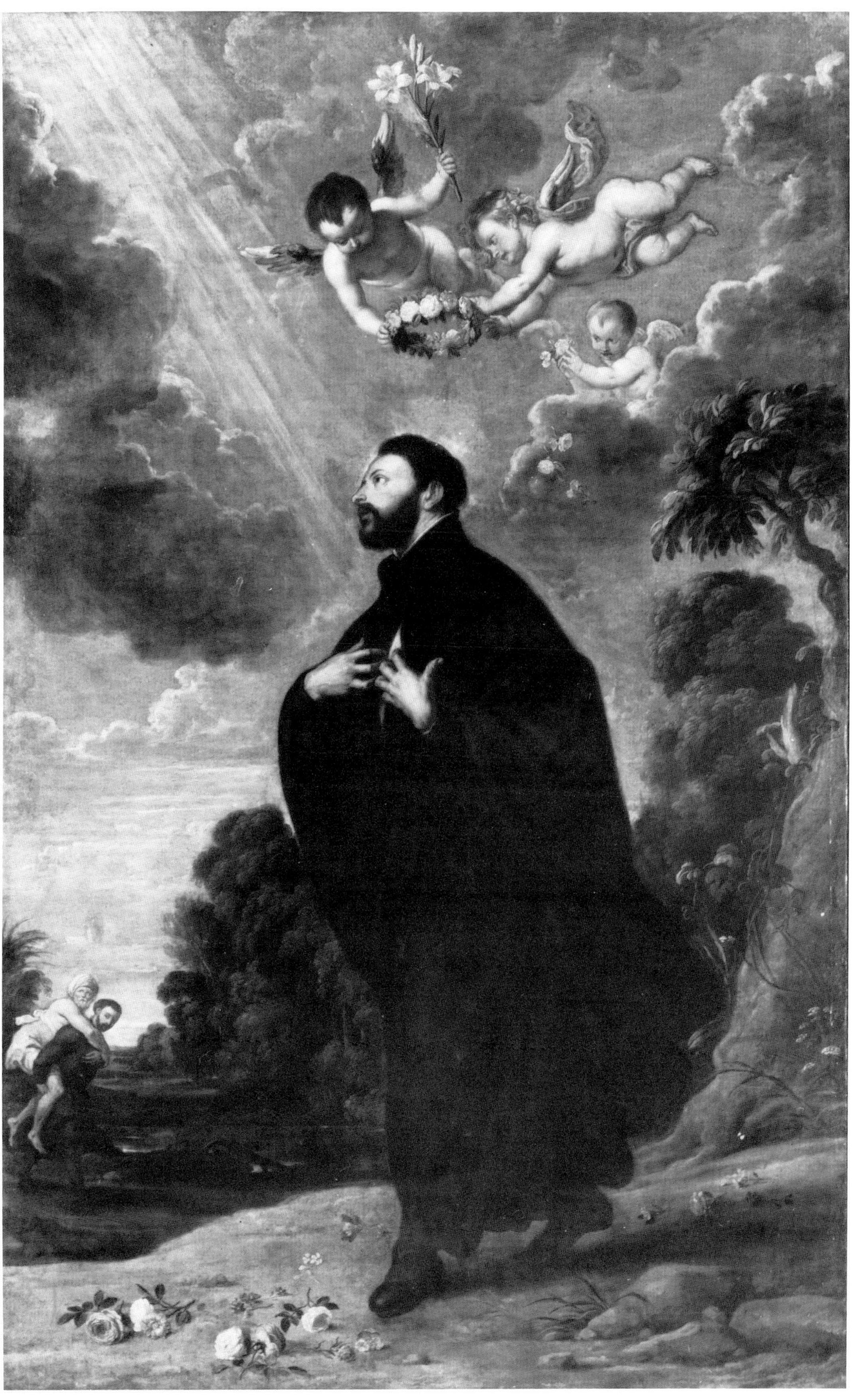

10. Gerard Seghers, *Saint Francis Xavier*, oil on canvas
Pinacoteca Vaticana, Vatican City

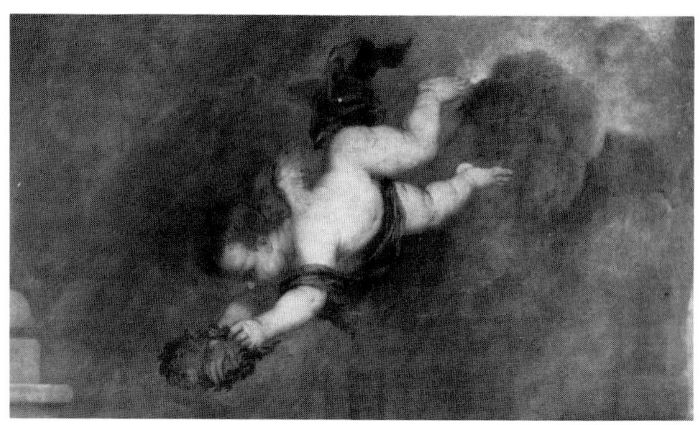

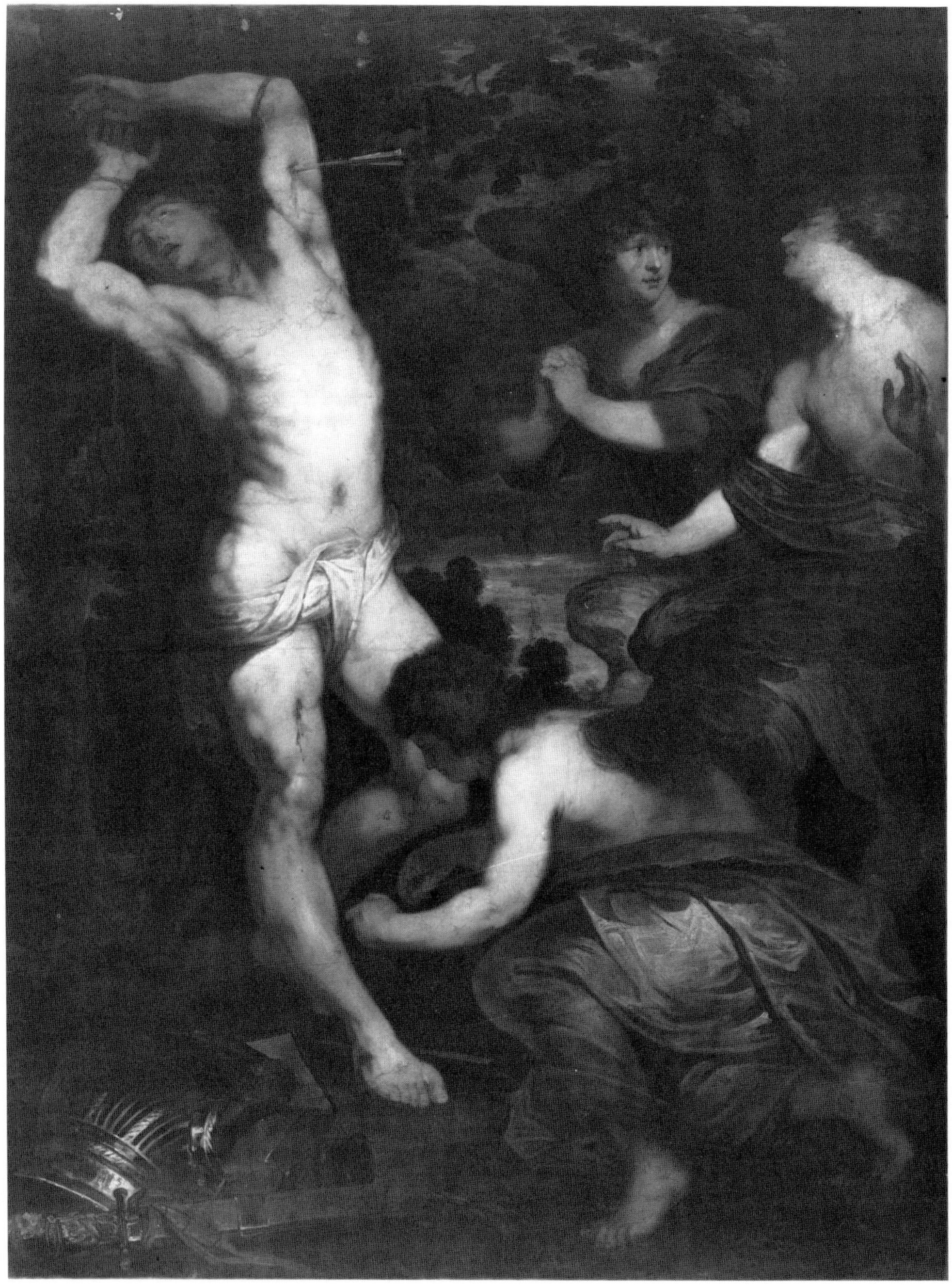

11. Gerard Seghers, *Putto Crowning Saint Yves* (detail), oil on panel
Saint James' church, Antwerp

12. Here attributed to Willem Panneels, *Saint Sebastian Assisted by Three Angels*, oil on canvas
Musées Royaux des Beaux-Arts, Brussels

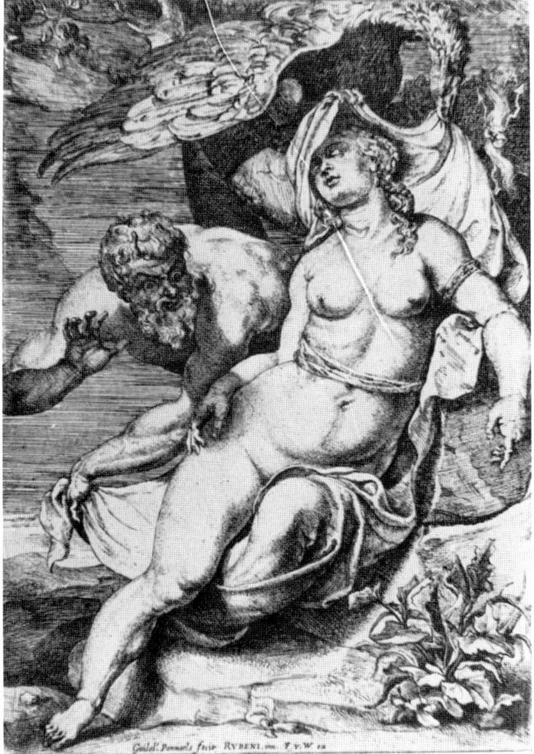

13. Willem Panneels, *Jupiter and Antiope*, etching

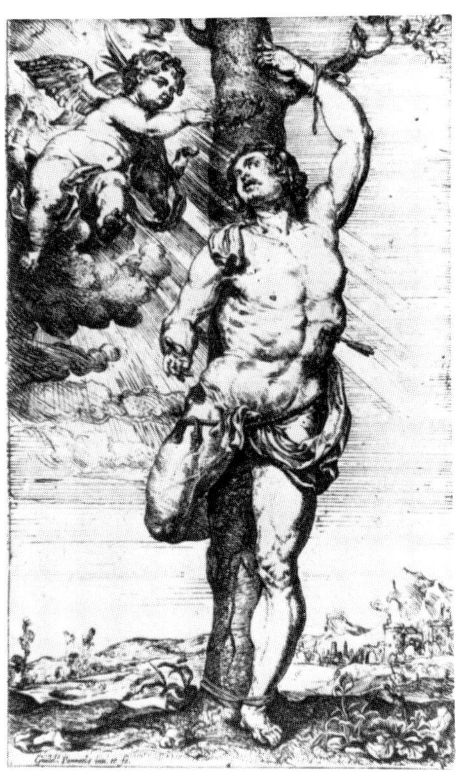

14. Willem Panneels, *Saint Sebastian*, etching

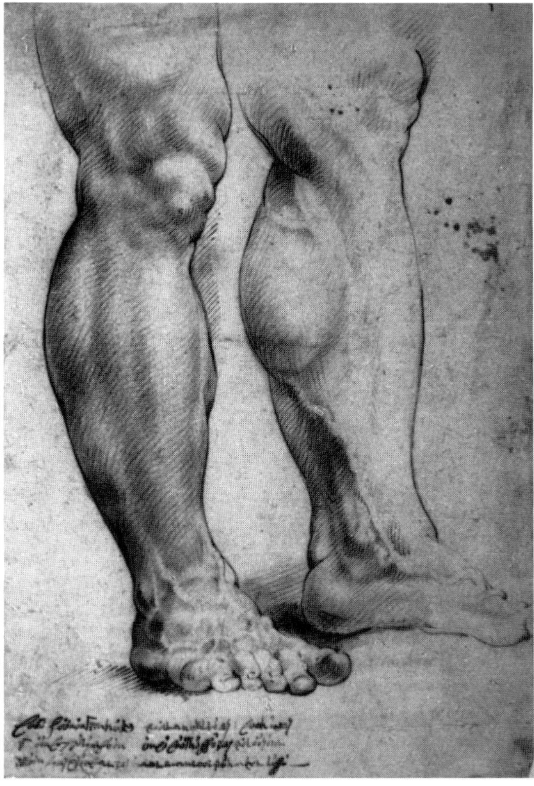

15. Willem Panneels, *Study of Legs*, c. 1628–1630, black chalk and pen
Statens Museum for Kunst, Copenhagen

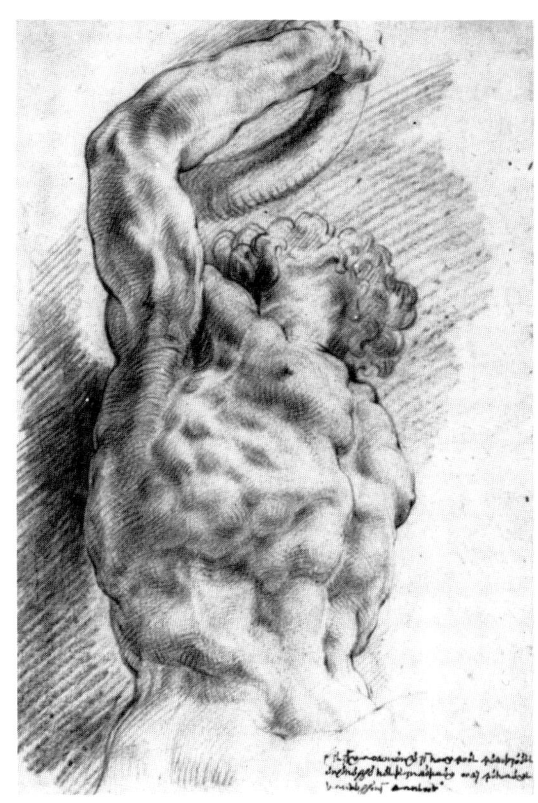

16. Willem Panneels, *Torso of Laocoön*, c. 1628–1630, black and red chalk
Statens Museum for Kunst, Copenhagen

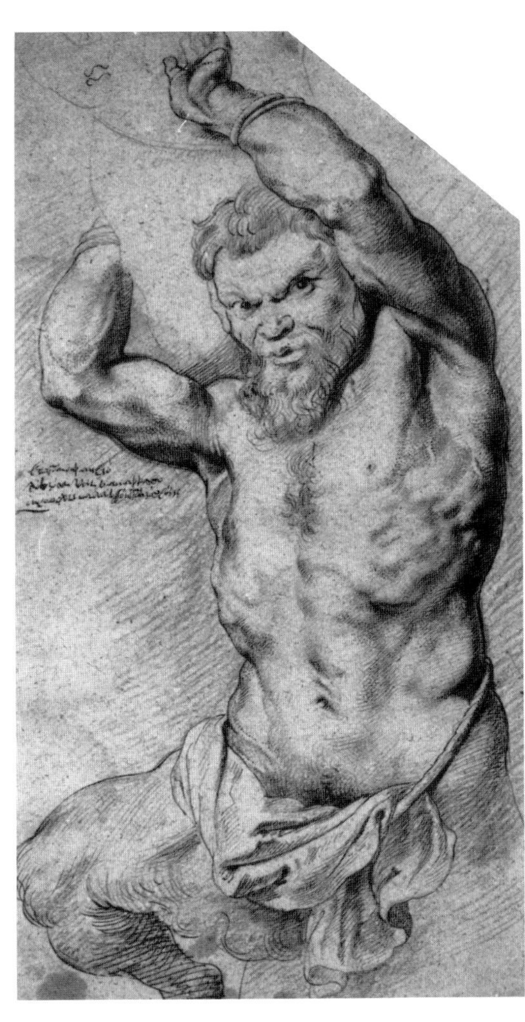

17. Willem Panneels, *Marsyas*, c. 1628–1630, black and red chalk and pen
Statens Museum for Kunst, Copenhagen

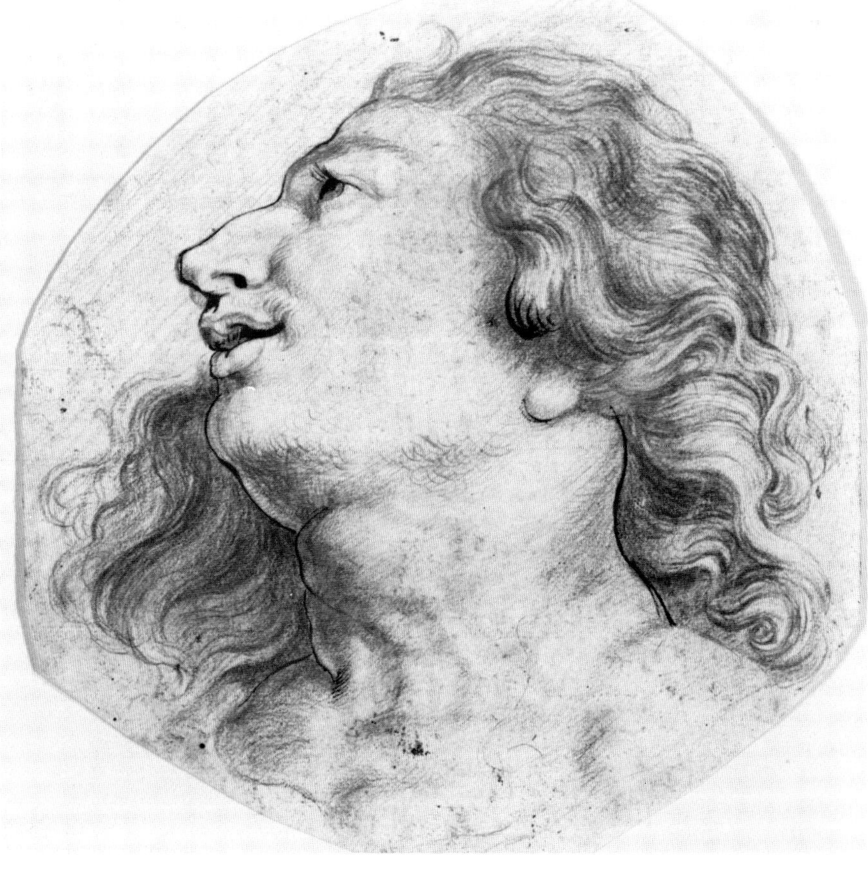

18. Willem Panneels, *Head of Saint John*, c. 1628–1630, black, red, and white chalk and pen
Statens Museum for Kunst, Copenhagen

1. Erik Larsen, *L'opera completa di Van Dyck*, 2 vols. (Milan, 1980); for a concise but sharp criticism see Justus Müller Hofstede, "Neue Beiträge zum Oeuvre Anton van Dycks," *Wallraf-Richartz-Jahrbuch* 48–49 (1987–1988), 131, with a list of 203 paintings he rejects; Erik Larsen, *The Paintings of Anthony van Dyck*, 2 vols. (Freren, 1988).

2. Gustav Glück, *Van Dyck. Des Meisters Gemälde*, Klassiker der Kunst, vol. 13, 2d ed. (Berlin and Stuttgart, 1931).

3. Inv. no. 866; 45 x 64 cm (an added strip at the top was removed in 1973); cradled. Provenance: probably Jodoc-Frédéric Hochhertz (d. 1786), Luxembourg; by descent to Eugénie Pescatore-Dutreux, who bequeathed it to the municipality of Luxembourg in 1902. It is executed in white, grays, and browns—less red and green in appearance than in the reproduction in Michel Lefèbvre, *"L'arrestation de Samson," esquisse d'Antoine Van Dyck. Etude historique et technologique* (Sterrebeek, n.d. [1980]). Some of the outlines seem to have been incised prior to being painted in, which would point to the use of a paper cartoon.

4. Inv. no. 512; 146 x 254 cm. See Glück 1931, 262; Larsen 1988, 2:295, no. 745. The original owner of the canvas is unknown; it figures in the 1659 inventory of Leopold Wilhelm (Adolf Berger, "Inventar der Kunstsammlung des Erzherzoges Leopold Wilhelm von Österreich," *Jahrbuch der Kunsthistorischen Sammlungen des Allerhöchsten Kaiserhauses* 1 [1883], 121, no. 112).

5. There is as yet no consensus among scholars as to which painted *modelli* for engravers (if any) are from Van Dyck's own hand. Horst Vey rejected all but one such highly finished grisaille paintings as not autograph (Horst Vey, "Anton Van Dycks Ölskizzen," *Bulletin. Musées Royaux des Beaux-Arts* [Brussels] 5 [1956], 205, n. 32; for Vey's one exception see note 11); he likewise rejected all the painted grisaille panels connected with the Iconography (Horst Vey, *Die Zeichnungen Anton van Dycks*, 2 vols. [Brussels, 1962], 1:48–50). More recently Christopher Brown and Julius Held have stood up for "the best" among the painted grisaille *modelli* for the Iconography (Christopher Brown, *Van Dyck* [Oxford, 1982], 134; see also Christopher Brown, *The Drawings of Anthony van Dyck* [exh. cat., Pierpont Morgan Library] [New York, 1991], 192; Julius Held, in Arthur K. Wheelock, Jr., et al., *Anthony van Dyck* [exh. cat., National Gallery of Art] [Washington, 1990], 339–340). Held (328–329) went even further and raised the question as to whether a few compositional grisaille sketches might also have been painted by Van Dyck himself as models for the engraver, "in view of their high artistic quality." Two of these were exhibited in Washington in 1990 and prompted considerable scholarly discussion. *The Lamentation* (Bayerische Staatsgemäldesammlungen, Munich; Washington 1990, no. 98) was, with its dry execution and "superimposed" modeling, the more disappointing of the two. The *Saint Augustine in Ecstasy* (Yale University Art Gallery, New Haven; Washington 1990, no. 94) I was at first inclined to accept, but critical discussion with colleagues and the opportunity to study this panel closely have caused me to change my view. I agree with Held (329) that "all the details, from human faces and hands to the intricacies of drapery have been done with . . . exquisite sensitivity," and that this is a work of the highest technical competence and of outstanding aesthetic quality. Yet there is something matter-of-fact in the very disciplined way the reddish-brown brushstrokes have been articulated and the white highlights have been laid on that seems, on closer inspection, alien to Van Dyck's temperament. A comparison can be made with the grisaille of *Rinaldo and Armida* (National Gallery, London; Brown 1982, fig. 125; Gregory Martin, *National Gallery Catalogues. The Flemish School circa 1600–circa 1900* [London, 1970], 37–41, no. 877B), which seems to me more acceptable as an autograph Van Dyck and is not unlike some of the Iconography grisailles in the quality of the brushwork (for instance, *Gaspard de Crayer*; Brown 1982, fig. 133). In the London panel the high definition in the rendering of every detail does not in any way impede the playfulness of the brush, which results in a more airy and at the same time more emotionally charged atmosphere, with a dynamic flow from the accented to the more suggestive areas. The New Haven panel is, by contrast, uniform throughout. Held rightly points out that an engraver would be unlikely to possess such painterly skills. Thus perhaps we should not look among the professional engravers for the author of the best of these *modelli*, but among the painters. When studying the *modello* of the *Saint Augustine*, I was somewhat reminded of Jan Boeckhorst. Here is a painter who, especially in small format, can be very precise without really becoming dull or spiritless; see, for example, his *Adoration of the Shepherds* (Statens Museum for Kunst, Copenhagen; *Jan Boeckhorst 1604–1668, medewerker van Rubens* [exh. cat. Rubenshuis], [Antwerp, 1990], cat. 5). However, we do not have any other *modello* by his hand painted in oils for comparison. His designs for the 1653 *Missale Romanum* (Museum Plantin-Moretus, Antwerp; Antwerp 1990, nos. 9–12) are painted on paper, but, I would contend, are not dissimilar in style from the New Haven grisaille. It is clear from the angels and putti in other works by Boeckhorst that this artist certainly had studied Van Dyck's *Saint Augustine* closely, although we should not make too much of this. In a drawing of the *Virgin of Sorrows* (Musée d'Art et d'Archéologie, Besançon; Antwerp 1990, no. 7), however, Boeckhorst almost literally borrowed the drapery on Christ's knees from the upper part of Van Dyck's *Saint Augustine*. I am aware that for the moment, for want of more appropriate comparative material, my attribution of the New Haven panel to Boeckhorst must remain highly hypothetical. (For connections between Boeckhorst and Van Dyck see Antwerp 1990, 13–14, 81–83. Michael Jaffé, review of Washington 1990, *Burlington Magazine* 133 [1991], 144, rejects the *Lamentation* but accepts the *Saint Augustine*.) As Burchard

pointed out (Van Dyck documentation, Rubenianum, Antwerp), it is likely that it was the New Haven *Saint Augustine* rather than any of the more sketchy versions (as Held suggested in Washington 1990, no. 93) that is mentioned in the inventory of Alexander Voet, 18 February 1689 (Jan Denucé, *The Antwerp Art-Galleries, Inventories of the Art-Collections in Antwerp in the 16th and 17th Centuries* [The Hague, 1932], 311). Indeed, we know from the journal of Nicodemus Tessin, who visited the Voet collection in 1687, that this grisaille was well finished ("treflich acheviret;" see *Oud Holland* 18 [1900], 203). Voet seems also to have owned the grisaille of *Rinaldo and Armida* now in the Musées Royaux des Beaux-Arts, Brussels (Martin 1970, 40, n. 19). Here also I am reluctant to see Van Dyck's hand, but the work is also different in style from the New Haven *Saint Augustine.*

6. Lefèbvre [1980]; Danièle Wagener, *Musée J.-P. Pescatore. Catalogue* (Luxembourg, 1984), 62, pl. 1.

7. Alfred von Wurzbach, *Niederländisches Künstler-Lexikon auf Grund archivalischer Forschungen bearbeitet,* 3 vols. (Vienna and Leipzig, 1906–1911), 1:473, no. 433 (as by Van Dyck); 2:634, no. 7 (as by Snyers). I studied the impression in the Stedelijk Prentencabinet, Antwerp; plate: 46 x 65 cm (composition: 43.5 x 63 cm); inscribed at bottom left: *Ant. van Dyck pinxit / Henr. Snyers sculpsit;* in the center, six lines of Latin, in three columns: *Vincula chara . . . instar erant;* at bottom right: *Abr. a Diepenbeke excudit Antuerpiae / Cum Priuilegio.* The print shows the composition in reverse and follows the Luxembourg grisaille in allowing for more space at the top than in the canvas in Vienna. There is a point-to-point correspondence with the Luxembourg panel. However, a few details shared by this engraving and the Vienna canvas are lacking in the Luxembourg panel in its present state: the knob on top of the helmet of the soldier to the right and the pair of scissors in the corner at bottom left. There is good reason to suspect damage and losses in these areas of the panel, as well as at the ill-defined right lower leg of Samson (see the photograph taken before restoration in Lefèbvre [1980], n.p.).

8. Frans Joseph van den Branden, *Geschiedenis der Antwerpsche schilderschool* (Antwerp, 1883), 784. Nine copperplates connected with this project were mentioned in the will of Van Diepenbeeck's daughter, Anna Theresia, 5 December 1701 (the "Samson" among them). Van den Branden, 1883, 784, n. 1, stated that four of these were preserved in the Museum Plantin-Moretus in Antwerp, but they can no longer be traced there.

9. Panel, 59.3 x 44.5 cm; it was published in the advertising supplement, *Burlington Magazine* (December 1989), xviii, with Michael Simpson Ltd., London, as by Van Diepenbeeck (attribution by Michael Jaffé; see also Michael Jaffé, *Rubens. Catalogo completo* [Milan, 1989], 165, under no. 88). Hans Vlieghe informs me that it has been acquired by the Staatliche Kunsthalle, Karlsruhe. The surface of this grisaille is squared for transfer, which is not the case with the Luxembourg panel, in which we find, however, inci-

sions along the edges, obviously intended as visual aids for a grid to be applied at some point (see Lefèbvre [1980], n.p.).

10. David W. Steadman, *Abraham van Diepenbeeck, Seventeenth-Century Flemish Painter* (Ann Arbor, Mich., 1982), nos. 42, 50, figs. 42, 47; see 25–31 for a general survey of Diepenbeeck's oil sketches for engravings.

11. The handling of the paint in all these grisailles is certainly a far cry from the marvelous fluency of Van Dyck's grisaille of *Rinaldo and Armida* in London, and is also more inhibited than the brushwork of the *Saint Augustine* in New Haven (see note 5 for both works).

As stated above (note 5), there is one grisaille *modello* for an engraving that Vey (Vey 1956, 186, fig. 15) did accept as painted by Van Dyck himself: a *Rest on the Flight into Egypt* (after Van Dyck's *Madonna and Child* in Buckingham Palace, with variations in the background; see Glück 1931, 225, for the latter painting). However, the engraving after this *modello* is also by Hendrik Snyers, and, pursuing the same line of thought as developed for the two other prints by Snyers, there is reason to suspect that here too Snyers worked from a model painted by his patron, Van Diepenbeeck, who here also acted as the publisher (Von Wurzbach 1906–1911, 2:635, no. 6; most likely the copperplate is the one mentioned as a "Charitas" in the will of Van Diepenbeeck's daughter Anna Theresia, for which see note 8). I have never seen the sketch referred to (it appeared at Christie's, London, 24 April 1981, no. 140, as by Van Dyck), but judging from the reproduction I am indeed inclined to attribute it to Van Diepenbeeck: it would seem to have the same solid, enamellike impasto as, for example, his grisaille of *Saint Albert* in Munich (Alte Pinakothek; Steadman 1982, no. 45, fig. 43), and the foliage of the tree in the backgound can be compared to that in his *Descent from the Cross* (National Museum of Wales, Cardiff; Steadman 1982, no. 49, fig. 46) and his *Conversion of Saint Paul* (formerly 2d duke of Westminster collection; Steadman 1982, no. 6, fig. 8).

12. Inv. no. 5861 (as school of Rubens), part of a hunting series; see *Catalogue of Western European Paintings, 2; The Netherlands, Flanders etc.* [in Russian] (Leningrad, 1981), 67. I will bear out Van Diepenbeeck's authorship in a forthcoming article.

Of this bearded head there also exists a painted study that was put up for sale in Munich (J. Böhler), 28 October 1937 (no. 36, pl. 16; oil on canvas, 34 x 27 cm; from the collection of Theodor Stroefer, Nüremberg); see Larsen 1988, 2:53, no. 102, who did not notice the relationship with the Vienna *Samson* and dated this head c. 1615–1616. Judging from the reproduction, the attribution to Van Dyck himself seems not unlikely, but should this work ever turn up again it would be wise to keep in mind that Van Diepenbeeck has used this head, too.

13. 245 x 170 cm. Provenance: sale, Galerie Georges Giroux, Brussels, 11 May 1925, no. 47, pl. 15, as by Van Dyck. See also M[ichèle] W[ilmotte] in *The 17th Century. The Golden Age of Flemish Painting* [exh.

cat., Tokyo Fuji Art Museum] (Tokyo, 1988), no. 23, who states that according to a Colonel Wegg the painting is by Van Dyck and is dated 1623 (both statements seem unacceptable). Suzanne Leclercq and Michèle Wilmotte, *La collection Coppeé* (n.p., n.d. [Liège, 1991]), 164–166, color repro., as studio of Van Dyck. I have in the meantime been informed by Hans Vlieghe that Danielle Maufort in her unpublished M.A. thesis on Pieter Thys (University of Leuven, 1986) has also argued for Thys' authorship of this painting. I had the occasion to see this painting in November 1987.

14. For Thys see Marie-Louise Hairs, *Dans le sillage de Rubens. Les Peintres d'histoire anversois au XVIIe siècle* (Liège, 1977), 265–276; for his relationship with Van Dyck see Alfons Monballieu, "Bij een aanwinst. Het portret van Cornelis Nutius (1589–1665) en zijn toeschrijvingen," *Jaarboek van het Koninklijk Museum voor Schone Kunsten Antwerpen* (1968), 234–238.

15. Hairs 1977, 272, fig. 81.

16. Hans Vlieghe, "Nieuwe toeschrijvingen aan Antwerpse schilders uit de zeventiende eeuw," *Gentse bijdragen tot de kunstgeschiedenis en oudheidkunde* 20 (1967), 165–173, fig. 11; Hairs 1977, 272.

17. Inv. no. 194; oil on canvas, 257 x 190 cm. See Hairs 1977, 273. The monk to the left has been identified as Saint Felix of Cantalice.

18. When in 1650 the Capuchin father Charles of Arenberg obtained from Pope Innocent XI the remains of ten early Christian martyrs (Saint Benedict among them), it was decided in Brussels to construct a new church with altars dedicated to them. These were installed in 1652 (Alexandre Henne and Alphonse Wauters, *Histoire de la ville de Bruxelles* [1845], ed. Mina Martens [Brussels, 1975], 4 vols., 4:56–57). The interior of this church, which was pulled down in 1803–1804, is described by several eighteenth-century sources: G. P. Mensaert, *Le peintre amateur et curieux . . .* (Brussels, 1763), 1:48–51; J. B. Descamps, *Voyage pittoresque de la Flandre et du Brabant* (Paris, 1769), 65–68; *Description de la ville de Bruxelles* (Brussels, 1789), 30–34. It included the *Martyrdom of Saint Benedict* by Pieter Thys (fig. 8), but no other painting by his hand or any other that could be identified with the one under discussion.

19. There is no mention of them in Larsen 1988, either in the catalogue or among the "Paintings wrongly attributed to Van Dyck" (2:413–515).

20. Inv. nos. 790, 775; both 345 x 213 cm. They used to hang in the Palazzo Pontifico at Castelgandolfo, and later in the Sala del Consistorio in the Vatican. It is supposed that they formed part of the goods confiscated from the Jesuits after the suppression of their order in 1773. See note 21 for references to such paintings in Il Gesù in Rome. See also E. Levy in Thomas M. Lucas, ed., *Saint, Site and Sacred Strategy* [exh. cat., Biblioteca Apostolica Vaticana] (Rome, 1930–1931), 224, no. 141, color repro. 225.

21. In the sources there are various references to images of both saints at various locations in Il Gesù, but it is not always clear whether the reference is to sculpture or to paintings, or again whether small portraits or monumental canvases are meant. In only two of the sources do we find a name connected with these paintings: in 1657 Scanelli (F. Scannelli, *Il microcosmo della pittura* [1657], ed. G. Giubbini [Milan, 1966], 205) attributed a pair of paintings with the two saints to Rubens and located them at both sides of the main altar; and in 1674 Titi (F. Titi, *Ammaestramento utile e curioso di pittura, scultura et architettura nelle chiese di Roma* [Rome, 1674], 127) knew of a pair (the same or a different one?) that used to hang in their respective chapels, and he attributed these to Van Dyck. The reference to Rubens has led to the rather ad-hoc hypothesis (first in Max Rooses, *L'Oeuvre de P. P. Rubens*, 5 vols., 2 [Antwerp, 1888]: 267, 286, but repeated by L. Burchard, "Die Seitenaltäre von Rubens für il Gesù in Rom," *Actes du XIIe Congrès International d'Histoire de l'Art* [Brussels, 1930], 1:127–128, and H. Vlieghe, *Saints* [Corpus Rubenianum Ludwig Burchard VIII], vol. 2 [Brussels, London, New York, 1973], 68–72, nos. 113–114) that two Rubens canvases with these saints, which at the end of the eighteenth century adorned the Jesuit church in Brussels, were in fact acquired some years earlier from Il Gesù in Rome. There is nothing to substantiate this, and Walter Scheelen has found documentary evidence that both works were from the start (1616) meant for the Brussels church (Walter Scheelen, "De herkomst en de datering van Rubens' voorstellingen van de H. Ignatius van Loyola en de H. Franciscus Xaverius," *Jaarboek van het Koninklijk Museum voor Schone Kunsten Antwerpen* [1986], 153–172, especially 159, 171: partial payment to Rubens for "twee stucken schildereye te weten BB.PP. Ignatium et Xaverium"). It may be that at some point copies after these Rubens originals adorned the Gesù church (as Scheelen suggests), but it is also very possible that Scanelli was mistaken in his attribution and that he was simply referring to the two Flemish paintings the authorship of which is under discussion here. These were first published by Redig de Campos, together with another pair of the same saints, of somewhat smaller dimensions and presumably of Italian workmanship and an earlier date (c. 1600 or soon after; they are also in the Vatican Museum; see Deoclecio Redig de Campos, "Intorno a due quadri d'altare del Van Dyck per il Gesù di Roma ritrovati in Vaticano," *Bolletino d'arte*, 3d ser., 30 [1936], no. 4, 150–165). Both these pairs may very well come from the Gesù. It would seem that they are sufficient to answer for all the references in the sources; but it is as yet not entirely clear which pair was where throughout the seventeenth and eighteenth centuries. For the fullest account of the sources and an overview of the literature see Ursula König-Nordhoff, *Ignatius von Loyola. Studien zur Entwicklung einer neuen Heiligen-Ikonographie im Rahmen einer Kanonisationskampagne um 1600* (Berlin, 1982), 76–96, 244. Her conclusions, however, both concerning Rubens and Van Dyck, seem to me unwarranted.

22. M. Vaes, "Van Dyck en Italie," *Bulletin de*

l'Institut Historique Belge de Rome 17 (1936), 326; A. Muñoz, *Van Dyck* (Leipzig, 1941), 22, fig. 24. See König-Nordhoff 1982, 79, 244, for references.

23. Frank van den Wijngaert, *Antoon van Dyck* (Antwerp, 1943), 64–66.

24. L. Van Puyvelde, "Les Saint Ignace et Saint François Xavier de Rubens," *Gazette des Beaux-Arts* 53 (1959), 234; P. Pecchiai, *Il Gesù di Roma* (Rome, 1952), 130, n. 1. See König-Nordhoff 1982, 87, 244, for references.

25. Larsen 1988, 1:214–215, figs. 162a, b; 2:174, nos. 428–429. Larsen had to admit that these canvases do not really fit into Van Dyck's oeuvre, but this seems not to have challenged him to rethink the problem: "We have to do here with paintings of mediocre quality, probably done with studio help, but certainly authentic and representative of Van Dyck's "Roman" manner at the time. . . . It is quite true that these paintings do not have the flavor of the more usual Van Dyck style. We simply have to admit a reconciling of the artist's Northern manner with autochthonous fashion." König-Nordhoff, too, felt somewhat uneasy about the stylistic evidence: "Bei der stilkritischen Betrachtung stösst man jedoch auf gewisse Schwierigkeiten" (König-Nordhoff 1982, 87). One is astonished to see that a source dating from thirty years after the death of the artist (and fifty years after the alleged installation of the paintings) should be granted such authority as to negate the impression of stylistic incompatibility.

26. Wildens came back from Italy to Antwerp in about 1616 (Wolfgang Adler, *Jan Wildens. Der Landschaftsmitarbeiter des Rubens* [Fridingen, 1980], 12). Redig de Campos 1936, 157, judged the landscape in the *Francis Xavier* to be different from that in the *Ignatius*, and in the former thought it to be the work of some specialized collaborator, given "la sapienza troppo spezializzata con cui questo paesaggio appare eseguito."

27. The profile of Francis Xavier may have been borrowed from an engraving by Schelte à Bolswert (König-Nordhoff 1982, fig. 191), and the face of Ignatius is remarkably close to his effigy in an engraving by Audran, in which we also find the same flamelike monogram of Christ in the sky and the depiction of the "storta-scene" in the background (König-Nordhoff 1982, fig. 139, in which the engraving is mistakenly labeled "unsigned;" there is a reference to it in the index of the book, s.v. "Audran, Claude I:" this should however read "Charles Audran;" see Charles Le Blanc, *Manuel de l'amateur d'estampes* [Paris, 1854–1888], 2:82, no. 105). The same face, but nearer to profile, is found in Schelte à Bolswert's print after Segher's *Vision of Saint Ignatius of Loyola*, 1631. See W. F. H. Hollstein, *Dutch and Flemish Etchings, Engravings and Woodcuts ca. 1450–1700* (Amsterdam, 1949–), 3:82, no. 242; Horst Vey, "Gerard Seghers: 'A Vision of Saint Ignatius of Loyola during the Writing of the Rules of the Jesuits,'" *Master Drawings* 2 (1964), 268–271, fig. 1; the *modello* for this print was sold at Sotheby's, Amsterdam, 26 November 1984, no. 30, as circle of De Crayer, illus.; gouache on paper, 36.5 x 27 cm.

28. For Seghers (or Zegers) see Van den Branden 1883, 879–885; Domien Roggen and Henry Pauwels, "Het Caravaggistisch oeuvre van Gerard Zegers," *Gentse bijdragen tot de kunstgeschiedenis* 16 (1955–1956), 255–301; Carl van de Velde, "De schilder Gerard Zegers," in G. van Brussel et al., *Een traditie met toekomst. Uitgegeven ter gelegenheid van . . . de reconstructie van de gevel van het Huis de Fraula* (Antwerp, 1986), 31–40. Jan Wildens, the painter who was responsible for the landscape background in these two paintings, was godfather to one of Seghers' children (Van de Velde 1986, 36).

Some very striking analogies are found in Seghers' *Christ and the Penitent Sinners* (which I know only from the engraving by Jacob Neeffs, reproduced in John B. Knipping, *Iconography of the Counter Reformation in the Netherlands* [Nieuwkoop-Leiden, 1974], 2: fig. 299); here we encounter the same sharply drawn profile as that of Francis Xavier (in the Prodigal Son) as well as the hands brought together across the breast (as in King David). The gesture of the uplifted hand of Saint Ignatius we find also in Seghers' *Vision of Saint Ignatius of Loyola* painted c. 1631 for the Jesuit church in Ghent (see the print by Bolswert mentioned in note 27).

29. 165 x 153 cm; see Théodore van Lerius, *Notice des oeuvres d'art de l'église paroissiale . . . Saint Jacques à Anvers* (Borgerhout, 1855), 111. The painting is not documented, but is traditionally attributed to Seghers (*Beschryvinge der bezonderste werken van de schilder-konste, ende beeldhouwerye . . . in de kerken . . . der Stad Antwerpen* [Antwerp 1765], 41, no. 11). It is indeed a typical work by this master. The chapel of Saint Yves was founded in 1636.

30. Van de Velde 1986, fig. 38; *Le Siècle de Rubens* [exh. cat., Musées Royaux des Beaux-Arts] (Brussels, 1965), no. 309, illus.

The difference of quality in the two Vatican paintings has often been commented upon (Redig de Campos 1936, 154–158; Van den Wijngaert 1943, 65–66; König-Nordhoff 1982, 87, and Susan Barnes [orally, 8 February 1991]). I have in the meantime had occasion to study not only the *Francis Xavier*, which has been on permanent display in the galleries for some time, but also the *Ignatius*, which was undergoing restoration in September 1992 (I would like to thank Fabrizio Mancinelli as well as the painting conservator at the Vatican museum for their assistance). Both are in my view by the same hand, namely that of Seghers, with the assistance of Wildens for the landscape.

31. For Seghers' dealings with the Jesuits see Van de Velde 1986, 35, 37; Hans Vlieghe, "Rubens's Activity for the Ghent Jesuits in 1633," *Burlington Magazine* 111 (1969), 427–435; J. Braun, "Gemälde von Rubens, Van Dyck und Gerhard Seghers in der Maria-Himmelfahrtkirche zu Köln," *Zeitschrift für Christliche Kunst* 18 (1905), 343–348. The two paintings for the former Jesuit church in Landshut were identified by Hans Vlieghe in a letter, 4 March 1975, to R. J. Reiter; see the Seghers documentation, Rubenianum, Antwerp.

32. Inv. no. 4112; 240 x 179 cm; entered the museum

with the bequest of Auguste Beernaert. See Fierens-Gevaert and A. Laes, *Musées Royaux des Beaux-Arts de Belgique. Catalogue de la peinture ancienne*, 2d ed. (Brussels, 1927), 97, no. 817; *Inventariscatalogus van de oude schilderkunst* (Brussels, 1984), 98, illus. With thanks to Willy Laureyssens for giving me the opportunity to study the painting, which is kept in storage. The canvas shows extensive damage and losses in various areas. The painter worked with broad and blended brushstrokes on a brown priming. The modeling is accentuated with dark brown. The carnations (especially in Saint Sebastian) are very varied: basically yellowish flesh colors, with shades of pink and gray (quite reminiscent of Rubens' technique). The angel in the front is dressed in a warm ocher with some red reflections; the two other angels wear blue and red. There is also red in the inside of the breast armor at bottom left.

33. Larsen 1988, 1:268, 437–438, fig. 250; 2: no. 677.

34. Various attributions to Panneels are on record, some of which carry more conviction than others. I will address this problem elsewhere.

35. For Panneels see especially Max Rooses in *Biographie nationale [de Belgique]* 16 (Brussels, 1901), 550–553; Zoege von Manteuffel in *Allgemeines Lexikon der bildenden Künstler . . . begründet von Ulrich Thieme und Felix Becker* 26 (Leipzig, 1932), 198 (with earlier literature); Hairs 1977, 44.

36. Philip Rombouts and Theodoor van Lerius, *De "liggeren" en andere historische archieven der Antwerpsche Sint Lucasgilde*, 2 vols. (Antwerp, 1864–1872), 1:649, 658.

37. Document first published by P. Génard, "Petrus Paulus Rubens en Willem Panneels," *Rubens-Bulletijn* 1 (1882), 220–223, and reprinted in Max Rooses and Charles Ruelens, *Correspondance de Rubens et documents épistolaires concernant sa vie et ses oeuvres*, 6 vols. (1877–1909), 5 (Antwerp, 1907): 295–298. Rubens declares that for five and a half years Panneels studied the art of painting with him, that he completed his apprenticeship and took care of Rubens' house while Rubens was in Spain and England. It is usually inferred from this that Panneels entered Rubens' studio in 1624 or 1625, but it should be pointed out that a different interpretation may be given to this statement: maybe Rubens meant to say that Panneels' apprenticeship, which came to an end on his becoming a master in 1627–1628, lasted for five and a half years, which would imply that he entered Rubens' service as early as 1622.

38. These dates and places we find on his prints; see note 42. G. Troescher, *Kunst und Künstlerwanderungen in Mitteleuropa 800–1800*, 2 vols. (Baden-Baden, 1954), 2:20, states that Willem Panneels died in Baden-Baden in 1634, but I have been unable to verify his sources. Additional documents concerning his stay in Germany are summarily quoted by W. K. Zülch, *Frankfurter Künstler 1223–1700* (Frankfurt-am-Main, 1935), 529: in 1631 Panneels tried (in vain) to obtain the citizenship of the town of Frankfurt, referring to a recommendation from the emperor (dated 10 November 1630) and an introductory letter from Rubens. (I owe the reference to this till-now neglected source to a note by Ludwig Burchard in the Panneels files at the Rubenianum, Antwerp). A date on one of Panneels' etchings, which in Hollstein (Hollstein 1949– , vol. 15, compiled by K. G. Boon and J. Verbeek [Amsterdam, n.d.], 116, no. 14, *Saint George*) figures as "1638" [last numeral is not clear], is usually read as "1631."

Recently Garff (in Jan Garff and Eva de la Fuente Pedersen, *Rubens Cantoor. The Drawings of Willem Panneels*, 2 vols. [Copenhagen, 1988], 1:20) has suggested that our Willem ("Gilliam," "Guilielmus") Panneels, who seems to have disappeared in 1634, might very well be the "Herman Panneels" who was active as an engraver in Madrid between 1638 and 1668 (for this last date and for a list of this engraver's work see Blanca Garcia Vega, *El grabado del libro español, siglos XV–XVI–XVII*, 2 vols. [Simancas-Valladolid, 1984], 1:87, 137, figs. 648–661; 2:345–348, nos. 2294–2312). Not only the different Christian name makes this unlikely, but also the fact that Herman seems only to have worked with the burin, a technique at which our Willem never tried his hand. And how are we to understand that at a certain point Willem's copperplates end up in Antwerp in the hands of Frans van den Wijngaerde (see note 43), which was not the case with those of Herman? The style of the latter does not seem to me to betray much influence of Rubens (except in one composition: Garcia Vega 1984, 1: fig. 649). Since the publication of J. A. Ceán Bermúdez, *Diccionario histórico de los más ilustres profesores de las Bellas Artes en España*, 6 vols. (Madrid, 1800), 4:42–43. Herman Panneels has, however, been called a pupil of Rubens, but maybe this is due to a confusion with his namesake.

Finally, there is also a Jan ("Joannes") Panneels, whose name we find on one etching ("fec. francfi.;" see Rooses 1901, 553; Hollstein 1949– , 15:108, no. 1, ill.). Rooses wondered whether this might not have been a son of our Willem. There is now some new evidence regarding a Jan Panneels: he is mentioned in the will of the Antwerp painter Willem van Haeght (1 July 1637) as his pupil (Erik Duverger, *Antwerpse kunstinventarissen uit de zeventiende eeuw*, 5 vols. to date [Brussels, 1984–], 4:90). The fact that Willem Panneels and this Van Haeght were friends (the former dedicating an etching to him: Hollstein 1949– , 15:112, no. 6. Van Haeght's name figures also on the back of one drawing in the "Rubens Cantoor;" see note 39; compare Julius S. Held, *Rubens. Selected Drawings*, 2d ed. [1986], 41) would seem to argue for a close relationship of the latter's pupil Jan Panneels and our Willem. There is one fact that seems to militate against Jan being Willem's son: in December 1628 the latter was admitted to the Sodality of the "bejaerde jongmans," which implies that at that date he was still a bachelor (Rombouts and Van Lerius 1864–1872, 1:649, n. 2). For more details on Willem Panneels see E. Duverger in *Rubens Cantoor* forthcoming [exh. cat., Rubenshuis] (Antwerp, 1993), 38–52.

39. Gustav Falck, "En Rubenselevs Tegninger," *Kunstmuseets Aarsskrift* 1918 (1919), 64–77, espe-

cially 66–69, was the first to formulate this hypothesis, taking as his starting point the close correspondence of one of these drawings to an etching signed by Panneels. For a full discussion of all Panneels drawings in Copenhagen see Garff and Pedersen 1988. As Nora De Poorter pointed out in *The Eucharist Series; Corpus Rubenianum Ludwig Burchard*, pt. 2 (London and Philadelphia, 1978), 1:230, not all these copies were executed during Rubens' absence.

40. The word "cantoor" ("comptoir," "contoir," "contoer," "cantoer," "cantoor," "kantoor") could designate two different things: the room in which a businessman did his accounting or writing, or the piece of furniture in which his papers and valuables were locked away. The latter we find mentioned especially in documents pertaining to the Antwerp art market; see Jan Denucé, *Kunstuitvoer in de 17e eeuw te Antwerpen. De firma Forchoudt* (Antwerp, 1930); Jan Denucé, *Na Peter Pauwel Rubens. Documenten uit den kunsthandel te Antwerpen in de XVIIe eeuw van Matthijs Musson* (Antwerp and The Hague, 1949); in these documents the Flemish word "cantoor" or its variants are usually used. See also Ria Fabri, *Zuidnederlandse pronkmeubels, 16de–18de eeuw* [exh. cat., Generale Bank] (Brussels, 1989). "Cantoor" meaning a room we find in countless inventories; see Duverger 1984– ; in these more formal documents the French term "comptoir" or its variants are most frequently used. In most of the houses of the better situated we find such a study, a "comptoir" or "cantoor." The use of the preposition "van" in Panneels' inscriptions (in all forty-two of his references to the "cantoor") seems to indicate—contrary to the now prevailing opinion—that he took his models from a particular *room* (Rubens' study) and not "out of" a specific secrétaire cabinet. In the last case we might have expected the preposition *wt* (*uit*). This "cantoor" may have been the "petit cabinet 2, au-dessus de la porte de la remise" referred to by François Mols in the eighteenth century; see Rutger J. Tijs, *P. P. Rubens en J. Jordaens. Barok in eigen huis* (Antwerp, 1984), 159, illus. Let me quote a few instances from other documents to substantiate this interpretation: in his will, 3 April 1622, Deodatus del Monte (a former pupil of Rubens) also refers to his "comptoor" as the room in which could be found everything pertaining to his art (his papers, paintings, plasters); see Duverger 1984– , 2:215–216, doc. 401. Similarly, when the inventory of Joos de Momper's deathhouse was drafted (6 March 1635), reference was made not only to two studios ("de lange Werckcamer," "de Schildercamer") in which he apparently did his painting and put to work his apprentices, but also to three more private studies ("'t Comptoir," "'t Comptoir boven," "'t Comptoirken met de Mannekens"), two of which contained plasters, drawings, and panels with figure studies (Duverger 1984– , 3:429–430, doc. 853).

41. Garff and Pedersen 1988.

42. See Hollstein 1949– , 15:109–127, where thirty-six etchings are listed (most of them reproduced). A few prints mentioned in previous publications as by Panneels have, however, not been included: see especially Rooses 1901, 552; Frank van den Wijngaert, *Inventaris der Rubeniaansche prentkunst* (Antwerp, 1940), 77–80, with further references.

43. In many instances Panneels takes care to inform us that he invented or painted the composition himself (although at times it is merely a paraphrase of a Rubens composition); in other cases Rubens is mentioned as the painter or inventor and sometimes Panneels states only that he executed the etching without giving details about the inventor. Presumably after Panneels' death the publisher Frans van den Wijngaerde (1614–1679) brought out most of these prints again, thereby changing many of the inscriptions and attributing more to Rubens than would seem to be justified. The use of "after Rubens" in Hollstein is thus not very reliable; more critical are the lists in Rooses 1901 and Van den Wijngaert 1940, but these also are in need of revision.

44. The first state with the inscription: "Guilels. Panneels Discip. RVBENI inu. et fe.;" the second state: "Guilels. Panneels fecit RVBENI inu. F.v.W.ex;" see Hollstein 1949– , 15:119, no. 20, illus.

45. Also typical of Panneels' sense of human anatomy is the etching *Christ at the Column*, signed: "Guil. Panneels fecit"; see Hollstein 1949– , 15:114, no. 11, illus. Even when he makes an effort to copy a Rubens figure closely, as is the case in innumerable drawings in the "Rubens-Cantoor" at Copenhagen, he does not succeed in grasping the vigor of his master's models, and the muscles have lost their tonus. The figures he shows us resemble bodybuilders who have neglected their condition for too long.

46. Signed: "Guilels. Panneels inu. et fe.;" see Hollstein 1949– , 15:116, no. 15, illus.

47. Garff and Pedersen 1988, no. 92, pl. 94 (Rubens Cantoor, box VI, 41).

48. Garff and Pedersen 1988, no. 166, pl. 168 (Rubens Cantoor, box III, 3).

49. Garff and Pedersen 1988, no. 61, pl. 63 (Rubens Cantoor, box V, 52); we know from a more personal drawing of his that Panneels was interested in this particular pose: compare Garff and Pedersen 1988, no. 258v, pl. 262.

50. Garff and Pedersen 1988, no. 198, pl. 200 (Rubens Cantoor, box I, 16). For Rubens' *Holy Trinity with Saint Paul and Saint John* see Rudolf Oldenbourg, *P. P. Rubens. Des Meisters Gemälde*. Klassiker der Kunst, vol. 5, 4th ed. (Berlin and Leipzig, 1921), 119, illus.

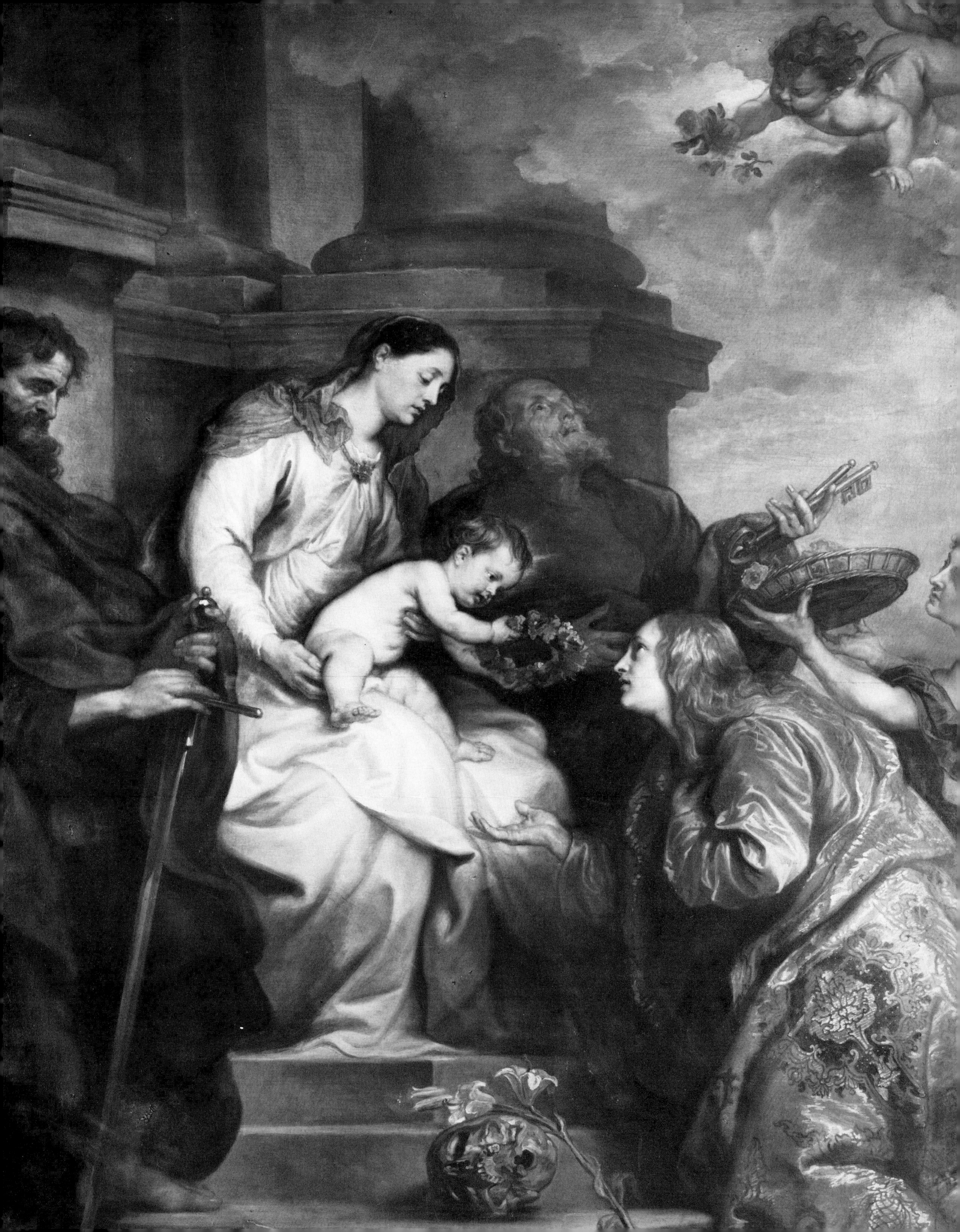

HANS VLIEGHE
Rubenianum, Antwerp
Catholic University, Louvain

Thoughts on Van Dyck's Early Fame and Influence in Flanders

A certain parallelism exists between the origins of Van Dyck's fame as a painter and that of Rubens. Both artists furthered their particular styles in Italy, where subsequently they also made their names; both also returned to Antwerp as renowned painters who immediately became overburdened with commissions. Van Dyck received many commissions for churches, not only in Antwerp but also from other Flemish towns, such as Mechlin, Ghent, Kortrijk, Lille, and Dendermonde.[1] And, of course, he could benefit from the circumstance that Rubens was absent from the southern Netherlands from August 1628 until March 1630.[2] With his specific emotional approach Van Dyck succeeded during these years in responding to an undeniable desire for a more sentimentally and emphatically defined religious imagery. Recently Frans Baudouin has been able to show how important this new conception had become in Flemish art from about 1640 onward.[3] But already as of the 1620s Rubens' oeuvre had also become more explicitly dramatic and emotional. The least that can be said is that Van Dyck with his personal sentimentalism arrived in Antwerp at a very auspicious moment.[4] He received, in addition, many portrait commissions from the nobility residing in the southern Netherlands and also from the wealthy Antwerp merchant class. The latter, especially, made the monumental full-length portrait fashionable outside aristocratic circles (in the strict sense of the words). Indeed, Van Dyck's Venetian-inspired styl-

ishness and sense of colorful decorum must have more than met the expectations of a rich bourgeoisie that increasingly aspired at this time to an aristocratic way of life.[5] Van Dyck's fame did not remain confined to Flanders; he also received portrait commissions from the Dutch stadholder.[6] Somewhat later, in 1634/1635, when he resided in Brussels for some months, nearly all the important representatives from the Flemish, Spanish, Italian, and German nobility linked to the Brussels court were lining up, so to speak, before his easel.

When, however, we consider these many commissions from the financial point of view, we may be led to the conclusion that there were important differences between Rubens and Van Dyck during the years immediately following their return from Italy. Indeed, it seems that Van Dyck did not receive exceptionally high payments for the altarpieces he painted between about 1627 and 1632. As far as documentary evidence informs us, he never seems to have received more than five to eight hundred guilders for altarpieces about 250 to 400 centimeters high, which is a rather average payment for any qualified Flemish history painter of the time.[7] Indeed, around the same time other artists in Flanders painted altarpieces for which they were not paid less than Van Dyck.[8] Only Rubens was the exception. Soon after his return from Italy he was able to command better terms: extant accounts and contracts make it clear that for the same type of altarpiece he could ask a much higher price.[9] Thus, during the years between 1627 and 1632 Van Dyck, although in great demand for religious imagery, may not have been considered a much more important master in Flanders than settled artists belonging to a somewhat older generation, such as De Crayer or other history painters who, at that time, were engaged in important artistic activities for churches and convents in various parts of the southern Netherlands.[10]

We are not informed about the details of payment with regard to Van Dyck's contemporary portraits. Thus we do not know whether for these, too, his prices were no more than average. Still, they must certainly have been high when in 1634/1635 he interrupted his stay at the British court to spend several months in Brussels. When in 1635 the city council of Antwerp wanted to have a portrait of the Cardinal-Infante Ferdinand by Van Dyck, as a prototype for the Spanish governor's depiction in the *Pompa Introitus* decorations, the artist's price was rejected as being much too high.[11] It must be added that the 1634/1635 clientele was mainly aristocratic, whereas the sitters during the second Antwerp period were members of the bourgeoisie. Certainly, given his exceptional rank as an artist, especially at the British court, Van Dyck was considered at the time of his death an artist of superior quality even in Antwerp. An early proof of this is the famous engraving by Paulus Pontius after Erasmus Quellinus (fig. 1),[12] which shows Van Dyck together with Rubens, almost as the princes of Antwerp painting. This fame was consecrated during the second half of the seventeenth century: in

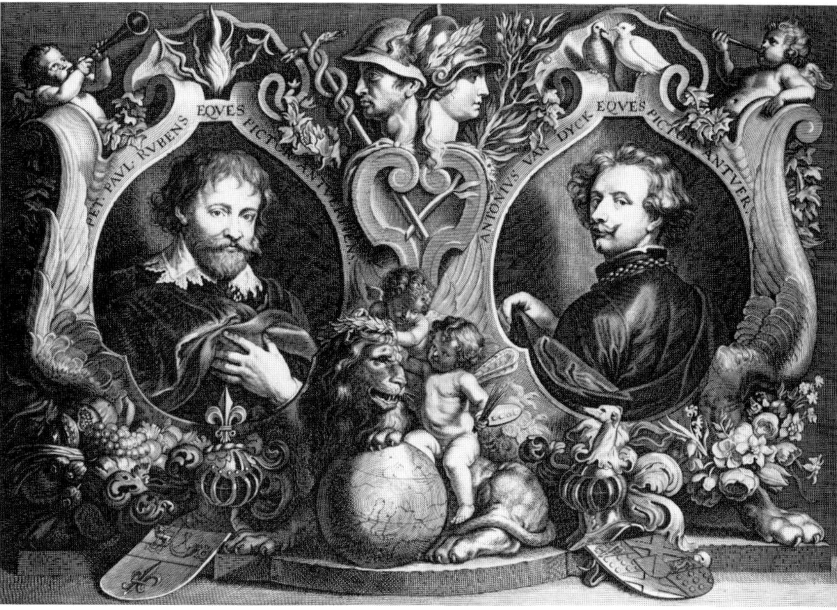

1. Paulus Pontius after Erasmus Quellinus, *Peter Paul Rubens and Anthony van Dyck*, engraving
Rubenshuis, Antwerp

1665 Theodoor Boeyermans depicted Van Dyck next to Rubens in his allegorical composition *Antverpia Pictorum Nutrix* (fig. 2),[13] as one of the two coryphées of Antwerp painting.

Another way to evaluate Van Dyck's early fame is to study his influence on the work of his contemporaries. Although Van Dyck's impact on his Dutch and English fellow artists has been studied to some extent, so far no research of this kind has been undertaken with regard to the work of his Flemish contemporaries. This paper is meant as a first survey. Horst Gerson once wrote that "Van Dyck's work was the most important source of inspiration for many of the generation born between 1600 and 1610."[14] I want to show that this is a somewhat oversimplified view, in need of correction.

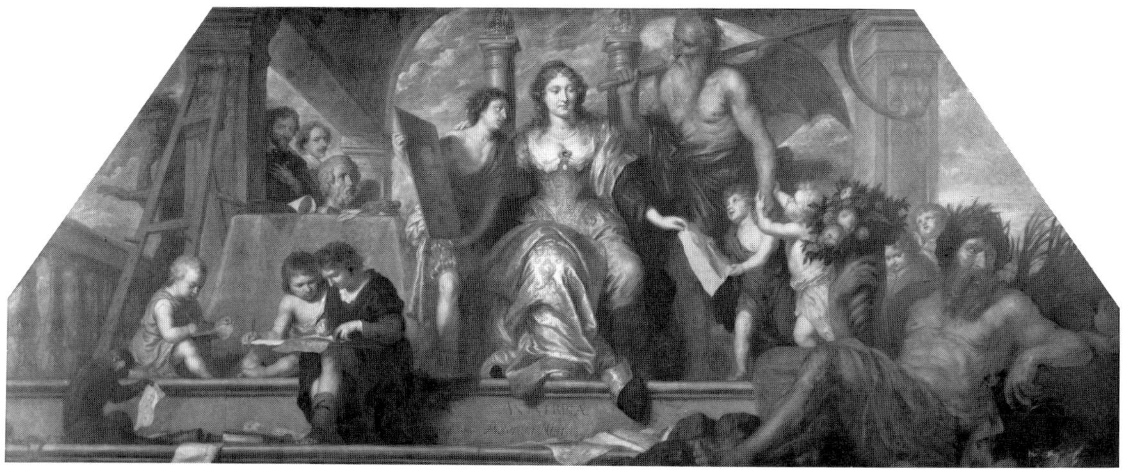

2. Theodoor Bocyermans, *Antverpia Pictorum Nutrix*, 1665, oil on canvas
Koninklijk Museum voor Schone Kunsten, Antwerp

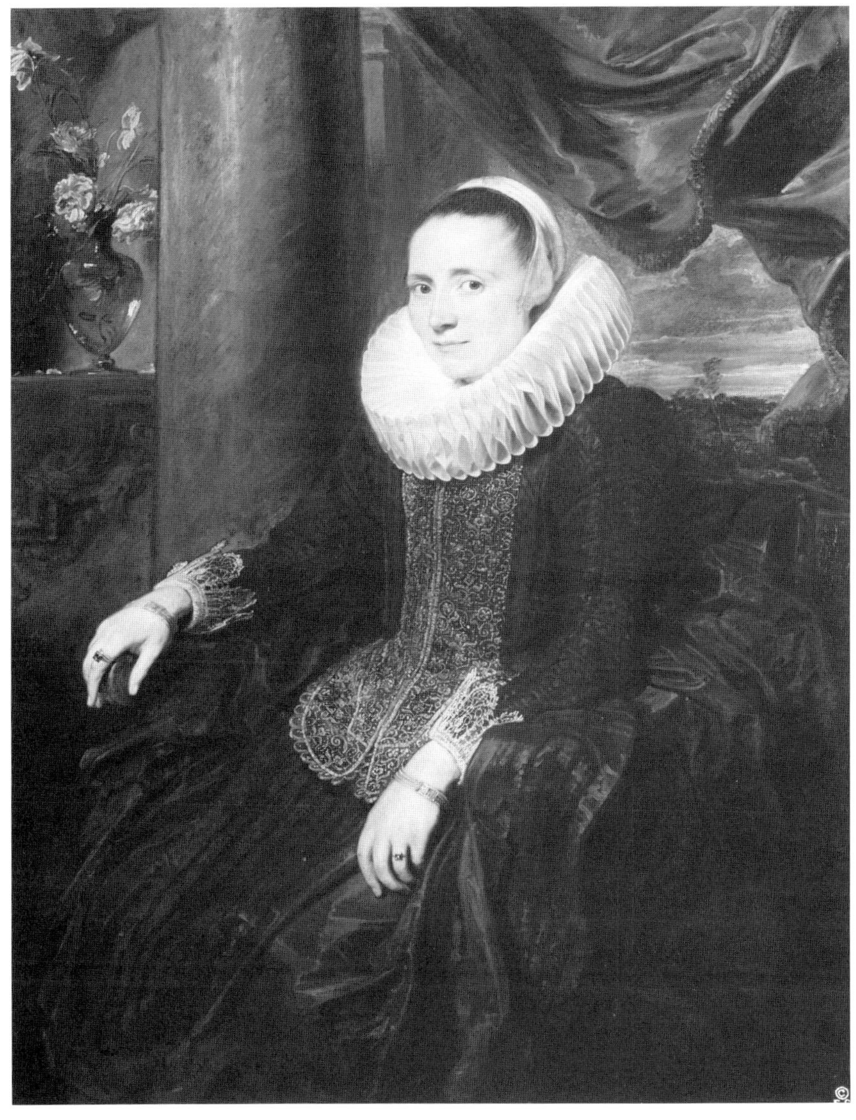

3. Anthony van Dyck,
Margaretha de Vos, c. 1620,
oil on canvas
Frick Collection, New York

Cornelis de Vos (1584/1585–1651) seems to have been the first painter to take over composition schemes used first by Van Dyck. Recently Katlijne Van der Stighelen demonstrated that Van Dyck's half-length portrait of Frans Snyders' wife Margaretha de Vos (fig. 3) was the inspiration for a series of female half-lengths painted by De Vos during the 1620s.[15] That this particular picture by Van Dyck could serve as a point of reference for De Vos can be explained first by the mere fact that Van Dyck's splendid portrait of De Vos' sister was visible in her own house. As De Vos closely collaborated with his brother-in-law Frans Snyders, it goes without saying that he must have been a frequent visitor at Snyders' home. And although the half-length

pose has a long tradition in Northern art, there is no doubt that De Vos must have been very receptive to Van Dyck's brilliant rendering of space and setting. In his *Antonia Canis* (fig. 4) of 1624, his background, enframed by a curtain, is opened up, uncovering vistas behind pillars. However, De Vos was not really able to adapt Van Dyck's sensitive brushwork; he remained tied to a more old-fashioned, somewhat stereotypical mode of expression. The difference becomes very obvious in the treatment of the curtain, where Van Dyck's lively play of folds is replaced by a somewhat dull and linear representation.

We see Van Dyck's work acting as a source of inspiration for De Vos in a more definite way soon after Van Dyck's return from Italy, late in 1627. Van der Stighelen explained that De Vos' full-length portraits made just before 1630, such as those of Charlotte Butkens (fig. 5) and Anna-Maria de Schotte (Museum of Fine Arts, Boston), were more deeply influenced by Van Dyck's contemporary style than were the earlier portraits.[16] Indeed, it is striking to see how from now on Van Dyck's aristocratic full-length pose, combined with a landscape vista *alla Veneziana* or enlivened with children or dogs, becomes fashionable with the members of the wealthy bourgeoisie. Although a rather severe style to some extent typifies these later portraits, it cannot be denied that De Vos now also wants to endow them with Van Dyck's sensitivity in the treatment of costume, especially in the more fluent rendering of folds and the delicate reflections of light. In some cases De Vos also seems to emulate Van Dyck's particular stylishness by representing his sitters with more elongated hands.[17] De Vos' stylistic development amply illustrates the growing aristocratization of the lifestyle of Antwerp's wealthy merchant classes in the course of the seventeenth century.[18]

Although Van Dyck made a portrait of Gaspar de Crayer (1584–1669) on two different occasions,[19] nothing is known about any personal contact between the two painters. Such contact, however, must have existed. There is sporadic mention of a Van Dyck painting in De Crayer's possession.[20] Of much more importance is the fact that in 1634/1635 Van Dyck spent some time in Brussels, where he must have had close con-

4. Cornelis de Vos, *Antonia Canis*, 1624, oil on panel
Thyssen-Bornemisza Collection, Lugano-Castagnola

tact with the court and the nobility residing there. The majority of Flemish and foreign nobles living near the Brussels court were portrayed by Van Dyck during these months. It can hardly be doubted that De Crayer, who then happened to be Brussels' most impor-tant painter, with good contacts in court cir-cles,[21] had personal connections with his younger fellow artist Van Dyck. However, De Crayer's interest in Van Dyck predates the 1634/1635 stay. Already in and even be-fore 1630, he made full-length portraits that

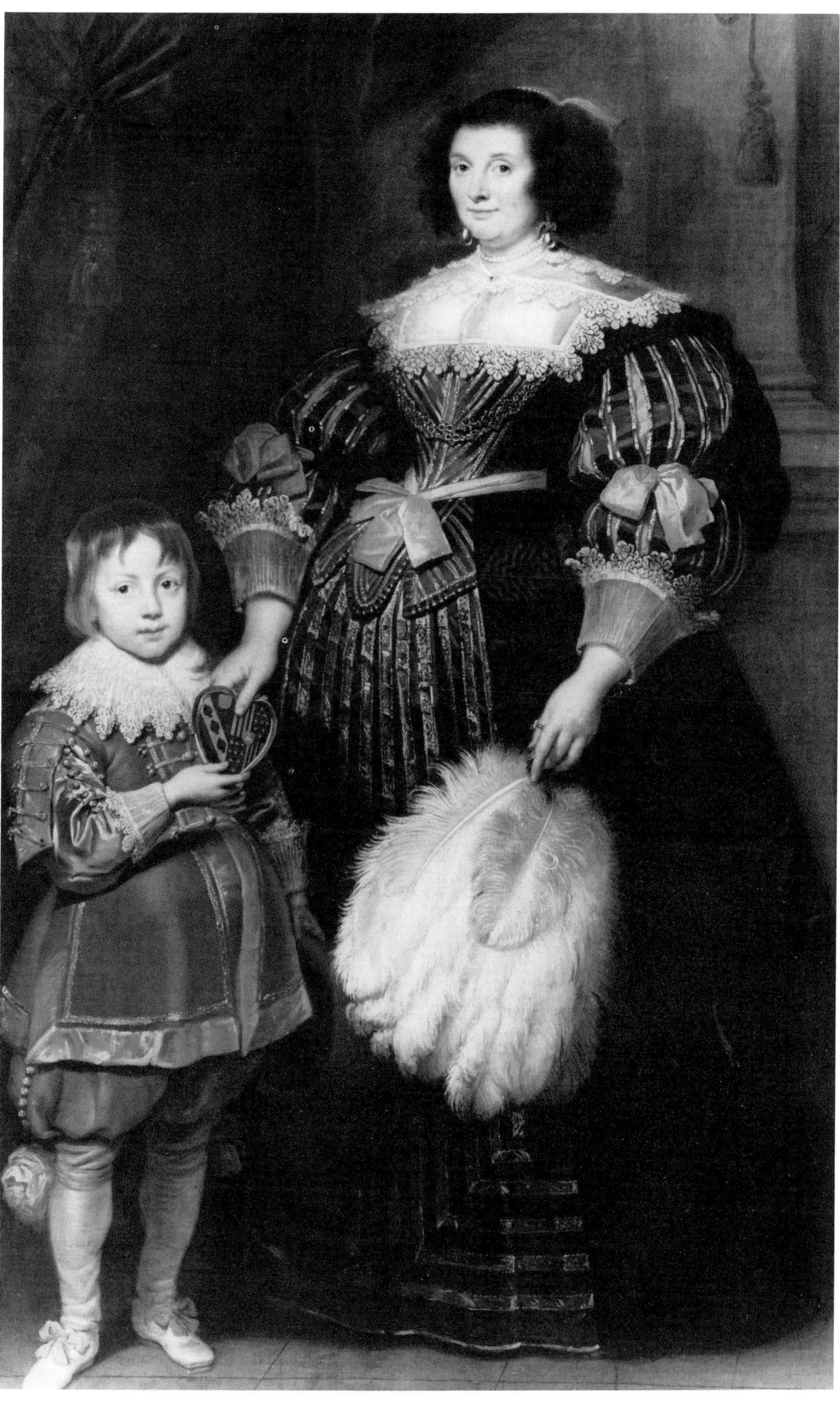

5. Cornelis de Vos, *Charlotte Butkens*, c. 1628–1630, oil on canvas
Schlossmuseum, Gotha

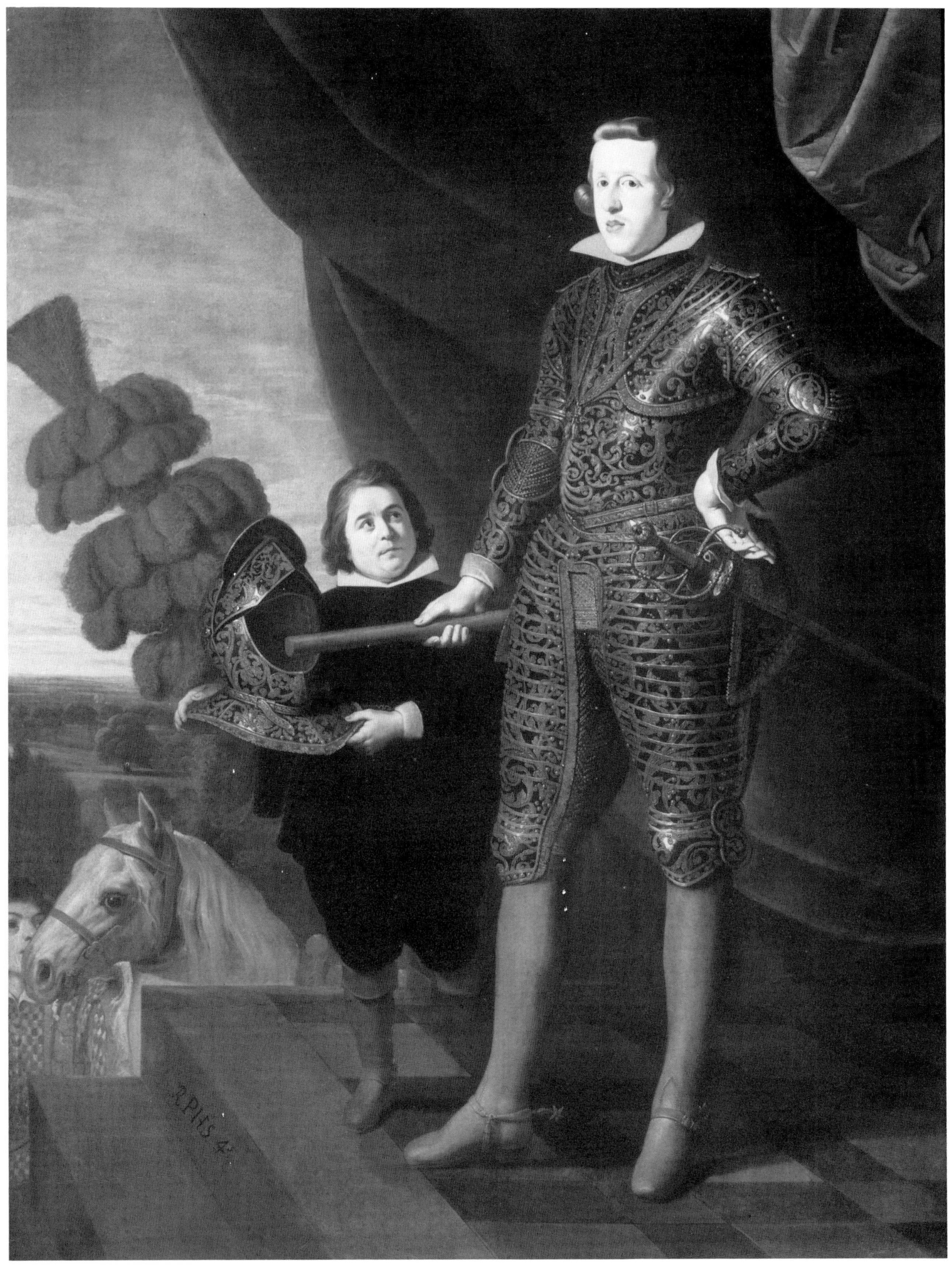

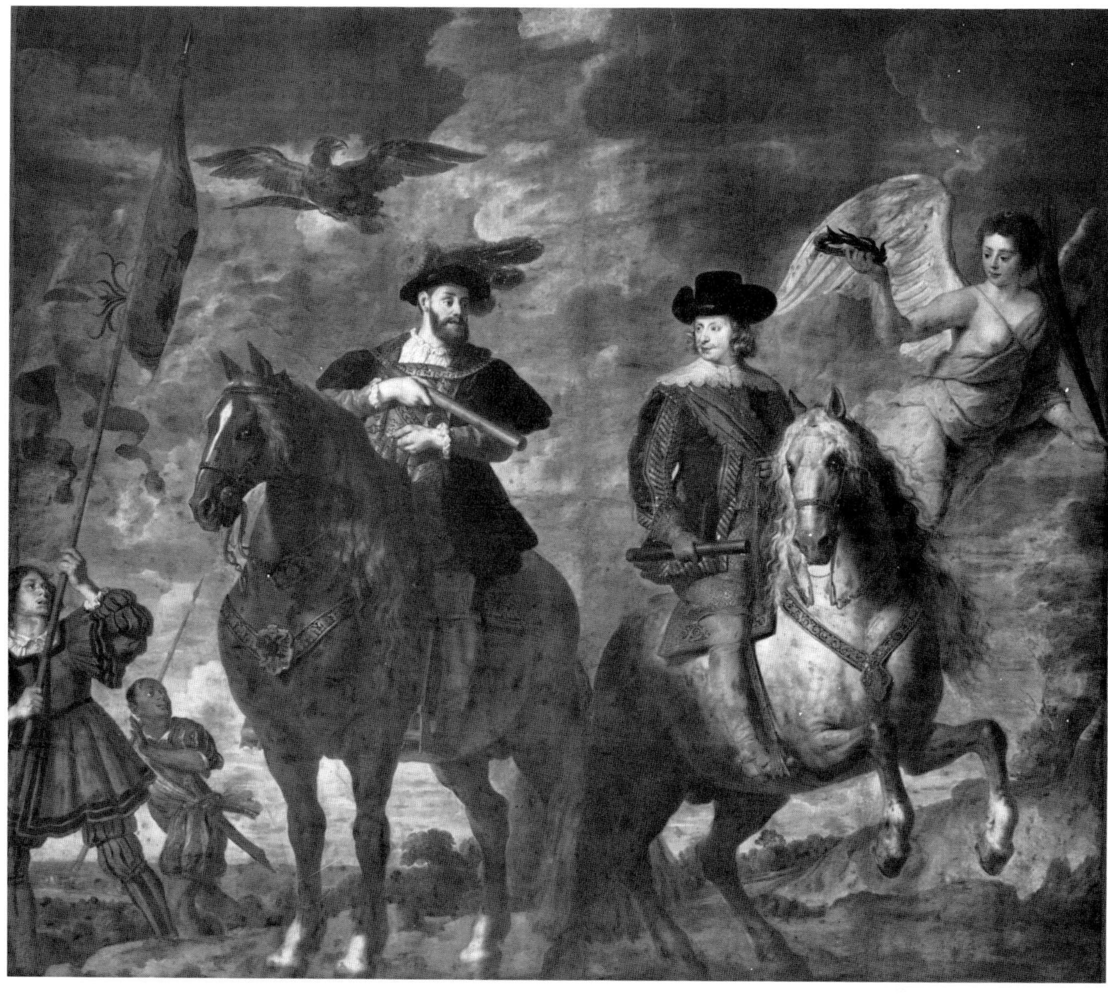

are unmistakably inspired by Van Dyck in their elongated pose, the seemingly unconstrained attitude, and the Venetian decorum with landscape vistas and colorful secondary figures. De Crayer's portraits of Philip IV (fig. 6)[22] and Ferdinand de Spoelberch[23] are good examples in this respect. Like Van Dyck, and in a similar way to De Vos, De Crayer must have understood how effectively the full-length could meet the need of the upper classes for self-representation and self-perpetuation.

De Crayer's sudden interest in Van Dyck has already been remarked upon by the anonymous eighteenth-century "Louvre compiler," who very pertinently writes:

Although he was already a famous painter at a time when Van Dyck had not yet used his brushes, Gaspar de Crayer owed to the portraits of our artist [Van Dyck] the strength and grace lacking in his own earlier works of this kind [his portraits]. This is confirmed by all the connoisseurs who have compared De Crayer's portraits painted before 1625 to those he painted after that date.[24]

However, in following Van Dyck's typology so closely De Crayer did not adapt his style to Van Dyck's specific *morbidezza* and rather nervous pictural treatment. On the contrary, what is striking in De Crayer's later portraits is their local coloring, their strong modeling, and their heavy impasto, thus linking them much more to Rubens' severe classicizing style of the years before 1620, which had been determinant for De Crayer ever since his beginnings. After all, outside Antwerp Rubens' works from the period 1612–1620 could nowhere be seen so well displayed as in the churches and public buildings of Brussels.[25]

Van Dyck's short stay in Brussels during the winter of 1634/1635 may only have fostered De Crayer's interest in the brilliant younger fellow artist. This interest is made clear by the groom in his 1635 portrait of *Charles V Exhorting His Great-Grandson Ferdinand to Follow His Example* (fig. 7), a motif that can only be understood as a direct borrowing from Van Dyck's *Henrietta of Lorraine, 1634* (fig. 8), visible to De Crayer in Brussels.[26]

De Crayer's first contact with Van Dyck's works was not confined to the field of aristocratic portrait painting. During the 1630s he also introduced into his devotional pictures those apparently neurotic, elongated figures with soulful expressions and theatrical gestures typical, it seems, of a new and more emotional religious approach.[27] The composition and motifs of De Crayer's *Raising of the Cross* (fig. 9) are undeniably derived from the altarpiece of the same subject painted by Van Dyck in 1631 for the church of Our Lady in Kortrijk (fig. 10).[28] Yet here again the stronger degree of sentimentality in the Van Dyck altarpiece was not "translated" by De Crayer into a weaker style, which would have corresponded better to the spirit of the piece. Also De Crayer's religious paintings are characterized by a rather descriptive pictural style, expressed by a stressed plasticity of forms and local coloring. Especially from the later 1640s onward Van Dyck's oeuvre would become important for De Crayer. From that time he would adopt a weaker manner, also coming closer to Van Dyck technically. But this change has to be understood within the context of the evolution of history painting in seventeenth-century Flanders in general. In addition to Van Dyck, the late Rubens and the sixteenth-century Venetians were sources of inspiration.[29]

The more or less contemporary reaction of Jacob van Oost the Elder (1601–1671) to Van Dyck's work is somewhat comparable to that of De Crayer. Van Oost was the most important artist of seventeenth-century Bruges, where in 1637 he executed a *Madonna with Saints* (fig. 11) destined for the decoration of the high altar of the chapel of Saint John's hospital.[30] This work is clearly based on Van Dyck's *Coronation of Saint Rosalie* (fig. 12), made in 1629 for the Antwerp Jesuit convent.[31] In spite of the very close relationship between the two paintings, it is once again the motif and not the style that Van Oost takes over, in his effort to achieve a more highly baroque, that is, a more ecstatically defined devotional art. The pictorial treatment remains Caravaggesque, imported from Italy in about 1628.[32] Van Oost continued to work in a very descriptive and colorfully realistic style, as is made clear by his fine *Portrait of a Theologian and His Secretary* (Groeningemuseum, Bruges) of 1668.[33] This portrait shows that, in one way or another, Van Oost must have known the composition

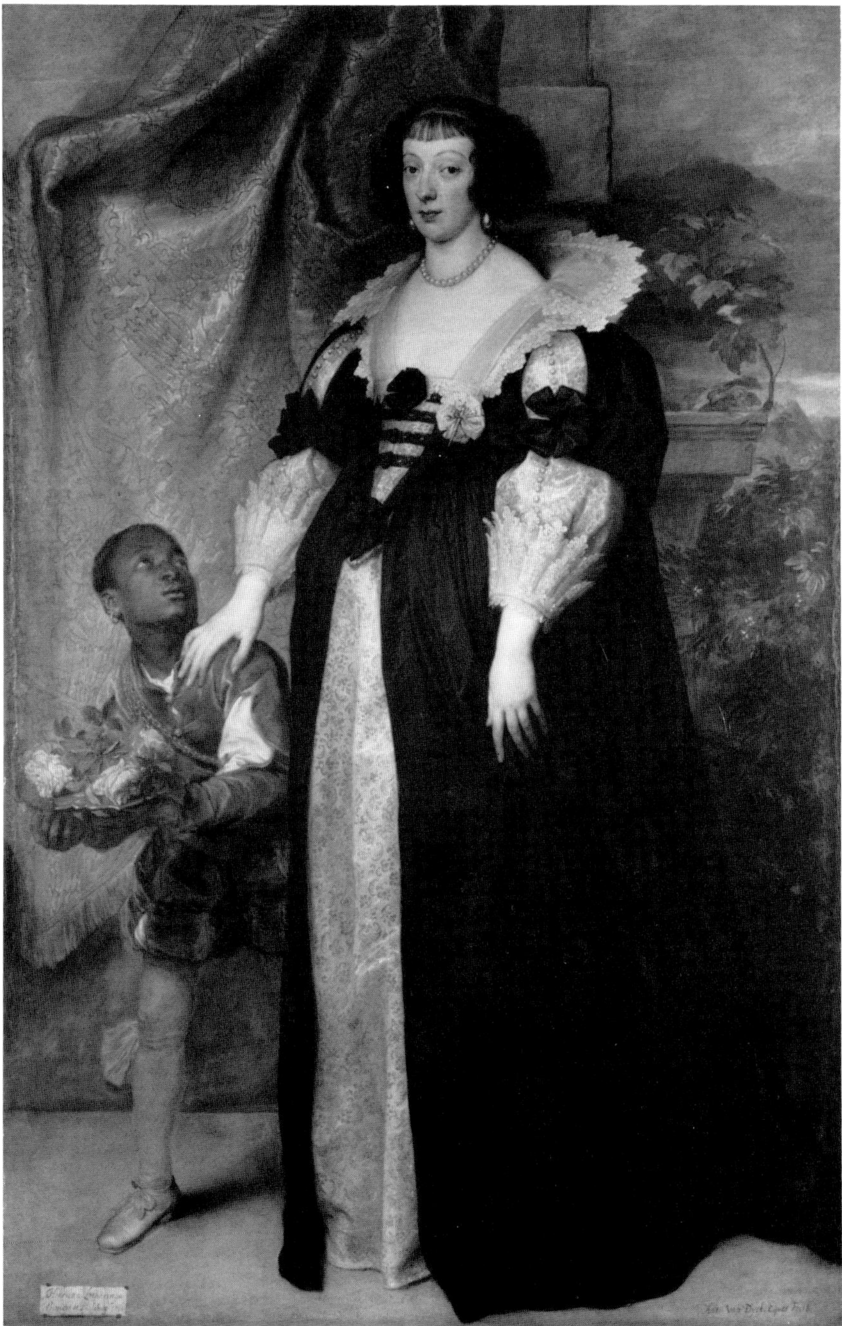

8. Anthony van Dyck, *Henrietta of Lorraine*, 1634, oil on canvas
Iveagh Bequest, Kenwood

of *Thomas Wentworth with Sir Philip Mainwaring* (Lady Juliet de Chair), painted by Van Dyck in England in 1640.[34] Nothing of the Venetian mood so characteristic of Van Dyck's picture enters into Van Oost's double portrait. On the contrary, its crude realism harks back to an old Flemish tradition. Only after Van Oost's death in 1671 would such a painter as Lodewijk de Deyster succeed in rendering Van Dyck's sensibility in pictorial terms.[35] Meanwhile, the provincial center of Bruges had become more familiar with Van Dyckian forms, thanks to the important commissions given in the 1650s and 1660s to Antwerp epigones of Van Dyck such as Jan Boeckhorst and Thomas Willeboirts Bosschaert.[36] These artists are representative of a younger generation of Antwerp painters whose artistic beginnings were not rooted in an older tradition. On the contrary, as Van Dyck's juniors they could as easily take the latter's more tender and emotional late style as their starting point.

Boeckhorst (1604–1668) must be mentioned first, since he was a transitional figure. His artistic career began shortly before 1630, somewhere in the shadow of Rubens' workshop. There was some collaboration between the two painters, and after Rubens' death Boeckhorst even retouched some of his master's works in order to make them more saleable. His early style seems to have been coined from Rubens' late works;[37] however, somewhat later in his career, in his *Martyrdom of Saint Lawrence* (fig. 13) of 1649, the weaker and less articulate anatomy, a more soulful and emotional mood, and the more expressive brushwork clearly demonstrate a reorientation toward Van Dyck.[38] Also striking in Boeckhorst's later style is the lighter tonality, with its unmistakable Venetian overtones. Again, this change fits well within a more general trend in Flemish art toward a lively and theatrical expressivity,[39] but it is striking that Boeckhorst achieves his aim by orienting himself toward the sensibility of Van Dyck's late style.

Boeckhorst's adaptation of Van Dyck's style brings us to a new phase in the evolution of Van Dyck's fame as seen in terms of artistic influence. Whereas in earlier years such painters as De Vos, De Crayer, or Van Oost were primarily interested in adapting motifs and schemes to their own, very different stylistic idioms, now we are confronted with a true *aemulatio* of Van Dyck's personal means of artistic expression. Boeckhorst was flexible enough to be able to "creep into" Van Dyck's brushwork. Indeed, there is evidence that Boeckhorst was very familiar with Van Dyck's painterly technique. An eighteenth-century statement that he was Van Dyck's pupil cannot be corroborated, but it may reflect a very specific aspect of Boeckhorst's artistic activity. Just as he did with some of Rubens' works, so he copied and retouched certain pictures by Van Dyck, very probably with the same commercial intentions.[40]

Born in 1604, Boeckhorst was only slightly younger than Van Dyck. We have to wait for the generation of painters born after 1610 to see some artists taking Van Dyck's specific *morbidezza* as a springboard for their careers. The first and most important of this younger group of "Van Dyckian" painters is Willeboirts Bosschaert (1614–1654). He became a master in Antwerp in 1637 and initially had close contacts with Rubens' workshop. Evidence for this is his collaboration in 1637–1638 in the Torre de la Parada project.[41] Another important proof of his close links to Rubens' workshop practice is his *Venus Withdrawing Mars*, his earliest known composition, made in the year of his enrollment in the Antwerp painters' guild and destined for the hall of the guild of Antwerp harquebusiers. The original painting of monumental size has long been lost, but can still be judged from an oil sketch (private collection, Germany), and from a late seventeenth-century copy (fig. 14) probably by Karel Ykens the Younger. Nora De Poorter has shown that this composition is directly inspired by Rubens' *Horrors of War* (Palazzo Pitti, Florence), painted in 1637 for the grand-duke of Tuscany.[42] Since this picture was only visible for a short time in Rubens' workshop before it was shipped to Florence,[43] evidently the young Willeboirts Bosschaert saw it in Rubens' atelier. He recast this Rubensian composition in a style entirely derived from Van Dyck. This stylistic connection is revealed in the somewhat weak yet graciously elongated figures, as well as in the stressed emotionality of Mars' facial expression. Most obvious, however, is the Van Dyckian character of the second putto from the left, who is seen raising his

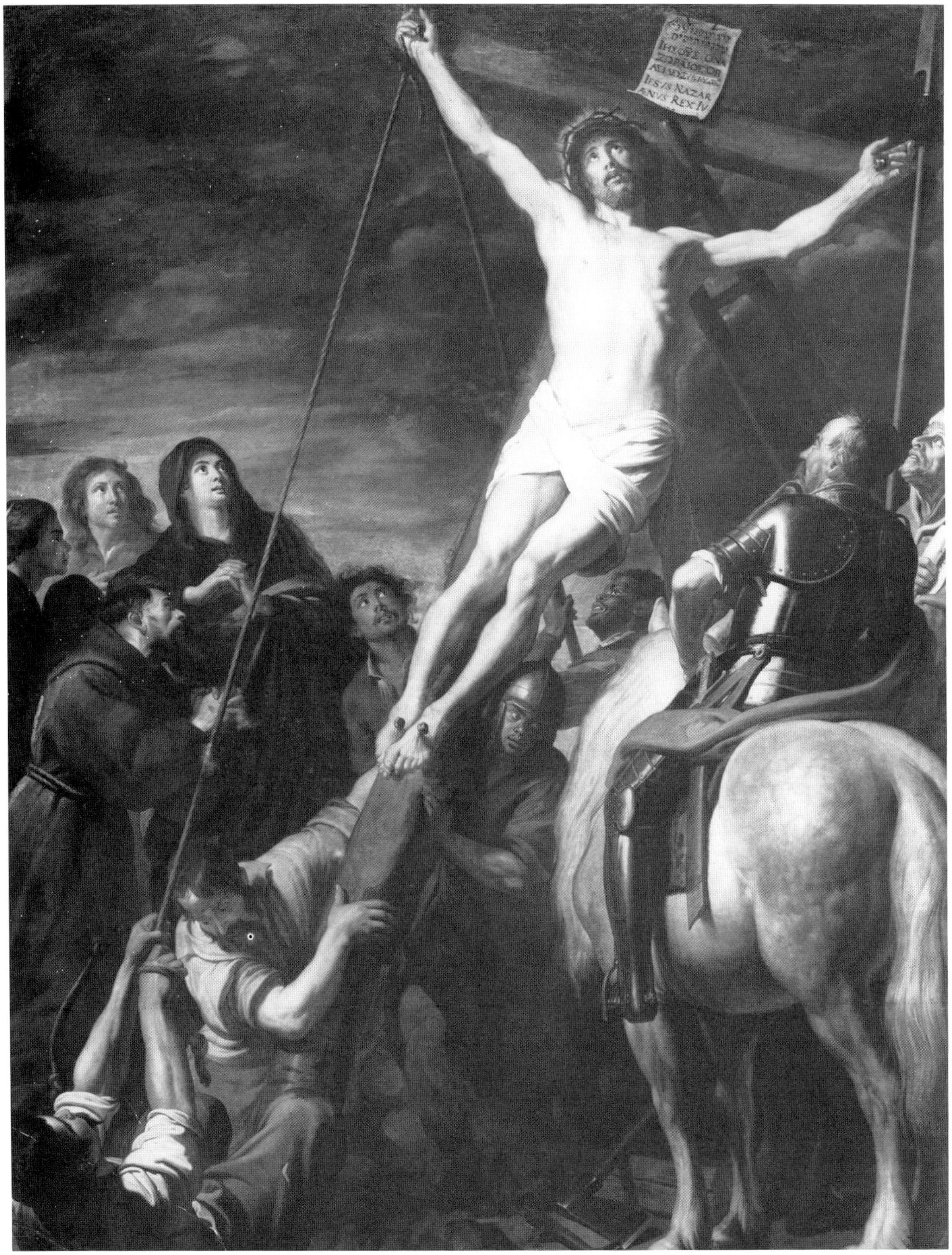

9. Gaspar de Crayer, *Raising of the Cross*, c. 1631–1635, oil on canvas
Musée des Beaux-Arts, Rennes

arms in a gesture of despair. Not only is the elegant *contrapposto* entirely in Van Dyck's mood, but the motif itself turns out to be a copy of one of the angels in Schelte à Bolswert's engraving after Van Dyck's famous *Madonna with the Partridges* (fig. 15).[44]

Willeboirts Bosschaert continued to produce this type of Rubensian composition in a Van Dyckian style until the end of his career. In large part Willeboirts Bosschaert's paintings, which consisted of allegorical and mythological compositions as well as

10. Anthony van Dyck,
Raising of the Cross, 1631,
oil on canvas
Onze-Lieve-Vrouwekerk, Kortrijk

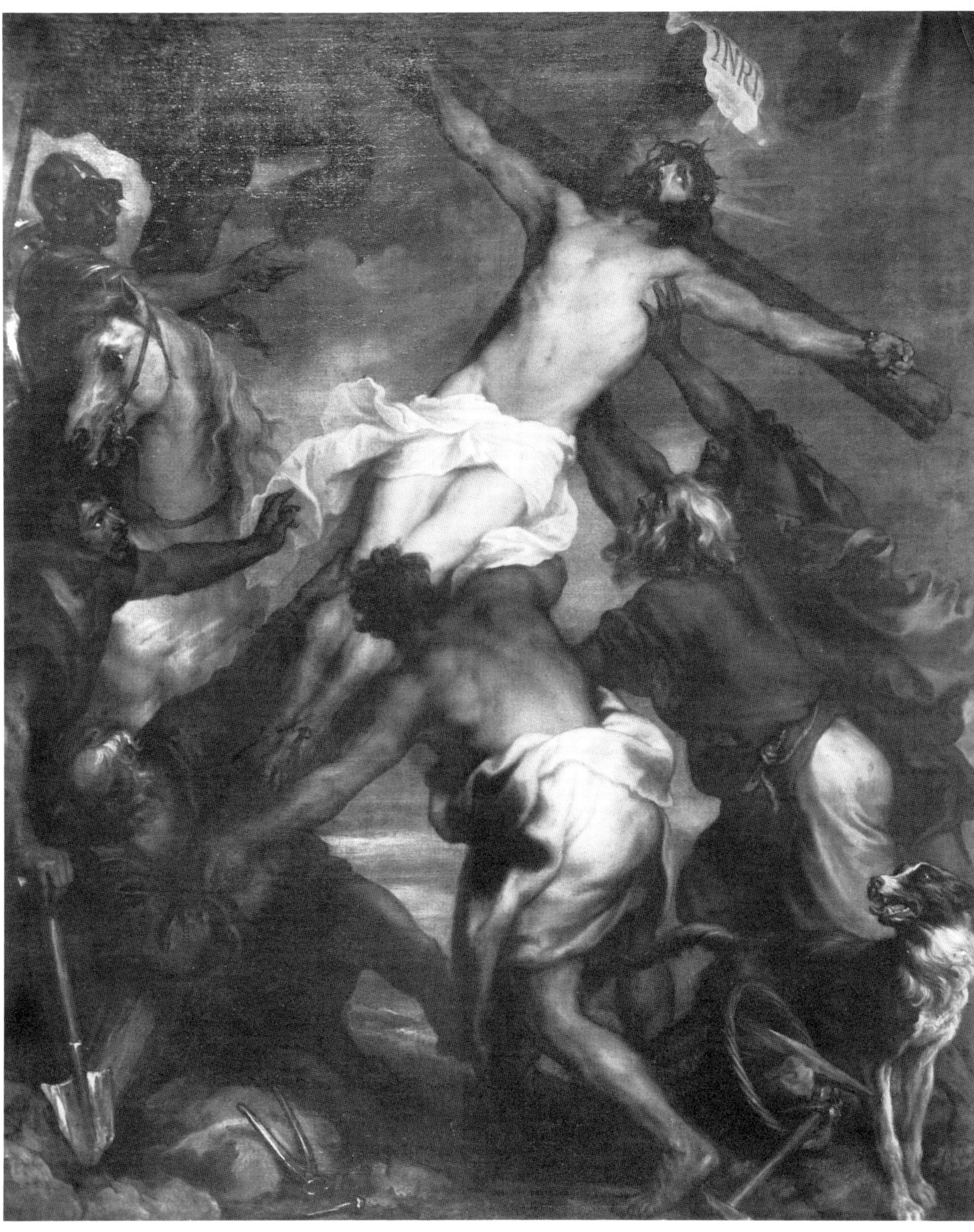

devotional subjects and *portraits historiés*, were commissioned by the Dutch stadholder Frederik-Hendrik and his wife Amalia von Solms. Already in 1641, the year of Van Dyck's death, Willeboirts Bosschaert had come into contact with the court at The Hague, and good relations in this quarter would last until his premature death in 1654.[45] It is well known that the princes of Orange greatly favored Van Dyck's work. They were the first princes in Europe to commission paintings by him immediately after his return from Italy: already in 1628 we see Van Dyck painting the portraits of the stadholder and his wife. When Van Dyck went to England in 1632 the princes continued to prefer portrait painters such as Adriaen Hanneman, for example, who had grafted their style onto that of Van Dyck. It is fair to question to what extent the princes of Orange considered Willeboirts Bosschaert's work an ersatz for that of Van Dyck.[46] Anyway, the elegant Van Dyckian style must have met the desire for pomp and circumstance in the court at The Hague.

The style of Willeboirts Bosschaert is so strongly dependent on that of Van Dyck that one wonders whether Willeboirts Bosschaert may not in some way have had closer contacts with Van Dyck's workshop. At first sight this does not seem likely: in 1628 Willeboirts Bosschaert became a pupil of Gerard Seghers,[47] and before his registration in 1637 as a master of the Antwerp guild[48] there is no further record of his training. We are not informed about the names of the disciples Van Dyck must have had during his very busy second Antwerp period. An explanation for this lack of evidence may be that when Van Dyck became a painter to the Brussels court in about 1628–1630, he got the same advantageous conditions as Rubens, namely, that he was exempt from registering his pupils. Unfortunately the detailed terms of his appointment are unknown, but it should be remembered that like Rubens Van Dyck continued to stay in Antwerp, despite his allegiance to the Brussels court.[49] Willeboirts Bosschaert need not necessarily have spent his entire training period in Seghers' workshop. He may, as so many did, have chosen another master. I raise the question as to whether, at some moment before April 1632, he may not have entered Van Dyck's studio.

Gonzales Coques (c. 1615–1684) is best known for his many cabinet-size portraits of family groups in a truly Van Dyckian style, for which he earned his sobriquet "petit Van Dyck."[50] Already in the poses of the two sitters in his earliest known work, the 1640 *Portrait of a Couple in an Interior* (fig. 16), this typical vein is apparent. Subsequently it may have been consciously developed, since Coques, along with Willeboirts Bosschaert and Pieter Thijs, was active at the Dutch court at least from 1645, both as a portraitist and a painter of political allegories.[51] He also worked for Leopold-Wilhelm and other princes: Cornelis de Bie stressed in 1661 the fact that Coques was much in demand in court circles.[52] Coques was slightly younger

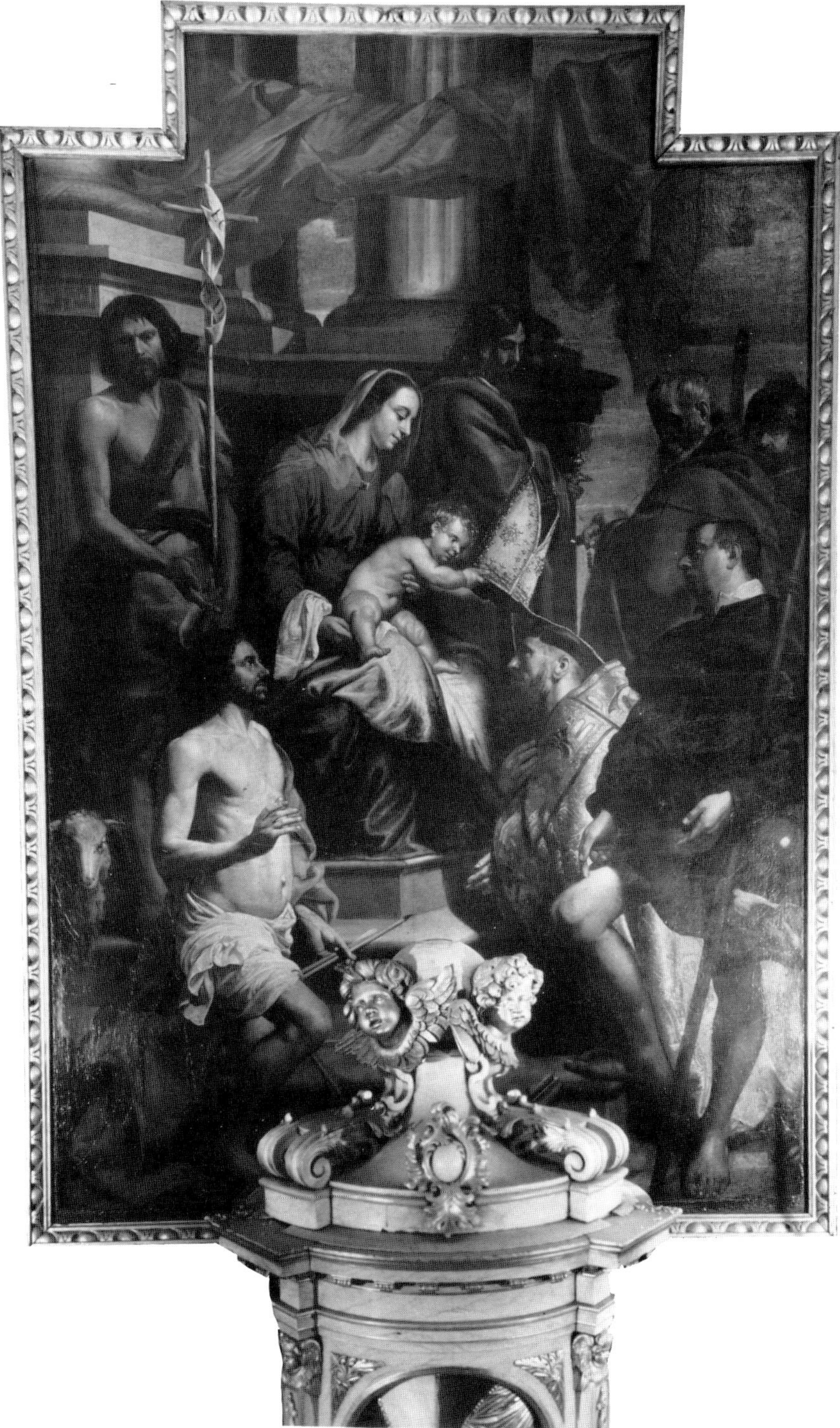

than Willeboirts Bosschaert, and became a pupil to Jan Brueghel II in 1626. He registered as a master only in 1641, and it has already been argued that in the meantime he may have worked as Van Dyck's pupil in

11. Jacob van Oost the Elder, *Madonna with Saints*, 1637, oil on canvas
Sint-Janshospitaal, Bruges

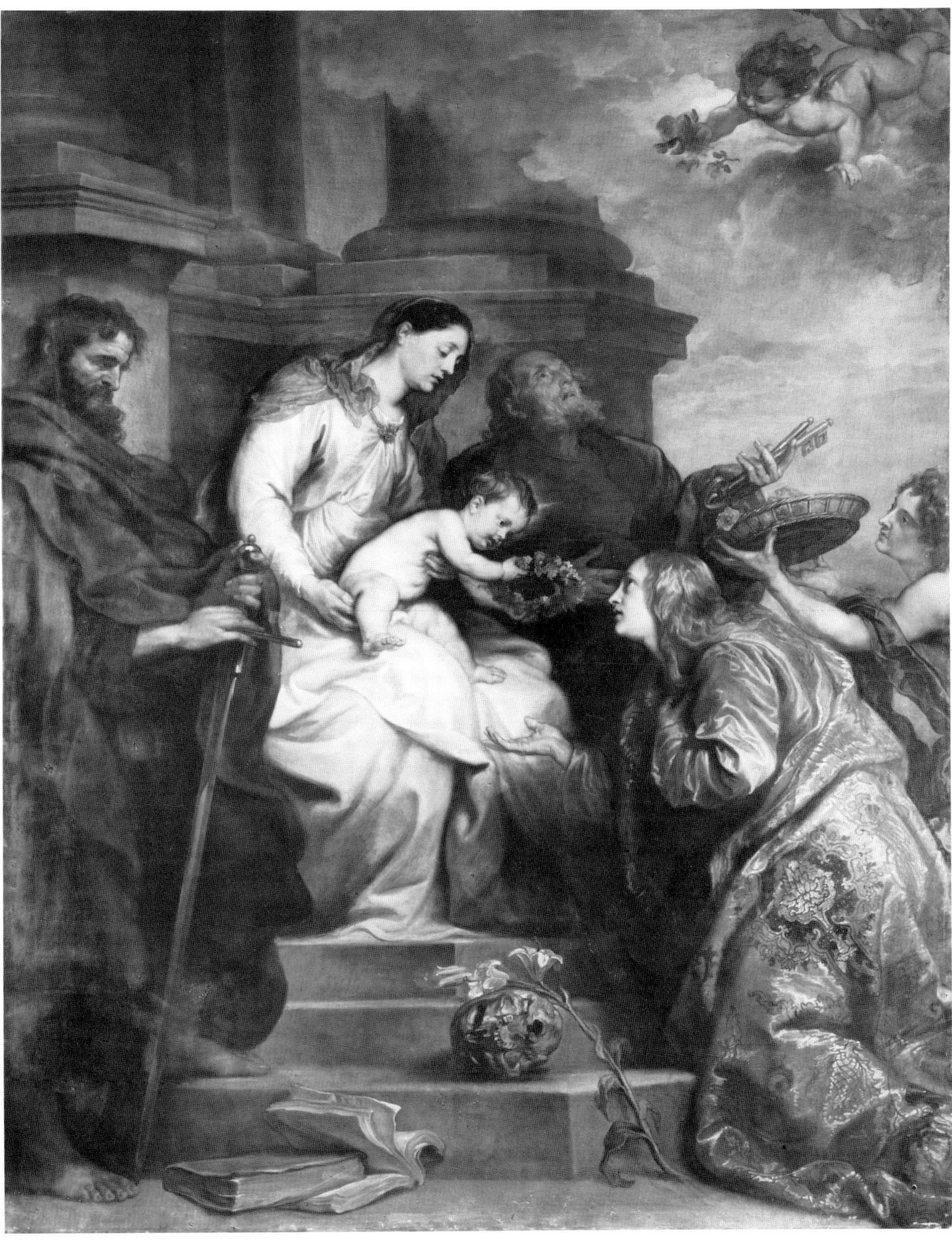

London.[53] There is no proof of this, but a stay in Van Dyck's workshop at some time between 1627 and 1632 may be considered a possibility for the same reasons as in the case of Willeboirts Bosschaert.

Thijs (1624–1677) is a third painter to have taken Van Dyck's late oeuvre as his starting point. It is striking to see that here, also, there is a certain link with the court milieu, at least in Thijs' early oeuvre. Immediately after having registered in the Antwerp guild in 1644/1645,[54] Thijs collaborated on the now lost decorations for Honselaarsdijk Palace.[55] Shortly thereafter he played a part

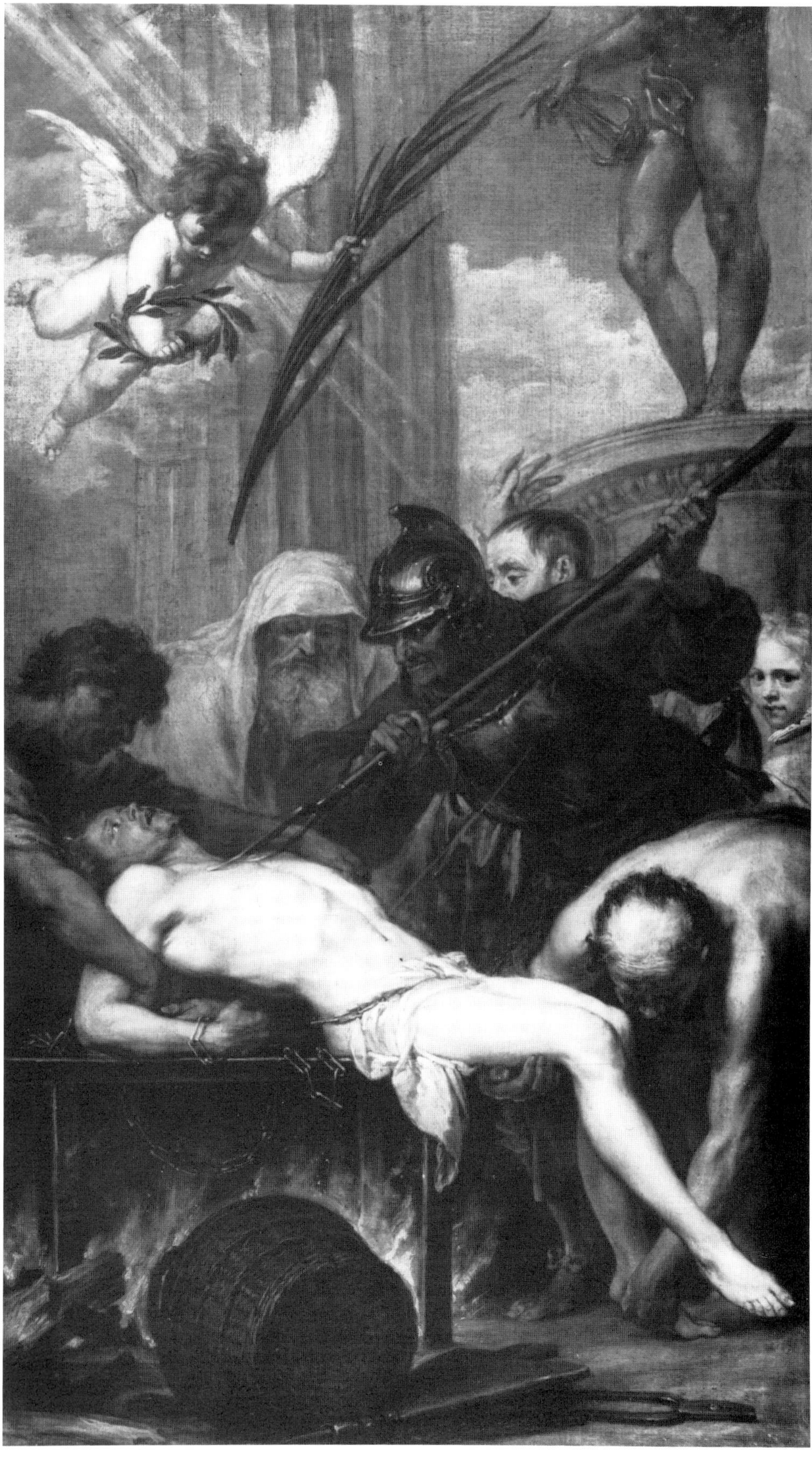

13. Jan Boeckhorst,
*Martyrdom of Saint
Lawrence*, 1649, oil on
canvas
Musée des Beaux-Arts, Bordeaux

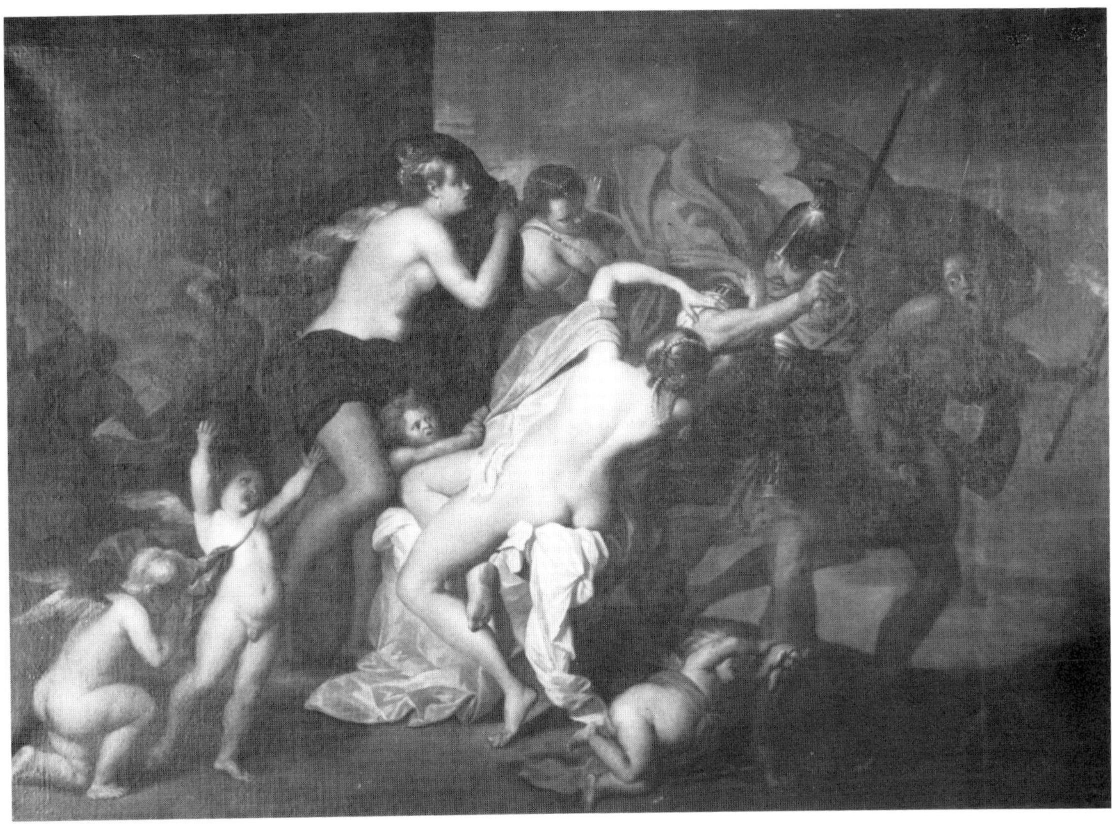

14. Karel Ykens the Younger (?), *Venus Withdrawing Mars*, oil on canvas
Musée des Beaux-Arts, Bordeaux

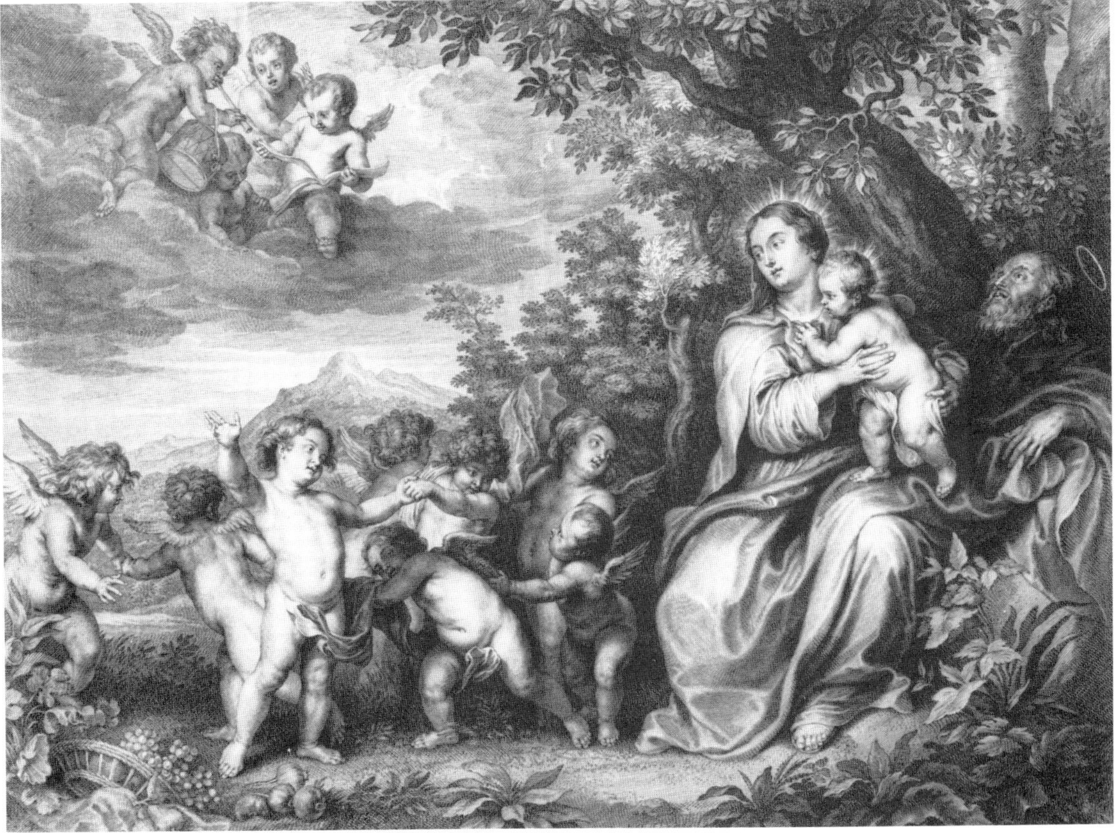

15. Schelte à Bolswert after Anthony van Dyck, *Madonna with the Partridges*, engraving
Stedelijk Prentenkabinet, Antwerp

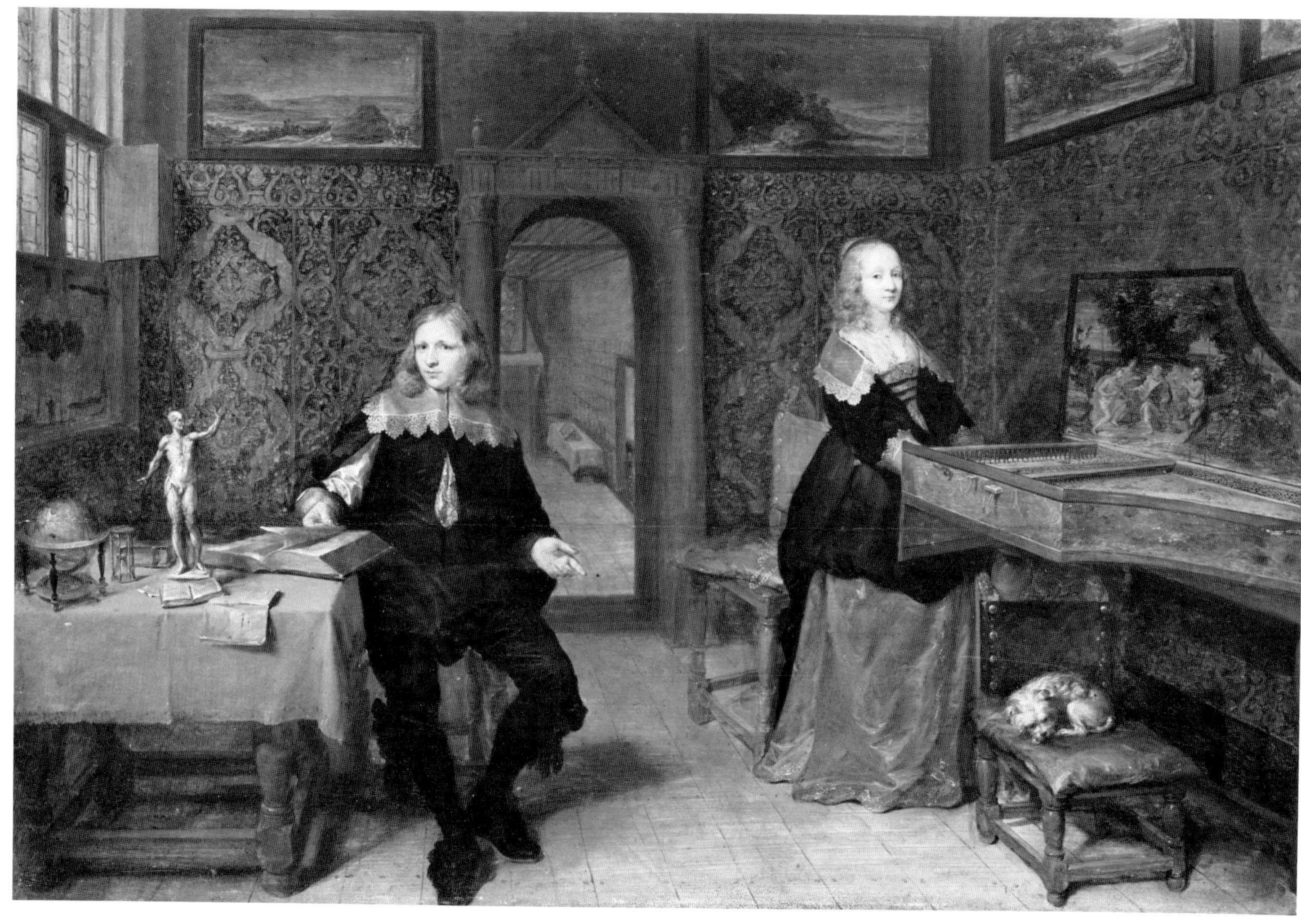

in the execution of tapestry cartoons for Archduke Leopold-Wilhelm.[56] He is also known to have painted a few mythological scenes, which found a place in the collection of the archduke.[57] Other early works include an altarpiece for the Brussels Capuchin church (fig. 17). This work was ordered by the influential Capuchin superior Charles d'Arenberg, an offspring of the famous family of that name and not without influence at the Brussels court.[58] It does not seem improbable to me that Thijs was instructed by Willeboirts Bosschaert or, at least, received strong artistic impulses from him. Not only was Willeboirts among those who were working for the princes of Orange and Archduke Leopold-Wilhelm, but we also find him active, at the same moment as Thijs, in the decoration of the Brussels Capuchin church.[59] Furthermore, it is striking to see how related some of Thijs' early works are to those of

Willeboirts Bosschaert: a good example is offered by his *Abraham and Isaäc* (fig. 18), a work from the mid-1650s,[60] in which the main character is directly inspired by Willeboirts' slightly earlier *Prophet Elijah in the Desert* (fig. 19).[61] From the late 1650s on, Thijs seems to have made mainly large-size altarpieces in a more "metallic" Van Dyckian style and of a rather repetitive character.[62] These, too, must have met the need for exalted religious imagery typical of the later decades of the seventeenth century. In his rather numerous portraits Thijs improvised on Van Dyck's dashing poses, which had been popularized by Van Dyck's Iconography.[63]

Willeboirts Bosschaert, Coques, and Thijs are the closest followers of Van Dyck in Antwerp. Willeboirts Bosschaert and Coques may have been trained by Van Dyck, while Thijs may rather have coined his style from Willeboirts Bosschaert's work. All three

16. Gonzales Coques,
Portrait of a Couple in an Interior, 1640, oil on panel
Staatliche Gemäldegalerie, Kassel

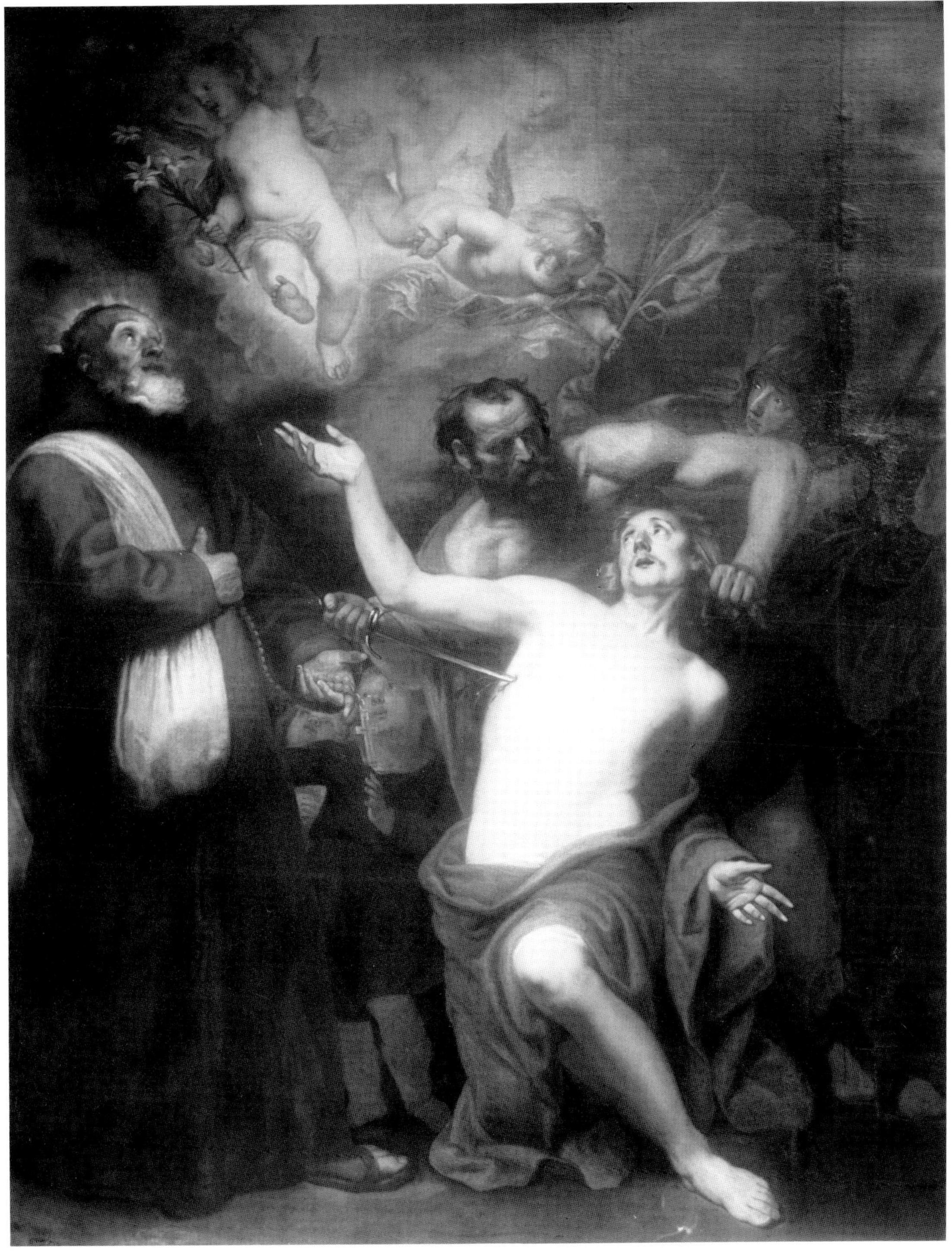

artists started their careers as painters in court service. The Orange court at The Hague played a particularly dominant role in this respect. It is thus fair to ask to what extent their deliberate choice of Van Dyck's "aristocratic" style was stimulated by this circumstance.

Outside Antwerp Van Dyckianism as a specific style found a very close follower in Lucas Franchoys II (1616–1681), the Mechlin painter who belonged to the same generation as Willeboirts Bosschaert and Coques and who, from about the 1650s onward, executed numerous altarpieces for his native town. By

orienting himself in that direction he may
have been stimulated by the circumstance
that Mechlin, the ecclesiastical capital of
the southern Netherlands, was a city in
which an emotionally loaded expressivity in
a particularly Van Dyckian vein must have
fully and entirely satisfied an undeniable desire for a triumphalist apology for the main
articles of the Roman Catholic faith. This
hypothesis seems all the more probable
when we consider that Alphonse de Bergues,
who from 1669 until 1689 was the powerful
and influential archbishop of Mechlin, was
Franchoys' patron.[64] Also as a painter of portraits (fig. 20) Franchoys was a true follower
of Van Dyck.

Certain Flemish history painters, such as
Abraham van Diepenbeeck (1596–1675)[65] or
Simon de Vos (1603–1676),[66] were occasionally influenced by Van Dyck's style but for
other important history painters who became active from about 1630 on, Van Dyck's
style was not influential at all. Until the
end of his career Cornelis Schut (1597–1655)
worked in a very lively high baroque style
of Italian origin.[67] Theodoor van Thulden
(1606–1669) came under Rubens' spell from
about 1635 on and continued to adhere to the
latter's late style until his death in 1669;
Van Thulden's fleshy figures, as in the 1654
*Flemish Provinces Paying Homage to the
Holy Virgin* (Kunsthistorisches Museum, Vienna), are clearly in a Rubensian vein.[68] A
different artistic personality was that of Erasmus Quellinus (1607–1678). His classicizing
style is very similar to that of his brother, the
sculptor Artus Quellinus, who was a disciple
and epigone of François Duquesnoy.[69] A special case is that of Jan van den Hoecke
(1611–1651), who in the *Way to Calvary*
(whereabouts unknown), an early work from
the beginning of the 1630s, comes very close
to Van Dyck in the depiction of the soldiers
in the background.[70] The strange thing is that
Van den Hoecke, from the time of his stay in
Italy—that is, from shortly after 1635—until
his death, adopted a severe Italianate classi-
cism strongly dependent on Guido Reni.[71]
The work of these and other masters shows
that Van Dyck's impact on Flemish seventeenth-century painting by artists of his own
and a slightly younger generation was an interesting artistic phenomenon, but certainly
not the only important one.

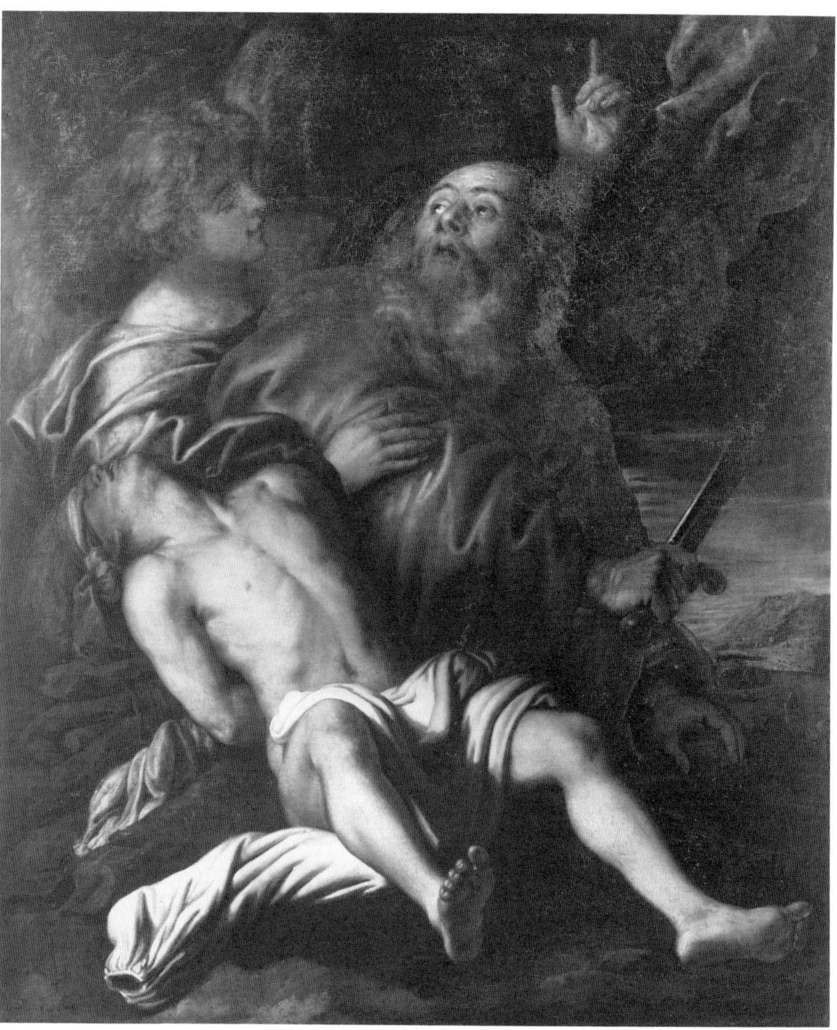

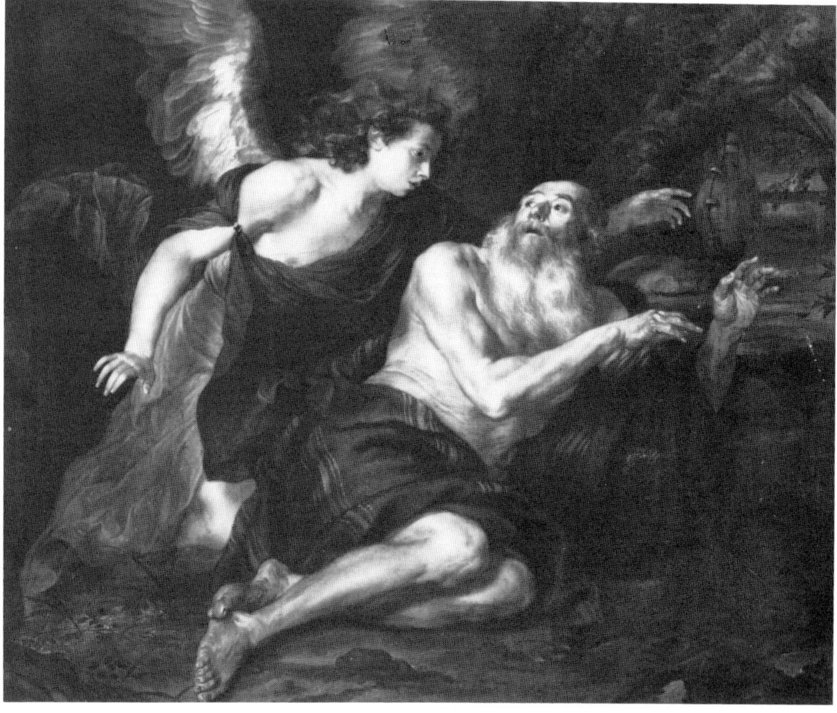

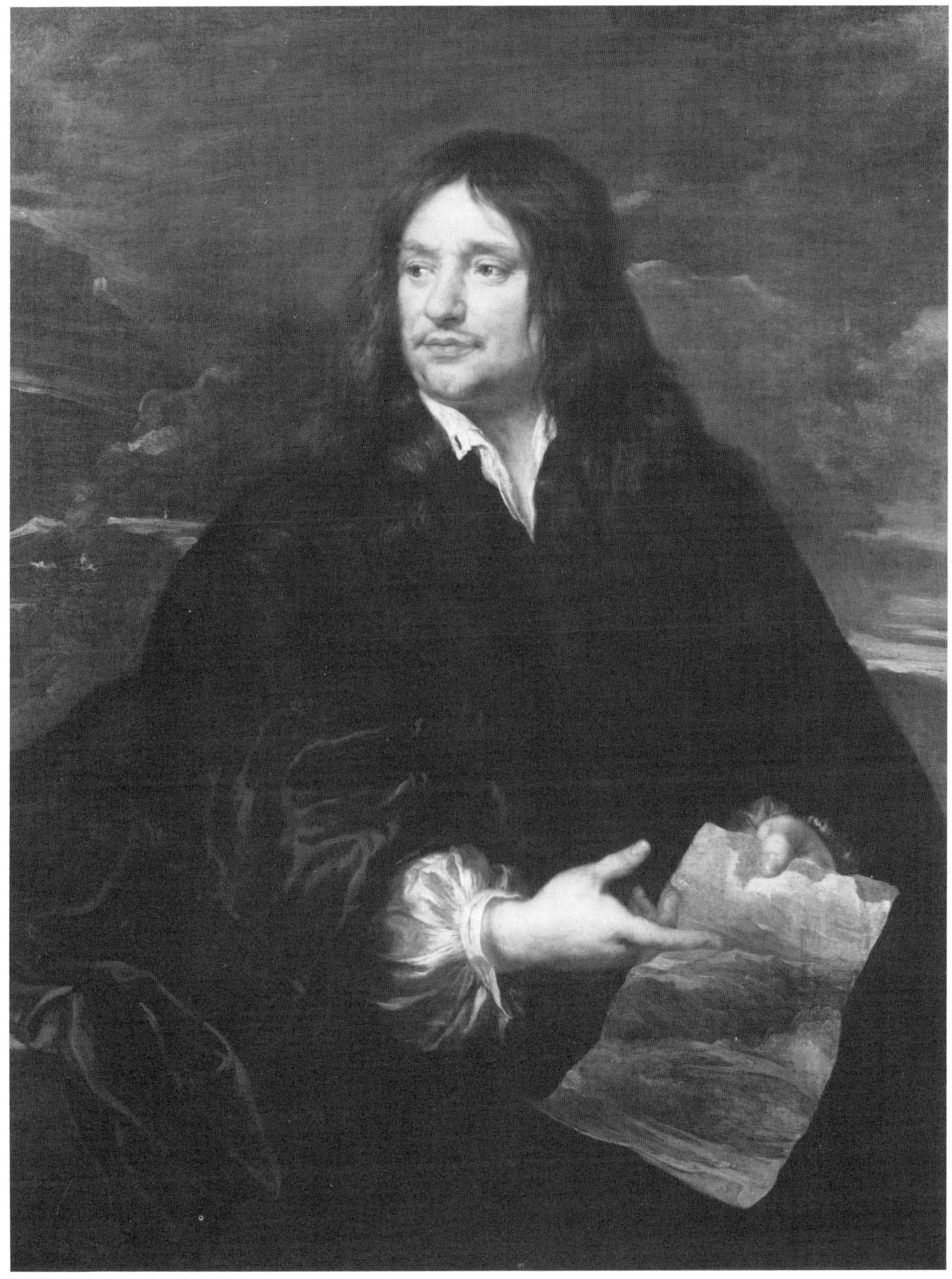

18. Pieter Thijs, *Abraham and Isaäc*, c. 1655, oil on canvas
Sint-Jacobskerk, Antwerp

19. Thomas Willeboirts Bosschaert, *The Prophet Elijah in the Desert*, c. 1650, oil on canvas
Kunsthistorisches Museum, Vienna

20. Lucas Franchoys II, *Portrait of a Landscape Painter*(?), c. 1660, oil on canvas
Musées Royaux des Beaux-Arts, Brussels

NOTES

1. See, for example, Gustav Glück, *Van Dyck. Des Meisters Gemälde*, Klassiker der Kunst, vol. 13, 2d ed. (Berlin and Stuttgart, 1931), 542–546; Christopher Brown, *Van Dyck* (Oxford, 1982), 100–136.

2. See Hans Gerhard Evers, *Rubens und sein Werk. Neue Forschungen* (Brussels, 1943), 70–72.

3. Frans Baudouin, "Iconografie en stijlontwikkeling in de godsdienstige schilderkunst te Antwerpen in de XVIIde eeuw," in *Antwerpen in de zeventiende eeuw* (Antwerp, 1989), 350–357.

4. See Hans Vlieghe, "Cornelis Schut in Italy," *Hoogsteder Mercury* 11 (1990), 38.

5. The question of the aristocratization of the merchant classes in the Southern Netherlands during the seventeenth century has been dealt with to some extent by Roland Baetens, *De nazomer van Antwerpens welvaart*, 2 vols. (Brussels, 1976), 1: especially 312–316.

6. See Jan G. van Gelder, "Anthonie van Dyck in Holland in de zeventiende eeuw," *Bulletin Koninklijke Musea voor Schone Kunsten van België* 8 (1959), 44–48; I am not convinced by Arthur Wheelock's proposal, in Arthur K. Wheelock, Jr., et al., *Anthony van Dyck* [exh. cat., National Gallery of Art] (Washington, 1990), 136–138, of 1632 as a more likely date for the Orange portraits.

7. Van Dyck was paid 500 guilders for the *Adoration of the Shepherds* (Onze-Lieve-Vrouwekerk, Dendermonde), 1631–1632, while he received 600 guilders for the *Ecstasy of Saint Augustine* (long-term loan, Koninklijk Museum voor Schone Kunsten, Antwerp), 1628, as well as for the *Raising of the Cross* (fig. 10) in Courtray, 1631. For his *Coronation of Saint Rosalie* (fig. 12), made in 1629 for the Confraternity of the Unmarried in the Antwerp Jesuit convent, Van Dyck only received 300 guilders, but here we may suppose that, being a member of the brotherhood himself, he may have been asked to reduce his price. The *Vision of the Blessed Hermann-Joseph* (Kunsthistorisches Museum, Vienna), made in 1630 for the same confraternity in Antwerp, brought Van Dyck only 150 guilders; apart from Van Dyck's membership of the lay brotherhood, in this case the difference may also be explained by the fact that the measurements of the *Hermann-Joseph* (160 x 128 cm) are considerably smaller than those of the *Saint Rosalie* (275 x 210 cm). According to documentary evidence, the *Calvary* in the Sint-Michielskerk at Ghent (1630) was Van Dyck's most expensive altarpiece: he received 800 guilders for it. Finally, Jean-Baptiste Descamps, in his famous travelogue *Voyage pittoresque de la Flandre et du Brabant* (Paris, 1769), 120, makes mention of the unbelievably high sum of 2,000 guilders that Van Dyck received for his *Crucifixion* made for the Recollects at Mechlin and now in Saint Rombouts Cathedral there. However, Descamps' statement cannot be corroborated and may well be based on an error of the eighteenth-century French author or his informant(s). See Glück 1931, 544–546, for the evidence regarding the above-mentioned altarpieces.

8. See, for example, Hans Vlieghe, *Gaspar de Crayer. Sa vie et ses oeuvres* (Brussels, 1972), 305; his later paintings seem also to have cost more or less the same price (Vlieghe 1972, 305, 317, 319, 321, 323, 329). See also in this context Hans Vlieghe, "Maatwerk en confectie. Over de functie van historieschilderkunst in de Vlaamse stad van de 17de eeuw," in *Stad in n Vlaanderen. Cultuur en maatschappij 1477–1787* [exh. cat., Gemeentekrediet, Brussels, and Schloss Schallaburg] (Brussels and Schallaburg, 1991), 260.

9. Apparently Rubens asked and received more or less double the sum paid to his fellow artists. With respect to Rubens' fees there are some relevant documents, such as a letter, dated 1611, mentioning him very explicitly as "diere," that is, expensive. See Adolf Monballieu, "P. P. Rubens en het 'Nachtmael' voor St-Winoksbergen (1611), een niet uitgevoerd schilderij van de meester," *Jaarboek Koninklijk Museum voor Schone Kunsten Antwerpen* (1965), 195; Vlieghe in Brussels and Schallaburg 1991, 260.

10. See, for example, Vlieghe 1972, 41–58. Further, in this respect, it is interesting to note that initially Van Dyck demanded 800 guilders for his Kortrijk *Raising of the Cross* (see note 7), but could not persuade his patron Canon Braye to pay him more than 600 guilders (see Frans Joseph Van den Branden, *Geschiedenis der Antwerpsche schilderschool* [Antwerp, 1883], 718–720). This fact, more than any other, may show that Van Dyck, unlike Rubens, did not yet have the means to impose his own terms on his clientele.

11. John Rupert Martin, *The Decorations for the Pompa Introitus Ferdinandi. Corpus Rubenianum Ludwig Burchard*, 16 (Brussels, London, and New York, 1971), 31.

12. See F. W. H. Hollstein, *Dutch and Flemish Etchings, Engravings and Woodcuts ca. 1450–1700*, vol. 16 (Amsterdam, 1976), 191, no. 123.

13. The painting was destined for the decoration of the recently founded Academy in Antwerp; see Marie-Louise Hairs, *Dans le sillage de Rubens* (Liège, 1977), 253.

14. Horst Gerson and E. H. ter Kuile, *Art and Architecture in Belgium 1600–1800* (Harmondsworth, 1960), 141.

15. Katlijne Van der Stighelen, "The Provenance and Impact of Anthony van Dyck's Portraits of Frans Snijders and Margaretha de Vos in the Frick Collection," *Hoogsteder-Naumann Mercury* 5 (1987), 37–47. Remarkable examples are, for example, Cornelis de Vos' portraits of ladies (Philadelphia Museum of Art and Wallace Collection, London), as well as his portrait of Antonia Canis in the Thyssen-Bornemisza collection, Lugano-Castagnola (Van der Stighelen 1987, figs. 5, 6, 9).

16. Katlijne Van der Stighelen, *De portretten van Cornelis de Vos (1584/5–1651). Een kritische catalo-*

gus (Brussels, 1990), nos. 56–58, illus.

17. Van der Stighelen 1990, 60.

18. See note 5.

19. See the painting in the Liechtenstein collection, Vaduz (Glück 1931, 308), and the engraving by Paulus Pontius in the Iconography (Marie Mauquoy-Hendrickx, *L'Iconographie d'Antoine van Dyck* [Brussels, 1956], no. 46).

20. See Vlieghe 1972, 312, document 61.

21. See Vlieghe 1972, 43–48.

22. Vlieghe 1972, no. A 258. The physiognomy of the Spanish king, who is here represented without a moustache, points to a date not much later than about 1628. Van Dyck's contemporary *Portrait of a Man with His Son* (Musée du Louvre, Paris) is a good point of comparison; see Glück 1931, 339; Arthur Wheelock in Washington 1990, no. 50.

23. University Library, Louvain, Spoelberch collection; see Vlieghe 1972, no. 260. The portrait as well as the companion piece representing Spoelberch's wife, Anne Grimaldi de Morosena, were executed in 1630; see Baron de Ryckman de Betz, *Les Livres de raison des Spoelberch, 1563–1873* (Tongeren, 1935), 55; with thanks to Jan Roegiers for this reference.

24. "Gaspar de Crayer quoique peintre déjà célèbre lorsque Vandyck n' avait point encore manié le pinceau, dut à la vue des portraits de notre artiste la force et les graces qu'il ne mettoit point auparavant dans ce genre de peinture. C'est l'aveu de tous les connaisseurs qui ont comparé les portraits que Crayer avait peints avant 1625 avec ceux qu'il peignit depuis cette époque." Quoted by Erik Larsen, ed., *La Vie, les ouvrages et les élèves de Van Dyck* (Brussels, 1975), 126.

25. It is striking that De Crayer, especially during the 1620s, has borrowed so many motifs and composition schemes from Rubens' works dating from the 1610s and then visible in Brussels; see Vlieghe 1972, 61–65, 81–105.

26. De Crayer's portrait of *Charles V Exhorting His Great-Grandson Ferdinand to Follow His Example* was painted by De Crayer in 1635 for one of the triumphal arches erected in Ghent on the occasion of the state entry of Cardinal-Infante Ferdinand of Spain; see Vlieghe 1972, no. A 50; Carl Van de Velde and Hans Vlieghe, *Stadsversieringen te Gent in 1635 voor de Blijde Intrede van de Kardinaal-Infant* (Ghent, 1969), no. 11. For Van Dyck's portrait and its initial destination see Glück 1931, 431; Arthur Wheelock in Washington 1990, no. 72.

27. Vlieghe 1972, 67.

28. Vlieghe 1972, no. A 66; see, for Van Dyck's altarpiece, Glück 1931, 249.

29. Vlieghe 1972, 68–71.

30. Jean-Luc Meulemeester, *Jacob van Oost en het zeventiende-eeuwse Brugge* (Bruges, 1984), no. A 12.

31. Glück 1931, 241.

32. For Van Oost's connection with Caravaggism see Roger-Adolf d'Hulst, "Caravaggeske invloeden in het oeuvre van Jacob van Oost de Oude, schilder te Brugge," *Gentse Bijdragen tot de Kunstgeschiedenis* 13 (1951), 169–192.

33. Meulemeester 1984, no. B 11.

34. Arthur Wheelock in Washington 1990, no. 86.

35. For De Deyster's life and work see Katrien van Damme (M.A. thesis, University of Louvain, 1988). See also Meulemeester 1984, 92–93.

36. For these commissions to Antwerp painters see Meulemeester 1984, 73–82; Hans Vlieghe, "De ontwikkeling van Boeckhorsts werk," in *Jan Boeckhorst* [exh. cat., Rubenshuis, Antwerp, and Westfälisches Landesmuseum für Kunst und Kulturgeschichte, Münster] (Antwerp and Münster, 1990), 69. Other Antwerp artists such as Theodoor van Thulden, Jan Cossiers, and Erasmus Quellinus the Younger were among this group.

37. See Vlieghe in Antwerp and Münster 1990, 63–64.

38. See Vlieghe in Antwerp and Münster 1990, 64–66.

39. See note 3.

40. See Vlieghe in Antwerp and Münster 1990, 81–83.

41. See Svetlana Alpers, *The Decoration of the Torre de la Parada. Corpus Rubenianum Ludwig Burchard*, 9 (Brussels, London, and New York, 1971), 34, 218.

42. Nora De Poorter, "Rubens 'onder de wapenen.' De Antwerpse schilders als gildebroeders van de kolveniers in de eerste helft van de 17de eeuw," *Jaarboek Koninklijk Museum voor Schone Kunsten Antwerpen* (1988), 227–231; for Rubens' picture see, for example, Rudolf Oldenbourg, *Rubens. Des Meisters Gemälde* (Stuttgart and Leipzig, 1921), 428.

43. For its early history see Max Rooses, *L'Oeuvre de P. P. Rubens*, 5 vols. (Antwerp, 1886–1892), 4: no. 827.

44. The Van Dyck original is in the Hermitage, St. Petersburg; see Glück 1931, 261. For Bolswert's engraving see Hollstein (1976), vol. 3 (n.d.), 76, no. 168.

45. Jan G. van Gelder, "De opdrachten van de Oranje's aan Thomas Willeboirts Bosschaert en Gonzales Coques," *Oud Holland* 64 (1949), 41–48.

46. Hans Vlieghe, "Constantijn Huygens en de Vlaamse schilderkunst van zijn tijd," *De zeventiende eeuw* 3, 2 (1987), 205.

47. Philip Rombouts and Theodoor van Lerius, *De "Liggeren" en andere historische archieven der Antwerpsche Sint-Lucasgilde*, 2 vols. (Antwerp, 1864–1876), 1:661.

48. Rombouts and Van Lerius 1864–1876, 2:87.

49. For Van Dyck's appointment as a court painter see Marcel De Maeyer, *Albrecht en Isabella en de schilderkunst* (Brussels, 1955), 193–197.

50. For a good characterization of his work see, for example, Katlijne Van der Stighelen in Arnout Balis, Carl Van de Velde, and Hans Vlieghe, eds., *Flemish Paintings in America. Selected by Guy Baumann and Walter Liedtke* (Antwerp, 1992), no. 92.

51. See Van Gelder 1949, 48–55; Vlieghe 1987, 202–204.

52. Cornelis de Bie, *Het gulden cabinet vande edele vry schilder const* (Antwerp, 1661), 316–318.

53. Rombouts and Van Lerius 1864–1876, 2:121; for the supposition of a stay in England see, for example, Francine-Claire Legrand, *Les Peintres flamands de genre au XVIIe siècle* (Paris and Brussels, 1963), 101; this apparently false assumption may be based on the fact that the inscription under Coques' portrait engraving, edited by Meyssens and used as an illustration in De Bie 1661, 317, reads rather cryptically: "le Roij d'Angleterre l'at emploijé pour avoir de ses pieces;" however, this activity in service of the British crown does not necessarily imply a stay in England.

54. Rombouts and Van Lerius 1864–1876, 2:162.

55. See Erik Duverger, "Abraham van Diepenbeeck en Gonzales Coques aan het werk voor stadhouder Frederik Hendrik, prins van Oranje," *Jaarboek Koninklijk Museum voor Schone Kunsten Antwerpen* (1972), 232, document 1; Vlieghe 1987, 202.

56. See Günther Heinz, "Studien über Jan van den Hoecke und die Malerei der Niederländer in Wien," *Jahrbuch der kunsthistorischen Sammlungen in Wien* 63 (1967), 140, 142.

57. See Adolf Berger, ed., "Inventar der Kunstsammlung des Erzherzogs Leopold Wilhelm von Oesterreich. Nach der Originalhandschrift im fürstlich Schwarzenberg'schen Centralarchiv," *Jahrbuch der Kunsthistorischen Sammlungen des Allerhöchsten Kaiserhauses* 1 (1883), 116, no. 21 (*Seven Putti in a Landscape*), 136, no. 397 (*Pyramus and Thisbe*); both paintings are now lost.

58. On behalf of Charles d'Arenberg, Thijs painted, c. 1650–1652, a picture representing *Saint Felix of Cantalicia and Saint Benedict Martyr*; this altarpiece formed part of a series of eight destined to decorate newly erected altars containing the relics of nine martyrs transported to Brussels in July 1652; see Father Hildebrand, *De Kapucijnen in de Nederlanden en het Prinsbisdom Luik. 5. De Vlaamsche kloosters* (Antwerp, 1950), 52.

59. See Hildebrand 1950, 52.

60. Hairs 1977, 272; see also Danielle Maufort, "De Antwerpse kunstschilder Peeter Thijs de Oude. Een benadering aan de hand van zijn historiestukken" (M.A. thesis, University of Louvain, 1986), no. R9.

61. Already mentioned in Leopold-Wilhelm's 1659 inventory as "No. 134. Ein Stuckh von Oehlfarb auf Leinwath, warin die Historia von Elia mitt seinem Engel. In einer schwartzen Ramen, hoch 9 Span 5 Finger unndt 11 Spann braith. Original von Thomas Willebordts, Mahler von Antorff" (Berger 1883, 122, no. 134).

62. See Hairs 1977, 265–276.

63. See, for example, Thijs' portrait of Archduke Leopold-Wilhelm (Kunsthistorisches Museum, Vienna); see Klaus Demus, ed., *Kunsthistorisches Museum Wien, Verzeichnis der Gemälde* (Vienna, 1973), 175, inv. no. 370, fig. 92.

64. For Franchoys' very Van Dyckian style and his patrons in Mechlin see Heidi Colsoul, "Lucas Franchoys de Jonge (1616–1681). Oeuvrecatalogus," *Handelingen van de Koninklijke Kring voor Oudheidkunde, Letteren en Kunst van Mechelen* 92 (1988), 117–283; 93 (1990), 197–257.

65. Van Diepenbeeck was one of the most flexible and eclectic among the seventeenth-century history painters. See, in general, David Steadman, *Abraham van Diepenbeeck. Seventeenth-Century Flemish Painter* (Ann Arbor, 1982); Van Diepenbeeck's strong and very specific ties with Rubens' workshop, where he was active as a copyist, are thoroughly discussed by Jeremy Wood, "Padre Resta's Flemish Drawings. Van Diepenbeeck, Van Thulden, Rubens and the School of Fontainebleau," *Master Drawings* 28 (1990), 3–53. Van Diepenbeeck's occasional emulation of Van Dyck is discussed by Arnout Balis in this volume.

66. Especially from the later 1640s on, Simon de Vos, in his many small-scale history paintings, adapted some Van Dyckian motifs and expressions in combination with a very idiosyncratic mannerism. A good example is the *Adoration of the Shepherds* from 1644, now in the convent of the Alexians at Boechout near Antwerp; discussed and reproduced by Katlijne Van der Stighelen in *Werken van Barmhartigheid. 650 Jaar Alexianen in de Zuidelijke Nederlanden* [exh. cat., Stedelijk Museum van der Kelen-Mertens] (Louvain, 1985), 256–258, no. 177, fig. 43.

67. Vlieghe 1990, 28–41.

68. Hairs 1977, fig. 36; for other examples of his work see *Theodoor van Thulden 1606–1669* [exh. cat., Noordbrabants Museum] ('s-Hertogenbosch, 1970).

69. See Hans Vlieghe in Antwerp and Münster 1990, 58.

70. See Hans Vlieghe, "Nicht Jan Boeckhorst sondern Jan van den Hoecke," *Westfalen* 68 (1990), 176–177, figs. 22, 23.

71. This style has been discussed in detail by Heinz 1967, 115–144; see also Vlieghe 1990 (note 70), 178.

AMY L. WALSH
Sherman Oaks, California

Van Dyck at the Court of Frederik Hendrik

On 28 January 1632, Constantijn Huygens, counselor to the Dutch stadholder Frederik Hendrik, noted in his diary that Anthony van Dyck had drawn his portrait.[1] This notation confirms that the Flemish artist was in the capital of the northern Netherlands just two months before he arrived at the court of Charles I of England.[2] Frederik Hendrik, the prince of Orange, was probably already an important collector of Van Dyck's work.[3] By the summer of 1632 his collection included the artist's portraits of Frederik Hendrik (fig. 1); his wife, Amalia von Solms (fig. 2); their young son, Willem (fig. 3);[4] four mythological paintings; as well as versions of portraits of Maria de' Medici and the archduchess of the Spanish Netherlands, Isabella Clara Eugenia. The stadholder may have acquired during his lifetime at least seven more portraits and four religious paintings attributed to Van Dyck.[5]

At the time of his visit to The Hague, Van Dyck was court painter to the archduchess of the Spanish Netherlands.[6] Because the Dutch were still at war with Spain, it is important to ask whether there was any political significance to the artist's visit to The Hague and to Frederik Hendrik's patronage of Van Dyck and choice of subjects. The Dutch stadholder was known to covet the works of Isabella's other famous court painter, Peter Paul Rubens, but Rubens' key diplomatic role as the Spanish negotiator prevented him from working at or for the Dutch court.[7] Van Dyck, however, had no official political posi-

tion and could travel more freely between the various courts of Europe. It appears, nevertheless, that he and his work, directly and indirectly, also played an important, if more subtle, diplomatic role in the often tense relations between the Dutch, English, and Flemish courts. In the concluding years of the long war with Spain, Frederik Hendrik's purchase of a devotional painting of the Madonna by the deceased Flemish master may even have been intended to signal to the Catholic Spanish Netherlands that the Protestant stadholder was willing to tolerate the practice of Catholicism in a reunited Netherlands.

When Van Dyck arrived in The Hague in late 1631 or early 1632, he found a lively and sophisticated court numbering as many as five hundred people. The court revolved around Frederik Hendrik (1584–1647) and his German cousin, Countess Amalia of Solms-Braunfels (1602–1675), whom he had married in 1625.[8] Frederik Hendrik was extremely wealthy and widely admired for his diplomatic and military feats as captain and admiral general of the Dutch forces during the final decades of the war with Spain from 1625 until his death in 1647.[9] He was, however, an elected official, not a sovereign.[10] His contemporaries recognized and frequently feared his acute ambition. As the number of his military successes and his influence grew, his desire to establish a Dutch dynasty became ever more evident in his actions and in his collecting. His conscious

goal was to promote an international image of a sophisticated, even royal Dutch court, with himself as lord.[11] Amalia, who had served as lady-in-waiting to Elizabeth, queen of Bohemia, spurred his ambition, particularly after the birth in 1626 of their first child, Willem.[12] The presence in The Hague of Frederik Hendrik's nephew, Frederick (1596–1632), Elector Palatine (1610–1620), and his wife Elizabeth Stuart, sister of Charles I, provided a particular challenge.[13]

As the exiled king and queen of Bohemia, they far outranked the elected Dutch stadholder. Frederik Hendrik, who had spent a period of his youth in the English and French courts,[14] was particularly impressed by the sophisticated "Winter Queen," who brought a new level of gentility to the Dutch court, introducing many of the entertainments for which the court of James I of England had been famous.[15]

Foreign leaders further encouraged Fred-

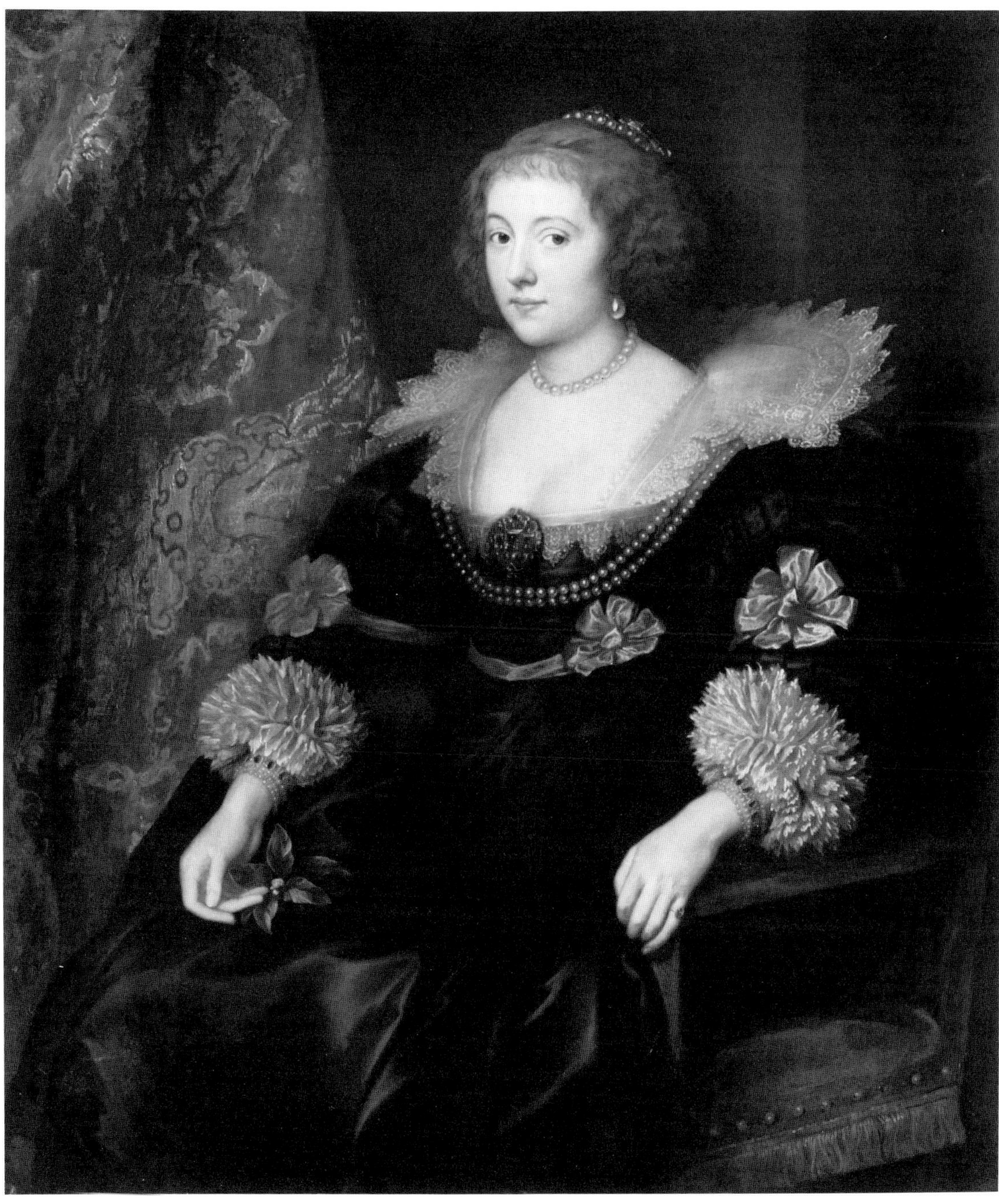

erik Hendrik's ambition. Unaccustomed to the Dutch republican government and often frustrated with having to negotiate with the multiple personalities of the States General, they recognized his unique position and sought to gain his influence. In 1627 Charles I made Frederik Hendrik a knight of the Order of the Garter,[16] and in 1637 Louis XIII of France flattered him by awarding him the title of "Highness." Four years later Willem, the fifteen-year-old Prince of Orange, mar-

ried Mary Stuart, daughter of Charles I. This was followed in 1646 by the marriage of Willem's sister Louise Henrietta to Frederick William, the "Great Elector" of Brandenburg.

Frederik Hendrik's avid patronage and collecting of art were closely tied to his political and personal ambition.[17] Emulating his godfather Henry IV of France,[18] he focused much of his attention on the construction and remodeling of palaces in and near The Hague.[19] Each residence was filled with paintings carefully selected or commissioned to suit the particular activity of the palace. A man of action, Frederik Hendrik preferred "modern" art, almost exclusively works by contemporary painters of both the northern and southern Netherlands. In sharp distinction to Charles I, with whom he shared an appreciation for the works of Rubens, Van Dyck, Gerard van Honthorst, and Cornelis van Poelenburgh, Frederik Hendrik owned only one Italian painting and virtually no works by early Netherlandish artists.[20] The arrangement of the stadholder's collection also differed significantly from that of the English king. Unlike Charles, who arranged his collection by artist, Frederik Hendrik hung his paintings according to general themes, suggesting that his primary concern was the subject rather than the artist. He was motivated largely by the political value of works of art—they could both bolster his image as a sophisticated prince, whose court could rival those of the major sovereigns of his day, and iconographically support his own personal claims to office.[21]

At Honselaarsdijk, the prince's hunting lodge, which was completed in time for the welcome of Maria de' Medici in 1638 and used for the entertainment of important guests during the summer months, the ceilings and walls were painted and hung with paintings by Jacob van Campen, Pieter de Grebber, Paulus Bor, Christiaen van Cowenburgh, and Moyses van Uyttenbroeck.[22] The themes appropriately related to hunting, the seasons, and pastorals. In the other rooms at Honselaarsdijk, as well as at the other palaces used for entertainment, Huis ter Nieuwburch in Rijswijk and the Oude Hof on the Noordeinde in The Hague, allegories and extensive portrait collections suggested both political and dynastic links to the major sovereigns of Europe. At Huis ter Nieuwburch Frederik Hendrik hung portraits of contemporary sovereigns and their consorts, paintings of their palaces, and allegories of their beneficent rule.[23] At Honselaarsdijk there was also a gallery of famous artists, scholars, and military heroes, modeled on the example of Paolo Giovio and dominated by the portrait over the fireplace of Frederik Hendrik's ancestor, Adolf of Nassau, holy Roman emperor from 1292 to 1298. Because of its proximity to the battle front, the ancestral castle of Buren was

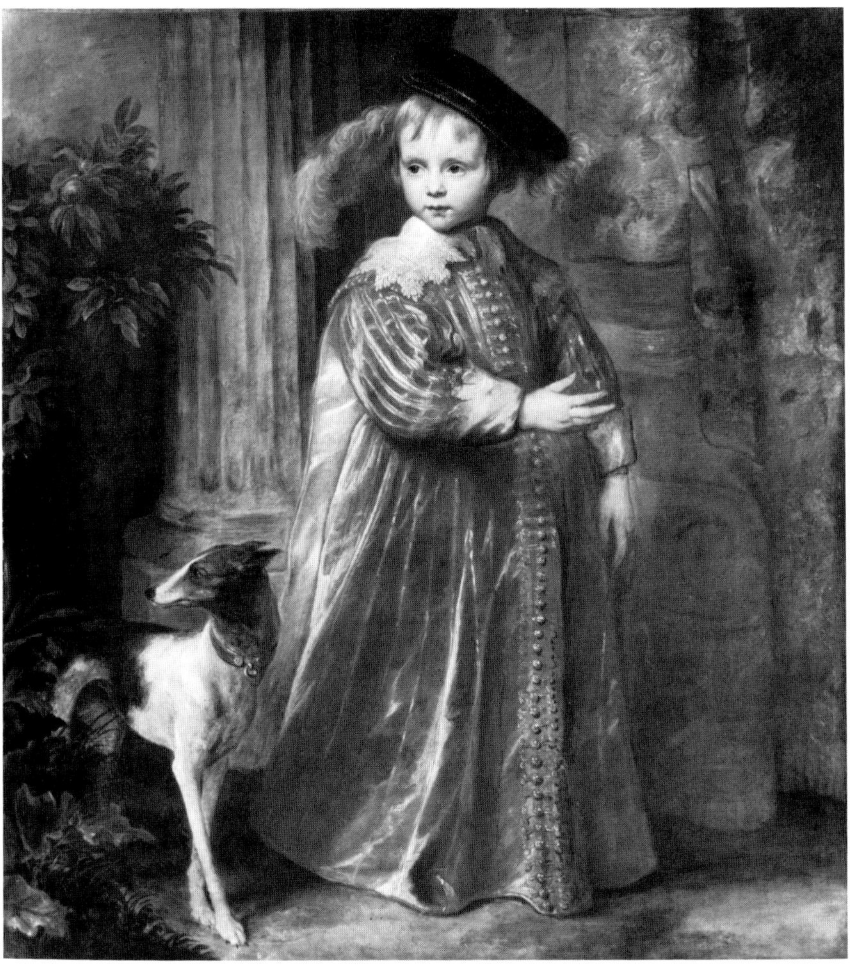

3. Anthony van Dyck, *Prince Willem II*, 1631–1632, oil on canvas
Staatliches Museum Schloss Mosigkau, Dessau-Mosigkau

used by Frederik Hendrik and his wife as their field headquarters during the 1640s. Here the "new long gallery" was decorated with thirteen paintings of famous sieges and battles alternating with pilasters on which hung eighteen paintings depicting military trophies. Over the mantelpiece hung Jacob Adriaensz Backer's *Allegory of Liberty of the Republic* (Jagdschloss Grunewald, Berlin).[24]

The Oude Hof on the Noordeinde, within the city of The Hague, was the private property of Frederik Hendrik.[25] Used as the court's guest house for visiting sovereigns, the palace was known for its rich furnishings.[26] Lacquer screens and other precious objects from the Indies elaborated on the theme of the worldwide influence of the Dutch Republic expressed in the paintings displayed in the ground-floor reception rooms.[27]

The main residence of the prince and his family was the small Stadholder's Quarters

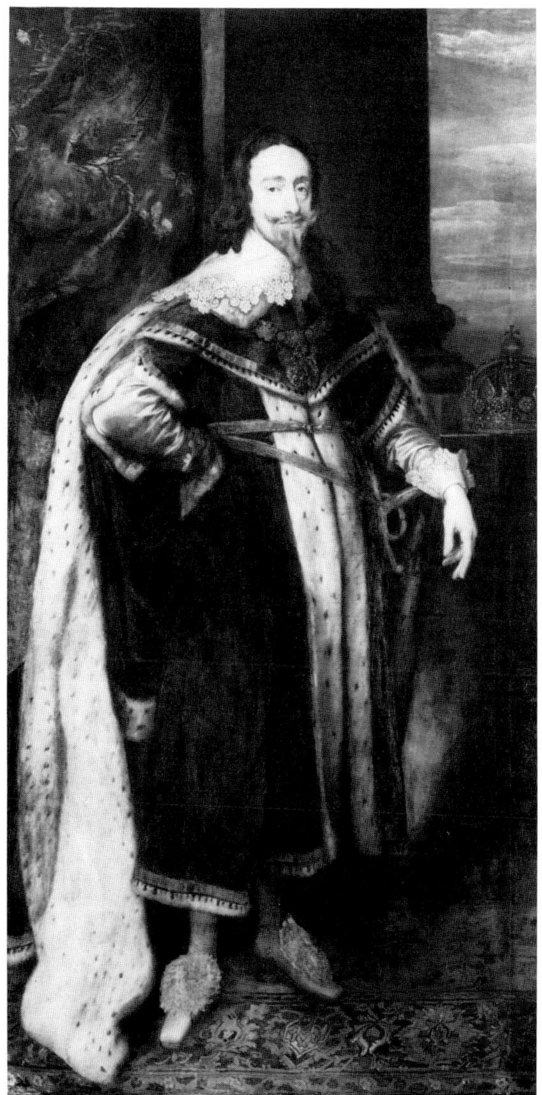

4. Anthony van Dyck, *King Charles I of England*, oil on canvas
Neues Palais, Potsdam

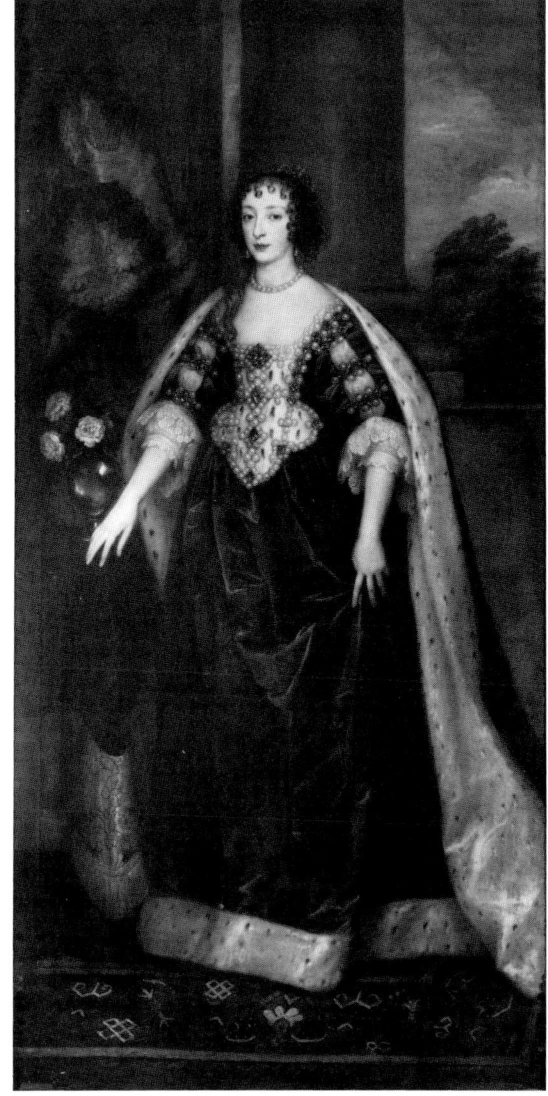

5. Anthony van Dyck, *Queen Henrietta Maria of England*, oil on canvas
Staatliche Schlösser und Gärten Potsdam-Sanssouci

in the Binnenhof, the seat of the Dutch government within The Hague.[28] Here hung the most precious and personal paintings in the collection. In the prince's gallery were portraits of the immediate family, pastorals by Honthorst, Poelenburgh, and Hendrik van Balen, as well as a large *Annunciation* by Rubens, perspectives by Bartholomeus van Bassen, and still lifes by Jan Brueghel.[29] In the bedrooms were four mythological paintings by Van Dyck. Following the death of Frederik Hendrik in 1647, most of the paintings in the Stadholder's Quarters moved with Amalia von Solms to Noordeinde and eventually to Huis ten Bosch.[30]

Distracted by political and military matters, Frederik Hendrik relied on others to recommend artists and iconography and to acquire works of art. Chief among his advisers were the humanist Huygens and the painter/architect Jacob van Campen.[31] The stadholder himself personally made the selection of at least some of the paintings. Having seen paintings by Thomas Willeboirts Bosschaert while on campaign in Bergen op Zoom in 1641, the stadholder sent for the painter, who soon assumed a privileged position with the prince, regularly sending him oil sketches of paintings available in Antwerp and elsewhere.[32] The final selection was made by the stadholder, who apparently also was involved in the specific definition of the commissions.[33]

Frederik Hendrik would have had many opportunities to know about Van Dyck. When he arrived in the Dutch court, Van

Dyck was already highly regarded among court circles as a portrait and history painter. He had returned from Italy to Antwerp in the fall of 1627 and by May 1630 had officially become court painter to Isabella, the governor of the Spanish Netherlands, and had fulfilled at least one commission for the king of England, Charles I.[34] In addition, Van Dyck's early English patrons, the duke of Buckingham, Sir Dudley Carleton, and Thomas Howard, earl of Arundel, all had close ties with the Dutch court and corresponded regularly with Elizabeth, queen of Bohemia, and with Huygens.[35] Huygens, who may have met Van Dyck in London in 1620/1621, also corresponded with courtiers in Italy and the southern Netherlands.[36] Charles I, Elizabeth, or Huygens could, therefore, have introduced the stadholder to the work of Van Dyck and encouraged him to invite the painter to the court, recognizing the desired prestige his works would bring the prince.

It may, however, have been Isabella herself who introduced Van Dyck to Frederik Hendrik. Gifts of works of art from artists, courtiers, and diplomats, flattering the recipient's taste in art, were popular means of gaining favor. The Infanta may have pursued such a plan, for she was determined during the years 1629 to 1631 to establish a new truce with the northern Netherlands as well as with England.[37] The Dutch had gained the upper hand militarily, their victory at 's-Hertogenbosch in September 1629 marking the turning point of the long war.[38] During the fall of 1631 Isabella established direct contact with Frederik Hendrik, who indicated his support of a truce.[39] In December 1631 Rubens arrived in The Hague on a secret mission from the archduchess to the prince of Orange. The visit was brief and apparently unsuccessful. After a matter of only a few days Rubens suddenly returned to Antwerp.[40] Was Van Dyck's arrival at the court of Frederik Hendrik within a month of Rubens' departure coincidental, or could the disappointed and frustrated Isabella have sent her court painter to placate, and indeed flatter the Dutch prince, having Van Dyck paint his portrait and that of his family? The idea that Van Dyck came with at least the blessing, if not at the instigation of the Infanta, is further suggested by the fact that he apparently brought to The Hague a version of his por-

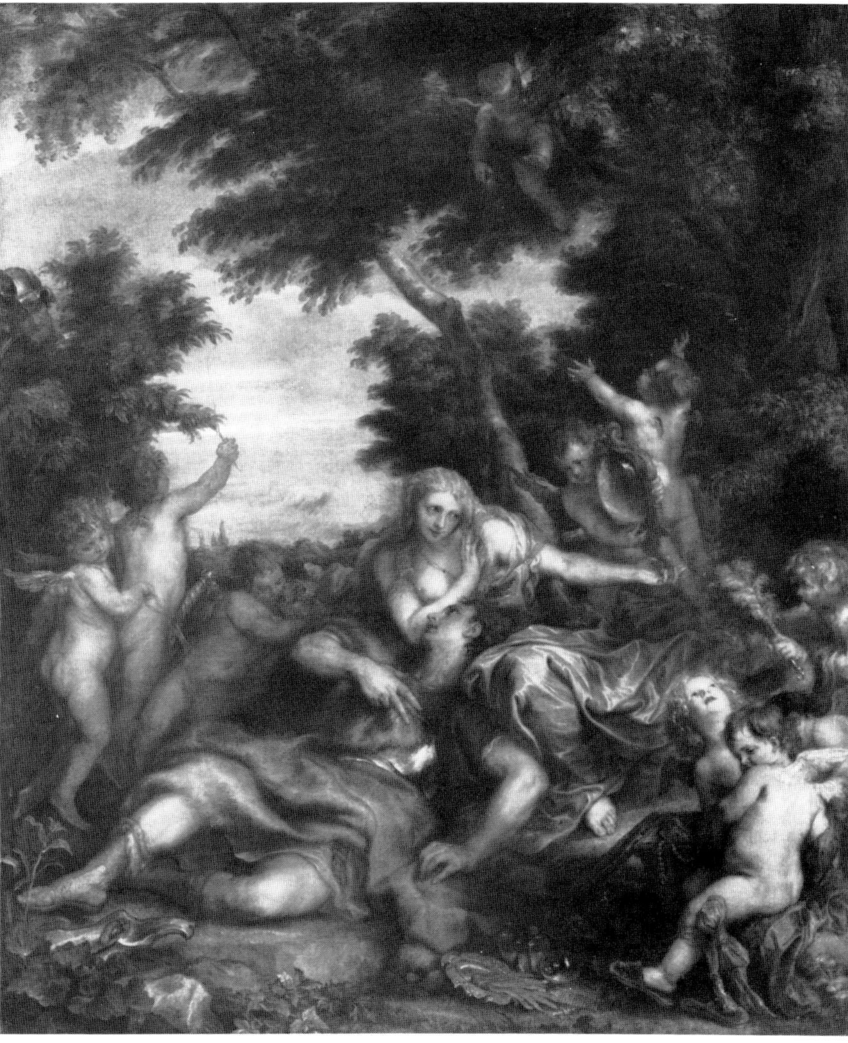

6. Anthony van Dyck,
Rinaldo and Armida,
c. 1630–1631, oil on canvas
Musée du Louvre, Paris

trait of the Archduchess Isabella (Musée des Beaux-Arts, Bordeaux) as well as a version of his recently completed portrait of the queen mother of France, Maria de' Medici (Jagdschloss Grunewald, Berlin), who was living in exile in Brussels.[41]

Van Dyck's primary purpose for coming to The Hague was probably to paint the three-quarter-length portraits of the prince and princess of Orange, as well as the full-length portrait of the not yet six-year-old Prince Willem (1626–1650).[42] Van Dyck's portrait of the stadholder portrays Frederik Hendrik in the full dress uniform of the commander of the Dutch forces rather than as a courtier. While in The Hague, Van Dyck also made small portraits of Huygens, Frans Hals, and several other artists for his planned Iconography.[43] Another important commission was

7. Anthony van Dyck,
Amaryllis and Mirtillo,
1631–1632, oil on canvas
Graf von Schönborn,
Pommersfelden

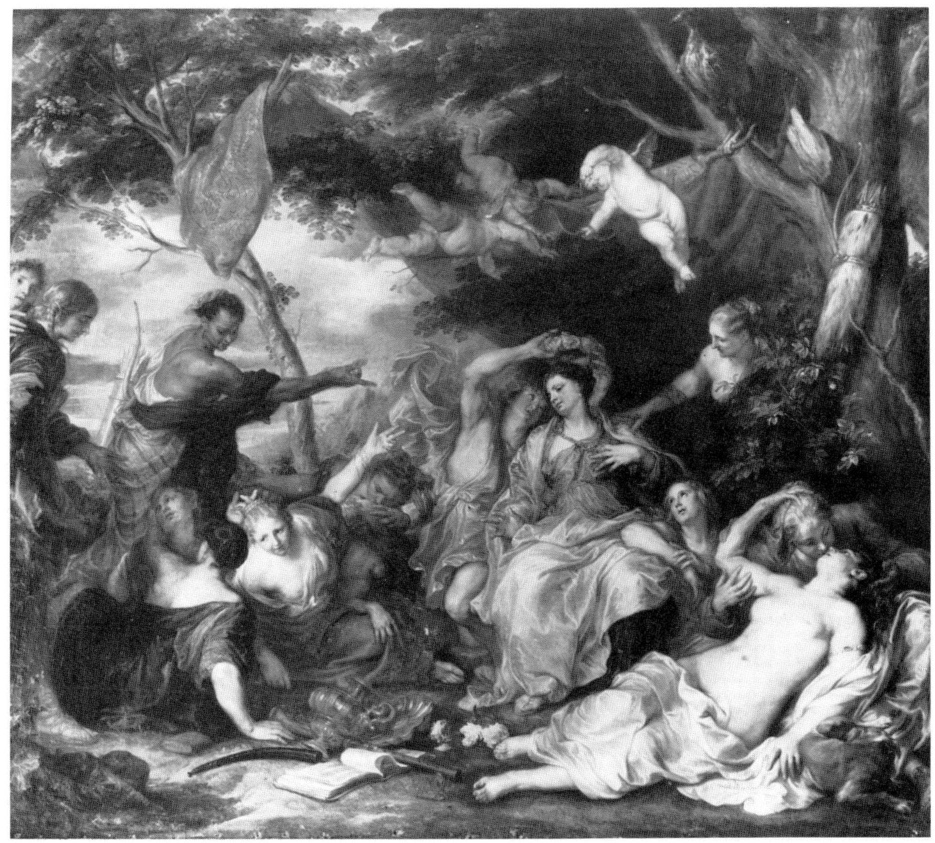

8. Anthony van Dyck,
*Achilles among the
Daughters of Lycomedes*,
c. 1628–1629, oil on canvas
Graf von Schönborn,
Pommersfelden

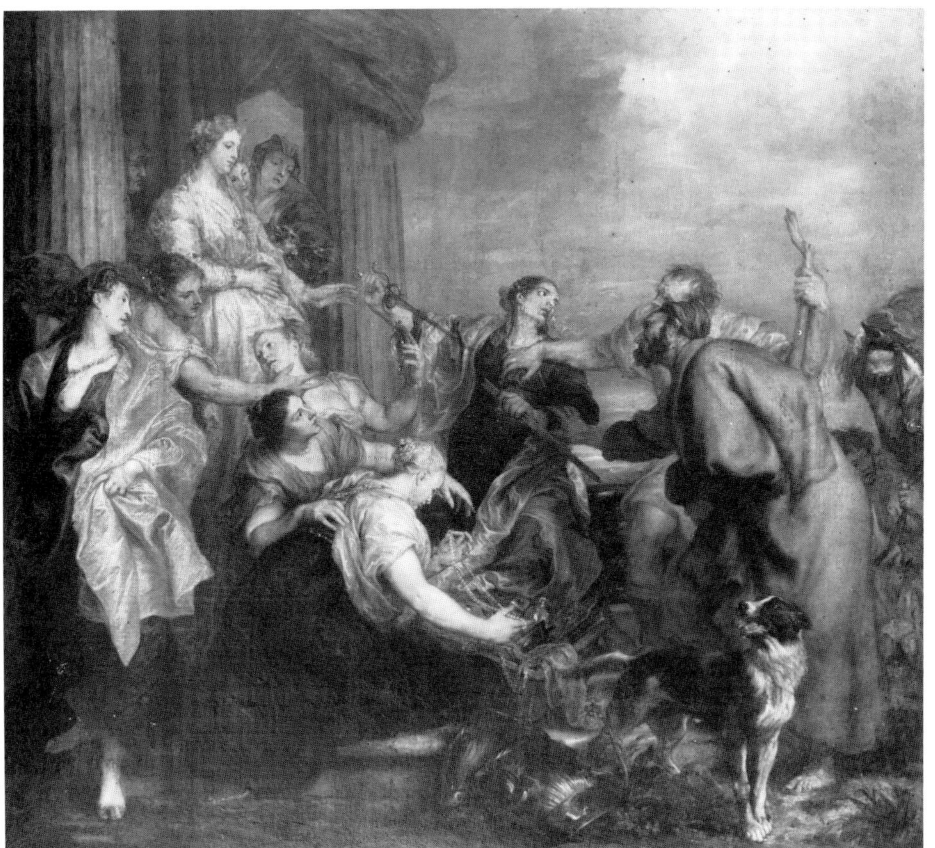

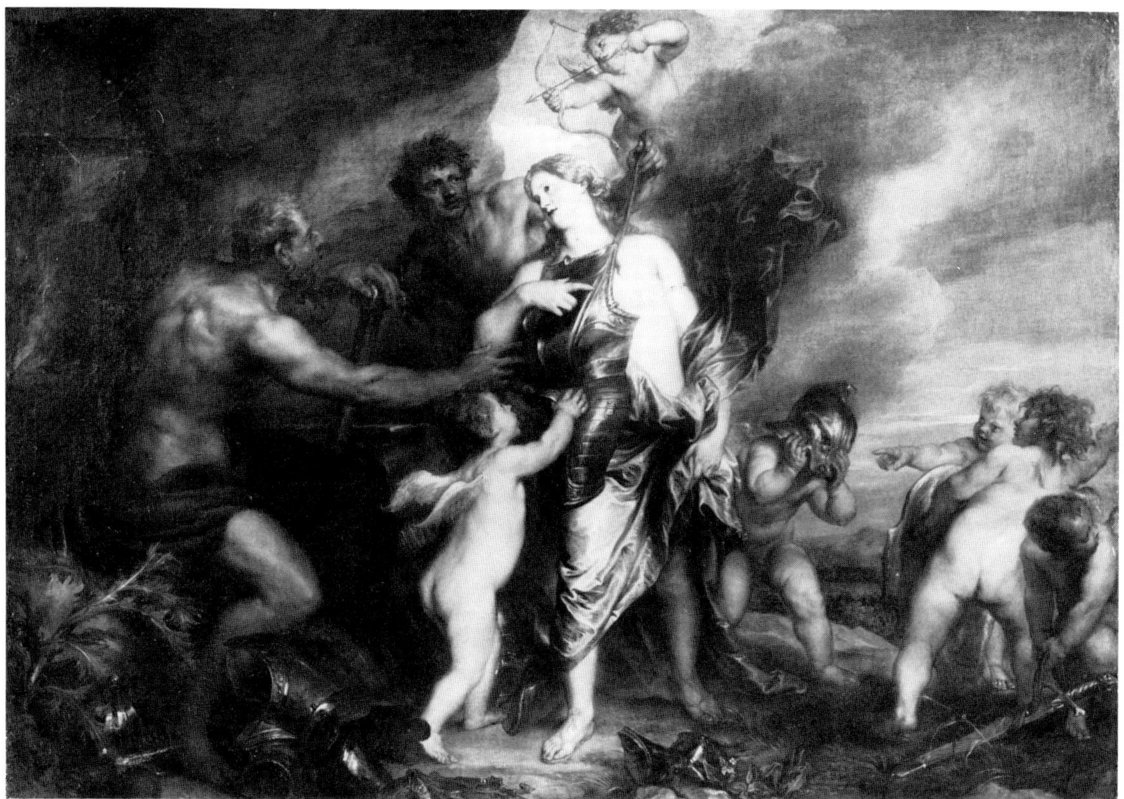

undoubtedly the full-length portraits of Karl Ludwig and Rupert, the two eldest surviving princes of the Palatinate.[44]

It is unclear for whom the portraits of the two young princes were intended. The paintings go without reference until 1866, when they appear in the collection of the earl of Craven, Elizabeth's long-devoted friend to whom she left her collection at the time of her death.[45] Although this seems to reinforce the most likely solution, that the portraits were commissioned by the parents of the teenage princes, the exiled family, which included thirteen children, was strapped for money and could ill afford the luxury of two full-length portraits by the most fashionable court painter of the day.

For whom, then, were the paintings made? The earl of Craven, himself, could have commissioned the portraits for the boys' parents or for his own collection. Craven, who had recently been appointed commander of the English troops in Germany, was in The Hague in January 1632, just prior to his departure with Frederick of Bohemia to join the war effort of Gustavus Adolphus, the Protestant king of Sweden. The possibility also exists that

Charles I commissioned the paintings of his nephews, which then passed into the collection of the earl of Craven after the dissolution of the English king's collection. There is no evidence in the records of his collection to support this theory, but in 1629 Charles had commissioned Honthorst to paint two portraits of members of his sister's family as Apollo and Diana for the Queen's Staircase at Hampton Court, and he later ordered a portrait of the king and queen of Bohemia and their children.[46] Furthermore, we know that in 1632 Van Dyck brought with him to England versions of portraits of Isabella and Maria de' Medici. On 8 August 1632, Charles paid Van Dyck for versions of the portraits of Frederik Hendrik and Amalia von Solms.[47]

Another possibility exists, that Elizabeth commissioned the portraits of her sons as a gift for her brother. Although the cost of the portraits would have been difficult for the financially restricted monarchs, political circumstances suggest that the clever and ambitious queen may have conceived of such a gift to remind the English king of his duty to his exiled nephews. The critical role that her brother played in their future was clearly on her mind in January 1632, when she wrote to Sir Thomas Rowe of her continuing fear that England would sign a separate peace with Spain and thus virtually eliminate any hope her sons would have of reclaiming their German patrimony.[48] In the same month, just prior to his joining a campaign with Gustavus Adolphus in 1632, the often melancholic Frederick of Bohemia wrote to Charles I, entrusting his wife and children to Charles' care.[49]

As court painter to Charles I, Van Dyck continued to serve the diplomatic needs of the Dutch as well as the English court. A letter written in 1638 by Huygens, who was at the front with Frederik Hendrik, informs Amalia of the receipt of Van Dyck's portraits of Charles I (fig. 4) and Henrietta Maria (fig. 5) and of his instructions that they be hung at Huis ter Nieuwburch (later transferred to Honselaarsdijk) with the portraits of the other heads of state.[50] Three years later, in anticipation of the marriage of Willem and Mary Stuart in 1641, Charles I sent Van Dyck's portrait of the young princess (private collection) in exchange for that of Willem by Honthorst, by then the court painter of Frederik Hendrik and also a favorite of the English king. A version of Van Dyck's portrait of the children of Charles I at Windsor had apparently preceded this to The Hague.[51] Van Dyck also painted the official portrait of the young couple at the time of their marriage in London in 1641.[52] The portraits of the immediate family were undoubtedly hung in the private chambers in the Stadholder's Quarters, where Van Dyck's portrait of Maria de' Medici was recorded in 1632.[53]

At least some of the four history paintings by Van Dyck listed in the 1632 inventory of the Stadholder's Quarters as overmantels either preceded or accompanied the artist to The Hague, perhaps one originally even arriving as a gift from the court in Brussels. There was simply too little time for Van Dyck to have executed all these pictures in the North. Two of the paintings were pastorals: *Rinaldo and Armida* (fig. 6) hung with Frederik Hendrik's most important paintings in his gallery, and *Amaryllis and Mirtillo* (fig. 7) hung over the mantelpiece in his dressing room.[54] A third painting, *Achilles among the Daughters of Lycomedes* (fig. 8), hung in Frederik Hendrik's new bedroom,

and another unidentified history painting hung over the carved mantelpiece in Amalia's New Room.[55] For reasons of iconography, and judging from later notations in the inventories, this last painting was probably the so-called *Venus at the Forge of Vulcan* (fig. 9), a version of a painting in Vienna.[56]

Van Dyck's sensual pastorals and mythologies, with their allusions to love and courtship, clearly suited the international taste of Frederik Hendrik, who already owned numerous pastoral subjects by Dutch artists and mythological paintings by Rubens, from whom he longed to acquire more works.[57] Yet because seventeenth-century court art typically used historical subjects to allegorize contemporary events or personalities, we must ask whether, in addition to the purely sensual pleasures of the paintings, there may have been other reasons for the selection of specific subjects. As we have seen, Frederik Hendrik's now-lost decorative schemes were motivated by his political ambitions. One must, therefore, consider the political significance for Frederik Hendrik of the paintings obtained from Van Dyck during a particularly ambitious period in the prince's political career.

In most cases, various levels of meaning can be attributed to these paintings. For example, the stories of Achilles and of Amaryllis and Mirtillo, in which the men disguise themselves as women to gain access to their lovers, relate, as Arthur Wheelock has noted, to the popular contemporary themes of transformation and hidden appearance as well as to clever intrigue.[58] But in addition to this, these paintings discuss other themes that were closely tied to Frederik Hendrik's personal ambitions. Specifically, Van Dyck's history paintings for the prince reflect Frederik Hendrik's desire to promote the image of his own importance and power as the founder of a Dutch dynasty. Throughout his career Frederik Hendrik, like many of his political contemporaries, was identified with various heroes of ancient literature, whose deeds and character could serve his own image by association.[59] The story of Achilles, the great hero of Homer's *Iliad*, was particularly popular at the court of the militant stadholder.[60] In addition to the military feats of Achilles, with which Frederik

Hendrik could identify, the outcome of Achilles' deceit, like that of Mirtillo, was the establishment of a new dynasty. Significantly, it was in 1631, just prior to Van Dyck's visit to The Hague and probably the date of these paintings, that the states of Holland and Zeeland joined Utrecht and Overijssel in granting the young prince Willem the right of survivance to his father's titles.

The previous year, 1630, the position of general of the cavalry, formerly his father's title, had been conferred on the four-year-old Willem. This significant event supports Wolfgang Prohaska's recent reidentification of *Venus at the Forge of Vulcan* as *Thetis at the Forge of Vulcan*, the story of a mother's quest for armor for her son.[61] Amalia's personal identification with the painting is reinforced by the fact that the picture hung in her private chambers.

Often multiple levels of interpretation or reference can be applied to history paintings. For instance, in addition to allusions to the stadholder's dynastic ambitions and past amorous reputation, Van Dyck's *Achilles among the Daughters of Lycomedes* may also have referred to the virtue and steadfastness of the stadholder/captain general, and by extension, of the Dutch state. By choosing the sword over the jewels, Achilles betrayed his disguise as a woman and revealed his true identity, abandoning safety and comfort for duty. Rather than the recently suggested warning to the captain general of the Dutch army not to shirk his duties,[62] the painting probably bore a specific, complimentary reference to the stadholder's virtuous willingness to forgo comfort and return to battle. This interpretation is especially convincing when one recalls that Frederik Hendrik probably commissioned the painting. Also, the theme of vigilance, found in images of the sleeping lion or Mars as well as in images of the hundred-eyed Argus, was especially popular in the northern Netherlands during anxious periods of truce and anticipated peace.[63]

The same theme of vigilant preparedness may also inform Frederik Hendrik's painting by Van Dyck of *Rinaldo and Armida* (fig. 6). In this erotic scene from Tasso's *Gerusalemme Liberata*, Rinaldo, the Christian Achilles, is discovered in the embrace of the nymph Armida and called back to battle by Carlo and Ubaldo, the upholders of virtue,

whom he willingly follows.[64] The stadholder's version differs significantly from that commissioned from Van Dyck in 1629 by Endymion Porter (Baltimore Museum of Art). That painting, the first of many works that Van Dyck was to complete for Charles I,[65] represents an earlier scene in which Rinaldo, entranced by the sorceress Armida, abandons warfare for the pleasures of love. Both paintings clearly must have appealed to the taste for sensuous pastorals and Titianesque manner shared by Charles and Frederik Hendrik. Yet, beyond this, was there any significance in the choice of these two closely related but clearly different scenes from Tasso's popular *Gerusalemme Liberata*? Could both Charles and Frederik Hendrik have wished through their commissions to convey a political message? The year 1629, the date of Charles I's pacifistic painting, was precisely the moment when Rubens, in London, and Isabella were urging Charles to sign a separate truce with Spain. Rubens himself would present Charles with his own allegory of peace, *Minerva Protects Pax from Mars* (National Gallery, London), before his departure from London in 1629/1630.[66] Approximately two years later, at the height of his success, Frederik Hendrik indicated his rejection of the idea of peace by his choice of a different episode in the story of Rinaldo and Armida, as well as by his commission of *Achilles among the Daughters of Lycomedes*. Both these pictures stress his dedication and his eagerness to fight.

Van Dyck, who died in 1641, did not work directly for the Dutch stadholder after 1632. Those artists who carried out the extensive decorations at Frederik Hendrik's palaces during the 1630s were Dutch, not Flemish.[67] But during his renewed push into Flanders in the 1640s, the prince continued to seek paintings by Van Dyck and turned increasingly to Flemish painters, in some cases apparently directly inspired by works he saw during his campaign. Willeboirts Bosschaert, whose paintings Frederik Hendrik had seen and admired during the siege of Bergen op Zoom in 1641,[68] and later another Flemish painter, Gonzales Coques, were important agents involved in Frederik Hendrik's acquisition of Flemish paintings.[69] The first Flemish paintings they acquired for the prince were mythological subjects,[70] but then on 7

December 1644 Coques wrote to Matthys Musson, the most prominent art dealer in Antwerp, noting that the stadholder wished to acquire a devotional painting of the Madonna. The artist suggested the Madonna by Van Dyck in the dealer's stock, adding that if that were not available, another work might suffice, but *not* a Christ.[71] During the mid-1640s Frederik Hendrik also acquired other paintings with Roman Catholic subjects, including a version of Van Dyck's *Caritas* (fig. 10) and a *Rest on the Flight into Egypt*, in which the children, the Innocenti, identify the painting as Roman Catholic.[72] In addition the prince acquired a *Madonna with Two Children* (location unknown) and an *Annunciation* (Staatliches Museum Schloss Mosigkau, Dessau-Mosigkau) by Willeboirts Bosschaert. The most significant of these pictures with Roman Catholic subjects was the large painting of a stone Madonna and Child by Willeboirts Bosschaert within a flower wreath by the famous Jesuit painter Daniel Seghers (fig. 11).[73]

What was the significance of the entry of these definitively Catholic images into the collection of the Protestant stadholder? No religious paintings of any kind appear in the collection of the Winter King,[74] whose chaplain, Scultetus, had ordered the removal of the crucifix and carved wooden statues of the Madonna and saints from the main bridge over the Moldau by which the monarch had entered Prague.[75] Another Protestant leader, Charles I, was severely criticized by the English Calvinists for his "papist paintings," most of which he probably acquired as examples of the work of famous Italian artists rather than as particular subjects, although the influence of his Catholic wife was always suspect.[76] Frederik Hendrik's request for a Madonna was clearly a desire for a specific subject, not an artist, as may have been the case when he earlier acquired Rubens' *Annunciation* (National Gallery of Ireland, Dublin), which hung in his gallery in 1632.[77] When Coques wrote to Musson, he first specifically requested a devotional painting, followed by the suggestion of the Van Dyck Madonna or, if that were not available, another devotional subject, but with few and beautiful figures. Frederik Hendrik obviously enjoyed the sumptuous beauty of Van Dyck's paintings, but in this case the subject was clearly his primary interest.[78]

The inventory of the Stadholder's Quarters shows that Frederik Hendrik already owned a number of religious paintings in 1632.[79] Many were narratives, but there were also paintings of the Annunciation, the Madonna, and the Crucifixion, which would have offended strict Calvinists and many, if not most Remonstrants.[80] Many of these paintings hung with other subjects in Frederik Hendrik's gallery in the Stadholder's Quarters, the showcase of his best works of art. They were also by popular, mostly contemporary artists—Poelenburgh, van Balen, and Rubens—whose mythological works Frederik Hendrik admired and collected.[81] Another small but significant group of religious paintings hung in Frederik Hendrik's private cabinet, a room adjacent to his gallery at the Stadholder's Quarters.[82] Over the fireplace hung an *Adoration of the Shepherds* by Honthorst (Wallraf-Richartz Museum, Cologne), next to which was the only nonreligious painting in the room, Honthorst's *Venus and Ceres with Satyrs* (probably Schloss Pommersfelden). The other paintings in the room included two anonymous paintings of the Crucifixion, an *Adoration of the Shepherds* by Van Balen (location unknown), and Rembrandt's *Simeon in the Temple* (probably Kunsthalle, Hamburg). Also listed in the room was a testament covered in sea-green leather with a skull and crossbones on top.[83] By all appearances this cabinet was a private chapel, one with significantly Catholic overtones. The presence of two *Crucifixions*, one of which was noted as small and therefore probably not a narrative, was highly unusual in a Calvinist household.[84]

In contrast to what is generally believed about the northern Netherlands after the split with Spain, in the early seventeenth century many of the oldest and most respected families were still predominantly Roman Catholic. That number swelled during the early 1620s after the Synod of Dordrecht condemned the more liberal attitudes of the Remonstrants.[85] At that time several hundred Remonstrants, including a number of patricians, adopted Catholicism.[86]

Although his biographer has suggested that Frederik Hendrik might have been willing to convert to Catholicism to head a united Netherlands, there is no indication that Frederik Hendrik was ever a Catholic.[87] Rather, he was probably a Remonstrant, a more liberal Calvinist. As such, he would have believed that God's sovereignty and man's free will are compatible and that Christ died for all, not just for the elect. Remonstrants were characteristically also much more tolerant of the practice of other religions than the notoriously conservative members of the Reformed Calvinist church. Raised by a Huguenot mother and tutored by the Remonstrant leader Johannes Uytenbogaert,[88] Frederik Hendrik was living at the French court in 1598 when Henry IV signed the Edict of Nantes, guaranteeing the rights of Protestants to practice their religion. Like his godfather Henry IV, a former Huguenot leader who converted to Catholicism to win the crown of France, Frederik Hendrik seems to have been a religious pragmatist. Thus, while maintaining a more tolerant attitude to Remonstrants and Catholics than his brother had, because of his constant need to juggle the war and peace factions and maintain the support of the Orthodox Calvinists as well as the Remonstrants, he never declared his allegiance. It may even have been for this reason that in 1632 the politically adroit stadholder employed the Orthodox Calvinist André Rivet to tutor his son.[89]

During two critical periods of intense discussions regarding the establishment of a truce or peace, around 1630 and in the mid-1640s, the Spanish, frustrated in their efforts with the disparate States General, engaged in secret negotiations with Frederik Hendrik, whom they felt was inclined toward peace for his own personal gain.[90] A major stumbling block had been the refusal of the conservative States General to budge on the issue of religion, and their consistent rejection of any attempt to improve the position of Dutch Catholics.[91] Frederik Hendrik seemed to be the Spanish king's best hope. In January 1643 Philip offered to recognize the prince and his heirs as the legitimate rulers of a "rump" northern Netherlands based in Holland, with a choice of new lands from either the Spanish king or the emperor. In return, among other major concessions, the stadholder was to guarantee Catholic worship in those territories under his control.[92] With polite and ambiguous responses, however, Frederik Hendrik dragged out the negotiations.

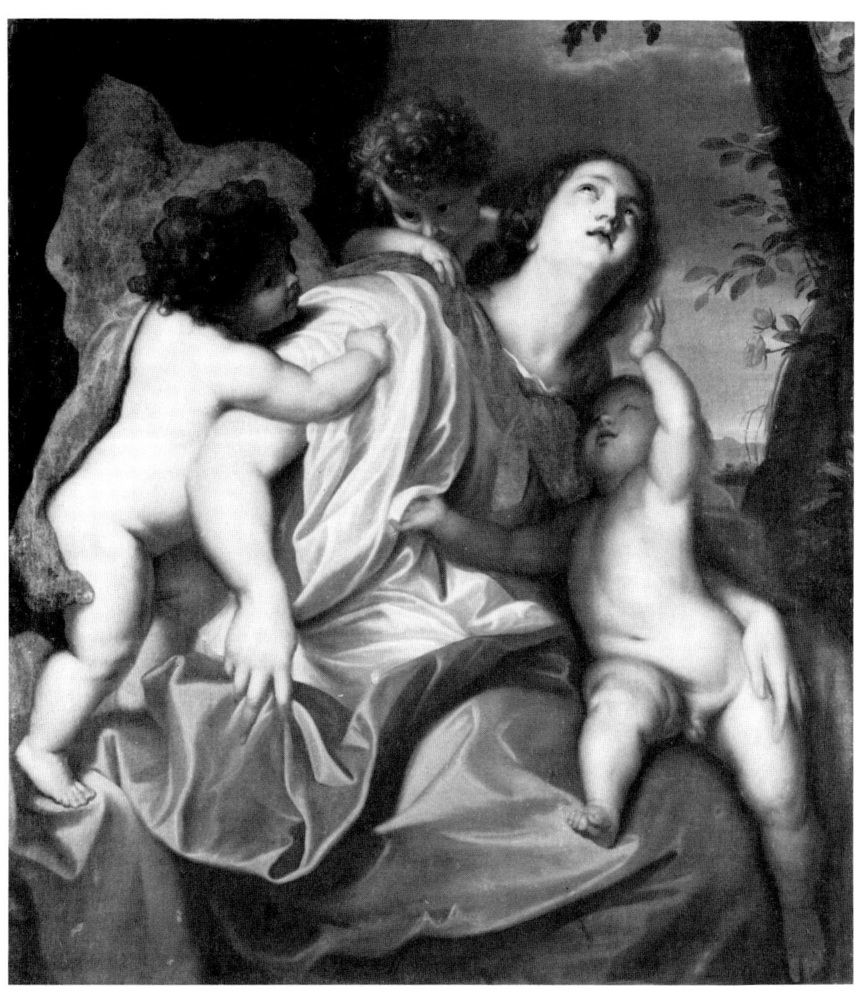

10. After Anthony van Dyck, *Caritas*, oil on canvas
Staatliches Museum Schloss Mosigkau, Dessau-Mosigkau

The negotiations reached a particularly intense level during the winter of 1644–1645. A stalemate caused by the long delay in sending Dutch plenipotentiaries to Münster again led to a number of secret meetings with Frederik Hendrik in The Hague. The Spanish hoped to break the Dutch alliance with the French and thus stressed the dangers to the Dutch of French expansion in the Netherlands.[93] Frederik Hendrik refused their overtures, citing treaty obligations to the French, but convinced Spain of his sincerity in desiring peace, at least for a while. By February 1645 the stadholder was preparing an assault on Antwerp; in response Philip offered him the addition of the northern district of Geldern in return for his aid in securing peace.[94] The prince remained evasive. Then, the following year, in the name of the States General with whom he had not conferred, Frederik Hendrik signed a secret agreement

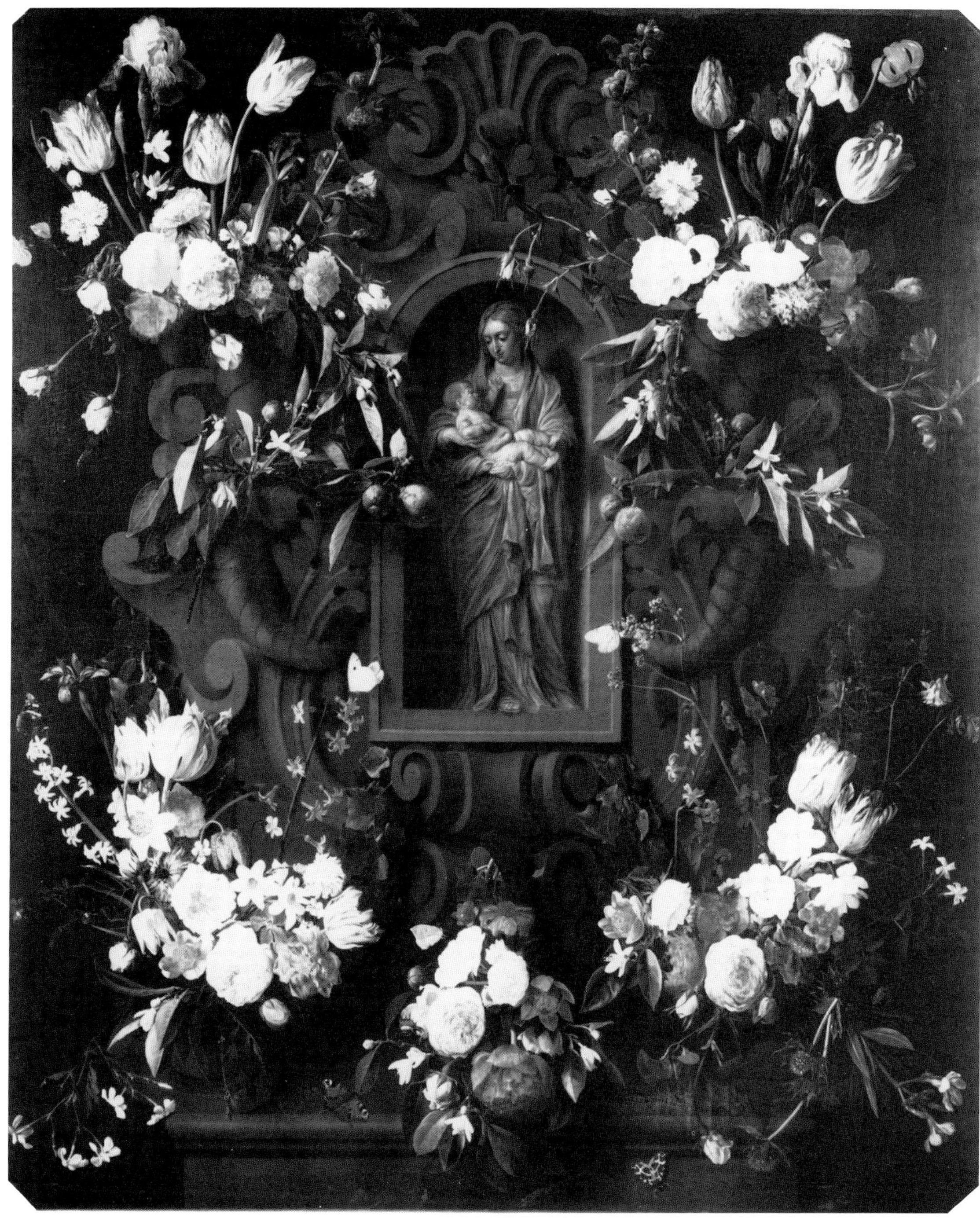

with the French for military assistance against Antwerp, with the condition that should the city fall, he would permit the public practice of Catholicism to continue.[95]

Frederik Hendrik's evasive answers led the Spanish constantly to question his sincerity.[96] A key issue for both the Spanish and the French negotiators was the practice of Catholicism. They had made dramatic concessions regarding trade and the Indies, but they remained insistent about the practice of Catholicism. Could Frederik Hendrik's request for the large painting of a Madonna in December 1644, during one of the most intense periods of negotiations, have been an attempt to assuage some of those fears, without committing himself and risking his position within the conservative factions of the northern Netherlands?[97] Certainly his ability to get the Jesuits to agree to his request for a painting by Seghers is significant. They had, in fact, refused his original inquiry of early 1645, shortly after his request for the Madonna from Musson, on the grounds that the Jesuit father's paintings were not for sale, that they were only to decorate their churches and for princes who supported the order.[98] Only after Willeboirts Bosschaert met with them did Conrad van Gavere, the head of the order in Antwerp, not only acquiesce, but also place Seghers at the service of the Protestant prince, sending him a still life of flowers by the artist as a gift from the order.[99] Could this reversal have been due to Willeboirts' assurance of the prince's Catholic sympathies? Within a year Seghers, in collaboration with Willeboirts, completed the large *Flowerwreath with the Madonna* for the Dutch prince.[100] Certainly these events did not go unnoticed, either in the Spanish Netherlands or in the north, where the paintings by Van Dyck and Seghers, whom the prince clearly admired for their abilities, were hung in prominent positions.[101]

A sage and pragmatic politician, Frederik Hendrik used his collections to create an image of a prosperous, idyllic "royal Dutch" court, dynastically related to heroes of the past and present and supported by the correspondence to mythological heroes and gods. Isabella undoubtedly recognized how Van Dyck's paintings could satisfy the prince's personal ambition and taste in art and thereby hoped that she might win his favor with the loan of her court painter. Frederik Hendrik himself was keenly aware of the status that his acquisition of works by the preeminent court painter would bring. He was also aware of the political impact that Van Dyck's individual works of art could have in creating an image of a dedicated, legitimate sovereign. An admirer of stories of transformation and hidden appearances, Frederik Hendrik knew that it was often only what appeared to be true, not reality, that was important, and that these perceptions could be manipulated. He avoided controversy within the Netherlands by his refusal to ally himself with either faction of the Remonstrant/Counter-Remonstrant debate, while leading each side to believe he favored them. Diplomatically he played similar tricks, encouraging the flirtations of the Spanish and Flemish negotiators to bolster his political stand, without jeopardizing his increasingly shaky relationship with the States General. Was his purchase of devotional, Catholic paintings, such as Van Dyck's Madonna from prominent sources in the south, part of this policy of clever diversion? One suspects that it was, and that Frederik Hendrik may have had the same intention when he hung a seemingly private collection of devotional works in his cabinet, an anteroom to his more public gallery. To this cabinet he could selectively lead his Catholic visitors,[102] such as the Venetian ambassador, who noted that the stadholder was certainly not averse to the Catholics.

1. J. G. van Gelder, "Anthonie van Dyck in Holland in de zeventiende eeuwe," *Bulletin, Musées Royaux des Beaux Arts, Brussels* 8 (1959), 50, quotes the passage from Huygens's diary: "Pingor a Van Dyckio cum arbor in aedes lapst esset." This notation confirms Houbraken's statement that shortly before he left for England in March 1632, Van Dyck had visited the northern Netherlands, where he saw Frans Hals. Arnold Houbraken, *De Groote Schouburgh der Nederlantsche Konstschilders en Schilderessen*, 3 vols. (The Hague, reprint, Amsterdam, 1976), 1:185.

2. Jacob Smit, *De grootmeester van woorden snarenspel: het leven van Constantijn Huygens* (The Hague, 1980), 167. Van Dyck was apparently in London by 1 April, when he paid for room and lodgings with Edward Norgate. On 5 July 1632 Van Dyck was knighted and made "principalle Paynter in Ordinary to their Majesties." Regarding Van Dyck's activities in London see Oliver Millar, "Van Dyck in London," in Arthur K. Wheelock, Jr., et al., *Anthony Van Dyck* [exh. cat., National Gallery of Art] (Washington, 1990), 53–58.

3. The collections of the House of Orange Nassau have been published in three volumes: *Inventarissen van de inboedels in de verblijven van de Oranjes en daarmede gelijk te stellen stukken, 1567–1795* (hereinafter *Inventarissen*), ed. S. W. A. Drossaers and T. H. Lunsingh-Scheurleer [*Rijks Geschiedkundige Publicatiën*, vols. 147–148] (The Hague, 1974). All references are to vol. 147.

4. There has been speculation that Van Dyck made an earlier trip to the northern Netherlands; see Arthur Wheelock in Washington 1990, no. 59, 236–238, in which he rejects the idea of an earlier trip and accepts 1632 as the date for these paintings.

5. See Van Gelder 1959, 43–86.

6. Van Dyck was named court painter by the Infanta in May 1630.

7. J. G. van Gelder, "Rubens in Holland in de zeventiende eeuwe," *Nederlandsch Kunsthistorisch Jaarboek* 3 (1951–1952), 106, notes the difficulty Rubens experienced in traveling in the north after the conclusion of the truce in 1621. The Dutch knew Rubens primarily from his paintings from the period of the truce (1609–1621).

8. On his deathbed, the bachelor stadholder Maurits had elicited a promise from his forty-one-year-old brother that he would marry. Amalia was Frederik Hendrik's current mistress. Regarding Amalia von Solms see Titia Johanna Geest, "Amalia van Solms en de Nederlandsche politiek van 1625 tot 1648, bidrage tot de kennis van het tijdvak van Frederik Hendrik" (M.A. thesis, University of Amsterdam, Baern, 1909); Arthur Kleinschmidt, *Amalie von Oranien, geborene Gräfin zu Solms-Braunfels: ein Lebensbild* (Berlin, 1902).

9. After the death of Maurits, Frederik Hendrik possessed all the property of Willem I, which he received in addition to twenty percent of the war booty and a share of the sea piracy. The major modern biography of Frederik Hendrik is J. J. Poelhekke, *Frederik Hendrik, prins van Oranje, een biografisch drieluik* (Zutphen, 1978); see also P. J. Blok, *Frederik Hendrik, prins van Oranje* (Amsterdam, 1924). An excellent summary of his life and significance is Herbert Harvey Rowen, "Frederick Henry: Firm in Moderation," in *The Princes of Orange: the Stadholders in the Dutch Republic* (Cambridge and New York, n.d. [1988]), 56–76.

10. In 1625 he had inherited his brother Maurits' title of prince of Orange and had followed him as the elected stadholder of the provinces of Holland, Zeeland, Utrecht, Gelderland, and Overijssel. In 1640 he was also named stadholder of Groningen and Drente. As stadholder, originally one who stood in place of the absent king, Frederik Hendrik was responsible to the six individual states that had elected him and could make no decisions without their counsel.

11. Regarding the tradition of princely collections see Ronald Lightbown, "Charles I and the Tradition of European Princely Collecting," in *The Late King's Goods*, ed. Arthur MacGregor (London and Oxford, 1989), 53–72.

12. Her father was steward to the court of the Elector Palatine. Frederik Hendrik may have first met Amalia when he served as godfather at the baptism in Heidelberg of Frederick and Elizabeth's first child, Frederick Henry, in 1614.

13. The marriage of the couple in London in 1613 was seen by many as a symbol of an international Protestant alliance. On 26 August 1619 the Protestant Diet of Bohemia deposed King Ferdinand and chose Frederick as king. As holy Roman emperor, Ferdinand had the support of Spain, Italy, and the Catholic League. Without the expected support of his father-in-law, James I of England, who refused to declare Spain his enemy, Frederick was forced to flee Prague on 2 November 1620. By February 1621 he and Elizabeth were in The Hague. The States General gave Frederick, the leader of the Protestant Union in Germany, a monthly pension of 10,000 guilders, while the English Parliament gave Elizabeth, princess royal of England, a pension of 26,000 guilders a month.

14. Frederik Hendrik had lived for about one year, in 1598, at the court of Henry IV and had visited in 1609. In addition to other visits before he was named stadholder in 1625, he was in England in 1613 to attend the wedding of Frederick and Elizabeth.

15. Each evening, members of the court played billiards or cards or watched a play or ballet performed at the palace on the Noordeinde. During the day there were games of pell-mell and balloon, as well as hunts and frequent excursions into the countryside or to the beach, where there were sailwagon races. The activities and spirit of the court are rendered in the lively drawing book by Adriaen van de Venne (British Museum); see Martin Royalton-Kisch, *Adriaen van de Venne's Album in the Department*

of Prints and Drawings in the British Museum (London, 1988). As Royalton-Kisch has convincingly suggested, this book of casual genre scenes of peasants and courtiers was a kind of *album amicorum*, which was probably presented by the king and queen of Bohemia to Frederik Hendrik and Amalia von Solms shortly after their marriage in 1625. The often emblematic drawings relate to the overall theme of the strength and glory of the Dutch republic and emphasize the close ties of the two courts. See also C.-A. van Sypesteyn, *Het hof van Boheme en het leven in den Haag in de XVIIe eeuw* (Amsterdam, 1886).

16. The investiture, which was encouraged by Elizabeth, was an attempt to placate Frederik Hendrik, who was angered by the news that the duke of Buckingham, on behalf of Charles I, was seeking a settlement with Spain through Gerbier and Rubens.

17. The most important treatment of this subject is still F. W. Hudig, *Frederik Hendrik en de kunst van zijn tijd* (Amsterdam, 1928); see also C. Willemijn Fock, "The Princes of Orange as Patrons of Art in the Seventeenth Century," *Apollo* 110 (1979), 466–475.

18. Frederik Hendrik's other godfather was Frederick II (1531–1588), king of Denmark.

19. Regarding the palaces of Frederik Hendrik see I. D. F. Slothouwer, *De paleizen van Frederik Hendrik* (Leiden, n.d. [1945]).

20. Regarding Charles I as patron and collector see MacGregor 1989, especially Francis Haskell, "Charles I's Collection of Pictures," 203–231. The only clearly identified Italian painting in Frederik Hendrik's collection was that by Franco Biagio Florentino of "four naked figures with a cupid," which hung over the fireplace in Frederik Hendrik's audience room (*Inventarissen*, 1632, Stadhouderlijk Kwartier, 186, no. 120).

21. Fock 1979, 471 and elsewhere, emphasizes the political motivation of Frederik Hendrik's artistic schemes.

22. The house was acquired in 1612 from the duke of Arenburg for 360,000 guilders. Remodeling began in 1620 and was extended in 1625. The place of honor in the large dining room was held by Rubens' *Crowning of Diana* (Staatliche Schlösser und Gärten Potsdam-Sanssouci) and in the grand stairway, painted musical merrymakers appear as if standing behind a balcony. See Slothouwer [1945], 39–88; D. P. Snoep, "Honselaersdijk: restauraties op papier," *Oud Holland* 84 (1969), 270–294; R. Meischke, "De grote trap van het huis Honselaarsdijk, 1633–1638," *Nederlands Kunsthistorisch Jaarboek* 21 (1980), 86–103; T. Morren, *Het Huis Honselaarsdijk* (Leiden, 1908). The earliest inventory of the collection of paintings at Honselaarsdijk is 1707, updated in 1713 and 1719 (*Inventarissen*, 521–538).

23. See H. H. Heldring, "De portrettengalerij op het Huis ter Nieuwburch te Rijswijk," *Jaarboek die Haaghe* (1967), 66. The collecting and commissioning of portrait series was a characteristic of late Renaissance and baroque patrons (see note 11). In these collections the interest was primarily in obtaining

likenesses of the sitters rather than in collecting examples of the work of particular artists. Many of these paintings of historic and contemporary personages owned by Frederik Hendrik were later transferred to Honselaarsdijk, where the 1694 inventory (*Inventarissen*, 1694, Honselaarsdijk, 470, nos. 422–427) notes they had come from " 't Huys te Rijswijk."

24. See *Inventarissen*, 1676/1712, Buren, 558, nos. 61–64. Backer's painting was incorrectly identified (no. 63) as a work by Honthorst. The Gothic castle at Buren was built in 1500 and had 170 rooms.

25. As a child Frederik Hendrik had lived for approximately two years (1592–1593) at the Oude Hof with his mother, Louise de Coligny. After 1593 he lived with his unmarried brother Maurits in the Stadholder's Quarters. The States General presented the Oude Hof to Frederik Hendrik in October 1609. The house remained his mother's residence until her death in 1620. The following February it became the home of the exiled king and queen of Bohemia and their family. Regarding the history of the palace and its inhabitants see Paul de Boer, *Het huijs int Noorteynde; Het Koninklijk Paleis Noordeinde historisch gezien/The Royal Palace Noordeinde in an Historical View*, trans. Rollin Cochrane (Zutphen, 1986). The inventory made of the collections at Noordeinde and the Stadholder's Quarters in the summer of 1632 are especially important as the only inventories actually made of the princely collection during the life of Frederik Hendrik. See *Inventarissen*, 1632, 181–201 (Stadhouderlijk Kwartier in the Binnenhof), 202–237 (Noordeinde).

26. Tapestries that decorated the walls during the winter were replaced in the summer by either damask or embroidered silk wall hangings and upholstery. A contemporary, [Jean-Puget] M. de la Serre (c. 1600–1665), *L'Histoire de l'entrée de la Reyne-Mère*, effused:

The residence belonging to His Highness and where Her Majesty was to stay was extraordinarily elegant, luxurious and beautifully furnished. All the rooms were hung with tapestries so lovely one could not look at them often enough. The Queen's own room had hangings woven with golden thread whose value was unimaginable: all the furniture was magnificent; the house had all the appearances of a royal palace . . . these effects and furnishings could never be put to the service of a greater queen
(Boer 1986, 148, n. 10). The royal visitors were apparently not always the best guests, however. During Maria de' Medici's visit in 1638 the palace sustained twenty thousand guilders worth of damage. Four years later, the visit of Maria's daughter Henrietta Maria reportedly cost the court a total of one million guilders for entertainment and repairs (Boer 1986, 43). Henrietta Maria had brought to The Hague her daughter Mary, who had been married as a nine-year-old child to the fifteen-year-old Willem.

27. In the entry room (*voorsaal*) hung paintings of a man standing with an Indian weapon, a horse from Breda, and four paintings representing the four ele-

ments (*Inventarissen*, 1632, Noordeinde, 202, nos. 483–485). In the large "downstairs room" (*de groote benedensael*) hung thirteen large paintings by François van Knibbergen representing the cities of Nova Batavia, Mexico, St. Maarten, Malaga, and other foreign ports, as well as paintings of ships and the city and castle of Breda, portraits of the admiral of Holland, Pieter Pietersz. Heyn, Admiral Chastillon, and his two brothers (over the fireplace) and of Prince Philip, and Rembrandt's (called Lievens') *Fortune-teller* (Gemäldegalerie, Berlin-Dahlem); see *Inventarissen*, 1632, Noordeinde, 202, nos. 489–498.

28. See *Inventarissen*, 1632, Stadhouderlijk Kwartier, 181–201. Regarding the history of the Stadholder's Quarters during the seventeenth century see D. J. Jansen, "Het Stadhouderlijk Kwartier in de 17de eeuw," in *Het Binnenhof van grafelijke residentie tot regeringscentrum*, ed. R. J. van Pelt and M. E. Tiethoff-Spliethoff (Dieren, 1984), 57–70.

29. *Inventarissen*, 1632, Stadhouderlijk Kwartier, 182–185, nos. 38–99.

30. T. H. Lunsingh-Scheurleer, "De woonvertrekken van Amalia's Huis in het Bosch," *Oud Holland* 84 (1969), 29–66. Amalia's apartments were reconstructed about 1650.

31. See J. H. W. Unger, "Brieven van eenige schilders aan Constantin Huygens," *Oud Holland* 9 (1891), 187–206.

32. During Frederik Hendrik's siege of Bergen op Zoom, Huygens wrote to Amalia von Solms on 3 October 1641: "Son Alt.ᵉ a trouvé goust icy à la peinture d'un certain jeusne, mais fameux peintre d'Anvers, nommé Willeboorts, duquel y a de belles et grandes pieces en c'est ville et S.A. desirant le faire travailler pour quelque cheminée vient de luy envoyer un passeport pour l'avoir icy en personne" (*De briefwisseling van Constantijn Huygens* [1608–1687], p. 3 [1640–1644], ed. J. A. Worp [The Hague, 1914], 241, no. 2883). Regarding Willeboirts Bosschaert see J. G. van Gelder, "De opdrachten van de Oranjes aan Thomas Willeboirts Bosschaert en Gonzales Cocques," *Oud Holland* 64 (1949), 40–56.

33. In a letter, 7 December 1641 (*De briefwisseling van Constantijn Huygens* 1914, 253, no. 2916), Willeboirts wrote to Huygens that he had not yet heard back from the prince, to whom he had sent a letter with some sketches of work that Frederik Hendrik had commissioned. He dared not go ahead without knowing the prince's specific intentions:

Het is nu ontrent vierthien daegen geleden, dat ick, toe Bergen op Zoom sijnde, UE een bryeff hebbe toegesonden, maer wete nijet, of hy wel ter handt is komen, waerinne ick UE badt van mij die twee bovenste schetsen van dat panneel te doen sagen, te weten de twee, dye syne Hoocheyt my heeft gecommandeert te schilderen, want ick soude nyet geerne voorsvaren, vooraleer dat ick de schetsen hadde, om nijet te missen van perfectelyck de intentie van sijne Hocheyt te volgen.

34. In 1629 Endymion Porter had commissioned Van Dyck to paint *Rinaldo and Armida* for Charles I (Baltimore Museum of Art).

35. Before his murder in 1628, Buckingham (b. 1592) had served as first minister to Charles I and traveled to the northern Netherlands on the king's behalf. In 1625 he had been an extraordinary delegate to the States General. A portrait of Buckingham later attributed to Van Dyck appears in the 1632 inventory of Noordeinde (*Inventarissen*, 1632, Noordeinde, 203, no. 522; *Inventarissen*, vol. 2, 1755/1758, Honselaarsdijk, 507, no. 94, as by Van Dyck); in other inventories it is listed with other portraits as an old copy. Sir Dudley Carleton (1573–1632) was ambassador to The Hague from 1616 to 1625. The earl of Arundel (1586–1646) was earl marshal of England and ambassador to the emperor in 1640.

36. Regarding Huygens see Hendrik Arie Hofman, *Constantijn Huygens (1596–1687); een christelijk-humanistisch bourgeois-gentilhomme in dienst van het Oranjehuis* (Utrecht, 1983), with full bibliography.

37. Frans Baudouin, *Pietro Pauolo Rubens*, trans. Elsie Callander (New York, 1977), 234–240. Rubens hoped that if England reached agreement with Spain, the northern Netherlands would follow (236–237).

38. Contributing factors were the fall of La Rochelle to the French; the diversion of Spanish soldiers to northern Italy; the growth of the Dutch army to 77,193 men by April 1629 (one and one half times the Flemish army); and the capture of the Silver Fleet by the Dutch. All this led to serious financial problems for Isabella and the initiation of intense diplomatic activity to establish a truce on the same terms as in 1609. See Jonathan I. Israel, *The Dutch Republic and the Hispanic World, 1606–1661* (Oxford, 1982), 176. The major Spanish demands remained essentially unchanged. They were that the Republic make at least a token acknowledgment of Spanish sovereignty; that the River Schelde be reopened; that the Dutch withdraw from the Indies; and that there be at least one Roman Catholic church in every town. In November 1625 Philip of Spain declared that his Dutch policy was motivated totally by religion; see Israel 1982, 224.

39. In January 1629 Philip granted Isabella the authority to conclude a truce with the northern Netherlands on terms similar to those of 1609; in August he gave her more independence. Prior to this any negotiations were severely restricted by the necessity of having to relay all proposals to Spain for a response.

40. Van Gelder 1951–1952, 117, cites a letter from Hugo de Groot, who was then in Holland, to Pierre Dupuy: "notre bon amy monsieur Rubens . . . n'a rien fait, ayant etté renvoyé par le prince d'Orange presque si tost qu'il fust arrivé." The secrecy was necessary because of the hostility of the Flemish nobility toward the special role assigned to Rubens and especially the influential positions held by Spanish noblemen. The ostensible purpose of Rubens' visit was to arrange for an exchange of prisoners and free fishing rights (for herring and other larger fish in the

oceans; Flemish fishermen were to retain the right to
the small fish near their coast). Apparently the real
issue was, however, the initiation of talks regarding a
truce or peace, for in December 1632, when Rubens
returned to The Hague with a delegation from the
States General of the Spanish Netherlands, it was to
renew the discussions of the establishment of a peace
or truce that had been begun the previous year. In
October 1635, in spite of Huygens' personal interven-
tion, Rubens was denied a passport for Holland. See
Huygens' letter to Rubens, 13 November 1635, delivered to D. de Wilhem, whom Huygens instructed to
hold the letter for eight days before delivering it to
Rubens (*De Briefwisseling van Constantijn Huygens*,
pt. 2 [1634–1639] [The Hague, 1913], 129, no. 1290,
132, no. 1301). Rubens had requested a passport to
travel through the northern Netherlands to England
(Resolutions of the States General, 11 October 1635).

41. In 1632, a portrait of "de infant, hertoginne van
Brabant" hung in "de voorcamer genaempt 't quartier
van de gravinne van Solms" at Noordeinde (*Inventarissen*, 1632, Noordeinde, 210, no. 673). In the
same room were an equestrian portrait of Charles V
and portraits of Philip II and Philip III of Spain, as
well as a portrait of Philip, the late prince of Orange
(*Inventarissen*, 1632, Noordeinde, 210, nos. 671, 672,
674, 675). The portrait of Isabella was later identified
as a work by Van Dyck in the context of the same
paintings of the Spanish kings, which had been
moved to the west gallery at Huis ter Nieuwburch
(*Inventarissen*, 1707, Huis ter Nieuwburch te Rijswijk, 541, no. 14). In contrast to the public display of
the portrait of the archduchess, the portrait of Maria
de' Medici hung in the family quarters: "de nieuwe
kamer van haer excellentie [Amalia]" in the Stadholder's Quarters (*Inventarissen*, 1632, Stadhouderlijk Kwartier, 190, no. 191). Versions of both paintings accompanied Van Dyck to London a few months
later. The inclusion of the portrait of Maria de'
Medici among the paintings in the family chambers
probably reflects personal ties with the widow of
Henry IV, Frederik Hendrik's godfather. The French
queen had been a close friend of his mother, Louise
de Coligny, who died in November 1620 while staying with her at Fontainebleau. In July 1631 the
French queen and her son Gaston d'Orleans took
refuge in Brussels, where the archduchess named
Rubens her representative to the court of the exiled
queen.

42. The portrait of Amalia shared the same provenance as that of the portrait of the stadholder until
1930, when it was acquired by Duveen Brothers,
New York. It was sold at Sotheby's, London, 12 December 1973, no. 42, by the Norton Simon Foundation, which had acquired Duveen's entire stock of
paintings in 1966, when the gallery closed. Regarding
the dating of the portrait of Willem, see note 4. None
of these portraits appears in the inventory made in
the summer of 1632, suggesting that the artist may
have taken the paintings with him to Antwerp,
where his workshop made the copies that would be
distributed to other courts. The portraits of Frederik
Hendrik and Amalia first appear in the family
archives in 1673, when they are mentioned in the

"dispositieboek" of Amalia von Solms, designated as
going to Henriette-Catherina, wife of George, prince
of Anhalt-Dessau (*Inventarissen*, 1673, Dispositieboek Amalia, 317, nos. 735, 736). At this time the
paintings hung in the Oude Hof on the Noordeinde
in the gallery of Amalia's alcove. The portrait of
Willem is first mentioned in the division of Amalia's
estate in 1676 (*Inventarissen*, 1676, Boedelscheiding
Amalia, 371, no. 1463), "Prinsje met een bonnet op,
door A. van Dijk." The painting was inherited by
Albertine Agnes, Vorstinne van Nassau.

43. See note 1. Drawings are known of Jan van
Ravesteyn, Cornelis Saftleven, and Jan van Goyen.
Prints of Willem Hondius, Michiel van Miereveld,
Gerard Honthorst, Palamedes Palamedesz, and Poe-
lenburgh, who all had connections with the court in
The Hague, suggest that Van Dyck also made studies
of these men at this time; see Van Gelder 1959, 50.

44. Vienna, Kunsthistorisches Museum, inv. nos.
484, 485. The first born of Elizabeth and Frederick of
Bohemia, Frederick Hendrick, drowned in 1629 when
the boat from which he and his father watched the
arrival of the Silver Fleet capsized.

45. The paintings first appear as nos. 4, 5, in the 1866
catalogue of the paintings in Combe Abbey, seat of
the earl of Craven. See Willem-Jan Hoogsteder, "De
schilderijen van Frederik en Elizabeth, Koning en
Koningin van Bohemen" (Ph.D. diss., Kunsthistorisch Instituut der Rijks Universiteit te Utrecht,
1986). From the late 1620s William Craven, later the
earl of Craven, was a devoted friend and patron of
Elizabeth, particularly after her husband's death,
when many speculated that they had secretly married. It was to the earl of Craven that Elizabeth left
many of her possessions at the time of her death. The
Craven sale at Sotheby's, 27 November 1968, included a number of pictures (mostly portraits) from
the collection of Elizabeth and Frederick of Bohemia.

46. Honthorst received the latter commission while
in England, but executed it in Holland, sending it to
Charles I on 22 May 1630. The painting stayed in the
royal collection until 1719, when it was taken to
Hannover by George I. It is now in the Herrenhausen
Museum.

47. Van Gelder 1959, 45, suggests that Charles I commissioned Van Dyck to paint replicas of the portraits
of the stadholder and his wife (possibly those now in
the Museo del Prado, Madrid, inv. nos. 1482, 1483)
and that Isabella may also have commissioned Van
Dyck to paint versions of the portraits for her. See Lionel F. S. A. Cust, *Anthony van Dyck. An Historical
Study of His Life and Works* (London, 1900), 99.

48. Elizabeth wrote to Sir Thomas Rowe, 13 January
1632, of her fear that peace would end her son's
claims in Germany, an ongoing concern of the queen
in letters to her brother and other friends in England;
The Letters of Elizabeth, Queen of Bohemia, compiled and ed. L. M. Baker (London, 1953), 82–83. Her
sons were a key factor in her attempts to gain her
brother's support. In a letter to Sir Thomas Rowe, 14
February 1630 (*Letters of Elizabeth* 1953, 80) she
notes that her sons had been sent to England at

Charles' request to inform him of their business; shortly after the death of her husband, Elizabeth wrote to Charles I, 24 December 1632, "I must intreat you to take us all into your protection, for after God, our sole resource is in you" (*Letters of Elizabeth* 1953, 87). Karl Ludwig and Rupert eventually entered the service of their uncle in 1636.

49. Josephine Ross, *The Winter Queen. The Story of Elizabeth Stuart* (New York, 1979), 105.

50. *De Briefwisseling van Constantijn Huygens* pt. 2 (1634–1639), 370–371, no. 1861, 26 June 1638. The previous year the States General had sent a gift, including a number of Dutch paintings, to the English king, at which time full-length portraits of Amalia von Solms and Frederik Hendrik by Honthorst may also have been sent.

51. It was first mentioned in the 1654 inventory of Amalia von Solms' collection at the Oude Hof on the Noordeinde (*Inventarissen*, 1654, Amalia von Solms, 286, no. 1246). The painting, which is now at Sanssouci, Potsdam, was inherited by the two princes of Brandenburg. Willem apparently referred to these two paintings when, after meeting the princess, he noted that she was even prettier than her painting (Van Gelder 1959, 70).

52. The primary version is now at Windsor Castle; a second version is in the Rijksmuseum, Amsterdam. The painting is first mentioned in the 1654/1668 inventory of Amalia von Solms' collection at Huis ten Bosch (*Inventarissen*, 282, no. 1188).

53. The paintings were later in the private chambers of Amalia at Noordeinde, where the princess arranged portraits of her then-grown children, leaving room for future portraits of her grandchildren. See Lunsingh-Scheurleer 1969, 61.

54. *Inventarissen*, 1632, Stadhouderlijk Kwartier, 182, no. 25. These paintings may be related to a power of attorney that Van Dyck signed on 12 February 1631 and sent to the painter Leonaert van Winde, who was to accept payment for paintings by Van Dyck that had been delivered. The wooden mantelpiece was gilded on a green ground. The room was decorated with tapestries of Vertumnus and Pomona, one of which had been removed to allow the painting to be hung over the fireplace.

55. *Inventarissen*, 1632, Stadhouderlijk Kwartier, 181, no. 11. The painting was placed over a mantelpiece with gilded festoons. The rest of the room was decorated with six pieces of Brussels tapestries of forests with various birds and animals (no. 10). No. 190 is "Eenen vergulden schoorsteenmantel met uytgesneeden werck daerinne een schilderie, d'historij van . . . gemaeckt door Anthony van Dijck van Antwerpen." Drossaers and Lunsingh-Scheurleur (*Inventarissen*), 190, n. "a," suggest that the painting was *Rinaldo and Armida*.

56. Kunsthistorisches Museum, Vienna. *Inventarissen*, 1654/1668, Amalia von Solms, 285, no. 1232, lists a painting of Pallas and Vulcan among the possessions of the princess at the palace at Noordeinde.

57. The prince apparently particularly enjoyed the story of Amaryllis and Mirtillo from Guarini's *Il Pastor Fido*, for he later commissioned a series of four paintings of the pastoral from Dutch artists for Honselaarsdijk. See J. G. van Gelder, "Pastor Fido-voorstellingen in de Nederlandse kunst van de zeventiende eeuw," *Oud Holland* 92 (1978), 227–263; Alison McNeil Kettering, *The Dutch Arcadia, Pastoral Art and Its Audience in the Golden Age* (Montclair, N.J., 1983), 107–119.

58. Arthur Wheelock in Washington 1990, 240.

59. For example, in the decorations for the arrival in Amsterdam of Henrietta Maria in 1641, Frederik Hendrik was portrayed both as Hercules and as Perseus freeing Andromeda who represented the Netherlands; see D. P. Snoep, *Praal en propaganda* (Alphen aan de Rijn, [n.d.]), 72. The marriage of Willem and Mary Stuart was typologically represented by the marriage of Peleus and Thetis, with the expressed hope that their union would bring the birth of a new Achilles.

60. The theme was represented in at least two tapestry series and several paintings. For example, a series of ten tapestries representing Ulysses hung in the *nieuwe sael* at Noordeinde (*Inventarissen*, 1632, Noordeinde, 211, no. 718, notes that they were normally in the *nieuwe sael* [one of the public rooms between the portrait gallery and the private rooms of the prince] at Noordeinde, but in the summer of 1632 the tapestries were, typically for that season, in storage in the attic). Rubens' *Mercury and Venus* hung over the mantelpiece in the *nieuwe sael* at Noordeinde (*Inventarissen*, 1632, Noordeinde, 207, no. 620). Vondel drew a comparison between the classical hero and Frederik Hendrik in his epiclike poem, *Zegesang ter eere van Frederick Hendrick, boschdwinger, wezelwinner, prince van Oranje*, in celebration of the prince's victory at 's-Hertogenbosch in 1629. The poem also calls Frederik Hendrik a second Hercules and identifies him with Apollo and Jupiter. The association with Achilles was also later made in the decorations in Amsterdam for the official visit of the queen of England in 1642 and in the Huis ten Bosch. Regarding the iconography of the Oranjezaal in Huis ten Bosch, Amalia's tribute to her deceased husband and his dynastic claims, see H. Peter-Raupp, *Die Ikonographie des Oranjezaal* (Hildesheim and New York, 1980); B. Brenninkmeyer de Rooij, "Notities betreffende de decoratie van de Oranjezaal in Huis ten Bosch," *Oud Holland* 96 (1982), 133–190. The prince and princess were also identified as Dido and Aeneas in a tapestry series at Noordeinde and painting by Willeboirts Bosschaert.

61. Wolfgang Prohaska, "Remarks on Van Dyck's Narrative Style," forthcoming. The story represents Thetis, who has come to Vulcan's forge to collect the armor he had made for her son Achilles. Moments later, wearing the armor, she would flee from Vulcan's amorous demands. As Prohaska points out, the newly identified scene therefore closely relates to Van Dyck's *Ulysses in Search of Achilles*, which was also in the prince's collection. Regarding the story and iconographic tradition of Achilles see Egbert

Haverkamp Begemann, *The Achilles Series. Corpus Rubenianum Ludwig Burchard*, pt. 10 (London, 1975).

62. Wheelock in Washington 1990, 240.

63. See Amy L. Walsh, "Vigilant Preparedness," in "Paulus Potter; His Works and Their Meaning" (Ph.D. diss., Columbia University, 1985), 370–374. This interpretation also agrees with the images discussed by Royalton-Kisch 1988, 93, where he cites prints that announced the people's acceptance of a resumption of war in 1621. In 1627 Vondel's eulogy on Frederik Hendrik's capture of Grol emphasizes a closely related theme, the stadholder's steadfastness (J. van Vondel, *De werken*, vol. 3 [Amsterdam, 1929], 124–152, especially 152, *Aeneis* X, v. 691). Brenninkmeyer de Rooij 1982, 140, 177, n. 23, cites Vondel in relation to the neostoic ideal of steadfastness and Gerard Honthorst's *Allegory on the Steadfastness of Frederik Hendrik* at Huis ten Bosch.

64. Regarding the theme and various versions by Van Dyck see Rensselaer W. Lee, "Van Dyck, Tasso, and the Antique," *Studies in Western Art, Acts of the Twentieth International Congress on the History of Art—Latin American Art, and the Baroque Period in Europe* 3 (1963), 21–26.

65. See Arthur K. Wheelock in Washington 1990, 221–222.

66. See R. Baumstark, "Ikonographische Studien zu Rubens' Kriegs- und Friedensallegorien," *Aachener Kunstblätter* 95 (1974), 125–134; Christopher Brown, *"Peace and War": Minerva Protects Pax from Mars* (London, 1979); A. Hughes, "Naming the Unnameable: An Iconographical Problem in Rubens' 'Peace and War,'" *Burlington Magazine* 122 (1980), 157–164.

67. The chief commissions were for the hunting lodge Honselaarsdijk. Jacob van Campen, Christiaen van Couwenbergh, Paulus Bor, Moyses van Uttenbroek, and Tyman Cracht decorated the staircase and banquet room. All had studied in Italy and were able to paint in the northern Italian illusionist style. Pieter de Grebber and Cornelis Vroom were also active at Honselaarsdijk. See note 22.

68. See note 32.

69. On 17 October 1641 Huygens wrote to Willeboirts Bosschaert regarding Frederik Hendrik's wish to acquire paintings and other works of art in Antwerp (*De briefwisseling van Constantijn Huygens* 1914, 246, no. 2894). On 7 December 1641 Willeboirts sent Huygens a letter with a number of drawings after paintings in the estate of Rubens (Rubens died 30 May 1640) and a panel with his own sketches of paintings Frederik Hendrik had commissioned (*De briefwisseling van Constantijn Huygens* 1914, 253, no. 2916). See van Gelder 1949, 42. Willeboirts purchased six paintings from Rubens' estate, as well as a fruit still life by Adriaen van Utrecht. In other transactions, Frederik Hendrik acquired works by Flemish sculptors, including Artus Quellinus and François Dieusart, who had, typically, been trained in Italy.

70. Van Gelder 1949, 42–53. For example, on 13 April 1642, Willeboirts delivered his paintings of *Dido and Her Sister* (location unknown) and *Venus and Adonis* (formerly Mauritshuis, The Hague; destroyed 1940); on 25 February 1645, *Mars and Venus* and *Flora* (location of both unknown); on 26 March 1646, *Aeneas and Dido* (Staatliche Schlösser und Gärten Potsdam-Sanssouci); on 11 January 1647, *Europa* (location unknown) and *Andromeda* (Schloss Schwedt an der Oder). A painting of *Jason and Medea* (Neues Palais, Potsdam) was not delivered until after the stadholder's death in 1647.

71. Jan Denucé, *Na Peter Pauwels Rubens, documenten uit den kunsthandel te Antwerpen in de XVIIe eeuw van Matthijs Musson*, vol. 5 of *Bronnen voor de geschiedenis van de Vlaamsche Kunst* (Antwerp and The Hague, 1949), 25–26:

Soo heft hy my in het nieu huys doen ghaen met den kamerlinck, deden my daer de mat nemen voor een schou die ik Ul hier seynt. Hy wenste it te hebben van divocie, een Livrou. Soo heb ik gedocht op Ul stuck de Livroiu van Van Dyck. Ul mach sien oft het past want ik heb hem daer van gesproken. Soo nit siet oft daer wat anders te bekommen is ten mach geenen Cristis syn en dat met hestel want hy ons voer het erst begint te proven, daer synder al veel van doen. Oft het sy een botschap Syn Hocheyt en sucket nit vel belden in het stuck en siet toch nae schoon tronien. Het stuck moet in de hoenden syn, het knoopken is de brede.

The present location of the painting, which is not further described, is unknown. A "Madonna after Van Dyck" is listed as over a fireplace at Honselaarsdijk in 1707 (*Inventarissen*, 1707, Honselaarsdijk, 521, no. 1). A Madonna by Van Dyck, possibly the same but noted as "door Anthony van Dijck gedaen," is also mentioned at Noordeinde in 1673 (*Inventarissen*, 1673, Dispositieboek Amalia, 319, no. 771). It is unlikely, however, that the painting was intended for Noordeinde, known as the Oude Hof, or Old Palace.

72. I appreciate Charles Dempsey's having pointed out this fact to me in Washington in 1991. Lunsingh-Scheurleer 1969, 50, suggests that since the painting was acquired in 1646, it was probably bought with the intention of hanging it at Huis ten Bosch. Van Gelder 1959, 73, cites a notation in the accounting books of the Nassausche Domeinen in the Algemeen Rijksarchief in The Hague (inv. no. 736, fol. 44) in which Frederik Hendrik instructs his accountant to pay Jan Caspeel for the painting by Van Dyck, which was purchased by her highness, Amalia von Solms. The question of Amalia's role in the selection and acquisition of paintings during the life of her husband has yet to be resolved. One cannot rely on the distribution of paintings following her death to determine which paintings she owned, since this painting, for example, was one of sixty-eight paintings that Willem III, rather than one of her daughters, inherited. It was customary for daughters to inherit from mothers and sons from fathers.

73. Regarding Seghers and Frederik Hendrik see A. J. J. Delen, "Daniel Seghers en het Huis van Oranje," in *Oude Kunst en Graphiek* (1943), 73–102.

74. The king and queen of Bohemia were never, apparently, true art collectors. Their collection con-

sisted primarily of portraits, many of which were probably gifts. See Hoogsteder 1986.

75. Ross 1979, 76.

76. See Oliver Millar, ed., "The Inventories and Valuations of the King's Goods," *Walpole Society* 43 (1972), xi–xii. For details of the iconoclasm in the chapel at Whitehall see *Historical Manuscripts Commission, Pourtland MSS*, 2 (1894), 132. Their suspicions were not totally unsubstantiated. The correspondence of Gregorio Panzani, the papal agent to Queen Henrietta Maria, reveals that presents of works of art, especially paintings, were considered by Rome to be a means of influencing Charles to assume a conciliatory policy toward his Catholic subjects. See R. Wittkower, "Inigo Jones—'Puritanissimo Fiero,'" *Burlington Magazine* 90 (1948), 50–51.

77. *Inventarissen*, 1632, Oude Hof, 185, no. 94. The inventory notes that the painting had been bought from the widow Verdoes. Apparently Frederik Hendrik was unable to acquire paintings directly from Rubens after the conclusion of the Twelve Year Truce in 1621.

78. Hans Vlieghe, "Constantijn Huygens en de Vlaamse skilderkunst van zijn tijd," *De zeventiende eeuw* 3–2 (1987), 200, places the emphasis on the prince's desire for beautiful faces, concluding that the only explanation for Catholic subjects in his collection is that the paintings served a purely decorative function. This commission should be seen in comparison with a letter, 2 July 1639, in which Huygens wrote to Rubens that the prince wanted a painting for the mantelpiece, of which he gave the dimensions but not the subject. In this case, in which the prince's primary concern was apparently to have a work by Rubens, Huygens noted that the subject was totally up to the artist, but that it must have only three or at most four figures and that the beauty of the women should be carried out "con amore, studio e diligenza" (Van Gelder 1951–1952, 142–143).

79. *Inventarissen*, 1632, Stadhouderlijk Kwartier, 182–186. Most of the religious paintings appear in "de galderije van zijne excellentie" and in "het cabinet van Zijn Ex^cie."

80. Regarding the Remonstrants' condemnation of papist attitudes toward idolatry and images of the Madonna and the crucifixion see "Disputation XXIII, On Idolatry," *The Works of James Arminius*, trans. James Nichols and William Nichols, 3 vols. (Grand Rapids, c. 1986), 2:289–306.

81. Among the seventy-six paintings in the prince's gallery were twelve paintings with religious themes [1632 inventory numbers are in parentheses]: (53) *The Discovery of Moses* by Lastman; (59) *Nativity* by Poelenburgh; (61)˙ *Madonna and Child* by van Balen; (65)˙ *Madonna in a Flowerwreath* by Jan Brueghel and van Balen; (67) *Landscape with Mary Laying the Child in Cloths and Angels* by Poelenburgh; (69) *Landscape with Cattle and a Herder and Tobias Sleeping* by Poelenburgh; (77) *Circumcision of Christ*; (79)˙ *Saint Martin on Horseback* (anonymous); (85)˙ *Mary Magdalene* by Goltzius (Staatliches Museum Schloss Mosigkau, Dessau-Mosig-

kau); (87) *Samson Having His Hair Cut* by Lievens (probably Gemäldegalerie, Berlin-Dahlem); (90)˙ *Madonna and Child* (anonymous); (94)˙ *The Annunciation*, Rubens (National Gallery of Ireland, Dublin). Six of these, denoted with asterisks, can be considered Catholic subjects because of their devotional potential.

82. *Inventarissen*, 1632, Stadhouderlijk Kwartier, 185–186.

83. *Inventarissen*, 1632, Stadhouderlijk Kwartier, nos. 101, 102, 108–111, 115. One could easily speculate that the stadholder might have added to this room the Passion series that Rembrandt began for him in 1633.

84. Neither painting agrees in description with a third Crucifixion, which Rembrandt painted for Frederik Hendrik in 1631. John Michael Montias, who kindly allowed me to read the manuscript of an article on the appearance of religious paintings in Amsterdam collections, notes that paintings of the crucifixion were relatively rare in Reformed households. He also notes that pictures of the Madonna were also rare but do occasionally appear. See John Michael Montias, "Works of Art in Seventeenth-Century Amsterdam: An Analysis of the Subjects and Attributions," *Art in History/History in Art: Seventeenth-Century Dutch Culture* (Santa Monica, 1991), 331–372.

85. Pieter J. J. van Thiel, "Catholic Elements in Seventeenth-Century Dutch Painting, Apropos of a Children's Portrait by Thomas de Keyser," *Simiolus* 20 (1990–1991), 52.

86. See van Thiel 1990–1991, 51. Sherrin Marshall, *The Dutch Gentry, 1500–1650. Family, Faith, and Fortune* (New York, Westport, Conn., and London, 1987), 91, stresses the central importance of religion for all Dutch people during this period. She discusses (81) the complex motivations for the adherence to the Catholic faith long after the revolt, noting (84) that "the gentry families clung to the appointments and sinecures which they regarded as their rightful possessions."

87. J. J. Poelhekke, "Een gefrustreerd Antwerpenaar Frederik Hendrik, Prins van Oranje, 1584–1647," in *Met pen, tongriemen papier, figuren uit een ver en nabij verleden* (Amsterdam, 1976), 54.

88. Uytenbogaert was the Calvinist preacher in The Hague who drew up the "Remonstrance," in which the group thereafter known as the Remonstrants set forth its creed. The Remonstrants rejected the doctrine of limited atonement, irresistible grace, and eternal perseverance of the elect in favor of free grace, conditional salvation, and a less specific doctrine of election. See Howard A. Slaatte, *The Armenian Arm and Theology. The Theologies of John Fletcher, First Methodist Theologia and His Precursor, James Arminius* (Washington, D.C., 1977), 15; see also Carl Bangs, *Arminius. A Study in the Dutch Reformation* (Grand Rapids, 1985), especially 332–355. The Synod of Dordrecht, which met in 1618–1619 and represented most of the Reformed Churches of Europe, denounced the five articles as

heresy and banished the Remonstrants. In 1619, just before the Synod of Dordrecht, Oldenbarnevelt, a leading Remonstrant, was beheaded.

89. Rivet (1572–1651), a Reformed Calvinist minister, served as chaplain to the Duchess de La Trémoïlle before being named professor at the University of Leiden. In 1631, through the intermediary of his friend Huygens, he was named governor of Willem. Rivet adhered closely to the Calvinist doctrine of predestination. His book *Apologia pro sanctissima virgine Maria matre Domini* (1639) may give further insight into the question of the Calvinist attitude toward the Madonna during the mid-seventeenth century. Regarding Huygens, another conservative Calvinist in the service of the prince, see Hofman 1983, especially chap. 2, 81–130.

90. Regarding the earlier negotiations, which involved Rubens, see page 6. Secret negotiations began with Frederik Hendrik in January 1641 and continued off and on in the succeeding years. See Israel 1982, 347–374.

91. Israel 1982, 355. The only major exception to this otherwise firm position occurred in May 1632, when the States General of the northern Netherlands issued a public manifesto calling on the people of the Spanish Netherlands to rebel and free themselves of the Spanish oppression. In return the States General promised to guarantee the practice of Catholicism in the southern Netherlands. The rebellion against Spanish domination, led by Hendrik van den Bergh, ultimately failed, largely because of the personal loyalty commanded by Isabella; see Israel 1982, 184–185.

92. According to the Spanish demands, Frederik Hendrik was to transfer both Zeeland and the Dutch-conquered zone of Flanders to the Spanish Netherlands to assure the security of free navigation to Antwerp; Dutch Brazil was to be restored to Spain; there were to be concessions in the Far East; and the Dutch were to concede liberty of Catholic worship; see Israel 1982, 351.

93. The French had formed an alliance with the Dutch in 1634 and had formally entered the war with Spain on the side of the Dutch the following year, bringing greater pressure on the southern Netherlandish, who feared that should they fall, they would be divided between their two neighbors. Not all in the north wished to see this happen. Many saw the value of an intact southern Netherlands, free of Spanish influence, as a buffer against the French.

94. Israel 1982, 358.

95. The young Louis XIV and Mazarin agreed to send six thousand French soldiers. The stadholder's agreement was later repudiated by Zeeland and Holland.

96. On 4 January 1645 the Marqúes de Castel-Rodrigo, one of the Spanish negotiators, commented: "Now I fear more than ever that the Prince mocks the king's authority and is deceiving those who are there on the part of his Majesty, diverting them with ceremonious and polite words to gain time and dispose of matters to his advantage" (Israel 1982, 353).

97. The Spanish were clearly aware of the precarious position Frederik Hendrik would be in if he accepted their offers. Israel 1982, 351, points out that the Spanish offer to make the prince a sovereign was made in an attempt to dislodge him.

98. See Delen 1943, 78–81. At the beginning of 1645 Frederik Hendrick, secretly and without identifying himself, inquired of the Jesuit fathers how much a painting by Father Seghers would cost.

99. Delen 1943, 81. In return for the gift from the Jesuits, Frederik Hendrik sent the artist a solid gold wreath with a letter of appreciation to the Antwerp Jesuits. The gift was delivered by Huygens, who later honored Seghers with Latin verses that had probably been commissioned by the Dutch stadholder.

100. See Delen 1943, 83. To show his appreciation, Frederik Hendrik sent the painter a solid gold cross, one palm high, weighing three pounds, three ounces, and worth approximately one thousand gulden. The total payment was far in excess of the cost of the painting.

101. In writing to Musson in 1644, Coques had noted that the Madonna was to be hung over a fireplace in the "New House," by which he may have meant the Huis ter Nieuburch, which was the only completely new palace. There is, however, no mention of the painting in the 1702 inventory of Nieuwburch, by which date the painting may have been moved to another house. See discussion, note 71. The painting by Seghers first appears in the 1654–1668 inventory of the possessions of Amalia von Solms (*Inventarissen*, 1654–1668, Huis ten Bosch, 281, no. 1179), in which it is noted as being for the mantelpiece of the cabinet.

102. Sebastian Dudok van Heel kindly informed me, in conversation, that it was a common practice for princes to have such anterooms to which they could withdraw privately with a visitor.

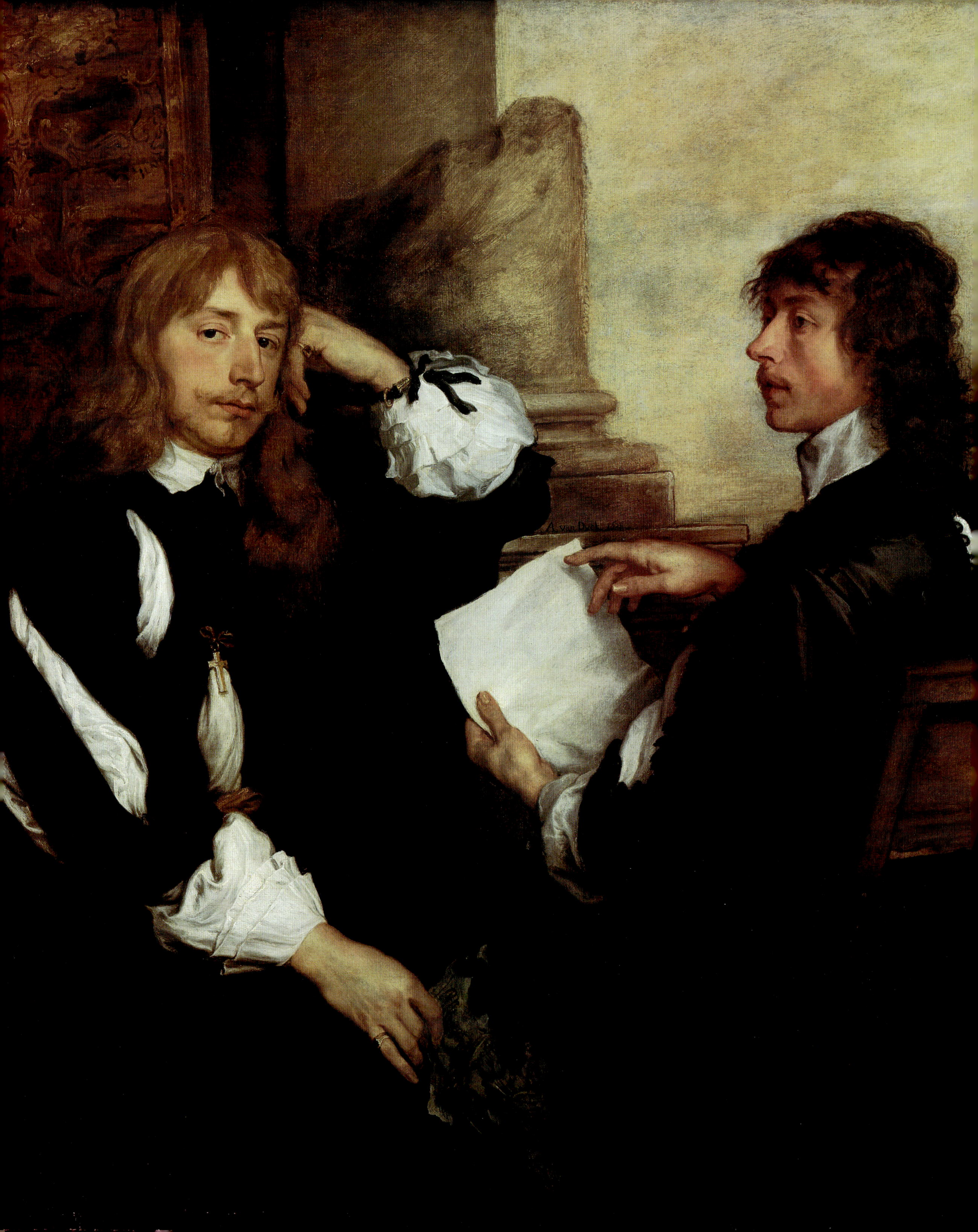

GRAHAM PARRY
University of York

Van Dyck and the Caroline Court Poets

It is commonly appreciated that Van Dyck's English paintings of the 1630s epitomize the new sophistication and refinement of the court of Charles I, and complement the so-called "Cavalier" poetry written by poets associated with the same court. In fact, it seems unlikely that Van Dyck, who spoke Flemish, French, and Italian but presumably very little English when he arrived in England in 1632, paid much attention to the poetry that pleased the court he served, although it is evident that the poets were alert to Van Dyck's innovations. The poets in question—Robert Herrick, Richard Lovelace, Sir John Suckling, Edmund Waller, Thomas Carew, Sir William Davenant, and Abraham Cowley—clearly accepted that Van Dyck was a denizen of their own imaginative world, and engaged in a common endeavor "to glorify the court," in Ben Jonson's phrase, and to project new images of the grace, wit, and virtue of the men and women of Caroline society. Certainly these poets referred to Van Dyck, and invoked his name with some frequency, using him as the highest standard of accomplishment in the sister art of painting. Indeed, it would appear that no other artist working in England received a mention in the verse of the Caroline poets, just as, among the poets of James I's time, there was a casual indifference to painting, only the miniaturists Nicholas Hilliard and Isaac Oliver attracting occasional comment and praise. Court painting in the first two decades of the seventeenth century, when Marcus

Gheeraedts, Robert Peake, Paul van Somer, Cornelius Janssen, and Daniel Mytens were the leading figures, simply did not interest the poets. With Van Dyck's appearance, attitudes changed. Poetry had always been the superior art in England, a country where painting did not much impinge on imaginative life, but when Van Dyck settled in and began to produce so many portraits of the royal family and the nobility, in a style more elegant, animated, and modern than anything seen in seventeenth-century England, then poets took notice of a fellow artist.

Van Dyck went about his usual business of setting the king and queen in poses that enhanced their majesty and gave them an authority of bearing as well as a refinement of sensibility and a mastery of fashion. His success accorded well with the comparable achievements of the poets. At the court of Charles I, poets were much more adulatory of the king and queen than the poets of the Jacobean era had been: they had more to be adulatory about, for one thing. Surprisingly few poems were addressed to James or Anne, whereas Caroline court poetry is notable for the quantity of verse praising the king and queen for their virtue, wisdom, statecraft, benevolence, mutual love, and fertility. The poetry of praise, compliment, or flattery reaches its height under Charles and Henrietta Maria, and the great increase in poems addressed to the royal couple must have been in response to a perceived approval by the monarch of this kind of elevating verse. Most of the poems refer to some occasion of

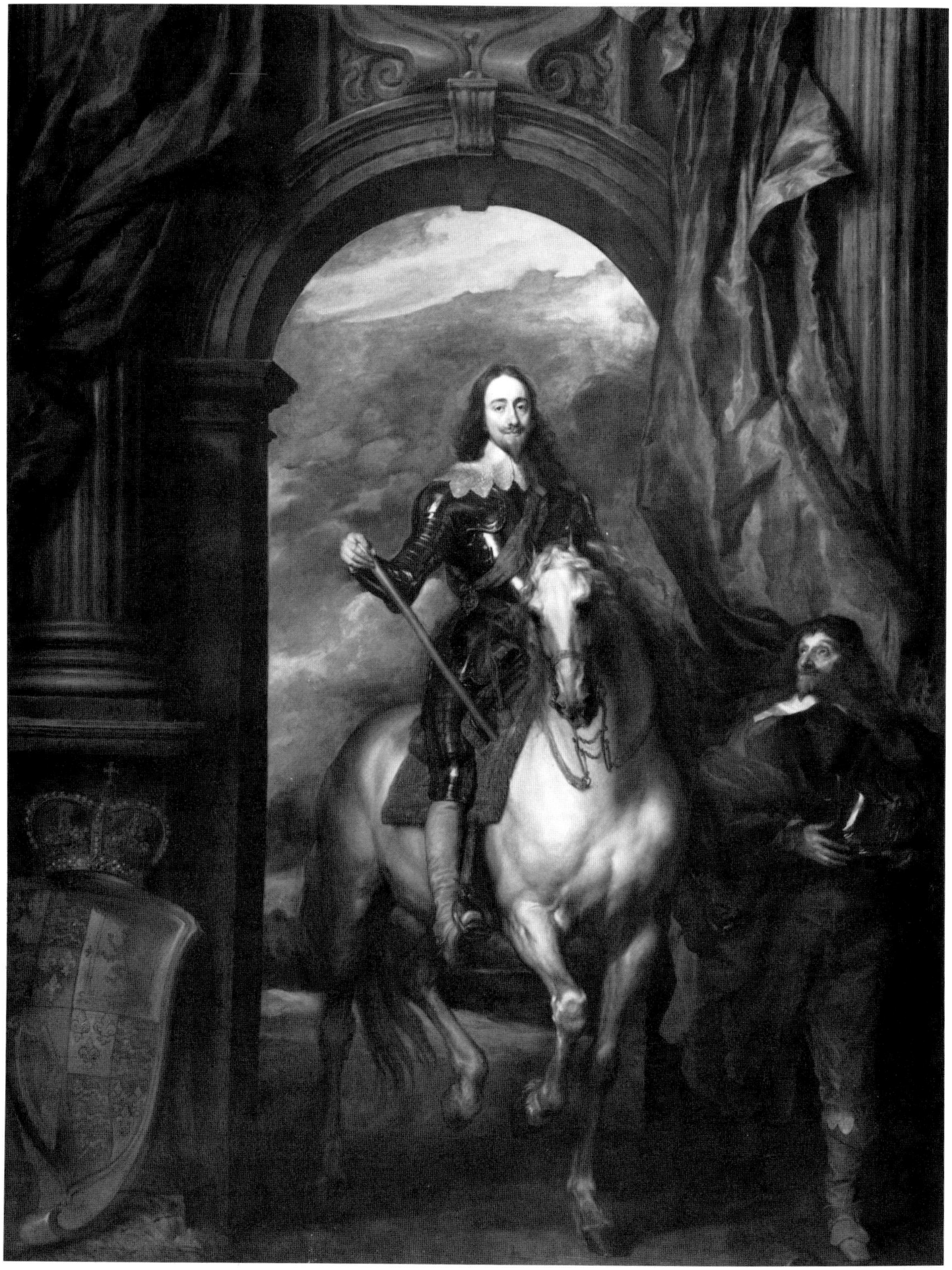

1. Anthony van Dyck, *Charles I Riding through a Triumphal Arch*, 1633, oil on canvas
Her Majesty Queen Elizabeth II

royal initiative or enterprise, the significance of which is assessed in flattering and optimistic terms.

We may take Edmund Waller as an example typical of the Cavalier poets. Writing from 1623 onward, Waller produced numerous poems addressed to the king, promoting an image of royal heroism or of patriotic magnanimity. Charles' escape from disaster at sea on his return from Spain and his stoical behavior on receiving the news of the duke of Buckingham's death provided mate-

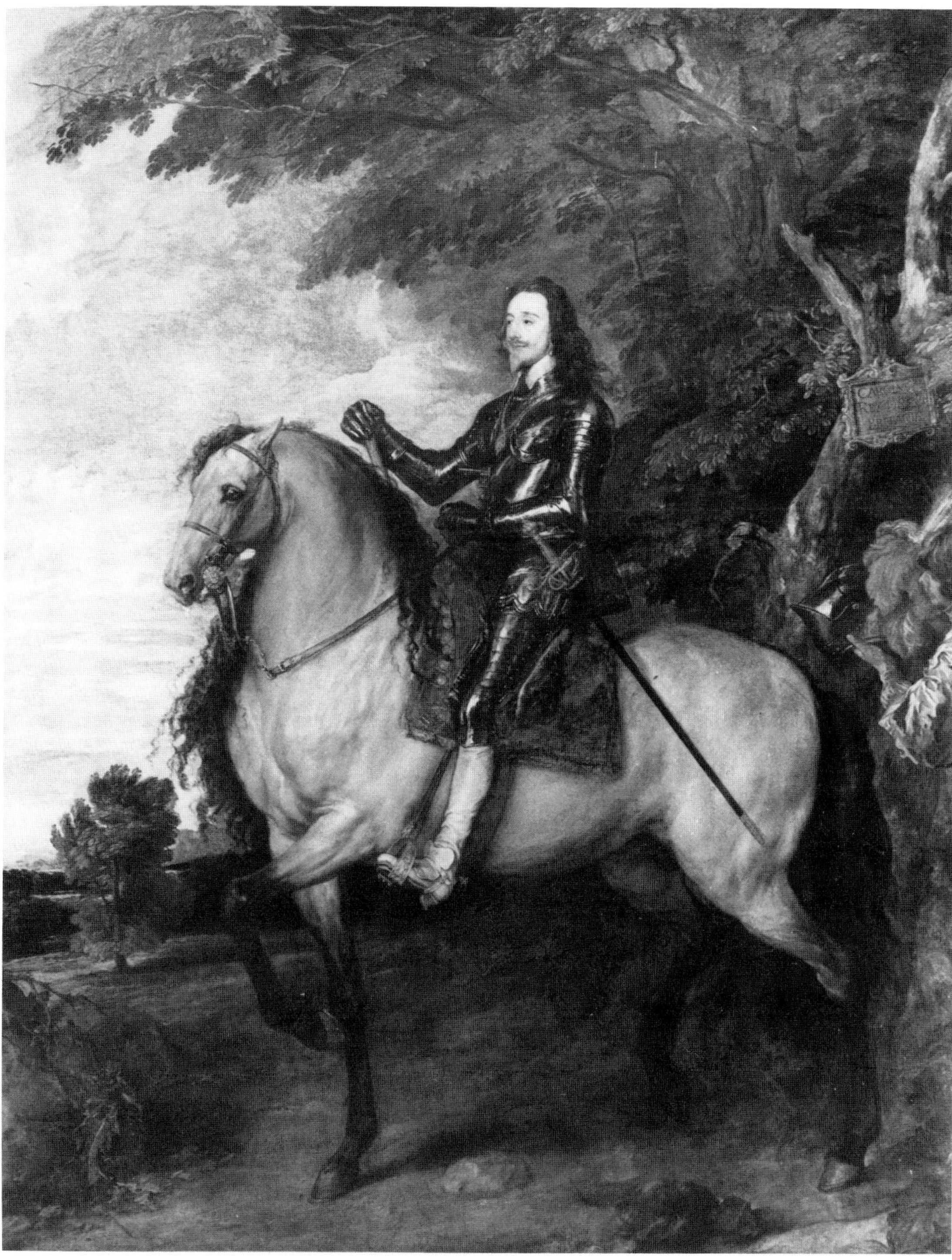

rial for poems that show adversity heroically overcome, the king's nobility of spirit asserting itself. Waller's titles ring with acclamation: "To the King, on his return from Scotland," "To the King, on his Navy," "To the King, on his repairing St. Paul's" all show the monarch actively enlarging his role as leader and inspirer of the nation.

Van Dyck soon came to understand how King Charles liked to be sustained by the elevating power of the arts. The three great full-length paintings of the king that he produced in the 1630s contributed to this impression of an active and enterprising monarch. The first of these, the famous portrait of 1633 of the king riding through a triumphal arch (fig. 1), projects an image of heroic activism. The king in armor on horseback (fig. 2) conveys a powerful sense of armed readiness: the king watchful and prepared. The third painting is the Louvre canvas of 1635, commonly known, from an early inventory, as *Le Roi à la Chasse* (fig. 3). Can this really be a picture of Charles out hunting? Did he hunt in a white satin jacket, with his Garter ribbon, and a wide-brimmed hat? Surely he is represented here as the First Gentleman of England. A man of peace this time, he surveys the estate of England. It is a pose that can be related to the country-estate poems of the 1630s, by Herrick or Carew, for example, in which the benevolent lord is seen presiding over his fertile and peaceful domain. This type of poem—exemplified by Herrick's "The Country Life," addressed to Endymion Porter, or the "Panegyric to Sir Lewis Pemberton," or Carew's "To Saxham" or "From Wrest"—praised the felicity of country life, described the harmless pleasures of the rural world, and took an admiring survey of the estate, where all was smiling prosperity, thanks to the good stewardship of the master. In Van Dyck's painting we see the source of the abundant peace and prosperity that made Britain one of the fabled Fortunate Isles: the king himself.

These paintings, then, are part of the same process of enhancing the royal image that the court poetry of the 1630s was engaged in, both arts responding to the king's desire to be seen as a stirring, watchful monarch in charge of events. In contrast, paintings of Charles' father, King James, showed him usually as an inert figure, seated on his throne or standing against a neutral background. Only Van Somer's portrait in the royal collection, showing him against the new banqueting house in 1620, attempts to provide an eventful depiction of royal authority, and even here we have a static, iconic king, stiffly holding an orb and scepter, demanding to be revered.

Charles' images are also related to the court masques, as Roy Strong made clear in the early 1970s.[1] Van Dyck's *Charles I Riding through a Triumphal Arch* (fig. 1) has obvious affinities with masque: the arch itself seems like a pasteboard affair, two-dimensional, and even lacking a base on the right; it bears an irregular, disproportionate display

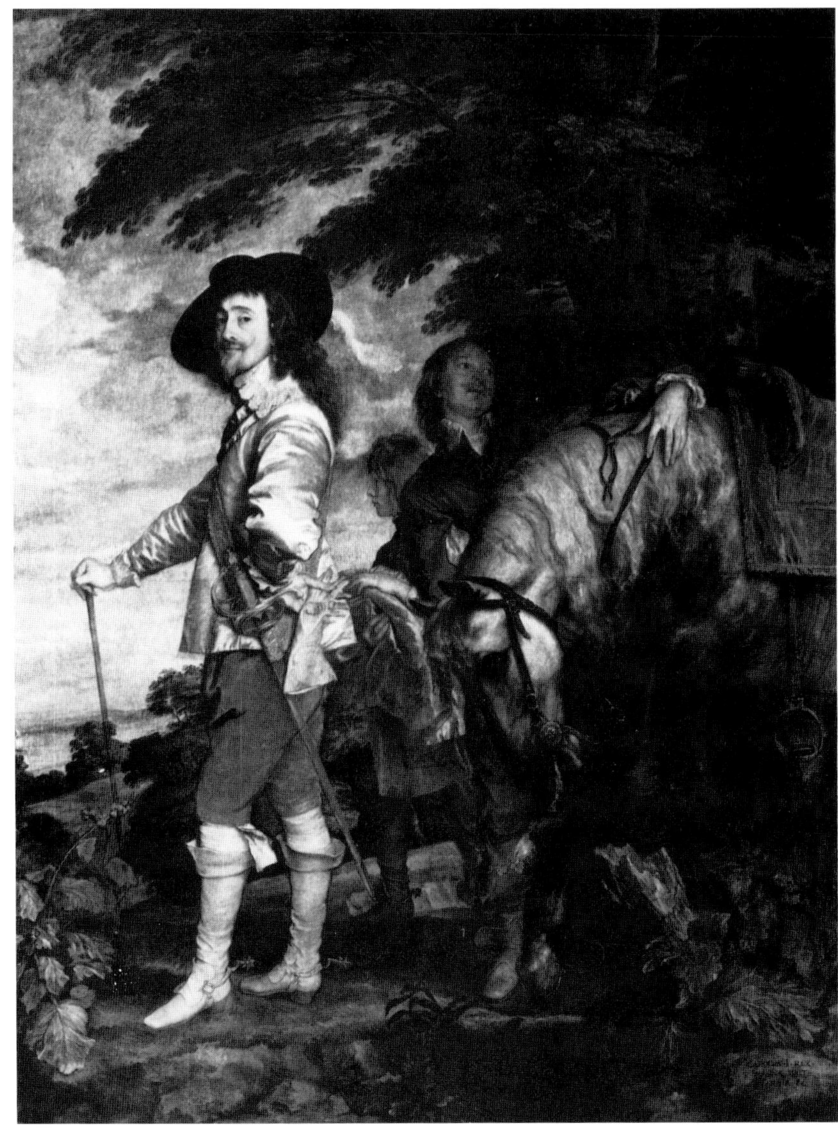

3. Anthony van Dyck,
Le Roi à la Chasse, c. 1635,
oil on canvas
Musée du Louvre, Paris

of classical motifs. The picture shows the king coming onstage, as it were, but his purpose and destination are unclear, and he has a vacant look in his eyes: "Where now?" he seems to say. As in a masque, it is the splendid entry that matters. Many of the masques of the 1630s were triumphant in character. Their titles convey their content: *Love's Triumph* (1631), *Albion's Triumph* (1632), *The Triumph of Peace* (1634), *Britannia Triumphans* (1638). A mood of effortless conquest is common to all of them. Typically, the king has only to appear in splendor and all his enemies, or those powers hostile to a successful reign, shrink and vanish. Charles, in an appropriate guise, "moves down the steps in stately pace to music," and all his

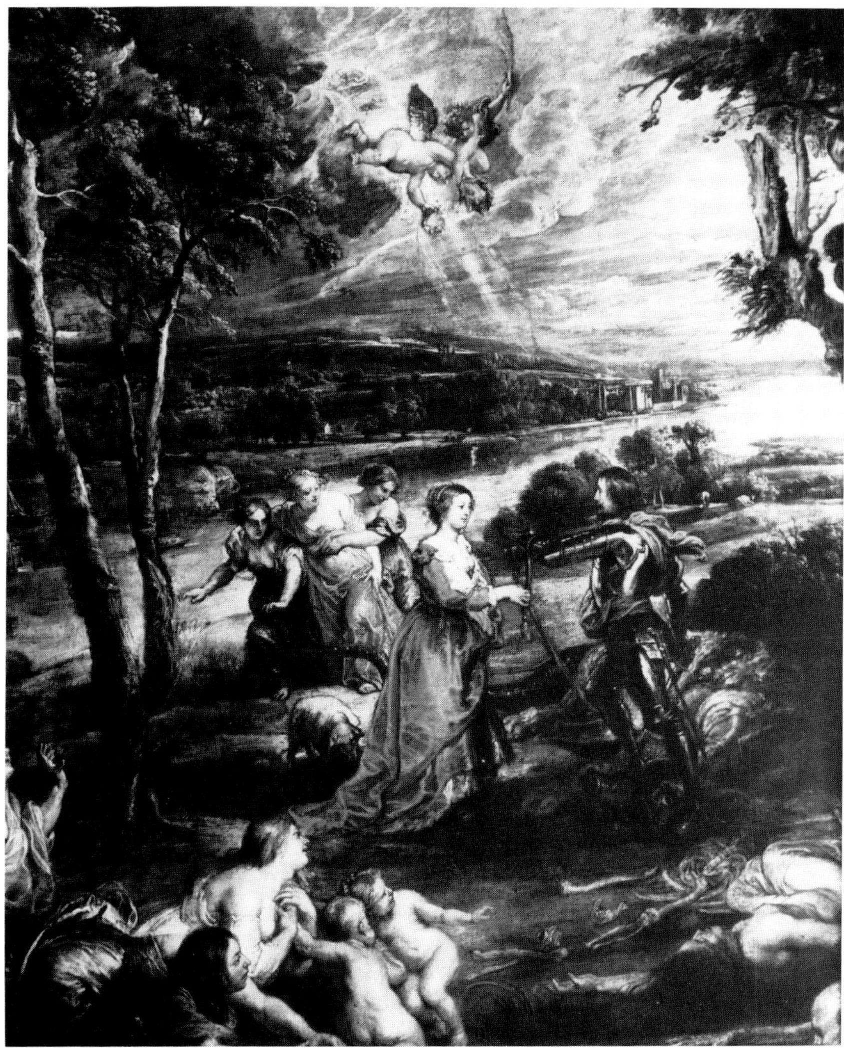

4. Peter Paul Rubens, *Saint George and the Dragon*, 1629, oil on canvas
Her Majesty Queen Elizabeth II

troubles are over, as Dissent, Discord, or Jealousy flee. So, with this painting, the king's heroic entry has sufficient force of itself to prevail over any opposition.

Charles is dressed in full armor. He liked to be portrayed in armor, in fact, which is a little strange when we consider the peaceful nature of England in the 1630s. "White Peace, the beautifullest of things, / Seems here her everlasting rest to fix," wrote Richard Fanshawe in his "Ode" of 1630, in praise of Charles' benign rule. Yet Charles has himself painted in full armor here and in the National Gallery picture (fig. 2) and in a half-length from a private collection. In 1632 he appeared on the Whitehall stage as a Roman emperor clad in armor in Aurelian Townshend's masque *Albion's Triumph*, even as the chorus of peaceful poets in that masque is loud in praise of the halcyon scene. Why did Charles adopt the military pose, in total contrast to King James' pacific stance? One could say that it was an international convention of painting in the sixteenth and seventeenth centuries that kings should be portrayed in armor. Charles would have had Titian's portrait of the Emperor Charles V in mind, or Velázquez' portraits of Philip IV, which he would have seen in Spain. The setting envisaged for the triumphal-arch painting effectively required Charles to be in armor, for the work was designed to hang at the end of a gallery in St. James's Palace, surrounded by portraits of Roman emperors by Titian and Giulio Romano. Charles himself, following his father, affected an imperial title as emperor of Great Britain.[2] The circumstances of Charles' time and place could justify his dressing in armor: the king was commander-in-chief of the army, although the English army was only a notional entity in the 1630s. At that time Europe was full of war, as the Catholic and Protestant armies fought to impose a military solution on the post-Reformation controversies. It was necessary for Charles to look watchful and prepared. Ironically, Charles was approached several times in the early 1630s to send military help for the Protestant cause in Europe, particularly in support of his nephew Charles Louis, who was trying to regain the Palatinate from the Catholic powers. Charles Louis and his brother Prince Rupert came in person to London in 1636 to seek military aid (and on that occasion they were painted by Van Dyck properly in armor), but they received no help. King Charles in armor was in fact a false and misleading image of readiness for war.

Nonetheless, given the midsummer hum of dozens of court poets as they sang of the peace of England throughout the decade of the thirties, Charles' preference for armor is strikingly discordant. The poets, dramatists, and masque writers at court favored a pastoral vision, and Charles spoke often of the blessings that peace brought to his kingdom. But for all his humoring of this fancy, Charles liked the idea of being a martial king. His particular fondness for the Order of the Garter, and his attentiveness to its composition and its costume, imply a self-dramatization as an armed prince, supported by his

faithful company of knights. The painting by
Rubens, *Saint George and the Dragon* (fig. 4),
which portrays Charles in the dragon-slaying
role in full armor, bears out this characterization. The desire to star as a military hero was
strong, and we should not forget that it was
Charles who first took up arms against Parliament, and when few men dreamed that
the disagreements between king and Parliament could lead to war, Charles raised his
standard at Nottingham in 1642.

King Charles no doubt carefully selected
his particular character for the big paintings,
just as he instructed his masque writers
about the roles he wanted for his stage appearances. The arts at court strove for royal
approval, which is why they are so useful a
guide to the king's intentions about how he
wanted to be perceived. The importance of
the arts for transmitting images of monarchi-
cal power and benevolence was at its height
in the 1630s when the king was ruling without Parliament, for during this decade poetry,
the masque, and painting were all being encouraged to send reassuring messages that
the control of the country was safe in the
hands of the Stuarts.

Courtiers, too, would give their instructions to Van Dyck to ensure a favorable
record with their contemporaries and posterity. They would often choose their costumes
and accoutrements to illustrate a salient trait
of character or some notable episode in their
lives. We can see how Van Dyck, once he
was in England, was soon drawn into producing occasional paintings that were the coun-
terparts of the occasional poems that were a
distinctive feature of court poetry in the
1620s and 1630s. These occasional poems
commemorated some incident, significant or
trifling, in the life of a friend or patron,
which was turned into an opportunity for
compliment or admiration. Of course, conventional expressions of congratulation or
mourning on marriage and death had been
part of the stock of poetry since Elizabethan
times, but the selection of suggestive moments of a life for poetic elaboration was
something new, and the rise of this kind of
occasional poetry virtually coincided with
the accession of Charles I. Almost all volumes of social poetry written throughout his
reign contain clusters of such poems, which
became an indispensable part of the poetic

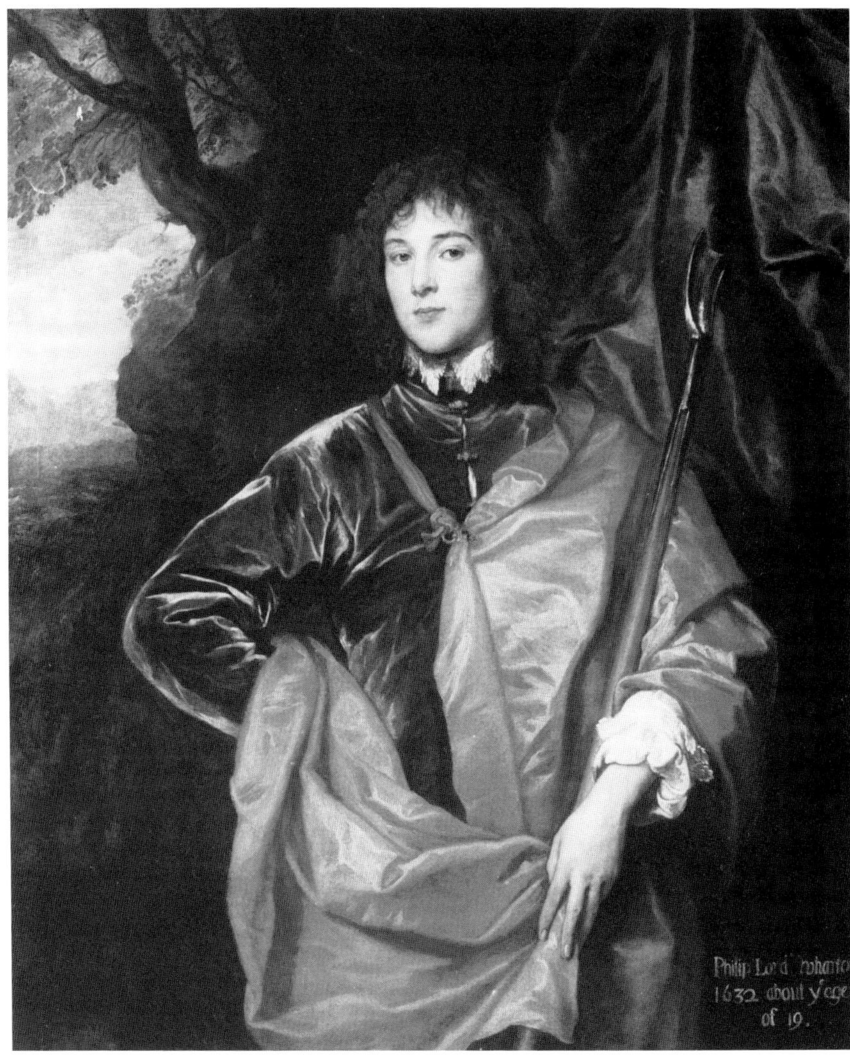

5. Anthony van Dyck, *Philip,
Lord Wharton*, 1632, oil on
canvas
National Gallery of Art, Washington

repertoire for the rest of the century. The in-
cidents selected, whether they were public
affairs such as the king's launching a new
flagship, private matters such as the recovery
of a friend from the smallpox, or odd circumstances of love or friendship, could form the
basis for poems that were aimed at consoli-
dating relations within the privileged group
of those concerned or of those who could understand the allusions. We can see how Van
Dyck was soon being commissioned to produce occasional paintings. Philip, Lord Wharton, chose to commemorate his involvement
in some court pastoral entertainment (fig.
5)—he had obviously won the prize for the
best-dressed shepherd of the year, 1632.
Suckling, as we can now appreciate, thanks
to Malcolm Rogers' decipherment of his portrait, wished to memorialize the production

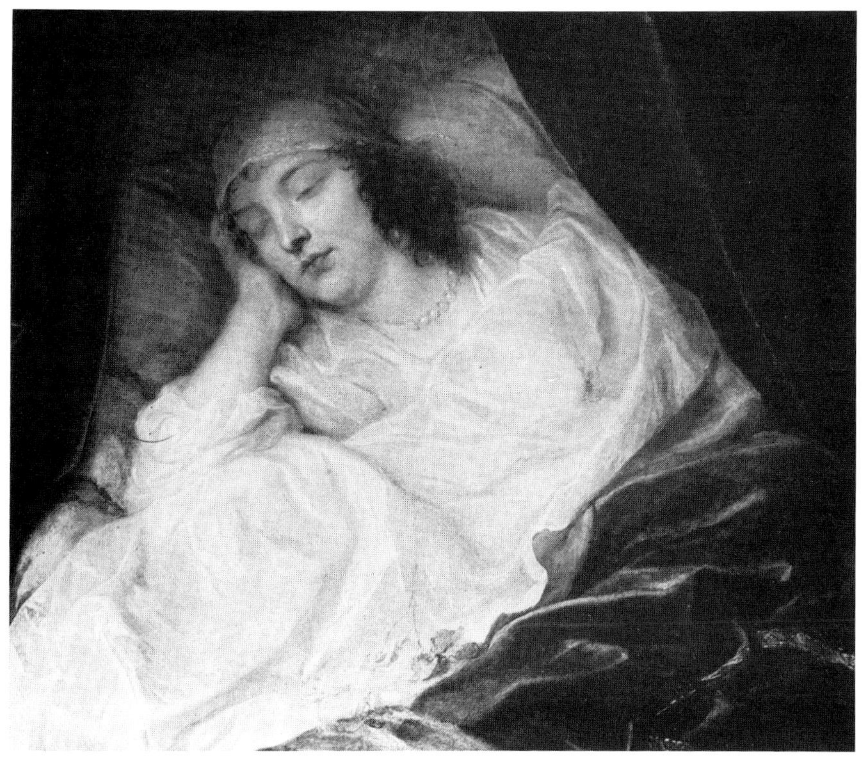

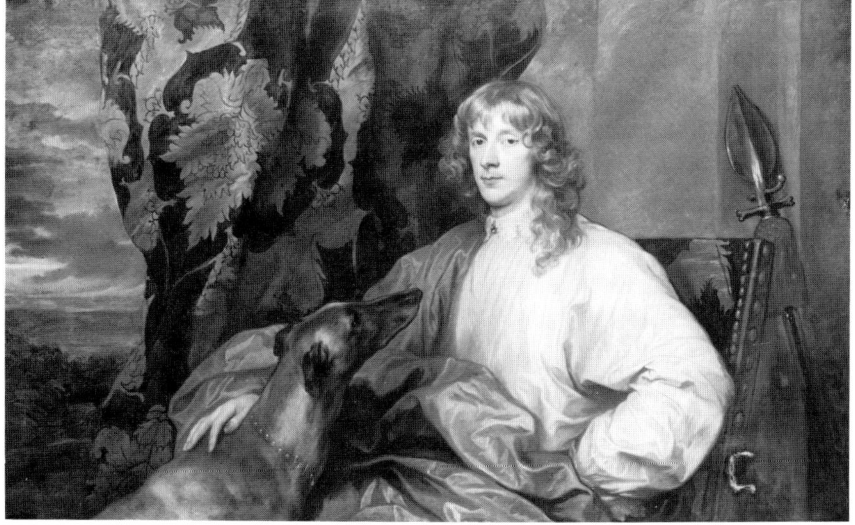

6. Anthony van Dyck,
*Venetia, Lady Digby, on
Her Deathbed*, 1633,
oil on canvas
Dulwich Picture Gallery, London

7. Anthony van Dyck, *James
Stuart, 4th Duke of Lennox
and 1st Duke of Richmond*,
c. 1632–1633, oil on canvas
Iveagh Bequest, Kenwood

ferred to recall his dog's faithfulness and courage in saving him from a boar when out hunting (fig. 7).[5]

An occasional painting of a more poignant kind is the double portrait in which the sitters have been identified as the poet and dramatist Thomas Killigrew and the courtier William, Lord Crofts, in mourning for the two sisters of Lord Crofts, one of whom had been Killigrew's wife (fig. 8).[6] As they sit together, remembering their defunct kin, Killigrew gazes at the viewer with a drained, expressionless look, as if too worn by grief to respond to any ordinary business of life. His hand lies heavily on his lap in a dead weight of sorrow, holding a crumpled paper on which two designs for funeral monuments can be made out. Discreet tokens of his love are displayed: his wedding ring on a black ribbon round his wrist, a crucifix with the initials of his dead wife. His friend and brother-in-law Crofts attempts to engage his attention, without success. Crofts, too, is distracted by grief: his gown is unbuttoned at the back, his hair hangs disheveled and unkempt. The tonality of the painting reinforces the mood of desolation. The black and white of the men's costumes are set against the washed-out coloring of the background. The broken stump of a pillar telling of life cut short occupies the central ground of the painting, while a region of featureless cloud hangs behind the scene. It is a masterly depiction of mourning, a painted elegy that shows the sorrowing survivors, not the object of their grief. It is also a painting that is a counterpart of a poem.[7] The Caroline elegy, so numerous a genre, commonly recorded the effects of loss on family and friends as well as praising the qualities of the departed. A significant part of a memorial poem by Carew or Waller, for example, is an exploration of the emotions aroused by death and the thoughts thereby provoked of our transience and mortality. Killigrew, himself a poet, must have appreciated the elegiac power of Van Dyck's achievement in this painting.

Perhaps the most memorable of Van Dyck's occasional paintings is the double portrait of the earl and countess of Arundel known as the Madagascar portrait (fig. 9), which was presumably painted as a record of Arundel's decision to undertake the colo-

of his Persian tragedy *Aglaura*, in 1637, by posing in pseudo-oriental costume and declaring his affinity with Shakespeare by perusing *Hamlet* among the rocks.[3] Sir Kenelm Digby had his friend Van Dyck record the beauty of his dead wife (fig. 6). (She died young and unexpectedly, thought by some to have been the victim of an experiment in cosmetic medicine by her husband, who had given her viper wine to preserve her beauty.[4]) James Stuart, later duke of Richmond, pre-

nization of Madagascar in 1639–1640. Arundel was dejected after the failure of the expedition against the Scots that he had led in 1639—the armor beneath his ermine and the baton prominently raised remind the viewer of his roles as captain general of the army and the earl marshal of England. As a result of his poor military showing, and perhaps also as a result of his great debts, Arundel thought of leaving England, and contemplated the settlement of Madagascar as a way out of his depressing circumstances. The project had originally been invented by Prince Rupert in 1636 as an outlet for his frustrated energies. The ambitious design had been celebrated by Davenant in his exotic poem "Madagascar," in which he foresaw the glorious rule of Rupert over the island of spice and treasure; but Rupert, like Arundel after him, never set sail. Calling on Van Dyck, whose patron he had long been, to put a fine gloss on events, Arundel sat with Aletheia his countess for a portrait to mark the new beginning. Aletheia holds the instruments of navigation somewhat in the manner of the muse of mathematics or astronomy, while Arundel casually covers the globe with his

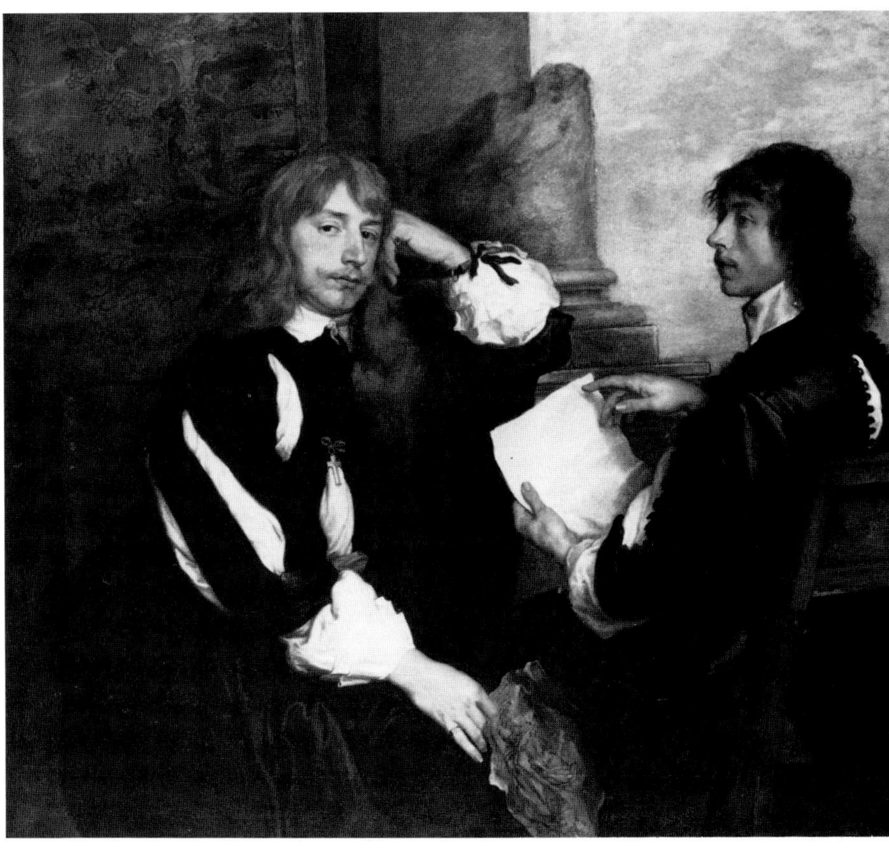

8. Anthony van Dyck, *Thomas Killigrew and William, Lord Crofts,* 1638, oil on canvas
Her Majesty Queen Elizabeth II

9. Anthony van Dyck, *Thomas Howard, 2d Earl of Arundel, with Aletheia, Countess of Arundel,* 1639, oil on canvas
Duke of Norfolk

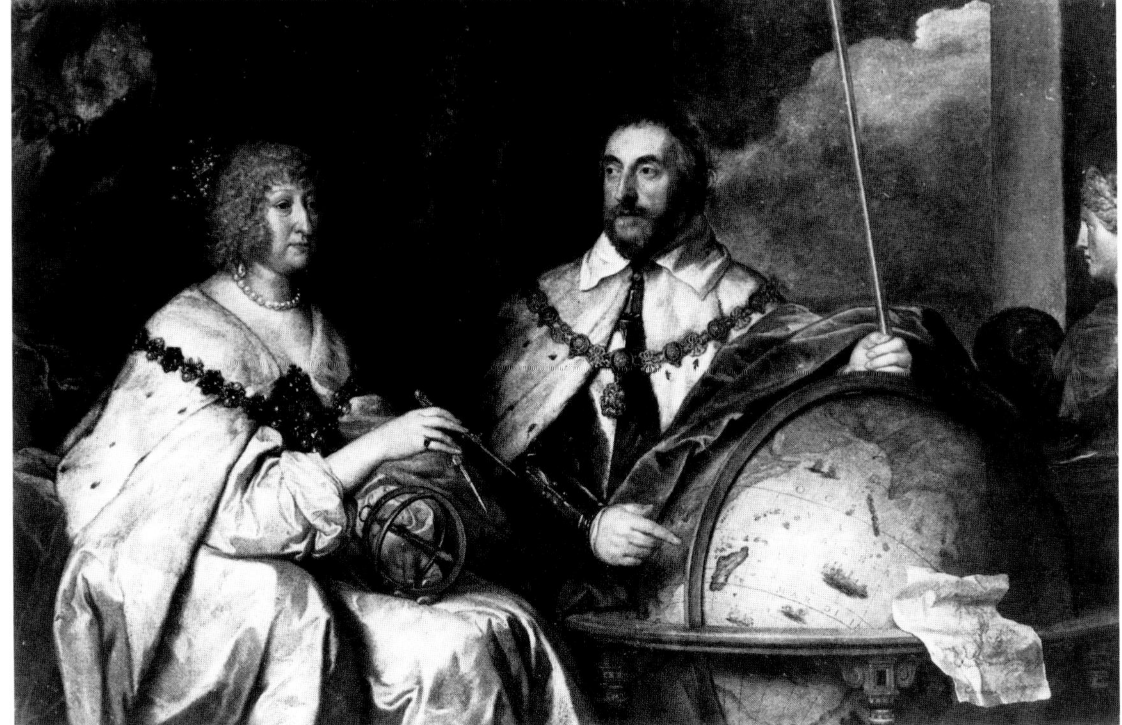

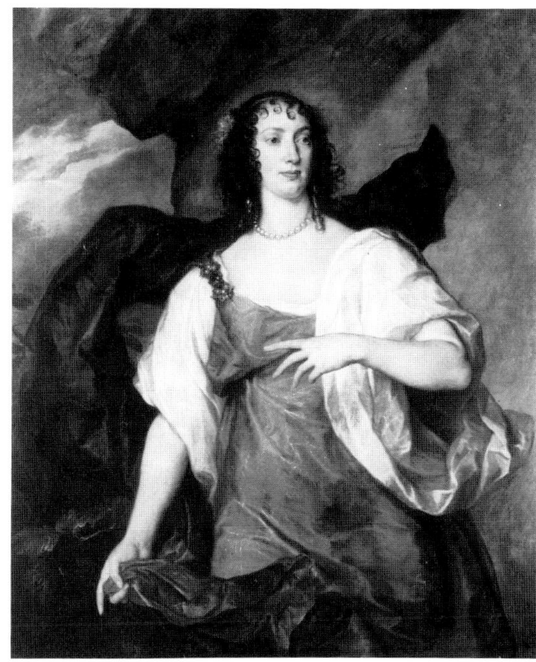

10. Anthony van Dyck, *Olivia Porter*, c. 1637, oil on canvas
Duke of Northumberland

11. Anthony van Dyck, *Sir Endymion Porter and Van Dyck*, c. 1635, oil on canvas
Museo del Prado, Madrid

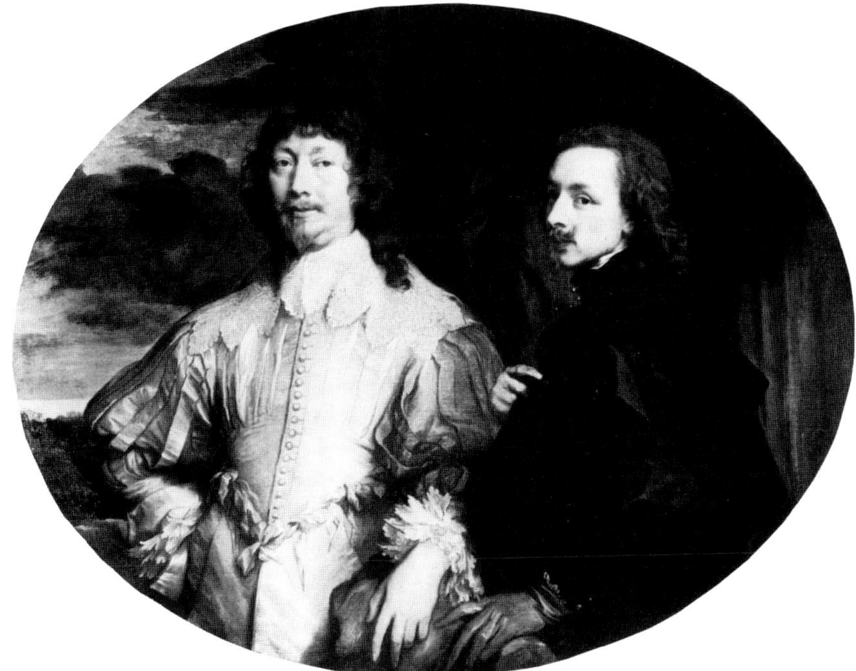

Turning now to another aspect of Van Dyck's work that complements the practice of the poets of Charles I's reign, I would like to consider Van Dyck's role in the advancement of civility. This involved the refinement of self-presentation among other things, and the cultivation of a more graceful and sophisticated mode of conduct than had been evident at the court of King James. The poet Ben Jonson, in particular, had addressed himself to the problem of improving the social smoothness of the English by means of his poems of conduct and comportment, and the so-called Sons of Ben, the Cavalier poets, with Herrick and Lovelace foremost, carried on the good work in the 1630s. When Van Dyck appeared on the scene, he gave pictorial form to the new aesthetic of grace that the poets were urging on the English court, and his skill in arranging the poses of his subjects so obviously fulfilled the ideal that it is understandable why the poets responded to him so favorably. Herrick is the poet who is closest to Van Dyck in his depiction of the new stylishness and grace in court life. Relevant here are several poems on the dynamics of female costume that express an appreciation of sensuous, flowing beauty, most comparable to Van Dyck's art. Some of Herrick's poems to Julia are animated Van Dycks; we hear the rustle of those bewitching silk dresses:

Whenas in silks my Julia goes,
Then, then (me thinks), how sweetly flowes
That liquefaction of her clothes.

Next, when I cast mine eyes and see
That brave Vibration each way free;
O how that glittering taketh me![9]

There are many poems in Herrick's volume *Hesperides* or in Lovelace's *Lucasta* that concern themselves with the appeal of stylish femininity. Natural beauty enhanced by art makes for an irresistible combination of charms in poems such as Herrick's "The Vision," "Delight in Disorder," "Julia's Petticoat," or "What kind of Mistress he would have," or in Lovelace's "Gratiana Dancing and Singing," or "To Lucasta: The Rose." (If we wish to find the male equivalents of these poems of graceful display, we probably should

red cape and points to Madagascar. Antique busts look on at this proposed advance of civilization into the unknown. A clearing sky behind suggests an improvement of the earl's fortunes. The optimistic painting is as full of promise as Davenant's poem to Prince Rupert had been, and equally fallacious:

Here in a calme began thy regall sway;
Which with such cheereful hearts all did obey,

look to the court plays of the 1630s with their elegant, finely spoken, mannered heroes.)

The very names that the Cavalier poets chose for their mistresses are a feature of the idealizing process of presenting female beauty; Julia, Ellinda, Ianthe, Lucasta, Aramantha, and the like are perfections of their kind, and Van Dyck, too, by the artifice of his compositions, painted the higher selves of his female subjects. You sat to Van Dyck to be elevated and transformed by art into the new fashionable ideal of admirable beauty. The portrait of Olivia Porter (fig. 10) catches the mood of these poems wonderfully well. Half court lady, half goddess, in the vaguely pastoral setting that was so often affected by the poets (and by the circle of Queen Henrietta Maria),[10] she stops and turns in a dance or chase, her animated drapery flying around her as a sign of spiritedness. Her noble carriage, lustrous eyes, and shapely arms tell of her breeding, and the ringlets that frame her face mark her unmistakably as a member of the Caroline court. *O dea certe!*

It was presumably Olivia's husband, Endymion Porter, who provided the main link between Van Dyck and the poets of the court circle. Porter had been acquainted with Van Dyck as early as 1620, on the painter's first visit to London. He was an important intermediary in securing Van Dyck's return to England, for it was he, on behalf of King Charles, who had commissioned the painting of *Rinaldo and Armida* (Baltimore Museum of Art) that had convinced the king that he should attract Van Dyck to his service. (Would it be too fanciful to imagine that the swirling drapery of Olivia Porter was a reminiscence of Armida's costume in the painting that had gained Van Dyck his fortune at the English court?) Porter became one of Van Dyck's closest friends in London, the testimony of this friendship being the outstanding double portrait in the Museo del Prado (fig. 11), in which for the only time in his career Van Dyck painted himself with a companion. A confidant of King Charles, a friend and patron of many of the Caroline poets, a connoisseur and collector, Porter was a key figure in the artistic and diplomatic business of the court. A considerable number of poems were dedicated to him, notably by Herrick, Davenant, and Randolph, and it is clear that he represented the *beau idéal* of

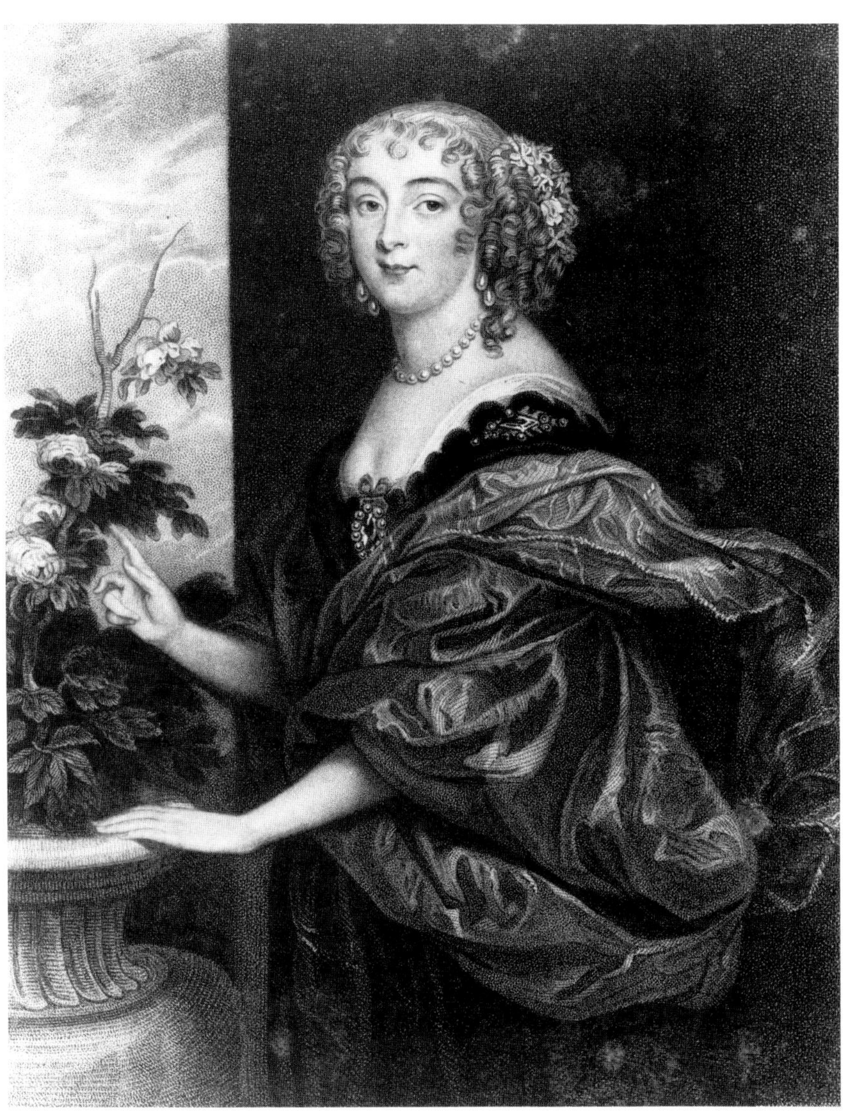

12. Engraving after Van Dyck, *Lady Dorothy Sidney*

courtiership for his contemporaries. His very name exemplified in a way the split personality of the Caroline courtier, part Greek shepherd, part solid Englishman. He was particularly close to Herrick, who wrote several poems of friendship to him, one of them amusingly exploiting the pastoral character of his name: "An Eclogue between Endymion Porter and Lycidas Herrick." In it Herrick complained of Porter's addiction to court life and described the countryside pining for his return. During his long stays in Whitehall Porter must have enlightened Van Dyck about the taste and topics current in the fashionable poetry of the time, and cued him to the particular affectations of English social life.

In turn, Cavalier poets responded to Van Dyck, who had rapidly become, in the words of Thomas Middleton, "a wondrous necessary man" at court. Those who praised him recognized their common endeavor. Waller, perhaps the most responsive of the poets to Van Dyck's art, somewhat ingenuously wrote of him: "So you the unfeigned truth rehearse, / (That I may make it live in verse)."[11] Waller and Van Dyck, both in their different ways, made their subjects live on an ideal plane. Waller's closeness to the painter's world is seen in the number of Caroline figures whom he celebrated in verse who were also painted by Van Dyck. There are at least eight, besides members of the royal family, and a list of them brings out the close-knit character of court life at Whitehall: Algernon Percy, earl of Northumberland, who was the Lord Admiral; Lucy Percy, countess of Carlisle, his sister; Northumberland's wife, Lady Anne Cecil; Lady Mary Feilding, the daughter of the earl and countess of Denbigh; Lady Anne Cavendish; Lady Rich; Lucius Carey, Viscount Falkland; Robert Sidney, earl of Leicester; and preeminently, Leicester's daughter, Lady Dorothy Sidney, who later became the countess of Sunderland. Dorothy Sidney (fig. 12) was painted at least four times by Van Dyck. To Waller she was Sacharissa, the nonpareil.

Let us look briefly at the two poems by Waller that address Van Dyck's portraits of his lady. "On my Lady Dorothy Sidney's picture" exclaims how the painter has been able to combine the love-provoking excellencies of this best of women into one enchanting face. Here the painter is superior to the poet, Waller maintains, because when Sir Philip Sidney (Dorothy's great-uncle) sought to show the full range of female beauty in his romance *Arcadia*, he had to divide its properties into two ideal portraits, Philoclea and Pamela:

The matchless Sidney, that immortal frame
Of perfect beauty on two pillars placed;
Not his high fancy could one pattern, graced
With such extremes of excellence, compose;
Wonders so distant in one face disclose!

But Van Dyck, inspired by the miracle that is Sacharissa, has caught all the varied glories of ideal beauty in a single face, and done full honor to her perfection.

The next poem in Waller's collection is the one addressed "To Vandyck," and it is clear from the setting that the poem primarily again concerns Van Dyck's painting of Sacharissa. What can we learn from it about

an interested party's response to his art? The emphasis is on the extraordinary, vital touches that Van Dyck can give to a face, so that the beholder is not only struck by its beauty, but inflamed by its fire. This is no mirror image of nature, but the painting has the force of nature to produce in the viewer just those effects that the woman herself arouses.

Strange that thy hand should not improve
The beauty only, but the fire;
Not the form alone, and grace,
But act and power of a face.

Waller smilingly suggests that Van Dyck must have detained the lady for many sittings in order to gaze on her beauty. Nature

. . . for many thousand years
Seems to have practised with much care
To frame the race of women fair;
Yet never could a perfect birth
Produce before, to grace the earth,[12]

until she contrived Sacharissa, her masterpiece. Astonished by her perfection, Van Dyck has surpassed himself, and found "immortal colours" to limn this deathless piece. How was it done? By a sublime mystery: to give such life to his art, Van Dyck "has climbed higher / Than did Prometheus for his fire."

Van Dyck's presence at the English court gave a new edge to the old debate about the supremacy of painting or poetry. Conventionally, the matter had been settled to the satisfaction of the poets, because they saw no painter who really challenged them in the portrayal of beauty, character, and presence. The capacity to move the viewer or reader to respond, as it were, to the living personality was an accepted criterion of excellence. Although this effect was commonly regarded in seventeenth-century England as one of the undisputed accomplishments of poetry or imaginative prose, we have seen that Waller was willing to grant Van Dyck supremacy over poets in registering the "act and power of a face."[13]

The contest between poetry and painting was fought with particular passion around the figure of Lady Venetia Digby, whose exceptional beauty, universally acknowledged, became a challenge to poets and painters alike. Which art could most convincingly capture the magic of her presence, the effects of her startling beauty, her intelligence and spirituality? Ben Jonson, the master of the Cavalier poets, who had been largely responsible for bringing together the components of this gallant and complimentary style of writing, had a particular devotion to Venetia, whom he honored as his muse. He composed a sequence of poems to her under the title of "Eupheme," or Fair Fame, the elegant name he bestowed on her. The sequence begins with a glamorized account of her childhood, and then we meet her in the prime of her beauty, awaiting the visit of a painter: "Sitting, and ready to be drawn." Jonson is above all conscious of the power of her beauty over him. It is so radiant, so vital a force, so sunlike that, although the mind may be delighted by it, it cannot be directly viewed. This is an experience of Platonic beauty. In order to capture this beauty, Jonson suggests that the painter frame it in emblematic terms, with Venetia's face like light breaking through clouds, and her garments not earthly but celestial:

Last, draw the circle of this globe,
   And let there be a starry robe
   Of constellations 'bout her hurled;
   And thou hast painted beauty's world.

An imaginative picture this, but in fact one that can only be painted by the poet. Next Jonson approaches the most difficult of tasks, how to represent the mind. Here, among ideas and abstractions, the poet feels confident of success: "Painter, you're come, but may be gone." The painter may only render the mind by images that offer analogy, not truth:

You could make shift to paint an eye
   An eagle towering in the sky,
   The sun, a sea, or soundless pit,
   But these are like a mind, not it.

No, to express a mind to sense
   Would ask a heaven's intelligence;
   Since nothing can report that flame
   But what's of kin to whence it came.[14]

It is the poet, who, inspired by his muse, can re-create through language the mysterious uniqueness of a mind and communicate its character to posterity. He can even preserve the charm of a voice, a feat quite beyond the powers of painting.

The voice so sweet, the words so fair,
   As some soft chime had stroked the air;

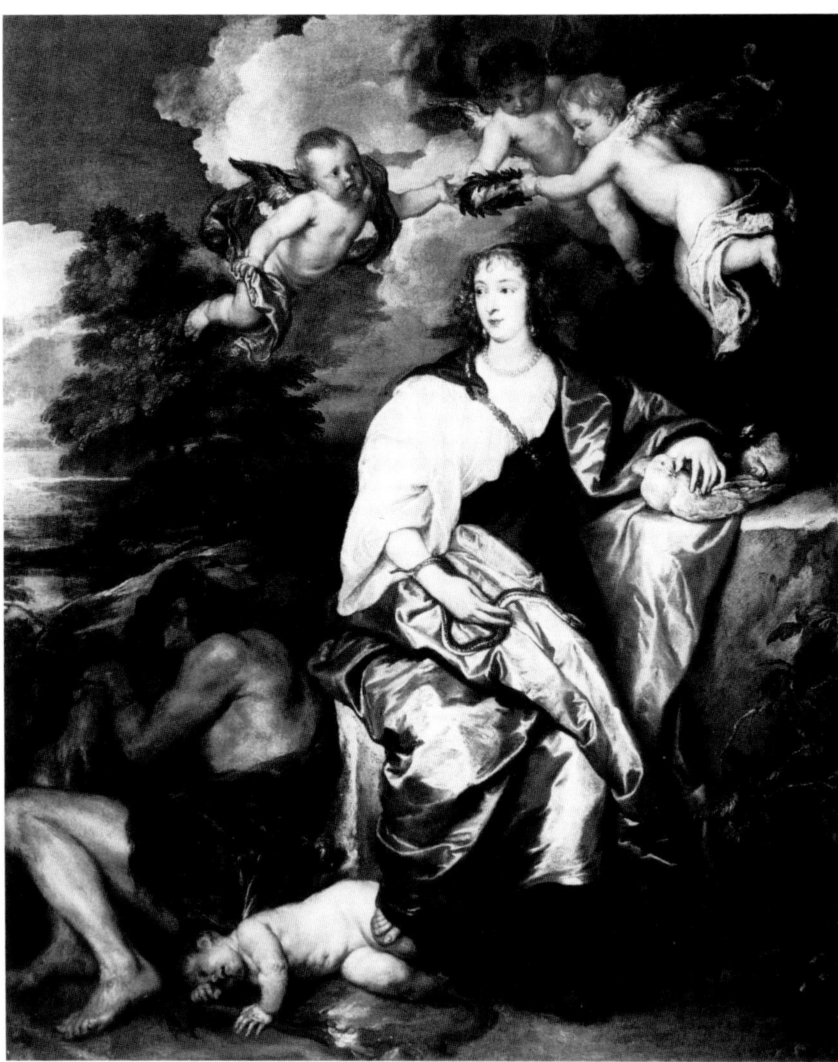

And though the sound were parted thence,
   Still left an echo in the sense.

13. Anthony van Dyck, *Venetia Stanley, Lady Digby, as Prudence*, 1633, oil on canvas
National Portrait Gallery, London

Jonson was adept at arguing for the superiority of the poet over the painter, for he had fought over this issue for years with his fellow masque maker, Inigo Jones. In the Eupheme poems he confidently strikes off the phrases of intellectual suggestiveness that he had developed for use in the masques to describe the Platonic ideas that informed the beauty and harmony of the masquers. His final poem in the sequence, "Her Apotheosis," is on Venetia's death, which occurred in 1633. He records first his own violent grief at her death, then moves into a serener state; he imagines her entrance into heaven, where, body and mind now left behind, she becomes a spiritual form, redeemed and sainted. Of her salvation there is no doubt, he reassures his reader, who in the first instance would have been Sir Kenelm Digby, her husband.

Digby, who as well as being Jonson's patron was also an intimate friend of Van Dyck (they were said to have undertaken alchemical experiments together in order to improve their fortunes), commissioned several paintings of his wife, two of which relate to her death. One is the overpoweringly sad image that Digby had Van Dyck make of Venetia two days after her death (fig. 6), showing her as if asleep, only the fallen rose with its scattered petals suggesting otherwise. So unassuming a portrait that avoids any stylistic devices succeeds by its unconventional naturalness. Van Dyck has set aside his studio arts to provide a memorial keepsake for his friend: its very unpretentiousness is moving. If this was the private memento for her husband, the public memorial was of an altogether different nature. I am inclined to believe that *Venetia Stanley, Lady Digby, as Prudence* (fig. 13) is a posthumous painting, commissioned as part of Digby's program of vindicating his wife's reputation after her death. (In her youth she had been notorious for her amours, but "after her marriage she redeemed her Honour by her strict living."[15]) Her pose in this painting could be described as monumental, and her crowning with laurel by cherubs has a posthumous air about it—virtue rewarded after death. The allegorical scenario and her fixed posture give the painting the feeling of a life summed up and justified. In character Van Dyck's painting is quite close to the description of a figure in a Jonsonian masque, and it is quite possible that Jonson devised the scheme for this work. It certainly makes a statement about Venetia's character, but as a composition it is too busy, distracting, and cluttered to rank as more than a curiosity in Van Dyck's oeuvre. In painting an overtly "poetic" picture Van Dyck has given up some of his most winning habits of portraiture: spontaneity of manner, gracefulness of pose, and vivacity of feature. In addition, he has sacrificed his usual economy of attendant detail, an economy that helps concentrate the viewer's attention on the face and stance of the subject.

In the case of Venetia Digby's "portrait," Van Dyck and Jonson come off pretty evenly. Neither artist is in top form, and each is conscious of the conventions and approaches of the rival art. The Caroline poets returned with some regularity to a consideration of the scope and powers of the respective arts. Usually, as one might expect, they are prejudiced in favor of their own art, as, for example, is James Shirley in "To the Painter preparing to draw Mistress M.H.," or Carew in "To the Painter." These are somewhat similar poems, both patronizing toward the artist, instructing him how to portray the lady to best advantage and in effect painting the portrait for him in verse, only to remind him of what cannot be drawn: her voice in the first instance, her virtue in the second. Both of these properties are claimed as the mysterious center of personality. In contrast to these poets and Jonson, Waller took the side of the painter, and his two poems about Van Dyck offer unusual and indeed unprecedented praise, a testimony to the high admiration that Van Dyck could command among the poets. Waller's poems are a recognition that, for the first time, here is a painter who can excel the poets of England on their own ground, in praise of a woman's beauty and grace and the portrayal of her mind and character.

Finally, let us glance at Van Dyck's elegy by Abraham Cowley, who was a poet on the edges of the court, just establishing himself in the late 1630s. He was twenty-two when Van Dyck died in 1641. Cowley echoes Waller in commending the power that Van Dyck's paintings possess to evoke the same emotions as did their originals:

Let's all our solemn grief in silence keep
Like some sad Picture which he made to weep,
Or those who saw it, for none his works would
*   view*
Unmoved with same Passions which he
*   drew.*[16]

The poem, unfortunately, has no real coherence. It reaches out awkwardly after witty conceits, including the notion that as in life he painted images after nature, now, being dead, he can paint the Platonic ideas in the divine mind. Cowley naively praises the perfection of Van Dyck's life—*De mortuis nihil nisi bonum*—and addresses finally his widow in an attempt at consolation, ending with the perversely ingenious trope that his last, best work has been his newborn daughter, his wife's image to the life. The elegy is not a good poem, not very informative about Van Dyck or about contemporary reaction to him; sadly, it is an inadequate response to the extinction of one of the main sources of light at the Caroline court.

A more satisfactory memorial was the one that King Charles ordered to be placed on Van Dyck's tomb in St. Paul's Cathedral: *Antonius Van Dyck, qui, dum viveret, multis immortalitatem donaverit vitam. Functus est Carolus Primus, Magnae Britanniae, Franciae et Hiberniae Rex, Antonio Van Dyck, Equiti Aurato* ("Anthony Van Dyck, who while he lived, gave immortality to many. Charles I, king of Great Britain, France and Ireland, provided this monument for Sir Anthony Van Dyck"). Not many people received a memorial from King Charles. None deserved it more.

NOTES

1. See Roy Strong, *Van Dyck: Charles I on Horseback* (London, 1972), 65–74.

2. For an example of Charles' style and titles most fully proclaimed, consider the dedication of the 1640 edition of Bacon's *Advancement of Learning*: "Sacratissimo Domino Nostro Carolo, Dei Gratia Mag. Britanniae Franciae et Hiberniae Regi. Terrae Marisque Potentissimo Principi. Oceani Britannici ad Quatuor Mundi Plagas Dispartiti Imperatori. Domino Virginiae et Vastorum Territoriorum Adjacentium et Dispersarum Insularum in Oceano Occidentali."

3. Malcolm Rogers, "The Meaning of Van Dyck's Portrait of Sir John Suckling," *Burlington Magazine* 120 (1978), 741–745.

4. *Aubrey's Brief Lives*, ed. Oliver Lawson Dick (London, 1950), 100–101.

5. Oliver Millar, *Van Dyck in England* [exh. cat., National Portrait Gallery] (London, 1982), 91.

6. For a discussion of the identity of the sitters and of the symbolism of the painting see Oliver Millar, *The Tudor, Stuart and Early Georgian Pictures in the Collection of Her Majesty the Queen* (London, 1963), no. 156; Arthur Wheelock in Arthur K. Wheelock, Jr., et al., *Anthony Van Dyck* [exh. cat., National Gallery of Art] (Washington, 1990), 313; and Malcolm Rogers' article in this volume.

7. The appropriate pendant to this painting is the elegy by Francis Quarles, "Sighs at the Contemporary Deaths of those Incomparable Sisters, the Countesse of Cleaveland and Mistresse Cicily Killigrue" (1640). The poem is emblematic in form, composed of twenty-four stanzas in the shape of pyramids, each erected, as it were, to the memory of the dead sisters. The emotional movement of the poem is from deep sorrow to assurance of the ladies' heavenly felicity. Addressed to the sisters' mother, Lady Crofts, the poem does convey a desolating misery at their death, but the change to a note of Christian optimism—"We'll teach your tears to smile"—is too facile. The stoical mood of Van Dyck's painting has no parallel in the poem. Indeed, Quarles positively repudiates the kind of hopeless grief communicated by the painting, for in his dedicatory letter he writes: "Religion moderates, and with the surplusage of Nature's teares, mollifies the Stoick's heart."

8. "Madagascar," lines 327–332, in Sir William Davenant, *The Shorter Poems*, ed. A. M. Gibbs (Oxford, 1972), 18.

9. "Upon Julia's Clothes," from *The Poems of Robert Herrick*, ed. L. C. Martin (London, 1965), 261.

10. See Erica Veevers, *Images of Love and Religion: Queen Henrietta Maria and Court Entertainments* (Cambridge, 1989), 39–50.

11. "To Vandyck," lines 25–26, in *The Poems of Edmund Waller*, ed. G. Thorn Drury (London, 1893), 45.

12. Waller 1893, 45.

13. For an illuminating discussion of the rivalry between poetry and painting in the seventeenth century see Claire Pace, "'Delineated lives': Themes and Variations in Seventeenth-Century Poems about Portraits," *Word and Image* 2 (1986), 1–17.

14. "Eupheme: Her Mind," lines 9–16, in Ben Jonson, *Poems*, ed. Ian Donaldson (London, 1975), 264–265.

15. *Aubrey's Brief Lives* 1950, 101.

16. Abraham Cowley, "On the Death of Sir Anthony Vandike," in *Works* (London, 1674), 9.

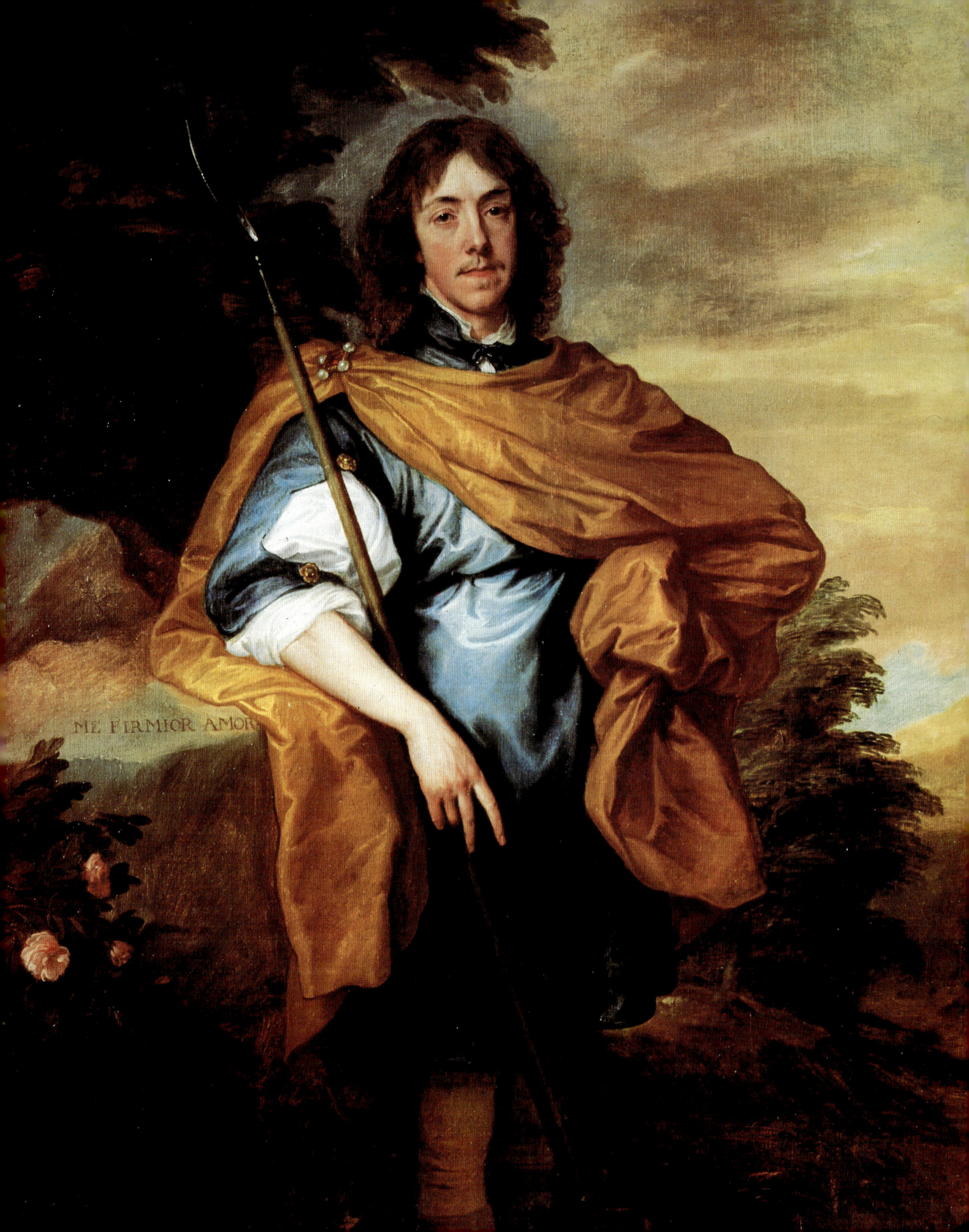
ME FIRMIOR AMOR

MALCOLM ROGERS
National Portrait Gallery, London

Van Dyck's Portrait of Lord George Stuart, Seigneur d'Aubigny, *and Some Related Works*

It is a truism that Van Dyck's style and tone as a portraitist were modified by the places and the societies in which he found himself; the works of one period are rarely mistaken for those of another. As a preface to my remarks about the artist's *Lord George Stuart, Seigneur d'Aubigny* (fig. 1) and related portraits, I will make some general points about Van Dyck's English period, some of which have direct relevance to the Aubigny portrait.

Encouraged by the fashions of the English court, Van Dyck adopts a wider palette in his English portraits than he uses at any other period. He continues to evoke the sonorous harmonies of black, red, and gold that he had deployed with such distinction in Genoa, Antwerp, and elsewhere, but a range of blues, pinks, yellows, and greens is now added to his repertoire. His color schemes are more diffuse and sophisticated: harmonies of contrasts, as in *Philip, Lord Wharton* or *Queen Henrietta Maria with Sir Jeffrey Hudson* (both National Gallery of Art, Washington). Heavy, embroidered materials are seen less frequently as the 1630s progress; the artist and his sitters favor light, shimmering silks, and the women wear diaphanous gauze stoles and lustrous strings of pearls and pearl-drop earrings as accessories.

As fabrics become lighter, so Van Dyck tends to abandon, except in portraits of the royal family, conventional day dress. William Sanderson, Van Dyck's near-contemporary, writes in his *Graphice* that

Van Dyck was the first painter "that e're put Ladies dress into a carelesse Romance,"[1] and the impact and originality of this step should not be underestimated. The same is true to an extent of Van Dyck's treatment of male dress: cloaks, for instance, which are so handsomely deployed in his earlier portraits, gradually give way to swags of less obviously utilitarian drapery. At their extreme—as in the *Sir John Suckling* (Frick Collection, New York) or the *Venetia Stanley, Lady Digby, as Prudence* (National Portrait Gallery, London)—Van Dyck's costumes (and they surely must be his inventions rather than his clients') resemble in a generalized way Inigo Jones' costume designs for court masques,[2] in which many of Van Dyck's sitters had themselves performed. Such outfits evidently gave an effect of timelessness and nobility that the artist's patrons favored.

Alongside the increasingly romantic treatment of dress is a perceptible change in attitude to characterization. Although Van Dyck is still capable of painting a haughty prince or an intense and intellectual statesman, he increasingly evokes a gentler, more reflective quality: an aristocratic *sprezzatura*. We do not look to Lady Mary Villiers (North Carolina Museum of Art, Raleigh) or to Lady Digby for intellectual qualities, and the mood of Van Dyck's female sitters ranges from the mildly flirtatious to one of soporific reverie. The aspect of his male sitters tends to be a shade melancholic and remote.

It is perhaps symptomatic that in this period the seated full-length portrait all but disappears from Van Dyck's repertoire, except in the case of a handful of allegorical portraits of women.[3] It is a format that Van Dyck had used throughout his earlier career to convey the forceful character of powerful men who ruled councils and noble women with large households at their command. His English women (and to a lesser extent his men) are very different from his earlier sitters in temperament. It is not surprising, therefore, that they favored the more intimate format of the standing three-quarter-length portrait, or that the double three-quarter-length of two friends or relatives—a form that Van Dyck virtually created—was so popular, stressing as it does subtle social and emotional intimacies and the closeness of the court circle. The range of accessories narrows: there are fewer gloves, fans, dogs, and, indeed, children in evidence. The favorites are flowers, above all roses—emblems of the pleasures and pains of love, of beauty and mortality—a motif infrequently found in Van Dyck's earlier portraits.

The English sitters, like their ancestors of the Tudor and early Stuart periods, show a fondness for symbolism of a more or less esoteric kind. This is especially true of the fashionable Roman Catholic converts who patronized Van Dyck in the later 1630s, and of whom Lord George Stuart was one. In the *Dorothy Savage, Viscountess Andover, and Her Sister Elizabeth, Lady Thimbleby* (fig. 2), painted about the time of Lady Andover's marriage in 1637, the lady is shown in the saffron robes of a Roman bride, while her sister adopts the veil and attitude of *Pudicitia*.[4] An attendant angel with a basket of roses is the attribute of Saint Dorothea of Cappadocia, and is included here as an allusion to the sitter's first name.[5] This allusion to the name saint would have been especially appropriate since Lady Dorothy converted to Roman Catholicism at the time of her marriage, amid considerable controversy.[6] The portrait is a particularly extreme example of Van Dyck's approach to characterization at this period, and it may be that Lady Andover's rapt expression is intended to convey the ecstacy of a saint of love who had married and embraced the Roman Catholic church against all opposition.

Patrons might well suggest quite complex

programs. An example of this is the *Thomas Killigrew and William, Lord Crofts* (fig. 3) of 1638. The brothers-in-law are almost certainly shown in mourning for Killigrew's wife Cecilia Crofts, who died on 1 January 1638, and for her sister Anne, countess of Cleveland, who died fifteen days later. Killigrew wears tokens of his late wife, and both men, who wear black, are also swathed in

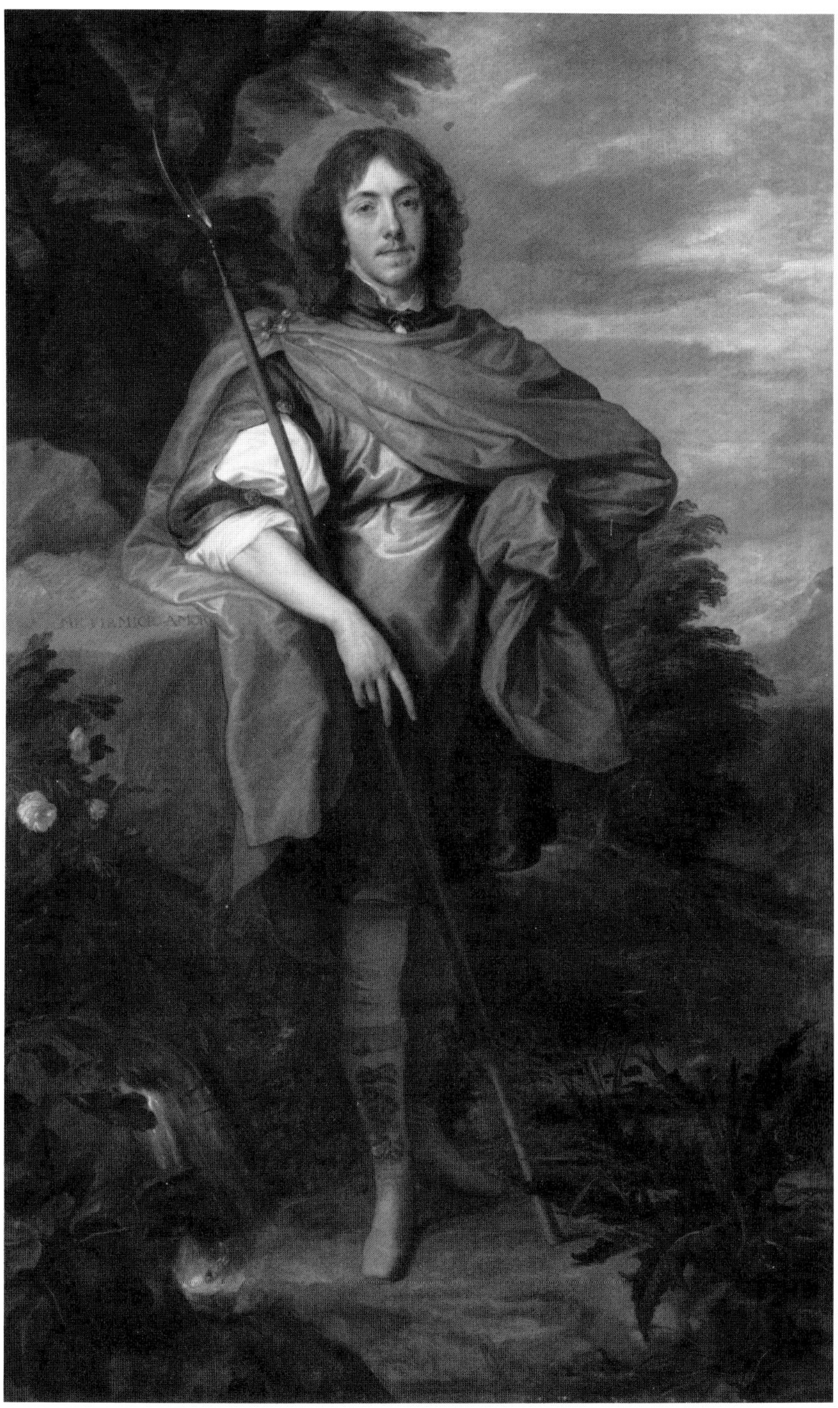

1. Anthony van Dyck, *Lord George Stuart, Seigneur d'Aubigny*, c. 1638, oil on canvas
National Portrait Gallery, London

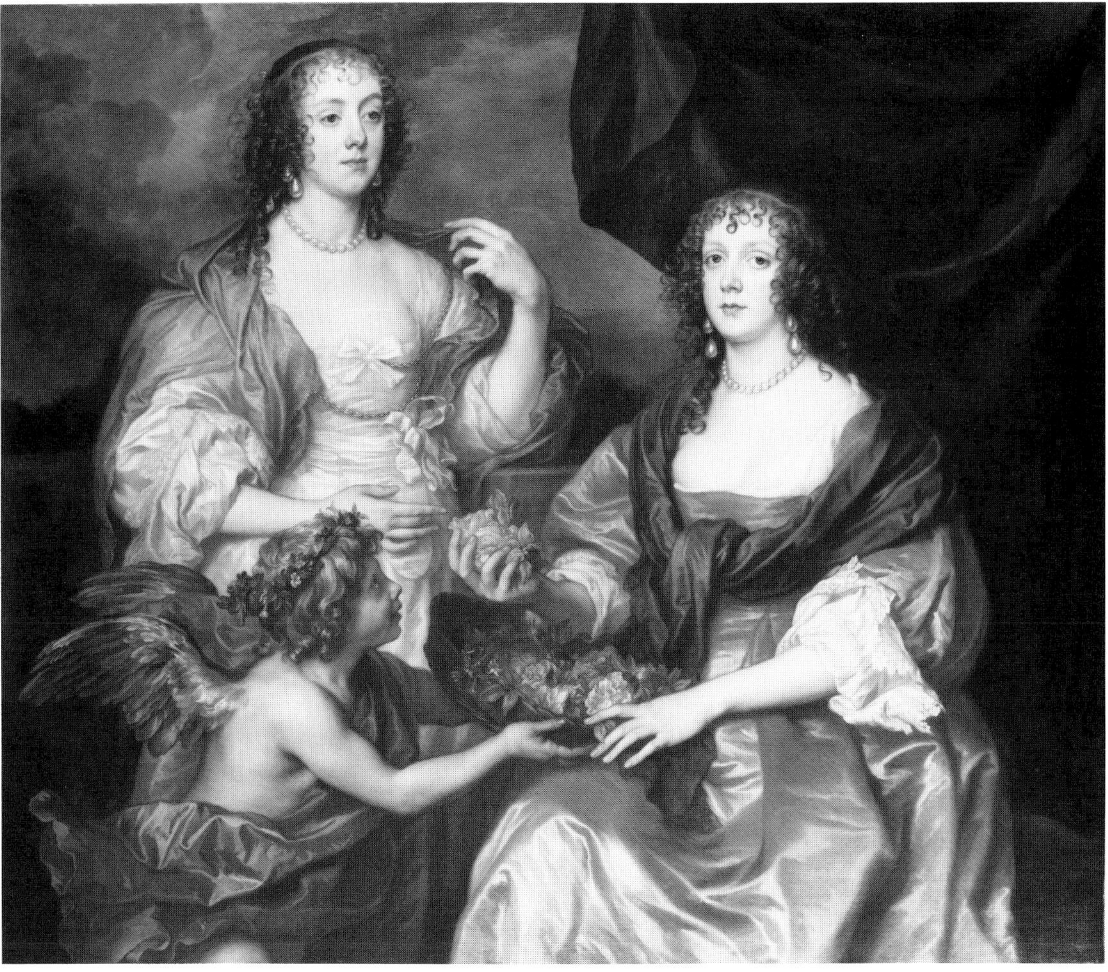

black drapery. A broken column, emblem of fortitude, is in the background. Sir Oliver Millar has given a masterly analysis of the painting,[7] but still a central point has not been emphasized. Killigrew almost lets slip from his hand a blue-gray sheet of paper, which is in shadow. On this is depicted a drawing of two female statues on pedestals— perhaps funerary sculptures; the one, with the figure of a child clasped to her side, may be intended for Cecilia Killigrew, whose son Henry had been born in April 1637; the other for Lady Cleveland. The drawing is no doubt intended to commemorate the dead women. The point, however, is made by Lord Crofts, a hot-tempered, quarrelsome youth who had been expelled from France for meddling in politics and who had recently converted to Roman Catholicism. He holds and gestures to a *blank* sheet of paper on which the light falls directly and which is at the center of the composition. The portrait is devised so as to contrast the present blank with what is past and gone. It has been suggested that Lord Crofts "attempts to bring him (*Killigrew*) solace."[8] He does not; he points out the absoluteness of the loss so that it may be more keenly felt. In the same spirit Sir Kenelm Digby, another Roman Catholic patron, commissioned Van Dyck to paint Lady Digby on her deathbed (Dulwich Picture Gallery, London): not to remind him of how she looked when living, but so as he might recall her aspect when dead. He kept the portrait by him, and at night meditated on it: "and by the faint light of candle, me thinkes I see her dead indeed."[9]

In his English period Van Dyck sets his sitters in open country for virtually the first time. In his earlier periods they are habitually seen in umbrageous interiors or on the terraces of palaces; there may be a suggestion

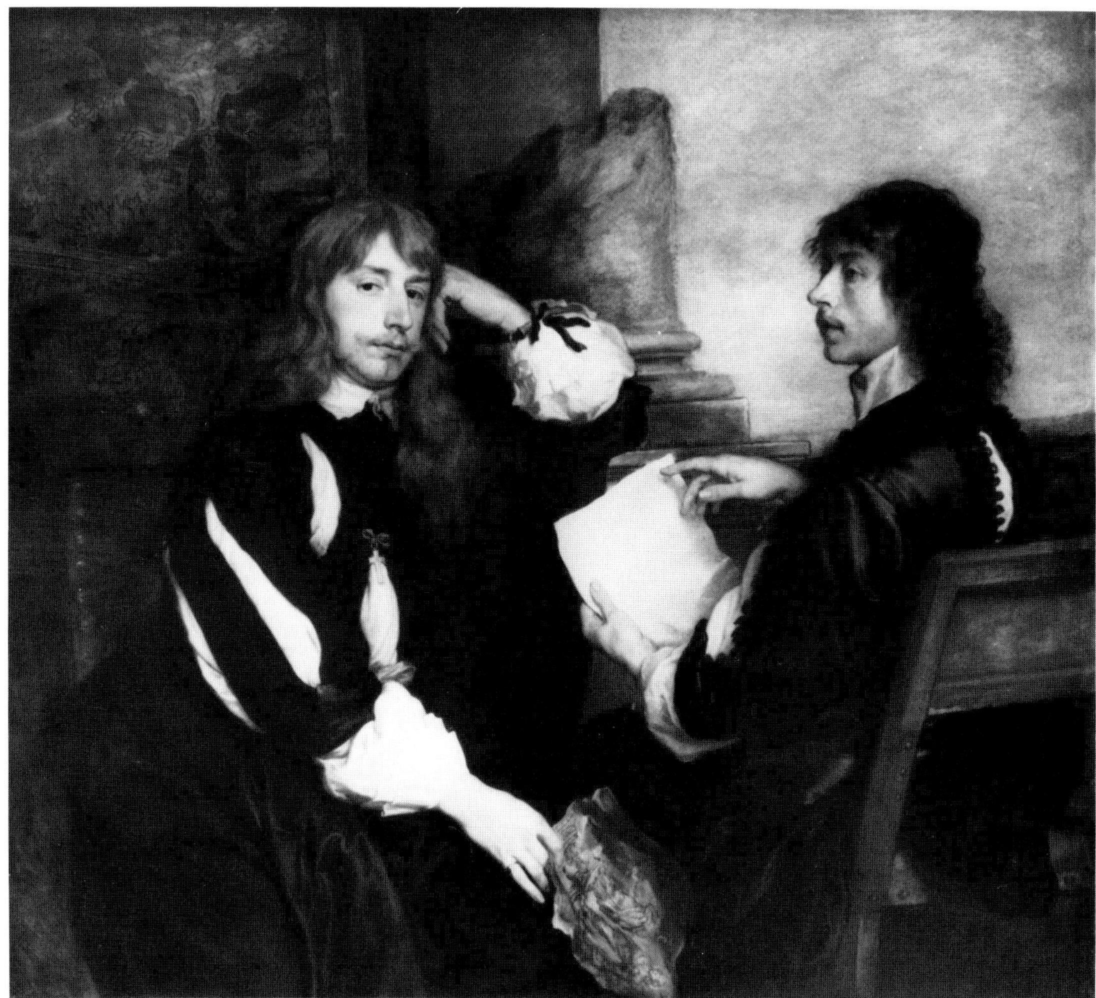

of landscape, but it is framed by a column or balustrade. Exceptions are the "Little To-bias" (Palazzo Durazzo Pallavicini, Genoa), c. 1623–1625; the *Count Henrik van den Bergh* (Museo del Prado, Madrid), 1626–1629, which once belonged to Charles I; and one or two equestrian portraits. In England Van Dyck made landscape drawings directly from nature, as well as studies of plants. He must also have been influenced by the character of London, with its parks and gardens, the vil-lages and rolling countryside nearby, so dif-ferent in scale and character from formal Genoa and bustling Antwerp, and also by the prevalent fashion for pastoral poetry and drama. His sitters move, each in his or her own way, through the countryside: *Charles I on Horseback* (National Gallery, London) as a great commander (which he was not), in a rich Titianesque landscape, or *Olivia Porter* (fig. 4), another Roman Catholic, on foot in

more barren terrain. It is hard to envisage the Marchesa Elena Grimaldi (National Gallery of Art, Washington) contemplating such a rash excursion among the rocks and bushes, wearing only her shift, a confection of draperies, and a simple string of pearls; or that the formidable marchesa would remain so utterly oblivious of the consequences of her actions. Yet Mrs. Porter appears a noble creature, bounding with energy and grace amid the stubborn rocks, emblems of the baser levels of creation.[10]

The National Portrait Gallery in London acquired its portrait of Lord George Stuart, Seigneur d'Aubigny (fig. 1) by purchase in 1987, shortly after it had been sold on the art market by the earl of Darnley. Lord George was the third son of Esmé Stuart, 3d duke of Lennox, and a second cousin of James VI of Scotland and I of England. Born in 1618, he succeeded to the seigneury of Aubigny-sur-

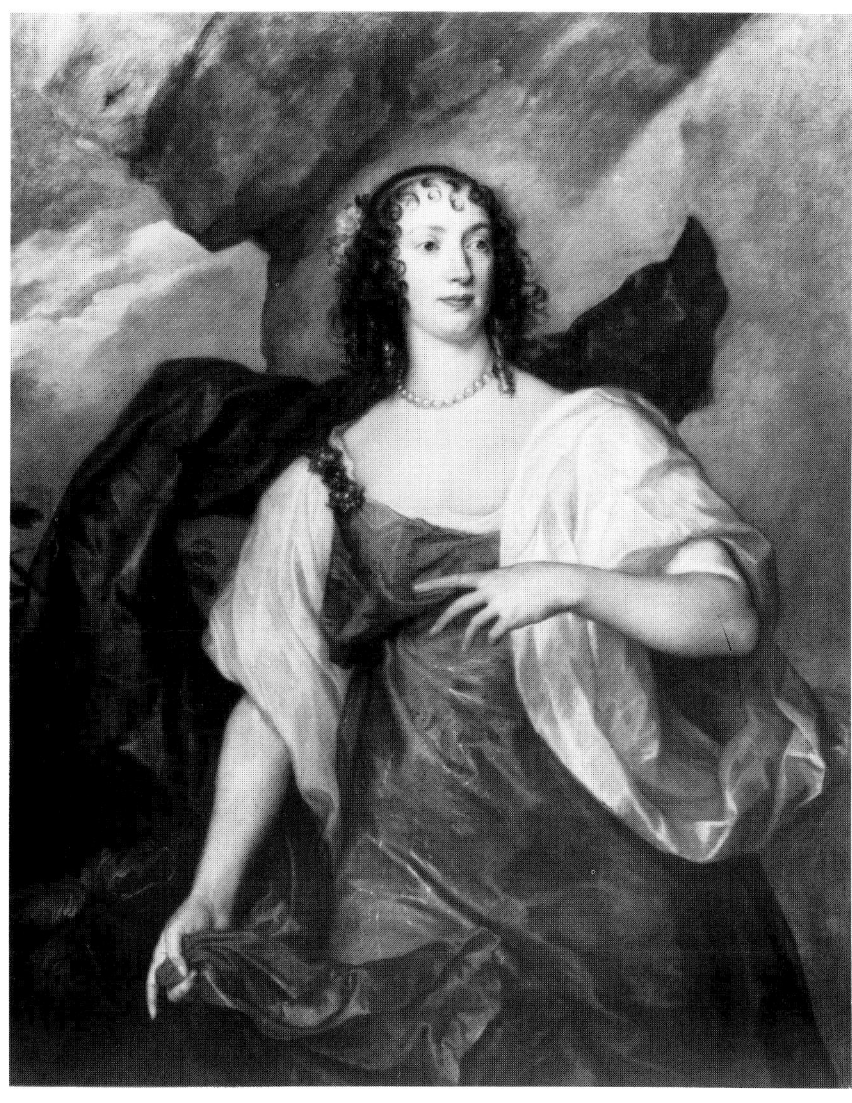

4. Anthony van Dyck, *Olivia Porter*, later 1630s, oil on canvas
Duke of Northumberland

Nère in Berry, close to the Loire, in 1632, at age fourteen, on the death of an elder brother. He was the ninth member of this warlike family to hold the seigneury, which had been awarded to Sir John Stewart of Darnley in 1423.

After the death of his father in 1624, Lord George, under the guardianship of Charles I, was brought up with his brothers and sisters in France by his French grandmother. He was Roman Catholic. References to his early career—indeed to his career as a whole—are scarce. In 1633 he is mentioned as a student at the College of Navarre in Paris. In October 1634 Charles I granted him license to travel for three years with six servants and £100 for expenses. In March 1636 he was a member of the suite of the earl of Arundel on an embassy from The Hague to the Emperor Ferdi-

nand II, but he was back in Paris by 5 August 1636, when he did homage to Louis XIII for his seigneury. Soon afterward he must have gone to England, where, like three of his brothers, James, duke of Richmond, and Lords John and Bernard Stuart, he was painted by Van Dyck. James, the eldest brother, sat to the artist on two occasions, first, a little before he was appointed a Knight of the Garter (1633), for the half-length with a greyhound belonging to the Iveagh Bequest, Kenwood, London (fig. 5). The head of this type reappears in the portrait of him as Paris (in his shirt, holding an apple) in the Musée du Louvre and in the full-length in the Metropolitan Museum of Art, New York (fig. 6), in which he wears the Garter for the first time and is again seen with his faithful hound.[11] The second sitting is represented by a full-length portrait in black in the collection of the duke of Buccleuch, in which Richmond again displays the Garter. His head is turned slightly to the right, and he wears a moustache, suggesting a later date, perhaps about 1635.

Lord John Stuart and Lord Bernard Stuart (later earl of Lichfield), Lord George's younger brothers, sat once, and probably twice, together to Van Dyck. First, for the double portrait (fig. 7) recently acquired by the National Gallery, London. The painting shares a provenance with the National Portrait Gallery picture of Lord George Stuart. One of Van Dyck's most haughty compositions, this was certainly painted before 1639, early in which year the brothers set off on a three-year Continental tour, when they were eighteen and seventeen years old respectively. The painting is, indeed, likely to have been executed a little earlier, for what may be a second, slightly later portrait of them also belongs to the National Gallery (fig. 8). This double portrait was identified in the later seventeenth century when it belonged to the 11th earl of Kent as Lords John and Bernard Stuart by Van Dyck, and as such was copied in the 1690s by John Closterman for the duke of Argyll.[12] In this century both identification and attribution of this once celebrated painting have been doubted,[13] but recent cleaning and conservation have revealed an original by Van Dyck. As for the identities, it seems reasonable, in the absence of positive evidence to the contrary, to accept the early tradition, for the likenesses are far from incompatible with the earlier painting. In both pictures the young men are portrayed in essentially stagy settings. Their costume, however, is treated with considerably more freedom in the later work, and great play is made with swags of drapery, falling in broadly classical forms, which elaborate and animate the composition. The effect is one of somewhat theatrical informality, emphasized by the simple vest worn by the figure on the left, his soft buskins, and his companion's slippers.

In the portrait of the Seigneur d'Aubigny (fig. 1) the costume is wholly fanciful, bearing no relation to contemporary day dress. Lord George is presented full length in a landscape, wearing a long blue vest and over this a deep-gold cloak. In the crook of his right arm is a spud or *houlette*. His fawn buskins are decorated with little blue bows. He leans on a rock from which a spring flows, and on the rock is inscribed the Latin motto: ME FIRMIOR AMOR. Over the spring grows a rosebush; in the right foreground is a thistle; in the background a wooded landscape with distant mountains. Aubigny's face wears an expression of intense melancholy. It is easy to understand why the eighteenth-century mount of the related drawing in the Victoria and Albert Museum (fig. 11) is inscribed: "Sir Philip Sidney in the character of ye author of ye Arcadia." In an earlier tradition of painting the portrait has close affinities in treatment and composition (in reverse) with Marcus Gheeraerts the Younger's *Captain Thomas Lee* (fig. 9) of 1594. Lee stands full length in a landscape, wearing the costume of an Irish soldier, and is accompanied by a Latin motto: *Facere et pati Fortia*. In format, costume, the use of a Latin motto, and, to some extent, in mood, the portrait is closest in Van Dyck's own oeuvre to his portrait of the courtier and dramatist Sir John Suckling (Frick collection, New York), a Roman Catholic convert who was later to revert to Protestantism. I have argued elsewhere[14] that this portrait illustrates a thematic program devised by the sitter, in collaboration with the artist, and dates from about 1638. Evidence suggests that the portrait of Lord Aubigny dates from the same period, and that, like the Suckling, it embodies a program of deep personal significance to the sitter.

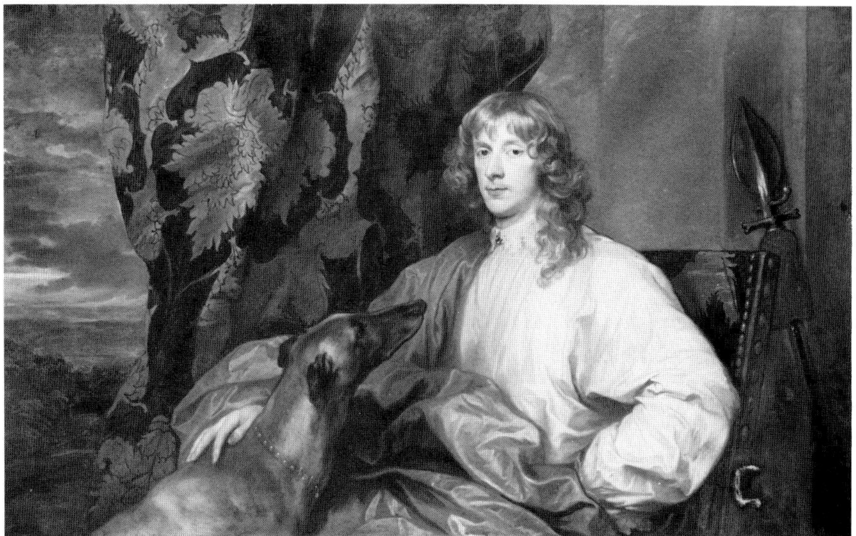

5. Anthony van Dyck, *James Stuart, 4th Duke of Lennox and 1st Duke of Richmond*, c. 1632–1633, oil on canvas
Iveagh Bequest, Kenwood

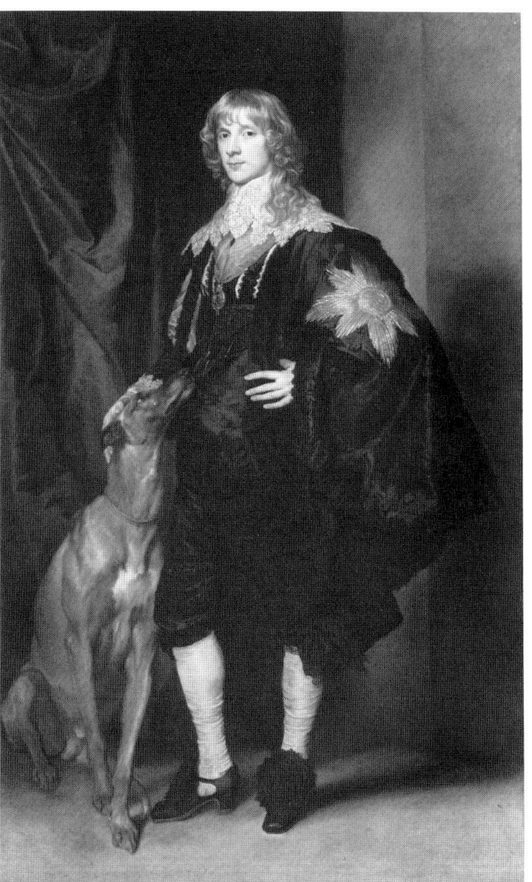

6. Anthony van Dyck, *James Stuart, 4th Duke of Lennox and 1st Duke of Richmond*, c. 1633, oil on canvas
Metropolitan Museum of Art, New York

Although the portrait of Lord Aubigny is likely to date from the later 1630s, it is closely related to an earlier portrait by Van Dyck, the three-quarter-length of Philip, 4th baron Wharton (fig. 10), the greatest beau of his time, which probably dates from 1632

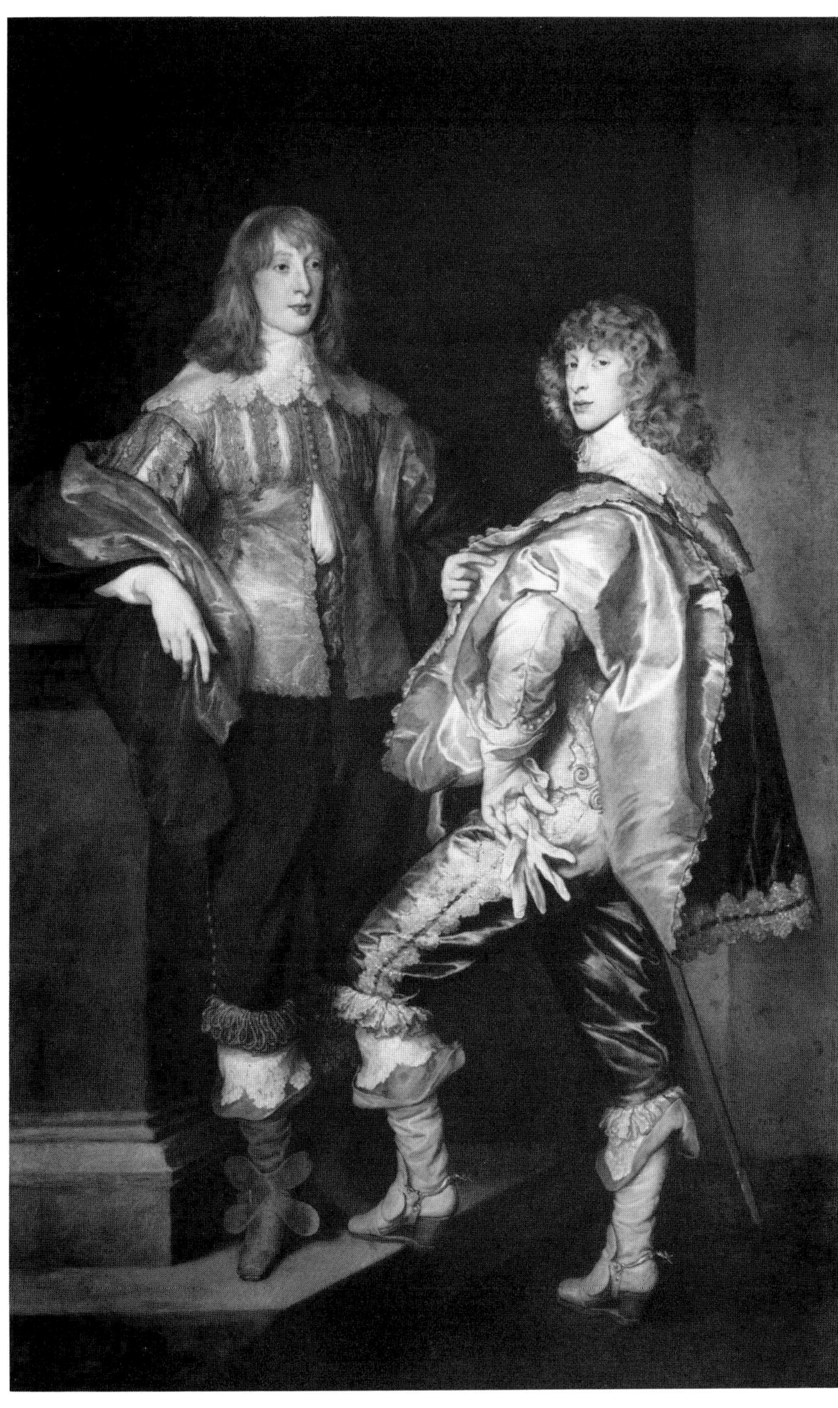

7. Anthony van Dyck, *Lord John Stuart and Lord Bernard Stuart, later Earl of Lichfield,* c. 1637, oil on canvas
National Gallery, London

the two portraits is obvious, but the point ought to be made that the pose of the *Aubigny* derives in reverse from the *Wharton,* with alterations to the tilt of the head and the spacing of the fingers. This argues that there was in Van Dyck's studio some record of the earlier composition preserved for future use.

The *Aubigny* is an excellent example of Van Dyck's late style, when the use of studio assistants was inherent in his practice. By this method, which Van Dyck described in a conversation with Eberhard Jabach,[16] he would at the first sitting sketch out his initial thoughts for the portrait, then set the sitter in the chosen pose and in the space of a quarter of an hour, on a "little piece of blue paper," produce a finished composition sketch. This sketch was then handed to studio assistants who would lay in the design on the canvas. At subsequent sittings Van Dyck himself would paint the head and hands of the portrait, while, between times, the assistants would bring the other parts of the composition to a fair stage of completion, ready for the master to add the finishing touches. The portrait of Lord Aubigny shows this process in the beautiful, melancholy head and expressive hand, both finely and carefully painted. The costume and landscape are finished with greater speed. In particular, the contours of the draperies over the left arm are put in with the greatest boldness and vigor, giving an almost sculptural effect. Sir Oliver Millar, when he catalogued the painting, missed "Van Dyck's characteristic freshness of touch in the foliage,"[17] but, though worn, the vegetation appears entirely autograph. Any weakness lies not in the quality of the painting, but in the unconvincing integration of these elements into the composition—notably the awkwardly placed thistle. Millar also notes that "the head . . . is slightly out of proportion" (that is, too large), which may suggest that the portrait was painted to hang high.

Although a number of composition and drapery studies for Van Dyck's English portraits survive, not one of his finished studies on blue paper for a whole composition is known. However, it may be worth reconsidering a drawing on blue-gray paper in the Victoria and Albert Museum, London (fig. 11), from the collection of Jonathon Richardson,

and is one of the earliest, perhaps the earliest, of the "outdoor" portraits that are such a feature of Van Dyck's English period. The sitter was nineteen, just a year younger than Lord George at the likely time of his portrait, and Arthur Wheelock has suggested that he was painted to mark his marriage in September 1632.[15] The general relationship between

who owned several drawings by Van Dyck.
This has been taken for a copy after Van
Dyck's portrait of Aubigny, and variously attributed. It is now very rubbed and, except in
the lower leaves of the thistle plant, lacks
that nervous angularity of line usually seen
in Van Dyck's composition sketches of a less
finished kind. Although the drawing for the
most part follows the design of the finished
portrait very closely, there are differences:
notably in the position of the sitter's right
foot, in the form of the folds in the drapery
below his right arm, and in the form of the
thistle. In the rock to the left of Aubigny's
elbow there appear to be the first thoughts
for a more rectangular form—a column or
pedestal. The drawing has been strengthened
(in wash?) in the shadows of the drapery and
hair and, most interestingly, along the contours of the drapery that falls over Aubigny's
left arm. The latter strengthening follows
closely alterations to the line of the drapery
visible in the finished painting, and it is con-
ceivable that these alterations were worked
out first on the drawing. The exact status of
the drawing remains unclear, but there must
be a possibility that it originated in Van
Dyck's studio, and that it played a part in the
genesis of the painting.

As in Van Dyck's portrait of Suckling, the
Latin motto of the *Aubigny*—ME FIRMIOR
AMOR, "love is stronger than I am"—is evidently the key to the "meaning" of the portrait. It is, of course, inscribed on a rock, and
it may be that a comparison is intended between the power of love and the rock, traditional symbol of constancy; but the primary
object of the comparison—the "I" of the
motto—must be Lord George himself. It is
possible that the motto is no more than a
general allusion to the amorous proclivities
of the sitter; it is, however, tempting to look
for some more specific significance, and a
case can be made of this.

On the evidence of the apparent age of the
sitter, the portrait must date from the later
1630s—Lord George was twenty in 1638. In
that year he secretly married Lady Katherine
Howard, daughter of the 2d earl of Suffolk.
The lady at that time converted to Roman
Catholicism, her husband's religion. Her portrait by Van Dyck in the National Gallery
of Art, Washington (fig. 12), was probably
painted shortly before their marriage. She

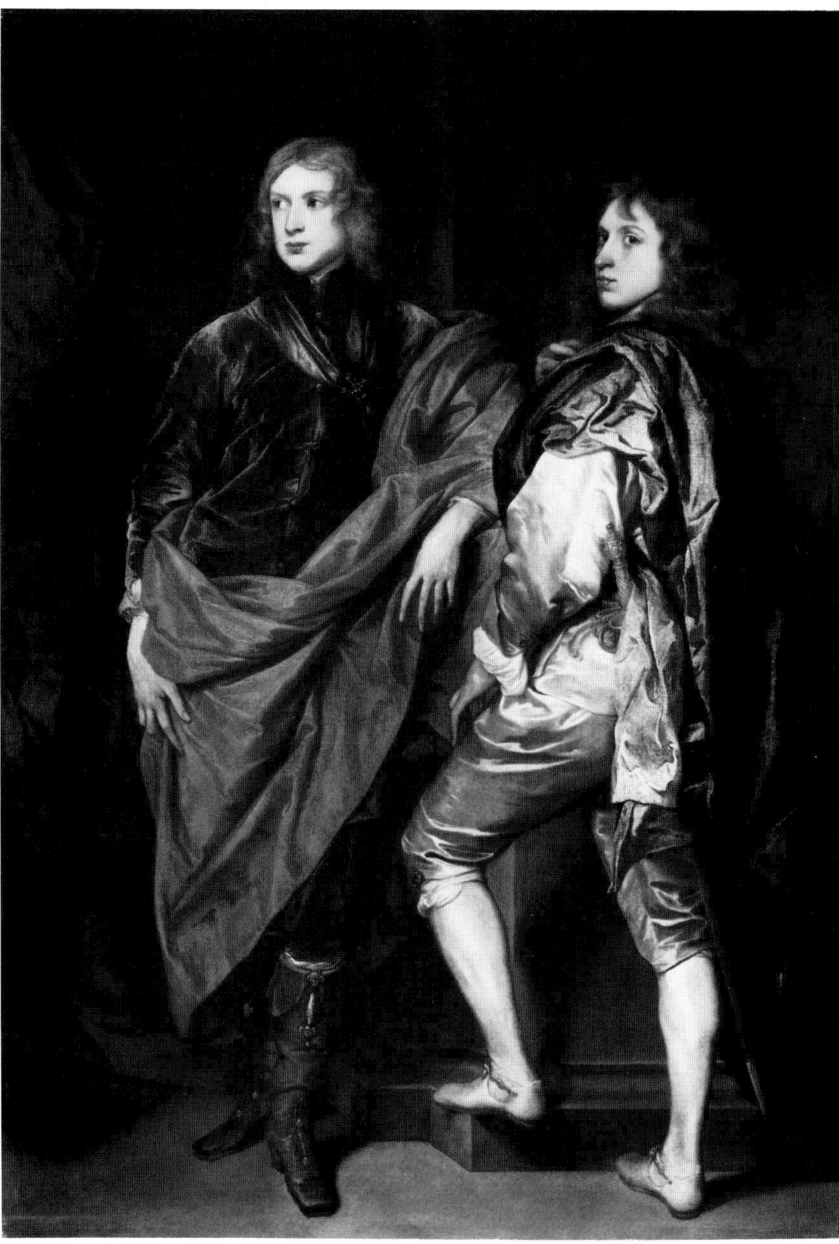

8. Anthony van Dyck,
*Lord John Stuart and Lord
Bernard Stuart, later Earl of
Lichfield,* c. 1638, oil on
canvas
National Gallery, London

holds a garland of roses and wears flowers in
her hair. The portrait is close in composition
to a three-quarter-length described somewhat unflatteringly by Sanderson:

*This figure (you see) side-way; perhaps her
body would not otherwise beare it out forward, with so much advantage as to the pleasing humour of Plumpnesse. She seems flat-
breasted; and therefore the Painter has done
what he can by Art, to hide defects of Nature,
and sets her out in such a posture best becoming her parts. Yet hath he given her Grace to
her good Face, which she turns from her bodies*

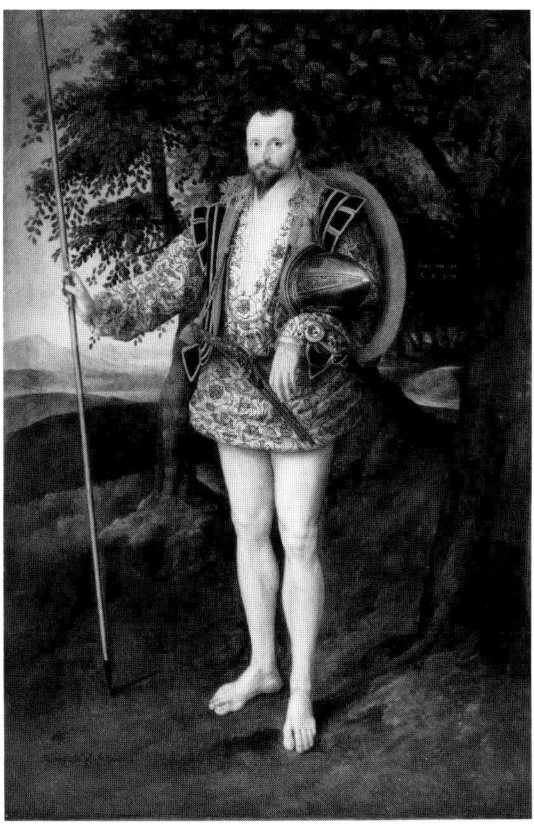

posture and shews it at the best, three-quarter.
*She is fair and full, not fat, plump enough, and
with good features to her length; Not over-tall,
nor too slender. See, see, how pretily she is
busied to wreath her Lilly-flowr'd branch into
a Chapelet which signifies her innocent mind
intent to Nature not Art, holding it forth as an
Embleme, that Solomon in all his Loyalty
came short of Nature's purity.*[18]

As Zirka Filipczak has pointed out,[19] the use
of this convention by Van Dyck was probably stimulated by his reading of Franciscus
Junius' *The Painting of the Ancients* (1638),
which makes repeated mention of "a most
famous picture" by Pausias of "a woman garland maker." The Reverend George Garrard
writes in one of his gossipy letters, dated 10
May 1638, to the earl of Strafford:

*Our great Women fall away every day. My
Lady Maltravers is declared a Papist; and also
my Lady Katherine Howard, but 'tis Love hath
been the principal Agent in her Conversion;
for, unknown to her Father the Earl of Suffolk,
she is or will be married to the Lord*

*d'Aubigny . . . who hath but a small Fortune,
under a thousand a Year, most of it in France,
where he hath been bred a Papist.*[20]

"My Lady Maltravers," Lady Katherine's
fellow-convert, was none other than Lord
George's sister, Lady Elizabeth Stuart
(d. 1674), wife of the eldest surviving son of
Van Dyck's great patron, the earl of Arundel,
whom she had married secretly, against
Charles I's wishes and to his intense displea-
sure, in 1626, over ten years earlier. Van
Dyck painted a modest half-length portrait of
her (private collection) in 1635. It is not surprising, therefore, that Lord George's own secret marriage angered his guardian, the king.
All those present at the ceremony incurred
Charles' wrath, and it is noteworthy that a
certain John Penruddock, a few months later,
presented a petition to Archbishop Laud beg-
ging him to intercede with Charles I on his
behalf, "being put in question in the Court of
High Commission" on account of this matter.[21] It seems reasonable to suggest in this
context that the *Aubigny* portrait was
painted in about 1638 to commemorate Lord
George's love for Lady Katherine Howard,
and that it may have been intended to convey the sitter's conflicting loyalties at this
time. "Love is stronger than I am," stronger,
it is implied, than his sense of duty to his
godfather, the king, and to his unwilling
father-in-law, Lord Suffolk.

Let us now turn to the question of whether
there is any symbolic significance to be attached to the rosebush, stream, and thistle in
the portrait. It is a subject that invites comment, but that cannot be fully resolved.
However, it may be useful to suggest some of
the associations that *might* be present. It
may be that the rose (in association here
with the thistle) with its traditional significance is an emblem of the pleasures and
pains of love. The supreme example of the
rose used with this significance in British
painting is Nicholas Hilliard's large miniature *A Young Man among Roses* (fig. 13), late
1580s, now doubtfully proposed as a portrait
of Robert Devereux, 2d earl of Essex, the
favorite of Elizabeth I. This bears the para-
doxical Latin motto, taken from Lucan's *De
Bello Civili*, VII.i.486: *Dat Poenas Laudata
Fides*, "My praised loyalty causes my sufferings." The parallels with the *Aubigny* need
not be underlined.

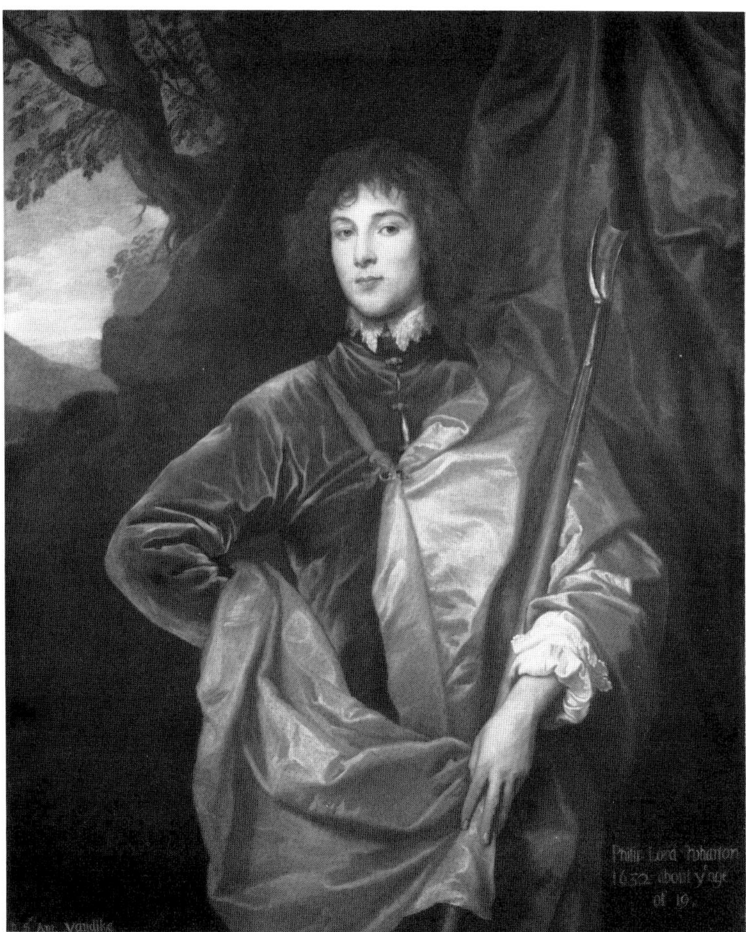

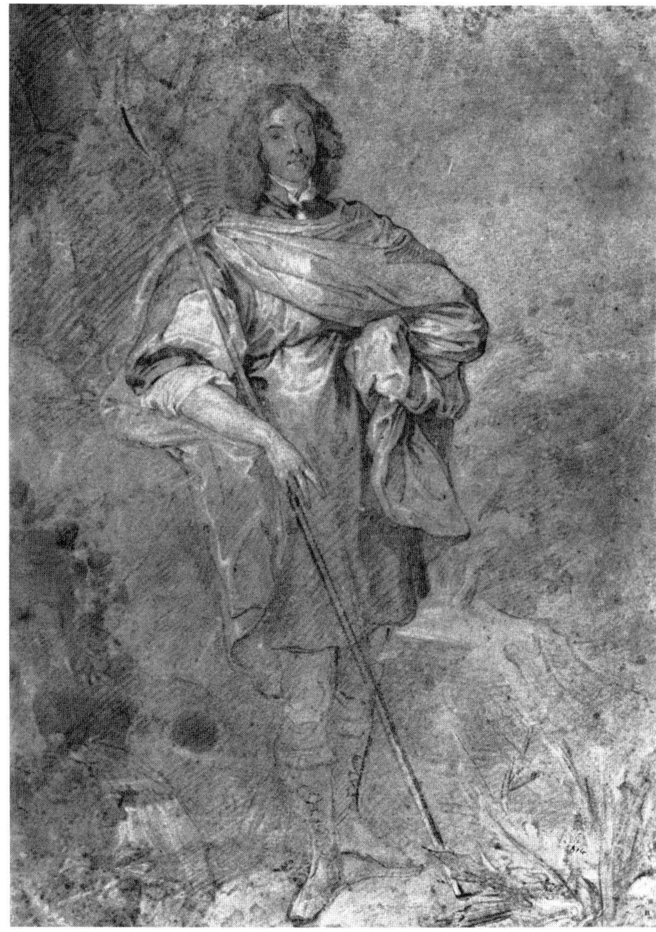

Millar, cataloguing the *Aubigny* portrait in 1982, suggested that it might illustrate the influence of contemporary emblem books.[22] In the case of the thistle he cites George Whither's *A Collection of Emblemes Ancient and Moderne* (1635), book 4, xxiv, where, he notes, "the thistle is seen as a symbol of affliction." Illustrating the motto *Duris gaudet patientia,* "Patience rejoices in adversity," is a woodcut of a peasant in buskins striding through the countryside picking thistles (fig. 14). The accompanying verses read, in part:

What meanes this Countrey-peasant, skipping here
Through prickling Thistles with such gamesom cheere.
And, plucking off their tops, as though for Posies
He gather'd Violets, or toothlesse Roses.
What meaneth it, but onely to expresse
How great a joy, well-grounded Patientnesse
Retaines in Suff'rings? and, what sport she makes,

When she her Journey through Affliction takes?
I, oft have sayd (and, have as oft, beene thought
To speak a Paradox, that favours nought
Of likely truth) that, some Afflictions bring
A Honey Bag, which cureth ev'ry Sting
(That wounds the Flesh) by giving to the Mind,
A pleasing taste of Sweetnesses refin'd.

Lord George is portrayed as a shepherd, a "Countrey-peasant," and undoubtedly patience in adversity was needed by this young man who had incurred the king's wrath and who was perhaps a patient wooer amid the pangs of love, ultimately rewarded by "a pleasing taste of Sweetnesses refin'd."

Millar also notes that the thistle and the rose growing together formed one of the emblems dedicated to the king (that is, James I of England and VI of Scotland) in Henry Peacham's *Minerva Britanna* (1612), one of the earliest and most popular of all emblem books. Although a compliment to the king

10. Anthony van Dyck, *Philip, Lord Wharton,* 1632, oil on canvas
National Gallery of Art, Washington

11. Studio(?) of Anthony van Dyck, *Lord George Stuart, Seigneur d'Aubigny,* c. 1638(?), black chalk (and wash) heightened with white on paper
Victoria and Albert Museum, London

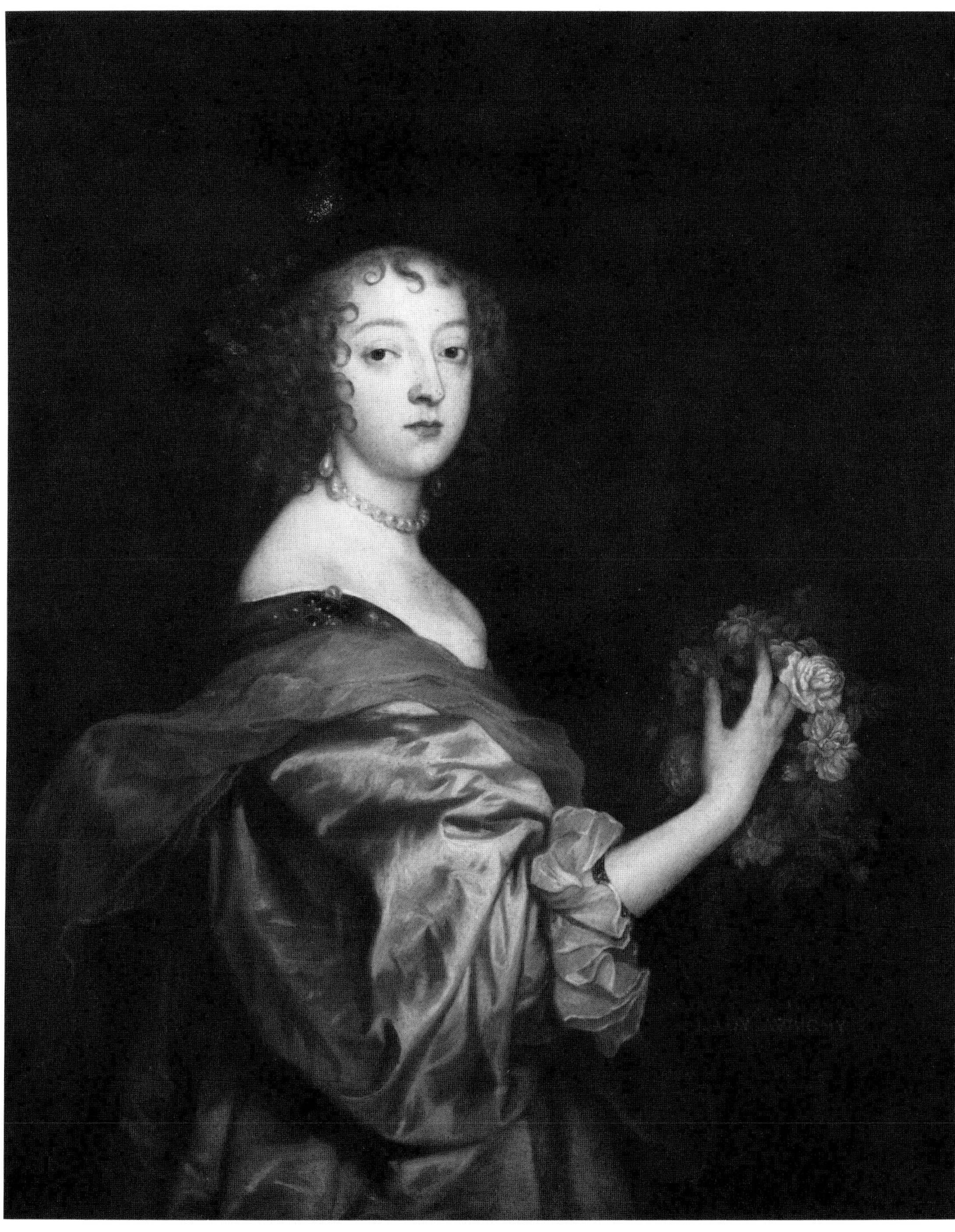

(in this case Charles I) might be appropriate, it is not especially so. A closer examination of the emblem (fig. 15) is, however, instructive. The whole device comprises a hand holding a watering can, which appears from a cloud to water alike the rose and the thistle that grow entwined below. This illustrates the Latin motto *Quae plantavi irrigabo*, "what I have planted I will water," referring to God's bounty in looking after the whole of his creation—both roses and thistles, England and Scotland. It is possible that this idea of God's bounty is embodied in the rosebush, thistle, and spring of the portrait (it is hard to imagine Van Dyck painting a watering can), God's bounty toward the seemingly unpropitious union of the two young people and the union of England (Howard) and Scot-

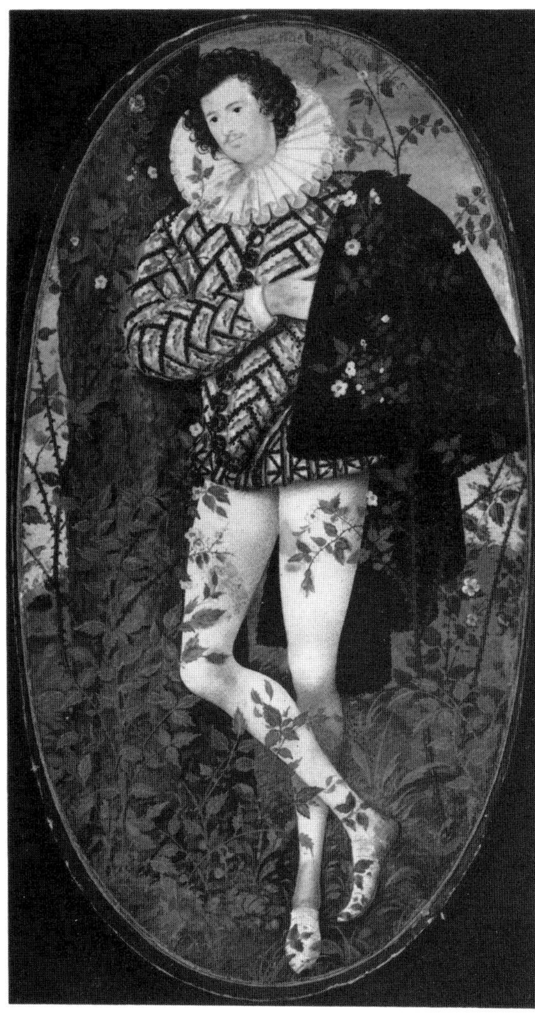

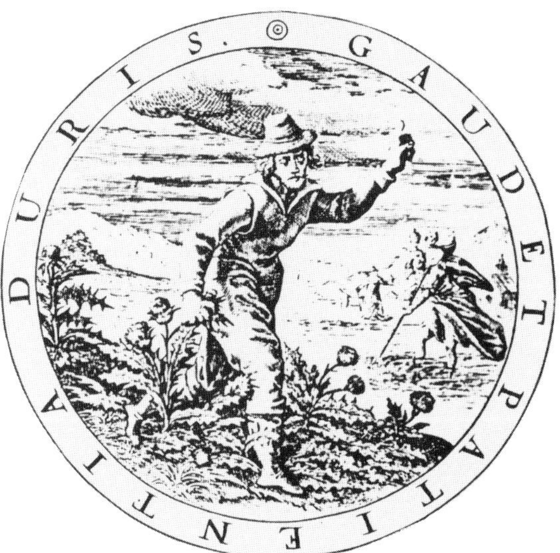

13. Nicholas Hilliard, *A Young Man among Roses*, c. 1587, watercolor on vellum
Victoria and Albert Museum, London

14. George Whither, *A Collection of Emblemes, Ancient and Moderne* (1635), book 4, xxiv

land (Stuart) implicit in it.

One other portrait by Van Dyck deserves comment in connection with the Aubigny picture: that is the double three-quarter-length portrait of Lord George's wife with her sister-in-law, Frances Stuart, countess of Portland, in the Hermitage, St. Petersburg (fig. 16). Because of the relationship between the sitters, the painting probably dates from after Katherine Howard's marriage and, indeed, it is likely that Lady Aubigny was pregnant at the time it was painted; on 7 March 1639 she gave birth to her first child, Charles, the last seigneur d'Aubigny and duke of Lennox of the Stuart line. He must have been conceived about June 1638, very close to the time of Katherine's marriage. That she was indeed pregnant is confirmed by the protective gesture of her hands resting on her stomacher. The portrait must therefore have been painted in the second half of

1638 or very early in 1639. Looped around Lady Aubigny's right wrist is a rope of pearls that may have some symbolic significance, for it is clearly not a bracelet of a type that might practically be worn—it is too long and loose. Pearls were the attribute of the virgin-martyr Saint Margaret of Antioch, and were appropriately enough emblems of purity, as has been shown by E. de Jongh.[23] In England the term "Margarite" was interchangeable with "pearl," and in Roman Catholic circles was associated with the Virgin Mary.[24] Saint Margaret was also the patron saint of those in childbirth. De Jongh writes:

The various Margaret legends were to enjoy a long life, particularly in the southern Netherlands, despite the fact that church-men . . . viewed them with a great deal of scep-ticism. . . . One reason for this was that St. Margaret was the saint to be invoked during pregnancy or if there were obstetrical compli-cations. She acquired this role due to one of the elements in the legend which related that shortly before she died God granted her the power . . . of ensuring that the pregnancies of those who venerated her came to full term. In the southern Netherland and in France writings on the life of the saint were used as amulets during labor.[25]

We may therefore hazard the suggestion that pearls in one form or another may have been worn by some of Van Dyck's Roman Catholic sitters during pregnancy as a means of invoking Saint Margaret's beneficent influence, and have been included in portraits because of this association.

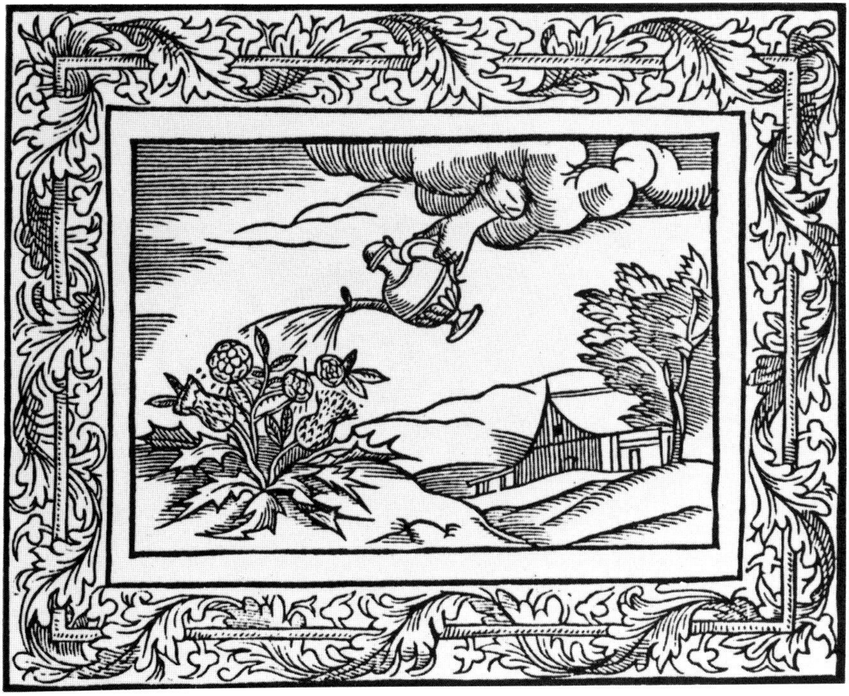

15. Henry Peacham, *Minerva Britanna* (1612), 12

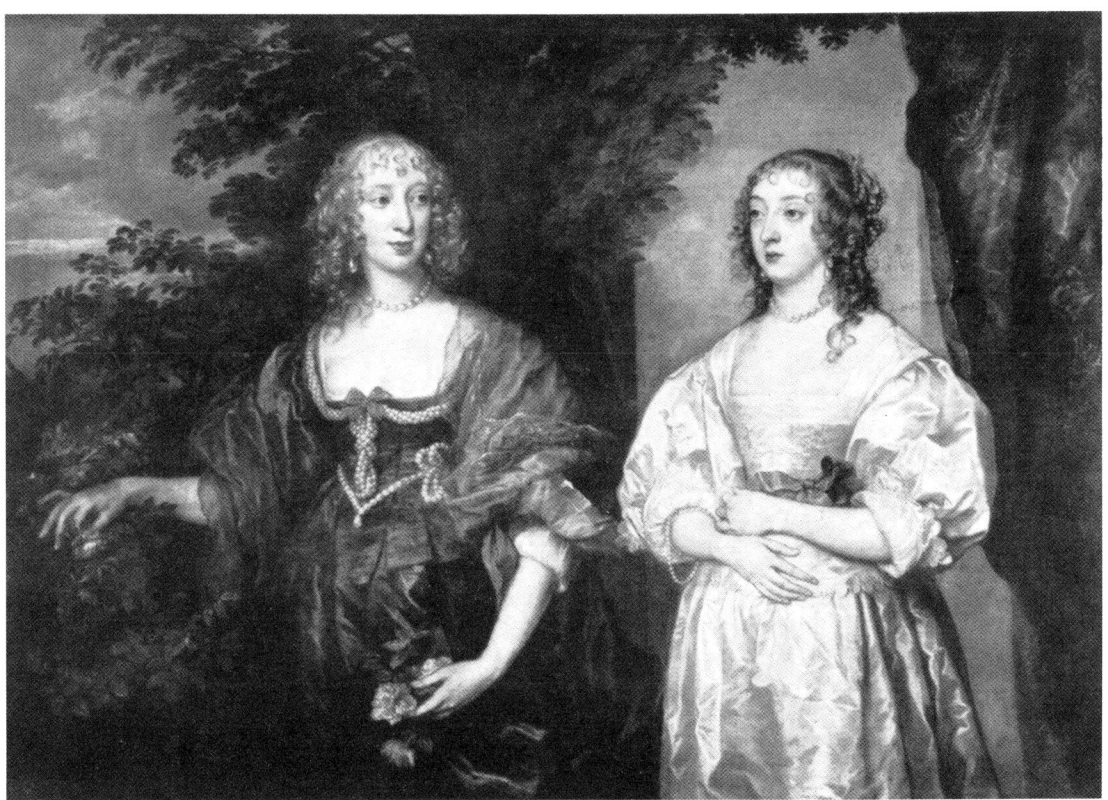

16. Anthony van Dyck, *Katherine Howard, Lady Aubigny, and Frances Stuart, Countess of Portland*, c. 1638–1639, oil on canvas
Hermitage, St. Petersburg

dant pearl on a single strand of pearls. She was also pregnant in 1638 and gave birth to a son and heir on 19 May 1639. In addition to the profusion of pearls, the twofold pregnancy may account for the especially intimate atmosphere of this portrait of the sisters-in-law.

The motif of a loose bracelet of pearls, combined in this case with a crucifix, is again used by Van Dyck in his portrait of another Roman Catholic sitter, his own wife Mary Ruthven (fig. 17), whom he married on 27 February 1640; their daughter Justiniana was born just over eighteen months later on 1 December 1641, eight days before Van Dyck's death. If the suggestion of the association of pearls with pregnancy is accepted,[26] it follows that the portrait is one of the artist's very latest works, painted in 1641. This theory also supports Oliver Millar's suggestion that Van Dyck's portrait of Queen Henrietta Maria, formerly in the Barberini collection, Rome, and now in a private collection, New York, painted in about December 1636, is intended to depict the queen pregnant with the Princess Elizabeth. Here we find the protective or cradling gesture of the hands and a stupendous rope of pearls. There are a number of other instances of the

Interestingly, Lady Portland also wears a double rope of pearls, twisted and knotted and attached to her bodice by a bow. Over her slightly bulging stomacher is suspended a pen-

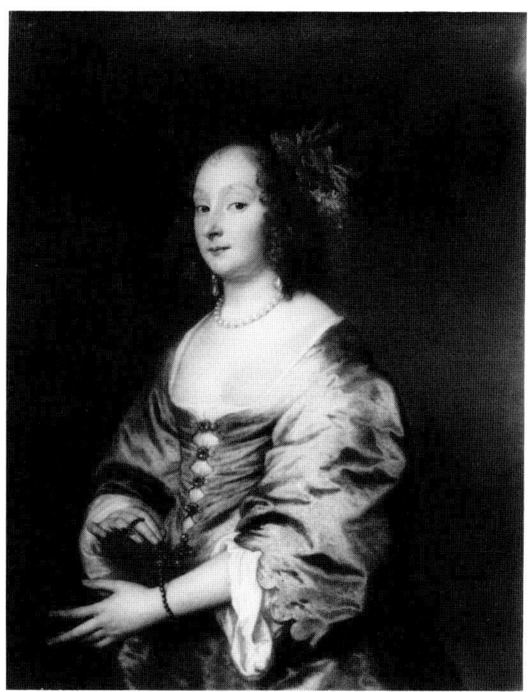

use of the rope of pearls as an attribute in the portraits of sitters who may be pregnant, though, in the absence of precise dates and the prevalence of pearls as a fashionable accessory, this is hard to prove.[27]

The story of Lord and Lady Aubigny ends sadly. At some time following their marriage they were reconciled with the king, and in the Civil War Lord George raised a band of three hundred horse, all gentlemen of fortune, worth some three hundred thousand pounds, for the royalist side. He fell, covered in wounds, at the Battle of Edge Hill on 23 October 1642, one of the first victims of the Civil War, and was buried in Christ Church, Oxford. Despite the romantic, pastoral aspect of Van Dyck's portrait, the evidence suggests that Lord George had inherited all the warlike qualities of his ancestors. His earliest biographer writes that he found it hard to understand how other young noblemen with the same privileges as himself were so backward in joining the royal cause, saying:

I would have all those that refuse serving in this War, served as they that were backward to engage in the Holy War, to each of whom was sent a Spindle and Distaffe, the upbraiding ensigns of their softness and effeminacy. . . . The delicacy of our mould and make, (speaking of Noblemen) the quickness of our spirits, the sprightliness of our faculties, the exact proportion of our parts, the happiness of our address, the accomplishments of our persons, the soundness of our constitutions, the difference of our souls, the happiness of our opportunities . . . And in fine, our being born happy . . . engageth us to do so much more than others, as we are more than others.[28]

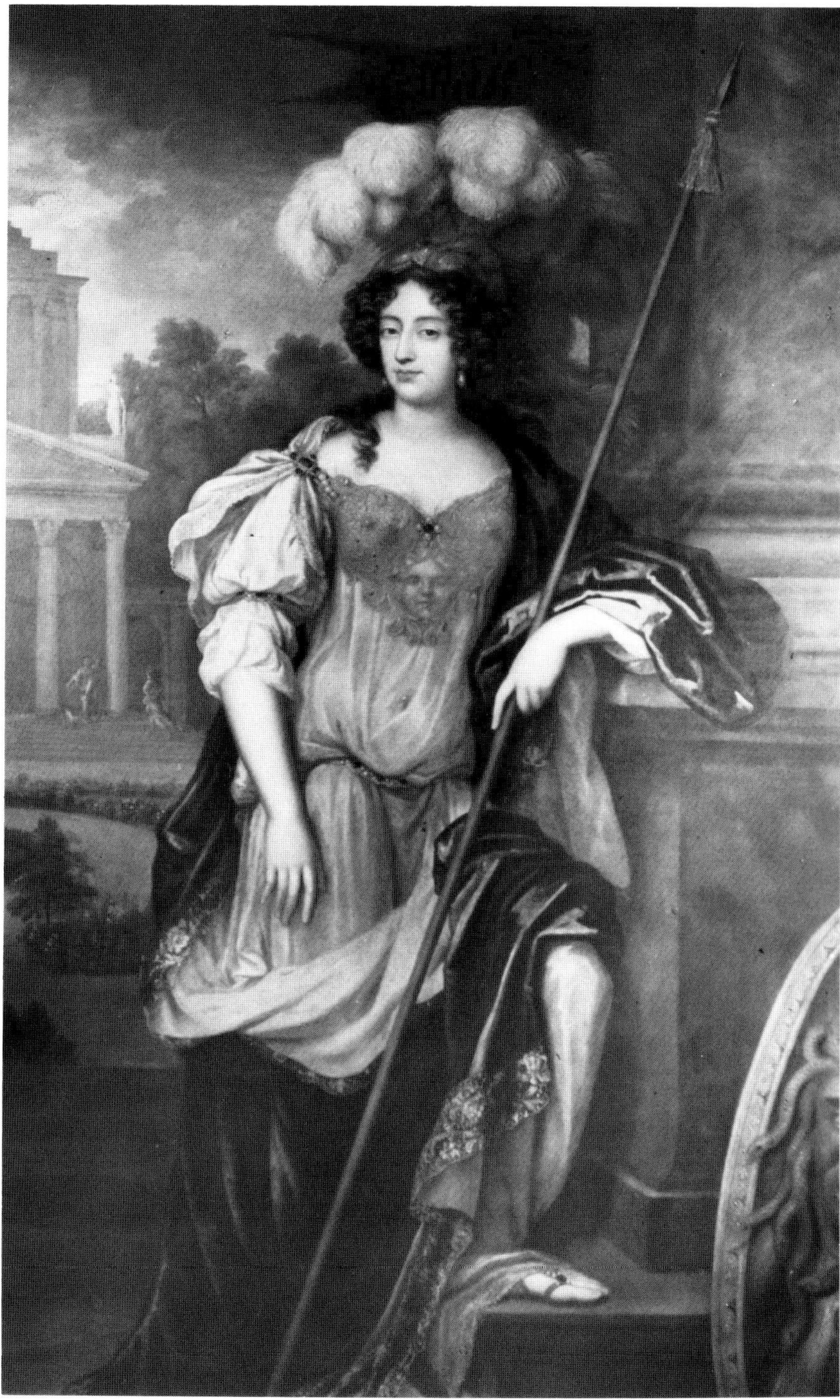

17. Anthony van Dyck, *Mary Ruthven, Lady van Dyck*, 1641(?), oil on canvas
Museo del Prado, Madrid

18. Henri Gascars, *Frances Teresa Stuart, Duchess of Richmond and Lennox*, c. 1678, oil on canvas
Goodwood House, Chichester, West Sussex

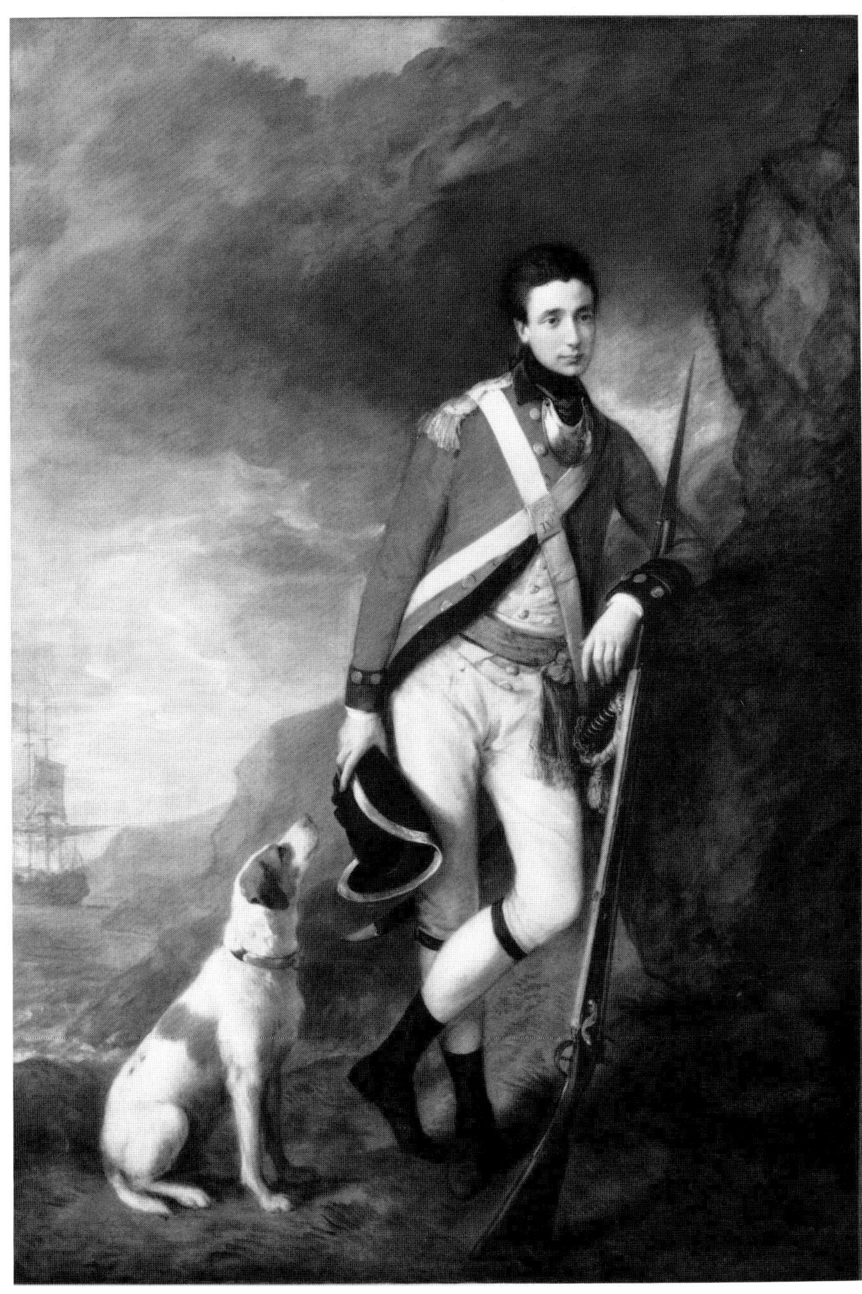

Lord Aubigny's portrait passed to his son, the 3d duke of Richmond, at Cobham Hall, Kent, and was bequeathed by him to his third wife Frances Teresa, "La Belle Stuart," who at her death in 1702 bequeathed it, according to her late husband's wish, to his sister, Katherine, Baroness Clifton in her own right, and thence to her descendants the earls of Darnley. "La Belle Stuart" was painted by a host of artists—by Sir Peter Lely, Jacob Huysmans, Willem Wissing and Jan Vandervaart in partnership, Samuel Cooper, and by the French artist Henri Gascars, who came to London in about 1675 under the patronage of the king's French mistress, the duchess of Portsmouth. He painted the duchess of Richmond as Minerva (fig. 18), with plumed helmet and gorgon shield, a strange, exotic metamorphosis of the pose of Lord Aubigny, in reverse, his spud now changed to a spear.

A century later Thomas Gainsborough visited Cobham Hall and painted there a copy of Van Dyck's *Lords John and Bernard Stuart* (City Art Museum, St. Louis). He must also have seen and admired the *Aubigny*, for a number of his late portraits of men, full-lengths and three-quarter-lengths, share its romantic pastoral mood. There may be an echo, in reverse, in the *3d Earl of Bristol* (Ickworth) of 1758. However, the portrait that shows the most obvious compositional influence (though like the *Bristol* it has a seascape background) is the full-length of an unknown *Officer of the 4th Regiment of Foot* (fig. 19) in Melbourne, painted in about 1780, the shepherd's spud now a musket with fixed bayonet. It may also be the influence of the *Aubigny* that accounts for the young man's expression of intense melancholy.

Lady Aubigny, after his death, continued to work for the royalist cause with great daring. She had borne him two children: Charles, mentioned above, and Katherine (born 1640).

1. William Sanderson, *Graphice* (London, 1658), 19.

2. See, for instance, M. A. Rogers, "The Meaning of Van Dyck's Portrait of Sir John Suckling," *Burlington Magazine* 120 (November 1978), 743.

3. For example, *Venetia Stanley, Lady Digby, as Prudence* or *Lady Southampton as Fortuna* (National Gallery of Victoria, Melbourne, and Fitzwilliam Museum, Cambridge).

4. See Zirka Zaremba Filipczak, "Reflections on Motifs in Van Dyck's Portraits," in Arthur K. Wheelock, Jr., et al., *Anthony van Dyck* [exh. cat., National Gallery of Art] (Washington, 1990), 63–64.

5. First pointed out by Alastair Smith, "A Van Dyck Double Portrait in the National Gallery," *Burlington Magazine* 119 (December 1977), 859. Christopher Brown, in discussion of this paper at the symposium "Van Dyck 350" at the National Gallery of Art (1991), defended his opinion that this figure represents Hymen, the god of marriage. This is erroneous. Hymen is usually depicted as a youth; wingless, he invariably carries a torch, wears a wreath of marjoram and roses, and is dressed in saffron robes. Here the figure is clearly a child-angel, lacks the torch, and is wearing a wreath of roses and violas and rose red drapery. Compare the analogous figure in Theodor Boeyermans' *Saint Dorothy* in the Saint Andrew Church, Antwerp. Ben Jonson's masque *Hymenaei* (1606), published in the folio of 1616, would have been familiar to English readers: "Hymen, the god of marriage, in a saffron coloured robe, his under vestures white, his socks yellow, a yellow veil of silk on his left arm, his head crowned with roses and marjoram, in his right hand a torch of pine tree." A pictorial treatment of Hymen familiar to the English court was that in Rubens' *Peace and War* (1629/1630), which the artist presented to Charles I and which is now in the National Gallery, London. In this, with the exception of saffron robes (the figure is virtually naked), all the above elements are incorporated.

6. See Filipczak in Washington 1990, 63–64, who suggests that the portrait's "extensive classical vocabulary. . . directed attention away from the issue of Catholicism." If the allusion to Saint Dorothy is accepted, then this point is undermined.

7. Oliver Millar, *The Tudor, Stuart and Early Georgian Pictures in the Collection of Her Majesty the Queen* (London, 1963), no. 156.

8. Arthur Wheelock in Washington 1990, 313.

9. Sir Kenelm Digby, letter to his brother, quoted by V. Gabrieli, *Sir Kenelm Digby* (London, 1957), 246.

10. See Filipczak in Washington 1990, 60.

11. Both Oliver Millar, *Van Dyck in England* [exh. cat., National Portrait Gallery] (London, 1982), no. 48, and Wheelock in Washington 1990, no. 66, argue that the Metropolitan Museum portrait with Garter predates the Kenwood picture. This is most unlikely, for it would be almost unthinkable to omit the Garter from a portrait, however informal, if the sitter

was entitled to wear it. Millar also suggests that the Kenwood portrait derives from a separate sitting. The head is, however, surely of the same type as the Louvre and Metropolitan Museum pictures, but antedates them. This accounts for the loss of vitality in the heads of these paintings.

12. See M. A. Rogers, "John and John Baptist Closterman: A Catalogue of their Works," *Walpole Society* 139 (1983), 224–279. The duke noted in his diary on 1 April 1698: "Thes hung in my room . . . My Lord John & My Lord Bernard Stewart/pictures done after Vandick by Mr/Closterman the Earle of Kent has the/originall." Closterman himself reused elements of the composition in several of his portraits, and earlier seventeenth-century quotations from it—especially of the left-hand figure—are also known.

13. See Millar in London 1982, no. 44; Gregory Martin, *The Flemish School c. 1600–c. 1900* (London, 1970), 63–67.

14. See Rogers 1978.

15. Washington 1990, no. 63.

16. There is a good account in Millar in London 1982, 29–30.

17. Millar in London 1982, 102.

18. Sanderson 1658, 39.

19. Filipczak in Washington 1990, 64.

20. William Knowler, *The Earl of Strafforde's Letters and Despatches*, 2 vols. (London, 1739), 2:165.

21. *Calendar of State Papers Domestic Series 1638–1639*, ed. John Bruce and W. D. Hamilton (London, 1871), 276.

22. Millar in London 1982, 102.

23. E. de Jongh, "Pearls of Virtue and Pearls of Vice," *Simiolus* 8, no. 2 (1975–1976), 69–97.

24. See H. A. [Henry Hawkins?], *Parthenia Sacra* (Rouen, 1633), 191–198.

25. De Jongh 1975–1976, 85.

26. Sanderson 1658, 38, in a somewhat *chargé* account of the portrait, does not comment on any such implications: "Hold Sir! Herself gives you the Ensigne of Religion; for having done her devotion, she wraps her Row of Beads about her Arm, lifting up the pendant crosse, as who should say: At the end of all. Look upon this Sir, and you shall never sinne."

27. For example, the portrait by Sir Peter Lely of Catherine Villiers(?), wife of the 5th earl of Pembroke (whom she married as his second wife in 1649), at Wilton, c. 1650 (this portrait, at some later date, was sewn to another female portrait of the later 1650s by Lely to form a double portrait); the Duchess of Cleveland by Lely, 1660s, National Gallery of Art, Washington; Mrs. Grinling Gibbons in the double portrait with her husband by John Closterman, 1692, which is known by a mezzotint by John Smith. De Jongh 1975–1976 reproduces (fig. 23) Cornelius Johnson's

portrait of Helena du Booys-de Sieveri, 1650, Centraal Museum, Utrecht.

28. David Lloyd, *Memoires of the Lives, Actions, Sufferings & Deaths of those . . . Excellent Personages, that suffered . . . for the Protestant Religion* (London, 1668), 322.

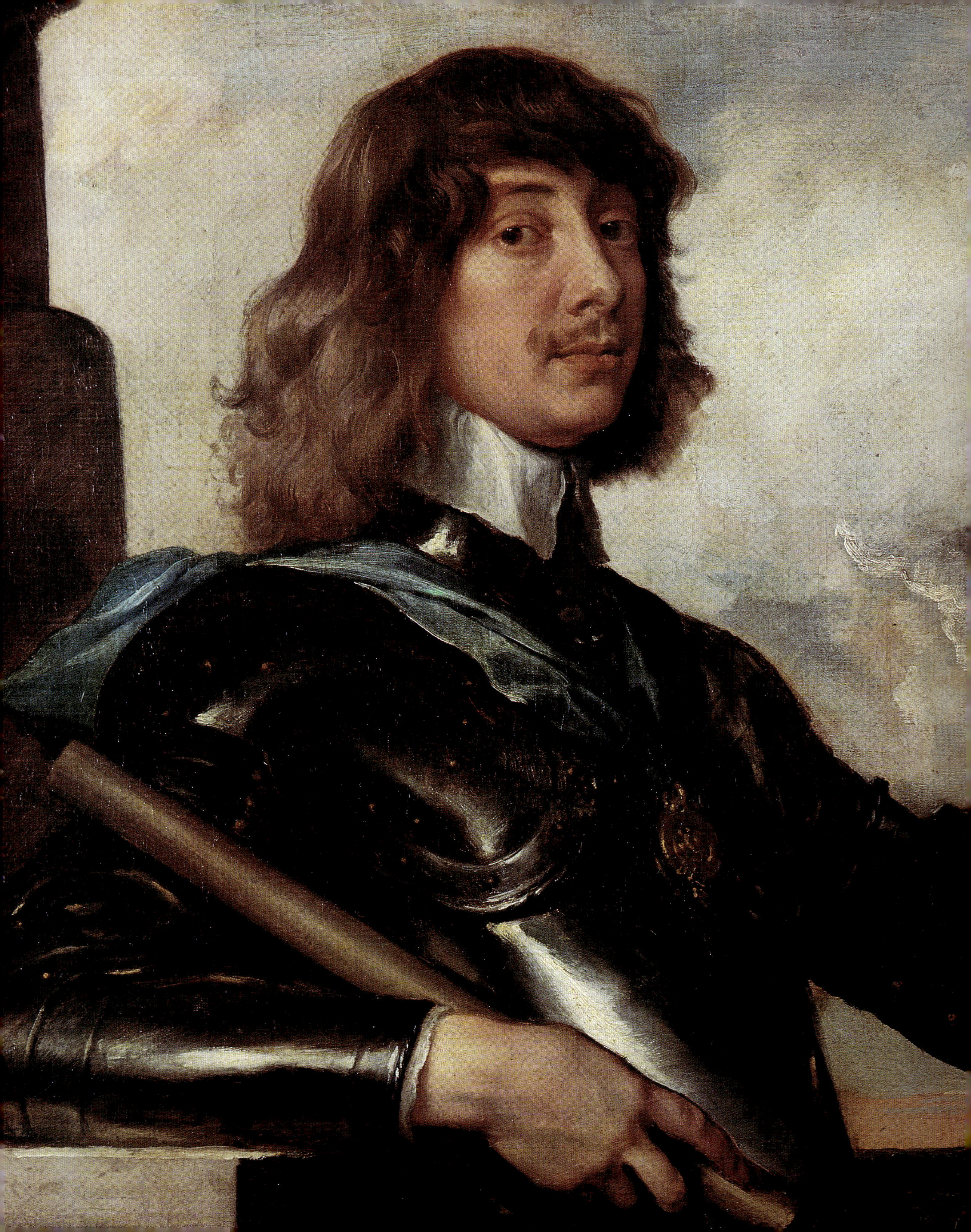

JEREMY WOOD
Oxford Brookes University

Van Dyck and the Earl of Northumberland: Taste and Collecting in Stuart England

In 1645 a curious tug-of-war over pictures took place between the House of Commons and Algernon Percy, 10th earl of Northumberland (1602–1668). The incident throws light on both the taste and the character of a man who remains the most neglected of the great Stuart collectors,[1] and who was also one of Van Dyck's most important patrons in England (fig. 1).[2] On 14 April 1645 two informants reported that York House, the London mansion of the duke of Buckingham that had been seized by Parliament as the property of a Royalist, was full of paintings worth £20,000, but that no money had been "browt into the State" because the earl of Northumberland, who then rented the house, "hath given a man £40 per annum to looke to the s.d goodes."[3] On 23 April the Commons found Northumberland intractable about having the pictures stripped from the walls of his rented mansion. "He had," he claimed, "as good [an] interest in them . . . as he had in any other Part of his Estate," but if Parliament insisted on selling the pictures and making the house "very unuseful for his Habitation," he wanted the rent paid so that it could be refurnished. He noted, though, that the state still owed him £360 from the sum voted to reimburse him for losses during the Civil War (the earl had proved a loyal and generous supporter of the Parliamentary cause), and he dropped a hint that he would be prepared to accept "some of the smaller Pictures in consideration of that money."[4] Finally, he asked that the family portraits be left in the house "being of no value," even though he must often have studied the great equestrian portrait by Rubens for which Buckingham had paid an astronomical £500.[5]

In the face of this obstruction the Commons set up a committee to investigate the "Quality and Condition" of the pictures at York House. On 23 July this body reported that all "superstitious" pictures of God the Father, Christ, the Holy Ghost, and the Virgin should be burned, and the remainder sold.[6] This arrangement was agreed upon by the Commons in an Order of 20 August,[7] but what happened next is not entirely clear. As early as April, according to an eyewitness account of the proceedings in Parliament, it was realized that if all the "superstitious" pictures were burned "ye residue would prove to be but of smale vallue."[8] Some that might have been liable for destruction, such as Andrea del Sarto's *Pietà* (Kunsthistorisches Museum, Vienna), have indeed survived.[9] Northumberland's intransigence seems to have saved some of the pictures, and, although a staunch Protestant, the earl had no compunction in accepting some highly "superstitious" pictures from York House for his own gallery. The importance of his seven years residence at York House, from 1640 to 1647, can hardly be underestimated as an influence on his own taste in art.

Although the Percys were among the greatest families of the realm, it was not until 1642 that they came to own one of the patrician mansions to be found in London be-

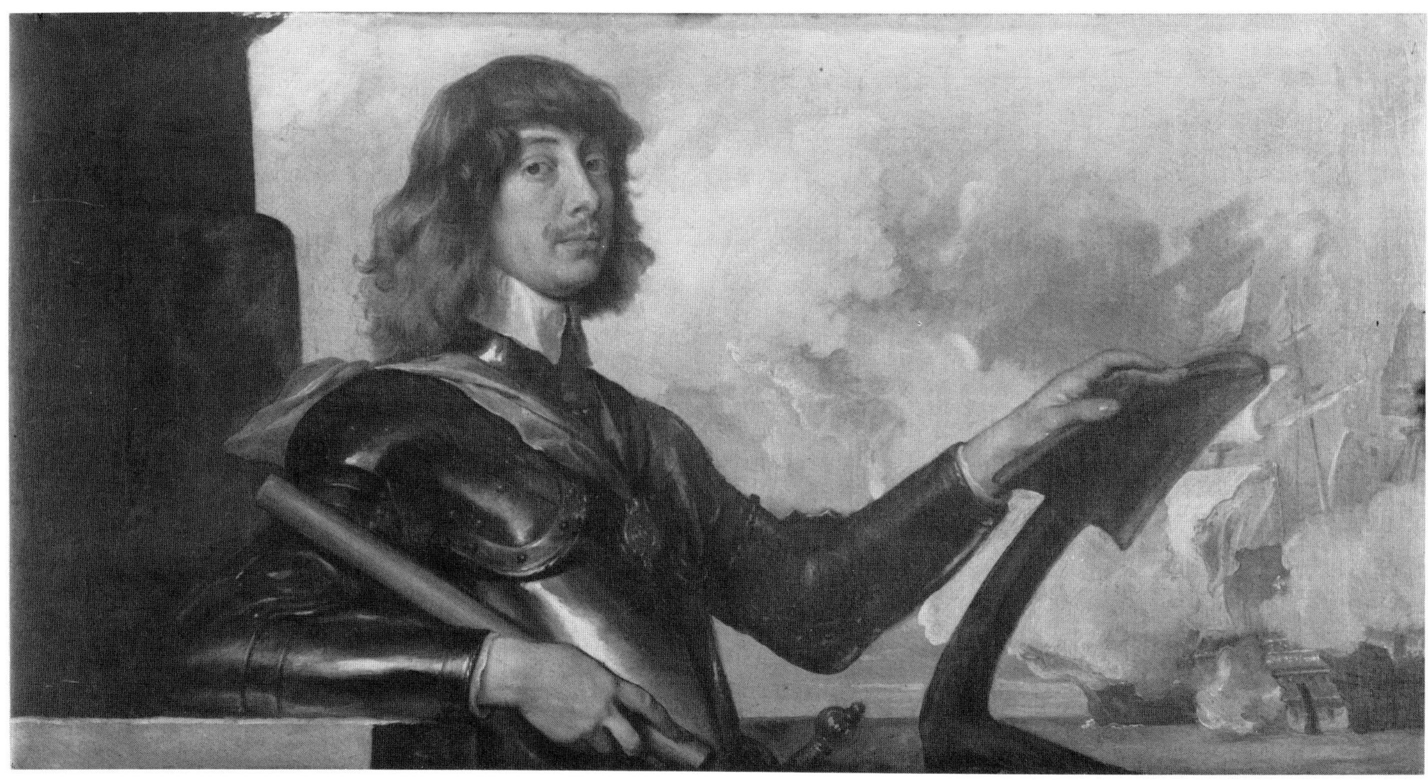

tween the Strand and the River Thames. When Northumberland reestablished the family at the court of Charles I, following his father's lengthy imprisonment on a charge amounting to technical treason,[10] the lack of an adequate residence became obvious and in the early 1630s he rented Dorset House on Fleet Street.[11] Within a few years, however, he was able to move to a grander address: the household accounts show that in midsummer 1640 Northumberland became the tenant of the duchess of Buckingham, five years after her second marriage to the earl of Antrim, at York House, for which he paid a substantial £350 a year.[12] During this period Northumberland, aided by Lord Denbigh and the earl of Pembroke, did much to protect the interests of the youthful 2d duke of Buckingham in London.[13]

The reasons for Northumberland's eventual departure from York House in 1647 are not difficult to establish. In 1642 his second marriage to Elizabeth Howard, daughter of the earl of Suffolk, had enabled him to buy Suffolk House from the 3d earl; the opportunity to acquire this residence may even have been a prime motive for his choice of bride, but in any event he needed a male heir. The great house, whose four towers dominated the skyline of the city, was not only close to Whitehall but adjacent to York House (fig. 2). Although Northumberland and his retinue stayed at Suffolk House from 14 October to 11 November 1643,[14] he continued to reside next door at York House, and many of the state papers that he received are addressed there. No doubt he preferred it because of its splendid furnishings, not least the picture collection, and his tenancy allowed him to refurbish Suffolk House, which soon became known as Northumberland House, in comfort and at leisure.[15]

Although little is known about the deal that Northumberland made with Parliament

1. Anthony van Dyck, *Algernon Percy, 10th Earl of Northumberland*, c. 1638, oil on canvas
Duke of Northumberland

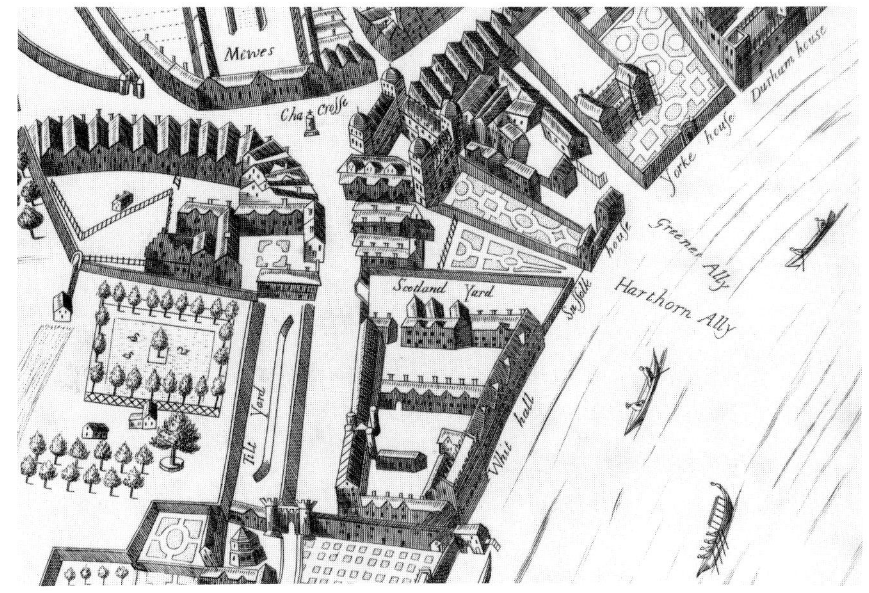

over the pictures at York House, the hint that he offered the Commons in 1645, namely that he would accept "some of the smaller Pictures" instead of cash, may explain how he obtained them. The selection is particularly interesting because he knew the collection so intimately. The greatest prize, according to the valuations in the 1671 Northumberland inventory (which provides detailed information about the collection shortly after the earl's death), was a set of "Eight Little Pictures in one Frame by Els-hammer," then valued at £250 (see Appendix III, no. 40). This series of saints and figures from the Old and New Testaments, which must once have been part of a piece of furniture, has descended with many other Northumberland pictures to Petworth.[16] Very different, but also highly prized, was the double portrait *Cardinal Georges d'Armagnac and*

2. Whitehall with Suffolk (Northumberland) House and York House, from Faithorne and Newcourt's *Map of London*, c. 1643–1647
University Library, Cambridge

3. Titian, *Cardinal Georges d'Armagnac and His Secretary Guillaume Philandrier*, oil on canvas
Duke of Northumberland

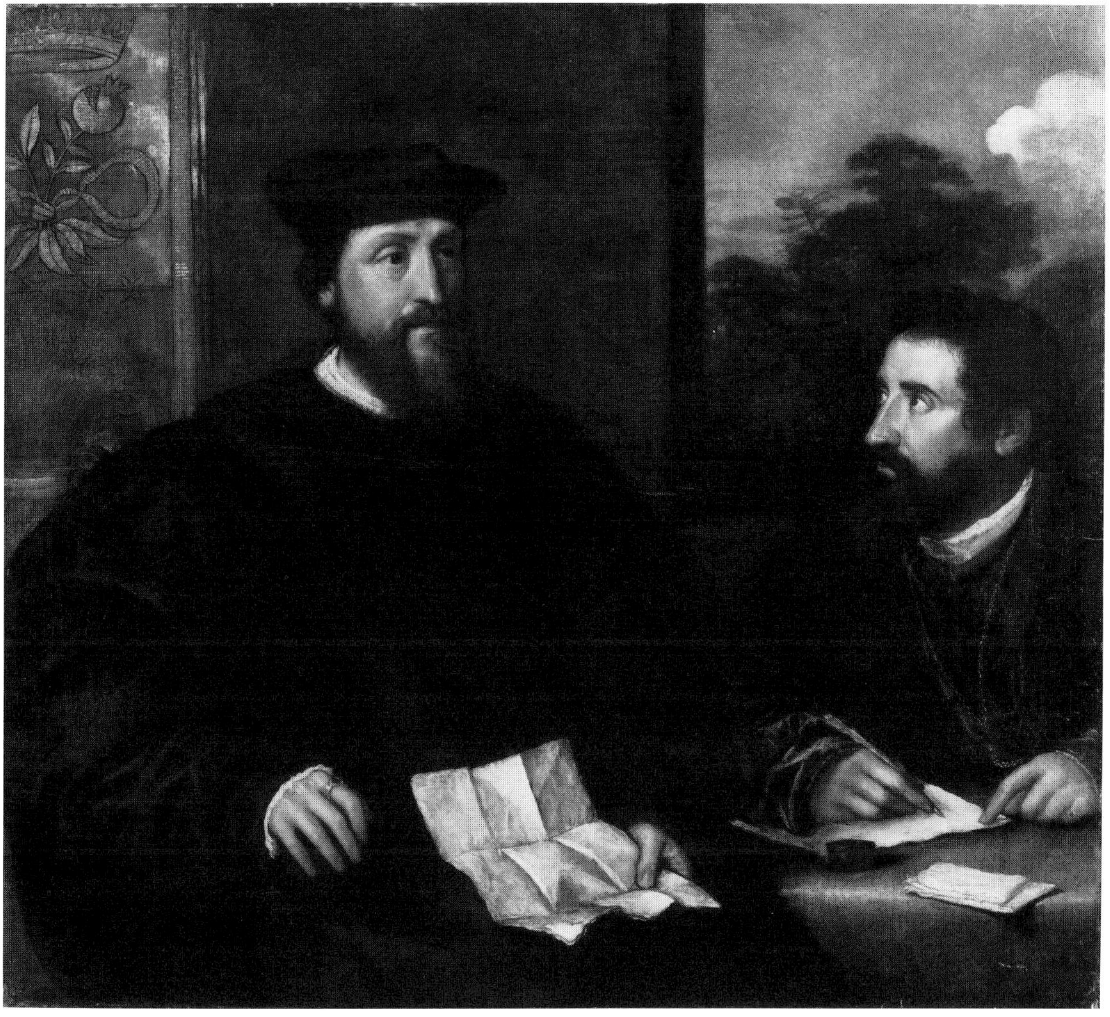

His Secretary Guillaume Philandrier by Titian (fig. 3), which today is to be found with another portion of the family collection at Alnwick.[17] This work was known and admired by Van Dyck who, as is well known, based his double portrait of *Thomas Wentworth, 1st Earl of Strafford, and Sir Philip Mainwaring* (Countess Fitzwilliam's Settlement and Lady Juliet de Chair) on it.[18] As will be shown, Van Dyck's opinion of Titian was of considerable importance to Northumberland, and may have influenced Northumberland's choice. When Richard Symonds visited Northumberland House in 1652 and made valuable notes on the pictures, the double portrait was simply called "A Senato[r] of Venice & his Secretary" (see Appendix I, no. 4), but by 1671 it was known as "The Duke of Florence and Machiavil" (see Appendix III, no. 4), probably reflecting Northumberland's own identification of the sitters. This title must have been established some time before 1671 because Symon Stone, who was employed by Northumberland as a copyist and as curator of the collection, sold a copy of the Titian under this title to the earl of Bath in 1661.[19] The work had been celebrated in England ever since its purchase for Buckingham in 1624 by Balthazar Gerbier, who, when the painting arrived in London, wrote that Inigo Jones "almost went down on his knees" before it.[20] Some of the other pictures that Northumberland selected were more "superstitious:" for example, two depictions of the Virgin and Child by Andrea del Sarto, one showing her as a Madonna of Humility with music-making angels, the other with Saint Elizabeth and the Infant Baptist. The pictures seem to have been hung by Northumberland as pendants, and were "esteemed both at £1000" when Richard Symonds visited the collection in 1652 (see Appendix I, no. 3), although this valuation dropped startlingly to only £200 in 1671 (see Appendix III, no. 5). One of the paintings, after a period of dismissal, has now been reinstated as an original of outstanding quality, while the other is considered an excellent workshop copy.[21]

"A Womans head with naked Breasts Done by Old Palma" (see Appendix III, no. 7) was much prized by Northumberland; he had a copy made of it in 1655 (see Appendix IV, no. 48), probably to give away or to use in an exchange of pictures, or even to hang in one of his other houses, and he had the work restored in 1657 (see Appendix IV, no. 51). The original can confidently be identified with Buckingham's "A Venetian Lady with naked

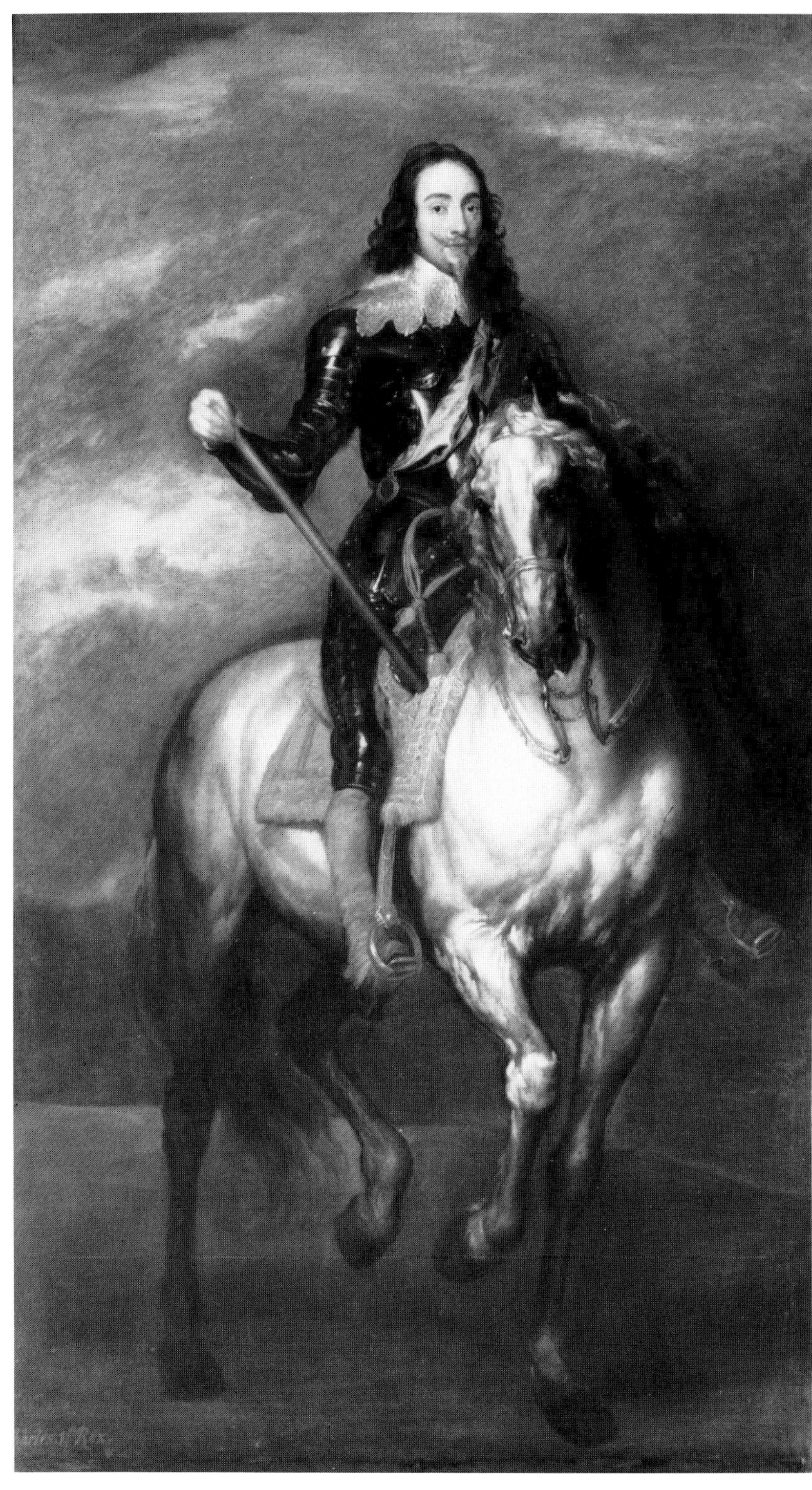

4. Anthony van Dyck and a later hand, *Charles I on Horseback,* c. 1633–1640, oil on canvas
Petworth House

Breasts" by Palma.[22] The painting left the Northumberland collection at an early date,[23] but there are some grounds for identifying it with a work now in the National Gallery, London.[24] It is less easy to be confident about what other works, if any, were obtained by Northumberland from York House, although Buckingham's "great Perspective" by Hendrick van Steenwijck could well be identical with the "rare Prospective done by Stenwick, the Figures by Pullenburke," inventoried at Petworth in 1671 (see Appendix III, no. 80), and recorded by Symonds at Northumberland House as early as 1652 (see Appendix I, no. 31). Other pictures by Bassano, Tintoretto, and Holbein could also have come from York House, but the evidence is incomplete. Northumberland's involvement with the estate of the 2d duke of Buckingham as late as 1650 makes it quite possible that he obtained pictures from the collection at different times, and by various means.[25] However, if the list of pictures obtained in 1645 was restricted to the eight small Elsheimers, the Titian, two Andrea del Sartos, and the Palma Vecchio, it is evident that the earl had an excellent bargain for £360.

In the same year that Northumberland obtained the pictures from York House, he set about getting hold of the two largest and most valuable Titians from Van Dyck's own collection: the *Vendramin Family* now in the National Gallery, London,[26] and the *Perseus and Andromeda* now in the Wallace Collection (see Appendix IV, nos. 24–25).[27] Following the legal chaos surrounding Van Dyck's estate, the artist's collection had been seized by several interested persons in a series of complicated maneuvers that I have discussed elsewhere.[28] A large part of the collection, including the two Titians, was acquired by Sir John Wittewronge of Rothamstead in Hertfordshire, in settlement of a debt.[29] A memorandum of Wittewronge's, dated 4 October 1645, establishes that he sold the *Vendramin Family* and the *Perseus and Andromeda* to Northumberland for £200.[30] At the same time Wittewronge accepted six small Netherlandish pictures from the earl in exchange for an unfinished version of Van Dyck's equestrian portrait of Charles I with M. de Saint Antoine, now at Buckingham Palace. Northumberland's ver-

sion remains at Petworth (fig. 4),[31] although considerably overpainted. As the face was described as incomplete in 1671 (see Appendix III, no. 11), the picture must have been repainted at some time after this date.

Another Venetian painting, then confidently attributed to Titian, is known to have been obtained by the earl before 1652, and seems linked to Van Dyck's connoisseurship of the great Venetian painter. Van Dyck's Italian Sketchbook contains a copy of a Titian *Mars and Venus* (fig. 5), inscribed as being in the Grimani collection.[32] The influence of this picture, particularly the pose of the female nude, can be traced in several Van Dyck mythologies, notably the *Amaryllis and Mirtillo* (Graf von Schönborn, Pommersfelden).[33] When Symonds visited Northumberland House in 1652 he noted, as by Titian, "A Venus lying along & Mars kissing her under a tree & naturall paese franco" (see Appendix I, no. 6). Rather surprisingly the same picture was listed in the 1671 Northumberland inventory as "A naked Venus & a Satyr Done by D⁰ [Titian]," valued at £100 (see Appendix III, no. 2). It can be found today at Petworth (fig. 6).[34] The transformation of a *Mars and Venus* into a *Venus and a Satyr* can be understood, however, through an examination of the X-radiographs of the surviving canvas (fig. 7).[35] Apparently in the interval between 1652 and 1671 the picture received a long vertical slash and was severely damaged. It appears that someone, when repairing the damage, not only altered the arms of the embracing figures, which in the underpainting were clearly identical with the pose of the figures copied by Van Dyck in the Sketchbook, but in the process transformed the subject.

It might seem that Van Dyck had made this copy in the Sketchbook from a version of the composition now in the Kunsthistorisches Museum, Vienna (fig. 8), thought to have been executed in Titian's workshop.[36] This painting, however, appears to have entered the collection of Rudolf II at Prague around 1621, when it was inventoried as "ein schoen stueck von Paolo Ferone" (that is, Veronese),[37] and has remained in the Habsburg collections ever since. If this identification is correct, the picture now in Vienna could not have been the version that Van Dyck saw in Italy during the early 1620s.

That a version of the *Mars and Venus* came to England in the early seventeenth century is confirmed by the discovery of a copy of it, based on one by Peter Oliver, at Kingston Lacy (fig. 9).[38] It is very likely that this copy derived from the picture owned by Northumberland—there can hardly have been another version in England at this time—and that it records the condition of the work before damage and repainting. It also seems reasonable to suggest that this is the same work that Van Dyck saw in the Grimani collection in the mid-1620s. Some means had to be found to transport the picture from Venice to Northumberland House, and, although this is conjectural, it is possible that the agent was Van Dyck. At the very least it seems likely that Van Dyck, who had studied the picture in Italy, advised Northumberland on its acquisition, and it could even have been one of the pictures that the artist brought back from Italy as part of the celebrated "Cabinet de Titien."

Northumberland obtained the *Vendramin Family* and the *Perseus and Andromeda*, as well as the group of pictures from York House, in 1645, at a time when he was least able to spend money freely. A newly found entry in the household accounts for this year, whereby one of the earl's servants, Lancelot

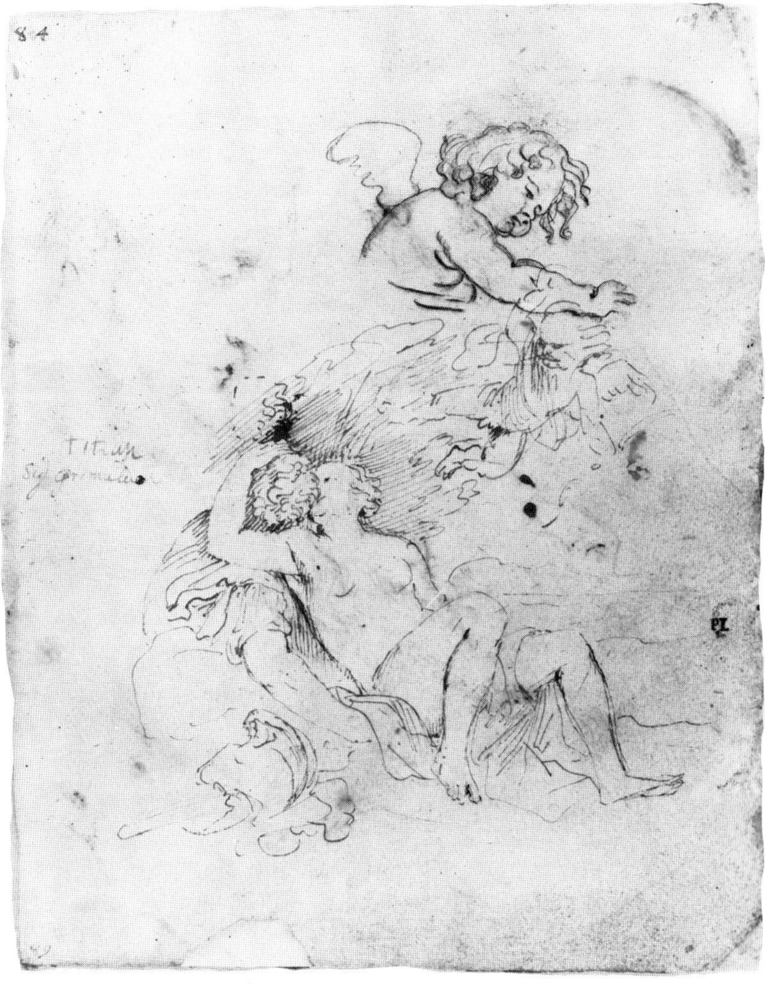

5. Anthony van Dyck after Titian, *Mars and Venus*, from the Italian Sketchbook, c. 1621–1627, pen and ink
British Museum, London

6. Attributed to Titian, *Venus and a Satyr*, c. 1570, oil on canvas
Petworth House

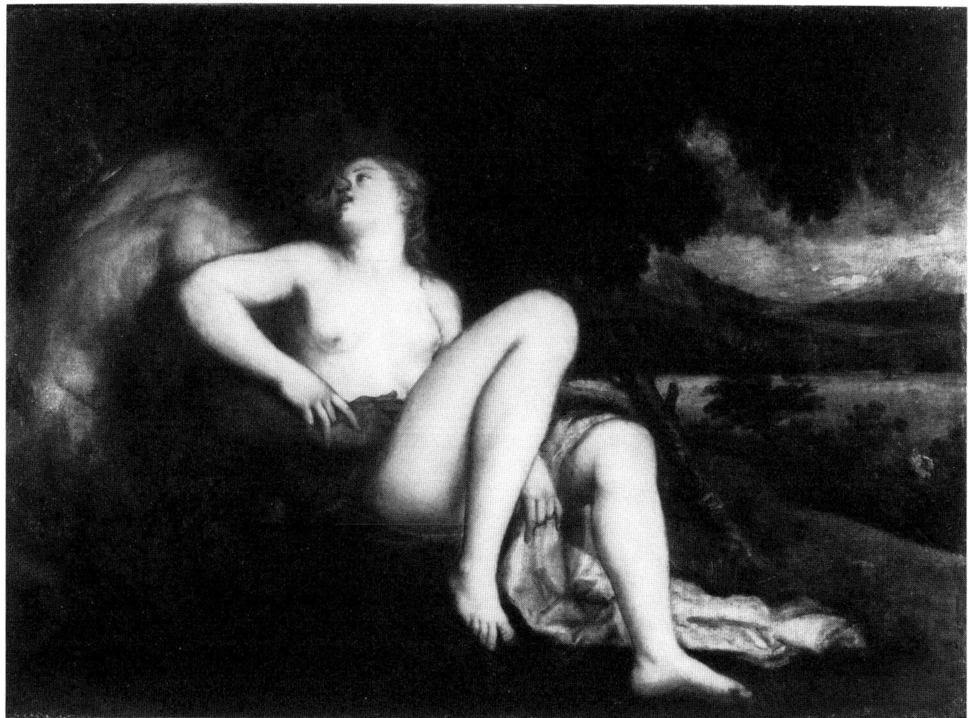

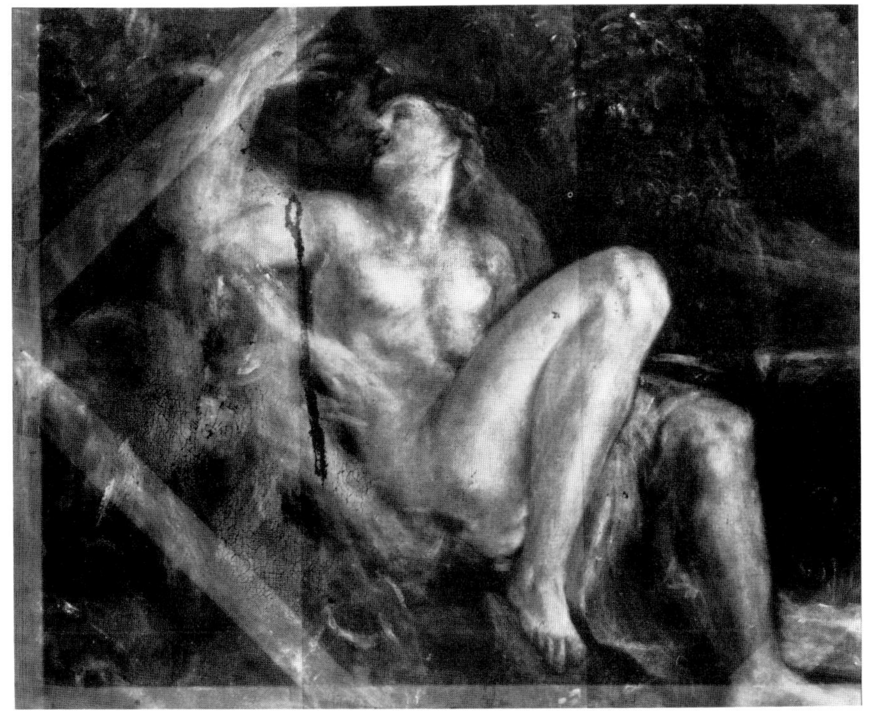

7. X-radiographs of *Venus and a Satyr*
Petworth House

8. Workshop of Titian, *Mars and Venus*, c. 1570, oil on canvas
Kunsthistorisches Museum, Vienna

Thorneton, sold pictures on his behalf for £439 (see Appendix IV, no. 24), indicates that the cost of the *Vendramin Family* was immediately recouped by the sale of the *Perseus and Andromeda*, which was not seen by Richard Symonds at Northumberland House in 1652 and which, some evidence suggests, passed to the Milanese painter Francesco Cairo.[39] The huge sums that the earl had advanced to Parliament, the disruption of his northern rents, and the somewhat unfriendly destruction of Wressel Castle meant that he faced bankruptcy in the 1640s. At this time the earl had to maintain Petworth, Syon, York House, and Northumberland House, where he had embarked on a costly building program. He was temporarily saved by a vote of £10,000 by Parliament, whose members were sensible of his loyalty and his authority as a spokesman when dealing with the king. They also realized that if Charles were to be deposed, Northumberland would, in all likelihood, become Lord Protector.[40] Despite

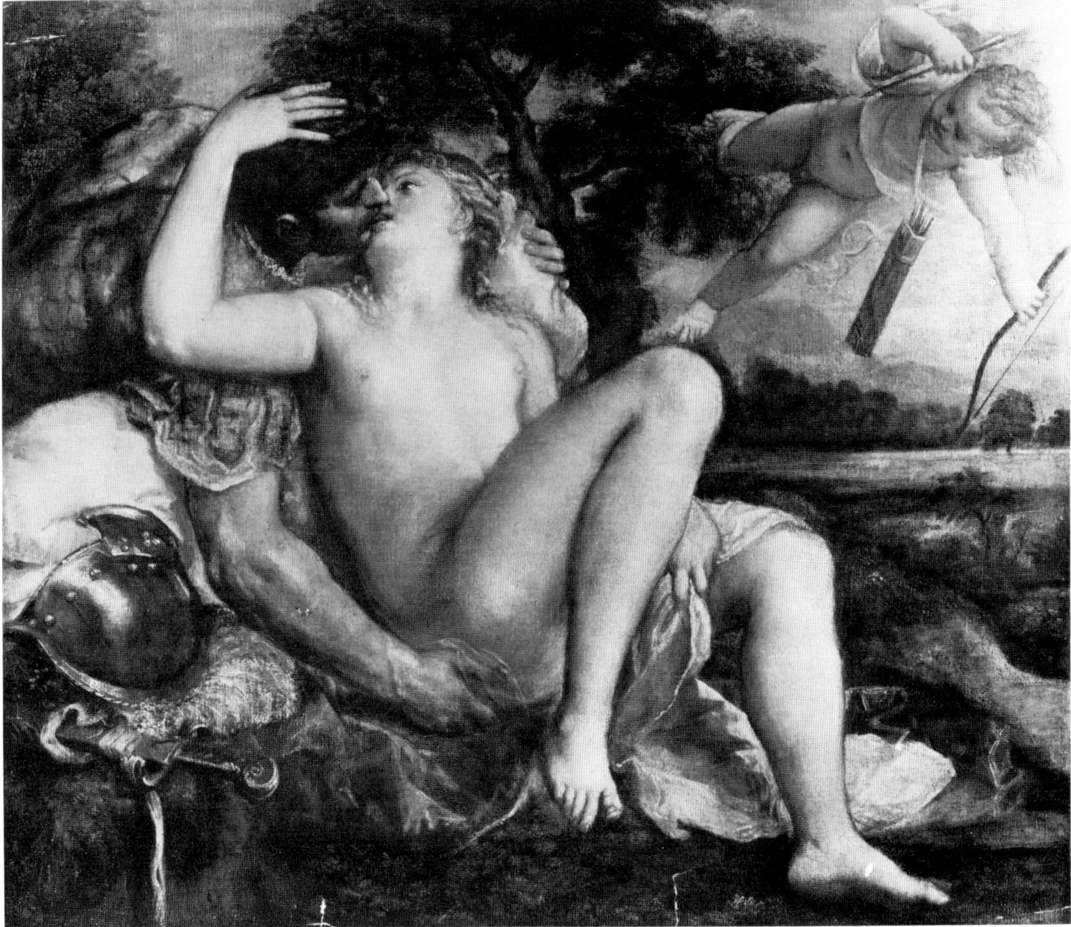

this grant of money, 1647 saw the dispatch of a consignment of the earl's pictures to the Netherlands, where they must have been sold (see Appendix IV, no. 30). A consignment of tapestries followed in 1648.[41]

Because one of Northumberland's first acts of lavish spending when he became earl in the 1630s was the purchase of "hangings," it is possible to compare these accounts with later inventories and make informed guesses about what was sold. It is very likely that the 1648 consignment contained five tapestries of the Story of Vulcan, probably woven at Mortlake, which had been purchased in 1633 for £225,[42] but that the earl kept six Brussels tapestries of the Story of David, which he had bought at the same time for £120.[43] Eight tapestries of the Story of Hester, which had hung in the 9th earl's closet and in the Green Bedchamber at Petworth at the time of the 9th earl's death in 1632,[44] also left the house during the 10th earl's lifetime. Northumberland's interest in the tapestry works at Mortlake is shown by a visit that he made there in 1635,[45] and by a payment "to the Dutchmen at Moreclake" in 1648, which was almost certainly connected with the consignment that he sent abroad.[46] The export did not go smoothly. The accounts show that the tapestries were seized by the Committee for the Navy, and that considerable trouble and expense were involved in getting them released, including "severall dinners for the Secretaries and Clarkes of the Committees of the Revenew and Navie and for the head searchers of London and Gravesend and severall of their friends."[47] A newsletter of February 1648 suggests that the political situation was so unstable that members of the House of Commons were suspected of sending their goods abroad intending "to fly from us," and it confirms that a consignment belonging to Northumberland had been prevented from going to the Netherlands.[48]

These were only relatively small financial measures, however, and the *Generall Accompte* for 1647 records that Northumberland sold plate to the value of £3,601 10s.7d.[49] This enormous sum must have meant that the earl had almost no plate left with which to entertain guests. Interestingly, he did not part with a silver "cesterne" that, newly found payments reveal, had been bought from the great Dutch silversmith

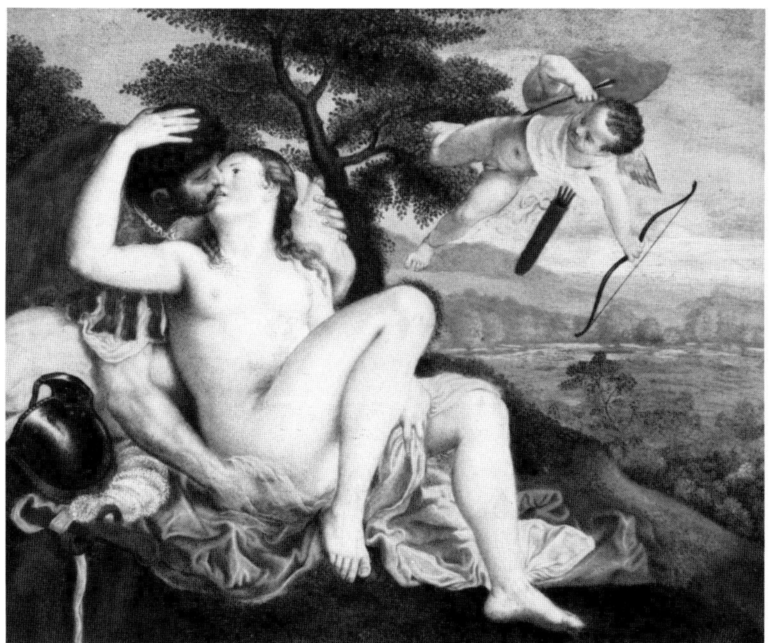

9. Unknown artist after Peter Oliver after Titian, *Mars and Venus,* vellum mounted on card
Kingston Lacy

Christian van Vianen in 1641 for the astronomical sum of £351 15s. 0d., as well as "sondrie peeces of engraven plate."[50] This was probably the largest sum that Northumberland ever paid for a single work of art. It must have been one of the last major pieces of silver that Van Vianen made before returning to Utrecht in 1643. Further newly discovered documents establish, in some detail, that Northumberland and his son, Josceline, made purchases from Van Vianen every year between 1662 and 1666,[51] incidentally providing some evidence to confirm the dates of Van Vianen's second stay in England and his death.[52] Northumberland's enthusiasm for this Dutch silversmith's work was perhaps only equaled, as an act of patronage, by his employment of Van Dyck.

It seems that Northumberland's collection began to take distinctive shape in the year 1645. Consequently I have focused on the acquisitions that he made from the collections of the duke of Buckingham and Van Dyck, in order to establish the character of Northumberland's taste. However, he had been buying pictures ever since he had succeeded to the earldom in 1632; the household accounts are tantalizingly brief and this phase of his activity is difficult to reconstruct. In 1631 he bought four pictures for £15 and had them put into ebony frames, which suggests that

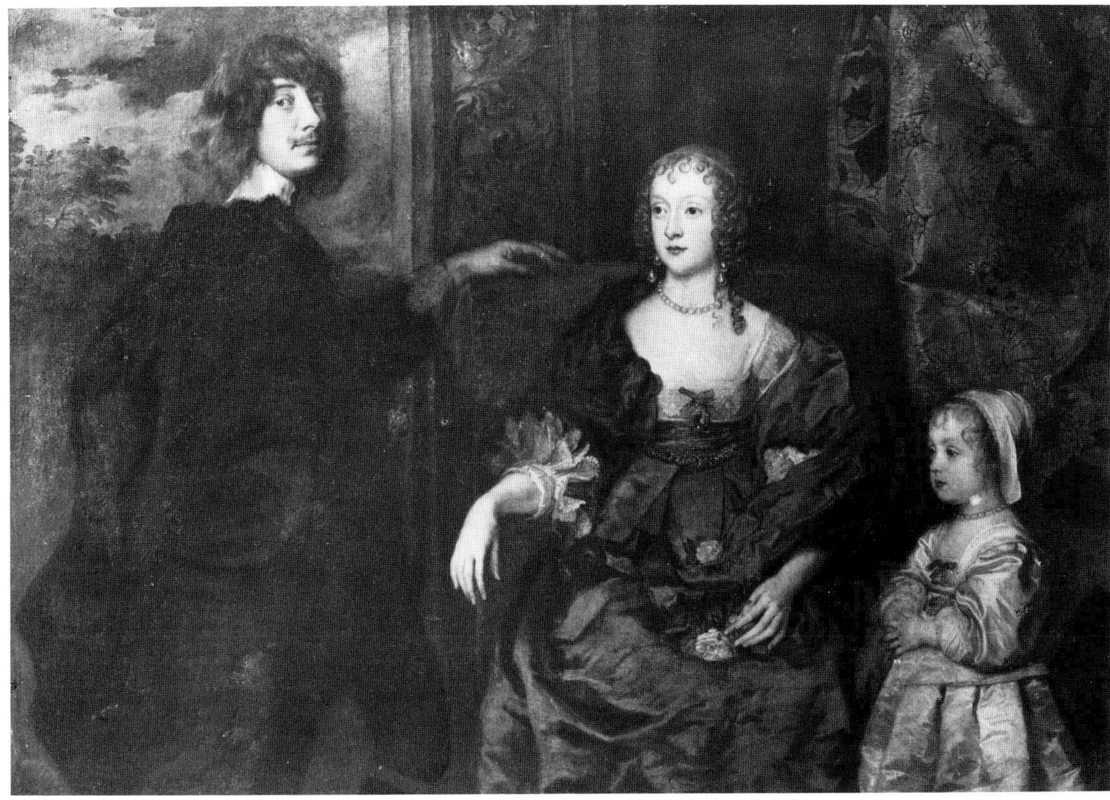

10. Anthony van Dyck, *Algernon Percy, 10th Earl of Northumberland, with His Wife, Lady Anne Cecil, and Daughter, Lady Katherine Percy*, 1635, oil on canvas
Petworth House

they came directly from the painter (see Appendix IV, nos. 1–2). On 22 March 1633 he spent £10 on a picture while staying at Essex House (see Appendix IV, no. 3). The year 1634 shows him beginning to collect in earnest, spending the large sum of £342 2s. 6d. on "Pictures of diverse kindes," and a more modest £9 on three pictures (see Appendix IV, nos. 5–6). Northumberland's early purchases were almost certainly motivated by the failure of his father to collect on a significant scale, but it should not be assumed that he had begun to buy Italian pictures at this date. We have seen that Northumberland unloaded a number of Netherlandish cabinet pictures on Wittewronge in 1645, and the 1647 consignment to the Low Countries may have contained northern works (see Appendix IV, no. 30). The development of Northumberland's taste in pictures was almost certainly influenced by his contact with Van Dyck in the mid-1630s. It might seem that the king's example would have been enough to encourage Northumberland's interest in collecting, were it not for his respectful but complex attitude to Charles I and the fact that he was not closely associ-

ated with the group of most avid collectors at court. Northumberland went to exceptional lengths, at a particularly difficult time, to trace the pictures by Titian that had been embezzled from Van Dyck's estate, and this suggests that they had a special importance for him.

Northumberland commissioned four family portraits from Van Dyck, and, as with many other English patrons, this seems to have opened his eyes to what the marquis of Hamilton called the bewitchment of "those intysing things," namely pictures.[53] In 1635 there was a payment to Van Dyck of £200 for "Pictures of his Lo^p. and Countesse & diverse others" (see Appendix IV, no. 8) that must refer to the group portrait at Petworth of Northumberland with his wife, Lady Anne Cecil, and one of their daughters (fig. 10), now identifiable as Lady Katherine (who died in childhood) on the basis of a later payment in 1660, when the earl commissioned a copy from his tame painter, Symon Stone (see Appendix IV, no. 60). Since Northumberland wears the Garter, visible in a raking light despite darkening and damage to the canvas,[54] the group portrait must date from after his installation on 16 May 1635, as the payment, mentioned above, confirms. The sum of £200 could also have covered the posthumous portrait of the 9th earl now at Petworth (fig. 13),[55] and Van Dyck's prices are probably reflected in the valuations found in Stone's 1671 inventory: £60 for the group portrait, £30 for the three-quarter-length (see Appendix III, nos. 12–13). It is most unlikely, however, that the payment included any of the three-quarter-length portraits of women by Van Dyck that later formed a striking group in Northumberland's collection.[56] These were almost certainly commissioned by the sitters. Symonds' account of the collection suggests that only four of these female portraits had been obtained by 1652 (see Appendix I, nos. 11–13, 17); there were eight at Northumberland House by 1671 (see Appendix III, nos. 14–17, 21, 24–25). Newly found entries in the accounts suggest that one of the two portraits of Northumberland's sister, Lucy, countess of Carlisle (1599–1660), was obtained in 1651 (see Appendix IV, no. 40).[57] In December 1661 William Russell, earl of Bedford, paid Symon Stone £10 for a copy of Van Dyck's portrait of his wife, Anne Carr (1615–1684),[58] which, if it was made from the version at Petworth,[59] suggests that Northumberland had obtained the portrait by this date. The picture may even have been the "Lady above in a light blew garmt" seen by Symonds in 1652 (see Appendix I, no. 17). The portrait of Lady Dorothy Sidney, countess of Sunderland (1617–1684), appears to have been obtained by exchange as late as 1662 (see Appendix IV, no. 62).[60] This was the year when Robert Spencer, 2d earl of Sunderland (1641–1702), attained his majority, and Northumberland may have obtained the portrait of Sunderland's mother in exchange for copies of Van Dyck's portraits of Henry, Lord Percy of Alnwick, and of Northumberland himself, which have remained at Althorp.[61] Some of these female portraits may have been acquired by gift, exchange, or purchase at any time over a period of more than thirty years.

Neither family bonds nor religious and political affiliation can explain why this group of portraits of beautiful women was assembled by the earl, and the conception of such a gallery does, of course, have its own history. It is possible that Van Dyck told Northum-

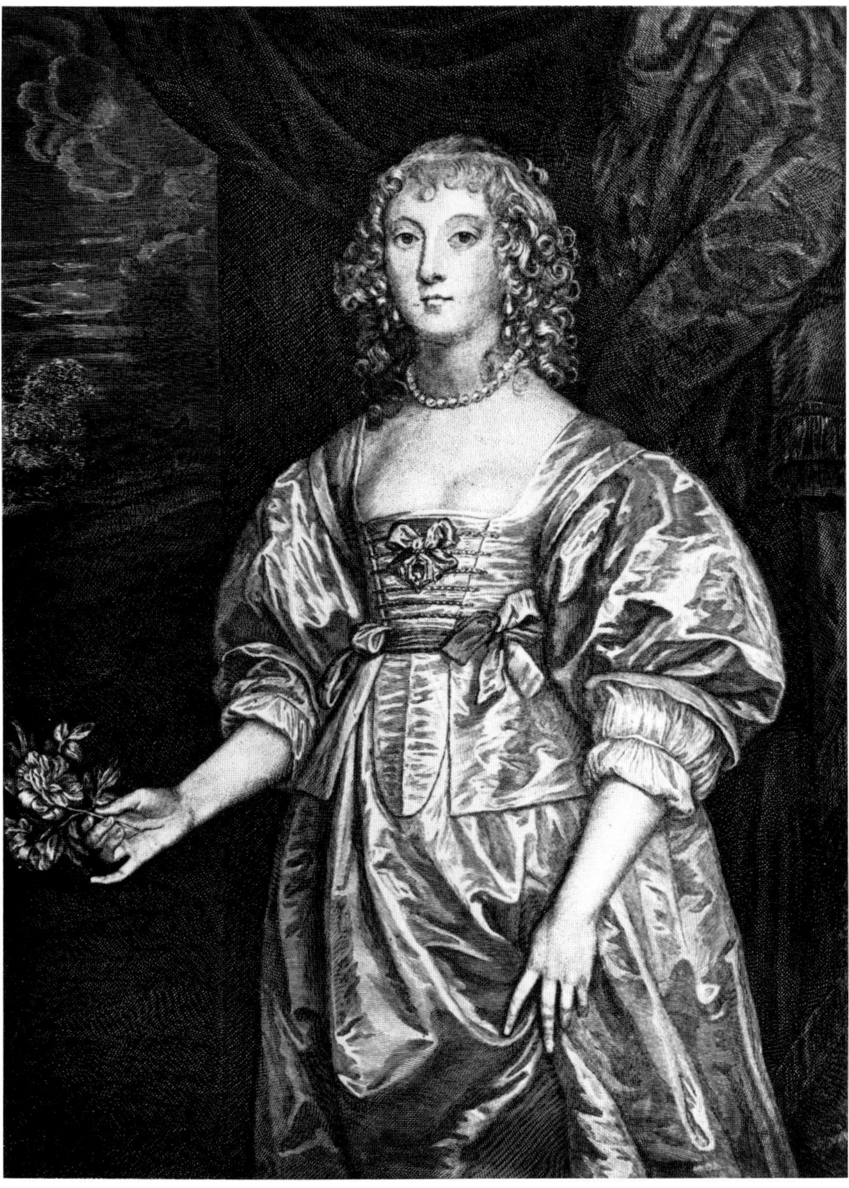

11. Pierre Lombart after Anthony van Dyck, *Elizabeth Cecil, Countess of Devonshire*, engraving

berland about the duke of Mantua's "Gallery of Beauties," for which Rubens was directed to travel to France shortly after his visit to Spain in 1603, although he did not in fact carry out the project. A more immediate precedent was the gallery of beautiful women by Van Dyck assembled by Philip, Lord Wharton, at Upper Winchendon. The inclusion of Northumberland's favorite sister, Lady Carlisle, in his gallery is self-explanatory; his other sister, the countess of Leicester, was only represented by a copy after Van Dyck that was not hung with the best pictures at Northumberland House but banished to Petworth (see Appendix III, no.

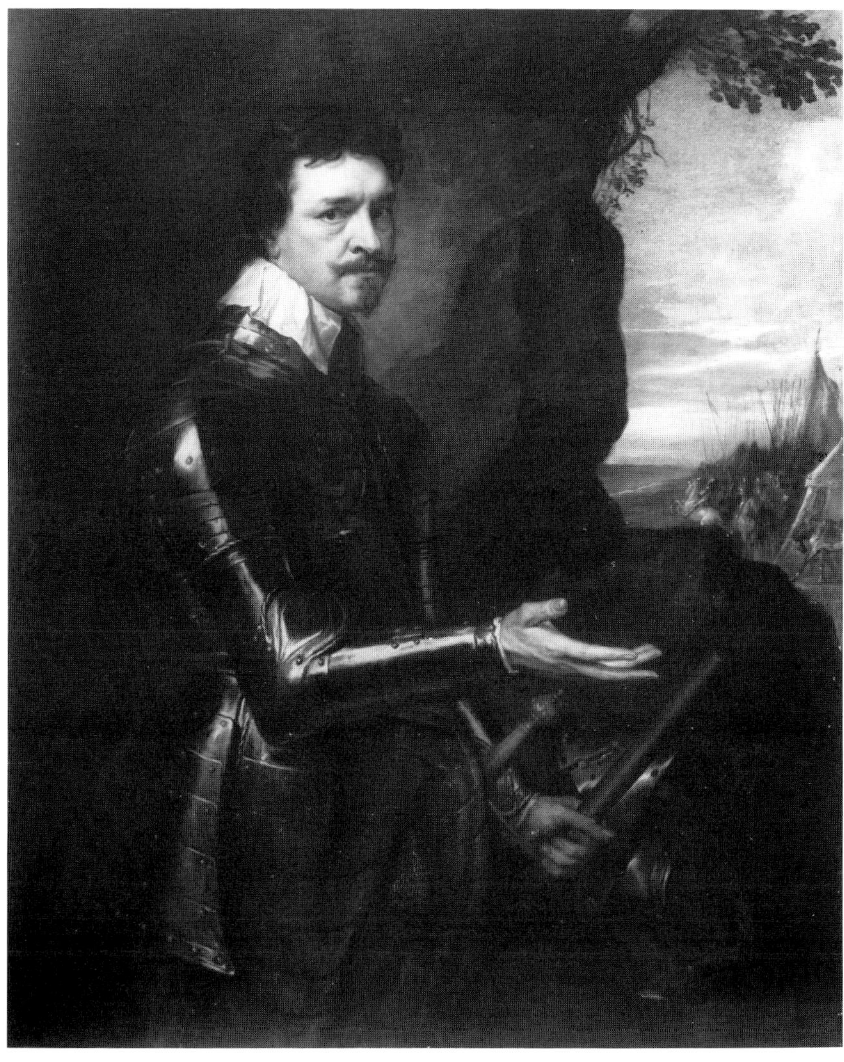

12. Anthony van Dyck, *Thomas Wentworth, 1st Earl of Strafford*, 1636, oil on canvas
Petworth House

78),[62] perhaps reflecting the earl's estrangement from the countess of Leicester and her husband. Elizabeth Cecil, countess of Devonshire, shown here in an engraving by Pierre Lombart (fig. 11),[63] may well have been included in the gallery because she was the younger sister of Northumberland's first wife. This family tie may explain the admission of a relatively dull Van Dyck into the pantheon. The organization of Richard Symonds' notes on the pictures in the gallery at Northumberland House suggests that a now lost or misidentified portrait of Anne Boteler, countess of Newport, hung next to one of her sister, Mrs. Endymion Porter (see Appendix I, nos. 11–12). Northumberland's reasons for owning portraits of these two Catholic converts, and zealous Royalists, are not clear—unless they were aesthetic.[64] It

seems that Northumberland, who had an eye for a bargain in pictures, was astute in obtaining good Van Dyck portraits from Royalists, such as Endymion Porter and the earl of Newport, who fell on hard times in the 1640s and found their estates sequestrated. This seems more likely than that Northumberland was given some of these portraits by the sitters in the 1630s, before the break between the king and Parliament. It was usual to give a copy, rather than the original, as a gift, unless a gesture of particular significance was being made, as was certainly the case when Strafford and Lady Carlisle exchanged their portraits by Van Dyck. It was surely from Lady Carlisle's estate that Northumberland obtained the second of his two portraits of his sister by Van Dyck (see Appendix III, no. 25), and it is also likely that he acquired the universally admired three-quarter-length of Strafford (fig. 12), which is now at Petworth (see Appendix III, no. 18), from the same source, since the sitter said, when discussing his portraits by Van Dyck, that "the shortt one is for my Ladye of Carlile."[65] However, either this work or a similar one must have been at Syon by 1637, because in that year the Reverend Garrard wrote to Strafford from that house that "I daily visit your Picture done by Vandike in Armour, which hangs in one of the Galleries here."[66] It may have been that Lady Carlisle loaned the portrait to her brother.

The portrait of Northumberland's father, the 9th earl (fig. 13),[67] is clearly a very different sort of commission, and has a very different iconography from any other of the Van Dycks in the collection. It had great significance for Northumberland, and in 1655 it was put into a new ebony frame and glazed (see Appendix IV, no. 48). It may well have been the only picture in the collection shown under glass, since there are no other payments for this. Symonds noted, probably because he was informed by Symon Stone, that it had been "done by an old picture" (see Appendix I, no. 10). Symonds' notes indicate that Van Dyck also painted a posthumous portrait of the 8th earl (1532–1585) in the same manner (see Appendix I, no. 9), although there is no trace of it in the 1671 inventory. The 9th earl had died in 1632 at sixty-eight, an advanced age in the seventeenth century, and he is shown by Van

Dyck looking somewhat younger than that.[68] It has also been rightly noted that the contemplative pose is related to Hilliard's miniature of the 9th earl, which dates from the 1590s (fig. 14).[69] According to the 1671 inventory Northumberland appears to have displayed the two portraits close to each other in his picture gallery (see Appendix III, nos. 19, 27). It is wrong to assume, though, that Van Dyck followed Hilliard's likeness, simply adding the beard that the 9th earl grew in later life and aging the features, as

has been claimed.[70] The 9th earl is known to have had his portrait painted on several occasions (see Appendix III, no. 42),[71] and it would be strange if Van Dyck had not used a more up-to-date likeness. The composition is also only loosely related to Hilliard's. Too much has perhaps been said about the association of the pose with melancholy,[72] and not enough about its link with depictions of philosophers, most famous among them the so-called Heraclitus from Raphael's *School of Athens.*[73] The pose is not unknown in Eng-

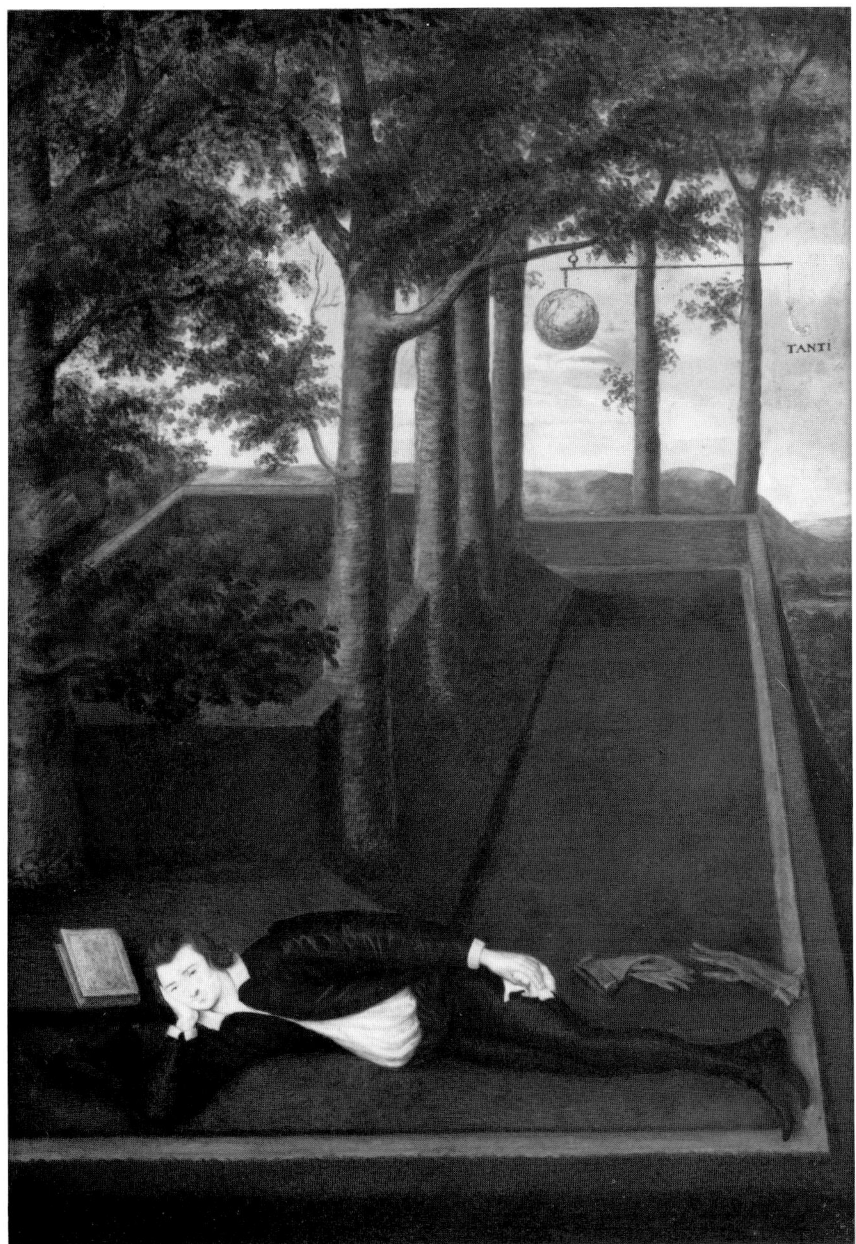

14. Nicholas Hilliard, *Henry Percy, 9th Earl of Northumberland,* c. 1590–1595, vellum mounted on card
Rijksmuseum, Amsterdam

15. Unknown artist, *Sir Henry Wotton,* c. 1630, oil on canvas
Eton College

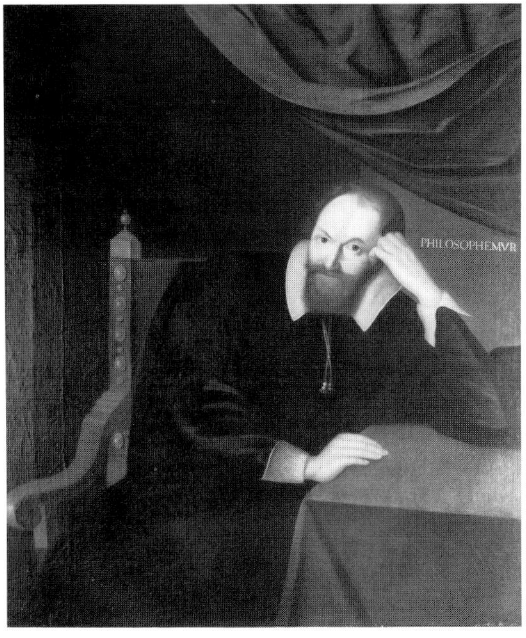

lish portraiture, and a version of it can be found in a likeness of Sir Henry Wotton at Eton College (fig. 15)[74] that is inscribed PHILOSOPHEMUR and shows the sitter similarly pensive, seated at a table resting his head on his hand. Another version of this pose can be found in a Hilliard miniature of an unknown young man that, as Erna Auerbach tentatively suggested, recalled the youthful 9th earl of Northumberland.[75]

A connection certainly exists between the emblem seen in the background of Hilliard's miniature and the inscribed paper under the earl's elbow in the portrait by Van Dyck. In the miniature a weighty sphere is balanced by a feather. As John Peacock has shown, the somewhat fractured Latin inscription in Van Dyck's portrait relates to Archimedes' proposition on the balancing of unequal weights,[76] although no one has yet established exactly what the inscription says. It contains a question and two statements. The question asks "What is the ratio of the distance of the heavier to the lighter weight?" (DIS[TAN-TIAE] / QUID / VERO AD [?GRAVE / ?LEV-IUS?] / RATIO GRAVIOR[IS] [?]). It is not really answered by two statements: "If they are of the same distance [then the weights must be equal]" (EADEM SIT DISTANTIA . . .), and "The weight is suspended at a distance at which the heavier one becomes balanced with it" (GRAVE APPENDITUR AD DIS-TANTIAM / IN QUA GRAVIUS FIET AE-QUILIBRIUM).[77] It seems that the emblem in Hilliard's miniature is transformed naturalistically onto an inscribed sheet of paper in Van Dyck's portrait, and the device is turned into a statement of a scientific principle. This is hardly typical of Van Dyck's portraits, and is obviously specific to the commission.

It is wrong to assume, as has been claimed, that the 9th earl devised this inscription himself before his death, six months after Van Dyck's arrival in England.[78] Because of the 9th earl's long imprisonment in the

Tower, from 1605 to 1621, it is sometimes thought that he was estranged from his son during Algernon Percy's childhood and adolescence. In fact, in 1608, at the age of six, Algernon Percy was sent to lodge in the Tower, where his father took his son's education in hand,[79] and the boy must have mixed with the exceptional group of scholars who attended the 9th earl. By 1632, however, there were few of these associates of his father still alive who could have given advice on the Latin inscription.[80] It seems that the emblem found in the Hilliard portrait of the 1590s, which was probably devised by the 9th earl himself, was revised in the posthumous portrait by Van Dyck to accord better with the earl's scholarly interests. The person best able to guide this was the earl's son. The Van Dyck portrait should be seen not as an *apologia pro vita sua*, but as an act of filial piety.

It is also worth considering how far the 9th earl was concerned with the visual arts,[81] and to what extent he created a picture gallery at Petworth. At the time of his death the Old Library there contained, in addition to a large quantity of books, some paintings, namely "twelve Turkes, twentyfoure Emperours, Hercules' labours twelve, of all other sorts of pictures twentie eight . . . [and] two large pictures of St. Lawrence and the Maccabees."[82] None of these is recorded in the 1671 Northumberland inventory and so must have been dispersed by the 10th earl, who otherwise respected his father's memory and kept his library intact. The twentyfour "Antick Pictures of the Emporers of Rome," bought for £24 between October 1586 and February 1587,[83] were among the first substantial items of expenditure made by Henry Percy when he became earl, together with some smaller payments "for drawing of little pictures or Embleames" and "for guyldinge the Picture of Cupide."[84] The 9th earl seems to have owned at least one very precious picture that he kept privately at Syon, because at the time of James I's visit on 8 June 1603 there is a payment "for a taffatye curten to hang on the picture in yor Lo: Chambre."[85] The earl seems to have preferred having framed maps hanging on his walls, however, and many were made for him during his expedition to the Netherlands in 1600–1602.[86] The earl's idea of a suitable

present for his son, when he went to Cambridge in October 1615, was a painting of a dissection of the human head.[87] The evidence suggests that the 9th earl valued pictures as visual information, and, unlike his son, was not much concerned with aesthetic pleasure.

Van Dyck's impact on Northumberland can be measured by the fact that the earl never again allowed himself to be painted by any other artist. In addition to the family group (fig. 10), Van Dyck provided Northumberland with two definitive likenesses that showed him as Admiral of the Fleet (fig. 1). A payment of £50 to Van Dyck in 1639 was probably for the full-length (see Appendix IV, no. 13).[88] It is striking that Lely was not asked to paint Northumberland, even though the earl recognized the artist's talents very early, and Lely supplied many portraits of the Percy family during the 1640s, 1650s, and 1660s (see Appendix III, nos. 31–34; Appendix IV, nos. 55, 57, 64–65, 67). Northumberland commissioned some miniature portraits of himself in later life, but these were always copied from Van Dyck's earlier likenesses; a signed Samuel Cooper of this kind is in the Victoria and Albert Museum, London.[89] The earl also liked to give away copies by Stone of the Van Dyck portraits, as can be seen from payments in 1655 for one given to Roger Boyle, Baron Broghill (see Appendix IV, no. 48), in 1658 for "Doctor Rainbow" (see Appendix IV, no. 55), and in 1659 for one "with the Anchor" for Elizabeth Percy, Lady Capel (see Appendix IV, no. 58).[90] In making these gifts Northumberland was clearly not concerned that he may no longer have looked or dressed like the man painted by Van Dyck twenty or so years earlier.

The picture gallery at Northumberland House is unlikely to have existed before 1647, when the earl moved out of York House, and it was probably under construction and decoration in the immediately preceding years. This chronology raises the question of where the 10th earl displayed his new acquisitions, not least the Van Dyck portraits, between 1632 and 1647. In 1632, at the time of the 9th earl's death, the few pictures that he owned were kept at Petworth, and the houses at Syon and in London were clearly treated as secondary residences.[91] In the early 1630s Northumberland may have housed his growing picture gallery at Dorset House, which he rented during these years and where, for example, he entertained on a lavish scale at the time of his investiture as Knight of the Garter on 16 May 1635.[92] The portraits would have been an important part of the public face that Northumberland turned toward the court. It is an open question whether in the years between 1640 and 1647 he moved his picture collection, including the Van Dyck portraits, to York House, which was one of his residences at that time.[93] Northumberland clearly considered York House his principal London residence, Syon then being in the country. Payments for "necessaries about packing vp of picktures" in 1647 (see Appendix IV, no. 31)[94] suggest that the earl moved his collection from York House to Northumberland House, next door, in that year. Richard Symonds' 1652 account of the collection then housed in the London mansion (Appendix I) establishes that the picture gallery had been organized by that date, and contained the nucleus of the works inventoried in 1671 (Appendix III). Frequent payments during the 1650s and 1660s for packing up pictures and for their dispatch to Petworth (see Appendix IV, nos. 38, 44, 47, 49, 51, 58, 61–62, 64) suggest that as new acquisitions were made the more minor works were removed and sent to the country. The 1671 inventory shows that the collection was not only housed in Northumberland House, but some good pictures and a number of copies were also then at Petworth, notably the Palma Giovane *Mars and Venus* now in the National Gallery, London (see Appendix III, no. 67),[95] which Symonds had seen in London in 1652 (see Appendix I, no. 28) and which was given the surprisingly low valuation of £15 in 1671. The picture with the highest valuation at Petworth, £100, was the large perspective by Steenwijck with figures by Poelenburgh (see Appendix III, no. 80), which Symonds reported having seen at Northumberland House in 1652 (see Appendix I, no. 31).

On one occasion, at least, a picture is known to have been sent to Syon rather than to Northumberland House. On 18 April 1649 Lely's group portrait *The Children of Charles I: James, Duke of York, Princess Elizabeth, and Henry, Duke of Gloucester* (fig. 16), now at Petworth,[96] was transported from Hamp-

ton Court to Syon, for reasons that are not entirely clear (see Appendix IV, nos. 35–36). Northumberland is known to have paid Lely for the double portrait *Charles I and James, Duke of York*, now at Syon,[97] in 1648 (see Appendix IV, no. 32), and though it has always been assumed that the two commissions were linked, there is no known payment for *The Children of Charles I*, which must have been painted while the princess and the princes were in Northumberland's custody. The ages of the children, which are inscribed on the picture, suggest that the group portrait was painted in 1647, and it may be that the double portrait was commissioned by Northumberland while the group was painted for Charles I, who would have kept it with him at Hampton Court during his enforced separation from his family. Following the king's execution on 30 January 1649, Northumberland could have been presented with the picture, and this would explain why it was sent from Hampton Court by William Smithsby, who was keeper of the Privy Lodgings and Standing Wardrobe. At any rate, it was soon sent to Northumberland House, where it was seen by Richard Symonds on 27 December 1652 (see Appendix I, no. 30).

On his 27 December visit to Northumberland House, Symonds was taken around the collection by "Mr Stone who coppyes." Stone seems to have entered Northumberland's employment in the late 1640s. The earl bought a picture from him in 1647 (see Appendix IV, no. 29), and Stone helped to send the consignment of the earl's pictures to the Netherlands (see Appendix IV, no. 30). In 1648 Stone traveled to Holland with another of the household servants, John Lamb, and must have been involved in negotiating the sale (see Appendix IV, no. 32). In 1648 Stone sold a picture of flowers to the earl (see Appendix IV, no. 33; Appendix III, no. 94), and in the same year he received the first of many payments for "necessaries about the picktures at Northumberland house" (see Appendix IV, no. 37). It is reasonable to assume that he was in charge of the hanging and organization of the collection at this time. However, it is only from 1654 that we find frequent detailed payments for "keeping cleane the picture roome a yeare, helpe to ayre and clense pictures, [and] charcoles for

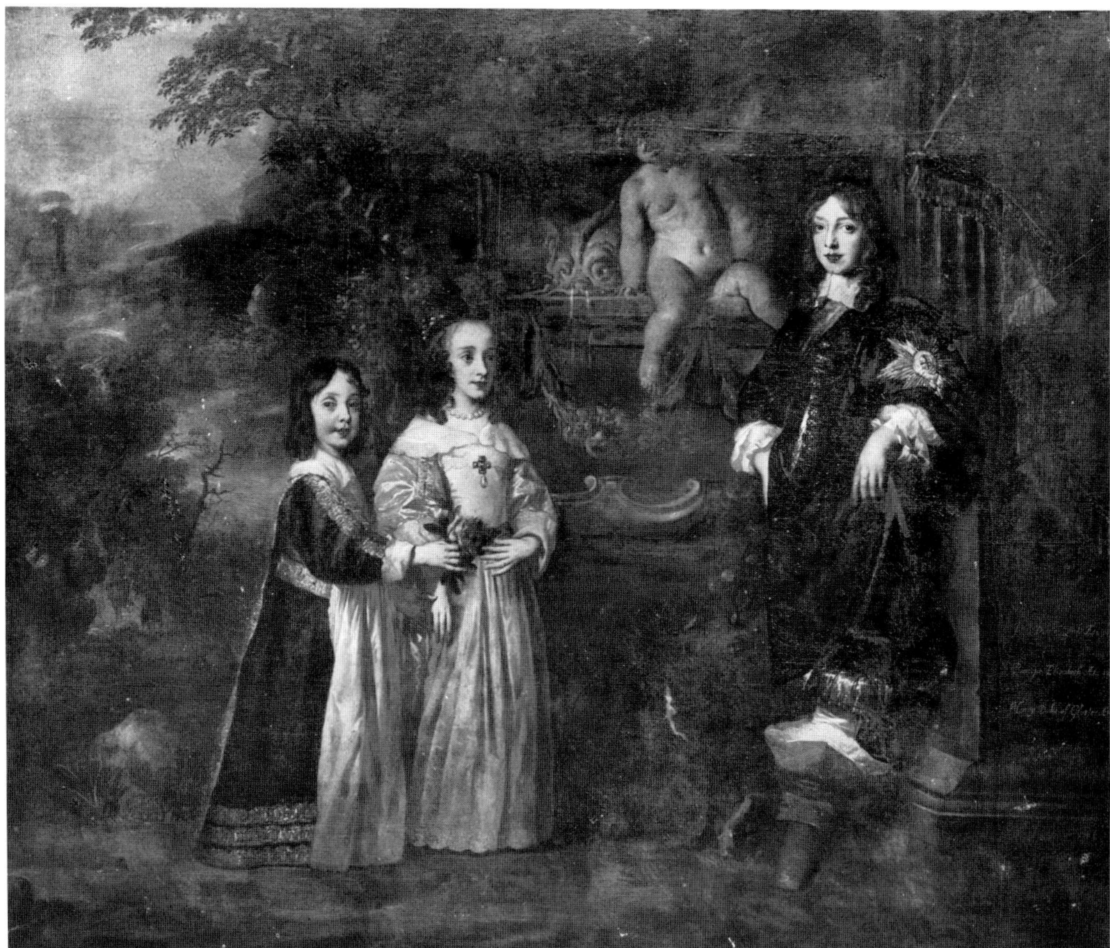

the picture roome" (see Appendix IV, no. 47). Despite Symonds' comment, it is also only from 1655 that we find detailed payments to Stone for copies after Italian pictures that were either added to the collection or, if made from pictures in it, given away by the earl. Stone copied the Titian double portrait (fig. 3) in 1655,[98] as well as a Palma Vecchio that was probably the woman with "rare fleshy breasts" (see Appendix I, no. 23; Appendix IV, no. 48.)[99] A "Coppy of Ecce homo" mentioned in the same payment, which cost £16, was almost certainly after Titian's *Christ Presented to the People*, now in the Kunsthistorisches Museum, Vienna, which had formerly been at York House,[100] because Stone's copy is mentioned in a manuscript inventory of the Buckingham collection.[101] Since the Titian original was sent to Antwerp in 1647–1648, Northumberland must have bought the copy from Stone's

stock. The earl's employment of the artist as curator of his collection and resident copyist is relatively unusual in England at this time, although Buckingham had, of course, employed Balthazar Gerbier to look after the pictures at York House.[102]

The early 1650s were not a time of rich acquisitions for Northumberland, and his finances were only kept afloat by an enormous loan of £10,000 at six percent interest from the distinguished physician Sir Theodore Turquet de Mayerne (1573–1655),[103] who had been friendly with both Rubens and Van Dyck and was an informed student of the methods and materials of painting.[104] Although the earl could have taken advantage of the dispersal of the king's collection in 1650, he chose not to, partly, no doubt, because of his personal refusal to endorse the execution of the king or profit from it, and partly because, although there were quanti-

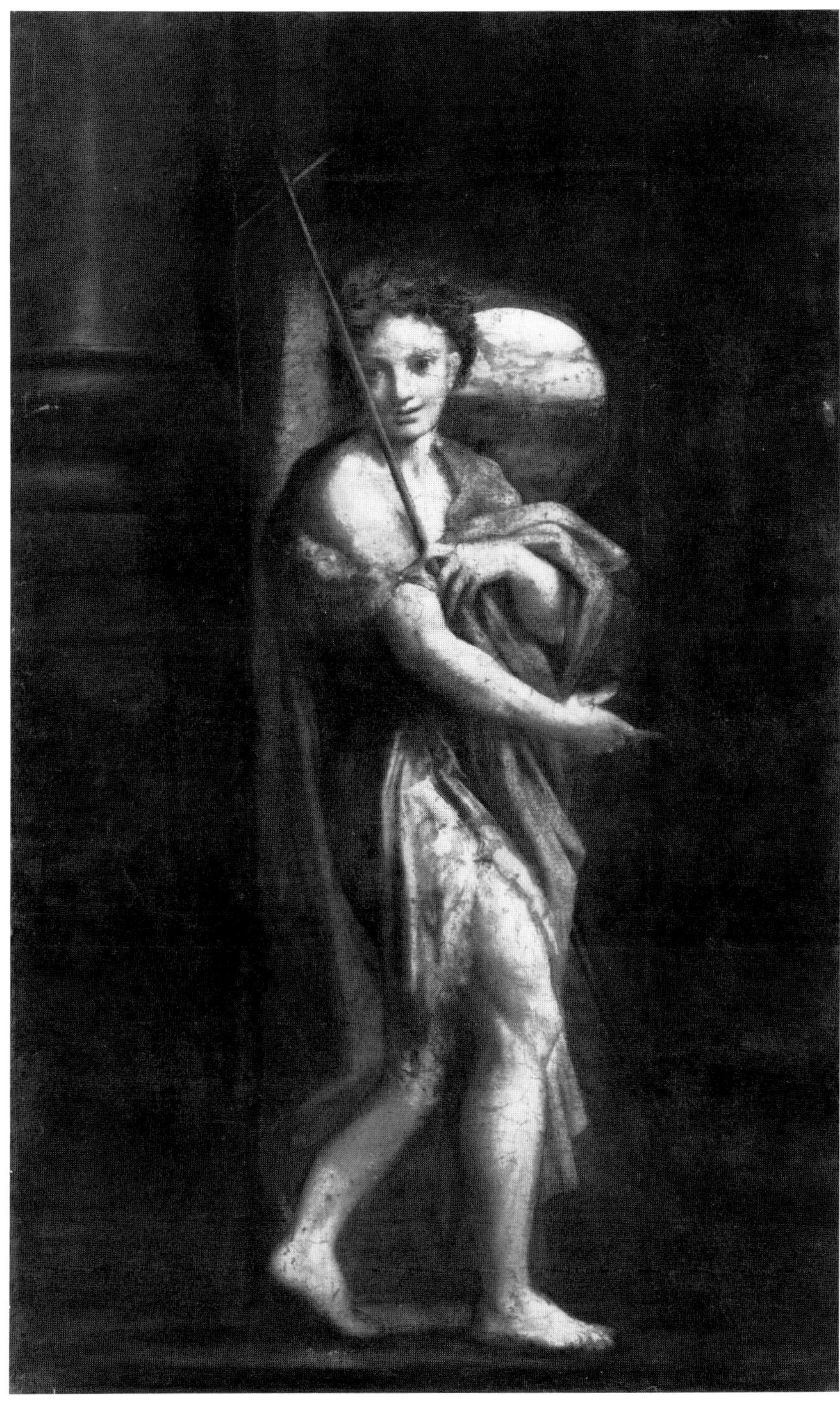

17. Workshop of Antonio da Correggio, *Saint John the Baptist*, c. 1530, oil on canvas
Royal Collection, Windsor Castle

known. His first purchases were three major Italian pictures that had been in the royal collection and that the earl bought from the elderly Jerome Lanier, who was a relative of Nicholas Lanier and also a musician (see Appendix IV, no. 51). Fortunately Lanier's receipt as well as detailed accounts survive in the Northumberland papers (see Appendix IV, no. 52). The earl bought a damaged picture of *Saint John the Baptist* (fig. 17), now at Windsor Castle, that had been bought by Charles I in Spain[105] and was then confidently attributed to Correggio.[106] Northumberland also obtained a panel of *The Sacrifice of a Goat to Jupiter* (fig. 18), now at Hampton Court, by Giulio Romano, that had originally hung in the Gabinetto dei Cesari in the Palazzo Ducale at Mantua.[107] The prize acquisition, however, was the panel by Polidoro da Caravaggio of *Psyche Abandoned on a Rock by Her Parents* (fig. 19), now at Hampton Court,[108] that had come to England with the collection of William Frizell, Arundel's agent who worked in partnership with William Petty.[109] The panel belonged to a series that must once have decorated a piece of furniture, possibly a bed. The various scenes had been split up between Jerome Lanier, Clement Lanier, and John Hadnott at the time of the sale,[110] although the largest portion of them soon entered the collection of Philip, viscount Lisle, and was displayed at his house at Sheen.[111] Lanier had bought the Correggio, the Giulio, and the Polidoro on 14 May 1650 for a total of £128,[112] so their sale seven years later to the earl of Northumberland for £120 represented a small loss. As we have seen elsewhere, the earl had a good nose for a bargain. He may well have bought the three pictures to get hold of the Polidoro, because, when he had to part with it in 1660, he employed Stone to make a copy, which, interestingly, was executed in the same materials as the original; it is described as "Done upon Board" (see Appendix III, no. 55; Appendix IV, no. 60). Following the Restoration Northumberland found it politic to return his three pictures by Correggio, Giulio, and Polidoro to the Crown,[113] together with an important group of antique statues and busts that he had bought in 1657 and 1658 (see Appendix IV, no. 60). In 1660, when he copied the Polidoro, Stone also copied the Correggio as a re-

ties of good paintings on the market, they still cost money, something in short supply in the Percy household.

In 1657, however, Northumberland felt able to resume his activities as a collector and made a series of important acquisitions that have, up to now, been entirely un-

placement for the original (see Appendix III, nos. 55, 118), but not the Giulio Romano, which suggests that it was less prized. Shortly afterward, in 1661, Northumberland employed Stone to copy five of the six *Friezes with Cupids* by Polidoro that had belonged to Lord Lisle;[114] these originals were also returned to the royal collection, and by having the copies made the earl partly reconstructed the series (see Appendix III, nos. 23, 64; Appendix IV, no. 61). He kept the copies in the picture gallery at Northumberland House until his death, although many others by Stone were relegated to Petworth (see Appendix III, nos. 111–116, 118). The additions to the collection made in 1657 precipitated a major rehanging, and the accounts give some idea of how the new installation appeared at this time: the pictures, which were hung on green silk strings, were placed alongside mirrors, which hung on red silk ones (see Appendix IV, no. 51).

The year 1657 also saw Northumberland purchase five antique statues for £107, as well as a *Bacchus* for £30, from Emmanuel de Critz, younger son of the Sergeant-painter (see Appendix IV, no. 51). De Critz and his syndicate had purchased many works at the dispersal of the royal collection, particularly antique sculptures.[115] His "disclosure" of those of the king's goods that remained in his possession in 1660 says that they had been "preserued by him wth great care & danger his now Matie haueing had oft notice from him of ye same."[116] De Critz, however, seems to have had no compunction about selling his purchases. These acquisitions transformed the earl's collection into one more like Buckingham's or Arundel's, in which fine sixteenth-century pictures coexisted with antiquities. Some details of their arrangement can be reconstructed. In 1656 the paving in the courtyard at Northumberland House was taken up and some bronze statues, which seem to have been obtained ten years earlier from Windsor Castle (compare Appendix IV, nos. 27–28), were removed (see Appendix IV, no. 50). The mason, Edward Marshall, constructed bases for six wooden pedestals, painted in oils, in order that the newly acquired statues could be displayed in the Terrace Walk of the gardens at Northumberland House (see Appendix IV, no. 54).

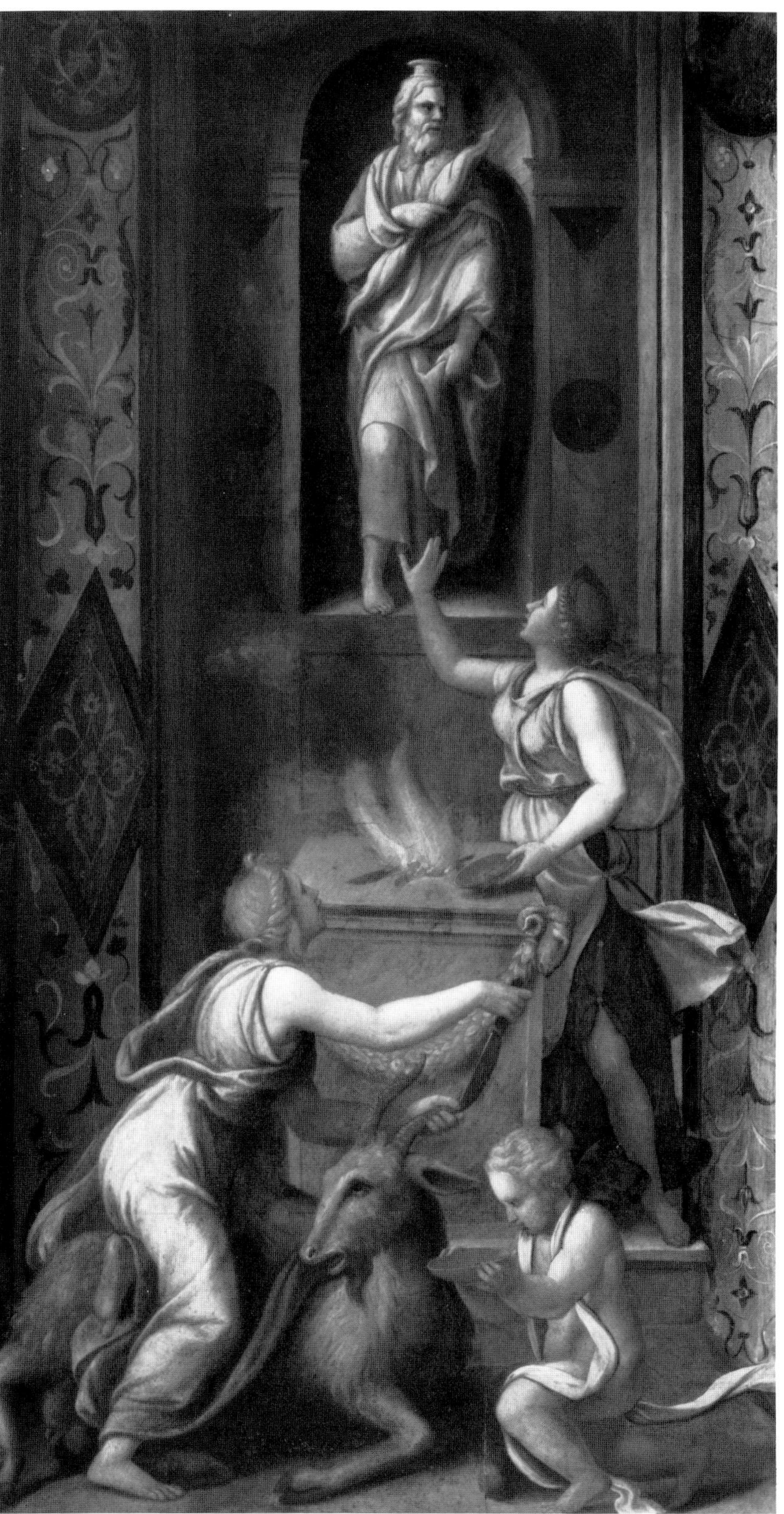

The earl was clearly pleased with this extension to his collection, because in 1658 he spent £190 on ten ancient marble busts and a

18. Workshop of Giulio Romano, *The Sacrifice of a Goat to Jupiter*, c. 1536, oil on panel
Royal Collection, Hampton Court

19. Polidoro da Caravaggio, *Psyche Abandoned on a Rock by Her Parents*, c. 1524–1527, oil on panel
Royal Collection, Hampton Court

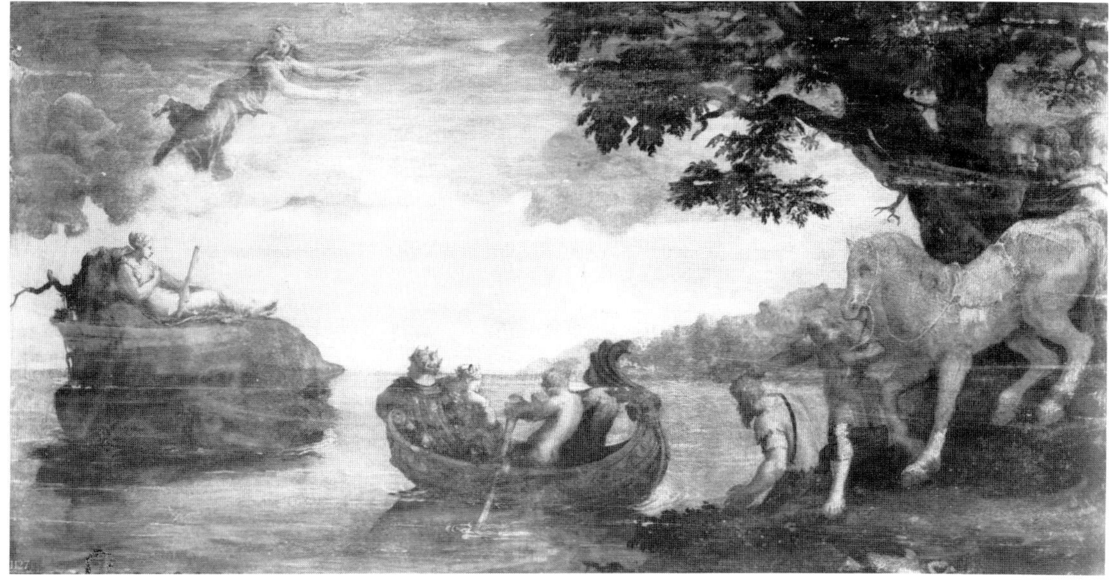

statue of Bacchus obtained from Thomas Beauchamp, who had been clerk to the trustees of the sale of the king's goods. Beauchamp accepted five bronze statues, presumably those recently removed from the courtyard at Northumberland House, to the value of £65, against this purchase. In addition Northumberland bought "a statue of a young Apollo, another of a Bachus and a head of Jupiter" from Beauchamp for £25 (see Appendix IV, no. 55). With these the earl had bought a total of twenty antique pieces, one of which, a *Bacchus*, had come with a pedestal. In 1659 he had nineteen new pedestals made to display the sculptures, and two of the statues recently placed on the Terrace at Northumberland House appear to have been moved indoors (see Appendix IV, no. 56). Robert Cleare made a black pedestal for the large sum of £5 for the most prized item and eighteen more at a cheaper price, six of which were carved by Richard Cleare with foliage, shields, and coronets; the upper moldings were enriched with lace (see Appendix IV, no. 59). The sculpture did not remain in the garden for long, however. In 1660, following the Restoration, the earl returned them to the Crown, together with the pictures by Correggio, Giulio, and Polidoro already mentioned, and there is a terse payment for "removeing pictures and Statues to Whitehall" (see Appendix IV, no. 60). The busts, which were probably displayed indoors, and the figures that were placed in the

garden can hardly have been at Northumberland House for more than two years.

The identification of the antique statues bought by Northumberland is made easier by the survival of two illustrated inventories now at Windsor Castle, one of the antiquities obtained by Charles I from Mantua, and the other of antique busts recovered at the Restoration.[117] The latter seems to have been partly compiled while the items were still at Northumberland House, because one of the sheets has an incomplete copy on the verso of the head of Lady Anne Cecil,[118] made from the group portrait by Van Dyck (fig. 10) then hanging in the earl's picture gallery. One of the pages from the Windsor album shows one bronze bust and three of the marble busts (fig. 20);[119] the latter may have come from Northumberland's collection. At the lower right is a *Jupiter* that can be identified with some certainty as a "Mantua peece" found in the earlier series of copies dating back to Charles I's acquisition of the collection, where it is described as *Giove Capitolino* (more correctly Jupiter Serapis).[120] It may well be identical with Northumberland's "head of Jupiter." The three statues of Bacchus and the *Young Apollo* were also almost certainly "Mantua peeces." These identifications are simplified because there were only three figures of Bacchus in the royal collection: a *Bachetto sotto vivo* holding up a bunch of grapes (fig. 21),[121] a *Bachetto* similar to the previous item in pose

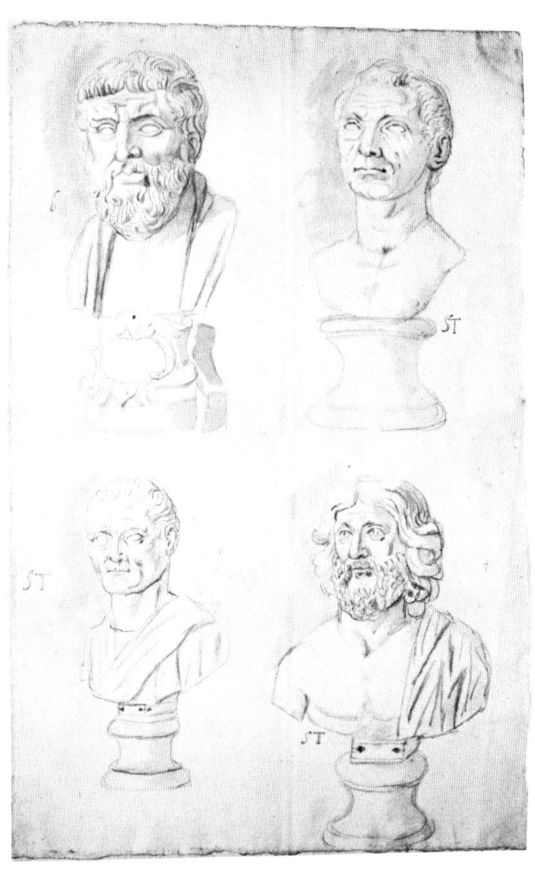

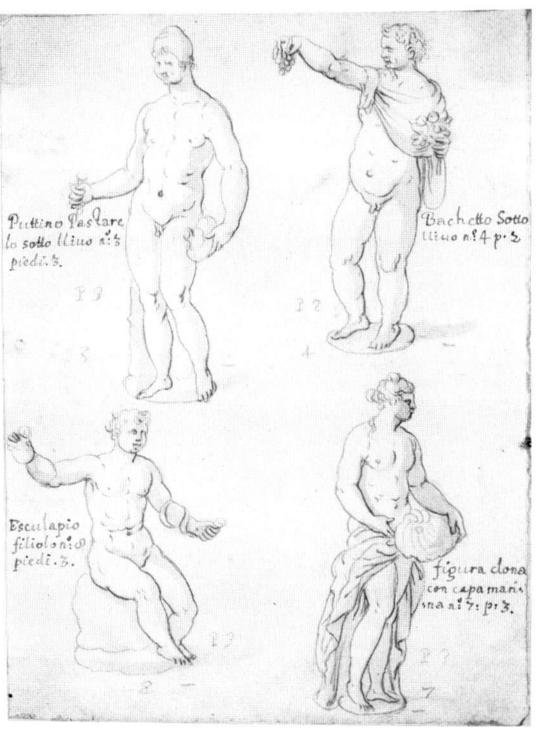

20. Unknown artist, *Three antique busts and one bronze bust by Hubert Le Sueur*, c. 1660, lead with brown wash
Royal Library, Windsor Castle

21. Unknown artist, *Four antique statues including a Bacchus with a bunch of grapes*, c. 1627, lead with pale brown wash
Royal Library, Windsor Castle

but shown as a child (fig. 22),[122] and another youthful statue of the god shown, in this case, as a genius of the harvests (fig. 23).[123] The *Young Apollo* was almost certainly an *Apollo del vivo* from the Mantua collection (fig. 24),[124] which, like the statues of Bacchus, was left without a purchaser's name in the valuations of the king's goods.[125] There are two other figures of Apollo in the inventories, but these were sold to Baggley and Houghton[126] and can therefore be eliminated. They are not known to have had any part in the sales to Northumberland. The fact that no purchasers' names are recorded for the relevant items at the time of the dispersal of Charles I's collection suggests that they were left unsold for several years in the early 1650s before being obtained by De Critz and Beauchamp, who were able to offer them to the earl at very modest prices.

During his long career as a collector Northumberland acquired works of art from many people. Payments to George Geldorp can be found throughout the earl's life, but

most come from the late 1630s. The first are purchases of unspecified pictures in 1638 and 1639 (see Appendix IV, nos. 12, 14), followed by the acquisition of a picture by Poelenburgh for £8 (see Appendix IV, no. 18), which was almost certainly a scene with a woman carried by two satyrs (see Appendix III, no. 90). This picture can be identified with one still at Petworth.[127] A payment to Van Dyck's servants for showing pictures at Lady Carlisle's house in 1640 (see Appendix IV, no. 19) is followed soon after by a payment in 1642 to Geldorp for finishing two pictures (see Appendix IV, no. 21). It may be that Geldorp completed some works from Van Dyck's studio after Van Dyck's death.[128] The likely candidates are not, however, among the better-known Van Dycks now at Petworth, but some of the studio works, such as the "Queen Dowager [Henrietta Maria] in Blue with an Angell holding a Crown over her head done by Van Dyke," as the picture was described in the Northumberland inventory (see Appendix III, no. 58), a little-known work now at Syon.[129] Another candidate could be the repetition of Lady Anne Cecil's portrait, presumably taken from the family group (fig. 10), which is described in the 1671 inventory and attributed to Van Dyck, but with a low valuation of £20 (see Appendix III,

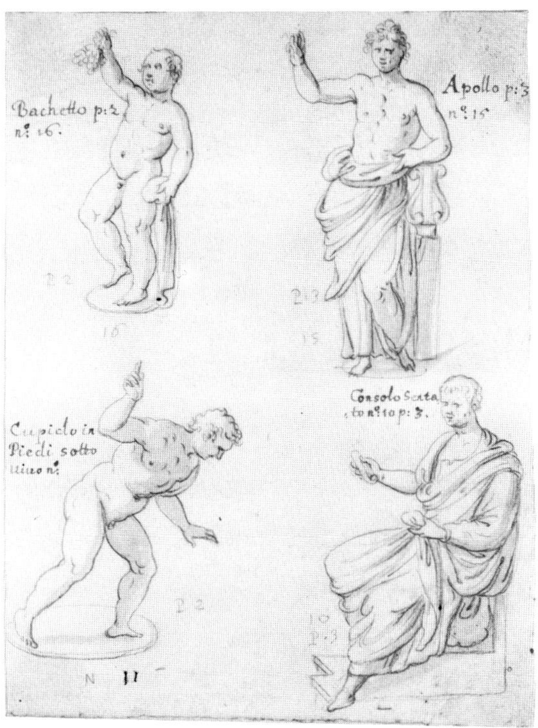

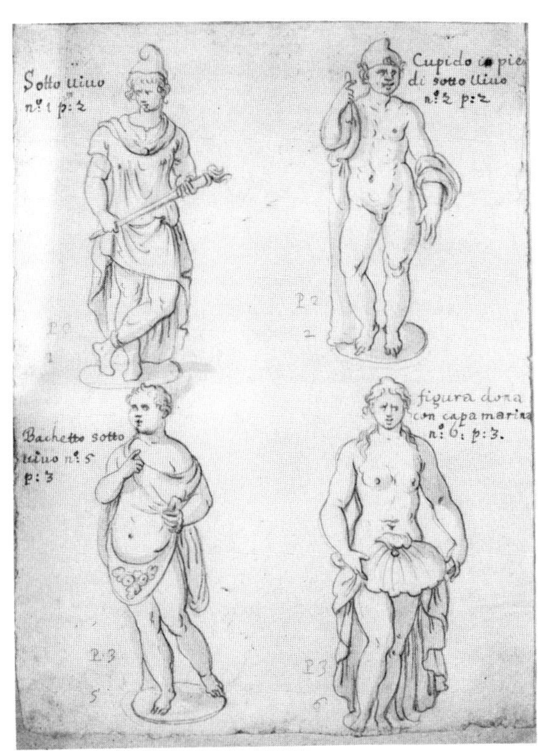

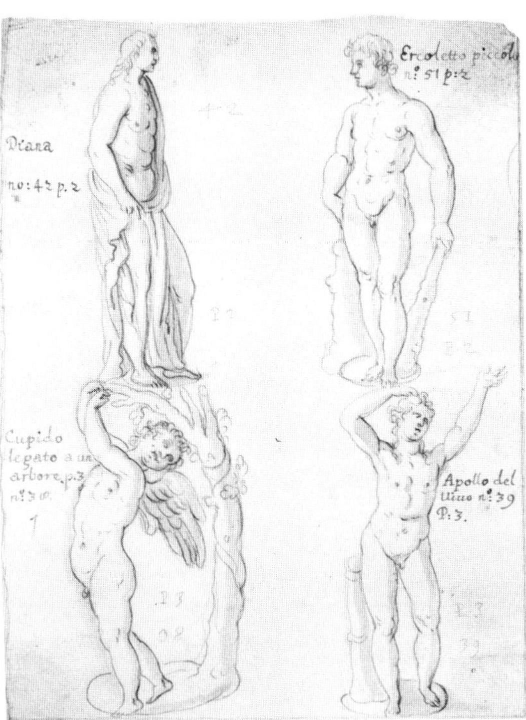

no. 74). Although the earl used Geldorp to advise on obtaining some bronze figures from Windsor Castle in 1645–1646,[130] he may have shared the general low opinion of Geldorp's work as an artist, and there is nothing attributed to him in the Northumberland inventory. Geldorp petitioned Parliament in 1645 as a "merchant stranger," incidentally establishing that he arrived in London in 1623.[131] Many of Northumberland's later dealings with Geldorp concerned exotic merchandise such as "a parcell of cheny plate,"[132] "29 pound of Permizan cheese,"[133] and some "Jessamin butter."[134] Geldorp may well have been more successful as a merchant than as a painter.

In 1640 the earl obtained pictures from Jan van Belcamp (d. 1652), the Dutch artist who was active as a copyist (see Appendix IV, no. 20), and he employed Remigius van Leemput (d. 1675), who had been a member of Van Dyck's studio in England, to repair a picture in 1654 (see Appendix IV, no. 47). In 1655 Northumberland bought a picture from Lely for £50 (see Appendix IV, no. 48). As this was too high a price for the work to have been a portrait by the artist, the piece was probably a good earlier painting. Lely is, of course, well known as a collector.[135] He bought works from the dispersal of the king's goods, including Van Dyck's *Cupid and Psyche*,[136] now in Kensington Palace, which is known to have been copied by Stone before 1661 and hence while in Lely's possession.[137] The purchase of a *Venus* by Rottenhammer from "Mr Webb" (see Appendix IV, no. 49) is almost certainly a reference to John Webb, the architect, who was in Northumberland's employ during the 1650s and who directed the earl's most ambitious building programs in his London house and at Syon.[138] A similar (identical?) picture had been at York House and this may explain why Webb offered it to Northumberland.[139] In the 1650s, as has been shown, the earl made substantial purchases from Jerome Lanier, Thomas Beauchamp, and Emmanuel de Critz.

The later part of Northumberland's life shows him as less active in buying works of art, although Stone remained in charge of the collection during the 1660s and was clearly a trusted member of the household. There are occasional payments to him for cleaning pictures and for arranging their hanging and transport (see Appendix IV, nos. 66, 68). He sold two pictures to the earl in 1665 for £40 (see Appendix IV, no. 66), and he also, perhaps surprisingly, supplied a copy after a portrait of Josceline Percy by Lely (see Appendix IV, no. 71), whose studio might have been expected to provide such things. During the 1660s Stone seems to have been asked less often to provide versions of Italian pictures. He did, however, become a person of some substance, and, like many of the earl's servants, he made substantial loans to him of between £200 and £600.[140] Stone was, however, frequently employed on relatively menial kinds of painting, such as "140 yardes of wainscott in the Lobby" at Northumberland House, for which he was paid £7 in 1658.[141] He appears to have taken over such tasks from John Gomersall, who had done this sort of work as well as jobs of decorative painting for the earl for many years. In 1661 Stone did over £20-worth of painting in Lord Percy's Lodgings in the London house,[142] and in 1664 he did over £80-worth of painting in oil in the Principal Lodgings and Hall at Syon.[143]

Although Northumberland's collection of pictures was smaller than those of some contemporaries at the Stuart court, it was unlike those of the king and the marquis of Hamilton, for example, in that additions to it were never made through large purchases *en bloc.* Indeed, the collection seems to have been put together very carefully over a long period of time. In 1645 Northumberland was at great pains to get hold of pictures from Van Dyck's collection, and negotiated with Parliament for works from York House at a time when he was faced with many pressing concerns, both political and financial. The loss of three of his finest sixteenth-century Italian pictures, as well as twenty antique sculptures, stripped the collection of its final phase of development. It remained, however, a very discriminating survey of sixteenth-century Italian art, which provided a magnificent frame for the four family portraits by Van Dyck that were at its heart. Northumberland's enthusiasm for Van Dyck's work is shown by the way that he continued to collect it, in particular the remarkable series of portraits of women by Van Dyck that he assembled over an extended period. A study of the earl as a collector must help dispel the assumption, sometimes found among art historians, that the opponents of the king were barbarians. Northumberland's final achievement, however, was not as a collector, but as someone who helped overthrow a willful and autocratic monarch and who, for reasons however complex, changed the relationship between monarch and Parliament.

Richard Symonds' notes on the pictures at Northumberland House in 1652. British Library, Egerton MSS 1636

fol. 91v.:

The Collection of y[e] Earle of Northumbl[d] in Suffolke house. 27. Dec. 1652
    M[r] Stone who coppyes showed y[m]

[1] A Paese of rocks & waters. by a spanyard.
[2] A Ritratto of an English Knight. by Holben. who sitts in a Chayre & a Table by him.[144]
[3] Sarto
    2 quadroes in Legno both of Mad & diverse putti esteemed both at 1000! [145]
[4] Titian
    A Senato[r] of Venice & his Secretary by him writing on a Table.[146]
[5]   3 Senato[rs] of Venice in their scarlets kneeling afore y[e] lofty altar. & six boyes. Ritrattoes all. & y[e] field are clouds. rarely done[147]
[6]   A Venus lying along & Mars kissing her under a Tree & naturall paese franco.[148]
[7] Tintoret
    A Ritratto of an old man[149]
[8] Another Ritratto rare colouring w[ch] Stone ssold me for x[l] I prize it afore Holbens his piece not far from it

fol. 92r.:

    Vandyke
[9] The Earle of Northumbl[d] that killd himselfe in y[e] Tower because y[e] King should not have his lands. Done by helpe of another Picture after the pty was dead.[150]
[10] Also Another of his Ancestores an old man sitting in a Gowne & leaning on a Table, done by an old picture[151]
[11] The Lady Newport[152]
[12] Mrs Porter[153]
[13] Mrs Murrey[154]
[14] L[d] Newport & Collonel Goring in one piece & a body doing on Gorings scarf rarely good. mezza figure[155]
[15] The Earle of Northumb[ld] halfe figure holding upon an anchor, & shipps in prospective[156]
[16] The Earl & his Lady & a daughter very sweet. & the rich blew vest of sattan of the Ladyes is Velato.[157]
[17] Another Lady above in a light blew garm̄t[158]
[18] The King Ch: mezza figura
[19] The King on horseback lesse than the life[159]
[20] A French Marquesse mezza figura
[21] Other Dutchmen mezze figure

[22] Lord H. Percy's picture[160]

fol. 92v.:

[23] Palma Vecchio
    Una femina mezza figura wth her hair loose. rare fleshy breasts upon a board w[ch] y[e] wormes have taken[161]
[24] Bassan Vecchio originali securo
    A Nativity. wth huge penellati longe narrow cloth
[25] O[r] Savio[r] at Emaus & the host sitting good & excell[t]
[26] A country farme.
[27] G. Vasari. a Ritratto wth a hatt on
[28] Palma Giovene
    A Venus whole body upon a bed & Mars a fat red colord knave w[ch] she pulls downe & cupid puls of his buskins.[162]
[29] Lilly
    The Duke of Yorke & King Charles done at Hampton Court[163]
[30] The sd Duke & Princesse Eliz: & duke of Glous. a fountayne by. y[m.164]

fol. 93r.:

    Maestri Fiaminghi
    Brughel [deleted]
[31] Stenwich. an inside of a church very rare & good. & y[e] figures are done by Po——[165]
[32] 6 Alpine paeses & ruines of Rome good
[33] An Alpe paes in brasse
[34] A small picture of Chinese worke
    3 figures good profiles of faces but no rilievo. & paese of Ruines w[th] boates
[35] L[od] Percy's picture young boy good
[36] 2 large quadro's of Madonna's & other psons Italian worke M[ers] unknowne [?]

APPENDIX II

*John Evelyn's account of the pictures at
Northumberland House in 1658*[166]

9 June 1658
I went to see the Ear[l]e of *Northumberlands*
Pictures, whereoff that of the *Venetian* Senators was one of the best of *Titians*,[167] & another of *Andrea de Sarta*, viz, a *Madona,
Christ*, St. *John* & an old Woman &c:[168] a St.
Catharine of *Da Vinci*,[169] with divers Portraits
of *V. Dyke*, a Nativity of *Georgioni*: The last of
our blessed Kings, & D: of *Yorke* by Lilly:[170] A
rosarie of flo: by the famous *Jesuite* of *Bruxells*
& severall more: This was in Suffolck house:
The new front towards the Gardens, is tollera-
ble, were it not drown'd by a too massie, &
clowdy pair of stayers of stone, without any
neeate Invention.

APPENDIX III

*The 1671 inventory of the Northumberland
collection. Alnwick 72, MS 107, GC 26,
compiled following the death of Josceline
Percy, 11th earl of Northumberland
(1644–1670)*

fol. [67]v.:

A Note of the Pictures att Northumberland
House, taken and appraised by M.r Symon
Stone The 30.th of June 1671

		£	S	D
[1]	The 3. Senato.rs done by Titian[171]	1000	00	00
[2]	A naked Venus & a Satyr Done by D.o[172]	0100	00	00
[3]	A Persion Bride holding a little Catt in her Hands, Done by Titian[173]	0080	00	00
[4]	The Duke of Florence & Machiavil Done by Titian[174]	0100	00	00
[5]	Two Pictures (the Story) of the Virgin Mary & Christ; and other Figures in them, Done by A. Dulcerto[175]	0200	00	00
[6]	A Womans head (St Katherine) by Leonardo Dulvincy	0050	00	00
[7]	A Womans head with naked Breasts Done by Old Palma[176]	0200	00	00
[8]	A Mans Picture Done by Holben[177]	0100	00	00
[9]	Another Mans Picture Done by Keyes	0030	00	00

fol. [68]r.:

		£	S	D
[10]	A Little Picture where one sitts Sleeping by a Cowe, with other figures in it Done by Old Bassano	0010	00	00
[11]	The King on Horseback, on a White Horse the face not finished by Van Dyke[178]	0015	00	00
[12]	The Earl of Northumberland with his first Lady & a Child by van Dyke[179]	0060	00	00
[13]	The late Earl of Northumberland's Father Done by Van Dyke[180]	0030	00	00
[14]	The Lady Devonshire by V:Dyke[181]	0030	00	00
[15]	The Countess of Newport by V:Dyke[182]	0030	00	00
[16]	M.rs Murray done by Van Dyke[183]	0030	00	00
[17]	M.rs Porter done by Van Dyke[184]	0030	00	00
		£2095	00	00

fol. [68]v.:

	£	S	D
[18] The Lord Strafford by Van Dyke[185]	0030	00	00
[19] The Earle of Northumberlands Grand=father Done by Van Dyke[186]	0020	00	00
[20] My Lord Goring and my Lady [sic] Newport in a piece with a Boy tying his Scarfe, Done by Van Dyke[187]	0060	00	00
[21] The Countess of Bedford by V:Dyke[188]	0030	00	00
[22] The Lord Henry Percy, by V:Dyke[189]	0030	00	00
[23] Three long Pictures coppyed after Polidore[190]	0015	00	00
[24] The Lady Sunderland, by V:Dyke[191]	0030	00	00
[25] Two Pictures of the Countesse of Carlisle, Done by Van Dyke[192]	0060	00	00
[26] The Countess of Northumberlands Picture in Water Colours, done by Hodgskine[193]	0030	00	00
[27] A little Picture of Henry Earle of Northumberland lying along[194]	0010	00	00

fol. [69]r.:

	£	S	D
[28] The late King and the Duke of York, Done by Lelly[195]	0020	00	00
[29] The Duke and Dutchess of York, by Lelly[196]	0020	00	00
[30] The Countess of Northumberland, by D.o	0010	00	00
[31] Three Pictures of Jocelin Earl of Northumberland, by Lelly when he was Lord Percy[197]	0030	00	00
[32] The Lady Essex Done by Lelly[198]	0010	00	00
[33] The Lady Stanhope Done by Lelly[199]	0010	00	00
[34] The Lady Strangford Done by Lelly	0010	00	00
[35] A Piece of O.r Lady and Christ & Joseph, Done by Coregio	0150	00	00
[36] A Picture of Grapes and a red spott in it Done by the Labouradore	0020	00	00
[37] A picture with 3 apples & a Bird &, a red spott, in it by the Labouradore	0010	00	00
[38] Another with Birds & a red spott in it by the Labouradore	0010	00	00
	£0615	00	00

fol. [69]v.:

	£	S	D
[39] A Picture of a Dutch Physitian and a woman standing by him Done by Dow	0060	00	00
[40] Eight Little Pictures in one Frame by Elshammer[200]	0250	00	00
[41] The late Prince of Orange Coppy'd after Van Dyke[201]	0010	00	00
[42] The Earl of Northumberlands Grand Father from head to foote[202]	0010	00	00
[43] Two Pictures of the Ly. Lisle; by Lelly[203]	0020	00	00
[44] The Lady Dorothy Saville, Done by M.rs Carlisle	0002	00	00
[45] The Lady Diana Rich, done by Lelly	0010	00	00
[46] An Italian Princess holding her hand on a clock	0003	00	00
[47] Two Dark Heads in a Picture	0005	00	00
[48] A greate Sebastian at length by Garrard Seager[204]	0020	00	00
[49] A Great Ecce Homo, Done by Titian[205]	0015	00	00

fol. [70]r.:

	£	S	D
[50] A Great heavey Picture on Board of our Lady & Christ, and an old Preist, by an Italian Master	0030	00	00
[51] A little Ecce Homo, Done by Titian	0005	00	00
[52] The Birth of Christ, by Bassaun	0020	00	00
[53] A Picture of the Earl of Pembroke and his Son, one done by Mytens and the other by Van Mole[206]	0002	00	00
[54] A Kitchen Piece where a Woman is beating in a Morter	0005	00	00
[55] A Coppy after Polidore Done upon Board the Story is Psiche lying upon a Rock[207]	0010	00	00
	£0477	00	00

fol. [70]v.:

	£	S	D
[56] A great Prospective	0010	00	00
[57] A great Kitchen Peece where there is a Hare hanging up by the heels with a Fowle	0010	00	00
[58] The Queen Dowager in Blue with an Angell holding a Crown over her head done by Van Dyke[208]	0030	00	00
[59] A Mans Picture with a Capp on his head, holding a paper in his hand, & a little statue by him	0003	00	00
[60] A little Coppy of S.ʳ Jocelin Percy	0002	00	00
[61] An Old Commanders Picture with a Staffe over his Shoulder	0002	00	00
[62] A Tawney moore Prince to the wast	0001	00	00
[63] A great Landskippe by Montford	0010	00	00
[64] Two narrow Pictures Coppyed after Polidore[209]	0010	00	00

fol. [71]r.:

	£	S	D
[65] The Earl of Suffolkes Picture	0005	00	00
[66] Some Sea Pieces	0012	00	00
	£0095	00	00

£	S	D
3282:	00:	00

Pictures Appras'd att Petworth by M.ʳ Symon
Stone the 30.ᵗʰ of July. 1671

	£	S	D
[67] A large Piece done by Young Palma of Mars Venus and Cupid[210]	0015	00	00
[68] A large Piece of the Birth of Christ Done by Bassaun	0010	00	00
[69] A Peece of Christ sitting at the well & a woman by said to be of Palma	0020	00	00

fol. [71]v.:

	£	S	D
[70] A Peece where there is a Boy clymbing of a Tree Don by Bassaun	0010	00	00
[71] Two Mens: Pictures Done to the Knees, by Tinterett[211]	0020	00	00
[72] Two Men's: Pictures done to the wast, one by Jerjone, yᵉ other by Titian[212]	0050	00	00
[73] A Picture of Apollo where there is men come to offer to him	0010	00	00
[74] A Picture of the late Countess of Northumberland, done to the waist, by Van Dyke[213]	0020	00	00
[75] A Picture of the Countess of Salisbury to the Waist by Mittens	0003	00	00
[76] A Picture of S.ʳ Jocelin Percy to the Knees	0005	00	00
[77] Three Pictures of the Earles of Northumberland to the Knees	0030	00	00

fol. [72]r.:

	£	S	D
[78] A Picture of the Countess of Leicester coppyed after V. Dyke[214]	0010	00	00
[79] A Large Landskipp done by Collantus	0020	00	00
[80] A rare Prospective done by Stenwick, the Figures by Pullenburke[215]	0100	00	00
[81] A Peece where there is a Cupp of Mother of Pearle in it, Done by Dehenme	0015	00	00
	£0338	00	00
[82] Another Picture, where there is a Glass of Roses in it: Done by Dehenme	0005	00	00
[83] A head Done by Sattocleave	0015	00	00
[84] A long narrow Picture by Bassaun	0005	00	00

fol. [72]v.:

	£	S	D
[85] A Landskipp where there is a Rock from where you may see into the sea, and see two Gallyes	0010	00	00
[86] A round Picture, where there is a Bunch of Grapes, Done by the Labouradore	0010	00	00
[87] A Picture of Grapes and a Red Pott, Done by the Labouradore	0015	00	00

		£	S	D
[88]	A Round Piece w.th a Boyes Head, Done by Bassaun	0003	00	00
[89]	A Picture of Appollo and Children Dancing	0040	00	00
[90]	A Batthanalio where there is a Woman Ryding upon Two Satyr's Shoulder, Done by Pullemborke216	0020	00	00
[91]	A Picture done by young Franck	0010	00	00
[92]	Two little Indian Pictures	0002	00	00
[93]	A little peece of a Sparrow Hawke	0001	00	00
[94]	A Picture of a Baskett of Flowers	0005	00	00

fol. [73]r.:

		£	S	D
[95]	The Dutchess of Richmond Done to the Knees, coppy'd after. V: Dyke217	0010	00	00
[96]	A Picture of the Lord Cranborne from Head to Foote218	0005	00	00
[97]	A Lady's Picture to the Knees	0005	00	00
[98]	A Landskipp Gloudilloraigne219	0030	00	00
[99]	A Peece with a Flaggon: a Musmillian and two peaches by Deheime	0020	00	00
[100]	A Peece of the Countess of Sunderland Coppy'd after Van Dyke220	0010	00	00
[101]	A Picture of my Lady Stanhope Done by Lelly221	0010	00	00
		£0231	00	00

fol. [73]v.:

		£	S	D
[102]	A Picture of the Queens Mother Done by Van Dyke222	0030	00	00
[103]	A Landskipp by Paul Brill	0012	00	00
[104]	A Little Landskipp w.th Figures in it & a Wind Mill in it Done by Mustard	0002	00	00
[105]	Eight Landskipps Done by Moncport	0005	00	00
[106]	A Picture of a Rocke where S.t Jerome is in by Moncport	0005	00	00
[107]	A Picture of Birds	0002	00	00
[108]	A Picture of the Circumcision of Christ, by George Versaillie223	0050	00	00
[109]	A Picture of the Duke of York, Duke of Gloucester & Princess Eliz.th by Lelly224	0040	00	00
[110]	A Picture of Cupid in a Storm done by Houseman	0005	00	00
[111]	A Picture of Titian & Aretine Coppy'd after Titian225	0010	00	00
[112]	A Picture of O.re Lady & Christ & Elizabeth, Coppy'd after Andrea Dulcerto226	0015	00	00

fol. [74]r.:

		£	S	D
[113]	Two Pictures of the Persian Bride after Titian227	0016	00	00
[114]	A Picture of O.re Lady & Christ and S.t Luke, after Titian228	0025	00	00
[115]	A Coppy of Guido, where Judeth Cutteth, off Holofurnes's Head229	0010	00	00
[116]	A Picture of Marques Dalquasto & his Lady coppy'd after Titian230	0015	00	00
[117]	A Picture of an Old Man Making a Baskett, and a Woman standing by him	0020	00	00
[118]	A Peece of S.t John from Head to Foote Done after Corregio231	0012	00	00
		£0274	00	00

fol. [74]v.:

		£	S	D
[119]	Two Landskipps over the Door in the Drawing Roome	0006	00	00
[120]	A Picture of my Lord of Alnwick	0010	00	00
[121]	The Story to Heliodorus Whipping out of the Temple being a Chimney Peece	0010	00	00
		£0026	00	00

£

869:00:0

Severall Pictures & Peeces at Syon now in use
of the R.t Hon.ble the Elder Countesse Dow.r
of Northumberland, Taken and appraised by
M.r Symon Stone the 10.th Day of July: 1671

In the Lobby

		£	S	D
[122]	A Picture of two men going for water and kill'd by a Draggon	0030	oo	oo
[123]	Greene=witch house & Castle	0002	oo	oo

fol. [75]r.:

		£	S	D
[124]	A Sea Peece where they are Canininge a Ship	0002	oo	oo
[125]	A Sea Peece where there is two Wind Mills upon the Torts at.	0002	oo	oo
[126]	A Citie of Holland upon the sea coast, with two Ships Riding before it and under Saile and the other not, prize at	0002	oo	oo
[127]	Two Peeces of Momport where there is Stags in one, & Rocks in the other at	0008	oo	oo
[128]	A Sea Peece with a Wind Mill upon the Banke at	0003	oo	oo
[129]	An Originall & a Coppy of Momports, at,	0007	oo	oo
[130]	Lord Henry Percys Picture in a Chimney Peece with two Doggs at	0005	oo	oo
		£0061	oo	oo

fol. [75]v.:

		£	S	D
[131]	A Landskipp in the same Roome over a Chimney	0003	oo	oo
[132]	Marquess Dell Quasto, and his Lady with Figures[232]	0015	oo	oo
[133]	Tarquin, and Lucretia	0010	oo	oo
[134]	Venus and Mercury teaching Cupid his booke[233]	0010	oo	oo
[135]	A Landskipp where there is a Castle and some Ships, and a Gally	0003	oo	oo
[136]	Two coppies after Monport	0003	oo	oo
[137]	A Sea-peece, where there is a great Gally, in the mouth of the haven	0001	10	oo
[138]	A coppy after Momport	0001	oo	oo
[139]	A Sea Peece where there is a Vessellus Coming into Harbour	0001	10	oo
[140]	A Landskip where there is a May Pole in it	0000	10	oo

fol. [76]r.:

	£	S	D			
Totall of the whole				0048	10	oo
Appraizement is	4260	: 10 :	oo	0061	oo	oo
				0109	10	oo

Sy: Stone

Excerpts from the household accounts of Algernon Percy, 10th earl of Northumberland, and his son Josceline, while Lord Percy, concerning expenditure on painting and sculpture[234]

1. Alnwick MSS: Syon House U.I.5 (unnumbered). *The Account of Peter Dodesworth from 22 January 1630/1631 to 21 January 1631/1632.*

To the painter for setting in Ebonye frames 4 pictures of his Lop.s xxvjs

2. Alnwick MSS: Syon House U.I.5 (unnumbered). *The Account of Peter Dodesworth from 12 January 1631/1632 to 12 January 1632/1633.*

Necessaryes for yor. Lop. vizt pictures [15-0-0 *above*]

3. Alnwick MSS: Syon House U.I.5 (unnumbered). *The Account of Henry Hearon for apparel and necessaries from 29 January 1632/1633 to 15 January 1633/1634.*

Money delived into yor. Lop.s private purse . . . at Essex house the xxijth of March [1633] . . . for a picture x.li

4. Alnwick MSS: Syon House U.I.5 (unnumbered). *The Account of Thomas Cartwright for reparations at Syon and Dorset House for the year ending 22 January 1634/1635.*

Wages of sondrie workmen vizt . . Joyners, making a frame for a picture of Ebonie . . .

5. Alnwick MSS: Syon House U.I.5 (unnumbered). *The Account of Henry Hearon for apparel and necessaries from 15 January 1633/1634 to 14 January 1634/1635.*

Sundry necessaries viz iij pictures ix.li

6. Alnwick MSS: Syon House U.I.5 (unnumbered). *The Account of Peter Dodesworth for foreign payments from 14 January 1633/1634 to 16 January 1634/1635.*

Pictures of diverse kindes cccxlijli ijs vjd

7. Alnwick MSS: Syon House U.I.5 (unnumbered). *The Account of Peter Dodesworth for foreign payments from 16 January 1634/1635 to 16 January 1635/1636.*

Pictures of diverse sortes and frames for pictures clvijli

8. Alnwick MSS: Syon House U.I.5 (unnumbered). *The Account of Henry Hearon for apparel and necessaries for the year ending 15 January 1635/1636.*

Pictures of his Lop and Countesse & divers others delivered by Sr. Anthony Vandyke as by his acquittance apps cc.li

For making cleene pictures lijs vjd

Making frames xxxviijs

9. Alnwick MSS: Syon House U.I.5 (unnumbered). *The Account of Peter Dodesworth for foreign payments from 16 January 1635/1636 to 16 January 1636/1637.*

Pictures vizt for 5 pictures & frames cliiijli viijs

10. Alnwick MSS: Syon House U.I.5 (unnumbered). *The Account of Peter Dodesworth for foreign payments from 16 January 1636/1637 to 16 January 1637/1638.*

Pictures twoe x.li

11. Alnwick MSS: Syon House U.I.5 (unnumbered). *The Account of Henry Hearon, Humphrey Tayler and Lancelot Thorneton for apparel and necessaries for the year ending 25 January 1638/1639.*

Pictures and frames bought of Sr. Anthony Vandyke and Mr. Gildrop xxj.li Pictures of the Princesse Mary & fower in pap. vijs iiijd

12. Alnwick MSS: Syon House U.I.5 (unnumbered). *The Account of Peter Dodesworth for foreign payments from 16 January 1637/1638 to 16 January 1638/1639.*

Pictures bought of Mr. Gildrope xlviij.li

13. Alnwick MSS: Syon House U.I.5 (unnumbered). *The Account of Peter Dodesworth for foreign payments from 16 January 1638/1639 to 16 January 1639/1640.*

Pictures bought of Sr. Anthony Vandyke [50li *above*] and Sr. Toby Mathewes [30li *above*] xx iiij.li

To Duckworth the Cabinet maker for 2 Cabinettes for his Lop. and for 5 picture frames and mending Ebony frames xxiiij.li xijs

14. Alnwick MSS: Syon House U.I.5 (unnumbered). *The Account of Lancelot Thorneton for apparel and necessaries for the year ending 24 January 1639/1640.*

Pictures had of Mr. Gildroppe [10li *above*] and for picture frames [10li-9-0 *above*] xx.li ixs

15. Alnwick MSS: Syon House U.I.5 (unnumbered). *The General Account for 1639.*

Pictures and picture frames xlv.li xijd

16. Alnwick MSS: Syon House U.I.5 (unnumbered). *The Account of Thomas Cartwright for reparations at Syon and his Lordship's house in Queen Street for the year ending 12 January 1640/1641.*

Buildinges & Repairacons at Syon: vizt . . Gilding a greate picture frame xxxs Money paid to Moses Glover the painter in part for worke done & to be done at Syon xvli

17. Alnwick MSS: Syon House U.I.5 (unnumbered). *The Account of Peter Dodesworth for foreign payments from 16 January 1639/1640 to 16 January 1640/1641.*

For mending a picture, making paper win-
dowes, & other worke done by his Lo^ps Cabi-
netmaker xxxiiij^s

18. Alnwick MSS: Syon House U.I.5 (unnumbered). *The Account of Lancelot Thorneton for apparel and necessaries for the year
ending 24 January 1640/1641.*
For a little picture of Pullingburg bought of
M^r. Gildropp viij^li[235] A gilt frame for a picture
xxij^s

19. Alnwick MSS: Syon House U.I.5 (unnumbered). *The Account of Edward Payler for
foreign payments for the year ending 20 January 1640/1641.*
To Sr Anthony Vandikes servantes at my La:
Carlisles howse they being there to view pictures x^s

20. Alnwick MSS: Syon House U.I.6 (unnumbered). *The Account of Peter Dodesworth
for foreign payments from 16 January
1640/1641 to 16 January 1641/1642.*
Three pictures bought of John Van
Bell. Campe xlv^li

21. Alnwick MSS: Syon House U.I.6 (unnumbered). *The Account of Peter Dodesworth
for foreign payments from 17 January
1641/1642 to 17 January 1642/1643.*
For your Lo^ps picture sent to the Trynitie
house vj^li To Mr Gildrop for finishing 2 pictures and for frames to them iiij^li x^s
To Patrick Grady for ayring pictures at Bay-
nardes Castle iiij^s

22. Alnwick MSS: Syon House U.I.6 (unnumbered). *The Account of Lancelot Thornton
for apparel and necessaries for the year ending
17 January 1643/1644.*
For cases to pack vp pictures iiij^li ij^s vj^d

23. Alnwick MSS: Syon House U.I.6 (unnumbered). *The Account of Peter Dodesworth
for foreign payments from 17 January
1642/1643 to 17 January 1643/1644.*
Sondrie other paymentes vizt for drawing her
La^pps picture l^li

24. Alnwick MSS: Syon House U.I.6 (unnumbered). *The General Account for 1645.*
Pictures sold this yeare by M^r. Thorneton iiij^c
xxxix^li
Two pictures bought the one called the Senators the other Andromeda cc^li[236]

25. Alnwick MSS: Syon House U.I.6 (unnumbered). *The Account of Peter Dodesworth
for foreign payments from 17 January
1644/1645 to 17 January 1645/1646.*
Sondry other paymentes vizt for 2 pictures
for his Lo^p one called the Senators the other
the Andromida cc^li[237]

26. Alnwick MSS: Syon House U.I.6 (unnumbered). *The Account of Lancelot Thorneton for apparel and necessaries for the year
ending 17 January 1645/1646.*
Necessaries about pictures vij^s

27. Alnwick MSS: Syon House U.I.6 (unnumbered). *The Account of Peter Dodesworth
for foreign payments from 17 January
1645/1646 to 17 January 1646/1647.*
To the Governour of Windsor Castle for some
brass pillers your Lo^p. had from thence cxvij^li[238]

28. Alnwick MSS: Syon House U.I.6 (unnumbered). *The Account of Edward Payler for
foreign payments for the year ending 17 January 1646/1647.*
To M^r. Bachelors man that brought a peece of
brasse from the Governor of Windsor Castle to
his Lo^pp x^s

29. Alnwick MSS: Syon House U.I.6 (un-
numbered). *The Account of Lancelot Thorne-
ton for apparel and necessaries for the year
ending 17 January 1647/1648.*
A pickture case of Eboney for the Countesse
of Northumberlandes pickture iiij^li
A pickture frame lxj^s vj^d
For the Duke of Yorkes picture lxxv^s[239] To
Mr Stone for a pickture his Lop gave to the
Earle of Manchester x^li

30. Alnwick MSS: Syon House U.I.6 (unnumbered). *The Account of Edward Payler, receiver of his Lordship's rents and revenues in
Sussex, for debts for the year ending 17 January 1647/1648.*
For expences on the Marchantes that carryed
the piktures v^s vj^d To Mr Stone for severall dis-
bursmentes about the said picktures xij^s
vj^d . . For a barge to carry his Lo^ps pictures to
the shipp xiiij^s . . To the searchers that
searched the picktures xx^s To the M^r of the
shipp v^s To him that went into holland to see
the picktures safe delivered c^s

31. Alnwick MSS: Syon House U.I.6 (unnumbered). *The Account of Peter Dodesworth
for foreign payments from 17 January
1646/1647 to 17 January 1647/1648.*
To Mr Lilley for drawing the Lady Anne Percys Pickture x^li[240] To Mr Stone the pickture
drawer c^s 10 pickture frames and necessaries
about packing vp of picktures lxxj^s ij^d[241]

32. Alnwick MSS: Syon House U.I.6 (unnumbered). *The Account of Peter Dodesworth
for foreign payments from 17 January
1647/1648 to 17 January 1648/1649.*
To M^r. Lilley for the king and the Duke of
Yorkes pickture in one peece xx^li[242] More to
him for the Lady Ann Percys pickture x^li[243]

Chardges of M[r] Stone and John Lambe into Holland in Aprill with 10[li] to them for their paines xiiij[li] x[s] viij[d] and of John Lambe in Decemb[r] with the rent of two Chambers at Middlebrough [Middelburg] and 5[li] for his paines xxij[li] xvij[s]

33. Alnwick MSS: Syon House U.I.6 (unnumbered). *The Account of Edward Payler, receiver of his Lordship's rents and revenues in Sussex, for debts in the year ending 17 January 1648/1649.*

Sondry other paymentes viz[t] To M[r] Stone for a pickture of fflowers vj[li][244]

34. Alnwick MSS: Syon House U.III.2. *The Account of Robert Scawen for defreying the charges of the building work and reparations at Northumberland House, ending 1649.*

For makeing Cases for picktures and helping to Carry them downe xxx[s]

For naileing pickture Cases . . . [and other expenses] xiij[s]

For a round piller to role a peece of painteing vpon, and making a Case for one of his Lo[pps] picktures xxx[s]

35. Alnwick MSS: Syon House U.I.6 (unnumbered). *The Account of Charles Kirke for foreign payments for the year ending 17 January 1649/1650.*

Guifts and Rewards viz[t] to M[r] Smithsbyes servante for bringing a pickture from Hamptoncourte to Syon xx[s] To the waterman that brought it v[s]

36. Petworth House Archives 617. *Miscellaneous accounts, 1633–1659*, fol. 40v.

1649

Given to M[r] Will: Smithsbys Seruant by his Lo[pps] Commaund for bringing a picture of 3 of his Ma[ties] Children from Hampton Court to Sion April 18th 1-0-0[245]

Given to the watermen that came with it Aprill 18th 0-5-0

37. Alnwick MSS: Syon House U.I.6 (unnumbered). *The Account of John Hay for foreign payments from 17 January 1648/1649 to 17 January 1649/1650.*

To M[r] Stone for necessaries about the picktures at Northumberland house vij[s] vj[d]

38. Alnwick MSS: Syon House U.I.6 (unnumbered). *The Account of Edward Payler (deceased), receiver of his Lordship's rents and revenues in Sussex, for debts from 17 January 1648/1649 to 28 February 1649/1650.*

For 3 picture cases to send pictures to Petworth lxvij[s] A frame for y[e] 3 Senators viij[s] For Custome and excise bringing a picture out of Holland xiij[s] vj[d]

39. Alnwick MSS: Syon House U.I.6 (unnumbered). *The Account of Lancelot Thorneton for apparel and necessaries for the year ending 17 January 1649/1650.*

Horsehire of M[r] Stone from Syon to London iij[s]

To M[r] Lilley the pictvre drawers servante v[s]

40. Petworth House Archives 5836. *The Account of Peter Dodesworth for foreign payments from 17 January 1650/1651 to 17 January 1651/1652.*

Mending the Senators [2-0-0 *above*], Perriwiggs [2-12-0 *above*] and severall other disbursm[ts] lxix[li] vj[s] x[d]

For a picture of the Countesse of Carliles xij[li]

41. Petworth House Archives 5843. *The Account of Lancelot Thorneton for apparel and necessaries for the year ending 17 January 1651/1652.*

A picture and case for my Lady Elizabeth lxij[s][246]

42. Petworth House Archives 5848. *The Account of Robert Scawen for reparations at Syon and Northumberland House from February 1651/1652 to February 1652/1653.*

For sondrie necessarie Chardges about Northumberland house vizt . . . to John Angier Carpenter for 43 whole deales at 15[s] a peece vsed for makeing picture frames and other worke where the pictures lie vij[li] xij[s]

43. Petworth House Archives 5852. *The Account of Lancelot Thorneton for apparel and necessaries for the year ending 17 January 1652/1653.*

Two picture frames lx[s]

To M[r] Stone the picture drawer xx[s]

44. Petworth House Archives 5854. *The Account of Peter Dodesworth for foreign payments from 17 January 1652/1653 to 17 January 1653/1654.*

A blacke frame for a pickture [1-10-0 *above*] and a case [0-18[s]-0 *above*] to send pictures to Petworth xlviij[s]

45. Petworth House Archives 5860. *The Account of Lancelot Thorneton for money by him received for the year ending 17 January 1653/1654.*

To M[r] Hoskin for a picture of his Lo[pp] in water Collours for my Lady xv[li] To a Jeweller that sett that picture in a lockett and necces to it C[s] To M[r] Stone for 2 pictures vj[li]

46. Petworth House Archives 5862. *The Account of Peter Dodesworth for foreign payments from 17 January 1653/1654 to 17 January 1654/1655.*

To Hoskines for a picture for my Lady xv.li247

47. Petworth House Archives 5869. *The Account of Lancelot Thorneton for foreign payments for the year ending 20 January 1654/1655.*

To Mr Leemput for mending a picture lxs

To Mr Stone for a case to send pictures to Petworth [0-3-6 *above*] keeping cleane the picture roome a yeare [5s *above*], helpe to ayre and clense pictures [5s *above*], charcoles for the picture roome [0-4-9 *above*], and carriage of pictures in London [0-2-0 *above*] xxs iiijd.

48. Petworth House Archives 5872. *The Account of Orlando Gee for foreign payments from January 1654/1655 to January 1655/1656.*

To Mr Bishopp for 2 large looking glasses xxxv.li To Mr Bolty for a frame of Ebony and a glasse to my Lordes fathrs picture [1-4-0 *above*], for 2 other picture frames [4-0-0 *above*], a frame for a looking glasse [3-10-0 *above*], a clocke case [2-10-0 *above*], and 2 standes [2-0-0 *above*] xiij.li iiijs To Mr Lelÿ for a picture l.li To Mr Hollibery for 2 Landskipps iiij.li To Mr Gibson for mending a picture Cs To Mr Stone for a Coppy of the Senator and his Secretary and another after Palma xx.li248 To him more for the coppy of his Lopps picture for my Lord Broghill iiij.li To him more for the coppy of Ecce homo xvj.li249 To him more for helpe to clense and ayre the pictures, keeping cleane the picture roome all the yeare and for charcoles for ayring the roome xxvjs To Norris the Joyner for 6 frames for pictures and 5 cases for pictures and looking glasses vij.li xiiijs

49. Petworth House Archives 5883. *The Account of Orlano Gee for foreign payments for the year ending 31 January 1656/1657.*

Carryages and portages vizt. . . portage of the Silver Cesterne,250 pictures, and other thinges in London xs vjd

To Thomas Stepney esqr. & John Stepney his son in full consideracon of their claimes to the picture of the Senatores iiijxx.li251 To Mr Webb for a small peece of painting of a Venus don by Rotten Hummer Cs252 To Mr Stone for the pictures of Tissian and Arratin a Coppie viij.li253 To him more to buy a picture frame by his Lopps order lxvs To him more for 3 cases to send pictures to Petworth [0-19-6 *above*], portage of them into Southwarke at severall times [0-3-0 *above*] his boathire with pictures to Syon severall times [0-12-6 *above*], charcole [0-7-6 *above*] and helpe to ayre the pictures [5s *above*], and for keeping cleane the picture roome one yeare in May 1656 [0-7-6 *above*] lvs

50. Petworth House Archives 5886. *The Account of Robert Scawen for reparations at*

Syon and Northumberland House for the year ending 10 January 1656/1657.

Also allowed to the said Accomptant for money by him disbursed and paid for charges about Northumberland house vizt . . . Mason to Edward Marshall for takeing vp the paving where the brasse Statues did lye and laying it downe againe,254 for helpe loding and vnloding 8 lode of stones out of the Coleyard, and for carryage of old free stone and paving stone to Thames side to be sent to Syon liijs ixd

51. Petworth House Archives 5893. *The Account of Orlando Gee for foreign payments for the year ending 31 January 1657/1658.*

To Mr Stone for keeping the pictures at Northumbland house a yeare Cs

Sondrie other payments vizt for 11 ounces of greene silke string [1-7-6 *above*], to hang vp pictures, and 10 ounces redd for lookeing glasses [1-5-0 *above*]lijs vjd For 2 large looking glasses vj.li

To Mr Stone Cs

To Mr Lanier for 3 pictures; one of St John, of Corregiores owne hand,255 another a sacrifice of a Goate to Jupiter,256 the third a peece of Pollidore painted in ffrisco Cxx.li257 To Mr Stone for coppying a Picture of our Lady and Christ xv.li To him more for mending the picture of old Palma [1-0-0 *above*],258 3 gilt picture frames [3-8-0 *above*], 5 stretching frames [2-10-0 *above*], a case for a picture sent to Petworth [0-5-6 *above*], and for spunges, and helpe to remove and make cleane pictures, to porters for carrying pictures into Southwarke and other places, and for his charges going to Greenwich to fetch 3 pictures ix.li vs viijd To Mr Bolty for 2 picture frames xvs

To Mr de Critz for 5 statues with 4li-10s-0d given him by his Lopps Command Cvij.li To him more for a Statue of Bacchus with a pedistall [30-0-0 *above*], and a peece of Olivers in Limning [25-0-0 *above*] lv.li

52. Petworth House Archives 319.

Aprill ye 18.th 1657

Then recd of ye right honoble ye Earle of Northumbld by ye hands of Mr Orlando Gee the sume of one hundred and and [sic] twenty pounds for three Picktures The first of St John at full length of Corregios owne hand the second a peece caled a sacrifice of a Goate vnto Jupiter the third a peece of Pollodore painted in ffrisco; I say recd by me

Jerom Lanier   120li: 00s: 00d

53. Alnwick MSS: Syon House, U.III.3. *The Account of Robert Scawen for the stone stairs and gardens at Northumberland House for three years ending 25 January 1657/1658*

[To Edward Marshall] for the greate Carved Pedistall and bringing it from ffetter lane to Northumberland garden ix.^{li} For 4 stones provided for the bodies of the round pedistalles 48 foote at 2^s-2^d a foote Ciiij^s

Sculpter to William Larson for Materialles [2-0-0 *above*] and workemanshipp in repairing the Statues [10-0-0 *above*] xij.^{li}

54. Petworth House Archives 5896. *The Account of Robert Scawen for reparations at Syon and Northumberland House for the year ending 20 January 1657/1658.*

For searches and a Coppy of Sr Thomas Widdringtons Report concerning pictures at Yorke house xvj^s ij.^{d}

Alsoe allowed to the said Accomptant for money by him disbursed and paid for Repairacones and other Charges for Northumberland house vizt . . Mason to Edward Marshall . . . repaireing the basies vnder the Pillers in the Tarries [=Terrace] walke [2-15-0 *above*], for 40 foote of Portland stepp for plinthes vnder the 6 timber pedistalles to keep them from rotting at 2^s-6^d a foote [5-0-0 *above*], for carryage of the Statues and for workemen and Labourers to help lode and vnlode them and set them vp [2-8-6 *above*], for 2 plinthes on the topp of 2 pedistalles to raise the marble Statues higher [1-4-0 *above*] . . . Painter to John Gomersall . . . priming and stopping the 6 pedistalles in oyle for the figures in the garden at 5^s a peece [1-10-0 *above*]

55. Petworth House Archives 5903. *The Account of Orlando Gee for foreign payments for the year ending 31 January 1658/1659.*

To Mr Stone for keeping the pictures at Northumberland house a year at X̄mas C^s

To a servant of my Lord Barckleyes that brought the fflorida Ambassadores picture to my Lord Percy xx^s

To Mr Lely for Drawing my Lord Percy's picture sent to Hadham xx.^{li}[259] For a carved and guilt frame for that picture lxx^s To Mr Stone for Coppying his Lo^{pps} picture given to Doctor Rainbow [3-0-0 *above*], for a coppy of my Lord Percys picture with a carved and guilt frame given to my Lady Drumond [7-5-0 *above*], for mending some pictures [2-0-0 *above*], for a large Ebbony frame for the picture of Stenwicke [4-10-0 *above*],[260] two greate cases for pictures [0-12-0 *above*], helpe to remove and hanging vp pictures [0-15-6 *above*], boathire to Greenwich and Dedford [6^s *above*], nailes and Springes [3^s *above*], and for severall cullours for my Lord Percy's Launces [0-18-9 *above*] xix.^{li} x^s iij.^{d} To Henry Norris for picture frames and stretching frames xxvij^s To Mr Beaucampe for 10 Marble heades and a figure called a Bacchus

190.^{li} whereof allowed for 5 brasse statues 65.^{li}[261] soe there was paid him in money Cxxv^{li} To him more for a statue of a young Apollo, another of a Bachus and a head of Jupiter xxv.^{li} and to him for the carriage of all these heads and statues lj^s

56. Petworth House Archives 5906. *The Account of Robert Scawen for reparations at Syon and Northumberland House for the year ending 7 March 1658/1659.*

Alsoe allowed to the said Accomptant for money by him disbursed and paid for Reparacones and other charges about Northumberland house vizt . . Masons worke vizt to Edward Marshall . . . removing two statues in the Garden [0-14-0 *above*]

57. Petworth House Archives 5911. *The Account of Orlando Gee for foreign payments for (Josceline) Lord Percy for the year ending 31 January 1658/1659.*

Coach-hire twice and Chairemen once waiting on my Lord Percy to Mr Lyllie's viij^s

58. Petworth House Archives 5913. *The Account of Orlando Gee for foreign payments for the year ending 31 January 1659/1660.*

Mr Stone for keeping the pictures at Northumberland house C^s

To Mr Stone for Coppying his Lo^{pps} picture wth the Anchor [6-0-0 *above*] and a frame to it [0-12-0 *above*] for my Lady Capell,[262] Coppying that picture [6-0-0 *above*] and a frame to it [1-5-0 *above*] for the Lady Diana Sydney, a Coppy after Coregio wherein there is a maide and a shocke dogg [8-0-0 *above*], and an ebbony frame for it [1-10-0 *above*], Exchanging a picture [5-0-0 *above*], painting 2 pedestalles [3-0-0 *above*], a frame and glasse [1-0-0 *above*], an ebbony frame for the Copy after Coregio [1-10-0 *above*], another for the peece of Pullenburke [8^s *above*],[263] a Carved and guilt frame for my Lady Capells picture [3-10-0 *above*], a stretching frame [0-6-0 *above*], severall cases to send pictures to Petworth and Hadham [0-14-0 *above*], and for Carryage of pictures into Southwarke and other places [0-7-3 *above*] xxxix^{li} ij^s iij.^{d}

Mending and clensing a brasse figure xvj^s

59. Petworth House Archives 5915. *The Account of Robert Scawen for reparations at Syon and Northumberland House for the year ending 28 February 1659/1660.*

Alsoe allowed to the said Accomptant for money by him disbursed and paid for Reparacōnes and other Charges about Northumberland house vizt . . Joyner to Robert Cleare for a blacke pedestall [5-0-0 *above*], 12 more at 30^s a peece [18-0-0 *above*], and 6 more at 20^s a peece

[6-0-0 *above*] xxix.li . . Carver to Richard Cleare
for 6 pedestalles inriched with fowleage
shieldes and Corronettes, and the vpper
mouldinges inriched with lace at 46s a peece
xiij.li xvjd Painter to John Peirce for painting
one of the pedestalles xxxs

60. Petworth House Archives 5931. *The Account of Orlando Gee for foreign payments for the year ending 13 February 1660/1661.*

Mr Stone for keeping the pictures at Northumberland house a yeare at Xmas Cs

To Mr Hodgkins for the Carryage of 2 pictures from Canterbury xviijs

Mr Hodgkines xls

To Mr Rawley's servant that brought a picture xxs

To Mr Stone for a Coppy of his Lopp with his first Lady and the Lady Katharine [20-0-0 *above*],264 a Coppy after Haniball Carratts [12-0-0 *above*], a Coppy of St John after Coregio,265 a Coppy after Pollidore [8-0-0 *above*],266 a peece of fflowers [2-5-0 *above*], vlta Marine & lake [1-5-0 *above*], painting 6 pedistalles [2-0-0 *above*], mending the picture of Andrea Dolseto [0-10-0 *above*],267 a large Ebbony frame for a picture [1-15-0 *above*], and for removeing pictures and Statues to Whitehall [0-8-0 *above*] lviij.li iijs

61. Petworth House Archives 5940. *The Account of Orlando Gee for foreign payments for the year ending 5 February 1661/1662.*

Wages of his Lopps Servants vizt . . Mr Stone a yeare at Xmas Cs

To Mr Stone for 5 Coppies after Pollidore xxx.li268 To Henry Norris for 3 Carved and guilt picture frames [6-10-0 *above*], a case to send a picture frame to Petworth [0-5-0 *above*], and for 3 daies worke altering a frame and hanging pictures [0-10-0 *above*] vij.li vs

62. Petworth House Archives 5752. *The Account of Orlando Gee for foreign payments for the year ending 9 February 1662/1663.*

Wages of his Lopps Servants vizt . . Pentioners vizt Mr Stone a yeare at Xmas Cs

To Monsr De-la-Sume for a picture iiij.li To Mr Stone for exchanging the Countesse of Sunderlandes picture [5-10-0 *above*],269 sending two Painters to Syon to view the Cisternes [0-10-0 *above*], and some other disbursmtes [0-8-10 *above*] vj.li viijs xd Mr Norris for a gilt frame for the Duke of Yorkes Picture [2-10-0 *above*],270 a case to send pictures to Petworth [0-7-0 *above*], and a days worke hanging pictures [0-3-0 *above*] lxs

63. Petworth House Archives 5762. *The Account of Orlando Gee for foreign payments for the year ending 5 February 1663/1664.*

Wages of his Lopps Servantes vizt . . Mr. Stone Cs

Mr Norris for . . . two cases for pictures [1-2-0 *above*], portage into Southwarke [0-3-6 *above*]

64. Petworth House Archives 5775. *The Account of Orlando Gee for foreign payments for the year ending 26 February 1664/1665*

Wages of his Lopps Servantes vizt . . Mr Stone for one yeares pencon at Xmas Cs

To him [Henry Norris] more 4 Carved and gilt frames [10-15-0 *above*], 4 stretching frames [1-4-0 *above*], and a case to send pictures to Petworth xij.li vs

To Mr Lilly for drawing my Lady Percy's picture xx.li271

65. Petworth House Archives 619. *Fragmentary account, dated 1664.*

To Mr Lilly for drawing my Lady Percys picture [20-0-0 *above*] and for severall picture frames [12-0-0 *above*] 32-0-0

66. Petworth House Archives 5788. *The Account of Orlando Gee for foreign payments for the year ending 2 March 1665/1666.*

Wages of his Lopps Servantes . . . Mr Stone for his yeares pention at Xmas Cs

To Mr Stone for two pictures [40-0-0 *above*], a picture frame [2-0-0 *above*], a case to send those pictures from London [0-7-0 *above*], and to Porters for hanging up and taking downe pictures for 3 yeares [2-0-0 *above*] xliiij.li vijs

67. Petworth House Archives 5796. *The Account of Orlando Gee for foreign payments for Josceline Lord Percy for the year ending 28 February 1665/1666.*

To Mr Lilly for drawing his Lopps picture xx.li272

68. Petworth House Archives 5801. *The Account of Orlando Gee for foreign payments for the year ending 22 January 1666/1667.*

Wages of his Lopps Servantes vizt . . Mr Stone for his yeares Pencon at Xmas Cs

Mr Stone for taking downe hanging up and clensing pictures xvjs vjd Mr Cleare for . . . cases for . . . pictures [0-3-6 *above*]

69. Petworth House Archives 5809. *The Account of Orlando Gee for foreign payments for Josceline Lord Percy for the year ending 16 January 1666/1667.*

Mr Stone for a gilt frame for a picture xxxs

70. Petworth House Archives 5814. *The Account of Orlando Gee for foreign payments for the year ending 27 January 1667/1668.*

Wages of his Lopps Servantes vizt . . Mr Stone for his yeares pencon at Xmas by Cs

John Norries for 10 Stretching frames for pictures [3-15-0 *above*], mending frames [1-1-0 *above*], and for nailes [0-3-0 *above*], iiij.li xixs

71. Petworth House Archives 5822. *The Account of Orlando Gee for foreign payments for Josceline Lord Percy for the year ending 20 January 1667/1668.*

To Mr Stone for a Coppie of his Lo.^pps Picture after Lilley [10-0-0 *above*], and for a gilt frame [1-10-0 *above*] xj.^li x.^s

NOTES

Permission to quote from documents in the Petworth House Archives has been kindly granted by Lord Egremont and P. Gill, county archivist for West Sussex. Permission to publish extracts from the papers at Alnwick Castle has been kindly given by the trustees of the 10th duke of Northumberland. I am particularly grateful to Alison McCann at West Sussex Record Office for help in consulting documents. Thanks are also extended to Caroline Armitage, assistant curator, and Colin Shrimpton, archivist, for assistance at Alnwick Castle. My warm thanks to John Adamson, Jaynie Anderson, Edward Chaney, Alastair Laing, Philip McEvansoneya, Oliver Millar, Elizabeth McGrath, Malcolm Rogers, Paul Shakeshaft, and Arthur K. Wheelock, Jr. for help and advice. An early version of this paper was much improved by Clare Tilbury.

1. No study has been published before now of Northumberland as a patron. Some material on the formation of his picture collection can be found in studies of the pictures at Petworth; see C[hristopher] H[ussey], "The Petworth Collection of Pictures—I," *Country Life* 58 (5 December 1925), 899–903; St. John Gore, "Three Centuries of Discrimination," *Apollo* 105 (May 1977), 346–357; St. John Gore, "Old Masters at Petworth: The background to the inventories recording the acquisitions of the 10th Earl of Northumberland and of the 2nd Earl of Egremont," in Gervase Jackson-Stops et al., eds., *The Fashioning and Functioning of the British Country House*, Studies in the History of Art 25, National Gallery of Art (Washington, 1989), 121–131. See also Gervase Jackson-Stops and C.H.B., *Petworth House, West Sussex*, 3d. rev. ed. (n.p., 1990). The most comprehensive, although still incomplete survey is Ralph Holland, *Noble Patronage. An exhibition devoted to the activity of the Percy family, earls and dukes of Northumberland, as collectors and patrons of the arts* [exh. cat., Hatton Gallery] (Newcastle upon Tyne, 1963). For Northumberland's life, which urgently needs a modern study, see Arthur Collins, *An History of the Ancient and Illustrious Family of the Percys, Barons Percy, and Earls of Northumberland. Collected from Records, Authentick Manuscripts, and our most approved Historians* (London, 1750); Edward Barrington de Fonblanque, *Annals of the House of Percy, from the conquest to the opening of the nineteenth century*, 2 vols. (London, 1887).

2. Christopher Brown, *Van Dyck* (Oxford, 1982), 201, cites an enthusiastic and friendly letter written by Northumberland to Van Dyck in 1637, signed "passionately your humble servant." I have been unable to trace this document. In Giovanni Pietro Bellori, *Le vite de' pittori, scultori e architetti moderni*, ed. Evelina Borea (Turin, 1976), 281, a *Crucifixion* painted for Northumberland, but now lost, is described: "Per lo conte di Nortumberland dipinse il Crocifisso con cinque angeli che in tazze d'oro raccolgono il sangue dalle piaghe, e sotto la Croce vi dispose la Vergine, San Giovanni e Madalena."

3. Public Record Office, London (hereafter P.R.O.), SP/99/15, "The Informat[ion] of Rob Stone and Rich. Vahan this 14th of Aprill 1645." Parliament urgently needed money at this time to pay Lord Fairfax's army and the Scottish troops in Ireland.

4. *Journals of the House of Commons, 4. From December the 25th. 1644, in the Twentieth Year of the Reign of King Charles the First to December the 4th. 1646, in the Twenty-second Year of the Reign of King Charles the First*, 120–121. See also Samuel R. Gardiner, *History of the Great Civil War, 1642–1649*, 4 vols. (London, 1893), 2:197–198.

5. "Given to Mr. Rubens for drawing his L^ps picture on horseback, 500l." W. Noël Sainsbury, *Original Unpublished Papers illustrative of the Life of Sir Peter Paul Rubens, as an Artist and a Diplomatist. Preserved in H.M. State Paper Office . . .* (London, 1859), 68 n.107a. For the destroyed original, formerly in the collection of the earl of Jersey at Osterley Park, see Hans Vlieghe, *Rubens' Portraits of Identified Sitters Painted in Antwerp. Corpus Rubenianum Ludwig Burchard*, vol. 19, pt. 2 (London and New York, 1987), 64–66.

6. *Journals of the House of Commons* (note 4), 4:216.

7. *Journals of the House of Commons* (note 4), 4:248.

8. L. Whitacre, *House of Commons Proceedings 1642–1647*, British Library, Add. MS 31,116, fol. 206v.

9. "Del Serto.-A great piece of our Saviour dead;" Randall Davies, "An Inventory of the Duke of Buckingham's Pictures, etc., at York House in 1635," *Burlington Magazine* 10 (1907), 382. For identification with the picture in Vienna see John Shearman,

Andrea del Sarto, 2 vols. (Oxford, 1965), 2:245–246, no. 56; Sydney J. Freedberg, *Andrea del Sarto*, 2 vols. (Cambridge, Mass., 1963), 2:90–91, no. 44.

10. See Gordon R. Batho, "The Wizard Earl in the Tower, 1605–1621," *History Today* 6 (May 1956), 344–351.

11. Repairs at Dorset House in 1633 are mentioned in *The Generall Accompte* for that year (Alnwick MSS: Syon House U.I.5). The earl received sums from his private purse there on 29 November and 18 December 1633, and 5 January 1634 (Account of Henry Hearon, 29 January 1632/1633–15 January 1633/1634). See also Petworth House Archives 478: "for the rent of the said house [Dorset House] for a year ended at the Lady day 1636 paid to the Lord Dorsett x[s]." The last reference to building work at Dorset House appears to be in *The Generall Accompte 1637* (Alnwick MSS: Syon House U.I.5).

12. Northumberland paid £150 for half a year's rent to the earl of Antrim in 1640 (Alnwick MSS: Syon House, U.I.5. Account of Thomas Cartwright for the year ending 22 January 1640/1641). Later documents (U.I.6) show that £350 was paid for a year's rent in 1641, and that the payments fluctuated during the mid-1640s. The earl's departure is suggested by a final payment of £250 in midsummer 1647 (Account of Robert Scawen, 30 March 1647/1648–30 March 1648/1649).

13. Some discussion of Northumberland's involvement with the dispersal of the York House collection can be found in John Walter Stoye, *English Travellers Abroad, 1604–1667. Their Influence in English Society and Politics* (London, 1952), 302–312. On 7 June 1650 the duke of Buckingham wrote to Lord Jermyn: "the whole bargain depends upon the Zealand pictures w[ch] cannot be delivered till order comes from my L[d] Northumberland." I am grateful to Philip McEvansoneya for this reference, who tells me that a letter datable July–August 1650 from Stephen Gough (or Goffe) refers to Buckingham's agent Peter Roberts who "must first go out to speake wth my L[d] Northumberland as I am told there is a debt upon them [the pictures] of over 4000[li]."

14. Alnwick MSS: Syon House, U.I.6. Account of Lancelot Thorneton for apparel and necessaries for the year ending 17 January 1643/1644.

15. Northumberland employed Edward Carter, the successor to Inigo Jones as Surveyor of the King's Works, to direct major alterations between 1642 and 1649; see John Bold, *John Webb. Architectural Theory and Practice in the Seventeenth Century* (Oxford, 1989), 162. It should be noted that Northumberland left York House at around the time that the duke of Buckingham petitioned Parliament to have the sequestration of his property revoked; the Order of the Commons is dated 4 October 1647; see Stoye 1952 (note 13), 304. For an account of the earl's building work at Northumberland House see Jeremy Wood, "The Architectural Patronage of Algernon Percy, 10th Earl of Northumberland," in John Bold and Edward Chaney, eds., *English Architecture, Pub-*

lic and Private: Essays for Kerry Downes (London, 1993), 55–80.

16. See C. H. Collins Baker, *Catalogue of the Petworth Collection of Pictures in the Possession of Lord Leconfield* (London, 1920), 33–36, nos. 272–279; Keith Andrews, *Adam Elsheimer. Paintings, Drawings, Prints* (Oxford, 1977), 147–148, no. 17 (in which "Symond Stowe" should read Symon [or Simon] Stone). For the presence of these pictures in the Buckingham collection see Davies 1907 (note 9), 382: "Ensen Hamor.- Eight little pieces."

17. See Michael Jaffé, "The Picture of the Secretary of Titian," *Burlington Magazine* 108 (1966), 114–126; Harold E. Wethey, *The Paintings of Titian. Complete Edition*, 3 vols. (London, 1969–1975), 2:78, no. 8. For the presence of this picture at York House see Davies 1907 (note 9), 380: "Titian.- A Picture of the French Ambassado[r] Enditeing [dictating]."

18. As noted by Jaffé 1966 (note 17), 126. See also Oliver Millar, *Van Dyck in England* [exh. cat., National Portrait Gallery] (London, 1982), 97, under no. 57; Arthur K. Wheelock, Jr., et al., *Anthony van Dyck* [exh. cat., National Gallery of Art] (Washington, 1990), 320–322, under no. 86.

19. British Library (hereafter B.L.), Add. MSS 27, 872, fol. 3.

20. See Lita-Rose Betcherman, "The York House Collection and Its Keeper," *Apollo* 92 (1970), 252.

21. Collins Baker 1920 (note 16), 113–114, nos. 320, 333. *The Corsini Madonna. The Madonna and Child with the Infant John the Baptist and Three Angels* is listed as "Andrea del Sarto.- A piece of Our Lady amongst the Children" in the 1635 Buckingham inventory (Davies 1907 [note 9], 380). It was considered an early copy (see Shearman 1965 [note 9], 2:217–219, under no. 32) until its recent restoration. For the acceptance of the work as an original see Antonio Natali and Alessandro Cecchi, *Andrea del Sarto. Catalogo completo dei dipinti* (Florence, 1989), 52, no. 18. *The Madonna and Child with Saint Elizabeth and the Infant John the Baptist* is listed as "Andrea del Sarto.- The Virgin Mary, our Saviour, St. John, and Anne" in the 1635 Buckingham inventory, and is discussed as a good early copy by Shearman 1965 (note 9), 2:227–228, under no. 39.

22. Davies 1907 (note 9), 382. It had reached Northumberland House by 1652; see Appendix I, no. 23.

23. It is not to be confused with a similar picture by Palma Vecchio, now at Alnwick, which was obtained by a later duke of Northumberland in 1857 from the Manfrin collection; see Philip Rylands in *The Genius of Venice, 1500–1600* [exh. cat., Royal Academy of Arts] (London, 1983), 197, no. 75. Symonds' mention of the picture establishes that it was on panel (Appendix I, no. 23) and thus cannot be the Paris Bordone *Cleopatra* at Petworth, which is on canvas (Collins Baker 1920 [note 16], 8, no. 191).

24. A copy of the London version was sold from Syon at Sotheby's, London, 26 March 1952, no. 109; it is not impossible that this was the copy painted for

Northumberland by Stone (see Appendix IV, no. 48). For the London picture (inv. 3939) see Cecil Gould, *National Gallery Catalogues. The Sixteenth-Century Italian Schools* (London, 1975), 187–188.

25. In 1657, when the duke of Buckingham returned to England, Northumberland obtained a copy of Sir Thomas Widdrington's "Report concerning pictures at Yorke house" (see Appendix IV, no. 54), which was almost certainly the Parliamentary report of 1645, as Philip McEvansoneya kindly pointed out to me.

26. See Wethey 1969–1975 (note 17), 2:147, no. 110; Gould 1975 (note 24), 284–287.

27. See Wethey 1969–1975 (note 17), 3:169–172, no. 30; John Ingamells, " 'Perseus and Andromeda': the provenance," *Burlington Magazine* 124 (1982), 396–400.

28. Jeremy Wood, "Van Dyck's 'Cabinet de Titien': the Contents and Dispersal of His Collection," *Burlington Magazine* 132 (1990), 682–686.

29. See Christopher Brown, "Van Dyck's Collection: A Document Rediscovered," in *Essays on van Dyck* (Ottawa, 1983), 69–72; Christopher Brown and Nigel Ramsay, "Van Dyck's Collection: Some New Documents," *Burlington Magazine* 132 (1990), 704–709.

30. Wood 1990 (note 28), 695, Appendix II.

31. Collins Baker 1920 (note 16), 32, no. 124; see also Erik Larsen, *The Paintings of Anthony van Dyck*, 2 vols. (Freren, 1988), 2:477, no. A 198/4. It is mentioned by Symonds in 1652 (see Appendix I, no. 19). For the large equestrian version see Oliver Millar, *The Tudor, Stuart and Early Georgian Pictures in the Collection of Her Majesty the Queen* (London, 1963), 94–95, no. 144; Millar in London 1982 (note 18), 50–52, no. 11.

32. See Gert Adriani, *Anton van Dyck. Italienisches Skizzenbuch* (Vienna, 1940), fol. 106r.

33. See Christopher Brown, "Van Dyck and Titian," in *Bacchanals by Titian and Rubens. Papers given at a symposium in the Nationalmuseum, Stockholm, March 18–19, 1987*, ed. Görel Cavalli-Björkman (Stockholm, 1987), 159.

34. Collins Baker 1920 (note 16), 130, no. 154; see also Wethey 1969–1975 (note 17), 3:217, no. X-29; Erica Tietze-Conrat, "Archeologia Tizianesca," *Arte Veneta* 10 (1956), 82–86.

35. X-radiographs were made at the Courtauld Institute of Art and were published by Gore 1977 (note 1), 351–352.

36. See Wethey 1969–1975 (note 17), 3:234, no. L-9, as "copy of a lost original." For a more favorable discussion see David Jaffé in *Rubens and the Italian Renaissance* [exh. cat., Australian National Gallery] (Canberra, 1992), 100, no. 25.

37. See William E. Suida, "Paolo Veronese and His Circle: Some Unpublished Works," *Art Quarterly* 8 (1945), 185, who retained the traditional attribution to Veronese of the picture in Vienna and provided incorrect dates for the inventories cited.

38. This miniature is described in the inventory of Ralph Bankes' pictures at Gray's Inn, dated 23 December 1659, as "A Peice of watercolours bought of mr Buttler, Coppy after Olivers Coppy after Titian [A Venus & Satyre *deleted*]." I am grateful to Alastair Laing for this reference.

39. See Wood 1990 (note 28), 684, 695.

40. In the period 1641 to 1646 Northumberland is believed to have lost £45,000 from damage to his property and the nonpayment of rents; see Gardiner 1893 (note 4), 3:196; for rumors that he would become Lord Protector, see 2:189, citing Salvetti to Gondi, March 21/31 1645.

41. For negotiations with the "Comittee of the Navie for an Order about releaseing the hangings" see Alnwick MSS: Syon House, U.I.6. The Account of Edward Payler for foreign payments for the year ending 17 January 1648/1649.

42. Alnwick MSS: Syon House, U.I.5. The Account of Peter Dodesworth for foreign payments, 12 January 1632/1633–14 January 1633/1634: "5 peeces of fine arras hanginge of the story of Vulcan 150 ells fflemish at 30s the ell. ccxxvli "

43. Alnwick MSS: Syon House, U.I.5. Account of Peter Dodesworth. . . 1632/1633 to . . . 1633/1634: "6 peeces Brissells hanginge 9 foote deepe cont 132 elles fflemish being the story of David cxxli " This item reappears in Alnwick MS 107 GC 26, "An Inventory of the late Right Honourable Jocelin, Earl of Northumberland's Personal Estate as it was at the time of his Decease, the 21/31 of May 1670:" "In the Wardrobe at Petworth. Six Peeces of hangings of the Story of David and Goliah 9 foote deepe £30 00 00."

44. Alnwick MSS: Syon House, H II. Ib; see Gordon R. Batho, *The Household Papers of Henry Percy, Ninth Earl of Northumberland (1564–1632)*, Camden Third Series, vol. 93 (London, 1963), 113, 116.

45. Alnwick MSS: Syon House, U.I.5. The Account of Edward Payler for foreign payments for the year ending 20 January 1635/1636: "given the bargemen when yor Lop went to Mortlake xxs "

46. Alnwick MSS: Syon House, U.I.6. The Account of Lancelot Thorneton for apparel and necessaries for the year ending 17 January 1648/1649.

47. Alnwick MSS: Syon House, U.I.6. The Account of Edward Payler for foreign payments for the year ending 17 January 1648/1649. Although not specified in the accounts, it is likely that the ship involved was the *Seaflower*, which failed to report to the customs on leaving London and was seized by an order dated 8 January 1647/1648; see P.R.O. SP 16/516/1.

48. See Stoye 1952 (note 13), 306.

49. Alnwick MSS: Syon House, U.I.6. *The generall accompte 1647*: "Plate sold at severall tymes by your Lops comand and not before accompted for m m m vj jcli xs. vijd "

50. Alnwick MSS: Syon House, U.I.6. The Account of Peter Dodesworth for foreign payments, 16 January 1640/1641–16 January 1641/1642: "ffor a silver ces-

terne bought of Christian Vianon, a dutch Goldsmith 35 1li 15s 0d." A salver and a covered bowl by Van Vianen have been published from the Northumberland collection and dated c. 1636–1642; see Ronald W. Lightbown, "Christian van Vianen at the Court of Charles I," *Apollo* 86 (1968), 435–436. The salver, which could be later in date, is decorated with Cupids and hounds, with, at the center, the embossed half-moon of the Percys in a Garter frame. This badge also occurs on the covered bowl, but here includes the anchor that Northumberland used as his device while Admiral of the Fleet between 1636 and 1642, and that was also included by Van Dyck in his full-length and half-length portraits of the earl. The covered bowl can thus be securely dated and is likely to be identical with Northumberland's "cesterne." It was among his most prized possessions. There are a number of later payments for cases made for its display and for "boyling and burnishing" it (Petworth House Archives 5872. The Account of Orlando Gee for foreign payments from January 1654/1655 to January 1655/1656).

51. See Petworth House Archives 5752, 5762, 5770, 5775, 5788, 5801, 5808.

52. See Lightbown 1968 (note 50), 436. The dates of Van Vianen's second period of employment by Northumberland correspond with the dates of his residence at Chapel Street.

53. Hamilton to Feilding, ⁸/₁₈ December 1636; see Paul Shakeshaft, " 'To much bewiched with thoes intysing things': The Letters of James, Third Marquis of Hamilton and Basil, Viscount Feilding, Concerning Collecting in Venice 1635–1639," *Burlington Magazine* 128 (1986), 123 (doc. xi).

54. Larsen 1988 (note 31), 2:362–363, no. 927, wrongly claimed that Northumberland does not wear the Garter in this work, and consequently that it must date from *before* Van Dyck's return to Flanders in 1634–1635. This detail, which does not seem to have been observed before, makes it almost certain that the portrait dates from the second half of 1635. For the work itself see Collins Baker 1920 (note 16), 30, no. 289.

55. Collins Baker 1920 (note 16), 29, no. 223. See also Millar in London 1982 (note 18), 53–54, no. 13; Larsen 1988 (note 31), 2:363, no. 928; and Wheelock in Washington 1990 (note 18), 256–258, no. 65.

56. Pace Oliver Millar, "Notes on British Painting from Archives—III," *Burlington Magazine* 97 (1955), 255; Millar in London 1982 (note 18), 83, under nos. 40–41. Millar again states in *The Treasure Houses of Britain. Five Hundred Years of Private Patronage and Art Collecting*, ed. Gervase Jackson-Stops [exh. cat., National Gallery of Art] (Washington, 1985), 139, under no. 64, as fact, that the "Four Countesses" were commissioned by Northumberland from Van Dyck. The Countesses (Carlisle, Bedford, Devonshire, and Sunderland) were engraved by Lombart at an undetermined date.

57. Collins Baker 1920 (note 16), 30, no. 225. See Larsen 1988 (note 31), 2:309, no. 781. Lionel Cust,

Anthony van Dyck. An Historical Study of His Life and Work (London, 1900), 271, under no. 35, mentions a copy at Syon (no. 191), which may be the second of the two portraits mentioned in the 1671 inventory (see Appendix III, no. 25), although the valuation suggests that both portraits were originals of good quality.

58. See Gladys Scott Thomson, *Life in a Noble Household, 1641–1700* (London, 1937), 290. Bedford may have commissioned Stone to copy the full-length of Anne Carr still at Woburn (see Larsen 1988 [note 31], 2:305–306, no. 771). A copy of the Petworth version is at Woburn attributed to Stone.

59. See Collins Baker 1920 (note 16), 29, no. 218; Larsen 1988 (note 31), 2:305, no. 768. See also Millar in London 1982 (note 18), 83–85, no. 41; Washington 1985 (note 56), 139, no. 64.

60. For the portrait at Petworth see Collins Baker 1920 (note 16), 31, no. 305; Larsen 1988 (note 31), 2:396, no. 1014. See also Millar in London 1982 (note 18), 83, no. 40.

61. See Kenneth J. Garlick, "A Catalogue of Pictures at Althorp," *Walpole Society* 45 (1976), 23–24, nos. 165–166. One of these copies of Northumberland's Van Dycks has an old attribution to "Henry Stone."

62. An unattributed portrait of Dorothy Percy, countess of Leicester, is mentioned in Sir William Musgrave's list of portraits at Petworth in 1775 and 1785; B.L. Add. MSS 5726 E, no. 6, fol. 26r. For the version now in the collection see Collins Baker 1920 (note 16), 29, no. 220; Larsen 1988 (note 31), 2:494, no. A 240/1.

63. Collins Baker 1920 (note 16), 30, no. 226; Larsen 1988 (note 31), 2:329, no. 838. For Lombart's engraving see Freeman O'Donoghue and Henry M. Hake, *Catalogue of Engraved British Portraits Preserved in the Department of Prints and Drawings in the British Museum*, 6 vols. (London, 1908–1925), 2:48.

64. Northumberland and his sister, Lady Carlisle, had been among the Puritan supporters of Henrietta Maria and had obtained political advantage from her; but unlike Anne and Olivia Boteler, they sided with Parliament. See R. Malcolm Smuts, "The Puritan followers of Henrietta Maria in the 1630s," *English Historical Review* 93 (1978), 26–45.

65. See Millar in London 1982 (note 18), 67, under no. 23, where he quotes Strafford's letter of 15 November 1636. See also Oliver Millar, "Strafford and Van Dyck," in Richard Ollard and Pamela Tudor-Craig, eds., *For Veronica Wedgwood. These Studies in Seventeenth-Century History* (London, 1986), 115–117. For the portrait at Petworth see Collins Baker 1920 (note 16), 31, no. 311; Larsen 1988 (note 31), 2:392–393, no. 1000.

66. William Knowler, *The Earl of Strafforde's Letters and Dispatches, with an Essay towards his Life by Sir George Radcliffe from the Originals in the possession of his Great Grandson the Right Honourable Thomas Earl of Malton, Knight of the Bath*, 2 vols. (London, 1739), 2:118. The Reverend Mr Garrard to

the Lord Deputy [Strafford] from Syon, 9 October 1637. I am grateful to Malcolm Rogers for this reference.

67. See note 55.

68. As observed by Wheelock in Washington 1990 (note 18), 256.

69. See John Peacock, "The 'Wizard Earl' portrayed by Hilliard and van Dyck," *Art History* 8 (1985), 139–157.

70. Peacock 1985 (note 69), 139.

71. See the portrait believed to have been painted in 1602 at Petworth; Collins Baker 1920 (note 16), 86, 590. Payments to Hubbard for a portrait of the 9th earl were made in 1585/1586; Alnwick MSS: Syon House, U.I.1. Account of Roger Thorpe, 1 September 1585–27 November 1586; and Account of Thomas Wycliffe, 1 August 1585–26 October 1586; see also Batho 1963 (note 44), 58, 65. See also Alnwick MSS: Syon House, U.I.3 (2). Account of Henry Taylor, 6 February 1607/1608–6 February 1608/1609: "for the picture drawer in drawinge yor. Lo: picture ij^s vj^d." This portrait appears to have been given to Lady Hutton; see Alnwick MSS: Syon House, U.I.3 (1), Edmund Powton's rough notes of payments, 1608: "for yor L. picture given to the Lady Hutton x^{li}"

72. See John Murdoch, Jim Murrell, Patrick J. Noon, and Roy Strong, *The English Miniature* (New Haven and London, 1981), 69–71; Roy Strong and V. J. Murrell, *Artists of the Tudor Court. The Portrait Miniature Rediscovered, 1520–1620* [exh. cat., Victoria and Albert Museum] (London, 1983), 158–159, no. 266; Roy Strong, *The English Renaissance Miniature* (New York, 1983), 108–110.

73. See L. Dussler, *Raphael. A Critical Catalogue of His Pictures, Wall-paintings and Tapestries* (London and New York, 1971), 73–74.

74. Two versions of this portrait survive; see Lionel Cust, *Eton College Portraits* (London, 1910), 65; David Piper, *Catalogue of the Seventeenth-Century Portraits in the National Portrait Gallery, 1625–1714* (Cambridge, 1963), 385–386 (inv. 1482).

75. Erna Auerbach, *Nicholas Hilliard* (London, 1961), 124: "The sitter's likeness . . . [is] in some ways near to that of the Cambridge miniature," that is, a version of Hilliard's portrait of the 9th earl now attributed to Rowland Lockey; see London 1983 (note 72), 92–93, no. 122.

76. Peacock 1985 (note 69), 139–140.

77. I am grateful to Elizabeth McGrath for help in interpreting this inscription.

78. Peacock 1985 (note 69), 150: "it seems likely that the project originated with Northumberland himself [the 9th earl], even though the picture was painted for his son." His father, however, had been confined to his estates following his release from the Tower, and died at Petworth; there is no evidence that Van Dyck visited Sussex until 1633, or that the earl was interested in his work or even knew of his existence.

79. See Gordon Batho, "The Education of a Stuart Nobleman," *British Journal of Educational Studies* 5 (1957), 131–143; Gordon Batho, "A Difficult Father-in-Law. The Ninth Earl of Northumberland," *History Today* 6 (November 1956), 745–746.

80. Of the celebrated "Three Magi," Thomas Harriot (1560–1621), famous for his work on optics and astronomy but also the author of studies on Archimedes, was the person best able to give this advice, but he had died some years prior to 1632.

81. The 9th earl was certainly interested in architecture and had one of the finest collections of books on the subject in England at this time. His annotated copies of Vitruvius, Alberti, du Cerceau, Palladio, and Vredeman de Vries survive at Petworth. He also rebuilt Syon and planned a gigantic enlargement of Petworth. He did not, however, own a copy of Vasari or any other sixteenth-century writer on art, such as Lomazzo or Armenini. For his books see Gordon R. Batho, "The Library of the 'Wizard' Earl: Henry Percy Ninth Earl of Northumberland (1564–1632)," *Library* 15 (1960), 246–261.

82. See Batho 1963 (note 44), 119.

83. Alnwick MSS: Syon House, U.I.1. Account of Thomas Wycliffe for foreign payments, 14 October 1586–14 February 1586/1587; see Batho 1963 (note 44), 75.

84. See Batho 1963 (note 44), 75. Around the same time the 9th earl spent £20 to have his portrait painted by Hubbard, the elusive artist patronized by the earl of Leicester and Lord Lumley (see Roy Strong, *The English Icon: Elizabethan and Jacobean Portraiture* [London and New York, 1969], 185). Hubbard also supplied the 9th earl with a portrait of "Madam Dundragoe" for £17; see Batho 1963 (note 44), 58, 65.

85. Alnwick MSS: Syon House, U.I.1 (2). Account of Gyles Grene, 28 March 1603–28 March 1604. This item is also found in *A note of Debtes dewe vpon this Audyte ended 21 Jnl: 1603*, Alnwick MSS: Syon House, U.I.3 (2).

86. For example, he paid £1 "to y^e: painter at Haye for mappes;" Alnwick MSS: Syon House, U.I.3 (1). Account of Roche Churche for foreign payments, 1 May 1600–27 March 1602. Documents from 1612 show that there were 5 "great mappes in frames wth Leather in his lo: great Clossett;" Alnwick MSS: Syon House, U.I.4. Account of Robert Flood, 7 February 1611/1612–7 February 1612/1613. Additional payments from 1614 show that he had maps of England, Italy, Spain, and the Netherlands framed, and that maps of the siege of Bergen-op-Zoom were mounted on rollers; Alnwick MSS: Syon House, U.I.4. Account of Robert Flood, 7 February 1613/1614–7 February 1614/1615.

87. Alnwick MSS: Syon House, U.I.4. Account of Robert Flood, 6 February 1615/1616–6 February 1616/1617: "for payntinge two peeces of the Desection of the skull with a case to carrie one to Cambridge viij^{li} iiij^s"

88. For the two portraits of Northumberland by Van Dyck, both now at Alnwick Castle, see Millar in London 1982 (note 18), 69–71, nos. 24–25.

89. See Daphne Foskett, *Samuel Cooper and His Contemporaries* [exh. cat., National Portrait Gallery] (London, 1974), 12.

90. This gift complicates our knowledge of the early history of Van Dyck's full-length of Northumberland, since it has been said that the original was given to Elizabeth Percy at the time of her marriage to Arthur, Lord Capel, in 1653, while a copy remained at Syon. See Millar in London 1982 (note 18), 71. It had certainly left the Northumberland collection by 1671 (compare Appendix III); it may be that the earl decided to keep Stone's copy and gave his daughter the original instead.

91. See Batho 1963 (note 44), xviii–xix.

92. Alnwick MSS: Syon House, U.I.5. Account of Peter Dodesworth for foreign payments, 16 January 1634/1635–16 January 1635/1636: "Chardges of his Lo.^{ps} installacon Knighte of the Garter . . . chardges of the feast at Dorsett House . . . $\overset{c}{vj}$ xlvij^{li} ix.^{s} ix.^{d}" According to this account the total spent was £2,585 0s. 5d.

93. See note 12.

94. This entry may simply refer to the removal of pictures formerly in the Buckingham collection, in which case the "10 pickture frames" may establish the number of works obtained from this source.

95. See Gould 1975 (note 24), 183–184.

96. Collins Baker 1920 (note 16), 73, no. 149. See Oliver Millar, *Sir Peter Lely, 1618–80* [exh. cat., National Portrait Gallery] (London, 1978), 38–39, no. 7.

97. See R. B. Beckett, *Lely* (London, 1951), 39, no. 78; Millar in London 1978 (note 96), 37–38, no. 6.

98. See note 17.

99. See notes 23–24.

100. See Wethey 1969–1975 (note 17), 1:79–80, no. 21.

101. B.L. Add. MSS 17, 915; see Jaffé 1966 (note 17), 120.

102. See Betcherman 1970 (note 20), 250–259. The year 1619 has been established as the date of Gerbier's entry into Buckingham's household by Philip McEvansoneya, "Some Documents Concerning the Patronage and Collections of the Duke of Buckingham," *Rutgers Art Review* 8 (1987), 28–29, 33.

103. For De Mayerne's receipts for payments see Petworth House Archives 319, 620. Further details can be found in Petworth House Archives 320, 617, 5829, 5838, 5847, 5856, 5864, 5876.

104. See Mansfield Kirby Talley, *Portrait Painting in England: Studies in the Technical Literature before 1700* (London, 1981), 72–149, for De Mayerne's interest in art, and 116–125 for information that he obtained from Van Dyck. For his portraits by Rubens see Frances Huemer, *Portraits. Corpus Rubenianum Ludwig Burchard*, vol. 19, pt. 1 (London, 1977), 176–180, nos. 46–47.

105. See John Shearman, *The Early Italian Pictures in the Collection of Her Majesty the Queen* (Cambridge, 1983), 80–81, no. 74.

106. See Oliver Millar, "Abraham van der Doort's Catalogue of the Collections of Charles I," *Walpole Society* 37 (1960), 15.

107. See Shearman 1983 (note 105), 123, no. 119.

108. See Shearman 1983 (note 105), 196, no. 198.

109. "Eleventh piece of the number of the 23 Italian collection pieces which your Majesty bought of Frezley" (spelling modernized); Van der Doort in Millar 1960 (note 106), 43. See also Brian Reade, "William Frizell and the Royal Collection," *Burlington Magazine* 89 (1947), 70–75.

110. See Oliver Millar, "The Inventories and Valuations of the King's Goods, 1649–1651," *Walpole Society* 43 (1972), 303, 314, 322.

111. See Penshurst MSS 1160/14, in G. Dyfnallt Owen, ed., *Historical Manuscripts Commission, 77. Report on the Manuscripts of the Right Honourable Viscount de l'Isle, V.C., preserved at Penshurst Place, Kent, 6. Sidney Papers, 1626–1698* (London, 1966), 502–503.

112. See Millar 1972 (note 110), 298, 303, 315.

113. See B.L. Add. MSS 17, 916: *A Booke containing severall of his Maties Goods brought into his Maties Closet & Wardrop by Coll: W^{m}. Hawley by ye order of A Comitte of Lords in Aprill: 1660: Whitehall June 1st 1660*, fols. 51v., 55r.

114. For the six horizontal panels by Polidoro, now at Hampton Court, see Shearman 1983 (note 105), 197–200, nos. 200–205. For Lord Lisle see note 111.

115. See B.L. Harley MSS 4898: *An Inventory of the Household Goods, Jewells Plate, &c, Belonging to the Late King. . . . With the Severall Contracts made by the Contractors for sale of the said Goods & c. From the year 1649, To the year 1652*, fol. 295r.

116. House of Lords Main Papers relating to the King's Goods, May 1660 to 11 June 1660, no. 87: *A pticular of such Goodes of his Late Maties remaining in safe custody of Ema: de Critz . . .* , 15 May 1660.

117. Royal Library, Windsor, A 49: *Drawings of Statues & Busts that were in the Palace at Whitehall before it was burnt, preserved by Sr John Stanley Bar^{t} who belonged to the Lord Chamberlaynes Office at the time the Palace was burnt down.* See A. H. Scott-Elliot, "The Statues from Mantua in the Collection of King Charles," *Burlington Magazine* 101 (1959), 218–227; David Chambers and Jane Martineau, eds., *Splendours of the Gonzaga* [exh. cat., Victoria and Albert Museum] (London, 1981), 229–231, no. 246.

118. Royal Library, Windsor, inv. no. 8920^{v}

119. Royal Library, Windsor, inv. no. 8917.

120. Royal Library, Windsor, inv. no. 8864.

121. Royal Library, Windsor, inv. no. 8903.

122. Royal Library, Windsor, inv. no. 8904.

123. Royal Library, Windsor, inv. no. 8901.

124. Royal Library, Windsor, inv. no. 8902.

125. See Scott-Elliot 1959 (note 117), 222–224, nos. 4, 5, 16, 39.

126. See Scott-Elliot 1959 (note 117), 223, nos. 15, 24.

127. See Collins Baker 1920 (note 16), 98, no. 231.

128. As proposed in Millar 1955 (note 56), 255.

129. See Larsen 1988 (note 31), 2:490, no. A 228/3.

130. Petworth House Archives 333, fol. 37r.: "Disbursments concerning the Stables and other expences," 17 January 1644/1645–17 January 1645/1646: "Decemb^r 9th pd for Mr Gildropes and my charges to Windsor and back againe. . . ." See also Appendix IV, nos. 27, 28.

131. *Journals of the House of Lords, Beginning Anno Vicesimo CAROLI Regis, 1644*, 7:591. House of Lords Main Papers, 28 August 1645–23 September 1645, no. 90.

132. Alnwick MSS: Syon House, U.I.6. Account of Lancelot Thorneton for apparel and necessaries for the year ending 17 January 1644/1645. First published by Millar 1955 (note 56), 255.

133. Petworth House Archives 5903. Account of Orlando Gee for foreign payments for the year ending 31 January 1658/1659.

134. Petworth House Archives 5783. Account of Orlando Gee for foreign payments for Josceline Lord Percy for the year ending 24 January 1664/1665.

135. See "Editorial: Sir Peter Lely's Collection," *Burlington Magazine* 83 (1943), 185–191.

136. See House of Lords Main Papers relating to the King's Goods, May 1660–11 June 1660, no. 86: endorsed "Mr Lilly of Covent Garden 18 May 1660."

137. See note 19.

138. See Bold 1989 (note 15), 162–164, 170; Wood 1993 (note 15), 72–74, 76–80. The picture can probably be identified with one still at Petworth; see Collins Baker 1920 (note 16), 111, no. 513.

139. See Davies 1907 (note 9), 382: "Rott^n Hamor.- Venus and Cupid." This work hung in the Red Closet, the same room that contained the Elsheimers that Northumberland is known to have acquired; see note 16.

140. See Petworth House Archives 620, 5754, 5764, 5777, 5790, 5800, 5803, 5816, covering the period 1663–1668.

141. Petworth House Archives 5906. Account of Robert Scawen for reparations at Syon and Northumberland House for the year ending 7 March 1658/1659.

142. Petworth House Archives 5934. Account of Robert Scawen for reparations at Syon and Northumberland House for the year ending 16 January 1660/1661.

143. Petworth House Archives 5765. Account of Robert Scawen for reparations at Syon and Northumberland House for the year ending 27 January 1663/1664.

144. See note 177; Appendix III, no. 8.

145. See note 21; Appendix III, no. 5.

146. Fig. 3. See note 17; Appendix III, no. 4.

147. See note 26; Appendix III, no. 1.

148. Fig. 6. See note 34; Appendix III, no. 2.

149. The following entry may also refer to a work attributed to Tintoretto; see Appendix III, no. 71.

150. An untraced portrait of Henry, 8th earl of Northumberland (1532–1585). Perhaps identifiable with Collins Baker 1920 (note 16), 32, no. 285 (as Sir Charles Percy); Larsen 1988 (note 31), 2:500, no. A261.

151. Fig. 13. See note 55; Appendix III, no. 19.

152. Anne Boteler, countess of Newport. See Appendix III, no. 15. This portrait was still at Petworth in 1764; see Petworth House Archives 6266, *An Inventory of furneture belonging To The R^t Honble the Earl of Egremont at Petworth in Sussex*, 24 August 1764; described as hanging in the Oak Room.

153. Alnwick Castle, collection of the duke of Northumberland. See Millar in London 1982 (note 18), 78, no. 36; Washington 1990 (note 18), 310–312, no. 83; Appendix III, no. 17.

154. Catherine Bruce, countess of Dysart, wife of William Murray (Petworth House). Collins Baker 1920 (note 16), 30, no. 295, wrongly identified as Mrs. Endymion Porter. See Millar in London 1982 (note 18), 78, under no. 36. Larsen 1988 (note 31), 2:486, no. A 221/2; see also Appendix III, no. 16.

155. *Mountjoy Blount, Earl of Newport (1597–1666) and George, Lord Goring (1608–1657)* (Petworth House). Collins Baker 1920 (note 16), 31, no. 300. Larsen 1988 (note 31), 2:361–362, no. 923. See Appendix III, no. 20.

156. Fig. 1. Alnwick Castle, duke of Northumberland collection. See London 1982 (note 18), 69, no. 24; Larsen 1988 (note 31), 2:362, no. 925; Appendix III, no. 13.

157. Fig. 10. See note 54; Appendix III, no. 12.

158. Possibly *Anne Carr, Countess of Bedford (1620–1684)* (Petworth House, Lord Egremont collection). Collins Baker 1920 (note 16), 29, no. 218; Larsen 1988 (note 31), 2:305, no. 768. See also Millar in London 1982 (note 18), 83–85, no. 41; Appendix III, no. 21.

159. Fig. 4. See note 31; Appendix III, no. 11.

160. *Henry, Baron Percy of Alnwick (1605–1659)* (Petworth House). Collins Baker 1920 (note 16), 31, no. 297; Larsen 1988 (note 31), 2:499–500, no. A 260; Appendix III, no. 22.

161. See notes 23–24; Appendix III, no. 7.

162. See note 95; Appendix III, no. 67.

163. See note 97; Appendix III, no. 28.

164. Fig. 16. See note 96; Appendix III, no. 109.

165. See Appendix III, no. 80.

166. Esmond Samuel de Beer, ed., *The Diary of John Evelyn*, 6 vols. (Oxford, 1955), 3:216.

167. See note 26; Appendix I, no. 5; Appendix III, no. 1.

168. See note 21; Appendix I, no. 3; Appendix III, no. 5.

169. See Appendix III, no. 6.

170. See note 97; Appendix I, no. 29; Appendix III, no. 28.

171. See note 26; Appendix I, no. 5.

172. See note 34; Appendix I, no. 6.

173. See Collins Baker 1920 (note 16), 130, no. 332; Wethey 1969–1975 (note 17), 2:187, under no. X-112. Formerly Robert Guggenheim, Washington (destroyed by fire).

174. See note 17; Appendix I, no. 4.

175. See note 21; Appendix I, no. 3.

176. See notes 23–24; Appendix I, no. 23.

177. Gore 1977 (note 1), 352, proposed that this was the *Portrait of Derich Berck*, formerly at Petworth but now in the Metropolitan Museum of Art, New York; however, it does not fit Symonds' description of 1652; see Appendix I, no. 2. For the *Derich Berck* see John Rowlands, *Holbein. The Paintings of Hans Holbein the Younger. Complete Edition* (Oxford, 1985), 143, no. 57.

178. See note 31; Appendix I, no. 19.

179. See note 54; Appendix I, no. 16.

180. See note 156; Appendix I, no. 15.

181. See note 63.

182. See note 152; Appendix I, no. 11.

183. See note 154; Appendix I, no. 13.

184. See note 153; Appendix I, no. 12.

185. See note 65.

186. See note 55; Appendix I, no. 10.

187. See note 155; Appendix I, no. 14.

188. See note 158.

189. See note 160; Appendix I, no. 22.

190. See also Appendix III, no. 64; Appendix IV, no. 61.

191. See note 60; Appendix IV, no. 62.

192. See note 57.

193. See Appendix IV, nos. 45–46.

194. Fig 14. Rijksmuseum, Amsterdam. See note 72 for recent literature.

195. See note 97; Appendix I, no. 29.

196. See Beckett 1951 (note 97), 66, no. 575. Sir William Musgrave's list of pictures at Petworth in 1775 and 1785 (see note 62), 25r., records a "D. & D^SS of York by Lely" in the "Red Room above Stairs." Collins Baker 1920 (note 16), 61, no. 433 (as Huysmans).

197. See Collins Baker 1920 (note 16), 73, no. 293; 75, no. 468; 76, no. 536. For portraits of this sitter at Syon and Alnwick see Beckett 1951 (note 97), 56, nos. 391, 393.

198. *Elizabeth Percy, Countess of Essex (1636–1718)* (Petworth House). See Collins Baker 1920 (note 16), 74, no. 524. For a portrait of this sitter at Syon see Beckett 1951 (note 97), 44, no. 178.

199. See also Appendix III, no. 101. *Anne Percy, Lady Stanhope (1633–1654)* (Petworth House). Collins Baker 1920 (note 16), 74, no. 525, as countess of Chesterfield. See Beckett 1951 (note 97), 62, no. 509. For payments to Lely see Appendix IV, nos. 31–32.

200. See note 16.

201. *William II, Prince of Orange (1626–1650) as a Child* (Petworth House). Collins Baker 1920 (note 16), 34, no. 313. Another version is in the Staatliche Museen Schloss Mosigkau.

202. See note 71.

203. *Catherine Cecil, Viscountess Lisle (1628–1652)*. Collins Baker 1920 (note 16), 74, no. 361, was formerly identified as a portrait of this sitter.

204. By Gerard Seghers. Collins Baker 1920 (note 16), 116, no. 601, as Giovanni Andrea Sirani.

205. The low valuation suggests that this was a copy known to have been made by Symon Stone from Titian's *Christ Presented to the People* (Kunsthistorisches Museum, Vienna), that was in the Buckingham collection at York House during the 1640s. See notes 100–101; Appendix IV, no. 48, for Northumberland's purchase of the copy in 1655.

206. The former may be identifiable with Collins Baker 1920 (note 16), 64, no. 532 (as Cornelius Johnson, but closer to Mytens).

207. See note 108; Appendix IV, no. 60.

208. See note 129.

209. See also Appendix III, no. 23; Appendix IV, no. 61.

210. See note 95; Appendix I, no. 28.

211. See Appendix I, nos. 7–8.

212. One of these portraits may be identical with Titian's *Man in a Black Plumed Hat* (Petworth House; no. 298); see Gore 1977 (note 1), 352.

213. Perhaps a studio repetition of Lady Anne Cecil's portrait from the family group; see note 54; Appendix I, no. 16; Appendix III, no. 12.

214. See note 62.

215. Perhaps the "great Perspective" by Steenwijck formerly in the Buckingham collection at York

House; see Davies 1907 (note 9), 379. Obtained by Northumberland before 1652; see Appendix I, no. 31.

216. Bought from George Geldorp for £8 in 1640; see Appendix IV, no. 18. Collins Baker 1920 (note 16), 98, no. 231.

217. A full-length portrait of *Mary Villiers, Duchess of Richmond (d. 1685)* is at Petworth; see Collins Baker 1920 (note 16), 33, no. 99, identified as Frances Howard, duchess of Richmond. Larsen 1988 (note 31), 2:505, no. A 279.

218. Seen by Sir William Musgrave in the Green Drawing Room in 1775, B.L. Add. MSS 5,726 E, no. 6, fol. 24r.: "Chas Cecil Ld Cranbourn—son of W^m 2^d E. of Salisbury & Bro. of Anne who marr^d. Algernoun 10 E. of North^d. wh. len. by van Dyke."

219. Presumably Claude Lorrain.

220. See note 60; Appendix III, no. 24; Appendix IV, no. 62.

221. See note 199; Appendix III, no. 33.

222. This entry is unlikely to refer to the mother of Catherine of Braganza. It might be a confused allusion to Maria de' Medici, but there is no record of such a portrait elsewhere in the Northumberland collection. It may be that Stone made a mistake and meant "Queen Dowager," as in no. 58, in which case there are two portraits of Henrietta Maria that might correspond with this entry: (1) Alnwick, duke of Northumberland collection. Larsen 1988 (note 31), 2:488, no. A 225/2, claims that this work is mentioned in Stone's 1671 inventory. It was described as at Northumberland House on 29 September 1738; see Sarah Markham, *John Loveday of Caversham, 1711–1789. The Life and Tours of an Eighteenth-Century Onlooker* (London, 1984), 524. (2) Petworth House. Collins Baker 1920 (note 16), 34, no. 478.

223. Almost certainly to be identified with the work still at Petworth but now attributed to Lambert Lombard; Collins Baker 1920 (note 16), no. 17, who notes that it was formerly given to Bronzino. This is likely to be the picture seen by Jeremiah Milles at Petworth in 1743; B.L. Add. MSS 15,776, fol. 228: "At top of ye stairs is an incomparable piece representing 5 or 6 of ye Apostles; (as I take them to be) in conference together; & pointing to a Golden Vase y^t stands on an altar at a little distance. I could not learn ye name of ye painter nor ye history."

224. See note 96; Appendix I, no. 30.

225. Bought by Northumberland from Stone for £8 in 1656; see Appendix IV, no. 49.

226. Presumably copied from Andrea del Sarto's *The Madonna and Child with Saint Elizabeth and the Infant John the Baptist* (see note 21). The original was owned by Northumberland and kept at his house in London; see Appendix I, no. 3; Appendix III, no. 5.

227. Presumably these were copies of the picture described in Appendix III, no. 3; see note 173.

228. Sold by the duke of Northumberland at Christie's, London, 24 November 1972, no. 120, as

Sir Peter Lely after Titian. The model was a *Virgin and Child, Saint Luke and a Donor* now at Hampton Court (Wethey 1969–1975 [note 17], 1:107, under no. 62), attributed to Palma Giovane but thought to be by Titian when in the collection of Charles I. See Van der Doort in Millar 1960 (note 106), 21; Shearman 1983 (note 105), 175–176, no. 176.

229. Abraham van der Doort records a painting of this subject by "Gwedo Bollonees" in the collection of Charles I; see Millar 1960 (note 106), 61.

230. Probably a copy of the *Allegory of the Marchese del Vasto, Alfonso d'Avalos* (Musée du Louvre, Paris) formerly in the collection of Charles I. See Millar 1960 (note 106), 16; Millar 1972 (note 110), 322. For Stone's copy see Collins Baker 1920 (note 16), 122, no. 348. For another copy of this work in the Northumberland collection, kept at Syon, see Appendix III, no. 132. This version appears to have been sold by the duke of Northumberland at Sotheby's, London, 24 March 1952, no. 96, as Lely after Titian.

231. Bought by Northumberland from Stone for £10 in 1660; see Appendix IV, no. 60. For the original see note 105.

232. Another copy of no. 116; see note 230.

233. Possibly a copy of Correggio's *Mercury Instructing Cupid before Venus ("The School of Love")* (National Gallery, London); at one time in the collection of Charles I. See Gould 1975 (note 24), 57–61 (inv. 10).

234. Some extracts from the manuscripts at Alnwick were first published in Millar 1955 (note 56), 255–256; see Appendix IV, nos. 8, 11, 12, 13, 14, 16, 19, 21, 25, 29, 31, 32, 33, 39.

235. Compare Appendix III, no. 90; see note 216.

236. Titian's *Vendramin Family* (National Gallery, London) and *Perseus and Andromeda* (Wallace Collection, London). See notes 26–27; Appendix I, no. 5; Appendix III, no. 1.

237. For a document establishing that Northumberland bought the paintings on 4 October 1645, see note 30.

238. This entry and the following one appear to relate to a visit paid by George Geldorp to Windsor on 9 December 1645; see note 130. It seems that he advised on the acquisition of these "brass [bronze] pillers," which were later placed in the gardens at Northumberland House; see Appendix IV, no. 50. John Adamson has kindly informed me that these "pillers," as well as the "peece of brasse" mentioned in Appendix IV, no. 28, were probably part of the remains of Wolsey's tomb, sculpted by Benedetto da Rovezzano and Giovanni da Maiano, and, by the seventeenth century, reused in the tomb of Henry VIII, situated in the Lady Chapel at Windsor. For the history of this work see Edward Chaney, "Henry VIII's Tomb: 'Plus catholique que le pape'?" *Apollo* 134 (October 1991), 234–238. For the sale of the metalwork from the "tomb-house" at Windsor in 1646 by Parliament see Howard Colvin, ed., *The History of the King's Works*, vol. 3, pt. 1, *1485–1660* (London, 1975), 321–322. See Appendix IV, no. 55, for the ex-

change of "brasse statues" from the gardens at Northumberland House for antique sculptures obtained from Thomas Beauchamp to a value of £65.

239. See Millar 1955 (note 56), 255, who identified it with a portrait by Lely at Syon dated 1647.

240. See note 199; Appendix III, nos. 33, 101.

241. Millar 1955 (note 56), 256, gave this payment as "Cxxi^{s} ij^{d}."

242. See note 97; Appendix I, no. 29; Appendix III, no. 28.

243. See note 199; Appendix III, nos. 33, 101.

244. Compare Appendix III, no. 94.

245. See note 96; Appendix I, no. 30; Appendix III, no. 109.

246. Lady Elizabeth Percy (1636–1718), daughter of the earl of Northumberland by his first marriage to Anne Cecil; married Arthur, Lord Capel (later earl of Essex) in 1653.

247. Perhaps identifiable with Appendix III, no. 26.

248. For the Titian see note 17; Appendix I, no. 4; Appendix III, no. 4. The Palma was almost certainly a copy after the portrait of a woman that Symonds saw in 1652 (Appendix I, no. 23); notes 23–24; Appendix III, no. 7.

249. See note 205; Appendix III, no. 49.

250. See note 50.

251. John Stepney had married Van Dyck's daughter Justiniana in 1653. Her inheritance had been embezzled by her stepfather Sir Richard Price. This payment suggests that Northumberland had a bad conscience over his astute purchase of works from the painter's collection, which had been dispersed during the 1640s. Further details of this settlement can be found in "The release of Jo: Stepney and his wife to the Earle of Northumberland of the Picture of the Senato^{rs}" (Alnwick MSS: Syon House, W.II.2). See Wood 1990 (note 28), 684.

252. Perhaps identifiable with Collins Baker 1920 (note 16), 111, no. 513.

253. See Appendix III, no. 111.

254. See note 238.

255. See notes 105–106.

256. See note 107.

257. See note 108.

258. Probably the work described by Symonds as "Una femina mezza figura wth her hair loose [and] rare fleshy breasts;" see Appendix I, no. 23; Appendix III, no. 7; notes 23–24.

259. Possibly to be identified with the three-quarter-length portrait at Syon House, in which the sitter is shown leaning on a Corinthian capital. Beckett 1951 (note 97), 56, no. 391, dated this work c. 1657. In 1658 Josceline Percy was aged fourteen, which is compatible with this likeness. See also Appendix III, no. 31.

260. See note 215; Appendix I, no. 31; Appendix III, no. 80.

261. See note 238.

262. See note 90.

263. Perhaps to be identified with Appendix III, no. 90; see also Appendix IV, no. 18.

264. For the original see note 54; Appendix I, no. 16; Appendix III, no. 12.

265. See Appendix III, no. 118; for the original see note 105.

266. See Appendix III, no. 55; for the original see note 108.

267. See note 21.

268. See Appendix III, nos. 23, 64; for the originals see note 114.

269. See note 60; Appendix III, nos. 24, 100.

270. See note 239.

271. See also Appendix IV, no. 65. The identification of this portrait is confused. It has been claimed (Beckett 1951 [note 97], 56, no. 394) that a portrait by Lely of Elizabeth Wriothesley, countess of Northumberland (wife of Josceline Percy), at Petworth (Collins Baker 1920 [note 16], 72, no. 125) has been wrongly identified as Elizabeth Howard, countess of Northumberland (wife of Algernon Percy, 10th earl). This seems confirmed by the inscription on a copy in the Sandwich sale, Christie's, London, 4 March 1927, no. 26. The face in the Petworth picture is not very like the one in Lely's well-known portrait of Elizabeth Wriothesley at Hampton Court (see Millar 1963 [note 31], 125–126, no. 261), usually dated to the late 1660s. There is, however, some resemblance to a miniature portrait of Elizabeth Wriothesley by Richard Gibson, dated c. 1662, in the duke of Buccleuch collection. Lely also produced a seated likeness of Elizabeth Wriothesley, usually dated c. 1668, of which the best version is in the collection of the duke of Northumberland. There is an early copy at Petworth (Collins Baker 1920 [note 16], 75, no. 485). Other versions are to be found at Althorp and at the Museum of Fine Art of the University of Kansas.

272. This entry is likely to refer to a seated portrait at Alnwick, but there is also a version by Lely at Chatsworth (see Beckett 1951 [note 97], 56, under no. 393), and a standing portrait in antique dress at Petworth (Collins Baker 1920 [note 16], 76, no. 536). The last mentioned, however, is probably a studio work, in which Lely may only have painted the head; it is unlikely to have cost as much as £20.

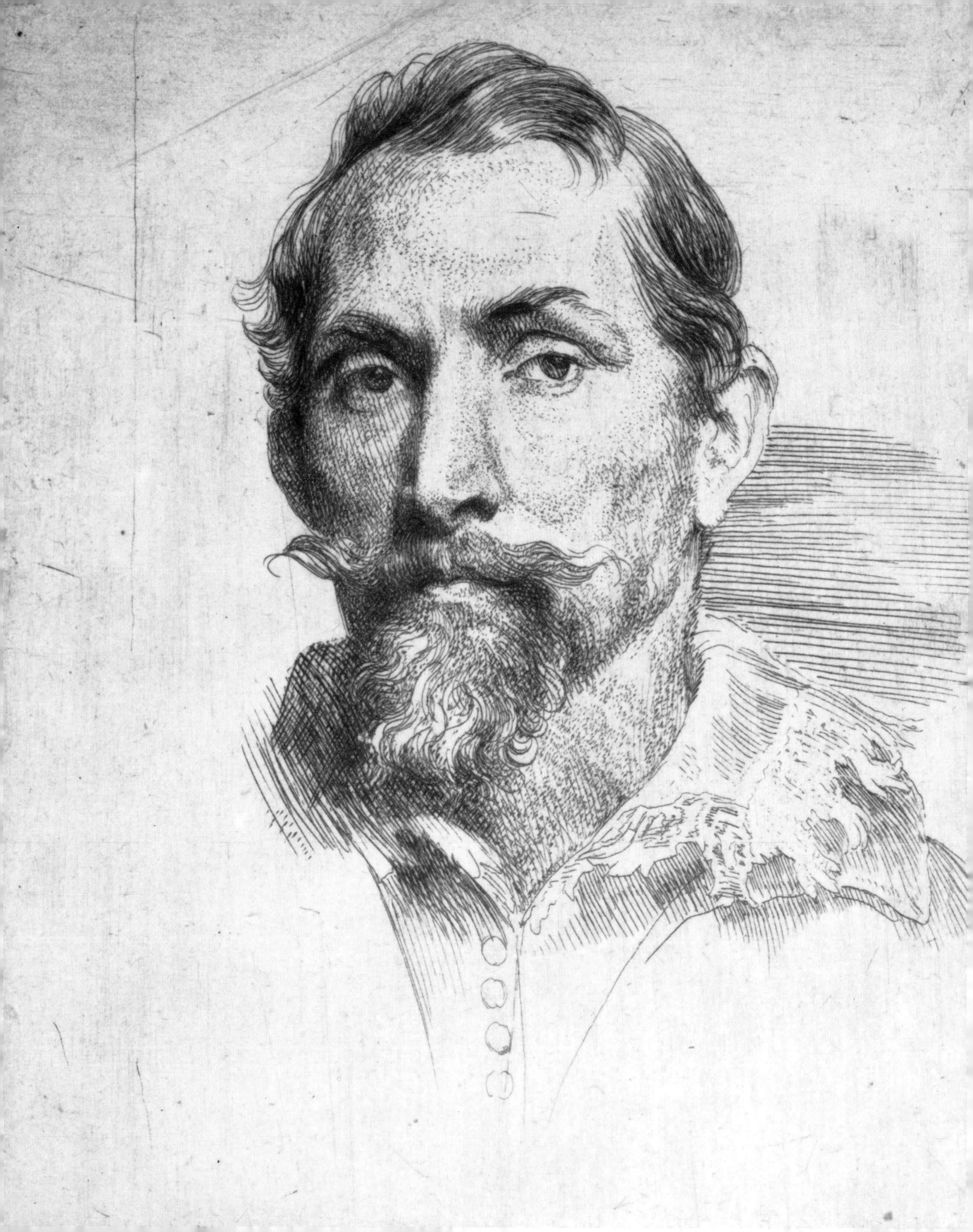

JOANEATH A. SPICER
Walters Art Gallery

Anthony van Dyck's Iconography: An Overview of Its Preparation

The group of portrait prints after Anthony van Dyck known as the Iconography or *Icones . . . Centum* is generally thought of in terms of the Latin title found on the title page printed by Gillis Hendricx in 1645, which reads in translation: *"One Hundred Portraits of Princes, Men of Letters, Painters, Printmakers, Sculptors As Well as Amateurs of the Pictorial Arts Done from Life By Anthony van Dyck, Painter, and Engraved at His Expense In Copper."*[1] These prints are one of Van Dyck's most important projects, but there is no consensus on how this "series" came into being, its purpose, or even its content.[2] In the literature on Van Dyck it is taken for granted that a specific publication as described on the title page actually existed. Since early in the century most scholars have assumed that *Van Dyck pinxit* inscribed on the engravings refers to the grisaille oil studies on panel as well as to Van Dyck's portrait paintings. The connection between at least some of the engravings and Van Dyck's paintings is acknowledged, though how to relate the drawings, oil studies (not always accepted), and indeed the etchings (eighteen are generally claimed) has perplexed scholars and has never been addressed systematically. Previous investigations proceeded either from the perspective of the prints or from that of the drawings. Integrating the prints, drawings, oil studies, and paintings (schematized in the Appendix) permits an overview from which patterns can be seen to emerge. Nevertheless, there are many lacunae in the existing material and the proposed reconfiguration is subject to revision.

This essay has two central propositions. The first is that whatever Van Dyck's intentions were, they were not realized. No edition as described on the quoted title page was issued. Neither the series by Hendricx—who printed the title page and 113 other plates, but apparently not as a single publication and probably not all the plates by 1645—nor that by his predecessor Martin vanden Enden represents Van Dyck's idea of a complete series. Van Dyck surely initiated the project, but his purposes evolved over time. At the outset he may have had in mind a series of portrait etchings after various sources, including his paintings.

The second proposition is that Van Dyck's purposes seem to have shifted to producing prints that would celebrate his paintings, as the prints promoted by Rubens did the latter's paintings. All the engravings published by Vanden Enden, the only one of the two publishers with whom Van Dyck actually worked, bear inscriptions claiming that they are based on Van Dyck's paintings (*Ant. van Dyck pinxit*). This inscription conveys the notion that the prints are based on Van Dyck's painted formal portraits; there is no allusion to the preparatory sketches, even to those in oil.

In support of these propositions, three types of evidence will be considered: the inscriptions on the prints, the genesis of the prints, and the compositional esthetic.

   i. A survey of the use of *pinxit* in the circle of Rubens and Van Dyck indicates that the phrase *Ant. van Dyck pinxit* on the majority of these prints was intended to convey that the legitimacy of the images derives from Van Dyck's paintings.

   ii. Analysis of the patchwork of prints, extant paintings, drawings, and oil sketches also leads to the conclusion that the relevant studies preparatory to the prints are, with one possible exception, after formal paintings. Of the 111 nonrepeated portraits (three others are duplicates) published by Hendricx, 55 depend on known portraits, while others can be posited.

   iii. Compositional curiosities exhibited by many of the engraved portraits can be explained by their adaptation from a different format.

First, let me give an outline of the Iconography as assumed in this essay. Eighty portrait engravings inscribed *Ant. van Dyck pinxit* were executed by nine printmakers, including Lucas Vorsterman, Schelte à Bolswert, and Paulus Pontius,[3] the finest of Rubens' collaborators, and printed by the Antwerp publisher Martin vanden Enden at least in part and most likely in full before Van Dyck's death in 1641.[4] While the portraits may have been printed by Vanden Enden in significant groupings—princes and generals (sixteen), statesmen and men of learning (twelve), artists and amateurs (fifty-two)[5]—the publisher put out no title page and no evidence has been presented that these eighty prints were ever issued or distributed as a set. The individuals included, at least among the princes, cannot represent Van Dyck's views of the great figures of the day, since his patrons Charles I, the Archduchess Isabella, and the prince and princess of Orange are absent.[6]

By 1645 Gilles Hendricx had acquired the eighty plates plus others printed by Vanden Enden[7] and began substituting his name or initials as publisher. Hendricx printed a title page, dated 1645 in the third state only and erased in the fourth, announcing a series of one hundred portraits (as above). This title page does not prove that a completed series was issued. There is a second, rarely cited title page printed by Hendricx that mentions neither a date, number of plates, nor the artist's financial involvement.[8]

Besides putting his initials as publisher on the plates published by Vanden Enden, Hendricx published 34 more plates for a total of 114 (not 100). These include 2 plates in other formats (N. Rockox [MH115] and J. LeRoy [MH112]), of which that of LeRoy was not added to the group until 1654,[9] together with Van Dyck's own 15 etchings (not 18), which were worked up by engravers. These 15 include 1 blemished, never completed plate, 3 that are virtual duplications of portraits published by Vanden Enden, and 1 of a person represented already in Vanden Enden's group by a different portrait. Not a tidy group. Though these prints are invariably referred to in the literature as if they formed a series published in 1645, Wibral, writing in 1877, seems to be the only one to cite specific bound copies[10] (as that of "1645/6" belonging to E. Dutuit), which in fact turn out to be later assemblages.[11] Subsequent writers refer to them simply, if at all, as "rare."[12] I have not been able to locate one. Neither, apparently, has anyone else.[13] Certainly a reference by Bellori, in his "Vita" of Van Dyck published in 1672, to a "book"["libro"] published by Anthony and printed in Antwerp, which includes a hundred portraits of illustrious men and in which there are representations of princes, men of letters, painters and sculptors,[14] would lead one to suppose the book's existence, even if one personally had not seen a copy. Nevertheless, there is no separate confirmation of it, and I suspect that Bellori saw one of the subsequent bound assemblages and took his information off the title page, not bothering to count the plates or check for inconsistencies. The subsequent bound assemblages examined by this writer vary enormously in number, selection, and ordering[15] (for example, beginning with the Archduchess Isabella or Maria de' Medici or the Swedish king and Protestant leader Gustav Adolphus—a loaded choice), including engravings published separately (later?) by Jean Meyssens[16] and Vanden Enden the younger. In this essay the term "Iconography" will encompass only the prints issued by Hendricx, thus those thought of as reflecting Van Dyck's wishes. Hendricx's group itself cannot, however, reflect Van Dyck's views on the great princes and art lovers of the day any more than did Vanden Enden's: Charles I is still not included, though his consort Henrietta Maria (MH108) is, and neither are the prince and princess of Orange.

Not only are the most illustrious of Van Dyck's princely patrons not included, but some of those portrayed in the prints published by Hendricx (and for whom there are no autograph preparatory studies) are not illustrious at all. They may simply have been the subject of an accessible portrait by Van Dyck (or his studio) of which Hendricx could commission an engraving. In this category fall the portraits of Van Dyck's English mistress Margaret Lemon[17] (MH111; private collection, England), painted around 1636–1638; Maria Ruthven (MH101; painting in the Museo del Prado), whom Van Dyck married in 1639; the unknown Jeanne de Blois[18] (MH103; Chatsworth) painted in about 1634–1635; and Hubert de Hot (MH106; painting formerly in a private collection, New York). The engravings do not differ from many others after some of the same and other portraits by Van Dyck inscribed *Ant. van Dyck pinxit*, printed by other publishers and assumed without query to reproduce paintings by Van Dyck or his shop.

As for a provisional chronology, the evidence suggests that Van Dyck began by experimenting with etchings in about 1630, after the return from England of Lucas Vorsterman, who must have taught him to etch, or at the earliest after his own return from Italy in 1627. At first he may have been undecided about the character of the series, thinking perhaps of focusing on Flemish artists and supporters of the arts. In 1632 Constantijn Huygens, who had just sat to Van Dyck in The Hague, wrote a few lines of verse "In libros iconum illustrium virorum."[19] The modeled drawings were likely made in a period centering on 1632–1634 when the artist was in London, and the oil studies begun around 1634 during Van Dyck's stay in Antwerp, 1634–1635. Apparently at this time he decided to include princes. In 1636 Van Dyck wrote to Franciscus Junius requesting a motto for the portrait of Sir Kenelm Digby;[20] this is the last known reference to the project. Once settled in London, Van Dyck may have had problems keeping the project going and his attention proba-

bly flagged. The only portraits published by Hendricx that were clearly done after 1635 are of Van Dyck's mistress and his wife; engravings after them were surely added by Hendricx after Van Dyck's death. In sum, the series was incomplete at the artist's death in 1641. After 1635 Van Dyck was caught up in court commissions and making money. This was one of his few personal projects and one in which the financial rewards were uncertain. It was sacrificed.

Pinxit

This discussion of *pinxit* (he painted it) and related terms is based on a survey of terms on prints published in Antwerp, the northern Netherlands (chiefly Haarlem), Prague, and Italy (Venice and Rome). In Antwerp Rubens, the first painter to focus on printmaking as a means of reproducing paintings,[21] was Van Dyck's primary model.

Ant. van Dyck pinxit (or *pinxcit*), inscribed on states of all the engravings after Van Dyck (as fig. 21) and on six of the etchings by him in the Iconography, is meant to convey that the portrayal is derived from a painting by Van Dyck.[22] It has been supposed (without examination) that *pinxit* indicates only that the artist involved was a painter, without indicating the exact nature of the prototype.[23] In prints after nonportrait paintings by Van Dyck that bear this inscription, the prototype is a formal painting. I find no instance in which the ultimate prototype for an engraving inscribed *Van Dyck pinxit* is an oil study.[24] In the only seventeenth-century reference known to me to the sources of the Iconography, Bellori describes the engraving of Sir Kenelm Digby as reproducing one of the portraits Van Dyck painted of his friend. The phrase does not indicate whether the original is exactly reproduced.

The use of *pinxit* should be juxtaposed with that of *Pictor*, the way Van Dyck is identified on the Hendricx title page, and *"Pictor Iconum"* (portrait painter) following the name on engravings of portrait painters,[25] and therefore of *Icones*,[26] on the title page. Since *Imagines* and *Effiges*[27] were both in use for series of images of noteworthy people—as in Pieter Soutman's contemporary *Effiges . . . Imperatorum* (Antwerp, 1644), which uses portraits by a number of artists

—the choice of *Icones* puts the emphasis on the portrait itself. The other terms put more emphasis on the subject or individuals portrayed.

The meaning of *pinxit* is clarified by the ten portraits published by Hendricx to which the term was never applied. They belong to the group of fifteen autograph etchings by Van Dyck himself.[28] These prints are inscribed *Ant. van Dyck fecit aqua forti* (as fig. 11), thus claiming only that Van Dyck was the author of the etching. Of these ten, the prototypes for three have been identified and are paintings by other artists: Hans Holbein's portrait of Erasmus[29] (MH5) and Rubens' portraits of Frans Francken I[30] (MH6) and Jan Brueghel[31] (MH1). In contrast, Van Dyck's etching of Frans Snyders (MH11; fig. 9), based on his own 1621 painting (fig. 10), is inscribed in the second state: *Ant. van Dyck pinxit et fecit aqua forti.* Five of the fifteen etchings are known in states (or in the duplicates by Vorsterman or others) bearing inscriptions also claiming a painted prototype by Van Dyck; four of these can be identified.[32] However, of the ten portraits whose inscriptions, as that on the Erasmus, make no reference to a painting by Van Dyck, only two, Paulus Pontius (MH9) and Jan de Wael (MH17), can be associated with portraits painted by him. Of course, it is not impossible that the publisher in certain instances intended the inscription to convey a false impression.[33] Still, of the twenty-one plates bearing *Van Dyck pinxit* added by Hendricx, every one can be connected with an extant painting.

Pinxit is not often encountered before the late sixteenth century; indeed, previously prints were not so commonly made after paintings, especially in the north. Even then one is more likely to see *invenit*,[34] which celebrates the composition rather than the specific work of art. *Pinxit* may well have been used if the painting were famous, as, for instance, is the case with the engraving Hieronymous Cock published after Frans Floris' *Allegory of Dialectics,* from a series of the Liberal Arts painted c. 1556 for the Antwerp merchant N. Jonclinc, which is inscribed *Franc Florus pinxit in*

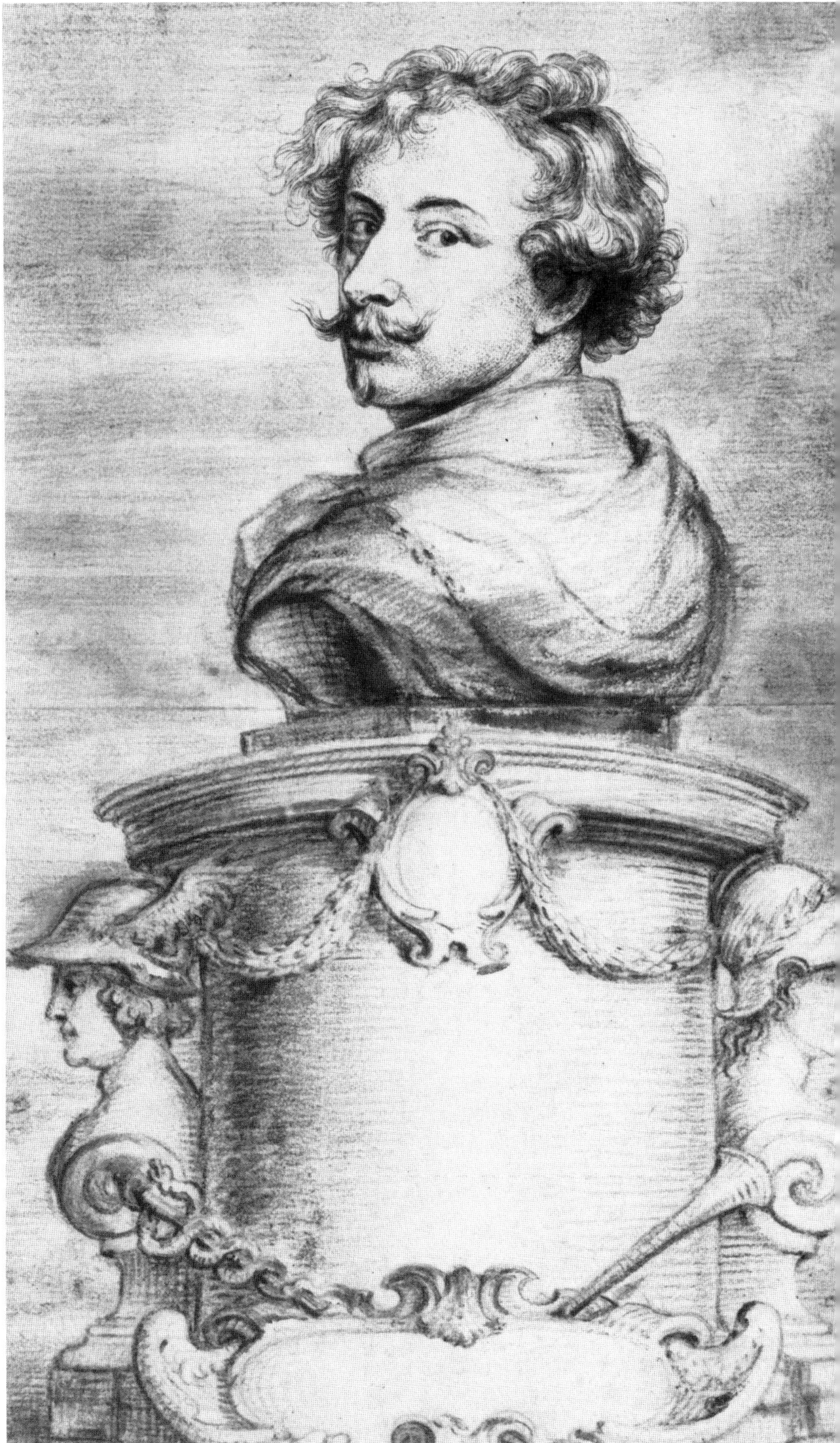

1. Anthony van Dyck, *Self-Portrait*, c. 1632, etching, reworked with black chalk by an unidentified hand
British Museum, London

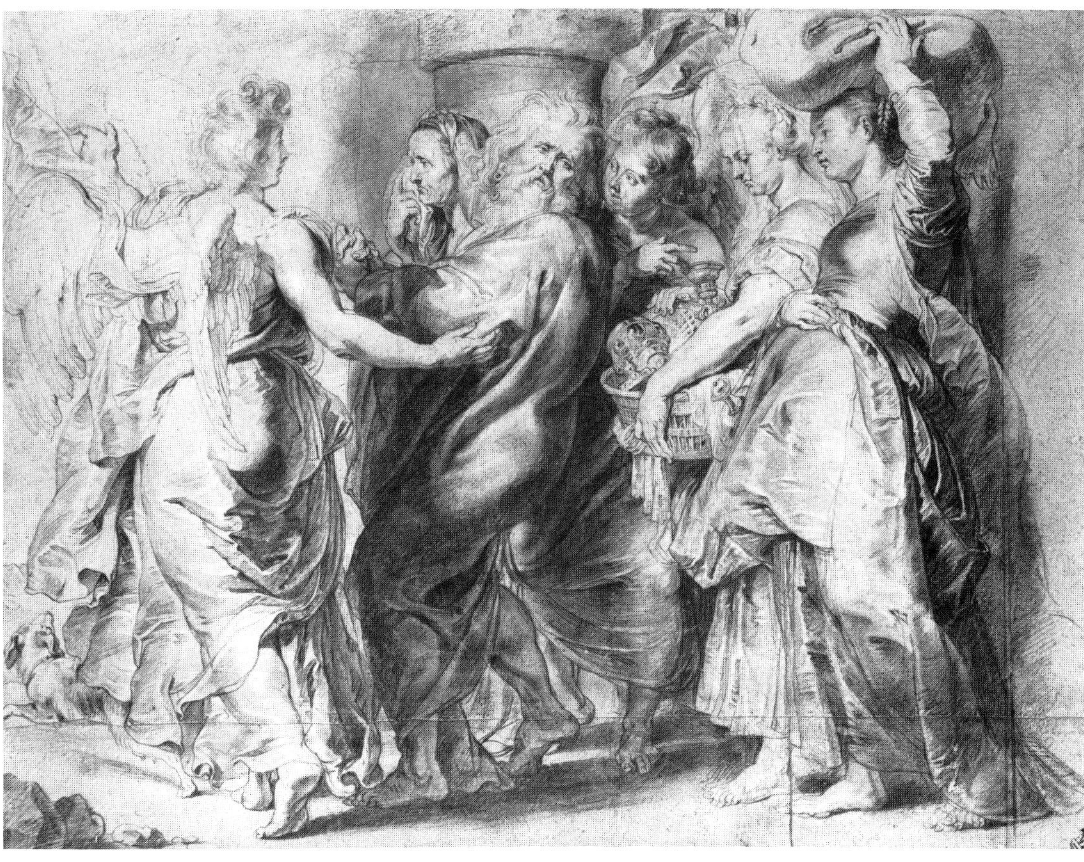

2. Anthony van Dyck after Pieter Paul Rubens, retouched by Rubens, *Lot and His Family Leaving Sodom*, c. 1620, black and white chalk
Musée du Louvre, Paris

suburbano Nicolai Iongelinc propeurbem Anverpia. . . .[35]

By the mid-sixteenth century, as the reproductive function of printmaking took on more importance than printmaking's earlier more creative role, *invenit* was the preferred verb to indicate responsibility for the *disegno*—as distinct from the execution—as a manifestation of the artist's *ingenuum* and thus his capacity for invention. In the overwhelming majority of cases of engravings published, for example, by Hieronymus Cock or, later, by Philip Galle, the prototype signaled by *invenit* was not a painting but an original drawing by Maerten van Heemskerck, Pieter Brueghel, or Frans Floris, made expressly to be engraved. This pattern is also true for the few examples of oil studies engraved by Antwerp printmakers, which were acknowledged by *invenit* or not at all.[36]

Straightforward portraiture (without an allegorical frame) is the one subject almost never accompanied by *invenit*,[37] and frequently by nothing more than the monogram of the printmaker, as in the portraits of famous artists in *Pictorum . . . Effigies*,[38] put together by Domenicus Lampsonius and Hieronymus Cock and published in 1572. Portraits were often valued more as images of specific persons than as works of art. It may also be that the claim of "invention" to the image of an actual human being would have been thought presumptuous.

When the significant prototype was an independent painting, it is so signaled; the intermediary printer's working *modello*—frequently by an assistant or the printmaker himself—rarely is. It makes no difference whether the intermediate *modello* is in oil,[39] as popularized by Rubens, or another medium. For example, Rubens' *Lot and His Family Leaving Sodom* (John and Mable Ringling Museum of Art, Sarasota)[40] of c. 1616 was copyrighted in an engraving by Lucas

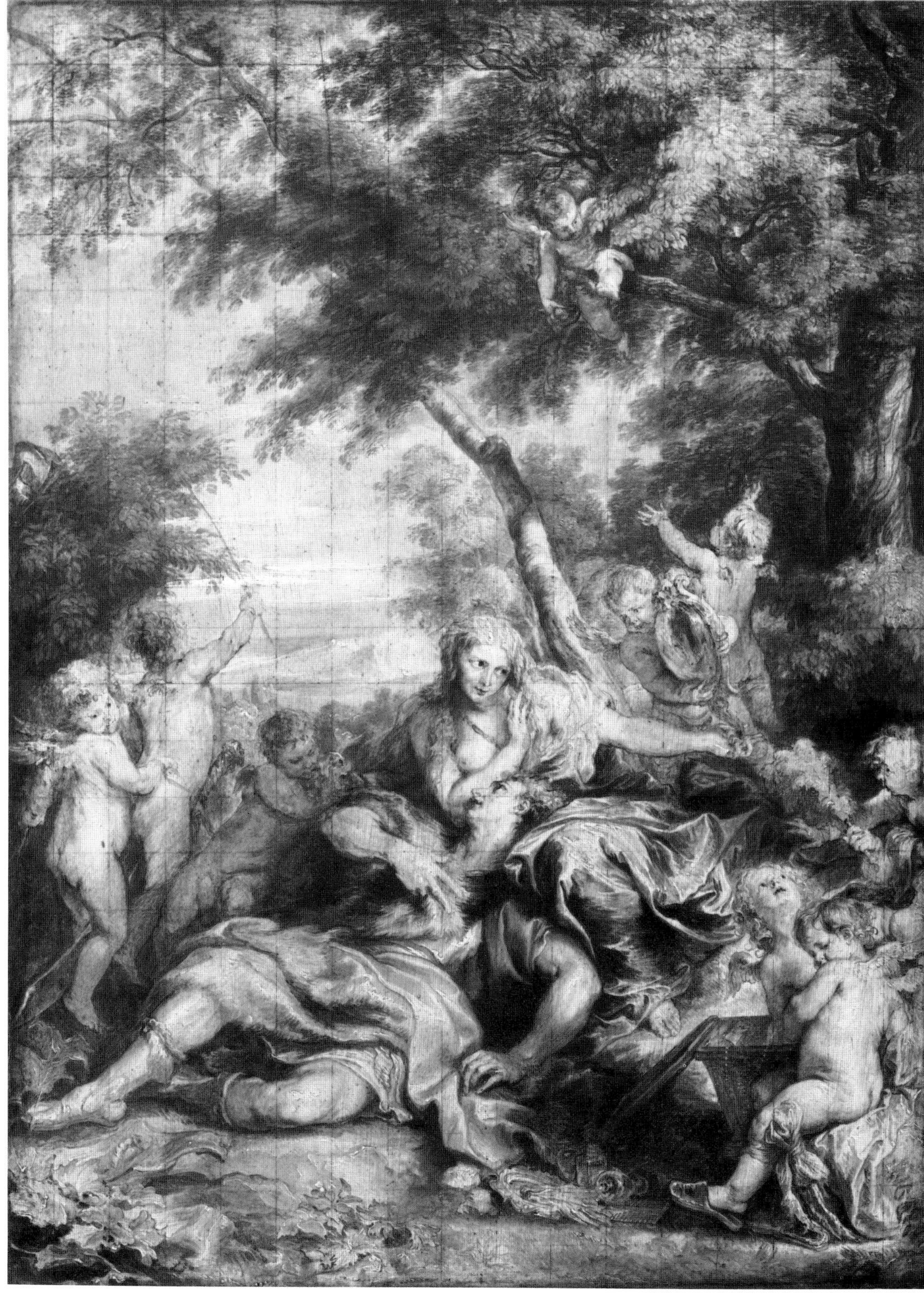

3. Anthony van Dyck,
Rinaldo and Armida,
c. 1632, oil on paper
National Gallery, London

Vorsterman[41] and inscribed: *P.P. Rubens pinxit. . . . Lucas Vorsterman sculp. et excud. An° 1620.* The engraver's *modello* is a highly modeled black and white chalk drawing in the Museé du Louvre (fig. 2), attributable to the young Van Dyck, though retouched by Rubens. Pieter de Jode the Younger's engraving[42] celebrating Van Dyck's masterpiece *Ri-*

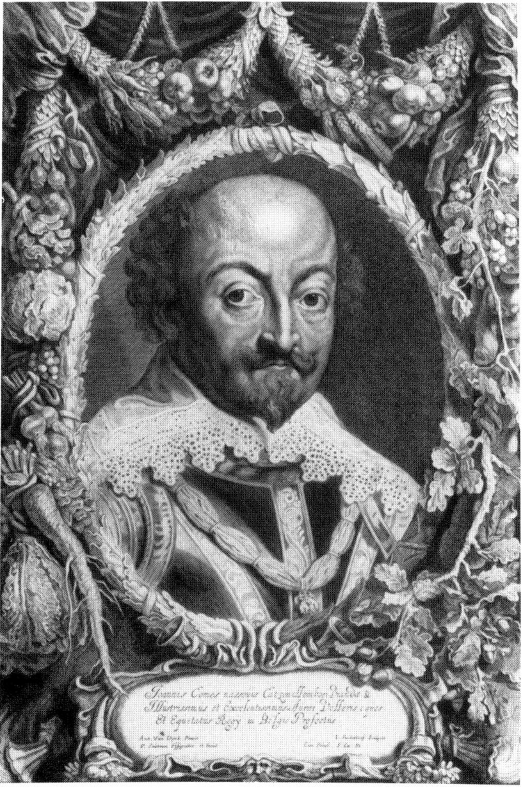

naldo and Armida (Museé du Louvre)[43] done for the prince of Orange in 1631–1632 is immediately based on Van Dyck's spirited oil study on paper (fig. 3).[44] Here *Van Dyck pinxit* refers to the princely commission and not to the engraver's *modello*, however fine the latter may be. I know of no instance in which it can be shown that *pinxit* on a print refers to a *modello* in oil rather than to the painting on which it is based.[45] As Julius Held has pointed out, "oil sketches were commonly referred to as 'disegni', 'desseins' or . . . 'teekeninge.' "[46]

If the publisher wanted to cite the author of the intermediate working model, then an additional designation was added, usually *effigiavit* (he made the image of it, represented it) or *delineavit* (he drew it). This happens if the artist was deemed noteworthy by the publisher—if he was famous (as is the case with Rubens' drawing after Leonardo's *Last Supper* etched by Soutman)[47] or if he was the publisher himself (as was Pieter Soutman or Theodoor van Thulden). *P.P. Rubens Pinxit. P. Soutman effigiavit et excud.* on the engraving[48] after Rubens' *Lamentation* (Kunsthistorisches Museum, Vienna) signals as

well Soutman's intermediary chalk and wash drawing (location unknown).[49]

Portraits are treated in a similar way. A three-quarter-length portrait by Van Dyck of *Count Johannes of Nassau-Siegen* (location unknown)[50] was among the portraits of rulers by various painters reproduced by Pieter Soutman (fig. 4) in his 1644 series *Effiges Imperatorum. . . .*[51] Here *Ant. Van Dyck Pinxit /P. Soutman effigiavit et Excud. /I. Suiderhof Sculpsit* signals not only Van Dyck's painting—the authority for the engraved image—but also the publisher's own incised drawing (Graphische Sammlung Albertina).[52] This drawing reduces the prototype to head and breast, including the order of the Golden Fleece and indications of armor—thus to the bare essentials for a "likeness." This alteration would not, for contemporaries, have affected the legitimacy of the claim *Van Dyck pinxit*. Similarly, Jean Morin's engraving commemorating the 1645 death of Cardinal Bentivoglio reduces Van Dyck's full-length 1623 portrait of the cardinal (Palazzo Pitti, Florence) to bust length, while maintaining in the inscription that *Antoine van Dyck pinx. / an. 1623.*[53]

If an idea is worked out only in an oil sketch or study, then this design is the significant prototype and is commonly cited with *invenit* or *delineavit*,[54] as it was in the sixteenth century. In about 1610 Rubens made an oil sketch of *The Miraculous Catch of Fish* (Wallraf-Richartz Museum, Cologne),[55] perhaps for a commission that was never realized, which was etched by P. Soutman and inscribed *P.P. Rubens invent. . . .*[56] The oil sketches made by Rubens as designs for the temporary arches for the 1635 entry of the Cardinal Infante Ferdinand into Antwerp later provided the prototypes for the plates in C. Gervartius' *Pompa Introitus Ferdinandi . . .*[57] (Antwerp, 1641–1642), etched and published by Van Thulden. The latter made his own working drawings from these oil sketches. The inscription on *Portico of the Austrian Emperors* after Rubens' oil sketch in St. Petersburg[58] via Van Thulden's own pen drawing (National Gallery of Art, Washington)[59] reads, in part, *P.P. Rubens Invent. C. Gevartius epigraphis Illustrab. Theod. a Thulden delin. sculps. et excu.* An example involving portraiture is provided by

Rubens' oil study in St. Petersburg[60] for an engraved *Allegorical Portrait of Carolus de Longueval, Count of Bucquoy* inscribed: *P.P. Rubens invent. / Lucas Vorsterman sculp. et excud.*

There were, however, no "rules," and printmakers and publishers had preferences or personal usages of *pinxit*[61] and related terms. In the case of Rubens the significant prototype for nearly all prints inscribed *Rubens pinxit* can be confirmed to be a formal painting; however, in a very few cases *pinxit* was applied eccentrically to Rubens' original oil sketches for title pages of books.[62] Rubens would not have done formal paintings of such compositions. Also, in Antwerp in the 1630s *invenit* could still refer to the execution of history paintings[63] consistent with sixteenth-century usage, but many examples involve significant reworking or the use of a drawing differing from the painting known today.[64]

In sum, by the early seventeenth century in Antwerp *invenit* lost its hegemony while references to the technique of the prototype or the division of responsibility gained in popularity. Rubens seems to have been the first to use the term *pinxit* so extensively. *Rubens pinxit* on engravings published by him after his own paintings celebrated his achievements as a painter. Van Dyck's intentions must have been parallel.

Preparation of Engraver's Models

The following analysis of the preparatory stages of the prints is complemented by the chart in the Appendix.

Possibly as a result of the passage of time during which the project took form, not to mention the artist's peregrinations, Van Dyck evolved different approaches to the problem of providing effective models for printmakers. I propose that Van Dyck experimented with etchings as well as the use of the more traditional drawings and the recently popularized oil studies as models for the engravers. Further, the three approaches apparently had two factors in common: they all began with a black chalk drawing (in all or almost all cases made from a painting) and ended with a highly modeled relief image "di chiaro scuro"—either a washed drawing, washed etching, or grisaille oil study—as an

immediate model for the printmaker *sculptor*, in the apt terminology of the inscriptions. In many cases the preparatory studies for the print, or the original painting, or both, are missing. Nevertheless a pattern emerges that will be assumed, for the sake of discussion, to apply to the group as a whole.

On essential points, specifically on the grisailles, my conclusions parallel those offered by Wijngaert in 1943,[65] but since ignored:

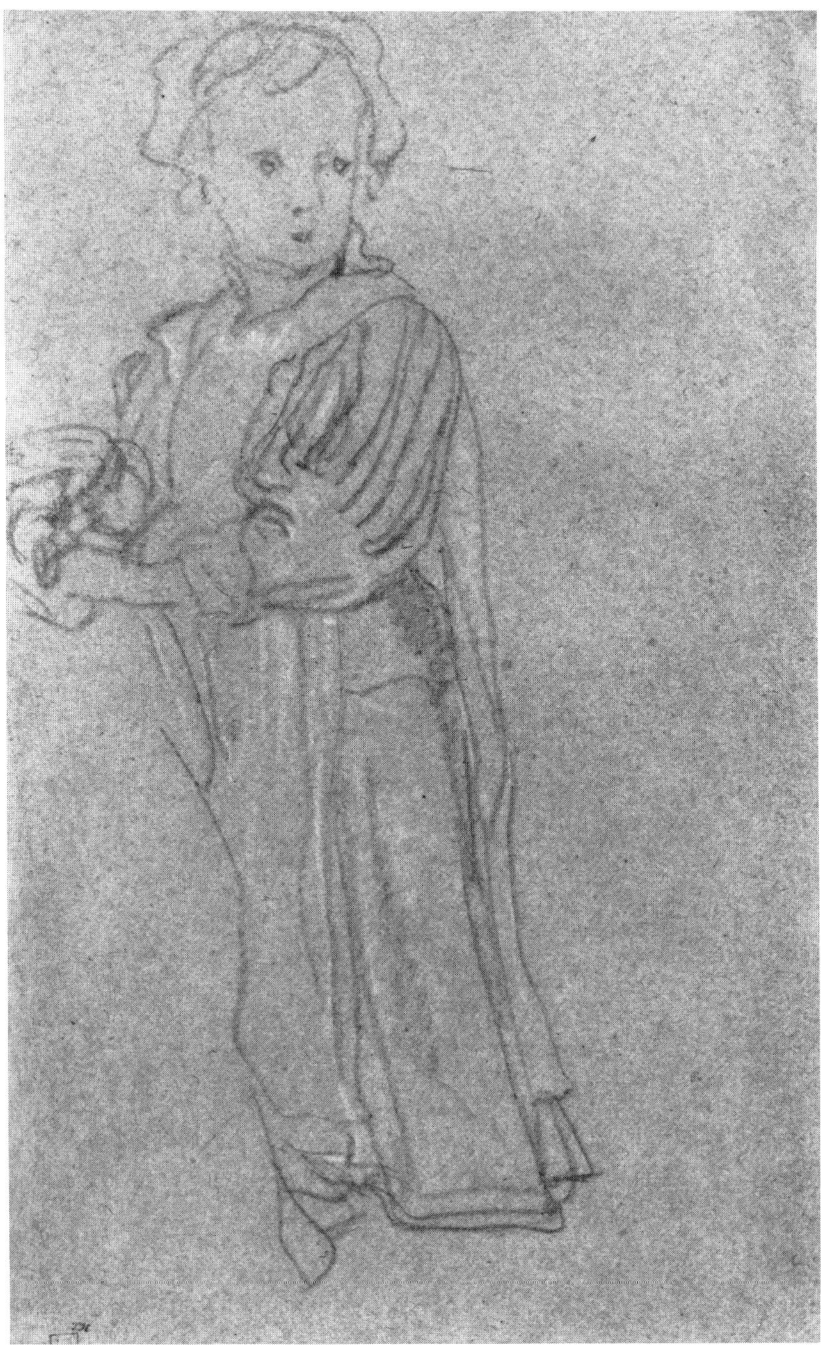

5. Anthony van Dyck, *Child*, c. 1635–1637, black chalk
National Gallery of Canada, Ottawa

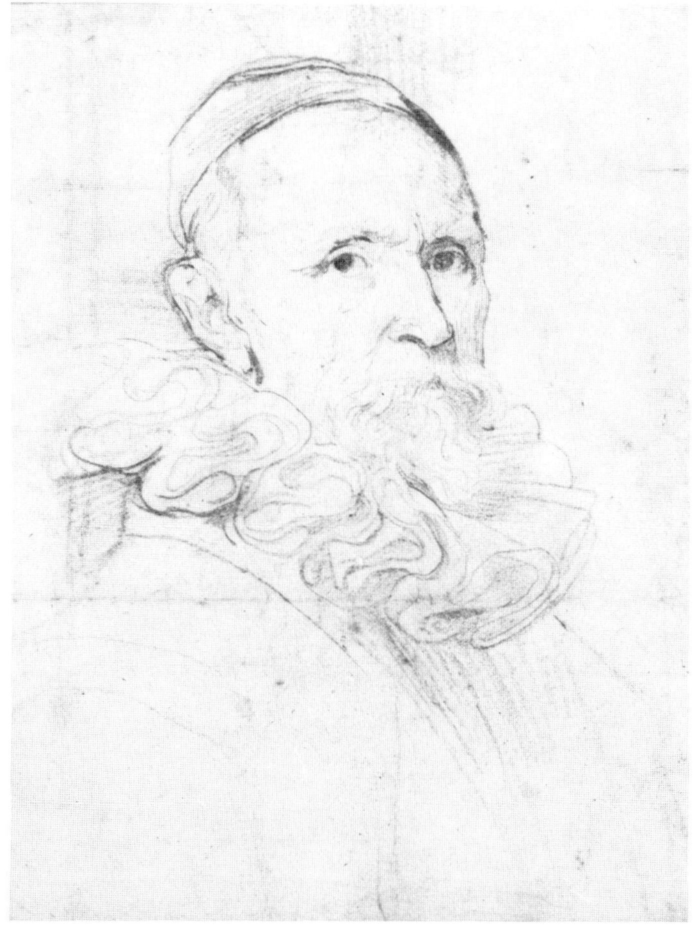

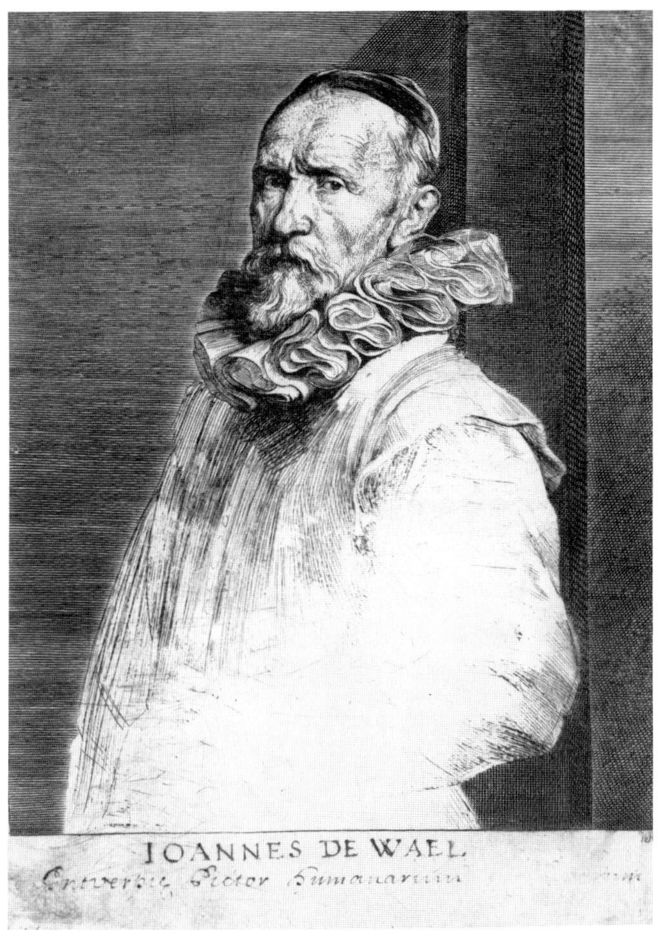

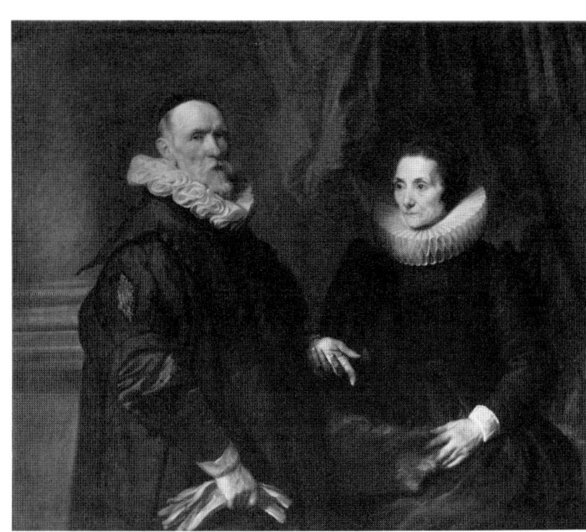

6. Anthony van Dyck,
Jan de Wael, c. 1630–1632,
black chalk
Cabinet Edmond de Rothschild,
Musée du Louvre, Paris

7. Anthony van Dyck,
*Jan de Wael and His Wife
Gertruide de Jode*, 1629,
oil on canvas
Alte Pinakothek, Munich

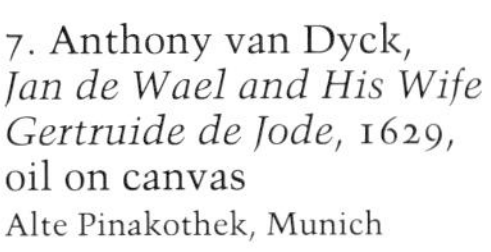

8. Anthony van Dyck,
Jan de Wael, c. 1630–1632,
etching and engraving
National Gallery of Canada, Ottawa

first a drawing of the person to be represented was made, not necessarily exactly like the painting from which it was derived; this drawing was transferred to the copper plate; if the drawing was not modeled with wash, then a grisaille oil study—autograph or not—was made for the printmaker.

This pattern suggests that for all the prints of which Van Dyck was involved in the preparation, the artist began with a black chalk study on white paper, focused on the face and then, to varying degrees, the upper body. From Van Dyck's 1629 double portrait *Jan de Wael and His Wife Gertruide de Jode* (fig. 7) the artist made a vigorous study of just De Wael's head (fig. 6), perhaps waiting for inspiration to adapt De Wael's pose to the self-contained image (fig. 8).[66] In contrast to this simplification of an image, Van Dyck's fully developed study of Inigo Jones (fig. 16) is adapted from a painting depicting only the head and shoulders (fig. 17). In a third variation the black chalk study of Karel de Mallery at Chatsworth (fig. 19) involves only a minimal compaction (the arms) and greater formality (the ruche collar) from the three-quarter-length portrait in Oslo (fig. 18).

Though Van Dyck's chalk studies of De Wael, Jones, and De Mallery are vivid and strikingly immediate, there is no reason to conclude that they are studied from life. If the drawings are from life and as well preliminary to the engravings (in the case of Jones, immediately so), so that the seemingly related paintings are irrelevant, then the inscription *Van Dyck pinxit* is meaningless as an indication of technique, as some scholars have supposed. Given the patterns adduced here, this pattern is unlikely. Many of the drawings for which related paintings exist are very close to the paintings, especially around the head, but include costume details that supersede the paintings and anticipate the engravings, as with the new formality of De Mallery's collar, which is preserved in the oil *modello* and engraving (figs. 20, 21). Due to these compositional factors, the drawings cannot precede the paintings; if, on the other hand, one imagines the drawings to have been made independently of the paintings, why did the artist almost always use the same attitude of the head? The vitality of the drawings is not a proof of their having been sketched from life; Van Dyck's remarkable capacity to create a lively portrait on the basis of another work of art, as in the portrait of Henry Percy (Petworth House), whom he never met, is well known.[67] The phrase "ad vivum expressae" on Hendricx' title page refers to the paintings on which the prints are based. The paintings were taken from life in the sense that the initial chalk compositional sketch for the painting (see below) and the actual painting-in of the head were done from the living model.

In general, these deceptively sensitive after-studies can be distinguished from Van Dyck's chalk sketches for his painted portraits. The latter are primarily executed in black and sometimes white chalk on blue or dun paper, the pose and costume roughly sketched in with, in most cases, little attention to the face. Two examples from the Antwerp and English years, both full-length sketches in black and white chalk on blue paper, are that in the British Museum,[68] made by the artist around 1628 for his full-length *Portrait of Wolfgang Wilhelm, Duke of Pfalz Neuberg* (Alte Pinakothek, Munich), and the sketch of perhaps 1635–1637 in Ottawa (fig. 5)[69] of an unidentified child at his

or her mother's knee.

While this relationship of technique to drawings preliminary to and after paintings can be confirmed by examining the drawings themselves, it is supported by the insufficiently heeded description of Van Dyck's working habits during his English years made by the artist's patron, the Cologne banker Everhard Jabach,[70] who comments on the use of quick compositional sketches on blue paper and makes it clear that in general Van Dyck expected to paint the faces directly on the canvas[71] with the subject in front of him. I suggest that it is only when this could

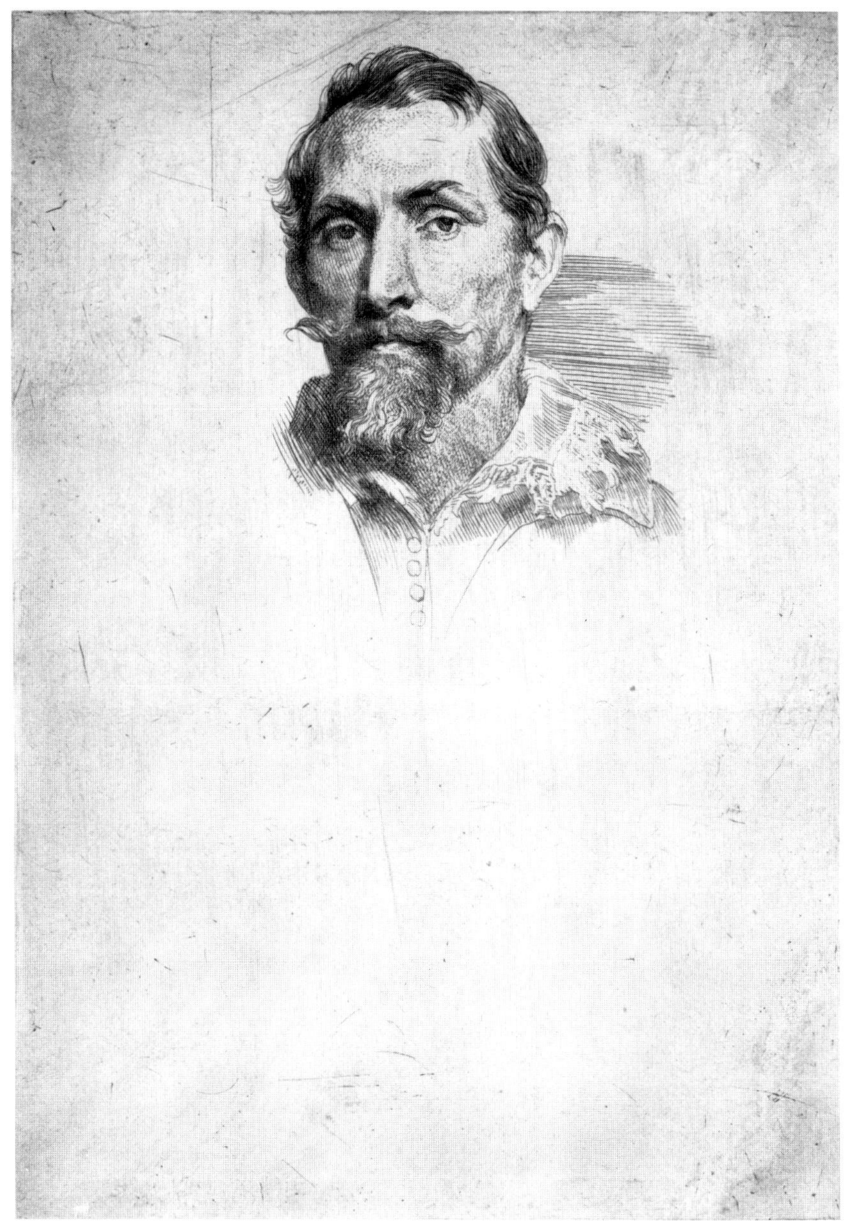

9. Anthony van Dyck, *Frans Snyders*, c. 1632, etching
National Gallery of Canada, Ottawa

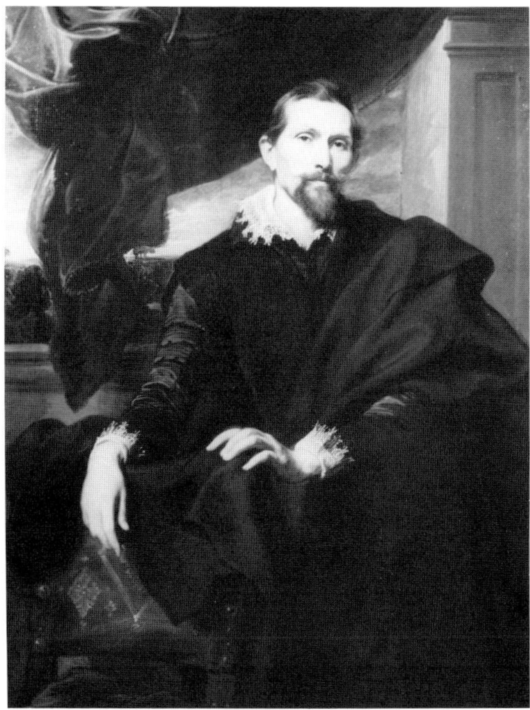

not take place in the studio that Van Dyck made careful oil studies of the heads from life. For example, in executing the *Five Eldest Children of Charles I* (Windsor Castle),[72] it may have been more practical for the artist to visit the royal nursery to make oil studies of the faces of the two infant daughters of Charles I[73] rather than to bring them to the studio for a "sitting."[74]

Perhaps the first kind of printer's *modello* with which Van Dyck experimented was an etching. The fifteen etchings[75] claimed in their inscriptions to be by Van Dyck himself were, in my view, very possibly intended from the beginning as guides for a professional engraver who would then work up the plate with the burin.[76] This applies as well to the etched portrait head of Philippe Le Roy (MH"C"), surely initially intended by Van Dyck for the same treatment as the others, but not included by either Vanden Enden or Hendricx and only engraved later.

The etchings are often summary and focused on the head, as is that of Snyders (fig. 9), very like the extant ten preliminary black chalk drawings that Van Dyck made for his etchings,[77] that of Jan de Wael, already noted, being taken from the 1629 portrait of De Wael with his wife. In the early states of

the ensuing print of De Wael (fig. 8), Van Dyck is at first indecisive in adapting the arm gesture in the painting to the new requirements. Four[78] of the drawings for his own etchings are lightly squared for transfer, as is none of the rest.

While various early seventeenth-century painters experimented briefly with etching, Van Dyck is the only one I know of to make use of the medium not as a creative end in itself but as a means to another end, a part of the process of producing an engraving. I suggest that rather than having worked out this approach himself, Van Dyck picked it up through his association with Vorsterman, from whom, around 1630–1631 (after the latter's return from England), he probably learned to etch. Indeed Vorsterman's innovation of making an etching as a sketch state (see fig. 14) before working up a composition as an engraving received admiring comment from John Evelyn, who refers to Vorsterman's portraits "which he engrav'd after a new way, of Etching it first, and then pointing it (as it were) with the Burine afterwards. . . ."[79] Van Dyck's two nonportrait etchings, *Ecce Homo* (MH"A") after his own painting[80] and *Titian's Self-Portrait with His Mistress* (MH"B") after a lost painting, were both completed by Vorsterman with the burin. In addition, the nine plates with an etched first state printed by Vanden Enden appear to be stylistically consistent and can probably all be attributed to Vorsterman.[81] I cannot find instances of Vorsterman using this technique before he began his association with Van Dyck, and it is not clear whether the etched *Ecce Homo* and *Titian's Self-Portrait* preceded or coincided with the first portrait etchings, or whether Van Dyck's or Vorsterman's portrait etchings actually came first. Thus it may be that the innovation evolved out of the two men working together, rather than being Vorsterman's own innovation, as Evelyn supposed. If the practice of an artist supplying an etched sketch to an engraver as a model was unprecedented in Van Dyck's day, it would later become common.

Van Dyck's etchings are here provisionally assigned to the years 1630–1632/1633,[82] thus entirely or nearly entirely before his departure for England and following Vorsterman's return from there. The etching of Jan van de

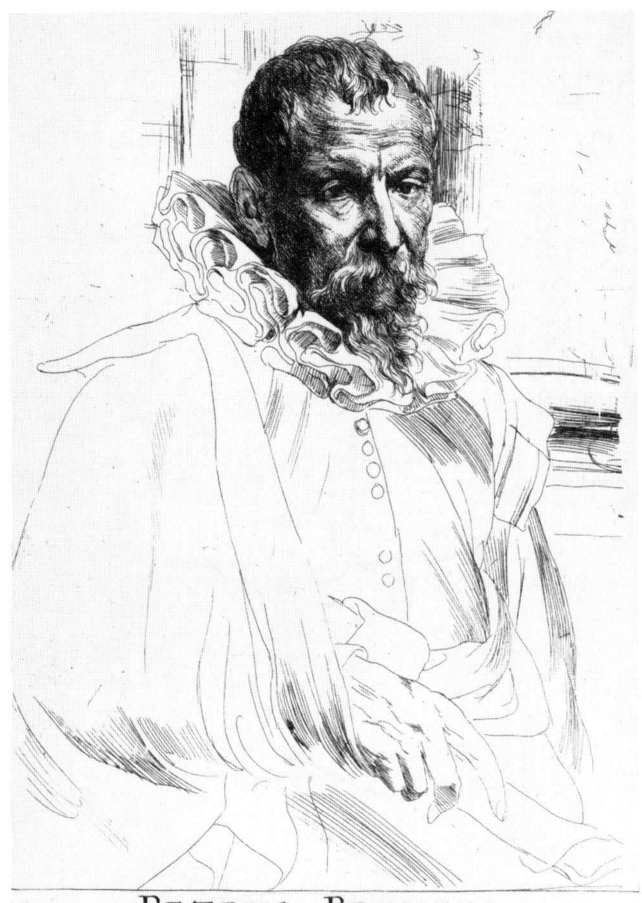

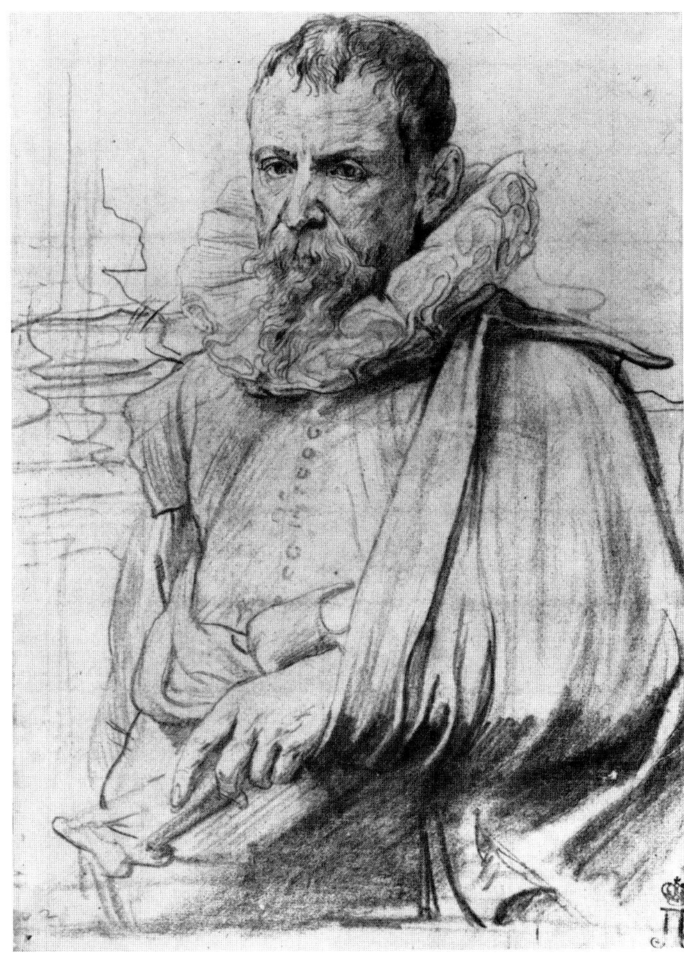

Wouver (MH18), attributed here to Vorsterman, is dated 1632 in the sixth (engraved) state. Van Dyck's two other etchings are dateable to about 1630–1632, and only his self-portrait[83] is open to a dating in the following year. That these etchings might be assignable to the beginning of the Iconography project is also suggested by their subject matter and the range of skill exhibited. All the works are of Netherlanders and, except in the case of Erasmus, are of Van Dyck's contemporaries and artists or supporters of the arts. There is some evidence that Van Dyck intended to etch a portrait of Rubens as well.[84] The portrait of Erasmus is by far the least skillful and was never completed, being left as an acid-pocked plate.[85] Thus, it may have been the first essay and therefore experimental. At this point the project had yet to find a focus: the etchings are based on portraits by Holbein and Rubens as well as on Van Dyck's own. There is also the etching of

Pieter Brueghel the Younger (MH2; fig. 11), which is one of the five signed only with *Van Dyck fecit aqua forti* and for which no prior painting by any hand is known. Although the black chalk drawing in St. Petersburg (fig. 12), published by the present writer,[86] was the immediate model for the etching, there is another autograph study at Chatsworth that depicts the sitter from a slightly different angle. While it is possible that these two studies are adaptations from a painting, probably by another hand, the existence of two variations makes it also possible that these were made from life. This is the only case in which this possibility presents itself.

Three of the sketch-etchings by Van Dyck and three by Vorsterman[87] are known in impressions retouched with wash or gouache, the touch suggesting Van Dyck's own, achieving a greater sense of light and dark for the benefit of the printmaker. Thus the basic pattern of black chalk sketch by Van Dyck

11. Anthony van Dyck, *Pieter Brueghel the Younger*, c. 1630–1632, etching
British Museum, London

12. Anthony van Dyck, *Pieter Brueghel the Younger*, c. 1630–1632, black chalk
Hermitage, St. Petersburg

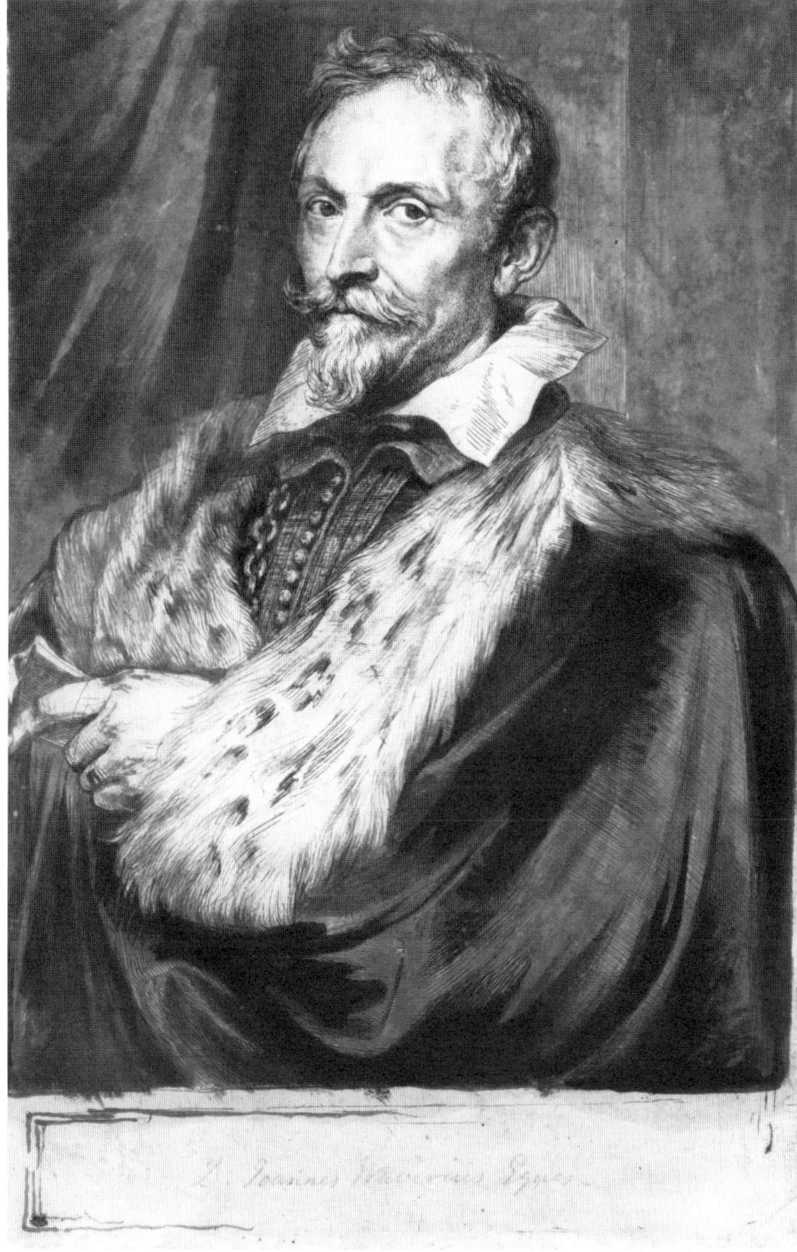

13. Anthony van Dyck, *Jan de Wouver*, c. 1630–1632, oil on canvas
Pushkin Museum, Moscow (from Erik Larsen, *The Paintings of Anthony van Dyck* [Freren, 1988])

14. Lucas Vorsterman after Anthony van Dyck, *Jan de Wouver*, c. 1632, etching, wash added by Van Dyck
British Museum, London

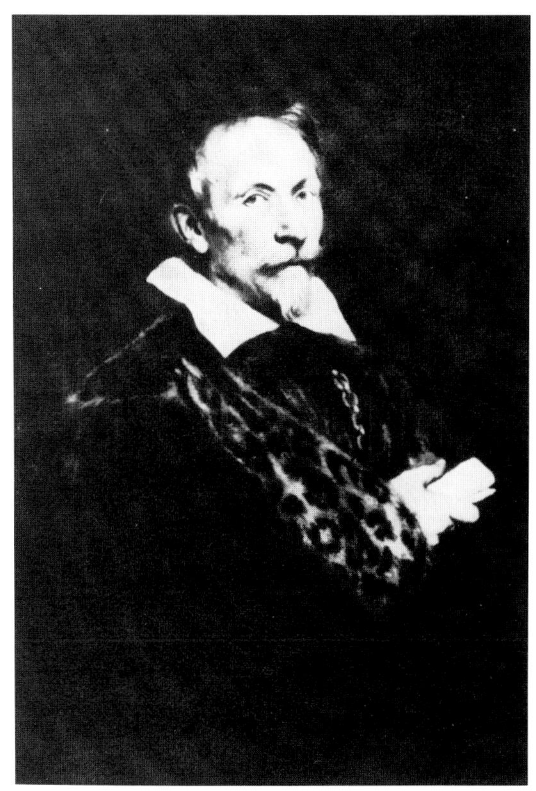

based on his own preexisting painting is developed to a chiaroscuro stage before completion as an engraving. In the eighteenth century Mariette wrote that he had seen an entire collection of the portraits in retouched proof impressions (later destroyed by fire).[88] Two impressions of the sketch-etching of Wouver (MH18) attributable to Vorsterman are extensively retouched in gray wash with a boldness suggesting Van Dyck's hand. In the impression of the first state in the Roth-schild collection (Musée du Louvre)[89] the hand is not yet actually etched but only indicated with the brush, revealing Van Dyck's indecision in adapting the gesture in the prototype painting (fig. 13). In an impression of the second state in the British Museum (fig. 14) the hand gesture has become more decisive, though again retouched in gray wash and gouache. One might imagine that an impression of the second state of the De Wael print, in which the arm gesture of the first state has been partially erased, was retouched in wash to work out shapes. A counterproof in the British Museum of Vorsterman's etching of Bishop Triest (MH13) has been vigorously washed, bringing out the deep contrasts found in the painted portrait (best extant version in the Blaffer collection, Houston). A drawing depicting Bishop Triest, formerly in the Deiker collection, Braunfels (or the lost original of which it would then be a copy), was used to adapt the painting for the etching. In addition, while four of Vorsterman's etched first states are derived from separate existing chiaroscuro studies— in chalk and wash (as Van den Eynden [MH80] in the British Museum) or oil (as De Mallery [MH86] at Boughton House)—none of Van Dyck's etchings can be associated with separate chiaroscuro studies.

In the cases of Frans Snyders (MH11; fig. 9), Paul de Vos (MH16), Van Dyck's self-portrait (MH4; fig. 1), and Philippe Le Roy (MH"C"), Van Dyck etched only the head, set high on the page. In my view these four are the most accomplished and may therefore be the last of Van Dyck's etchings to have been executed. Visually satisfying as these isolated heads are to modern tastes, they appear not to have been thought of by Van Dyck as anything other than preliminary sketches to be completed, as to garments and setting, by a professional printmaker, a procedure paralleled by the work of assistants on the painted portraits.[90] Indeed all four etchings are derived from extant formal portraits and in each case there is a state of the etching or of the duplicate inscribed *Van Dyck pinxit....*

Van Dyck's etched head of Paul de Vos follows the painted portrait head, at one time in the Herner collection, Vienna, whereas the half-length drawing of De Vos, formerly in the V. Koch collection, London, includes a graceful hand gesture. The rigid composition of the engraved states is adumbrated in a counterproof of the etched state in the Rothschild collection (Museé du Louvre),[91] which was competently but less imaginatively worked up in black chalk and incised only in the added portions, presumably by the unidentified etcher (Jean Meyssens) who completed the image before it was reworked with the burin by S. à Bolswert. Similarly, I propose that the black chalk half-length study of Le Roy in Antwerp[92] is not a copy of a lost study for the full-length portrait of 1630 in the Wallace collection, London, as was proposed by Vey, but a copy of Van Dyck's initial half-length formulation for a projected engraving, to be complemented by the artist's exquisite etching of the head alone.[93] For unknown reasons the work was later engraved and published anonymously in an oval format.

Van Dyck's sensitive etching of Snyders (fig. 9) was adapted from the 1621 three-quarter-length painting in the Frick Collection (fig. 10) and was surely again complemented by a half-length compositional study. If we accept for the moment that the etching was probably done around 1631–1632, then

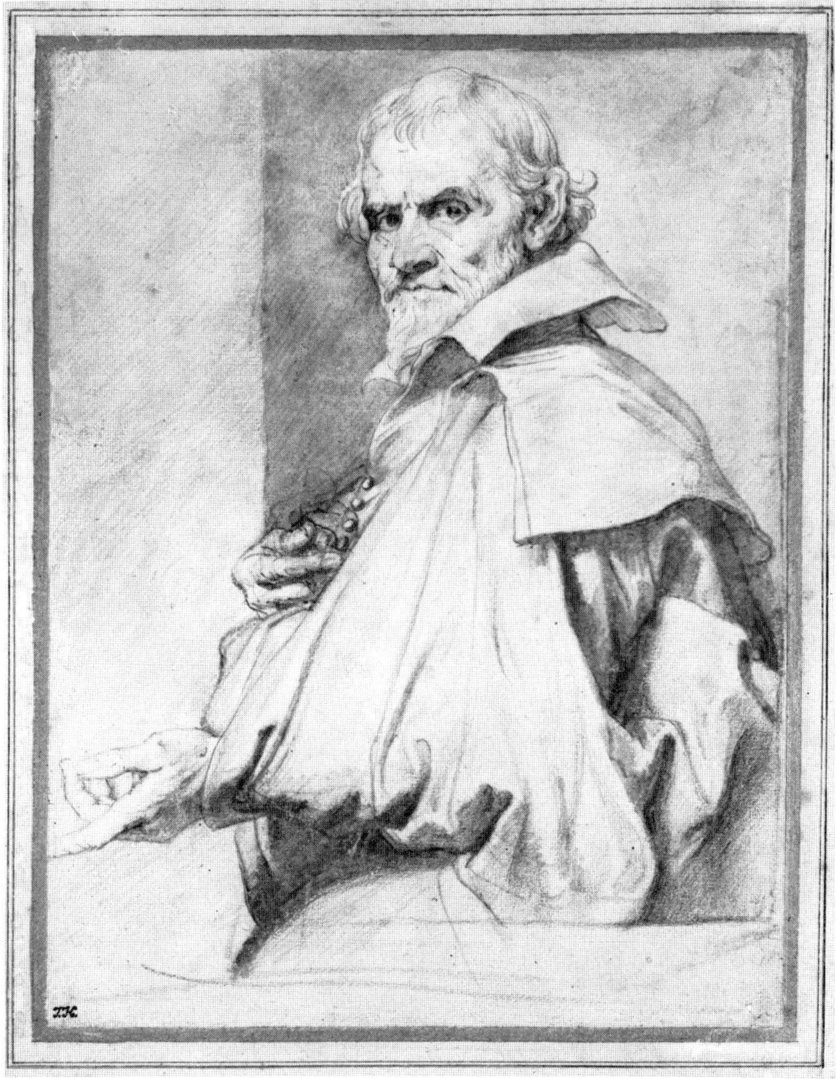

15. Anthony van Dyck, *Orazio Gentileschi*, c. 1632–1634/1635, black chalk and gray wash
Devonshire Collection, Chatsworth

we must assume that Van Dyck, having decided that he wanted to include Snyders in his pantheon, sought out the painting he had done years before in order to prepare an etching from it.

The pattern developed here suggests that Van Dyck's splendid etched self-portrait was not intended as an independent work. It was not intended either, at its inception, for the design of the frontispiece. The frontispiece, as is evident from an impression (fig. 1) of Van Dyck's etching, was designed at a later date by an unknown draftsman from the circle of Rubens.[94] I suspect instead that the etched self-portrait was intended, like the other etchings, as the initial state of an engraving reproducing a painting, in this in-

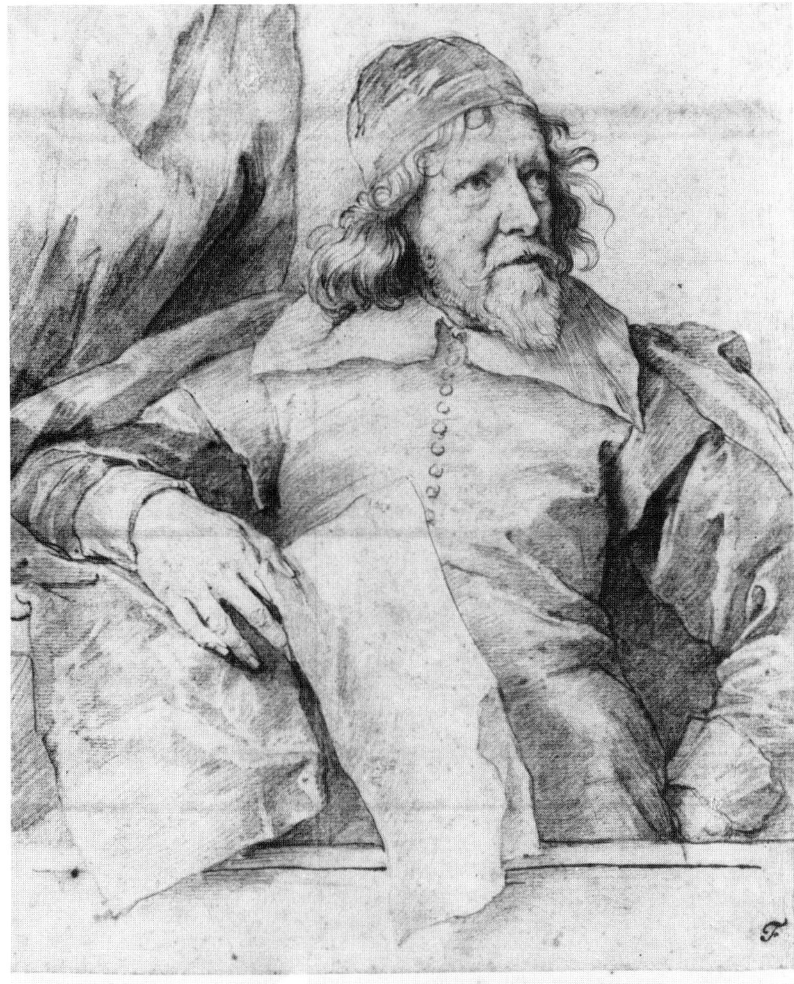

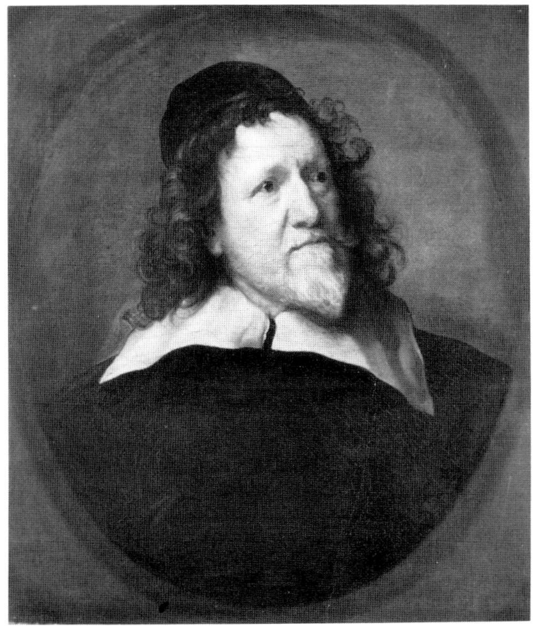

16. Anthony van Dyck, *Inigo Jones*, c. 1632–1634/1635, black chalk
Devonshire Collection, Chatsworth

17. Anthony van Dyck, *Inigo Jones*, c. 1633, oil on canvas
Hermitage, St. Petersburg

stance Van Dyck's *Self-Portrait* in a Swiss private collection. The latter was separately engraved by Vorsterman (M79) for Vanden Enden, apparently on the basis of a monochrome oil study at Boughton House, possibly attributable to Van Dyck himself.

Around 1632–1634/1635 Van Dyck appears to have essayed a second method of preparing an image for an engraver. For at least twenty-four of the engravings of artists, amateurs, and scholars the immediate model was a drawing broadly modeled in light and shade—either in black chalk with a brown or gray wash, as in Van Dyck's magnificent study of the Italian painter Orazio Gentileschi (fig. 15), or in black chalk alone, as in the drawing of Inigo Jones (fig. 16)—in brief, a highly modeled study similar in its relief character to the washed etchings and monochrome "grisaille" oil studies. Such studies are incised, as the simple black chalk studies preliminary to the etchings and the oil studies are not. For this group there was no need for another preparatory stage unless a further alteration in the composition was made.[95]

The drawing at Chatsworth of Inigo Jones provides an example of those drawings worked up in black chalk alone. It is incised and corresponds to the engraving. The lower portion incorporates a parapet readied for an inscription, which is neatly accommodated by the device of the papers in the architect's hand falling over the edge. Vey proposed that this "nature study,"[96] as he characterized it, had served first as a preliminary study for the bust-length painting of Jones (fig. 17). However, the drawing shows no signs of having been worked on in two campaigns and the composition is evidently calculated for the format of the engraving—including the standard parapet or plaque. While many of Van Dyck's painted portraits show the subject leaning on a side support, such as the base of a column, the only use by Van Dyck known to me of a parapet or tablelike support extending the width of the picture postdates the work on the Iconography and may well have been influenced by it.[97] In sum, it is more logical to see the painting as the point

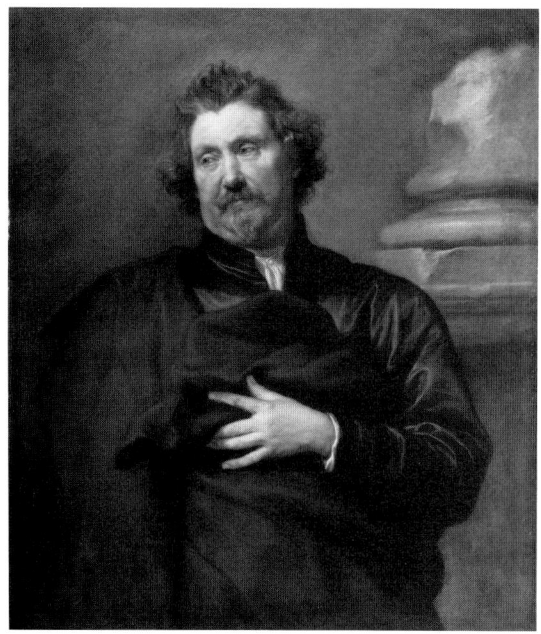

of departure for the more complex composition of the drawing, the one similarity being the head and collar. The suggestion[98] that the Chatsworth drawing might alternately be based on a separate study from life does not address the issues raised here. In other instances, as well, Van Dyck takes little more than the head and collar from the earlier painting and then in the drawing enlivens the composition, frequently through gesture. The black chalk and brown wash study in the British Museum of the Louvain professor Eyricius Puteanus in his study (engraved by Pieter de Jode [MH36]) is, in parallel fashion, based on a bust-length portrait in Raleigh.

Besides that of Inigo Jones, the other four extant studies by Van Dyck associated with his years in England—those of Orazio Gentileschi (MH83), Robert van Voerst (MH73), Hendrick van Steenwick (MH67), and Daniel Mytens (MH56)—are all chiaroscuro drawings. While the studies of Mytens[99] and Gentileschi were engraved by Pontius in Antwerp, the same exigencies of logistics need not have influenced the choice of model study for the portraits of Jones and Van Voerst,[100] which, like that of the English diplomat Sir Kenelm Digby (MH71), were engraved in England by Van Voerst himself before his death in 1636. Thus one might postulate that the intermediary study between the engraving of Digby and the painting (private collection, England), and the study pre-

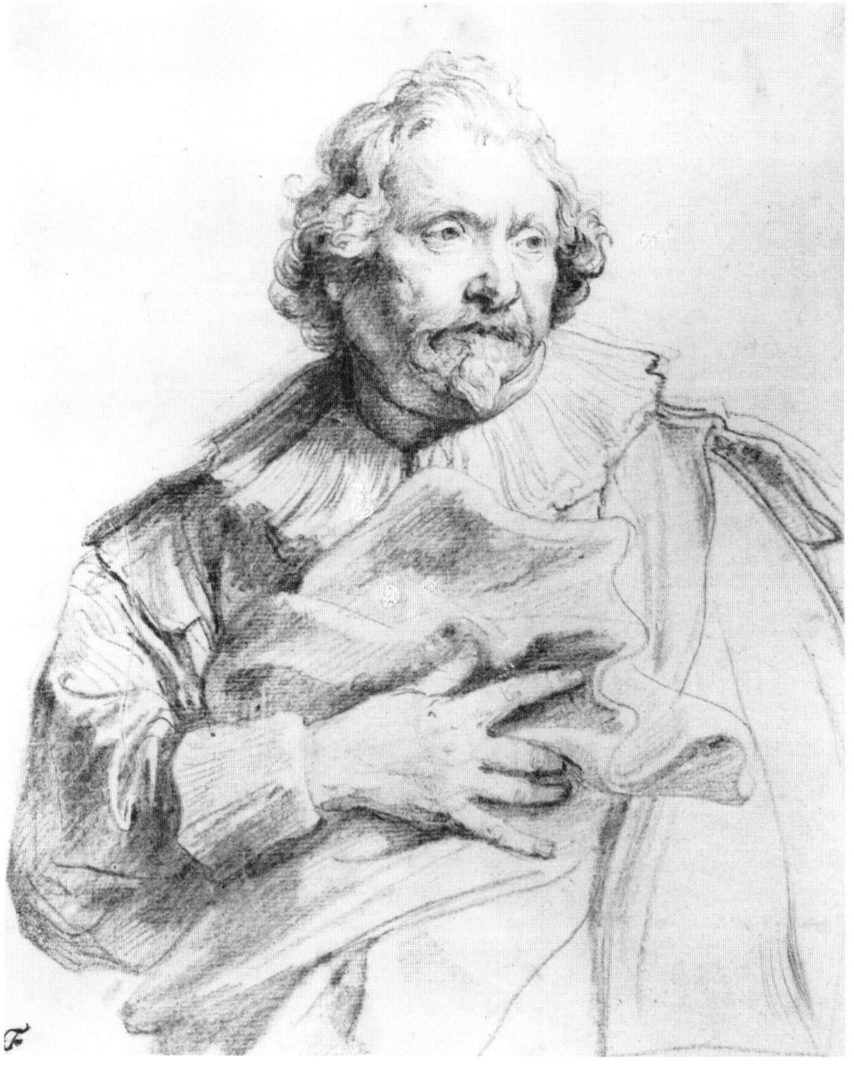

ceding Van Voerst's engraving of Van Dyck's portrait of the French painter Simon Vouet (MH74),[101] were also chiaroscuro drawings. Of the eleven extant chiaroscuro drawings developed from portraits surely executed in Flanders, five can be associated with extant paintings, as those of Puteanus (MH36) or Cachiopin (MH75).[102] The beautifully washed drawing of Cachiopin (Cabinet Rothschild, Museé du Louvre) is dated 1634, thus not long after Van Dyck's arrival from London. The artist's involvement in the engraving process while in Antwerp is seen in his work-up in pen and brown ink of Van Thulden's chain on the proof of De Jode's engraving (MH38) in the British Museum.

These monochrome preparatory model drawings recall those, such as the *Lot and His Family Leaving Sodom* (fig. 2), that the

18. Anthony van Dyck, *Karel de Mallery*, 1634–1635, oil on panel
Nasjonalgalleriet, Oslo

19. Anthony van Dyck, *Karel de Mallery*, c. 1634–1635, black chalk
Devonshire Collection, Chatsworth

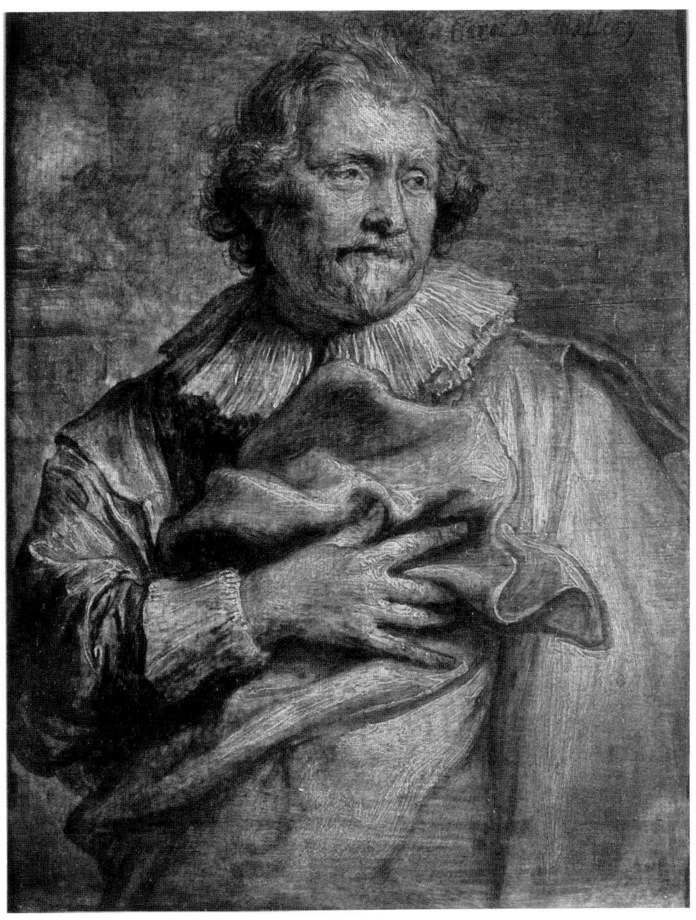

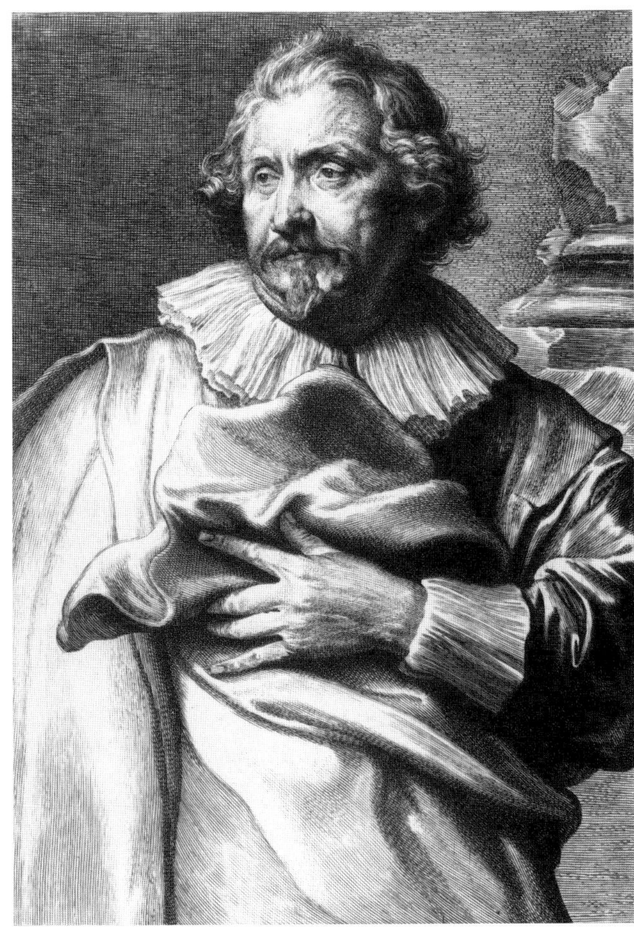

20. Anthony van Dyck,
Karel de Mallery,
c. 1634–1635, oil on panel
Duke of Buccleuch, Boughton House

21. Lucas Vorsterman after
Anthony van Dyck, *Karel de
Mallery*, c. 1635, etching
and engraving
British Museum, London

young Van Dyck made after paintings by Rubens. That experience must have informed the portrait drawings technically. The comparison clarifies as well the *reproductive* function of the drawings.

The third type of preparatory model with which I propose Van Dyck experimented—perhaps around 1634–1635—was a monochrome oil study[103] "de chiaroscuro," as thirty-two were first described in a 1655 sale of the Arundel collection,[104] in which, as well, the author is given as Van Dyck (as in other early references). From the chalk drawing of De Mallery (fig. 19) Van Dyck worked up a freely brushed grisaille in reddish browns and gray (fig. 20), which was engraved by Vorsterman (fig. 21). The immediate *modelli* for at least fifty engravings published by Hendricx must have been monochrome oil studies, though some of these were not exe-

cuted by Van Dyck himself. For twenty-two of these, related paintings exist. Of Vanden Enden's eighty plates, forty-five were based on known oil studies, of which sixteen are derived from identified paintings. Five more oil studies were prepared by or at the behest of Van Dyck, of which four were separately printed. Of these, the formal portraits of Charles I and the prince and princess of Orange can be identified.

The reproductive function of the portrait *modelli* in oil is clarified by looking at Van Dyck's print *modelli* as a whole. As noted above, all other nonportrait oil studies for prints attributed to Van Dyck himself are based on paintings, for example the grisaille oil study on paper of *Rinaldo and Armida* (fig. 3), based on Van Dyck's painting (Musée du Louvre) of 1631/1632 and later engraved by Pieter de Jode the Younger.

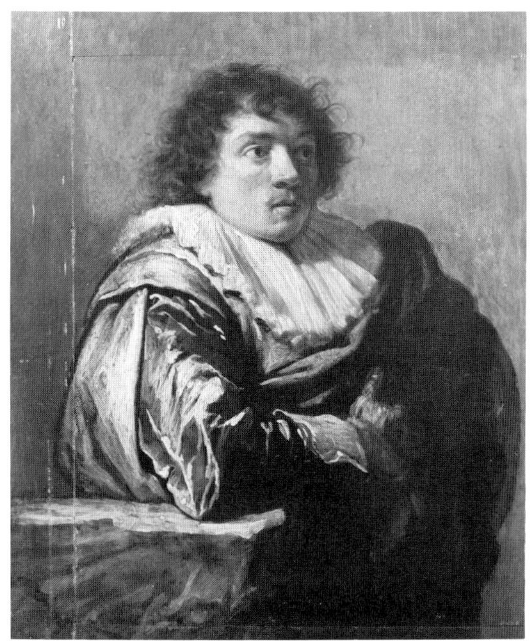

The preparation of studies in oil probably took place around 1634–1635, at a time when Van Dyck was preparing other *modelli* in oil for Antwerp printmakers. In addition, of the seven paintings[105] executed in 1634–1635 of which engravings for the Iconography were prepared, all were adapted via oil studies and all depict members of the nobility. Indeed, all engravings of the nobility for which we have preliminary studies were developed from oil studies (although others are represented as well). Portraits of Charles I and the prince and princess of Orange are not among the prints published by Hendricx, but are represented in oil studies at Boughton House. These are derived from extant easel paintings and were separately engraved and published by Jean Meyssens.[106] Undoubtedly Van Dyck intended them to be included. After returning to England in 1635 Van Dyck must have found it hard to keep control of the project, and, without his presence in Antwerp, it languished.

The problem of separating the oil studies attributable to Van Dyck from those by assistants, by printmakers, or by later copyists is beyond the scope of this essay. For the lines of reasoning pursued here it is not always critical whether an oil study was done by Van Dyck or on his instructions or behalf. There are two major collections of applicable

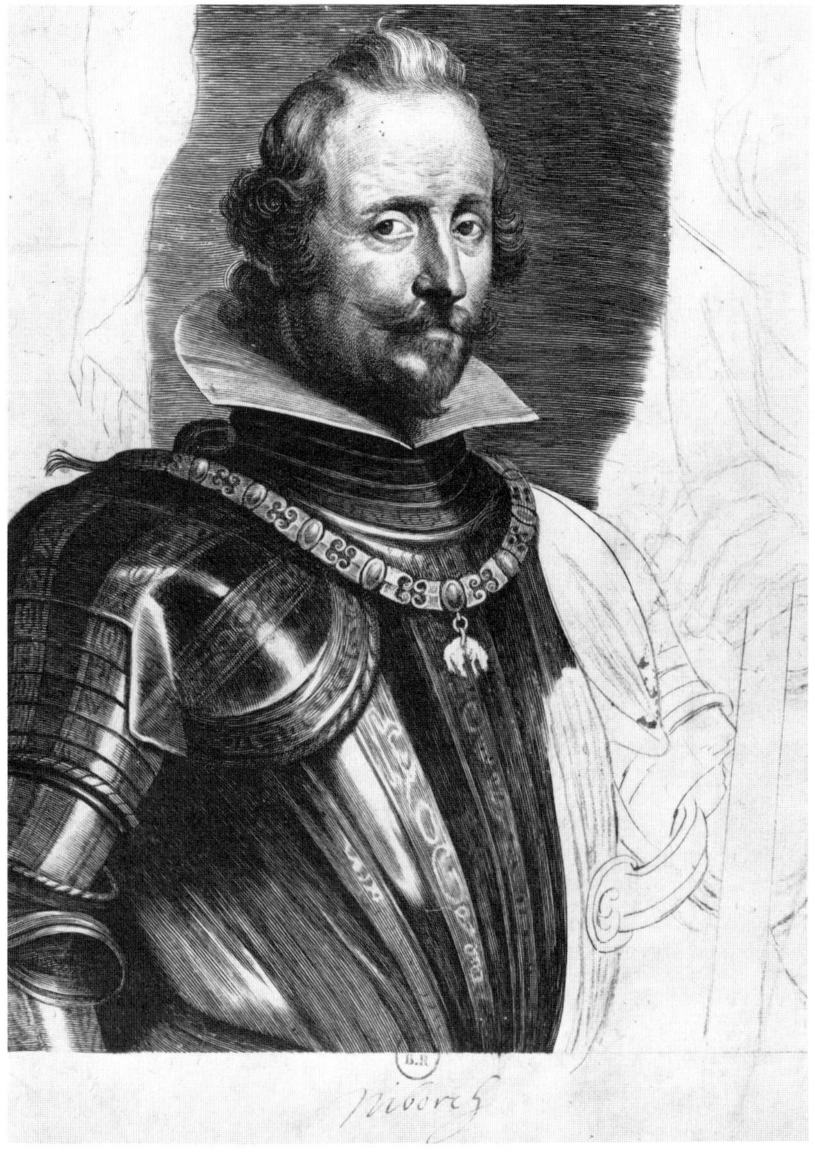

oil studies: one belongs to the duke of Buccleuch at Boughton House,[107] which collection was acquired in 1680,[108] and the other is in the Alte Pinakothek, Munich. Of the forty-two oil studies at Boughton House at the beginning of this century, the great majority are by Van Dyck. Others are copies, and possibly a few are by assistants or the engravers. Those at Munich range from undistinguished to very coarse. There are others in scattered collections.[109] The pattern suggests that not only the apparently autograph studies at Boughton but also those studies in Munich served as *modelli*. It also strongly suggests that other extant, inferior oil studies (that are the only or the best versions known)

22. Workshop of Anthony van Dyck, *Palamedes Palamedesz*, c. 1635?, oil on panel
Alte Pinakothek, Munich

23. Lucas Vorsterman after Anthony van Dyck, *Wolfgang Wilhelm, Duke of Pfalz Neuburg*, c. 1635, engraving, proof state, reworked in black chalk by Van Dyck(?)
Bibliothèque Nationale, Paris

24. RIGHT: Anthony van Dyck, *Wolfgang Wilhelm, Duke of Pfalz Neuburg,* c. 1628–1630, oil on canvas
Alte Pinakothek, Munich

25. BELOW: Anthony van Dyck or Lucas Vorsterman (?), *Wolfgang Wilhelm, Duke of Pfalz Neuburg,* c. 1635?, oil on panel
Malcove Collection, University of Toronto

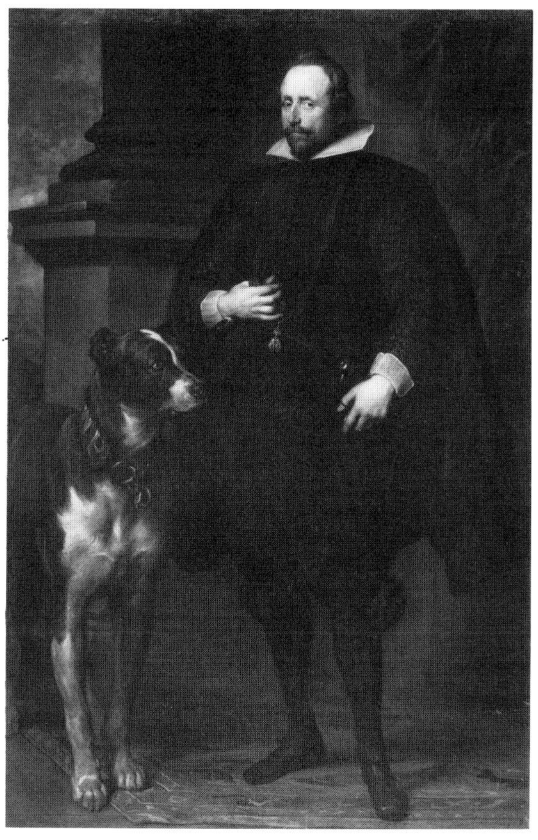

may be the engraver's actual models or copies of lost versions that were. In addition, of the fifty-plus functional oil studies, nineteen are associated with preliminary drawings. For two more engravings, the existence of an unincised drawing[110] points to the initial existence of an oil study. Finally, there are three black chalk portrait drawings by or after Van Dyck apparently composed with the preparation of oil studies and prints in mind, but no further stage of execution is known. Perhaps Van Dyck changed his mind about including Henri Liberti,[111] who would have been the only musician.

Some of the extant oil studies are neither obviously attributable to Van Dyck nor obviously copies, and yet they must have served

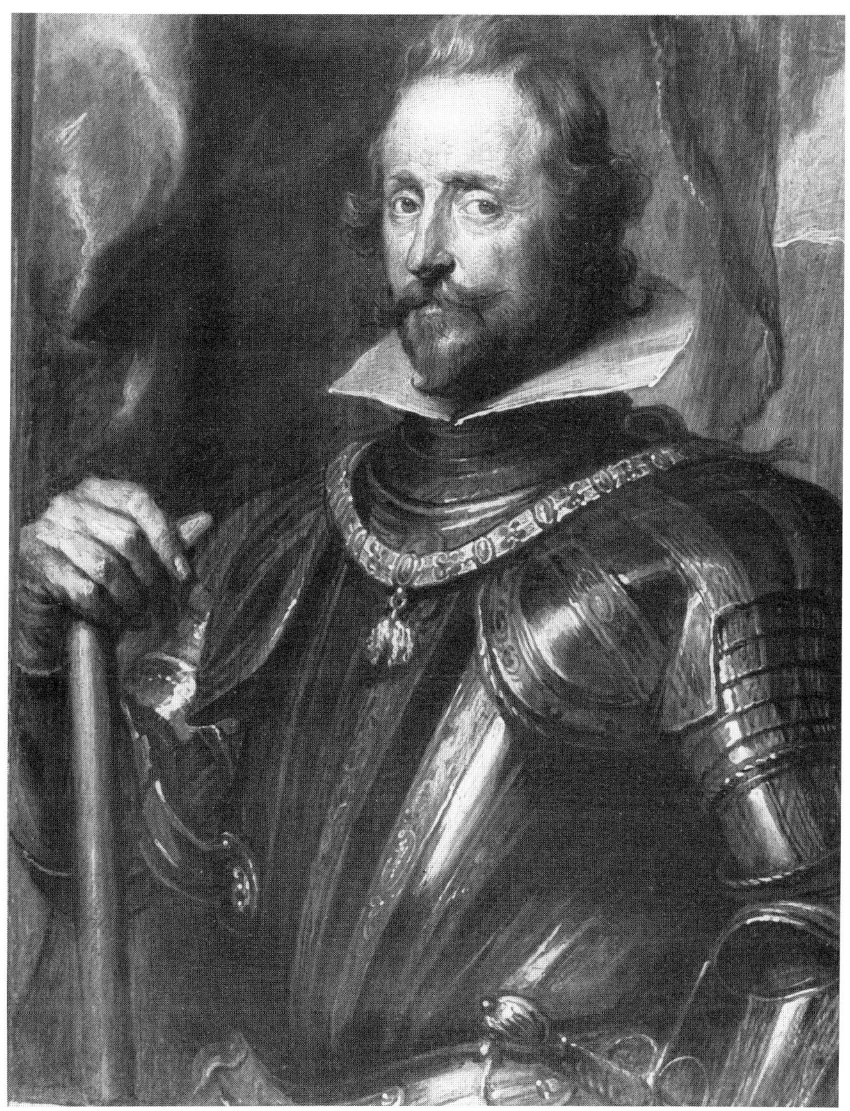

as the printer's *modelli*. For example, the oil study in Munich of Palamedes Palamedesz (MH58; fig. 22) lacks the deftness of that of Adam de Coster (MH31; fig. 29), but it incorporates pentimenti, such as a visible shifting of the hand, that were followed by Pontius in the engraving. Lucas Vorsterman's engraving of Wolfgang Wilhelm, duke of Pfalz Neuburg (MH118; fig. 23), printed by Hendricx, looks back to the full-length painting of the duke c. 1628/1630 in Munich (fig. 24). From this portrait type was derived the face and collar, but now the duke wears armor and wields a baton for a more aggressive demeanor, a transformation like that of the Emperor Ferdinand (MH105) and the marquis of Leganes (MH50) and indicative of the enhanced status of the military image.[112] The brushwork in the oil study of Wolfgang Wilhelm now in Toronto (fig. 25)[113] is much tighter and more precise (notable in the skin and armor) than in the study of De Coster, and the panel may be one of those by another, supervised hand, possibly Vorsterman's[114] own. Alternately, this stylistic variation may reflect a shift, over time, of Van Dyck's approach to the ex-

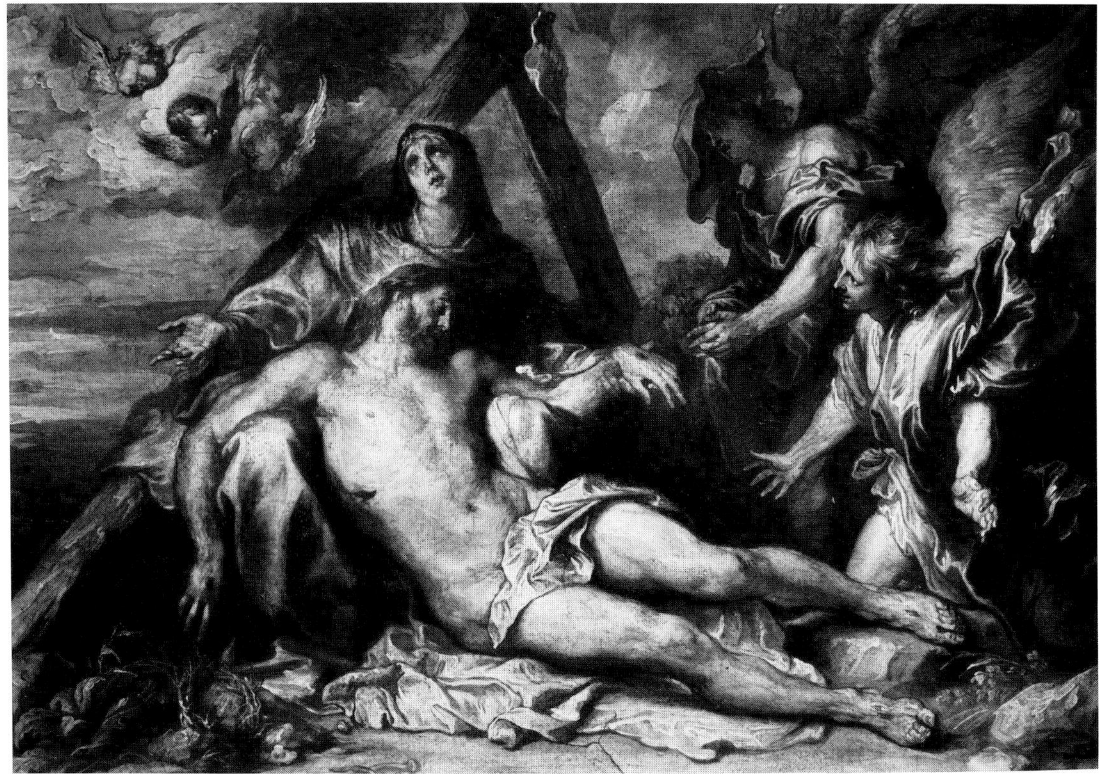

ecution of oil studies, from a looser to a tighter manner, as shown in a comparison of Van Dyck's execution of the engraver's *modello* of *Rinaldo and Armida* (fig. 3) with his more precisely brushed study of the *Lamentation* (fig. 26),[115] based on the painting (Alte Pinakothek, Munich) of 1634 and engraved by Vorsterman. A monograph on the oil studies as a whole could clarify these issues.

The careful execution of the study of the duke of Pfalz Neuburg draws attention to an alteration that points, in any case, to Van Dyck's involvement. In raking light it can be seen that the duke's hand was originally sketched about two centimeters higher than its final placement in the oil study, the latter agreeing with the completed engraving. In the proof state of Vorsterman's engraving the area around the hand is not worked up. On the impression in the Bibliothèque Nationale (fig. 23) the two corresponding positions of the hand have been sketched in black chalk. The handling suggests Van Dyck, not Vorsterman.

Among the engravings for which no preparatory model is known are those made in Holland of the Dutch engraver Willem Hondius (MH29), which he engraved himself, and Michiel van Mierevelt (MH26),[116] states of which are attributed to both Hondius and William Delft. The absence of a preparatory model suggests that the portraits were in Holland; thus I assume that the engraver was responsible for his own working model.

Composition

The third feature of these prints that points to their derivation from preexisting formal paintings concerns compositional problems. Those of imposed conformity have already been mentioned. In Van Dyck's formal painted portraits hand gestures[117] off to the side of the body are typically purposeful and relate to something—a person, object, or prospect. While an arm or hand may be cut at the bottom edge of the picture plane in a half- or three-quarter-length portrait, such gestures are not cut at the side, neither do hands brush the edge or acknowledge the physicality of the frame.[118] However, some of the men included in the Iconography have suffered a procrustean amputation: the tip of one or more fingers is cut by the edge of the image field, as in Gentileschi (MH83; fig. 15),

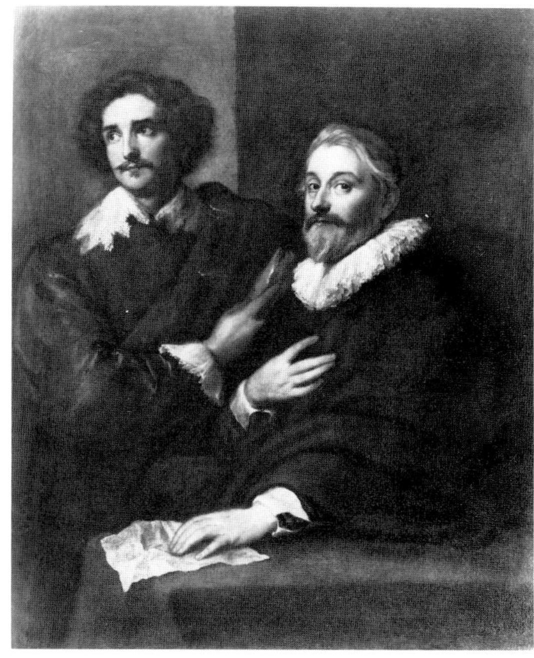

27. Anthony van Dyck,
Pieter de Jode and His Son,
c. 1628–1632, oil on canvas
Musei Capitolini, Rome
Photograph: Archivi Alinari

28. Anthony van Dyck,
Pieter de Jode, c. 1634–1635,
oil on panel
Duke of Buccleuch, Boughton House

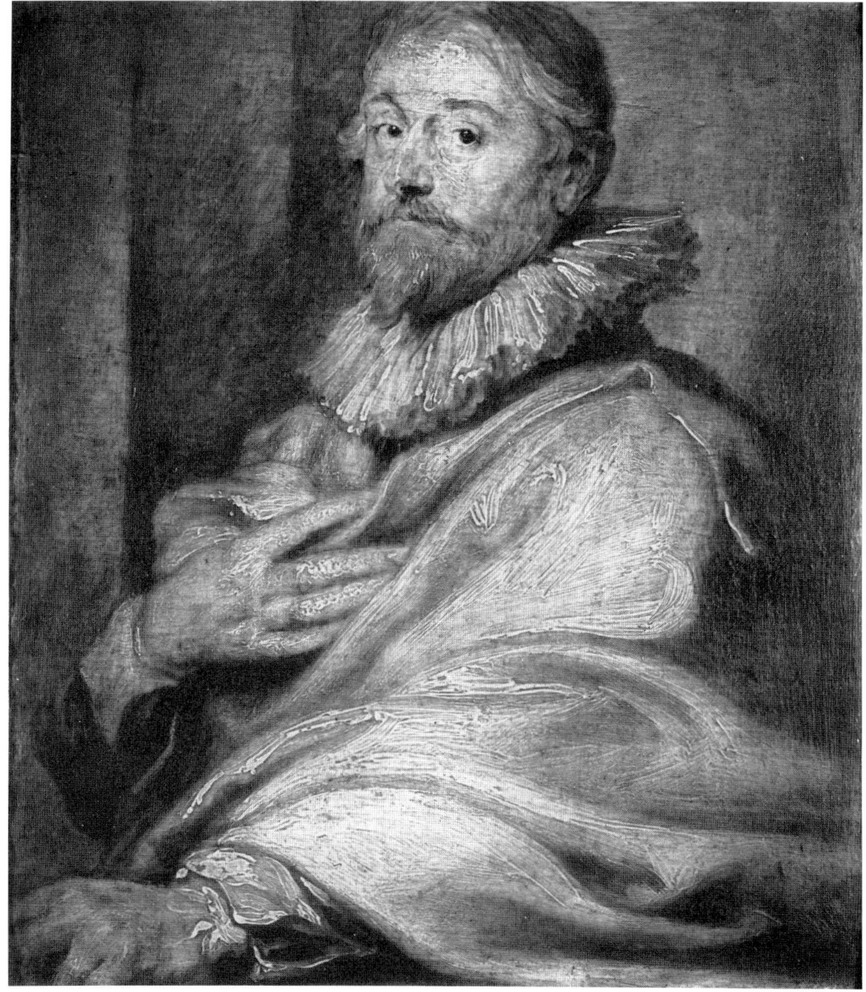

Theodoor Rombouts (MH61), Van den Eynden (MH80), and De Jode (MH84; fig. 28).
Less dramatically, both Antonie Cornelissen
(MH3) and Justus Lipsius (MH22) touch the
framing edge of the picture plane. Such proximity to the edge creates cramping foreign to
the dignity and elegance of Van Dyck's portraiture.

If Van Dyck had designed the models for
the Iconography from scratch, I suspect they
would exhibit the decorum of his paintings.
Compositional problems result from the
need to standardize the proportions of the
portraits to meet the series format. If these
half-length portraits are all or nearly all derived from preexisting formal paintings of
varying proportions, then in the majority of
cases the image field had to be cut down.
This pattern is demonstrable in cases in
which the formal painting-prototype is
known, as in the double portrait of Pieter de
Jode with his son (fig. 27), the source for the
oil study and engraving of the father alone
(fig. 28). Experiments with Van de Wouver's
index finger—which caused no difficulties in
the amply spaced painting—are visible in the
washed etching state (fig. 14). In a second
washed proof (Musée du Louvre, Paris) the
hand is drawn with the index finger tucked.
These cases may be contrasted with those of
Van den Eynden or Jones, in which the composition has been expanded; in such instances problems do not arise.

The portrait of Adam de Coster (MH31) is
my last example. The composition of the
black chalk study (copy?; Städelsches Kunst-
institut, Frankfurt am Main), presumably derived from a lost painting, is followed in Van
Dyck's oil study (fig. 29), though a strip for
the inscription is roughed in, forcing a
change in the hand. De Coster's gesture
would be effective in the pictorial space of a
three-quarter-length painting, but could not
be easily accommodated to the new requirements: the fingers of his open palm—as an
extension of the arm akimbo, a characteristic
gesture of male self-confidence—extend awkwardly out of the picture field. In a proof
state of Vorsterman's engraving (fig. 30) the
problem is unresolved: the hand remains in
outline, with the extended fingers cut off. In
the finished engraving (fig. 31) the fingers
have been unnaturally curled into the corner.
De Coster's elegance and boldness are com-

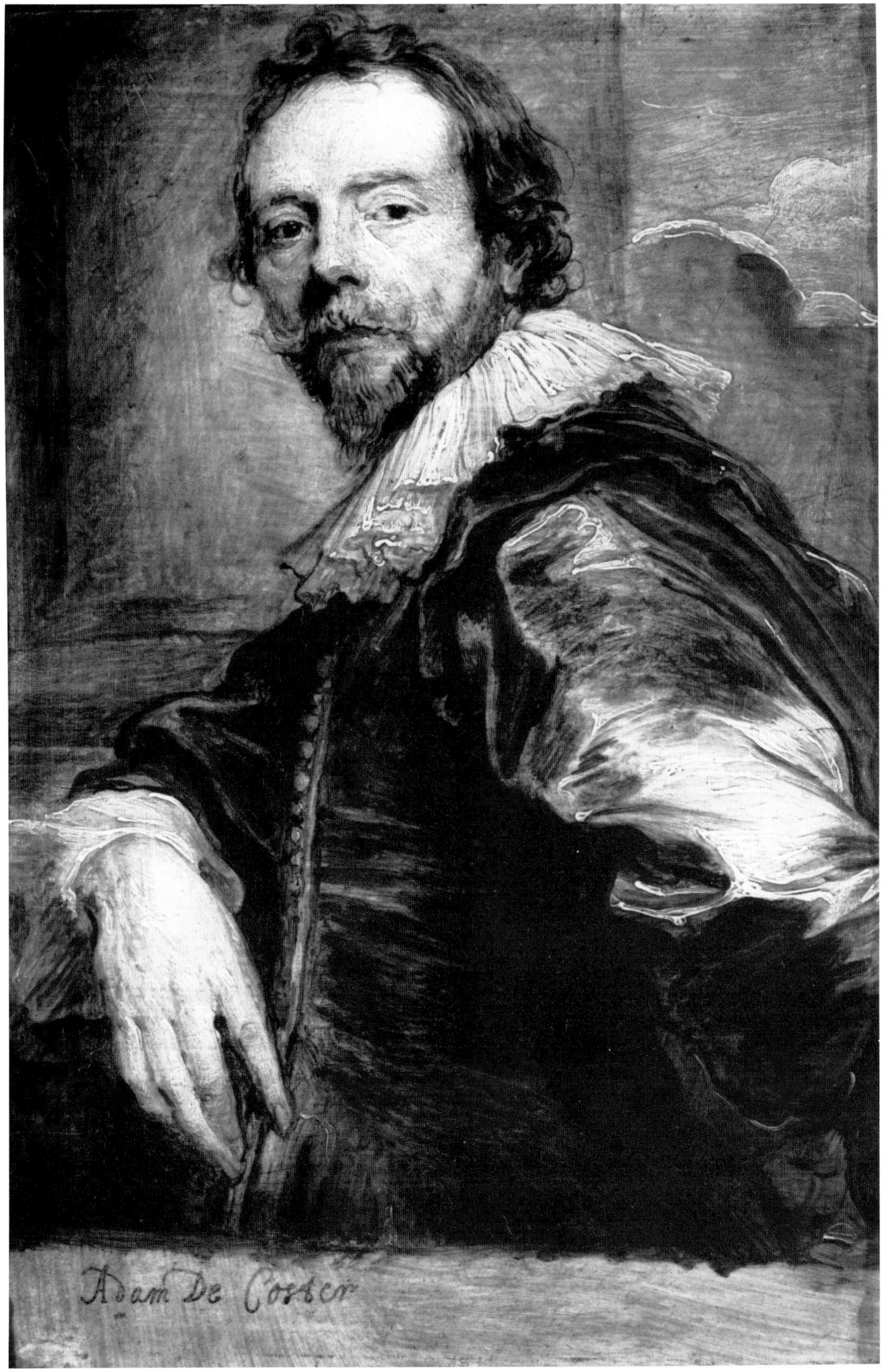

29. Anthony van Dyck,
Adam de Coster, c. 1634–
1635, oil on panel
Duke of Buccleuch, Boughton House

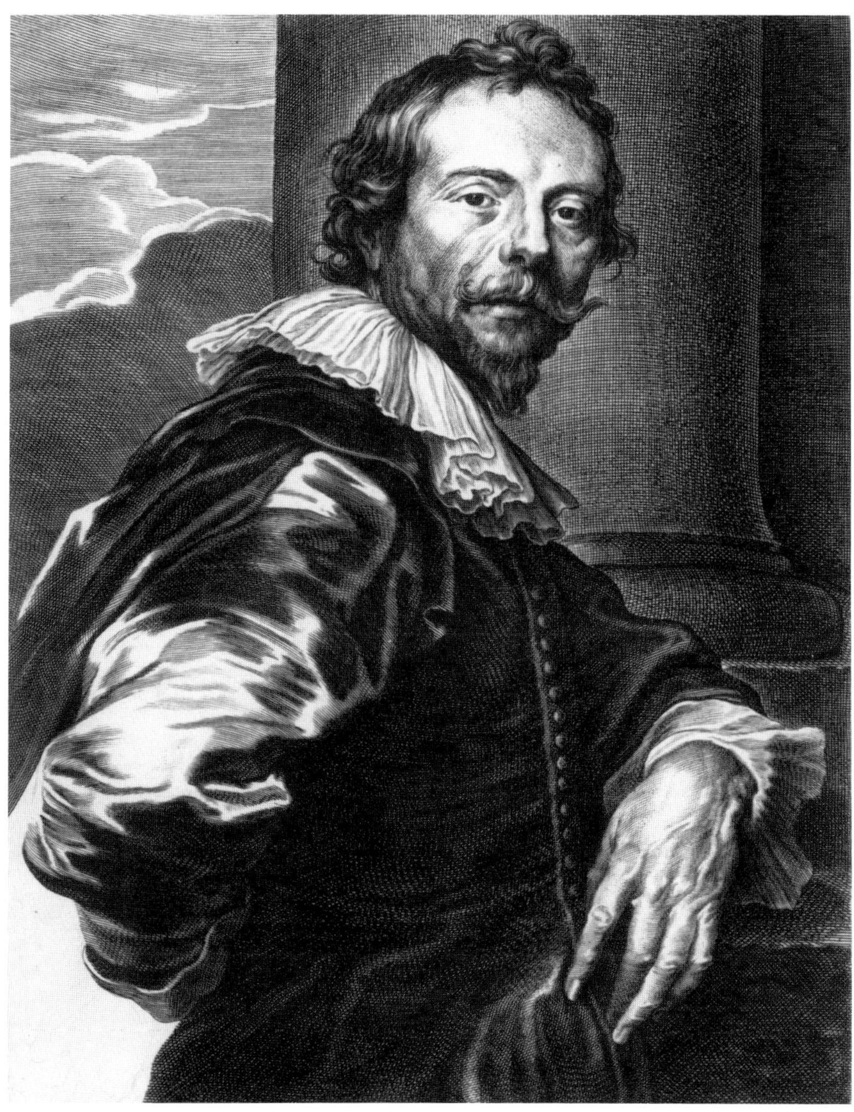

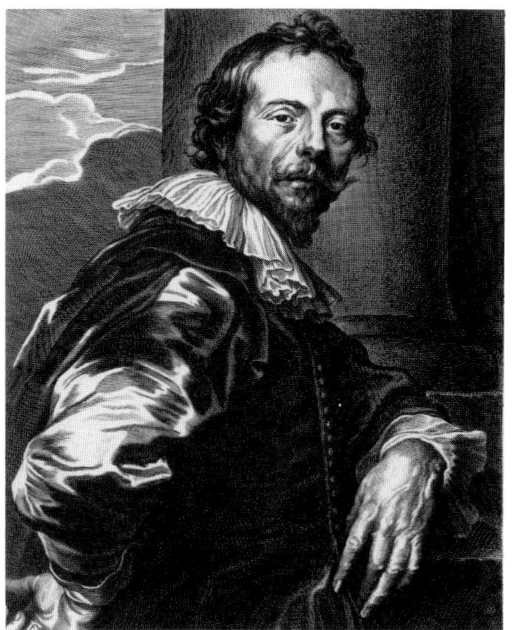

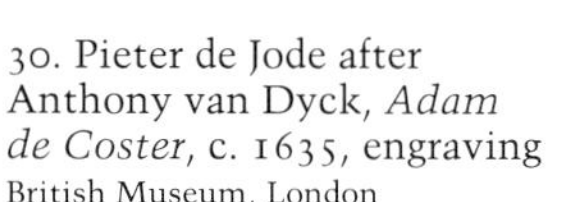

30. Pieter de Jode after
Anthony van Dyck, *Adam
de Coster*, c. 1635, engraving
British Museum, London

31. Pieter de Jode after
Anthony van Dyck, *Adam
de Coster*, c. 1635, engraving
British Museum, London

promised for the sake of the standardized format.

In conclusion, even if there is no one set of prints that can be described as "Van Dyck's Iconography," the extant prints remain an important segment of Van Dyck's oeuvre, no less revelatory of the artist's strengths and weaknesses for being incomplete. Van Dyck never executed a series of monumental history paintings such as those for which Rubens is famous. The Iconography was to be his great enduring ensemble, directly celebrating the status of artists in the company of princes and statesmen, and indirectly celebrating Van Dyck's own achievements as a painter. Even as the Iconography reveals Van Dyck's weakness in carrying through a complicated project on his own, it also makes clear an unexpected degree of ingenuity and innovation.

NOTES

My thanks to Kimberly Turner for help with the initial research, funded by a grant from Canada Council, and to Arthur Wheelock, Anne-Marie Logan, and Elizabeth Cropper for their helpful comments on earlier drafts.

1. *Icones / Principum / Virorum Doctorum / Pictorum Chalcographorum / Statuariorum nec non Amatorum / Pictoriae Artis Numero Centum / ab / Antonio van Dyck Pictore ad vivum expressae / eiusq: sumptibus aeri incisae./ Antverpiae / Gillis Hendricx excudit./ Anno 1645 / Ant. van Dyck fecit aqua forti / Iac. Neeffs sculpsit.* The title appears in the third state; *Anno 1645* is erased in the fourth state.

2. The two most important, sustained examinations of the Iconography are Marie Mauquoy-Hendrickx, *L'Iconographie d'Antoine Van Dyck* (Brussels, 1956; partially rev. ed. 1991), cat. nos. cited hereafter as MHxx; this is invaluable as a catalogue of the prints; and A. M. Hind, "Van Dyck: His Original Etchings and His Iconographie," *Print Collector's Quarterly* 5 (1915), 2–37, 220–252, a thoughtful analysis of the preparatory process, recognizing the primacy of the paintings and a function for the oil studies as engraver's *modello*. Until very recently Hind's insights on these oil studies were taken up only by the unjustly ignored Frank van den Wijngaert, *Antoon van Dyck* (Antwerp, 1943).

Further bibliography, cited chronologically: Fr. Wibral, *L'Iconographie d'Antoine van Dyck, d'après les recherches de H. Weber* (Leipzig, 1877); M. Delacre, *Recherche sur le role du dessin dans l'Iconografie de Van Dyck* (Brussels, 1932); Horst Vey, "Anton van Dycks Ölskizzen," *Bulletin des Musées Royaux des Beaux-Arts* 5 (1956), 167–208; Horst Vey, *Die Zeichnungen Anton. van Dycks* (Brussels, 1962), cat. nos. cited hereafter as V.xxx; A. McNairn, "Van Dyck's Iconography," *Journal of the National Gallery of Canada* 38 (September 1980), 1–8; Oliver Millar, *Van Dyck in England* [exh. cat., National Portrait Gallery] (London, 1982); H.-J. Raupp, *Untersuchungen zu Künstlerbildnis und Künstlerdarstellung in den Niederlanden im 17. Jahrhundert* (Hildesheim, 1984); Joaneath Spicer, "Unrecognized Studies for Van Dyck's 'Iconography' in the Hermitage," *Master Drawings* 23–24 (1985–1986), 537–543; Erik Larsen, *The Paintings of Anthony van Dyck*, 2 vols. (Freren, 1988), cat. nos. cited hereafter as L.xxx; E. Haverkamp-Begemann and Stephanie Dickey, "Iconography," in Christopher Brown, *Anthony van Dyck* [exh. cat., Sogo Museum of Art] (Yokohama, 1990); Arthur K. Wheelock, Jr., et al., *Anthony Van Dyck* [exh. cat., National Gallery of Art] (Washington, 1990); Christopher Brown, "Drawings for *The Iconography*," in *The Drawings of Anthony Van Dyck* [exh. cat., Pierpont Morgan Library] (New York, 1991), 190–193; Alfred Moir, "The Iconography," in Alfred Moir et al., *Antoon Van Dyck (1599–1641) & Antwerpen* [exh. cat., Museum Plantin-Moretus] (Antwerp, 1991). Moir's catalogue appeared after this article was submitted; nevertheless, an attempt has been made to insert Moir's conclusions as they relate to the issues raised here.

3. Other prints are signed by Pieter de Jode and Nicolas Lauwers working in Antwerp, Robert van Voerst in England, and in the United Provinces, Willem Hondius and Willem Jacobsz. Delff.

4. The 1641 death of Abbot Scaglia is noted on the fifth state of Pontius' engraving (MH64); the publisher is still Vanden Enden. Vanden Enden was still working with the plates in 1641.

5. For the watermarks see Mauquoy-Hendrickx 1991, chap. 6.

6. The consequences of such absences in both Vanden Enden's and Hendricx's series were queried by Spicer 1985–1986, 537, but not addressed by more recent essayists.

7. The other plates after paintings by Rubens, as those engraved by Schelte à Bolswert, which were issued by Vanden Enden and subsequently by Hendricx, were probably acquired at the same time.

8. The title reads: *Icones Principum Virorum Doctorum Pictorum Chalcographorum Statuariorum nec non Amatorum Pictoris Artis ab Antonio van Dyck ad vivum Expressae* (Mauquoy-Hendrickx 1991, pl. 2).

9. Hendricx's address appears first in the third state, along with the date 1654 and a reference to Le Roy's death in 1653.

10. Wibral 1877, 16.

11. *La Collection Dutuit: livres et manuscrits* (Paris, 1899), no. 179; E. Dutuit, *Manuel de l'amateur d'estampes* 1 (Paris, 1881), 155.

12. Hind 1915, 14, refers to the "extreme rarity" of bound copies of the 1645 edition, without citing one.

13. The two authors of the major modern research, Marie Mauquoy-Hendrickx and Horst Vey, have generously let me know that they actually never found one either. More recent writers have apparently assumed that these two had seen copies.

14. G. P. Bellori, *Le vite de pittori, scultori et architetti moderni* (Rome, 1672), 260–261. A newly translated and extensively annotated version is conveniently included by Brown in New York 1991, 17–23.

15. The issue of the ordering lies outside my concerns here. Later assemblages examined begin most often with the Archduchess Isabella. They may also begin with Maria de' Medici or the Swedish king Gustav Adolphus. Rulers are followed by generals. The second major grouping is men of letters, with Justus Lipsius and Alexander Scaglia among the first. The artists almost always begin with Rubens, then Van Dyck, followed by Margaret Ruthven with Gerard Seghers, Jacob Jordaens, and Adriaen Brouwer frequently among those who follow. The last places are often taken by the etched plates that duplicate other portraits.

16. For the later publishing history see Mauquoy-Hendrickx 1991, 37–49.

17. Yokohama 1990, 30, previously unpublished, dated by Brown c. 1636–1638.

18. Another argument against Van Dyck's selection of this portrait is the way the full-length painting is cut off through a hand, without adjustment. See the discussion of "Composition."

19. For the verses see Vey 1962, 46.

20. W. H. Carpenter, *Pictorial Notices: Consisting of a Memoir of Sir Anthony van Dyck* (London, 1844), 55–56.

21. On Rubens and printmaking see K. Renger, "Planänderungen in Rubensstichen," *Zeitschrift für Kunstgeschichte* 37 (1974), 1–30; K. Renger, "Rubens Dedit Dedicavitique, Rubens' Beschäftigung mit der Reproduktionsgraphik," *Jahrbuch der Berliner Museen* 16 (1974), 122–175, and 17 (1975) 166–213; see also *Bilder nach Bildern. Druckgraphik und die Vermittlung von Kunst* [exh. cat., Westfälisches Landesmuseum für Kunst und Kulturgeschichte] (Münster, 1976); *Peter Paul Rubens, Maler mit dem Grabstichel, Rubens und die Druckgraphik* [exh. cat., Wallraf-Richartz Museum] (Cologne, 1977); D. Bodart, *Rubens e l'incisione* [exh. cat., Gabinetto Nazionale delle Stampe] (Rome, 1977); Ingeborg Pohlen, *Untersuchungen zur Reproduktionsgraphik der Rubenswerkstatt*, vol. 6 of *Beiträge zur Kunstwissenschaft* (Munich, 1985), informatively reviewed by A.-M. Logan in *Print Quarterly* (March 1988), 78–81.

22. L. de Pauw-De Veen, *De Begrippen 'Schilder,' 'Schildrij' en 'Schilderen' in de zeventiende Eeuw* (Brussels, 1969) barely touches on the question, and it has otherwise hardly been addressed as applied to prints, perhaps because, relative to *fecit*, it seemed obvious.

23. This general assertion by Mauquoy-Hendrickx 1956, 10 (1991, 3) is commonly cited by later writers. While Hind 1915, 22, 37, thought of Van Dyck's painted portraits as constituting the significant prototype in cases in which they could be identified, he still thought that *pinxit* referred to the oil studies. For Moir 1991, 65, *pinxit* implies that the images were "probably derived from painted portraits made as ends in themselves." He is uncertain what to do with the grisailles.

24. The one print after Van Dyck that to me appears from its style to be after a sketch is Soutman's etching *Taking of Christ* (F. W. H. Hollstein, *Dutch and Flemish Etchings, Engravings and Woodcuts c. 1450–1700* [Amsterdam, 1949–], 5, ill. [cited hereafter as Holl. xx]), inscribed *Van Dyck invenit* and apparently after an early preliminary pen drawing close to but not identical with one in Berlin (V. 79) by Van Dyck for the paintings at Corsham Court and in the Museo del Prado. For the known studies see Washington 1990, nos. 13, 14; Brown in New York 1991, 128–143.

25. For example Michiel van Mierevelt (MH26).

26. My rendering of *Icones* in the title (kindly reviewed by Elizabeth McGrath) as "Portraits" was influenced by the use of *Pictor iconum* for portrait painters within the series. Begemann and Dickey render *Icones* as "Images." Moir does not discuss the title.

27. For example, the series of images of famous artists entitled *Pictorum . . . Effiges*, published by H. Cock and D. Lamsonius (Antwerp, 1572) with no indication of who made the portraits.

28. There are thirteen etchings simply inscribed *Ant. van Dyck fecit aqua forti*, but three (MH4, 7, 10) exist in duplicate prints inscribed *Ant. van Dyck pinxit*. See note 32 and Appendix.

29. An early copy of Holbein's lost original is in the Galleria Nazionale at Parma (J. Rowlands, *Holbein* [Oxford, 1985], 128–129) and is surely recorded in an engraving by Frans Huys (Holl. 132, ill.). McNairn 1980, 3, suggests Van Dyck saw it in the collection of the Antwerp printer Jan van Meurs. In the traditional view, as in Haverkamp-Begemann and Dickey in Yokohama 1990, no. 34, Van Dyck worked from a version of the painting (in which Erasmus' book is treated differently) seen in England belonging to the earl of Arundel (eventually to the earl of Radnor; Rowlands 1985, pl. 26). Though impressions are found in compilations assembled after Van Dyck's death, that the plate was never cleaned of its acid-pocking indicates that Van Dyck ceased to be interested in its inclusion.

30. Musée Fabre, Montpelier; Hans Vlieghe, *Corpus Rubenianum: Portraits II, Antwerp—Identified Sitters* (London, 1987), no. 105. Mauquoy Hendrickx 1956 (and 1991) confuses the portraits of father (MH6) and son (MH28).

31. Alte Pinakothek, Munich; probably a copy of a lost original.

32. The portraits of Snyders (MH11; Frick Collection, New York) and P. de Vos (MH16; formerly in the Herner collection, Vienna) bear inscriptions on the etching: *Ant. van Dyck pinxit et fecit aqua forti*, while three more exist in duplicates by Vorsterman that are inscribed: *Ant. van Dyck pinxit*; see self-portrait (MH4, 79; private collection, Switzerland), Joos de Momper (MH7, 88; no clearly related portrait), Jan Snellincks (MH10, 37; private collection, England).

33. Six of the engravings already published by Vanden Enden and inscribed *Ant. van Dyck pinxit* depict men with whom it is difficult to imagine Van Dyck having contact. Two were dead: Jacques de Breuck (MH44), a sixteenth-century architect (not the elusive nephew [as recently proposed by Brown in New York 1991, no. 57]), for whom see M. Mauquoy-Hendrickx, "Précisions sur le portrait de Jacques du Broeucq . . . ," *Revue Belge d'Archéologie et d'Histoire de l'Art* 60 (1991), n.p.; and Justus Lipsius, who died in 1606. There are also four generals of the Thirty Years War—Jan de t'Serclaes de Tilly, d. 1632 (MH30); Albert von Wallenstein, d. 1634 (MH40); L. Brancaccio d. 1637 (MH41); and Gustav Adolphus, king of Sweden (MH51)—who are not known to have ever been in the same place as Van Dyck.

Since I know of no instance in which there is evidence that Van Dyck concurred in a false claim to authorship, either Vanden Enden had these engravings prepared after Van Dyck's death and misrepresented the authorship of the paintings so that he could include them in the series, or else Van Dyck or his shop did in fact paint portraits of these men, based on existing portraits by others, something we know Van Dyck did, for example in the case of the intimate portrait of Henry Percy (Petworth House), c. 1633, who died before Van Dyck could have met him. Van Dyck's portrayal of Lipsius is derived either from Rubens' *Justus Lipsius with His Pupils* (Palazzo Pitti, Florence) or, more likely, from a 1605 portrait by Abraham Janssens, known from an engraving by Pieter de Jode (J. R. Judson and C. Van de Velde, *Corpus Rubenianum: Book Illustrations and Title-Pages* [London, 1978], 2: figs. 104–107), which must also have been Rubens' source. There are oil grisaille studies for Lipsius at Boughton House and for Tilly and Wallenstein in Munich, the last two surely not by Van Dyck himself.

34. For another perspective see Münster 1976, 74–94 ("Inventio").

35. Münster 1976, 47, illus. For the series see *In de Vier Winden, De prentkunst van Hieronymus Cock* [exh. cat., Museum Boymans van Beuningen] (Rotterdam, 1988), nos. 85–86. An Italian example would be Marcantonio Raimondi's engraving after Raphael's *Parnassus* in the Stanza della Segnatura, inscribed: *Raphael pinxit in Vaticano/ MAF* (*Illustrated Bartsch*, vol. 14, 200–201, 247), for which see Innis H. Shoemaker, *The Engravings of Marcantonio Raimondi* [exh. cat., Spencer Museum of Art] (Lawrence, Kansas, 1981), no. 48b.

36. For example, the Antwerp engraver Jan Sadeler's five engravings after original monochrome oil studies on paper by Dirck Barendsz. of c. 1580, the engravings being inscribed *T. Bernard invent . . .* , for which see *Kunst voor de Beeldenstorm, Noornederlandse Kunst 1525–1580* [exh. cat., Rijksmuseum] (Amsterdam, 1986), no. 303, Sadeler's engraving illustrated. The inscription is not discussed.

37. For example, while Jacques de Gheyn's engravings after his own portrait drawings are inscribed *JDGheyn fe*, other subjects are commonly inscribed with *invenit*. For a catalogue of De Gheyn's prints see J. P. Fildet Kok, "Jacques de Gheyn II, Engraver, Designer and Publisher," *Print Quarterly* 7, no. 4 (1990).

38. For which see Rotterdam 1988; Raupp 1984, 17–44.

39. A sustained discussion of this issue would be welcome. For the present see the literature on Rubens and printmaking (note 21) or on oil sketches, as J. S. Held, *The Oil Sketches of Peter Paul Rubens* (Princeton, 1980); *Schilderkunst uit de eerste hand, Olieverfschetsen van Tintoretto tot Goya* [exh. cat., Museum Boymans-van Beuningen] (Rotterdam, 1983); J. Müller Hofstede, "Zur Grisaille-Skizze in der Flämischen Malerei des XVII. und XVI. Jahrhun-

derts," in *Beiträge zur Geschichte der Ölskizze vom 16. bis zum 18. Jahrhundert*, ed. R. Klessmann (Herzog Anton Ulrich-Museum, Braunschweig, 1984), 45–58.

40. R.-A. d'Hulst and M. Vandenven, *Corpus Rubenianum, The Old Testament* (London, 1989), no. 5.

41. Pohlen 1985, no. 32. It is now generally accepted that after Van Dyck left for Italy in 1621, Vorsterman took over from him the task of producing modeled working drawings after Rubens' paintings for the engravings Vorsterman was to produce, for example the *Adoration of the Kings* (Pohlen 1985, no. 41; Rubens' painting of 1617/1618 in Lyon; the drawn *modello* slightly enlarging the composition in the Musée du Louvre [Renger 1974, fig. 2, as by Rubens]), inscribed *P.P.Rubens pinxit . . . Lucas Vorsterman sculp. et excud. A 1621.* See also Cologne 1977, 39.

42. Holl. 26.

43. L.742.

44. L.744.

45. In the inscription *P.P.Rubens pinxit. H. Witdouc sculpsit A 1638* on the engraving of Rubens' *Raising of the Cross* (Antwerp Cathedral), *pinxit* refers to the famous triptych and not to the engraver's *modello*, an oil study on paper in the Art Gallery of Ontario, Toronto (Held 1980, no. 351), attributed to Rubens himself. It is the renown of the altarpiece, cited in the dedication "Ex tabula Walburgensis Ecclesiae," that prompted the print and would attract the buyer. *Pinxit* has no bearing on the authorship of the engraver's model.

46. Held 1980, 11.

47. Holl. 4; Münster 1976, fig. 135.

48. Holl. 7.

49. Black and red chalk with gray wash, heightened with white gouache, retouched in brown ink, probably by Rubens, 26.6 x 39 cm, sold by Sotheby's, London, 22 November 1974, no. 111.

50. The original painting of this portrait (or a copy) was sold by Fievez, Brussels, 25–26 June, 1924, no. 29, illus. The sitter is older and wears different armor from that in the full-length portrait in a private collection, Switzerland (Yokohama 1990, no. 14 [or the better known version in the collections of the prince of Liechtenstein, Vaduz Castle]), dated by J. Müller Hofstede c. 1628–1629 and from which was made the engraving by Pontius (MH57) via the half-length oil study in Munich (L.917).

51. Pt. 2, pl. 22 (H. Hymans [from M. J. Wussin], *Jonas Suyderhoef* [Brussels, 1862], 78–79, no. 42).

52. In the same series Suyderhoef's engraved portrait of the Archduchess Isabella is derived from Rubens' three-quarter-length portrait in Vienna, which is similarly adapted in Soutman's incised drawing at Windsor (Vlieghe 1987, nos. 65a, 69).

53. Also Pieter de Jode II's similarly reduced engraving of the portrait (Holl. 49) with a parallel inscription.

54. Christoffel Jegher's woodcuts after Rubens inscribed with a variation of *P.P.Rubens delineav. et excud . . . Christoffel Iegher sculp.* appear to be based on pen drawings or oil sketches by Rubens instead of the related paintings. For example, Jegher's woodcut of the *Coronation of the Virgin* (Holl. 10), related to the destroyed ceiling paintings of the Jesuit church in Antwerp, has been shown to be based on Rubens' oil sketch in the Musée du Louvre, and Jegher's *Hercules Overcoming Discord* (Holl. 15) to be based on the oil sketch in Boston (Held 1980, no. 141) used already for the Whitehall ceiling painting. While scholars generally suppose Jegher's working models to have been pen drawings by Rubens or possibly by Jegher himself, W. Vomm in Cologne 1977, 11, proposes that Rubens may have drawn directly on the wood block. This is hard to disprove, but I suspect the term *"delin."* refers to a separate model. The pen drawing *Susanna and the Elders* in the Musée du Louvre appears to be related to the execution of Jegher's woodcut, though not strong enough to be by Rubens. *Delin.* offers no precisions as to whether the "drawing" was made with a pen or a brush; it is the working design.

55. Held 1980, no. 335.

56. Holl. 2. Contrast to the inscription *Rubens pinxit . . .* on Schelte à Bolswert's engraving (Holl. 11; Pohlen 1985, no. 8) of the same subject, based on Rubens' oil sketch in the National Gallery, London (Held 1980, no. 336), and derived from an altarpiece in the church of Nôtre Dame in Mecheln.

57. Münster 1976, 222–224; Cologne 1977, 98; John R. Martin, *Corpus Rubenianum; The Decorations for the Pompa Introitus Ferdinandi* (London, 1972).

58. Held 1980, no. 150–166.

59. Martin 1972, no. 22.

60. Hermitage, St. Petersburg (Held 1980, no. 294; Vlieghe 1987, nos. 81, 82). The head alone was carefully worked up in a more graphic pen drawing by L. Vorsterman (British Museum; J. Held, "Rubens and Vorsterman," *Art Quarterly* 32 [1969], 125–127, fig. 4). Rubens was commissioned to do a commemorative print of Bucquoy shortly after Bucquoy's death in 1621 in Hungary. No formal portrait of Bucquoy by Rubens is known, though it might be inferred from the very fact that he was in a position to produce an up-to-date and unidealized portrait of Bucquoy on short notice and after Bucquoy's death when no similar portrait is known, and by the notation made by Vorsterman on the oil study itself: *P.P. Rubens fecit Et Pinxit Ao 1621.* See Vlieghe 1987, no. 82, with the suggestion that Rubens very likely did such a portrait (no reference to Vorsterman's notation) and Held 1980, no. 294.

61. For example, *Raphaello Urbin Pinxit* inscribed on Soutman's print after Raphael's carefully painted cartoon in full color for the tapestry *Christ's Charge to Peter* (Holl. 3; D. Freedberg, *Corpus Rubenianum VII. The Life of Christ after the Passion* [Oxford, 1984], fig. 57) indicates that though the cartoon was executed as a model for tapestry makers, it was appreciated as a painting.

62. For example, the title page of *M. Bonacina, Opera Omnia,* published and engraved in 1632 by Cornelius Galle the Younger and inscribed *Pet.Paul Rubens pinxit./ Corn. Galle sculpsit,* is based on Rubens' oil sketch of a printer's device for Jan van Meurs in the Plantin-Moretus Museum, Antwerp (Held 1980, no. 307; Judson and Van de Velde 1978, no. 60a, figs. 205, 206).

63. For example, Pontius' engraving (Holl. 13) after Van Dyck's *Lamentation* (Museum voor Schone Kunsten, Antwerp; L.718) or possibly Van Dyck's etching (MH"A"IV) after his own painting of the *Ecce Homo* (Art Museum, Princeton University; L.699) inscribed *Anton. van Dyck invenit et fecit.*

64. For example, Soutman's etching (Holl. 16) *A Turkish Prince on Horseback,* inscribed *Adam Elsheimer Invent. . .* is based on a Rubens drawing in the British Museum made after a few figures in Elsheimer's *Stoning of Saint Stephen* (National Gallery of Scotland, Edinburgh).

65. Wijngaert 1943, 106. This sequence is a refinement of Hind 1915, 22, who gave the chief stages as "Van Dyck's original sketch" (in many cases after a larger oil painting), "an oil grisaille," and the etching or engraving. Mauquoy-Hendricx 1956 and 1991 does not attempt to resolve the problem, while Vey 1962, 44–50, sees only the drawings, most of which were made from life, as preparatory. According to Haverkamp-Begemann and Dickey in Yokohama 1990, 28, "If a painted portrait was to serve as the source, engravers worked from drawings made either before or after the painting. If the portrait was made specifically for the Iconography, Van Dyck began with a drawing in black chalk/or pen and ink taken from life. He then prepared a grisaille (monochrome) oil sketch that served as the engraver's model." According to Held in Washington 1990, no. 92: "Van Dyck began making drawings in a variety of media, most frequently chalk but also in pen and ink and washes, and in most cases from life. For people who were unavailable or dead . . . he had to rely on whatever portraits were at hand. Vey lists forty such drawings, and some others have been added since. . . . The engravings agree—though generally, as one would expect, in reverse—with the drawings except that they complete what in the drawings is often only outlined or occasionally even missing. . . . It is precisely these details that were provided by small grisaille panels, and I believe we must accept the fact that the engravers mostly worked from such panels, done in oil. . . . Even those at Boughton House differ in quality. The question of whether any of them were painted by Van Dyck himself, and if so which, has never found a unanimous answer." Besides my differences with the above views, discussed in the text, I do not know of any authentic pen drawings by Van Dyck that can be construed as preparatory to the Iconography. Moir 1991 does not analyze the preparatory stages beyond assuming a function for the drawings.

66. Hind 1915, 24, notes that sometimes Van Dyck "varied his subject so as to bring it within the form of his series (taking the figure of Jan de Wael from

the picture of *Jan de Wael and his Wife* in Munich)."
This observation was not taken up in the literature
and the possibility that the drawing was after the
painting was not recognized.

67. See, further, note 33.

68. Vey 1962, no. 190.

69. Spicer 1985–1986, 543; Brown in New York 1991,
no. 82. The striped sleeves point to this being an Eng-
lish royal prince still in "coats," perhaps Charles II as
Prince of Wales, made in 1632 preliminary to Van
Dyck's *Charles I and Henrietta Maria with Their
Two Eldest Children* (Buckingham Palace).

70. Jabach's commentary on Van Dyck's working
habits during the English years was recorded by
Roger de Piles in *Cours de Peinture* (Paris, 1708;
reprint, 1766), 229–231.

71. In some cases, as in *Cesare Alessandro Scaglia*
(Viscount Camrose; Washington 1990, no. 70), a
boundary between the head and immediate surroundings and the rest of the painting can be quite visible.

72. L.809; London 1982, no. 26.

73. British Rail Pension Fund; Washington 1990, no.
101.

74. Van Dyck's individual oil sketches of the heads
of those to be depicted in his *Magistrates of Brussels*
(L.577, 578) may fall into this category. From this
pattern it is logical to suppose that Van Dyck did an
oil sketch of Charles I (now lost), which he used to
produce countless formal portraits. This is more consistent with his practices than the assignment (by
Brown in New York 1991, no. 69) to Van Dyck of the
black chalk drawing of Charles I in Amsterdam
(Rijksmuseum; Vey 1962, under no. 204, as a copy). I
know of no other example of Van Dyck doing such a
study, and the drawing is flat and labored. In reject-
ing the possibility of Van Dyck having made an oil
study of the head of Charles, Millar in Washington
1990, 56, makes the puzzling statement that "there
is no evidence that Van Dyck ever made an oil
sketch of a sitter's head."

75. Though Hind, and Mauqoy-Hendrickx following
him, accepted only fifteen, leaving out Antoon Cornelissen (MH3), Antoon Triest (MH13), and Jan van
de Wouver (MH18) for stylistic reasons and because
their inscriptions do not include a reference to Van
Dyck as the etcher, Haverkamp-Begemann and
Dickey in Yokohama 1990, 28, and Brown in
New York 1991, 190, cite the number as eighteen
(MH1–18) without discussion. Dickey mistakenly describes Van de Wouver as inscribed *Ant. van Dyck
fecit aqua forti* (under no. 31). Moir 1991, 101, and
under no. 8 considers the three questionable. His reference to them under no. 7 as autograph must be a
mistake.

76. Hind 1915, 22, 243–46, raised this option but
thought Van Dyck would not have wanted the aesthetic effect of his etching obscured by the (less talented) engraver; thus he saw them as having a "more
purely artistic aim." Mauquoy-Hendrickx 1991, 25,
is caught between seeing them as a group of portraits

Van Dyck wanted to reserve for himself, or as a later
"protestation muette" against the insensitive prod-
ucts of the engravers. Vey 1962, 47, simply notes the
above options. The issue has not really been addressed since.

77. Studies are known for Brueghel II (MH2);
Francken I (MH6); Van Noort (MH8); Snellinck
(MH10); Vorsterman (MH14); W. de Vos (MH15); P.
de Vos (MH16); De Wael (MH17), Le Roy (MH"C").
See Appendix.

78. Brueghel (MH2), Van Noort (MH8), Snellinck
(MH10), De Vos (MH15).

79. John Evelyn, *Sculptura or the History and Art of
Chalcography* (1662; London, 1769), 73–74, cited by
Mauquoy-Hendrickx 1956, 33 (1991, 19), only in reference to Vorsterman. Evelyn implies that a large
number of portraits were prepared by Vorsterman
this way.

80. Art Museum, Princeton University; L.699.

81. Cornelissen (MH3), Triest (MH13), Van de Wouver (MH18), Snellinck (MH37; distinct from Van
Dyck's etching MH10), Delmont (MH78), Van den
Eynden (MH80), Mallery (MH86), De Momper
(MH88; distinct from Van Dyck's etching MH7), and
Stevens (MH93) have been variously attributed, including some to Vorsterman (see Hind 1915,
228–238; Mauquoy-Hendrickx 1991, 16–22). I suggest
they are likely by Vorsterman, who worked up six of
them as engravings.

82. Mauquoy-Hendrickx 1991, 26, suggests a dating
of before 1632 or 1634–1635.

83. See note 29 for a discussion of the Holbein portrait of Erasmus. The only painting to which Van
Dyck's etched self-portrait head relates is a bust-
length piece in a private collection, Switzerland. The
prominent golden chain could be the one awarded by
the duke of Mantua in 1622, rather than that
awarded by Charles I in 1632, if it refers to a princely
gift at all. For the chain in Van Dyck's self-portraits
see Arthur Wheelock in *Masterworks from Munich*
[exh. cat., National Gallery of Art] (Washington,
1988), no. 20. That a monochrome oil study was
made from this painting for Vorsterman's engraving
(MH79) suggests that it was in Antwerp.

84. A portrait of Rubens etched by Jan de Visscher
and inscribed *Ant. van Dyck Delin.* relates to a lost
drawing by Van Dyck, reflecting the character of the
drawings for the Iconography in the work-up of the
head. The pose is casual, with the head turning away,
and does not suggest a formal portrait. The same is
true of a lost drawing of Jan van Goyen copied by
Ploos van Amstel (see Appendix).

85. See Mauquoy-Hendrickx 1991, 26.

86. Spicer 1985–1986, 539–540, illus.; Brown in New
York 1991, no. 55.

87. Van Dyck: W. de Vos (MH15; British Museum;
Holl. 15, illus.); F. Francken (MH6; Chatsworth), and
L. Vorsterman (location unknown; E. Göpel, *Ein
Bildnisauftrag für Van Dyck* [Frankfurt, 1940], 152).

By Vorsterman: Triest (MH13, 13.1), proof and counterproof (both Chatsworth); Van de Wouver (MH18; Rothschild collection, Musée du Louvre; P. Jean-Richard, *Maitres de l'eau-forte des XVIe et XVIIe siècles* [Musée du Louvre, 1980], no. 51; British Museum [see fig. 14]); Snellinck (MH37; Chatsworth); also Lievens (MH85), engraved proof (Stichting Custodia, Paris).

88. Wijngaert 1943, 106. The only proof impression touched with gouache known to me is that of Constantijn Huygens (MH53) in Amsterdam.

89. See note 87.

90. Noted as well by Haverkamp-Begemann and Dickey in Yokohama 1990, 28.

91. Inv. 2545 L.R.

92. Vey 1962, no. 179.

93. The proof state (pure etching) in the British Museum has been roughed out in brown ink with a plaque at the bottom inscribed *PHILIPPUS LE ROY EQUES' Antonius Van Dÿck fecit*. The half-length format consistent with the drawing was engraved by Vorsterman (MH185) but not published by either Vanden Enden or Hendricx.

94. This artist drew in black chalk on Van Dyck's etching the pedestal and flanking figures of Minerva and Mercury (Wisdom and Eloquence), which he derived from a device designed by Rubens in about 1631. The frontispiece was then engraved by Neefs for Hendricx. See also note 64. Moir 1991, 77, suggests an attribution to Neefs himself.

95. The splendid washed drawing for A. Wolfaert (MH27) in the Graphische Sammlung Albertina is executed in the same technique, though not incised. Wolfaert's right hand, lightly outlined in black chalk, does not appear in the engraving, the composition of which corresponds instead to an oil study at Boughton House ascribable to Van Dyck.

96. Vey 1962, no. 271. M. Varshavskaya, *Van Dyck Paintings in the Hermitage* (Leningrad, 1963), no. 13 (in Russian), offers the same assertion. Millar in London 1982, no. 79, considers it drawn for the engraving, but is cautious: "It also has the air of having been drawn from life and is very close in type, with slight variations in detail, to the painted image of which the best, but not necessarily the original, version is in The Hermitage."

97. See Van Dyck's portrait of Thomas Wentworth, 1st earl of Strafford (Duke of Grafton, Euston Hall), dated 1636–1640 by Millar, Washington 1990, 54, fig. 4.

98. Brown in New York 1991, no. 72.

99. Hind 1915, 31, n. 2, cites an oil study of Mytens among ten then belonging to the countess of St. Germans and which he had not seen; in fact it represents the marquis de Moncada. Judged from photographs, all ten studies appear to be copies of other extant ones and are therefore not listed in the Appendix.

100. A rather hesitant black chalk drawing of Robert van Voerst in half-length made by Gerard ter Borch, Jr., in 1635 in England, while staying with his step-uncle Van Voerst, is completely in Van Dyck's style. Either it is a copy of a lost drawing by Van Dyck or, less likely, an attempt to mimic his manner (see Alison McNeil Kettering, *Drawings from the Ter Borch Studio Estate in the Rijksmuseum* [The Hague, 1988], no. GJR60).

101. The grisaille oil study of Vouet cited at Port Eliot early in this century actually depicts Caspar Gevartius. See note 99. The original painting of Vouet, now lost, could have been executed in Rome in 1622 or 1624. Van Voerst was working in England by 1624, so the engraving was executed there after Van Dyck's arrival in 1632. Since Van Dyck watched over the execution of Van Voerst's engravings for him, the inscription *Van Dyck pinxit* may be taken to reflect a painted portrait, even though one is not now known. Either Van Dyck brought a study after the painting to England, or the painting was itself in England by 1636. Van Dyck's portrait of Justus Sustermans (MH12) was surely made in Italy. Of course, another hand could have made the engraver's model, as in the case of Van Dyck's *Cornelis and Lucas de Wael* (Capitoline Museum, Rome; L.347), painted c. 1626, of which Wenceslaus Hollar's engraving was probably based on an anonymous oil study in Kassel (see Washington 1990, no. 42).

102. Those executed in Flanders: Puteanus (MH36), Van Thulden (MH38), De Breuck (MH44), Seghers (MH65), Wildens (MH70), Cachiopin (MH75), Van den Eynden (MH80), Saftleven (MH90), Schut (MH91), Coeburger (MH77), and Rombouts (MH61). The fine drawing in Leningrad for Pontius' engraving of Rombouts appears to me close in style to Pontius' own drawings, and thus in 1985 I published it as by the engraver. The similarities still strike me; however, having in the interim found no other examples of model drawings for these engravings by the printmaker, I have to regard the attribution as in question.

103. Hind 1915 accepted many of the oil studies as autograph and as immediate models for the engravers, but his views were rejected without real discussion by scholars through Vey 1962, 48–50, except for Wijngaert 1943, 105–106. Brown in New York 1991, and Haverkamp-Begemann and Dickey in Yokohama 1990 stress a role for the oil studies, though without specifics; however, in their respective catalogue entries they do not cite the related oil studies in their discussion of the preparatory process. Moir 1991 notes the existence of oil studies in his catalogue entries of engravings (as under no. 32) but does not attempt to analyze their role. In his essay (65) he, like other recent authors, limits himself to suggesting that a preparatory function "must also be considered."

104. For the Arundel sale in Amsterdam see L. Cust and M. L. Cox, "Notes on the Collection Formed by Thomas Howard," *Burlington Magazine* 19 (1911), 324. Other early references in Vey 1962, 48–49.

105. Margaret of Lorraine (MH23), Count Johannes of Nassau-Siegen (MH57), Thomas de Savoie-Carignan (MH63), Abbot Scaglia (MH64), Gaston de France (MH82), Cardinal Infante Ferdinand (MH105), Marquis de Moncada (MH117).

106. See Appendix.

107. The oil studies at Boughton House vary in brushwork and color (grays and browns, the latter ranging from ocher to reddish) but all or nearly all, other than the copies, may be by Van Dyck. The script recording the name on several of the panels is not obviously Van Dyck's own, so its importance is unclear. The promise of a study of these by Christopher Brown is welcome. The oil study of the marquis de Moncada (location unknown; see Appendix) appears from a photograph to be of the same group.

The nearly round grisaille study of Nicolas Rockox (private collection, Washington 1950, no. 100) apparently used for the engraving by Pontius (MH115) published by Hendricx, must be by Van Dyck himself; its unique character underlines the differences in format that separate this engraving from the others and make clear that it was not conceived as part of the Iconography, though the existence of an autograph black chalk sketch composed consistently with others for the series makes it clear that Van Dyck himself intended Rockox to be represented (see Appendix). Van Dyck's intentions for the oil sketch of Lucas van Uffel (private collection; Washington 1990, no. 92) are not clear; it is more loosely brushed than those studied here and was not engraved. The grisaille study of Franciscus Junius in Oxford (Millar in London 1982, no. 64) is not related to the Iconography.

108. Hind 1915, 30.

109. See note 99 and Appendix.

110. Brancaccio (MH41), Van Mildert (MH87). The engraved portrait of Brancaccio is so stiff that one suspects an oil study by another hand, like those in Munich.

111. The black chalk study of Hendrick Liberti in half-length in Stockholm (see Appendix) is not a copy of a lost preparatory study for the formal three-quarter-length portrait (Alte Pinakothek, Munich), but of a lost preparatory study for a projected engraving for the Iconography, to be followed by a monochrome oil study. The version engraved by De Jode (MH172) of the entire picture is not related.

112. This is paralleled in the greater formality of prints and their *modelli* of a few artists and art lovers, who are less elegantly attired in the paintings. For instance, a ruche collar has been added to the print portraits of De Mallery (MH86) and Cachiopin (MH75; Washington 1990, no. 69). While Cachiopin's hands are as well adjusted in the print as in the painting to accommodate the parapet, the real difference between the painting and print is the facial expression of the sitter. As Wheelock remarks (Washington 1990, 269), the melancholy of the more personal painting gives way to the neutral expression of the public print.

113. Sheila D. Campbell, ed., *The Malcove Collection* (Toronto, 1985), no. 473, as L. Vorsterman (by J. Spicer). Probably the study of Wolfgang Wilhelm cited by Hind 1915, 30, n. 1, as belonging to the duke of Buccleuch.

114. While there are careful but dull drawn *modelli* for Vorsterman's engravings after paintings by Rubens that have reasonably been attributed to Vorsterman, there are no other studies in oil known to me.

115. Washington 1990, no. 98.

116. For the perplexing status of this engraving see Mauquoy-Hendrickx (under MH26) and J. W. Salomonson, "A Self-Portrait by Michiel van Mierevelt: The History, Subject, and Context of a Forgotten Painting," *Simiolus* 20, no. 4 (1990/1991), 240–286. It is not clear how to explain the similarities in the head of Mierevelt's unfinished *Self-Portrait Painting His Son-in-law Willem Delft* and that described as based on a painting by Van Dyck in the engraving (MH26). Since Salomonson (248) points to aspects of the *Self-Portrait* that are consistent with a dating no earlier than the late 1630s, it is not excluded that Mierevelt (1576–1641), then in his sixties, was content to use as his model the portrait of him made earlier by the famous Anthony van Dyck.

117. See Raupp 1984, 96–136, for the gestures of the artists depicted, though he is unaware of the adaptations from paintings.

118. This problem does not occur in the engravings after portraits of women, due to the socially restricted range of gestures in the original paintings. By extension, none is depicted with a parapet, much less would be so brazen as to rest a hand on one. See also J. Spicer, "The Renaissance Elbow," in H. Roodenberg and J. Bremmer, eds., *The Cultural History of Gesture* (Oxford, 1991), 84–128.

APPENDIX

Data for each print as numbered by Marie Mauquoy-Hendrickx, *L'Iconographie d'Antoine van Dyck: Catalogue raisonné*, Brussels, 1991. Abbreviations at end.

MH NAME	PRINT	PAINTING	DRAWING	OIL STUDY	MISC.
dates *initial publisher(s)/ etcher, engraver(s)/ sense/ location of touched state*	*inscription/ L.#/date/ sense*	*location, location, V.#/ sense*	*medium/ (best)/ sense*	*location*	
1. J. Brueghel 1568–1625	*vD f*/H/ vD-e/<	Munich, [by Rubens]/>			
2. P. Brueghel 1564–1637	*vD f*/H/ vD-e/>		1) bl,i,sq./ St. Petersburg, Spicer 1985– 1986/< 2) bl/Chatsworth V.242/<		
3. A. Cornelissen 1565–1639	*vD p*/E,H/ LV-e,LV/>		bl/Bayonne, V.243/<	Boughton/<	
4. A. van Dyck 1599–1641	*vD f*/H/ vD-e,JN/>	Switzerland, p.c. L.1017/c. 1633/<			79 same source with *pinxit*
5. D. Erasmus 1469–1536	*vD f*/H/ vD-e/>	*Padua [by Holbein]			unfinished
6. F. Francken, I 1542–1616	*vD f*/H/ vD-ew/>	*Montpelier [by Rubens]/<	bl/Sotheby's, Amsterdam, 18 April 1977, lot 89, copy/<		
7. J. de Momper 1564–1635	*vD f*/H/ vD-e/>	(Dresden)			88 same image with *pinxit*
8. A. van Noort 1562–1641	*vD f*/H/ vD-e/<		bl,sq/Amsterdam, V.244/>		
9. P. Pontius 1603–1658	*vD f*/H/ vD-e/<	loc. unk. L.564/c. 1630/>			59 other image
10. J. Snellinck 1549–1638	*vD f*/H/ vD-e/<	Jersey, L.614/>	bl,sq/Chatsworth, V.245/>		37 same image with *pinxit*
11. F. Snyders 1579–1657	*vD p+f*/H/ vD-e/JN/<	New York, Frick, L.67/c. 1621/>			
12. J. Sustermans 1597–1781	*vD f*/H/ vD-e/<				
13. A. van Triest 1576–1637	*vD p*/E,H/ LV-e,w/PJ/> Chatsworth	*Houston Blaffer coll. L.A134–1/<	bl/Braunfels, Deiker coll., copy/<		
14. L. Vorsterman 1595–1675	*vD f*/H/ vD-e/>		bl/Cambridge, V.246/<		
15. W. de Vos d. after 1629	*vD f*/H/ vD-ew/SB/< London,BM		bl,sq/Amsterdam, V.247/>		
16. P. de Vos c. 1596–1678	*vD p,f*/M,H/ vD-e/?JM-e/ SB/<	Vienna, Herner coll., formerly/ c. 1628/>	bl/London, Koch coll., formerly, copy?/>		MH181/ AL same image with *pinxit*
17. J. de Wael 1558–1633	*vD f*/H/ vD-e/<	Munich, L.525/>	bl/Paris, V.248/>		

MH NAME	PRINT	PAINTING	DRAWING	OIL STUDY	MISC.
dates *initial* *publisher(s)/* *etcher,* *engraver(s)/* *sense/* *location* *of touched* *state*	*inscription/* *L.#/date/* *sense*	*location,* *location, V.#/* *sense*	*medium/* *(best)/* *sense*	*location*	
18. J. de Wouver d. 1636	*vD p*/E,H/ LV-e,w/PP/< Paris, CR	Moscow L.635/>			
19. A. de Arenberg 1600–1674	*vD p*/E,H/ SB/>	Holkam Hall, L.497/1628–1632/<			
20. J. B. Barbé 1578–1649	*vD p*/E,H/ SB/>		bl/Bayonne, V.249/<	loc. unk., L.481/<	
21. A. Brouwer 1605–1638	*vD p*/E,H/ SB/>			Boughton/<	
22. J. Lipsius 1547–1606	*vD p*/E,H/ SB/>	PJ engraving after after A. Janssens/>		Boughton/<	
23. M. de Lorraine 1615–1672	*vD p*/E,H/ SB/<	Florence, L.904/1634/>		Munich, L.905/>	
24. M. Pepyn 1575–1643	*vD p*/E,H/ SB/>	Antwerp, L.563/1632/>		Boughton/<	
25. S. Vrancx 1573–1647	*vD p*/E,H/ SB/<		bl/London, BM, V.250/<	Boughton/<	
26. M. van Mierevelt 1567–1641	*vD p*/E,H/ WH/WD/>		modello was the responsibility of Delft (or Hondius) in Holland		
27. A. Wolfaert 1581–1641	*vD p*/E,H/ CG/>		bl,g/Vienna V.251/<	Boughton/<	
28. F. Francken, Yr. 1581–1642	*vD p*/E,H/ PJ/WH/<		bl/Chatsworth, V.252/<	Boughton/<	
29. W. Hondius 1597–1658	*vD p*/E,H/ WH/<		modello was the responsibility of Hondius in Holland		
30. J. T'Serclaes de Tilly 1559–1632	*vD p*/E,H/ PJ/>	(LV engraving after N. Vanden Horst)		Munich/>	
31. A. de Coster c. 1586–1643	*vD p*/E,H/ PJ/>		bl/Frankfurt, V.253, copy/<	Boughton/<	
32. P. Halmal 1596–1643	*vD p*/E,H/ PJ/<		bl/Chatsworth, V.254/>	Augsburg/>	
33. J. Jordaens 1593–1678	*vD p*/E,H/ PJ/<				
34. A. C. Nolé 1590–1638	*vD p*/E,H/<			Boughton/>	
35. C. van Poelenburgh 1586–1667	*vD p*/E,H/ PJ/<			Copenhagen/>	
36. E. Puteanus 1574–1646	*vD p*/E,H/ PJ/<	Raleigh, L.566/1629–1630>	bl+b,i/London, V.255/>		
37. J. Snellinck 1549–1638	*vD p*/E,H/ LV-ew/PJ/< Chatsworth	Jersey, L.614/>	bl,sq/Chatsworth, V.245/>		10 same image

MH NAME	PRINT	PAINTING	DRAWING	OIL STUDY	MISC.
dates *initial publisher(s)/ etcher, engraver(s)/ sense/ location of touched state*	*inscription/ L.#/date/ sense*	*location, location, V.#/ sense*	*medium/ (best)/ sense*	*location*	
38. T. van Thulden d. 1645	*vD p*/E,H/ PJ/^,reversed		bl+b,i/Paris, V.256/^		
39. G. de Urfé b. 1598	*vD p*/E,H/ PJ/>	loc. unk., L.505/c. 1628/<		Boughton/<	
40. A. von Wallenstein 1583–1634	*vD p*/E,H/ PJ/<			Munich, L.633/>	
41. L. Brancaccio 1560–1637	*vD p*/E,H/ NL/>		bl,w/Vienna, copy		
42. H. van Balen 1575–1632	*vD p*/E,H/ PP/>		bl/Malibu, V.257/<	Boughton/<	
43. A. Bazan d. 1646	*vD p*/E,H/ PP/<		bl/Rotterdam, V.258/>	Boughton/>	
44. J. de Breuck 1500/ 1540–1584	*vD p*/E,H/ PP/<		bl+b,i/New York, p.c., Spicer 1985–1986/>		
45. C. de Colonna 1573–1637/ 1643	*vD p*/E,H/ *PP*/>		bl/Cambridge, V.259/>	Boughton/>	
46. G. de Crayer 1584–1669	*vD p*/E,H/ PP/>		bl/Chatsworth, V.261/<	Boughton/>	
47. Count of Feria d. 1646	*vD p*/E,H/ PP/>	1) Germany, p.c., L.530/ 2) Vienna, ABK	bl/Chatsworth, V.261/<	Boughton/<	
48. C. van der Geest 1577–1638	*vD p*/E,H/ PP/<	(London)	bl/Stockholm, V.262/>	Boughton/>	
49. G. Gevartius 1593–1666	*vD p*/E,H/ PP/<		bl,i?/Vienna, V.263(i)/>	Boughton/>	
50. Marq. of Léganes d. 1655	*vD p*/E,H/ PP/>	1) Tokyo, L.827 /1634/> 2) Madrid, BU,L.826		Boughton/>	
51. Gustav-Adolphus 1594–1632	*vD p*/E,H/ PP/<			Munich, L.A98/>	
52. G. Honthorst 1590–1656	*vD p*/E,H/ PP/<				
53. C. Huygens 1596–1687	*vD p*/E,H/ PP-bl+g/< Amsterdam	painted in Holland, 1631–1632			
54. Maria de' Medici 1573–1642	*vD p*/E,H/ PP/<	Bordeaux, L.511/1631/>		Munich, L.514/>	
55. A. Miraeus 1573–1640	*vD p*/E,H/ PP/>	Woburn Abbey, L.543/<			
56. D. Mytens 1590– before 1648	*vD p*/E,H/ PP/<	Woburn Abbey L.543/>	bl,i/Bayonne, V.264/>		
57. J. von Nassau Siegen 1585–1638	*vD p*/E,H/ PP/>	Vaduz/1634/>		Munich, L.917/>	

MH NAME	PRINT	PAINTING	DRAWING	OIL STUDY	MISC.
dates *initial publisher(s)/ etcher, engraver(s)/ sense/ location of touched state*	*inscription/ L.#/date/ sense*	*location, location, V.#/ sense*	*medium/ (best)/ sense*	*location*	
58. P. Palamedesz 1607–1638	*vD p*/E,H/ PP/<			Munich, L.565/>	
59. P. Pontius 1603–1658	*vD p*/E,H/ PP/<			Boughton/< also Chris- tie's, London, 24 July 1936, lot 11/<	9 other image
60. J. van Ravesteyn c. 1576–1657	*vD p*/E,H/ PP/<		bl/Vienna, V.265/>	Boughton/>	
61. T. Rombouts 1597–1637	*vD p*/E,H/ PP/>		bl,i/ St. Petersburg [by Pontius?], Spicer 1985–1986/<		
62. P. P. Rubens 1577–1640	*vD p*/E,H/ PP/>			Boughton/<	etching by J. Visscher after lost drawing of other image
63. T. de Carignan 1596–1656	*vD p*/E,H/ PP/<	Turin, L.986/1634/<		Munich, L.988/<	
64. C. A. Scaglia d. 1641	*vD p*/E,H/ PP/>	Lord Camrose, L.989/1634–1635<		Munich, L.990/<	
65. G. Seghers 1591–1651	*vD p*/E,H/ PP/<		bl+bg,i/Paris, EdBA,V.266/>	(Christie's, London, 1 August 1963, lot 82)	99 other image
66. A. van Stalbemt 1580–1662	*vD p*/E,H/ PP/<		bl/Paris, Petit Palais, V.267/<	Boughton/<	
67. H. van Steenwijk c. 1580–1649	*vD p*/E,H/ PP/>		bl+g,i/Frankfurt, V.268/<		
68. T. van Loon 1585–c. 1660	*vD p*/E,H/ PP/>		bl/London, B.M. copy/<		
69. S. de Vos 1603–1676	*vD p*/E,H/ PP/>		bl/Paris, V.269/<	Boughton/<	
70. J. Wildens 1586–1653	*vD p*/E,H/ PP/>	(Vienna)/>	bl+gb,i/London, V.270/<		
71. K. Digby 1603–1665	*vD P*/E,H/ RV/>	Luton, p.c., L.840/c. 1633/<			
72. I. Jones 1573–1651	*vD p*/E,H/ RV/<	St. Petersburg, L.885/>	bl,i/Chatsworth, V.271/>		
73. R. van Voerst 1593–1636	*vD p*/E,H/ RV/<		bl+b,i/Paris, V.272/>		
74. S. Vouet 1590–1649	*vD p*/E,H/ RV/<				

MH NAME	PRINT	PAINTING	DRAWING	OIL STUDY	MISC.
dates	*inscription/*	*location,*	*medium/*	*location*	
initial	*L.#/date/*	*location, V.#/*	*(best)/*		
publisher(s)/	*sense*	*sense*	*sense*		
etcher,					
engraver(s)/					
sense/					
location					
of touched					
state					
75. J. Cachiopin 1578–1642	*vD p*/E,H/ LV/>	Vienna, L.502/1634/>	bl+b,i/Paris, CR,V.273/1634/<		
76. J. Callot 1592–1635	*vD p*/E,H/ LV/<				
77. W. Coeberger 1561–1634	*vD p*/E,H/ LV/>	(Paris, MJA, L.21/>)	bl+b,i/Amsterdam, AHM, V.274/<		
78. D. Delmont 1582–1644	*vD p*/E,H/ LV-e/LV/>				
79. A. van Dyck 1599–1641	*vD p*/E,H/ LV/>	Switzerland, p.c., L.1017/c. 1633/<		Boughton/<	4 same source
80. H. van d Eynden d. 1661	*vD p*/E,H/ LV-e/LV/>	loc. unk., photo at NGA/>	bl+g,i/London, V.275/<		
81. T. Galle 1571–1633	*vD p*/E,H/ LV/>				
82. G. de France 1608–1660	*vD p*/E,H/ LV/>	Chantilly, L.929/1634/<		Boughton/<	
83. O. Gentileschi 1563–1638?	*vD p*/E,H/ LV/>		bl+g,i/London, V.276/<		
84. P. de Jode, Sr. 1570–1634	*vD p*/E,H/ LV/>	Rome, L.507/<		Boughton/<	
85. J. Lievens 1607–1674	*vD p*/E,H/ LV/<				
86. K. de Mallery 1571–1636	*vD p*/E,H/ LV-e/LV/<	Oslo* L.510/<	bl/Chatsworth, V.277/<	Boughton/>	
87. J. van Mildert d. 1638	*vD p*/E,H/ LV/>		bl/Chatsworth, V.278		
88. J. de Momper 1564–1635	*vD p*/E,H/ LV-e/LV/>	(Dresden)			7 same image
89. N. Peiresc 1580–1637	*vD p*/E,H/ LV/<			Boughton/>	
90. C. Saftleven 1607–1681	*vD p*/E,H/ LV/<		bl+b,i/ Amsterdam, AMH, V.280/>		
91. C. Schut 1597–1655	*vD p*/E,H/ LV/>		bl+b,i/ St. Petersburg, Spicer 1985–1986/<		
92. A. Spinola 1571–1630	*vD p*/E,H/ LV/<	Edinburgh, L.A71/>		Boughton/>	
93. P. Stevens b. c. 1590	*vD p*/E,H/ LV-e/LV/>	The Hague, L.617/1627/<	bl/Vienna, inv. 8660 not in Vey/<	Boughton/<	
94. L. van Uden 1595–1672	*vD p*/E,H/ LV/>		bl/Amsterdam, V.281/<	Munich, L.629/<	
95. C. de Vos 1584–1651	*vD p*/E,H/ LV/>				

MH NAME	PRINT	PAINTING	DRAWING	OIL STUDY	MISC.
dates *initial publisher(s)/ etcher, engraver(s)/ sense/ location of touched state*	*inscription/ L.#/date/ sense*	*location, location, V.#/ sense*	*medium/ (best)/ sense*	*location*	
96. T. Bosschaerts 1613–1654	*vD* p/E(ygr.)/ ?		96–99 published by neither Vanden Enden, Sr. nor Hendricx		
97. C. Howard d. 1650	*vD* p/E(ygr.)/ Arnold de Jode				
98. P. Snayers 1582–1666	*vD* p/E(ygr.)/ André Stock				
99. G. Seghers 1591–1651	*vD* p/E(ygr.)/ L. Vorsterman, Jr.				
100. A. van Eertvelt 1590–1652	*vD* p/H/ SB/>	*Augsburg/<			
101. M. Ruthven m. 1639	*vD* p/H/ SB/>	Madrid, L.983/c. 1639/<			
102. H. Rich 1590–1699	*vD* p/H/ PC/<				
103. J. de Blois ?	*vD* p/H/ PJ/>	Chatsworth, L.821/ c. 1634–1635/<			
104. P. de Jode, Ygr. 1606–1674	*vD* p/H/ PJ/>	Rome, L.507/<			
105. Ferdinand of Austria 1609–1641	*vD* p/H/ AL/<	Madrid, L.766/1634/<		Boughton/<	MH 159 same image
106. H. de Hot ?	*vD* p/H/ AL/^	New York, p.c., formerly/^			
107. A. de Faille 1589–1653	*vD* p/H/ AL/>	Brussels, L.508/>			
108. Henrietta Maria 1605–1669	*vD* p/H/ AL/<	England, p.c., L.860/1632/<			
109. Z. van Hontsum d. 1643	*vD* p/H/ AL/<	Buckingham Palace, L.623/>			
110. C. Howard d. 1650	*vD* p/H/ AL/<	loc. unk., L. fig. 436 [as Lely or VDJ/<			97 reversed
111. M. Lemon ?	*vD* p/H/ AL/>	United Kingdom, p.c., Yokohama 1990, no.30/ 1636–1638/<	w,i?/Paris, FC [by Lely], Millar in London 1982, no. 80		
112. J. LeRoy c. 1569–1653	*vD* p/H/ AL/1654/<	Lugano, L.545/1631/>			dated 1654 other format
113. M. Ryckaert 1587–1631	*vD* p/H/ JN/>	Madrid, L.609/<		Zurich, with Koester in 1962/<	
114. A. Tassis d. 1651	*vD* p/H/ JN/<	Vaduz, L.520/>			

MH NAME	PRINT	PAINTING	DRAWING	OIL STUDY	MISC.
dates *initial publisher(s)/ etcher, engraver(s)/ sense/ location of touched state*	*inscription/ L.#/date/ sense*	*location, location, V.#/ sense*	*medium/ (best)/ sense*	*location*	
115. N. Rockox 1560–1640	*vD p*/H/ PP/1639/>	St. Petersburg, L.55/1621/>	bl/Windsor, V.193/<	p.c., Washington 1990, no.100/ round	engraved image is oval but drawing is right format
116. Archduchess Isabella 1566–1633	*vD p*/H/ LV/>	*Turin, L.491/c. 1628/<		Boughton/<	
117. Marquis de Moncada 1586–1653	*vD p*/H/ LV/>	Vienna, L.828/1634/<		Paris, Hotel Drouot 8 March 1982/<	
118. Wolfgang Wilhelm 1578–1653	*vD p*/H/ LV/>	Munich, L.562/<		Toronto (Boughton) [by vD or LV/<	

Portraits not published by Hendricx but which Van Dyck apparently intended to include, given the existence of preparatory work

MH NAME	PRINT	PAINTING	DRAWING	OIL STUDY	MISC.
C P. Le Roy 1596–1679	*vD d+f*/ vD-e/>	London, WC, L.546/1630/<	bl/Antwerp, V.179(copy)/<		MH 185 same image LV/PP/< *pinxit*
119. Charles I 1600–1649	*vD p*/JM/ ?JM-e/?JM/<	*Phoenix, L.785/>		Boughton/>	
127. Graf zu Papenheim 1576–1641	*vD p*/JM CG/>			Boughton/>	
151. Frederick Henry 1584–1647	*vD p*/JM/ CW/<	*Baltimore, BMA, L.554/>		Boughton/>	MH161/ PP, GHpub. same image
152. Amalia v. Solms 1602–1675	*vD p*/JM/ CW/>	loc. unk., L.557/<		Boughton/<	
172. H. Liberti 1600–1640	*vD p*/?/ PJ/<	Munich, L.548/>	bl/Stockholm, V.184, copy/>		

Portraits never engraved but apparently thought of as potential engravings

MH NAME	PRINT	PAINTING	DRAWING	OIL STUDY	MISC.
1. L. van Uffel		Braunschweig, L.417/1622/>		London, p.c., L.419/>	
2. Aristocrat in armor				Boughton/>	
3. Aristocrat in armor			bl/Stockholm, inv.1974–1863/<		
4. Scholar			bl/Van Beuningen, formerly, V.183/>		
5. Jan van Goyen			bl?/ loc. unk., copy by Pl. van Amstel, 1821/<		

Abbreviations

AL	Adrien Lommelin, engraver
b	brown wash
bl	black chalk
Boughton	collection of the Duke of Buccleuch, Boughton House
CG	Cornelius Galle, Sr., engraver
city	major public collection unless indicated; abbreviations used for Akademie der Bildenden Künste (ABK); Amsterdams Historisch Museum (AHM); Baltimore Museum of Art (BMA); Banco Urquijo (BU); British Museum (BM); Cabinet Rothschild, Musée du Louvre (CR); Ecole des Beaux-Arts (EdBA); Fondation Custodia (FC); Musée Jacquemart André (MJA); National Gallery of Art, Washington (NGA); Wallace Collection (WC)
vD p	*Ant. van Dyck pinxit*
vD f	*Ant. van Dyck fecit aqua forti*
E	published by Martin vanden Enden, Sr.
-e	etched state
g	gray wash
H	published by Gillis Hendricx
i	incised
JM	etched or published by Jean Meyssens
JN	Jacob Neefs, engraver
L	E. Larsen, *The Paintings of Anthony van Dyck* (Freren, 1988)
loc. unk.	location unknown
LV	Lucas Vorsterman, engraver (-e, etcher)
NL	Nicolas Lauwers, engraver
PC	Pieter Clouwet, engraver
p.c.	private collection
PJ	Pieter de Jode, engraver
PP	Paulus Pontius, engraver
RV	Robert van Voerst, engraver
SB	Schelte à Bolswert, engraver
sq	squared
V.	Horst Vey, *Die Zeichnungen Anton van Dycks* (Brussels, 1962)
w	washed etched state (gray or brown wash)
WD	Willem Delff, engraver
WH	Willem Hondius, engraver
<,>,^	directional sense of image
*	best of known examples
( )	uncertain as source

Anthony van Dyck: *An Afterword*

The publication of these papers seems an appropriate occasion to reflect on what we as curators of the *Anthony van Dyck* exhibition learned from the experience. As is always the case, judgments had to be formed and the catalogue written before the paintings themselves were assembled. Seeing the paintings together and in good light, many of them only recently restored, proved to be a vastly different experience from viewing them over time and in different circumstances. Struggling with the installation and determining in which sequence paintings worked best also enhanced enormously our sense of the relationships between the individual works.

In the catalogue we decided to propose, when possible, a somewhat tighter chronological sequence for the paintings than previously had been done. Traditionally, most of Van Dyck's paintings have been placed within one of his generally recognized periods, rather than given to a more particular moment of execution. Van Dyck's chronology is particularly complex during the 1610s since, as was abundantly clear in the exhibition, he worked in a wide range of styles during these formative years. Chronological issues, however, are not limited to his first Antwerp period; marked variations of technique occur throughout his career when he painted different types of subjects.

We hoped that at the very least our effort would stimulate discussion about the relative sequence of Van Dyck's paintings, and discussion about Van Dyck's early chronology did take place at the Van Dyck seminar held at the time of the opening of the exhibition. Reinhold Baumstark, who maintains that Van Dyck did not enter Rubens' workshop until about 1617, questioned whether Van Dyck executed the *Saint Jerome* (cat. 2) and *Saint Sebastian* (cat. 3, fig. 1) as early as 1615.[1] He prefers a later date of c. 1617, just prior to Van Dyck's entry into the Saint Luke's Guild. While no consensus was arrived at in this discussion, the exhibition did reveal that *Susannah and the Elders* (cat. 16) was dated too early in the catalogue. It belongs, as Gustav Glück had already noted, to Van Dyck's Italian period, and should be dated c. 1622. Not only does the canvas have a nubbly texture comparable to that of his other Italian works, the modeling of Susannah's face can be compared closely to that of *Teresia, Lady Shirley* (cat. 29), which Van Dyck painted in the summer of 1622.

One of the most interesting discoveries during the exhibition was the number of Van Dyck's paintings that had been enlarged by others at later dates. Strips had been added to one or more sides of at least seven paintings (cats. 11, 12, 21, 23, 32, 51, 56). The most significant later additions to a Van Dyck painting, those on three sides of his portrait of *Marchesa Elena Grimaldi* (cat. 36), were removed during the dramatic restoration of the work just prior to the exhibition. The reasons for these additions undoubtedly vary, but the underlying motivation for a number of them may have been to place images more conventionally within the picture plane. Van Dyck often cropped his forms quite tightly, which adds to the emotional intensity of the image.

Another revelation in the exhibition was the fact that Van Dyck was a superb colorist. This aspect of his work was brought out by the optimum viewing circumstances, but even more so by the large number of paintings expressly cleaned for the exhibition (cats. 11, 17, 34, 35, 36, 39, 40, 43, 63, 85, 88, 91). Unfortunately, the glorious colors and nuances of brushwork revealed in a number of these restorations cannot be seen in the catalogue, since the restorations were concluded only after the catalogue was in production. Some paintings, such as the marvelous *Cupid and Psyche* from the Royal Collection (cat. 85), were still being worked on while the exhibition was being installed! Various interesting discoveries from these restorations thus were not included in the catalogue. Two among them seem quite significant. As Christopher Brown reported during a lecture at the College Art Association meeting in Washington at the time of the exhibition, x-radiographs of the Dulwich Picture Gallery's *Samson and Delilah* (cat. 11) indicate that Van Dyck changed his composition by adding the Dionysian ewer that so delightfully describes the root causes of Samson's drunken sleep. At the same time Van Dyck adjusted the poses of the figures that flank the ewer, to give it more emphasis. The restoration of the Christ Church oil sketch, *Armed Soldier on Horseback* (cat. 88), revealed the remnants of a figure at the right edge, which indicates that this already large-scale sketch is a fragment of a still larger image.

As always in such exhibitions, pentimenti become apparent that offer insights into an artist's working procedure and evolving ideas. In the Edinburgh *Saint Sebastian Bound for Martyrdom* (cat. 22) it could be seen that the foot of the rider on horseback initially came quite close to Sebastian's left knee, precisely in the position of the oil sketch in the exhibition (cat. 91). A pentimento in *George Gage with Two Men* (cat. 30) suggests that Van Dyck first painted a curtain behind Gage's head, similar to that seen in his portrait of *Lucas van Uffel* (cat. 31). It may well be that when Van Dyck de-

cided to eliminate the curtain he also decided to change the character of the portrait by enlarging the canvas to the right to accommodate the two men dealing the sculpture. The fact that the canvas weave and preparation on the right section differs from that on the left seems to indicate that the painting was not conceived in its present shape, but was expanded during the course of execution. Another interesting pentimento occurs in the double portrait of *Lady Mary Villiers with Lord Arran* (cat. 78). Lady Mary was initially dressed in a loosely fitting garment similar to that of *Olivia Porter* (cat. 83): a blue robe fluttering to the left can be seen through the thinly painted background. Trees also underlie the clouds above Lord Arran's head. It appears that after painting Lady Mary in appropriate attire for her guise as Venus, the artist was asked to change the dress, with the result that the allegory was vested in Lord Arran alone.

A number of colleagues have kindly shared with us the following information that has helped us correct mistakes and oversights. We are particularly grateful to Alastair Laing for his long and thoughtful letter, which brought to our attention much new information about the history and provenance of paintings belonging to the National Trust and the Royal Collection.

Cat. 13. Alastair Laing notes that by 1896 the title of Lord Egremont had become extinct. Nor is there a record of this picture at Petworth. He suggests that it may have belonged to the collections dispersed in 1892, which had been put together by the 4th and last earl of Egremont at Silverton (Devon) after Petworth passed to the eldest illegitimate son of the 3d earl.

Cat. 14. According to Alastair Laing, "[George] Vertue was a careful observer and a good Christian, so he would hardly have mistaken a large oil of *The Betrayal of Christ* for a gouache or tempera of *Christ before Pilate*. What is more, he was writing in 1722 and never mentions Van Dyck. So it is only the 1747 receipt that refers to this painting."

Cats. 26, 27. Correction: Piero Boccardo hypothesized that the couple might be the *parents* of Senator Luca Giustiniani, the father himself having been a senator.

Cats. 28, 29. Alastair Laing has found an early reference to the joint provenance of these pendants. Both are recorded in the 1764 posthumous inventory of the 2d earl of Egremont (†1763), who probably purchased them on the open market. He challenges the notion that *Lady Shirley* was alone in the collection of Charles I and proposes that this picture was in fact a different one by another artist. Christopher Brown caught the omission that Lady Shirley's monkey was taken from Van Dyck's sketchbook study, fol. 59v.

Cat. 74. Marianne Michel was the first of several colleagues to correct our interpretation of Benoit Cize's letter to the duke of Savoy. Charles I was angry at Van Dyck for *not* having painted the children in the aprons that they regularly wore to protect their fine garments. Cize reported that the queen had written to her sister to have the aprons *added* ("qu'elle enscriproit à Madame sa soeur, pour le leur faire mettre"), as indeed she did. One can see that the fine white lace borders running down the sides and across the lower hems of Mary's and James' dresses are mere allusions to the heavy lace aprons that the children actually wore and that Van Dyck included in the later group of the same three belonging to Her Majesty Queen Elizabeth II (cat. 74, fig. 1). This oversight on Van Dyck's part offers proof of the accounts of the practice whereby he and his assistants worked up portraits in the studio using costumes but not the posed sitters. Apparently Van Dyck had been sent the children's costumes, but not the aprons.

Cat. 80. While Laing agrees that the sitter of this portrait could not be Sir Thomas Chaloner the Younger, as Walpole had indicated, he believes the correct identity to be Sir Thomas' son and heir, Sir William Chaloner, Bart. (c. 1592–1640), who alone pursued the military career suggested by the sword and ban in this portrait.

Finally, while most paintings included in the exhibition fit comfortably within Van Dyck's oeuvre, the attributions of certain works were debated by a few colleagues. The most controversial painting in the exhibition was undoubtedly the double portrait of *Sir George Villiers and Lady Katherine Manners as Adonis and Venus* (cat. 17). The discussion in this instance included both subject and attribution. While the consensus was that the figures represented Villiers and Katherine Manners, whether they represented Adonis and Venus is less certain. They could depict figures drawn from a masque or, as suggested by Laing, they could represent Corydon and Phyllis. As for the attribution, we remain convinced that Van Dyck executed the figures, but now believe that he had an assistant complete the landscape, which seems far more schematic than, for example, that in his *Saint Jerome* (cat. 8) from c. 1618, in Dresden. Another painting that elicited a number of comments was the *Venus at the Forge of Vulcan* (cat. 58) from the Kunsthistorisches Museum, Vienna. A number of stylistic discrepancies in this work, particularly in the comparatively smooth execution of the armor, suggest that the picture may be by a member of the workshop.

In the complex area of the oil sketches, so ably analyzed by Julius S. Held, the most controversial work was *The Expulsion of Adam and Eve from Paradise* (cat. 90), which has been recently attributed to Jan Boeckhorst by Anne-Marie Logan. The elongated and rather formless figures do share a resemblance to Boeckhorst's. Another possibility, now favored by Held, is that the Ottawa sketch dates from the end of Van Dyck's career, as was already proposed by J. Douglas Stewart in the exhibition catalogue *Master Drawings from the National Gallery of Canada* (Vancouver Art Gallery, 1988–1989, no. 39). Various colleagues also suggested that *The Assumption of the Virgin* (cat. 96) was by Boeckhorst. Here, we continue to believe, the intensity of the expressions and the angular rhythms of the gestures are totally characteristic of Van Dyck.

SUSAN J. BARNES and
ARTHUR K. WHEELOCK, Jr.

NOTE

1. Arthur K. Wheelock, Jr., et al., *Anthony van Dyck* [exh. cat., National Gallery of Art] (Washington, 1990).

Contributors

Arnout Balis is a member of the Nationaal Centrum voor de Plastische Kunsten van de 16de en 17de Eeuw, Antwerp. He is a senior research associate at the National Fund for Scientific Research, Brussels. He has published books and articles on Flemish painters and tapestry designers of the sixteenth and seventeenth centuries, and is a member of the editorial board of the Corpus Rubenianum Ludwig Burchard, to which series he contributed the volume on Rubens' hunting scenes (1986).

Susan J. Barnes is deputy director and chief curator at the Dallas Museum of Art. She was co-curator of the exhibition *Anthony van Dyck* at the National Gallery of Art, Washington. Her publications include articles on El Greco, Van Dyck, and European portraiture, as well as *The Rothko Chapel.*

Piero Boccardo is curator of the Galleria di Palazzo Rosso and of the Gabinetto Disegni e Stampe in Genoa. His 1989 doctoral thesis focused on the patronage and art collecting of the Genoese aristocracy. He has also published studies on the social and historical context of the arts in Genoa from the fifteenth to the eighteenth century, including *Andrea Doria e le arti, committenza e mecenatismo a Genova nel Rinascimento* (1989).

Marzia Cataldi Gallo is an art historian and a director with the Soprintendenza per i Beni Artistici e Storici della Liguria. Her research focuses on the history of textiles and dress. Recent works include *Cotoni stampati e mezzari dalle Indie all'Europa* (1993), with Maria Bellezza Rosina; and a CD-ROM, *Tessuti genovesi del Seicento,* with the Centro Nazionale delle Ricerche.

David Freedberg is professor of art history at Columbia University. Previously he taught at the Courtauld Institute in London and has been Slade professor at Oxford University. He has written widely in the field of sixteenth- and seventeenth-century Dutch, Flemish, and Italian art, as well as on the problems of iconoclasm, censorship, and response both in the past and the present. His many books include *Dutch Landscape Prints of the Seventeenth Century, Rubens: The Life of Christ after the Passion*, and *The Power of Images: Studies in the History and Theory of Response.*

Julius S. Held is professor emeritus of art history at Barnard College, Columbia University. Among his many books are *The Oil Sketches of Peter Paul Rubens, Rubens: Selected Drawings, Rembrandt Studies, Seventeenth- and Eighteenth-Century Art* (with Donald Posner), *Anthony van Dyck* (with coauthors), and *Rubens and His Circle.*

Michael Jaffé is director emeritus of the Fitzwilliam Museum and professor emeritus of the history of western art, University of Cambridge. He is an honorary foreign member of the American Academy of Arts and Sciences. He has published widely, especially on seventeenth-century Flemish painting and drawing and on Titian. He is the editor of *Van Dyck's Antwerp Sketchbook,* 1956, and in 1992 contributed the section on paintings and drawings in *The Boughton House Book,* much of which treats of the grisaille oil sketches preparatory to Van Dyck's Iconography in the collection of the duke of Buccleuch.

Justus Müller Hofstede is professor of art history at the University of Bonn. He received his Ph.D. from Freiburg im Breisgau in 1959. He has taught at the Kunsthistorisches Institut der Universität Bonn since 1969. He has published on artists of the sixteenth century including Pieter Bruegel the Elder, Jacques de Backer, Otto van Veen, Johann Rottenhammer, Hendrick Goltzius, and Jacopo Bassano, and on artists of the seventeenth century such as Peter Paul Rubens, Anthony van Dyck, Abraham Janssens, Cornelis de Vos, Jan Brueghel the Elder, Gerard van Honthorst, and Hendrick ter Brugghen. He also wrote the catalogue for the exhibition *Rubens in Italy 1600–1608.*

Graham Parry received his Ph.D. from Columbia University and is currently reader in English at the University of York, England. His interests lie in the relationships between literature and the visual arts in the seventeenth century. He has published several books, including one on Wenceslaus Hollar's English career and *The Golden Age Restor'd* on the culture of the Stuart court. He is completing a book on the English antiquarian movement in the seventeenth century.

Malcolm Rogers is deputy director and keeper of the National Portrait Gallery, London, where he is also curator of the sixteenth-, seventeenth-, and early eighteenth-century collections. He has published on Van Dyck, William Dobson, Sir Peter Lely, and John Closterman, as well as on other aspects of British art in all media and on royal portraiture and photography. He is the author of the *Blue Guide* to the museums and galleries of London and has recently edited David Piper's *The English Face* and *The Companion Guide to London.*

Joaneath A. Spicer is James A. Murnaghan curator of Renaissance and baroque art at the Walters Art Gallery, Baltimore. She has published on topics that include the interpretation of gesture, Christian and Jewish iconography, and issues in collecting and connoisseurship of paintings, drawings, and sculpture in the Netherlands and at the court of Rudolf II in Prague. Upcoming publications include studies on bronzes in the Walters Collection.

Katlijne Van der Stighelen received her Ph.D. from the Catholic University of Louvain. Since 1988 she has been a senior research assistant at the National Fund for Scientific Research, Brussels, and since 1991 has lectured at the Catholic University of Louvain and at the University Faculties of Saint Ignatius in Antwerp. She has written on Anna Maria van Schurman and Cornelis de Vos and has a particular interest in Flemish portraiture of the seventeenth century.

Hans Vlieghe was trained as an art historian at the universities of Ghent, Munich, and London, and received his Ph.D. in 1967. He is a senior research associate at the National Fund for Scientific Research, Brussels, and a member of the managing committee of the Nationaal Centrum voor de Plastische Kunsten van de 16de en 17de Eeuw and the editorial board of the Corpus Rubenianum Ludwig Burchard. He is also a part-time professor of art history at the Catholic University of Louvain and a member of the Royal Academy of Belgium. He has published several books and articles in European and American art-historical periodicals, and has made many contributions to exhibition catalogues, especially dealing with Flemish seventeenth-century painting.

Amy Walsh is an independent art historian living in Los Angeles, where she has taught part-time at the University of Southern California, Occidental College, and California State University, Northridge. She received her Ph.D. from Columbia University and formerly worked at the Metropolitan Museum of Art, New York, where she coauthored volume 2 of *American Paintings in the Metropolitan Museum of Art*. She is currently writing a monograph on the Dutch painter Paulus Potter. Her research has focused on the philosophical and political implications of the depiction of nature and the natural in the Netherlands during the mid-seventeenth century. She has also written on the history of collecting and is currently researching the collection of Frederik Hendrik and Amalia von Solms.

Arthur K. Wheelock, Jr. is curator of northern baroque painting at the National Gallery of Art, Washington, and professor of art history at the University of Maryland. He was co-curator of the exhibition *Anthony van Dyck* at the National Gallery of Art. He has published widely on Dutch and Flemish art. Recently he completed a book on Johannes Vermeer as well as the catalogue of Dutch seventeenth-century paintings at the National Gallery of Art.

Jeremy Wood is senior lecturer in history of art at Oxford Brookes University. He has written on the influence of Italian art in northern Europe during the seventeenth century, in particular concerning the work of Van Dyck, Rubens, and Inigo Jones, and he has worked on the history of collecting in this period. He is currently collaborating on the preparation of volume 25, part 2, of the Corpus Rubenianum Ludwig Burchard, on Rubens' copies after Italian art.

vande[n] [...] advocaten [...] noemen ende dat hij [...]
[...] hij sal [...] maer alleene[n] de [...]
oft de [...] tot betalinge bedvonge[n] [...]
[...] dat alhier bij [...] sal voordts [...]
[...] onder [...] [...] [...]
tot datter [...] [...] [...] onder [...] ende dat [...]
[...] met [...] sal voordts [...] [...] metten advocaten daer voer [...]
advocaet bij bet te noemen [...] [...]

[Inne] heer Borgem[eeste]r ende Scepen[en] [...] advocaet [...]
[...] om [...] der name vande[n] [...] voer de [...] [...] [...]
[...] prommitteert alle[s] te doen naer [...] [...]
Actu[m] [...] Sept[embris] a[nn]o [15]61 [...] J[acobus]

[...]

[...] [...] bij miller [...] dat hij [...] gebeurt[...] [...]
maer [...] was [...], alguis [...] [...] [...] [...]
tege[n] mijn [...] van Luir daer [...] [...] [...] [...] dat[...]
geapp[oi]nct[eert] te [...] ende dijs volgende des saecke [...]
[...] vi das om [...] de voorg[aende] [...] int tegenwoerde[...]
Borgem[eeste]r [...] [...] dat hij op [...] rapporteur alle[...]
mij te [...] [...] beproeven[...] [...] [...] dat[...] [...]
tot [...] meerder [...] [...] sij [...] [...] tot [...]
Biddende tot[...] voorg[...] rapporteur noch tve[...] andere [...]
[...] te committeren[...] ende [...] namentlijck [...] gu[...]
[...] [...] om bij [...] de saecke[...] [...] [...]
[...] rapport [...] ende [...] [...] [...] [...]
voordts naer behoire[n] [...] [...]
[...] mijn heer Borgem[eeste]r ende de Scepen[en] [...] rapport[...]
dat de saecke[...] [...] sal voordts geapporteert [...] [...]
[...] [...] absentie van de[n] [...] party[...] A[ctum] 23 Septemb[ris]
[...] J[acobus]